SOULS *for* SALE

The Diary of An
EX-COLORED MAN

Conflict and Compromise of Second-Generation Advocacy In the Post-Civil Rights Era

ANTHONY ASADULLAH SAMAD

$ $ $ $ $

Souls For Sale

The Diary of an Ex-Colored Man

Conflict and Compromise of Second-Generation Advocacy In the Post-Civil Rights Era

Anthony Asadullah Samad

KABILI PRESS
LOS ANGELES, CA
www.kabilipress.com

SOULS for SALE

Copyright © 2002
Anthony Asadullah Samad

All rights reserved. No part of this publication may be reproduced in any manner whatsoever without written permission from the publisher, except in the case of brief quotations embodied in critical articles or reviews.

Requests for permission to make copies of any part of the work should be mailed to: Kabili Press, Permissions, 3870 South Crenshaw Blvd., #408, Los Angeles, CA 90008

Library of Congress Cataloging-in-Publication Data

Samad, Anthony Asadullah (Born Anthony Maurice Essex) 1957-
Souls for Sale: Diary of an Ex-Colored Man/Anthony Asadullah Samad
p.cm ISBN 0-9723880-0-1
1. United States--Race Relations 2. African-Americans--Social Conditions, 1984 to 1992
3. United States--Autobiography

First Edition, August, 2002

Printed in the United States of America

1 2 3 4 5 6 7 8 9 0

In the Name of Allah, the Beneficent, the Merciful,
the lord of all the worlds to whom Praise is Due Forever;

This book is dedicated to my children: Kellie, Gabrielle, Anthony, Jr. And DeShawn. May they never have to live in a compromised existence.

To my wife, Debra Ward-Samad, who reached out and caught my hand...just as I had let go of the merry-go-round, and saved me from crashing. Your love has pulled me back on the pedestal of progress and, has given me the strength (by Allah's permission) to reach out to the vision God has put before me. May our love be a testament to those of a lesser faith that in trial is trust, in trust is truth and in truth is a real victory... one that only those who demonstrate their faith, in the midst of trial and tribulation, can come to know. A victory that redeems the failures of our past with accomplishments of our future. A redemption we all pray for, and to which I am a living witness to the power, the grace and the mercy of Allah.

Acknowledgements

I first give praise and acknowledgement to the one God, Allah, the beneficent, the most merciful. I humbly thank thee, the lord of all the worlds, for blessing me with your grace and mercy in putting my life back together in a manner that shows the disbeliever the truest power of God. Praise is due forever. I thank Allah for the Nation of Islam and the work of the most Honorable Elijah Muhammad, whose works, through men like Malcolm X and Minister Louis Farrakhan have healed the lost, despised and rejected in America, for over 60 years now. God bless "the Nation" and its continuing works, under the leadership of the Honorable Louis Farrakhan. Thank you for your spiritual guidance. The Nation is forever in my prayers as the salvation for Africans in America, as the truest example of rising up "the dead," and in helping all who seek real truth, freedom, justice and equality.

I thank all who contributed to the production of Souls..." including my enemies. If not for their betrayal, I would not have had (as much of) a story to tell. A'udhu Billahi Mina Shaytanir Rajim. May Allah guide you on the right path. I thank my wife to whom this book is partially dedicated, for being the driving force behind its release. It is a better book, because we held it. History is the truest teller of all tales. (Remember when you told me that?) I thank my mother for her prayers and support over the years. To people over the years that helped this go from paper to computer, and from computer to page. Ola Boykin, Marcia Clark. My first editor, Lisa M. Sanchez, my second editor and proofer, Katherine Newton. Thank you for your hard work. It hasn't been forgotten. To Third World Press, for your editorial guidance, and for making me do what God always intended for me to do, publish this book on his time (not mine). And last, but certainly not least, to Kamau Ramsey, for getting the final manuscript into shape for publication under very severe timelines, and for "making it all happen," including final book product, before the end of summer (smile). Looks like a life long relationship ahead. God bless you. Thank you to my childhood friend, Kisasi Ramsess, for using your brilliant mind's eye for the book cover rendering, "Prisoner of Compromise." If a picture is worth a 1,000 words, yours is worth 10,000. Can't wait for the next one. Thank you, Akaili Ramsess, for the set-up shot. Thank you

Charles Essex, Jr. Aloma Quon, and Rene Cross Washington for the dust cover concepts and ultimate design. Thank you, Carmen Hawkins, Esq. for your friendship, and your help in organizing Kabili Press, and for your legal review of the manuscript. We "know what we know," don't we (smile)?

To my friends. Two sets. Ten who helped me during the toughest time of my life, and ten who have helped me get on with my life. To Ron Carter, Floyd Frazier, Fred Rasheed, Daryl Sweeney, Minister Wazir Muhammad, Sharon Clerkley, Debrah Fontenot, Jayne Reese, Marie LaFargue and Janet Caldwell. I can never thank you enough for standing with me, defending my integrity and literally "carrying my spirit" in the midst of my wilderness experience. Because of you, I know what true friendship is. To Atty. Arthur Morris, Atty. Linda Bernard, Carter Womack, Greg Brandon, Kisasi Ramsess, Joe Powell, Oscar Morgan, Connie Bass, Deborah Morrisette, Suzanne Jett and Dr. Anyim Palmer. I will never forget your constant concern and care for my well-being. God bless you all. To the many people that played a key role in building Samad and Associates (you know who you are) to help others, and my newspaper publishers for letting me write in my column whatever God puts in my heart to say. Thank you for letting me "be myself, again."

Lastly, there are several people who significantly influenced my life in a positive way, but never got to see this book. May your legacy and memory live on through those good works Allah may bestow upon me; Gilbert Lindsey, Charles Wright, Henry F. Davis, Jr., Kevin Thomas, Gil Fernandez, and Horace Waters, III. May God bless your souls. You all showed me how to never "sellout. Your souls were never for sale. I will love you forever.

This is the story of my life, as I recall the events, my thoughts, feelings and reactions, as they occurred during a very tumultuous period in time. I have recollected these events based on my memory of personal observations and discussions, written in the contexts which I conveyed them, received them and perceived them to occur by virtue of my direct involvement and my knowledge of conversations, comments and opinions held and expressed to me by others directly involved in the events during this period of time. The contents of this book, both fact and feeling, have been reflected as accurately as possible.

CONTENTS

1

The Last Dinosaur....For Real!!!!

"If now isn't a good time for the truth,
I don't see when we'll get to it."

- Nikki Giovanni

Examining race and class disparities in America's four and one half century social construct causes one to examine the historical social advocacy approaches that were integral to social change. Civil rights groups played a significant role in the 20th Century, using protests to bring about policy initiatives that would, by and large, set the table for racial equality. But setting the table and making someone "eat" are two different things, and as the "civil rights" generations of the 1950s and 1960s found out, you can't legislate social attitudes and behaviors. By 1980, America's desire to make up the racial differences born out of Jim Crow and de jure segregation was clearly in retreat. With former U.S. President Lyndon Johnson's War On Poverty incomplete, desegregation in education called into question with the 1976 Bakke Decision, economic, employment and health disparities were still largely in effect. The legislative support for "equity" policy initiatives had begun to reverse itself with one significant historical event--the election of Ronald Wilson Reagan. America's second reconstruction period ended much like its first, with the country socially stigmatized and in a deep racial divide over what to do with what Abraham Lincoln called "the negro problem." Even as ethnic minorities began to witness the retreat of the social change agenda, that was thought to be the impetus for economic, social, and most critically, racial parity, Blacks still heavily relied on the civil rights community to lead them to "the promised land." After the period of social change (1954-1970) ended, the civil rights community became partners with many of their civil rights adversaries. This disqualified them to be the Black community's primary vehicle for addressing social and economic change in the late 1970s, entire 1980s and the early 1990s. Moreover, the tactics (some would even call them, antics) of civil rights period advocates were perceived to be obsolete and outdated.

Community advocacy has always been a complex mix of organized and less than organized (grassroots) involvements. More times than not, urban and rural communities would look to what many perceived as the "organized" or more "traditional" forms of advocacy. So, when asked, who does one look to resolve community "race problems," in most cases, the response would be "the NAACP," the most recognizable of the civil rights period advocacy organizations. That recognition is based on its leading role in the legal redress to end segregation (particularly, Brown vs. Board of Education), and its grassroots connection in local community "race problems." Even in the light of Blacks' political maturation born out of the presidential campaigns of Jesse Jackson in 1984 and 1988, the NAACP was seen as the focal point to address the reversal of fortunes and race problems that stemmed from the policy and constitutional challenges ushered in under the second post reconstruction mission of the Reagan-Bush legacy. Yet, while the NAACP has surely contributed to the erosion of racism through its effective litigation and civil rights advocacy during the past century, it had, by and large, continued to hold a national spotlight on issues of social significance based on a fading legacy.

As a young player in Los Angeles during the 1980s, I chose the NAACP above other community involvements because of its historical tradition, choosing to ignore "the problems" caused from time having passed it by. While this book discusses and examines community and inner-race conflict in the 1980s,' it also examines the broader conflicts of leadership succession in the African American, Black, negro, colored culture. No place is this issue ever more prevalent than in the NAACP. Because my experience of conflict and compromise was centered in the NAACP, the NAACP will serve as the center of this discussion. The same discussion could be applied to any Black organization, on any level. Twelve years after my experience, the issues of generational conflict and advocacy compromise are still the same. The NAACP is symptomatic of the larger problem, a stalled advocacy agenda with no real direction. The question of the NAACP's current relevancy and effectiveness is never more evident, than when examining its leadership grooming philosophy (or lack of one), its organizational structure and its (lack of) processes for leadership at its varying national, state and local leadership levels.

The national NAACP structure is highly concentrated with freedom fighters from ages past and philanthropic sympathizers who steer corporate guilt money in the direction of the organization. It is headed by a sixty-four member Board of Directors, as cumbersome as you would ever want to see. One-third of the board is elected by its 400,000 members. The rest are appointments as deemed appropriate by the board itself. Most of the time, the membership never even knows a vacancy has opened before it's closed.

Responsibility for the day-to-day operation of the organization is relegated to a national staff, under the direction of its National Executive Director (now called the President, in the Mfume administration). Traditionally, the executive director had served as the national spokesperson for the organization. However, in recent years, there has been an increasingly intense focus on the national organization's board leadership, the direction of the organization, and ensuing conflict, with respect to the NAACP Chairman and the Executive Director. The battles between Benjamin Hooks and "his first" chairperson, the highly respected Margaret Bush Wilson, were historic. Through a very shrewd and calculating power play, Hooks prevailed, when the board removed Ms. Wilson from the chairmanship over her criticism of Hooks, and her apparent unhappiness with the organization's progress (or lack of it). Hooks asked for more time and received it. However, fifteen years later, the same questions were being raised again about Hooks' effectiveness by Wilson's successor, Dr. Gibson, when Hooks allegedly orchestrated a coup attempt to remove Gibson, and failed. Gibson then became the NAACP's "kingmaker," eventually backing Hooks' successor, the Reverend Benjamin Chavis. Chavis was relatively an outsider unfamiliar with the NAACP compromise (some call it "cut- throat") politics. Fired for using $82,000 of NAACP money to settle a sexual harassment allegation, Chavis claimed that the group rejected his views toward progress (which was probably true). Maryland Congressman Kweisi Mfume, in replacing Chavis in the newly created President and CEO position, assumed (and has since eliminated) a five million dollar debt. He has faced a difficult time in facilitating a much needed restructuring of the organization, particularly at its branch levels.

Following Chavis' ouster, Gibson was then accused of financial impropriety, and was displaced in his role as chairman, by Myrlie Evers-Williams, the widow of the late NAACP martyr and Mississippi State chairman, Medgar Evers. The in-fighting was not completely over, given that a renegade faction of the board that pushed for Gibson's ouster was looking to retain power. Gibson, who stayed on the board until 1996, retained much influence despite the conflict. Below the Chairman and President position, the perception by many is that the board and intermediate leadership is still very much polarized. So much so that the organization's programs and future direction are likely to be stalled in the political battles at the board level. Gone are many of the key senior staff players that built the infra-structure in the 1980s.' They were prepped for successorship, only to be turned out, turned down, turned away, or turned off by the NAACP's vigilante politics. Fred Rasheed, architect of the NAACP's most successful program," The Fairshare Project," and co-administrator of the NAACP in the post-Chavis firing, was gone. So was Earl Shinholster, another co-administrator, and the organization's most grassroots-connected regional director. Earl was the architect of the NAACP's $50 million, six-state community economic development center partnership with Nationsbank (Earl lost his life in an automobile accident, in August of 2000).

Wade Henderson, the NAACP's Legislative Director (out of Washington, D.C.), was published in several periodicals (prematurely) as having the inside track to Chavis' replacement. The NAACP Mfume inherited was tantamount to receiving a classic car without an engine. The value of the car is in "the guts" of the car and its ability to run after it's restored. Like the value of a classic car, the value of the NAACP won't be known until it's restored and you can see what's "actually under the hood." Once it is restored, the NAACP still has major internal combustion problem at its inner core, with its lifeline, a largely volunteer branch system.

What is most distressing is its lack of support and trained expertise at the branch level, and its tendency to still take on "soft issues" that carry no real consequence, in terms of changing the racial behaviors of institutions and corporations. The national leadership structure continuously seems to have trouble implementing sustained strategies for issues, (many of which could equal or exceed the impact of its glory years of the '50s and '60s). Even today, many accuse the

NAACP of siding with the enemy on key issues. Two thousand or so branches are expected to support the activities of the national organization, over and above the limited resources of those branches. However, when it comes to supporting the branches, "National" (as the insiders call the headquarters operation) suppresses and constrains the activity of the branches. The result is that many of the branch communities receive compromised services and little resolution of local problems.

Because the NAACP still heavily relies on untrained volunteers, many of the people involved do not have the necessary skills or tenacity to handle the highly sophisticated institutional racism that has replaced the overt discrimination of the past thirty to fifty years. It's like sending a 1940s fighter plane to fight a twenty first century war. Many of the volunteers are sitting ducks for the well-trained, suited-down racist who have traded their hoods for a judicial robe or corporate briefcase. Discrimination at the branch level is now not a social aberration, but a way of life, countered by reverse discrimination proponents, who feel they should not have to carry the burden of their forefather's discriminatory behavior. The "Angry White Men" of the Republican Party, who took over Congress in 1994 felt that 30 years of reciprocity for 450 years of compromised equality and injustice, was enough and that the "equality" slate should be seen as even. Never mind that every advantage they inherited and continue to enjoy was a result of the injustices and indignities perpetuated against Blacks. With this type of attitude growing across the country, civil rights advocacy cannot be effectively addressed on a part-time volunteer basis, at most local branch levels.

Given the staunch realities of a society driven by capitalism and opportunism, civil rights advocacy is highly sensitive to compromise, and even sabotage, when volunteers are forced to be the vanguard for social, economic and political change at the risk of life, limb and reputation, with no opportunity for compensation and in most cases, little recognition. More than a few members have told me during my time with the organization, "Everybody has a price, it's just a matter of finding it." The price, as I have witnessed, was to see the sell out of a position of principle for a meaningless compromise, a formal acknowledgment and a check made out to the NAACP. In other cases, it was assurances that certain individuals would get some play down the line. Many times, it was before they even left the organization. The NAACP representative is every adversary's showpiece at banquets, conferences and advisory meetings where Blacks were generally persona non-grata. While these parties are all too willing to play the gracious host for the sake of equality, the wink and smile passed on to their colleagues and counterparts are indicative of the oppressors of justice doing what they have to do to pacify the natives, while his discriminating practices continue to persist. The newest forms of discrimination play more of a conciliatory role toward the idea of equality and fairness. This demonstrates that Jim Crow did learn some lessons in the racial confrontations of the '50s and '60s, where being labeled "overtly racist" was extremely damaging. Many corporations can hardly afford high-profile discrimination claims. So in effect, Jim Crow, Jr., in watching his forefathers closely, has recognized that a somewhat softer, but equally effective strategy must be implemented to stem the tide of justice and equality. What better way to do this than to treat Blacks as human (rather than the subhuman behaviors that refused to even discuss the thought of racial equality). By elevating Blacks to human status, the oppressor is forced to sit at the table with his confronter, as they did with Russia, Germany, Japan and now the Middle East, and intelligently discuss the merits and demerits of each position. But as with all of the others, America continued to strategically plot against those who recognized America's hypocrisy of democracy. Meanwhile, America advances itself on the world stage as a so-called democracy and "land of opportunity." Negotiation with African Americans for America has always been a stalling tactic to buy time, while it reinforces an illegally acquired, corrupt system of racial advantage that funds its wealth, its courts, and its access to power. This is all done under the guise of a preferred "citizenship," the ultimate "entitlement" question.

The NAACP's system of "indiscriminate volunteerism" plays right into a social oppressor's new strategy of economic oppression. Jesse Jackson, under his "Wall Street Initiative" advances that economic racism is the next battleground of the civil rights movement. Well, racism has always been economic, and indiscriminate volunteerism is highly vulnerable to economic illiteracy, because you can't talk what you don't know. You can't get what you don't ask for. In the NAACP, anybody who is willing to put in the time, often can represent the organization at the branch committee or officer levels, qualified, or not. In many cases, I've seen NAACP representatives, in meetings in which they had absolutely no business, facing an oppressor's lead negotiator, who oftentimes was a high level executive or legal representative, trained and prepared with a game plan. Corporate oppressor's seduction strategy sucks the NAACP representative right up. Some NAACPers who came in ready to scream and holler (a throwback to the '60s), were stunned when the oppressor came at him in soft, conciliatory tones with proposals to "look into your allegations, because they're extremely concerned about the possibility of any form of discrimination existing in his company." This is usually the line that comes from the highest level executive attending that meeting, who knows damn well what is going on at his company. At some point, these executives have to know that they are discriminating. Even if it's doing nothing more than looking around the table at management meetings and asking, "What's wrong with this picture?"

The representative of Colored People's Association (as I started calling them after I left the organization) interprets the oppressor's sympathetic tones and reassurances as sincere, and ends up thanking him before he's done anything. "Thank ya, Mista Charlie. Thank ya. We are sorry to have troubled you, Mista Charlie." Before they can ask him to respond to specifics, setup response timelines or anything else, they go tell the rest of the community how Mr. Charlie is really our friend, that he didn't know what was going on, and that he's gonna fix it. The Colored People's rep sends all his friends to Mr. Charlie, whether they can help him or not, and Charlie gives them some play. Pretty soon the Colored People and Mista Charlie are real close. Mr. Charlie creates an advisory board (as long as you don't cause no real trouble), for you to sit on, and you put one of his people (not him though) on your executive committee or your dinner committee. But what has happened to the issues initially raised a year ago, i.e., Blacks in management, money the company spends with Black firms and Black professional services, etc.? Nothing.

The NAACP may have gotten a little money, or one or two people known to you may have gotten in the door to discuss some business. They may have even put a five-year plan in effect (of course, to start next year). But no real gains materialize for the yearlong effort. No substantive gains for Blacks and other minorities for the short run, or the long run for that matter, because tomorrow rarely comes from these efforts of change. Many times, this activity is an exercise in futility, often caused by the seduction of a volunteer, or inexperience in one of the NAACP's 2,000 or so branches. Most NAACP branches have no paid staff or full-time location. Less than two dozen branches have paid directors or executives.

While volunteerism can be the basis for emotional mass movements, and even boycotts and other forms of momentary rallies and demonstrations (which the NAACP rarely evokes these days), volunteerism is the sustaining foundation of the NAACP's organizational branch structure. "Gratis activism" has made the NAACP weak and ineffective in addressing the thousands of day-to-day discrimination complaints received around the country by its branches. Other civil rights organizations, The Urban League, the Southern Christian Leadership Conference (SCLC), the American Civil Liberties Union (ACLU), the National Organization of Women (NOW), Anti-Defamation League, the Mexican American Legal Defense and Education Fund (MALDEF), and even the NAACP Legal Defense Fund (now a separate organization) do not run solely, or rely primarily on volunteers. In fact, most of them have fewer branches, but are considered more effective in their respective charges, because they have paid trained staff, and a full-time focus on the issues. But the nation's largest civil rights organization continues to expect that the country's most flagrant social ill, racism, is going to be turned back on a "catch-when-catch-can" basis. The rope is slipping fast, and the misapplication of volunteerism is the primary weight.

In taking a magnified look at the problems that have accelerated the Colored People's obsolescence, one would have to take a close look at its membership makeup, to assess why there appears to be a time warp in its ideas and mentality. Looking past the fact that the membership renewal rate is estimated at about 55 percent per year, the NAACP has sheer capabilities of maintaining its overall numbers by acquiring new members or past members (who didn't renew in the immediate prior year). The organizations' growth rate over the past 10 years has been sub-zero. It has, in fact, lost members. One has to wonder what the reasons are for such significant reclamation failures. What does the organization do with such a vast resource pool, based on its past and present membership, that it cannot effectively utilize the magnanimous individuals and collective talent of its membership to regenerate an aging warrior.

These questions are addressed in three very simple but critical reasons: First, most of the members of the NAACP are veterans of the Civil Rights era. They were marchers and freedom riders, now over 60 years of age, and have long worn tired of the struggle, fighting on the front-line, as such. Most of them come to conventions to reminisce about old times and support the new wave of freedom fighters in the organization they dedicated their lives to, only to find out there are few new faces, relatively speaking. This "age factor" is reflected at every level of the NAACP hierarchy. The NAACP, if a study were to be done, would have one of the oldest memberships of an organization of its size in the country, other then senior citizens groups. While these members are still very committed to the struggle, and have a fighting spirit, the fight has grown much too complex for the rank-and-file NAACPers with their antiquated strategies of the Civil Rights Movement. Plus, because of the many issues that need to be addressed and the time required to resolve them, the energy level is just not there to deal with issues with the intensity necessary to effectuate changes. This is the equivalent of asking our World War II veterans to fight the "war on terror." While many of them would probably be willing, chances are they would be ineffective against younger environmentally adapted, strategically prepared troops that outnumber them. They're in for a tough day at the office, to say the least. Because the NAACP has largely failed in its efforts (or lack of effort) to bring in second and third generation legacies, (other than on a check writing basis) to take over the fight under the wisdom and guidance of the older players, many of them are forced to retain leadership long after their effectiveness has run its course. Where are the successors to the struggle?

With the exception of ACT-SO and Fairshare (started in 1980 and terminated in the Mfume administration), there has been no significant departure from its traditional civil rights focus. Operationally, you'd have to go back decades to find out when a significant organizational and procedural restructuring of the NAACP occurred. To try to change constitutions and bylaws at the national level, without first kissing the proverbial "rings of power," is to risk life, limb, credibility and, would most likely bring about ridicule. This resistance to change, of even the most outdated policies, keeps the organization in a rigid posture, insensitive to the needs of the branches. With little or no communication flowing upward (only commands flowing downward) fresh ideas rarely get to the board and executive levels. The branches must then think of creative and innovative ways to continue the programs, at the risk of reprimands, suspensions, and everything else, to overcome resistance from the national organization.

Much of the annual 45 percent loss of NAACP memberships can be directly attributed to the frustration of people getting involved with the organization. New members full of energy witness the cumbersome and sometimes insane processes that take place to get even the most routine business handled. To deal with anything else of any social or community significance is another world altogether. In this day and time, when people have options, they don't have time to waste, because "that's the way we have always done it." Again, much of that has to do with the conflict between the autocratic charge of the national organization's influence over the branches, and the democratic charge of the branch to do what it has to do to serve the interest of the branch and its community. New members either don't want to understand this, or don't see the purpose in this exercise, and have very little patience for it. It's easier to just write a check. Can you blame them? Others would just as soon leave the NAACP alone. That brings us to the third and last point--commitment to the struggle in general and the NAACP in particular.

Many Blacks have apparently forgotten how they got where they are. Even today, while many economic opportunities developed, as a result of agreements pursued by the NAACP, PUSH and others begin to dissipate in the face of a "return to yesterday," a great number of Blacks still refuse to acknowledge that advocacy produced those opportunities. They think they just fell out of the sky, or came looking for the first Black man they saw to buy a beer distributorship. There are now over 10 million Blacks in the American mainstream "so-called" middle class. While Blacks are still earning significantly less than whites, comparatively, they are still making more than they've made before in corporations and agencies that wouldn't have hired them as janitors or mail clerks 30 years ago. And if you made the money 30 years ago, where were you going to spend it? Not in the hotels, restaurants and stores you patronize now!

For no other reason than this, whether you agree with the organization and its leadership or not, there should be 10 million life members taken out in deference to the Colored People's accomplishments. The people that struggled and died paid the ultimate price in getting our people to the day of equal accommodations and the right to vote. There is not one single day in the life of an African- American where you do not encounter some form of American freedom that was restricted just fifty short years ago. That, of itself, is worth $500 a year, especially since we can afford it now. But many, many Black people, most of whom know and understand what the NAACP has done, won't even write a $25 check in consecutive years to support a cause to which they owe so much. The $25 membership doesn't even cover the cost of a bimonthly mailer. It always sickened me to ask someone whom I knew could afford it (most who earned $30,000 or above), only write a $10 check, (the price of a membership then), or even decline. Hell, most people give $10 to street beggars during the course of a year, but won't give $10 to the group that made it possible for them to work where they work. We are a very dysfunctional race of people when it comes to establishing priorities for maintaining collective interests.

Everyone over the age of 40 should recognize and acknowledge this organization for nothing more than breaking down racial barriers. Then, there are those who are 35 years and younger who weren't even alive during the "March on Washington" and the signing of the 1964 Civil Rights Act, or the 1965 Voting Rights Act. They think public accommodations have always been in effect, as well as, equal education, fair housing and all the other comforts of life that the "me" generation now takes for granted. Many of them don't identify with a "civil rights" struggle, or the need for the NAACP. Neither are they willing to acknowledge that the organization is doing something that has been in effect all of their lives.

The point is that Blacks now have no more than a sentimental attachment to the so-called "civil rights" struggle, and unless reminded (often) what it once stood for (given its relative inactivity over the past 20 years). Most Blacks have not gotten actively involved in any organization, beyond writing a small donation, while others will not get involved at all--neither physically, nor financially. What are the incentives? No pay. Blacks, by and large, are making it (so we think) and don't want to worry about someone less fortunate. Many qualify their participation by asking, "What are the Urban League, NAACP, or the SCLC doing now?" Or they reason, as a justification to withhold their helping hand or their check: "Why would I want to be involved with an organization that still goes by "Colored People," anyway?"

This lack of support has so weakened groups like the NAACP, which was my involvement of choice, that it has now forced them to heavily rely on corporate donations for almost 70 percent of their income. Can you blame the reluctance of these organizations to bite the hand that feeds them? Our largest organization now rolls over nightly and kisses our open oppressor before he goes to sleep.

In assessing the impact of such lack of support, do you ever wonder what would be the possibilities, if the NAACP were supported like they should be? Maybe it wouldn't be as slow to transcend the changes of time. Maybe it could recapture the vigor of its litigious dynamism of the Marshall years, the legislative tenacity of the Mitchell years, and certainly, the advocacy spirit of the White years. While much of this is wishful thinking at this point, maybe the transition from the civil rights years could have been quicker with the support of the masses. And maybe the old times may have attracted the young warriors it so desperately needs, if it had money to restructure and pay them to fight, so as not to go to work for the multinational corporations that drain their talent and stall their professional growth. Yes, Blacks have to take some responsibility for their sick old pup. But the old pup also resisted learning a new trick or two that would have created the interest and loyalty from succeeding generations. Now, there is a perception, sometimes imagined, sometimes real, that the NAACP is a present day enigma. It lives on the sentimental attachments of its glorious past. Caught in a 30-year vacuum, changing times and philosophies find it groping for a relevant niche in dealing with the highly complex sophisticated racial sentiments of this generation's oppressors.

Civil Rights groups now finds themselves as willing partners, and have to play into the oppressor's hand of conciliatory negotiation. This breeds passivity and a false sense of security amongst the Colored People that allows for sustained discrimination practices to be camouflaged right under their noses. Yet, the NAACP claims it wants to continue to be the impetus for discrimination reform in this country. These philosophical entanglements pose a vile and even bitter conflict for a new generation of Blacks, who are catching the brunt of a renewed spirit of racial intimidation, spurred on by the country's conservative resurgence and growing sentiments that sufficient reparations have been met, as far as civil rights are concerned. With each hesitant step that the NAACP takes in confronting this newfound bedfellow, Blacks across the board, in every industry and section of American life, fall victim to newer, bolder, and more permanently damaging forms of racism. This happens while the NAACP entertains the oppressor's denials and constant breaches of good faith and fair dealings. Blacks, particularly young professionals, recognize that the NAACP is not willing to challenge the oppressor openly, for fear that the oppressor will expose the organization. The Chavis episode brought many revelations to the NAACP. It demonstrated the organizations' financial vulnerability when outsiders (non-Blacks) are the primary contributors. It discovered that it has a generation gap to mend (when many young NAACPers walked when Chavis was ousted). As a result, young Blacks have recognized that they have become the sacrificial lambs of the organization's willingness to serve two masters. It gives lip service to injustice, and superficially protects its legacy. It honors its promise to the devil, to maintain a passive posture as he moves swiftly to reinstitute a racial advantageous society to the detriment of Blacks. Young Blacks are being kept on the sidelines to watch their future compromised by old-timers, who don't know when to pass the baton.

If a new civil rights revolt campaign were to take place, (as it did in the 1990s), the tactics once used to shame white folk into a position of self-guilt and remorse over their treatment of Blacks, would be no longer effective. Whites no longer feel guilty over what many say "they" weren't responsible for, even though, many were around thirty years ago, and quite involved with maintaining the status quo of the time. Millions and millions of whites longed for this day to return, and they now refuse to be shamed into conceding anything different. Reagan's eight years in the White House reinforced what many whites privately held to during the late '60s and '70s, that Blacks have nothing else coming to them, and that race relations can go out the window if Blacks expect anything else to change. This attitude has almost bred contempt for Blacks who even try to raise legitimate issues of fairness and equity.

The very mention of race sets them off into an anti-race denial. Whites become vehement over the most evident issue of discrimination, because Reagan, Bush and other right-wing extremists (like former House Speaker Newt Gingrich), have put in the people's minds that they have been over bludgeoned with "Black rights," affirmative action, set-a-sides, quotas and other strategies to bring Blacks into the mainstream, after 400 years of exclusion. Truth to be told, this country still hasn't done even a fraction of what it should still be doing to correct the disparity between Blacks and whites.

Whites, once willing to take a "give till it helps" posture, when it came to resolving social welfare and racial equity issues, no longer have the desire or patience to help until the problem is corrected. Especially, if they started to feel the hurt or discomfort Blacks have long felt. Giving until it hurts wasn't in the plan for white America. So their position becomes (and has most often been), "You can get yours, but not at our expense. If you can rightfully qualify for this position you can have it, otherwise, it's up for grabs at my discretion."

These same whites completely ignored the fact that everything they got, was at the expense of Blacks in America. They either refused to allow us to compete, when we were qualified, disqualified us, when we were overqualified, underpaid us, when we did qualify, never promoted us, when we were justified, and fired us first, when it was not justified. But now they want this without any hurt or pain. It was back to business as usual. And business as usual, for a regressionist president like a Ronald Reagan, was to "make people feel comfortable with their prejudices," as former first lady Rosalyn Carter once quoted.

This attitude combined with the refined strategies implemented to reinforce the oppressor's new status quo, has put the NAACP in the vicarious position of cooperative obsolescence. They neither have the ability to strategically respond to this new fight, because of its failure to depart from passive resistance, nor the support and confidence of the masses in the NAACP as the vehicle for change at this critical point in history. The courage, tenacity and technical expertise of a younger generation, which not only is needed, but is necessary to its survival, is just not present in significant numbers. The Post-Civil Rights Era generation cannot avoid feeling maligned by the organization's often weak, compromising and/or non-responsive positions to issues that may affect them for the rest of their lives. Organizations like the NAACP can't move forward, and they can't go backward. They can only wait and hope that there is a change in perception from its own, before there is a change of attitude by the hand that is currently feeding them. Until then, they are not about to bite that hand by speaking out against them. And there's no organization more emblematic of this predicament than the NAACP. While trying to convince a highly cynical Black community to give it another shot, this dinosaur is playing dead when it should be trying to learn how to roll over, get up and attack. If it has any attack left.

* * *

2

A Tribute to Brother John

"Time is neutral and does not change things. With courage and initiative, leaders change things."

- Jesse Jackson

I became involved with the Los Angeles NAACP in the fall of 1983. I had read about the resurgence of the organization by a group of young professionals. Many in the community called them "the civil rights pups," perceived as second-generation freedom fighters. They were being credited for implementing some revolutionary strategies in fighting the more sophisticated forms of discrimination that were beginning to take shape in the 1980s. Much of this sophisticated discrimination was a direct result of the then Reagan administration's neo-conservatism and "guru" economics. It was a period when both social and economic fortunes of the country were recast to set the tone for a second post-reconstruction period. The first post-reconstruction period (1877 - 1919) was a re-establishment of the race divide. The second post-reconstruction would be a division based on race and class.

The NAACP (in years past) had preached that it was making the change from active demonstrations in the streets and the courtrooms, to Fair Share negotiation in corporate boardrooms. The transition was very slow, and failed to grab the imagination of the second and third generation civil rights advocates born after Brown vs. The Board of Education.

Under the braintrust and leadership of a young man named John McDonald III, all of this was about to change. The Los Angeles NAACP branch was rollin' over everybody and everything. John was assembling some of the most brilliant young brothers and sisters, from virtually every arena in the city, trying to convince them that this old dinosaur deserved one more shot at the big time. It was a tough sell.

I had already rejected two invitations to get involved in early 1983, right after John's election. John was trying to recruit from the Black Greek-letter organizations. Someone had identified me as the youngest (age 26) regional director of any Greek-letter group in the country. I had been involved with the NAACP in the late '70s, when Phi Beta Sigma, raised some 500 NAACP memberships in support of a fraternity brother, Kevin Davis. Kevin was then a youth member on the national board. He had fired up a few "young guns," to the point that we attended about a half-dozen meetings at the headquarters offices of Golden State Mutual Life Insurance in Los Angeles. But, after seeing some of the petty discussions and arguments that ensued meeting after meeting, we soon became very discouraged. Our disgust came to a boiling point, when we witnessed the leadership of the branch involved in a fistfight. I left that NAACP meeting with the intent to never get involved with that kind of foolishness again. The first time John asked me to get involved, that memory was too fresh in my mind. I promised I'd stay in touch, wrote him a $10 check, and left.

Around June 1983, I met Irma Brown. I had decided to join First AME Church the previous year. Irma approached me and asked if I had decided how I would be involved in the church. I told her I had not decided. She asked me if I had thought about the NAACP. I told her that I really wasn't sure about that. She sat with me for about 30 minutes defending the branch's current activities. I still remember how she ended the conversation, because of its stinging relevance to the condition of our people. Not relenting in my abstinence to join the "Dinosaur Club," I expressed serious doubt that the NAACP could be turned around, and that I couldn't see myself wasting any more time with another stagnant organization. She proceeded to tell me that it would never change, if those who had the power to move it don't get involved. If I did get involved and it still didn't move, then I should not blame the organization, but myself.

I thought about that for a long time. I prided myself as a mover and a shaker, one who doesn't wait for things to happen, but made things happen. None of my involvements had the potential to help oppressed people like the NAACP... if it could come alive again. I never thought the same about the NAACP nor Irma. I saw them both in a very different light. While I wasn't completely sold on the NAACP, I didn't totally dismiss it. I just stayed on the peripheral until my cynicism could be relieved.

After a few months of reading about some of the other branches' activities, I felt the least I could do was support them financially. My buppie generation was often accused of not giving back. I wrote a $500 check for a life membership to dispel that theory. That was the extent of my involvement..for about five months. I did not hear from anyone about my check, neither did I receive a membership card, or even a thank-you note. Nothing. I ended up having to go to a meeting to track my money. That didn't do much for my cynicism. Same old "niggah" shit was the first thing that came to my mind.

When I got to the church, it became worse, when I inquired about who I should speak to about my membership. I got directed to about seven or eight people. I was finally directed to a brother named Ralph Crabbe, who was the life membership chair. I saw Ralph as a good brother, and we eventually became associates. Ralph sometimes had a sarcastic personality, which could be offensive, if you didn't know him. Well, I didn't know him and I got offended.

It was one of those days. After being shuffled from one person to the next for 45 minutes, I wasn't particularly in the mood to deal with any sarcasm. I explained to Ralph that I had forwarded a check to the branch about five months earlier for a life membership, and had not received any notification. Ralph proceeded to tell me how I couldn't have sent a check in the mail, because he definitely would have seen it. Then he asked me what was the amount of the check. When I told him $500, he really went on and on about how he didn't recall the name, how it must have gotten lost, and a bunch of other excuses.

Somehow, I knew I'd have to go through all of this. I had dealt with a Negro organization or two at that point in my life. I pulled out a copy of the canceled check, with the NAACP bank stamp on the back. No, the check had not been lost. Yes, the check was cashed by the NAACP and, yes, it had gotten by ole' eagle-eyed Ralph. He proceeded to tell me that he would have to research the branch to see if he could find it, and he'd have to get back to me later. I was so exasperated that I could barely concentrate on the meeting.

I was somewhat impressed with what I was able to pick up. I was particularly impressed with John's facilitation of the meeting and the way he handled people. We talked for a minute after the meeting. He said Irma had told him of our dialogue and that he was glad to see me out. I didn't have the heart to tell him why I was really there. At that point, it really didn't matter. I was impressed.

That was the first time I gave some affirmative indication that I might be willing to work with the branch. We agreed to get together within the ensuing weeks to discuss how I could get involved. I never heard from Ralph, but I called the branch a few weeks later, and John's assistant, Joanne Robertson, helped me. She found my information in a matter of days. She arranged a meeting with John and me to work out details of my involvement.

In mid-May 1984, John appointed me to the branch's Executive Committee, as Chairman of the Small Business Council. This was a vehicle John had designed to help small businesses with procurement opportunities being developed by the "Fair Share agreements" the branch and national were initiating. While the Council was still in the conceptual phase, there was a lot of interest in the Council's ability to foster economic opportunities for minority businesses. The committee didn't become functional until late September, when several businesses sent checks to join the Council. The branch had a lot going on -- fashion shows, private movie screenings, radiothons, elections, a Coors and McDonald's Fair Share negotiation, and a big battle with national over undermining our fundraising base by proposing to have the Spingarn Award dinner in Los Angeles. John wanted monthly breakfast meetings to have corporate executives talk to minority small businesses about procurement opportunities. He felt that with all that was going on, and with the end of the year coming, we should plan the first meeting for January 1985. Only he wouldn't live to see it.

* * *

"One of the saddest days in the history of Los Angeles," I heard one of the old timers say. "Certainly, one of the most shocking," said another. What they were talking about was the unexpected death of Los Angeles Branch President, John McDonald III. He died in the middle of the night of a massive heart attack on December 20, 1984, at the young age of 36 years old. As a result of his death, he took with him the heart and spirit of one of the most successful resurrections in the history of the organization.

From all who could recall, it was certainly one of the greatest comebacks the NAACP had seen. He had increased a branch membership which had fallen from an average of 5,000 to a low of 1,500 in 1982, to over 15,000 in less than two years. National claimed they never received more than 10,000 but who was counting in our time of bereavement. What was so amazing about that feat was that most of those people had sworn off the NAACP forever. He brought together grassroots types, high-level corporate executives (Black and White), and politicians on the local, county, state and federal levels. He developed the most unlikely coalitions, and forced them to forget about personal feuds (and there are a lot of them in Los Angeles) and deal with the issues at hand.

The most impressive accomplishment of the John McDonald legacy was that these groups all came together in such a short period of time. The reinstitution of the Freedom Fund (the Roy Wilkins Dinner), the successful Coors boycott, the acceleration of the Fair Share Program, the original focus on Black on Black youth violence, can all be attributed to John's vision, energy and tenacity. Not to mention that he had to fight the national office every step of the way in trying to address relevant issues, without having to deal with the many irrelevant constrictions that the organization puts on its branches. Most importantly, he assembled the most professionally astute, aggressive and diverse group of people, who, because of their significantly different interests, attitudes, cultural values and motives, would not have come together otherwise. John's charisma and dynamism created the prototype for a new generation branch.

Once John started grabbing national headlines on several projects, and his young guns started showing up at conventions in unprecedented numbers, branches all over the country started taking a younger, fresher look and fashioned their branches after those "renegades" (as national called us) in Los Angeles. To a certain degree, they were right--but who cared. Due to John McDonald's influence, the NAACP got its second chance for just a moment. The old timers who had retained their seats from prior administrations were in for a hell of a ride. And a hell of a ride it was. But just as fast as it started, it stopped.

Men and women who had turned the city and the country on its ear, and people who ran some of the biggest corporations, agencies, and private businesses in California, sat in the branch conference room helplessly lost. They offered strength and support to each other and to Irma, who was engaged to marry John within the coming year.

A chapter's Executive Committee that was never short on confidence and self-assurance, was now crumbled with grief and insecurity, trying to emotionally grasp the last fleeting contrasts of the memories we all so vividly shared. Some of the memories included: the branch Christmas party at John and Irma's just a week earlier, John's re-election, the stirring state of the branch speech at the general membership meeting only six days prior, and John dressing as Santa Claus at the branch's Christmas Toy Giveaway just the day before his death. The brother was full of life, so full of energy, and had a great sense of humor.

The city of Los Angeles in the mid-1980s, in all its political and philosophical diversity, paid a fitting tribute to its fallen warrior. Regardless of one's persuasions or differences, respect for John couldn't be faded, as the youth say (meaning you couldn't argue with his success). Irrespective of the fact that his tenure was short, the city godfathers (Negro and white) and the community generals acknowledged his role as being an effective power player, by giving John "his propers" for a valiant effort, posthumously.

The Los Angeles NAACP Executive Committee served as the honor guard for their fallen leader by posting 24-hour vigils with the body in state, and with Irma in her time of bereavement. This admirable show of unity and strength, in a time of crisis was not indicative of the things to come. It was a sincere attempt to express the love we all had for the man who had brought us all together to breathe life into a branch that was virtually breathless.

For many of us who had been knighted by Brother John as stewards of a newer, more sophisticated struggle, this would be this group's most courageous moment collectively. It was the last time we would all be on the same page, at the same time, agendas and motives aside. It was also one of the group's last time for reflection. However, we didn't recognize it while it was happening, nor did we realize that it could only happen once. It's like taking a picture; it only happens once. You were either in it or you weren't. You may take a similar picture but not with the same spontaneity, same natural flavor or accentuation of the moment.

It was definitely a first shot type of experience, both for the NAACP, and for a new generation of freedom fighters who didn't quite know where they fit, until a brother that God had touched fashioned an unlikely group of soloists and bit players into a highly respected and well-rehearsed orchestra. It was a two-year success unparalleled. Just that quick he was there, and in the camera's next click he was gone. In the flash of an eye and in between shots, John McDonald proved to believers and disbelievers alike that even dinosaurs deserve, and can get a second chance.

The power struggle that ensued to fill the branch's vacant presidency set the tone for betrayal and unrest, that would continue through the end of my involvement (and beyond). Forty-five supposedly intelligent individuals, most of whom only had one thing in common, which was a loyalty to John McDonald and his memory, were now left to choose a successor from a group of people none of us really knew. This process only gave greater credibility to John's ability to put together such a diverse group of personalities (and egos), and be able to succeed, in most cases. John hadn't been buried two weeks, and you'd swear that many of these people never knew, or had ever worked with each other. Furthermore, the Executive Committee was now being asked to select a President from individuals, whose personalities were as extreme from John's as they were from each others. John had managed to entrench players of his liking (and apparent philosophies) by formulating a slate, in the previous election, that would allow for his progressive influence and philosophies to be maintained for some time to come. While incorporating some of the so-called "NAACP lifers" in the slate at the lower officer and board levels, all of the higher officers were considered John's people, or progressives.

In the First Vice President spot, John basically fulfilled a political promise, by allowing Ray Johnson, an local attorney, to succeed him, after Ray withdrew from seeking the branch presidency two years prior. Ray Johnson supported John's candidacy, when it became apparent that he didn't have what it took to oust the preceding Jess McClendon administration. This allowed a consensus candidate (John) to eventually beat McClendon. The rest was history. John rewarded Ray by playing his incumbent First Vice President, Larry Aubry, out of pocket. Shocked by the fact that John's nomination committee brought Ray's name forth, in an obvious slight of support, Larry declined when he was nominated from the floor the following month, at November general membership meeting. Larry quickly recognized that he could've beaten Ray, if it was Ray he was running against. It was the McDonald election machine he was running against, which he chose not to oppose.

In the Second Vice President spot was a real ringer, Melanie Lomax. Also an attorney, Melanie was a legacy from a civil rights family, who was very sharp and even more aggressive. Melanie had (and still has) the tenacity of a pit bull. She was very straightforward, not particularly friendly (which intimidated most everybody, including Executive Committee members). She enjoyed her role as an antagonistic negotiator for the branch's initial Fair Share disputes. You had to pick your days with Melanie. Perceived as very unpredictable, she may let you get near one day, and snap at you the next. More than a few people have caught Melanie Lomax on the wrong day. But make no mistake, she was clearly the best of the lot after John. Her being in the second spot had nothing to do with Raymond. It was her deference to John's wishes.

Melanie had a lot of respect for John. He was the only one who could handle Melanie, who was labeled a maverick, and was not especially noted as a team player, in the eyes of many. However, she was seen as John's successor. John wouldn't have been able to control the reality of Melanie's succession, not because he wouldn't have been able to hold Melanie back, but because his magic would have run out on Ray. Ray's lackluster personality and weak leadership qualities wouldn't have stood up to Melanie's overbearing personality and very capable leadership qualities. John may have had to back away from that one. Melanie's only hindrance had been her handling of people. But given the choice of handling people or getting something done, you'd be surprised of what would win out. Melanie would have dusted Ray given a fair and equal opportunity, but Melanie played along with John, for the moment.

With John deceased and not there to manage the delicate coalition that he had masterminded, to keep the diverse personalities outwardly focused, and to intercede when the personalities clashed (and they did clash, frequently), it was just a very short time before the "civil rights pups" were turning on each other. As far as some were concerned, without John in the picture, all deals were off. They weren't necessarily compelled, or even inclined to hold themselves to promises made to John (based on their relationships), and transfer them to Ray. Others had a "do it for John" (let's wait and see) attitude, while the NAACP traditionalists (the lifers) were trying to bind all actions constitutionally, so that the business of the NAACP could move forward. What they failed to see was that to most of those involved, John was the business of the NAACP, which was the major reason they were involved. Before John, the NAACP hadn't any real business to interest the Los Angeles Black community, in almost fifteen years. Not any that was particularly relevant to issues most of us were concerned about.

While it was critically important that the progressive direction of the Los Angeles branch continue, the coalition that made it so diversely effective was quickly unraveling over the question of leadership succession. The two primary issues were: what process would be used to select a successor, and what leadership style would be most effective in continuing the work that McDonald had started in a similarly progressive fashion?

In most organizations, officer succession is a constitutional question. If the President is not able to fulfill his duties for whatever reason, the Vice President or the next in line succeeds the President. Simple enough, right? What made this situation different was that McDonald died six days after the election, so while he was President-Elect, and all of the other officers were Officers-Elect, nobody had been sworn into office. Complicating the situation even more was that, technically, the only person who had a right to succession was Larry Aubry, who was First Vice President, and would continue to be, until the new officers were sworn in at the January 1985 general membership meeting.

The correct process would have been to allow Larry his right of succession for the remainder of John's first term. Then the issue could have been taken to the membership in January, so the membership could decide whether it wanted to invalidate the election and hold new ones, thereby allowing the presidency to be opened up to all qualified members. Or they could have sworn in the new officers, including John (posthumously), declared his office vacant, then allowed the constitutionally mandated succession to take place. That would have given Ray the presidency with the general memberships' acclamation. Either way, the branch's general membership should have had the opportunity to make that decision. As one would surmise, that is far removed from what actually happened.

John had turned the Los Angeles NAACP presidency into a prize plum for both advocacy and publicity. It had the attention of the nation as one of the NAACP's largest and most active branches. Much was at stake, in terms of how mainstream, or how proactively radical the branch would become with the two most obvious choices before us. While there was extreme concern about whether Ray could internally lead such an independent group of activists, there was actually fear in the hearts of the mainstream at the possibility of Melanie becoming President. Melanie, while always commanding respect, wasn't very well-liked in some business and community circles. She was outright despised by our national organization. Melanie's conflicts and criticisms of the national branch were well known, and they let her know (even though she was right in many instances) that they didn't appreciate the open criticism from one of its branch officers. But love her or hate her, there was no doubt that she was a fighter for the people, and was relentless and indiscriminate with whom she fought. This was bad news for many proponents of racism, who, coincidentally, may have been contributors to the organization, and expected the organization's silence in return for money. National watched this branch dilemma very closely.

Melanie, of course, was pushing for an invalidation of the election, which was a reasonable request. No one had been sworn in, so no one had any full-term claim to the seat. Of course, Ray, having the most to lose (other than that which Aubry had already conceded) by having to run for his seat, was pushing for succession. At that point in time, Melanie had certainly been more recognized for her work in the organization, and certainly, would have presented a more forceful leadership heir than Ray. In an election, she would have won hands down. Ray wanted no part of that, so the old-fashioned manipulative NAACP politics went into effect.

First of all, the Executive Committee invoked its power to act in the absence of, and on behalf of the general membership, which limited the participation of the members. In some instances, their actions would be appropriate, but limited to the discussions of the day. The only thing that was even appropriate to decide on was how the branch would operate in the interim of the next general membership meeting.

The issue of the Presidential succession was too crucial to be discussed, in light of the confusion over the swearing-in ceremony. In addition to that issue, the membership was now getting ready to receive a totally different leadership package than that which they had voted. It was certainly within the members right to accept or reject that. Those forty people really didn't know either candidate, and now were acting, not just on emotion, but on an array of self-serving motives. Yet, the committee proceeded to address that question by finishing the hatchet job on Aubry. Since he had apparently abdicated the throne (by declining the re-election nomination) so to speak, many felt he had no claim to it now, and that the branch, in the interim should allow Ray to represent it as President-Elect. Ray would represent the branch at John's funeral, until it was decided what course of action would be pursued. This kept the debate from getting too messy before John's burial. Succession would be addressed at an Executive Committee meeting in two weeks.

The question of process was now at hand. By this time, lines of support had been clearly drawn, and constitutional interpretations had been solicited. There was really only one interpretation that counted, national's. Since this situation was apparently unprecedented, Ray sided with branch lifers John Mance and Henry Dotson, both of whom had influence with the national organization. Both men could manipulate the committee better than most (a relative group of newcomers), with their knowledge of history, procedure and organizational protocol (which is famous in the NAACP). This is where old-timers make up stuff, under the guise that the NAACP doesn't do it this way or that way, which puts newcomers at a disadvantage, because they can't discern fact from fiction. It's usually some verbal recollection of some simple member trying to apply the circumstances to something that happened in 1945. It may be relevant, and it may not, but it's almost never in writing, and almost always unverifiable.

After relating Mance and Dotson's analyses of the situation, national concluded that the swearing in was simply a "formality," and to ease the pain and suffering of the branch, succession should take place based on the newly elected board. It was decision that was rather predictable, given that national didn't ignore the fact that Melanie was waiting in the wings to jump Ray in an election. I'm also sure Melanie knew that if she had to depend on a decision from national to get a shot at an election, she was in trouble. While national really didn't know Ray, they sure as hell knew Melanie. All objectivity went out of the window from there.

Still, national's opinion was “just” a recommendation, and it presented an interesting dilemma for the L.A. branch. Historically, predating to Celes King's administration in the mid-60s, the Los Angeles branch had been perceived as rebellious and out of step with the national charge. Many of the constraints put on the branches proved to be an additional burden on us. Geography, greater racial tensions by West Coast conservatives (often disguised as liberals, no less) and, a greater fundraising capacity kept the Los Angeles branch and the national organization in constant disagreement.

Conversely, Los Angeles was more apt to act contrary to an opinion from national than any other branch in the country. These conflicting philosophies and styles were rekindled under the McDonald administration. Los Angeles hadn't been receptive to national's input in the prior two years. Now it was asking them to mediate its leadership succession process, which in effect would choose its next leader -a real act of blind faith.

Because the timing of this situation was so intermixed with the emotions of John's passing, the branch's Executive Committee was emotionally drained. They just were not up to fighting anybody at this point in time, not national, and certainly not each other (not yet at least). With an impending battle between Melanie and Ray, emotional burnout soon followed. There were those who felt that Ray deserved a chance to serve, and that while John couldn't have anticipated a tragedy such as this, he thought enough of Ray to at least position him as his successor. Whether he could win an election would be incumbent upon him.

These sentiments worked for Ray and against Melanie. Even John's bereaved fiancee, Irma, who really liked (and even preferred) Melanie, wanted to see this situation resolved, as quickly as possible. A new election would prohibit this from happening. Melanie effectively lost her first opportunity to be Branch President, due to untimely circumstances. Her second loss a year later would be a pure power play--with concurrence from her organizational adversary, the national office. The most unlikely successor had become the President, and the waiting game for Melanie had begun. Only Ray's insecurity coupled with Melanie's ambivalence toward the resolution of the situation would curtail both the unique mix of the "pups," and any continued collaboration of the McDonald dynasty. But for this last moment, branch solidarity, in a final tribute to John, would be shown in a rather magnanimous manner -- a unanimous affirmation of Ray's ascendancy to the branch presidency.

Although there was no way to know it then, a golden chance had passed for many of us. The impetus for sustaining a second chance to redeem a fading legacy had now died. Still, not knowing what would happen, many of us would try to keep the renewed effort alive, if in nothing more than to keep the spirit of John alive. We knew that, even if just for a short time, we had won, as none thought we could. And it was all due to a brother named John.

* * *

The pomp and circumstance that surrounded the branch installations, in January 1985, was in no way indicative of the disarray that would follow. The installation was held at West Angeles Church of God in Christ, and was witnessed by almost 500 people -- the most to attend an NAACP meeting in years. Mayor Tom Bradley made some comments. It was the last time he would set foot in a branch meeting for the next two and a half years. The late Gil Lindsey, then City Council-man of the "great Ninth District," had the audience rolling with laughter with his unique swearing-in ad-lib. All in all, it was a solemn, but lighthearted tribute to the commitment to continue what John had started.

However, after it was over; confusion reigned. Ray proved to be every bit as indecisive as some had predicted. That's being nice. Many others perceived him as being weak. Several members who headed committees were ready to get back to work, only to find out that Ray hadn't appointed any committee chairs. This, in spite of the fact, that many expressed willingness to continue serving, as they had in the prior administration.

Ray hardly knew any of them, and they hardly knew him. Ray was trying to evoke a commitment to himself, and from people who were extremely loyal to John, or who were organization loyalists (lifers who were supposedly committed to the ideas of the NAACP). This was something that would haunt Ray during his entire presidency. While most acknowledged, and even admitted that a President needed to surround himself with his own players, some of the extremes that Ray went to, to try to secure loyalties were not earning him any brownie points with many of the members. The litmus test of where you stood with Ray was how you felt about Melanie Lomax, who in the first month, was rolling in her position as First Vice President. That only fed Ray's paranoia.

While many of us tried to separate ourselves from this question, it was obvious that the lines were being clearly drawn. Melanie had her supporters, and Ray intended to make sure that as few of them, as possible, would end up on the Executive Committee. So, many committee persons either resigned, or were held in abeyance, until Ray could decipher their loyalties, or at least, observe how they interacted with Melanie. That made things wild and woolly.

At times you thought there were two Presidents. Melanie organized a "Say No to Drugs" march with the Los Angeles Unified School District, on the steps of City Hall. She was clearly in charge. It was extremely funny watching Ray compete with her, in his attempts to show the public that he was the new President. He had little stage presence in comparison to Melanie. She simply outshined him.

Juxtaposed against Melanie's aggressive advocacy style, and subsequently, John's past achievements, Ray's identity was taking a "hell of a licking." If that wasn't enough, the branch then discovered that it was $80,000 in debt from unexplained expenses. Of course, the past President was not there to defend himself, or render any explanation. There were some receipts, here and there, from events that had lost money, and some bills that had been incurred over the preceding year. It was nothing that appeared out of the extreme ordinary. The only real impropriety was that the Executive Committee hadn't approved any of the expenses, which appeared to be the norm back then. While the committee appeared to be distressed by this revelation, they didn't appear ready to lay the responsibility on anyone, even though, malfeasance by all the officers was obvious.

They just kind of hushed the issue, closed ranks and bit the bullet. The prevailing attitude was "This is what John had to do to get this dinosaur up off the ground," which probably contributed to the stress he was under that eventually killed him. (In fact, as a past President, I suspect it was). But clearly the process had been circumvented, and the pieces were now in Ray's lap.

The branch held a retreat at the offices of accounting firm, Coopers and Lybrand, thanks to a man named Colin Mitchell, then a partner and also a branch Executive Committee member). The retreat sought to address the branch's immediate, mid-range and long-term goals and objectives. Again, the absence of leadership was evident. Many of the proposals (including mine) that addressed the financial shortfall fell on deaf ears. Everybody concurred with what needed to be done, but very few concurred as to who would do the work. Many saw the branch's plans conflicting with other events, which would make it difficult for the branch to fund raise.

The major obstacle was the Spingarn dinner, which national was to hold later in the month. This would make it virtually impossible to have a Roy Wilkins fundraising dinner for the rest of the year. But the branch saw fit to try because of its enormous debt. A proposal would be presented at the upcoming Executive Committee meeting by a sister named Carolyn Webb-DeMacias, then a senior executive with Pacific Bell. She was unequivocally, the sharpest, most culturally conscientious corporate person I met during my entire tenure with the Los

Angeles NAACP. I felt if anybody could pull this off, Carolyn could.

Another issue that needed to be addressed was the Fourth Vice President vacancy, which was created when everybody moved up during the succession. While seeking the position was something that I had momentarily considered, I had responsibilities with a couple of other organizations, which required some significant time commitments. I had my job at the Founders Savings, which was increasing in scope, and two very young daughters, whom that I was crazy about, who were growing by the day. While I had an interest in helping people that had been nurtured during my short involvement with John's administration, I couldn't see where I'd find the time, and didn't give it another thought until the night of the Spingarn dinner.

Mayor Tom Bradley was being honored with the 69th Spingarn Medal, the organization's highest award. During the cocktail hour, I saw Irma Brown with an Executive Committee member Ellen Deshazer and branch office manager Joanne Robertson on their way to their table. I hadn't seen Irma for a couple of weeks. She looked good, rested, relieved and detraumatized from the events of the past couple of months. We carried on small-talk for a moment, then the conversation turned to the branch. I brought up the V.P. vacancy. My opinion was that since she literally lost the most that caused the void, I thought her input would be invaluable in filling the void. I told her I had heard some names being mentioned to fill the Fourth Vice President slot. I asked her if she had anybody in mind. Irma looked at me with her characteristically incredible stare -- one that pierced steel and usually meant business -- and said, "Do you?"

I was a little taken by her response and replied, "No, I don't."

She then looked at me, with what I perceived as a look of reflection of all the conversations that she, John and I had about my involvement. She said, "Well, you should know somebody that could fill the gap." Then, she and her entourage vanished, leaving me to contemplate the conversation.

While sitting at my employer's table, my mind kept drifting back to one of the last conversations I had with John. He, Irma and I were standing in the hallway of the branch waiting for Bill Penn, the national director of branches, to arrive for an emergency Executive Committee meeting. John mentioned earlier in the year that he had heard that I was interested in the executive director position, which the branch was seeking to fill. He wondered why I never applied for the position. I told him that I did, but never heard anything. John looked surprised, saying he never saw the application. He asked to whom did I give it. I told him I gave it to Charles Jackson, the branch treasurer. I had left my previous employer in June of that year, and happened to see the search announcement. I mentioned to Irma, after church one day, that I had seen it, and she encouraged me to forward a resume. After dropping one off at the branch, and not hearing a response, I concentrated on three other offers I had, eventually accepting a Vice President's position at a Black-owned S & L, over two larger, more secure ones that offered similar positions. This would be the biggest mistake of my life as I will discuss later. Still, at the time, I was excited about working for a Black institution, and in the community. I just presumed that I didn't get the NAACP position, and John assumed that I never applied.

It wasn't until our conversation that we both realized that Charles never gave John the resume. John called Charles over and asked him, "Did Anthony give you his resume to give to me a few months back?" Charles looked at me and Irma like, "What's up?" and acknowledged that I had. John just shook his head, told Charles thanks and excused him. John then let me know that the position was only being filled temporarily by Donald Fields until a more suitable candidate could be found. He asked me would I still be interested. I told him that I was committed at that time to turning Founders around. He said, "Well, my acquisition of Family Savings is almost complete. I'm gonna need help turning it around, too. That may make it a little easier for you to come over here (to the branch)."

I told him, "I may be open to that. Let's talk when the time comes. Anything's possible."

However, less than two weeks later, John was gone.

Irma knew that John wanted me involved in a significant way, and I knew that. It was always a matter of how I would be involved. If I was going to become involved in a major way, now was the time. Joanne came back over to the table later that night and asked me point blank, "Some people want to know if you want the spot?" She never mentioned "people" by name, but she knew that I knew who wanted to know. I told her that I thought I wanted the spot. She looked at me in mocked astonishment and said, "You think you want it? You either want it or you don't?"

"OK," I said, "I want it!"

Joanne smiled at me and said, "That's better. We'll be in touch."

The wheels were now in motion. When the next Executive Committee meeting was held, my candidacy for Fourth Vice President was very subdued. Irma and Joanne had contacted a few key people on the committee, and I had talked to a few others. That was the extent of my campaigning.

In the meantime, the branch leadership was totally out of step with what was about to happen. Both Ray and Melanie had somehow reached a consensus on their candidate for Fourth Vice President: an attorney named Joseph Massengale. This was probably the only thing they would agree on during the rest of their joint involvement. Ray nominated Joseph, and Melanie seconded the nomination. Both gave a little speech on what a great guy Massengale was. When Colin Mitchell nominated me, neither appeared particularly surprised or worried. However, when the votes were announced, both were very surprised. It wasn't even close. I was now the new Fourth Vice President.

At the end of the meeting, neither Ray nor Melanie said anything (even though Melanie later commended me on pulling off "a coup" as she put it). As members came by to congratulate me, I saw Irma heading for the door. She looked back, made eye contact with me and winked. I lipped, "Thank you" to her. She nodded, smiled and left. I knew that it was Irma who was most responsible for my selection to that post, even though she never stepped out front or took credit. She just did what she had to do. A world class act, and one final favor to her lost love, John. Because of how I was elected, I was committed to making a significant contribution to the branch for our people, for the organization, and to continue the legacy of John McDonald III.

* * *

It wasn't long before the feuding between Melanie and Ray reached outrageous proportions. Many perceived Ray as a very insecure man, who was dropped into a position for which he wasn't ready. Make no mistake about it. However, when Melanie got her steam up, she could and would roll over even the most confident man. Or, she would try. This part of her personality is what earned and perpetuated her perceived reputation as a "loose cannon." Many people supported Melanie's activities, because she was on point, most of the time. It was the way she went at an issue that upset people. Many times the branch would know nothing about it, until it was in the paper, or on television. The branch Executive Committee perceived this as disrespecting Ray, who was trying to establish his own identity as the new "leader of the branch."

Melanie's dynamic presentation, and the fact that she often chose more substantive issues to deal with, made her visibility more justified. Ray had the position. Melanie had the issues. The public and the press really didn't care who you were. They just wanted to know what you were about, and how were you addressing the problems. Ray was never an "issues man." He shunned substantive issues for ones he thought would bring publicity -- real lightweight stuff. When it was time to act, Ray was indecisive, or altogether invisible. So, Melanie moved and dealt with the issues. As the issues evolved, the press would call Melanie instead of Ray, or whomever was handling the issue.

It gave the impression that there was more than one leader, made you wonder, "Who's the Boss?" How else could it have been handled? It became a bone of contention that only increased Ray's insecurity, and fueled his paranoia beyond belief. He began to outwardly accuse Melanie of trying to sabotage him. I don't believe that was the case. It was just that Melanie didn't have a great deal of respect for Ray, nor would he ever earn it, because of his continuing attacks on her. Having experienced it firsthand two years later, I'm sure Melanie took ideas and updates of her projects to Ray, who either didn't respond, or summarily dismissed them. After doing the work, Melanie just moved on with her program. Later, Ray would profess that he wasn't in concurrence, or that he had no knowledge of her actions. A couple of times it got pretty ugly in Executive Committee meetings. Once Ray outright accused Melanie of trying to embarrass him, when he, in fact, had no intention of cooperating with her by ignoring her calls and conciliatory efforts. With a preponderance of evidence against her (like quotes in the paper), Melanie had no choice but to sit through the committee's admonishments. At the same time, the Executive Committee tried to show its support for Ray by instituting motions like "all statements from the branch will come through the President," etc. Melanie wasn't the type to do all the work, and "bring the catch home to daddy." It was ludicrous to think that one would work an issue, and refer inquiries to Ray, who either wouldn't know or couldn't adequately respond.

Ray had totally convinced himself that Melanie's involvement was disruptive. He began to make plans to eliminate her involvement, and he had to do it before next year's election, where everyone saw Melanie's candidacy as very problematic for Ray, to say the least. Very few knew how Ray was manipulating branch sentiments against Melanie, and exactly how he intended to carry out his plan. I knew, because Ray had confided in me that he was going to need my help in assuming a greater role in the branch's activities. As an enthusiastic new player, I was willing to put in more time to be included "in the loop," not knowing, at that time, that Ray had intended to use me and a few others to dilute Melanie's role in the branch. By delegating the branch's projects to people other than Melanie, Ray thought he could effectively eliminate her from the total scheme of things.

Ray prioritized projects based on the amount of press he thought they would get, not the substantiveness of the issues. Substantive issues required time to research, to develop the facts, to strategize and to plan. When developed properly, the substantive issues could have a greater overall impact on the community, and get five times the press coverage (if press is what one is seeking), as the reactive "quick hit" statement that often came about, as a result of some event of the moment. The reactive "hits" would get some immediate TV coverage, very little print coverage, and rarely any follow-up coverage. Ray would take the "quick hit" stuff, because it kept his face out front, and required little follow-up. This is partially how the NAACP in Los Angeles developed a reputation for taking on "soft issues," a perception consistent with that of the National organization.

Melanie, on the other hand, had been the branch's "real issues" person. There was nothing "soft" about any issue she took, often the most substantive and controversial issues the branch had. When she would get an issue, she would work it magnificently, and to a successful conclusion. The press would follow up on the issue until it was concluded, which may be a dozen different coverage spots (both TV and print).

If Melanie was working two separate issues simultaneously (which is low given the branch's case load at the time), she would be in the media eight to ten times a month. Ray would have had to tackle eight to ten "quick hits," which happened when they happened. You can't predict "quick hits." They often were some publicly discriminating acts that called for a rebuking response. They may hit once a month, twice a month, every other month, etc. So, while Melanie would just work the process, and let the attention come to her in its normal course of "doing the work," Ray was killing himself to find issues to address that didn't require a lot of work. He even forced a few hits, just to get the press.

By forcing a hit, you call attention to an issue that may not have gotten the press attention any other way. Sometimes it had merit, other times it didn't. What it did was to make the press suspicious of how and when to respond to a NAACP press conference. Much of the community began to accuse Ray of publicity seeking. Much like the boy crying "wolf," the community was afraid that if there was ever a real critical issue that needed to be covered, the press wouldn't respond. The running joke in the community was, "we saw Ray on TV again today being 'outraged and appalled.' Are you guys going to do something about it?" That was because Ray would almost always start every press conference with "The NAACP is outraged and appalled..." with whatever the issue was. This would dog Ray during his entire tenure because his "issues people" (Melanie and later myself) always had a greater media presence, because of the substance of the issues we addressed. Also, we were willing to put in the time to do the work.

In order for Ray to stifle Melanie's public presence, he stopped giving her issues to address. He shifted her workload to me, not necessarily because of any great ability I possessed (I was still an unknown factor with respect to civil rights work), but because, as far as, his Vice Presidents were concerned, Ray had very few options.

His Second Vice President, a gentleman named Mr. Richard Jones, was 80 years old, and was there basically, because Second Baptist Church, the branch's largest church membership put him there. Nobody wanted to alienate Second Baptist. To tackle issues the branch was facing, at that time, may have been a little much for Mr. Jones. The Third Vice President, Skip Cooper, who was also President of the Black Business Association, was hesitant to go out front on NAACP issues, because of potential conflicts with his role in the BBA. He was mainly a strategist for the NAACP, due to his great community awareness. Ray could have gone outside of his Vice President's realm (which he did every now and then) to address issues. However, such a move would potentially create a bigger problem for the branch and himself. The public (particularly the press) often called on branch leadership to facilitate local issues. If the officers were unaware of the issues, then it caused credibility problems (which the branch suffered from anyway). Some of the other more experienced Executive Committee members, who could handle issues management for the branch, were perceived as potential opposition. Ray wasn't going to do anything to increase their visibility.

My selection was, at this point, the only sensible option. I was well spoken and had the younger image the branch wanted to continue to portray. I wasn't perceived as a threat to Ray, and wasn't particularly interested in his politics with Melanie. He didn't perceive me as particularly loyal to Melanie, or disloyal to him. This was an accurate assessment because I really didn't know either of them that well. I was as bewildered as the rest of the Executive Committee, when it came to the Ray-Melanie thing. Nevertheless, I did want a greater role in the more substantive branch issues. Ambition was never my short suit, and Ray played to that need. Even if it was to be at Melanie's expense, which I would soon find out.

It was a subtle move over a few months. Under the guise of greater officer accountability, Ray asked me to be more accountable, and allowed Melanie to be less accountable by simple omission. I began attending more meetings on behalf of the association, making more reports to the Executive Committee, and taking a greater overall role in branch affairs. It wasn't long before Ray would put me in the middle of his and Melanie's conflict.

In the Los Angeles branch, the President chairs the meeting. Ray wasn't able to attend one particular Executive Committee meeting, early in his administration. In the absence of the President, the First Vice President would chair the meeting. Ray knew this but for this particular meeting, he chose to ignore this rule. After calling me at my office, he requested that I chair the meeting. I reminded him that Melanie was next in line, and he should contact her. He flatly said, "No, Anthony. I want you to chair the meeting. Just do it!" When meeting time came, I called the meeting to order and called for additions to the agenda. Melanie was in her usual seat in the first row, farthest to the left (as opposed to sitting at the head table to the right of the President).

Melanie quickly recognized something was up and asked, "Where is Ray?"

I told her, "He will be late, and might not show tonight."

She appeared to be disgusted that Ray would do something like this, but calmly said, "Well, I'm the First Vice President, shouldn't I be chairing this meeting?"

I told her, "As far as I know you are," and yielded the gavel. Most of the Executive Committee and I realized that Ray and Melanie were no longer communicating, and were not even pretending to be amicable toward each other.

The degree of Ray's animosity toward Melanie finally surfaced at the branch's 1985 Roy Wilkins dinner. The program was over, and Ray had a couple of drinks under his belt. He began to talk about where he wanted to take the branch. Then out of the clear blue sky he said, "Anthony, I want you to be the next President of the branch. I'm gonna make sure that you are. Melanie will never be President. Over my dead body. She won't."

I found it very peculiar that Ray would say this to me. It was like dangling a carrot in front of a rabbit and waiting for him to jump. I often wondered if Ray was "bad" enough to say what he was saying to me to Melanie. I doubted it. But from that night on, I knew Ray was going to try to eliminate Melanie from the branch's political scene because he was not able to shoulder her critical eye during his very vulnerable term as President. For as long as she was there, she presented the branch with an alternative in the event Ray stumbled. If she wasn't there, then he had some margin for error and could still maintain the confidence of the Executive Committee and, to a larger degree, the community.

Ray began to challenge Melanie's speaking on the branch's behalf. The Executive Committee, under Ray's prodding, issued a warning to Melanie that Ray would be the only spokesperson for the branch. Ray had not given her any new assignments, so Melanie (who was Chair of the branch's Fair Share committee) began to develop her committee activities. Given her ability to get to the source of the problem, Melanie began to tap issues that were highly sensitive and meritorious of media coverage. Since Melanie was doing the work, she had to respond to the inquiries from the press. That was just a necessary evil that the Executive Committee would have to accept.

In July 1985, an article appeared on the front page of the *Los Angeles Times* criticizing the record industry for excluding Blacks from their organizations. This article was not responding to any independent discovery by the press, but appeared to be initiated by Melanie under the guise of being the Southern California coordinator of the National NAACP's Fair Share program. In this way, she didn't have to receive branch approval to address the press. She did, however, have to get national approval from the national director of economic development, under whose auspices the Fair Share program was initiated.

The NAACP was preparing a two-year investigation of the record industry's hiring practices of Black professionals. The objective was to negotiate Fair Share agreements with the seven major record companies: Capitol Records, EMI, Inc., CBS Records, RCA Records,

MCA Records, Inc., Warner Brothers Records, Inc., and Polygram Records, Inc. With National NAACP Economic Development Director, Fred Rasheed heading the effort, a campaign task force was assembled (including Melanie) to gather data to be used in the negotiations. Melanie was a key component, because she was closest to Hollywood, where much of the negligence was occurring. She had an abundance of information, including data that stated Blacks buy more records than any other race of people, but receive the lowest return of participation in the industry. Ironically, the biggest stars in the industry, at that time, were some of the biggest excluders of Blacks from their respective companies.

However, what set off a major internal stir was that Melanie accused only Black artists of committing this offense. That made it look like Blacks were discriminating against Blacks, instead of the larger issue, that the industry discriminated against Blacks. Furthermore, based on the information that she had amassed from the negotiations, Melanie went on to name five artists she felt were most guilty of excluding Blacks. Tina Turner, Michael Jackson, Lionel Richie, Diana Ross and Prince -- were the artists she identified, largely because of their perceived independence to control their own organizations. The article reflected the need to hire more Blacks in the industry, and asked why these five Black entertainers didn't have more Blacks in their respective organizations. It was perceived as promoting a "Blacks against Blacks" theme.

The national organization was livid. Fred Rasheed had not approved the statement, and did not concur with its context. His position was: Why make five Black artists the focus of an industry wide problem? Black artists represent less than 20 percent of the total industry. What about the other 80 percent of the non-Black artists who exclude Blacks? Blacks, by the way, also buy some of their records because many go through great lengths to sound Black and appeal to the lucrative "Black" market. Cross-over in reverse, if you look at it that way.

It was the opinion of the National NAACP that Melanie was premature in releasing this information, and *The Los Angeles Times* article didn't reflect the true intent of the overall campaign. Melanie Lomax had jumped ahead of national on a campaign they had intended to wage later in the year. By pre-empting the announcement, she had put the industry "on notice" about the details of the investigation. She had now alienated many of the industry insiders that the organization had intended to use as "allies" to facilitate progress, including the five artists named in the article. National Executive Director, Ben Hooks was out on the first thing smokin' to hold follow-up interviews, in an effort to "clear the air" on Melanie's statements. Ray was in seventh heaven. He confided to several of us that Hooks was coming out to "bury the hatchet in the middle of Melanie's forehead," as he termed it.

Hooks did censor Melanie from talking to the press on any national project. Ray now saw this as an opportunity to follow suit at the branch level. But even more importantly to him, he had a reason to remove Melanie from a highly visible position as the branch's Fair Share negotiator. The Los Angeles branch was one of the few in the country allowed to pursue Fair Share agreements, because of its past success with them. Melanie had been in that position since the Coors agreement was signed. She had continued to represent the branch on most of national's investigations and future efforts, particularly if they had a West Coast presence. She also sat on existing Fair Share monitoring committees to evaluate the participating company's progress. She had the ability to provide public "updates" on Fair Share issues, which is outside the parameters of so-called "branch issues." While Ray could limit branch members from interfacing with the press on local issues, there was little he could do on press statements on national issues. But now that Melanie had been silenced on the national level, she was more vulnerable to the politics of the Los Angeles branch and its President.

In light of Ben Hooks' actions toward Melanie, Ray lost no time in getting the branch's Executive Committee to implement a "gag order," complementing the one national had imposed. While this should have been the extent of Melanie's so- called "punishment" for her statements, Ray used this event to totally strip Melanie of her involvement in the branch. The last bit of Melanie's branch activity was centered on her appointment as Fair Share negotiator. Ray knew that if he removed Melanie at this point, her recourses were few. On the heels of her recent censoring by both the branch and the national office, Melanie would be effectively silenced in the NAACP. Ray used this situation to finally rid himself of the one thing that intimidated him most, Melanie Lomax.

Ray called an officers meeting to get some support on his decision. Melanie took it as a declaration of war and wrote everybody and their mother. Literally! She wrote the mayor's office, the national office, the Executive Committee and selected branch members. Melanie talked to everybody she thought could influence the process and reverse Ray's decision. The letters that were flying scared the hell out of Ray, especially the ones to the mayor. Ray, most times, seen by myself and others as the proverbial "ass-kisser," didn't want his triviality to reach the mayor. Yet the damage had been done. Ray couldn't afford to relent now. All credibility with Melanie had been destroyed and, moreover, any trust that existed between them was now gone.

There were many of us who were sensitive to Melanie's plight. I called Melanie over to the bank to discuss her embattlement with Ray. She was trying to size me up, and determine if I was sincere in my inquiry, or if I was pumping her for information. I assured her that I supported her involvement, and didn't agree with Ray's actions against her. We talked approximately one hour about what was happening. While I knew what Ray's intent was, I told Melanie to hang in there, and that she had the support of the branch, though not on the Executive Committee. I suggested that she just lay low until the next election in December 1986. Melanie's position was that she wasn't going to be Ray's doormat, and be "shit on" for the next year and a half.

Melanie was poised to fight and had no inclination that Ray had done all he could do. Now it was incumbent upon her to show the branch that she was a team player, and develop her own strategy to deal with Ray. I emphasized that no one would be particularly intimidated by her verbal counterattack against Ray. He already had everyone thinking that he was just defending his presidency. To continue to attack it would be misperceived by most. This ended up being the case.

As Ray appointed another local attorney named George Mallory to replace Melanie as the branch's Fair Share negotiator, there was barely a whimper about her displacement. The only objection voiced was Mr. Richard Jones, who everybody wrote off as a crazy old man. He was the only one to vocally come to Melanie's aid. Some of us, including myself, voiced disapproval of Ray's decision in the meeting, but everyone remained silent while Ray dismissed Melanie's impassioned plea for reconsideration.

From that day, while Melanie never formally resigned her position, she was never directly involved in the branch again. Instead, she limited her involvement to giving an annual scholarship in the name of John McDonald, to the branch's women's auxiliary. Mr. Jones called everyone in the meeting "chickenshit," and vowed that if we let Melanie walk, he'd walk too. This would also be his last NAACP meeting. Many saw Ray's actions against Melanie as harsh, but just as many saw it as justified, or as what the late Roy Wilkins called the risks of leadership: fifty percent will be with you, and fifty percent will be against you, on any one issue. A leader has to make a decision and live with it, regardless of the outcome. Melanie did bring some baggage that was hard to defend, and while the personal feud ran much deeper, Ray made a decision he was prepared to live with. It was a decision based on split sentiments, for which he knew he had some support. When people are looking for a reason to oust you, it doesn't take much to create support for it. Melanie's ouster was cold, calculated and really unnecessary, as is the case with most issues of conflict amongst Blacks. The compromise of Melanie was the compromise of all of us in the branch's leadership. Once the first compromise goes unbridled, other forms of compromise will follow, as I would find out three years later.

* * *

With Melanie out of the way, Ray began to rely more on my involvement. My responsibility would be to develop and implement a budgetary process and a spending policy for the Executive Committee. It was a process that allowed the Executive Committee to plan its expenditures, and to authorize and track spending on a regular basis. These procedures were basically derived to prevent a re-occurrence of what was discovered after John's death. However, after the processes were in place, the branch still had problems with unauthorized expenditures.

The budgetary process was always circumvented under the guise of "an emergency," or some other urgent insistence that required an inappropriate departure from the approval process. While the Executive Committee would be aware of the expenditures, most would be approved after the fact. There would, from time to time, be a selective application of this policy, whenever the committee slept an inexplicable expense. And there were many. The process would have to be refined, when it was discovered that expenditures were being hidden in the budgetary line items. An explanation of each expense had to be given by check number. Still that didn't prevent the spending manipulation. It just gave the illusion of accountability, which suited Ray's purpose.

My first assignment on branch issues dealt with replacing Melanie on the Southern California Gas Company's Minority

Advisory Panel. Even before Melanie had left the branch, the Gas Company had become totally exasperated with her combative style. Eventually, they requested that she not be allowed to continue participating on the panel. While the panel represented a cross-section of ethnicities and community interests, there were several critical issues that weren't being addressed. I stepped in right away, and brought those issues to the forefront in a manner that was confrontational, but not adversarial or divisive. I was very well-received and invited to participate on several other public utility panels and advisory committees. Most of those advisory committees are stacked with people who are perceived as having a community presence. But many of them lack the business acumen to raise substantive questions that would bring about changes in the company's policies, particularly with respect to minority involvement. Most of these panels are used as sounding boards for companies to find out what the community is thinking, rather than forums for company change. I developed a "knack" for moving past this process and forcing discussions for promoting change.

The first real issue that I had the ability to influence came in September 1985. Minister Louis Farrakhan had announced an appearance in Los Angeles. It was the first major appearance in the city, since the alleged anti-Semitic statements attributed to Minister Farrakhan regarding the existence of Israel, and the Jewish community's allegation that he called their religion "dirty." Minister Farrakhan had traveled the country to bring clarity to the actual comment, and to announce a self-determination program sponsored by the Nation of Islam entitled "Power."

The Jewish community in Los Angeles, whose population in this city is second in number only to the Jewish population in New York, was infuriated with his appearance, largely because of where he was appearing. The Los Angeles mosque had managed to secure the city's largest indoor venue, then called "the fabulous Forum," in Inglewood, California. The idea of Minister Farrakhan speaking to 19,000 people sent the Jewish community into a state of hysteria. It was well known that Jewish money elected Tom Bradley as mayor, and that there was a heavy Jewish influence in the Black community via Black organizations, including the NAACP.

Ray had painstakingly cultivated a relationship in the Jewish community by serving on joint commissions and other co-sponsored projects. The question always existed as to how equitable was the Black community's relationship with the Jewish community. The

Black community was always the vehicle by which Jewish economic exploitation had been allowed to persist. The extent of Jewish commitment had been their support of a Black mayor, and token contributions to Black civil rights organizations, as well as the commonality of our experiences in dealing with racially oppressive regimes.

The Jewish community apparently felt that this support was sufficient enough to justify dictatorship over the Los Angeles Black community. Jewish leaders approached every Black civic and community leader, and issued a demanding ultimatum: "Repudiate Farrakhan, or else." The brash, bold manner in which the Jewish community confronted Black leaders exposed how vulnerable our community was (and still is) to Jewish manipulation. The community response to the Farrakhan appearance was so positive that Black leaders were forced to respect the wishes of the people, and acknowledge Farrakhan's right to be heard. This wasn't the position the Jews expected, so they intensified their efforts by focusing on the civil rights organizations. The Brotherhood Crusade's President, Danny Bakewell, and then-executive director of the SCLC-West, Mark Ridley-Thomas, immediately refuted the demand. Ridley-Thomas, who was no Farrakhan supporter, didn't take to being given an ultimatum without the benefit of discussion. Bakewell, who was a supporter of Farrakhan, argued the right to listen to whom he wanted, and reserved the right to agree with some opinions of Minister Farrakhan and disagree with others. The Los Angeles NAACP and Urban League made no public position known, but both were rumored as siding with the Jewish community on a repudiation statement.

Inside the branch, the issue was hotly debated. When a group of us brought the hearsay to Ray's attention, he admitted that he was undecided on what to do. However, a few of us had gotten firsthand knowledge of a meeting between the civil rights leadership. Ray was, in fact, very close to signing a repudiation statement. When asked what I thought, I told him that I felt it would be a big mistake to go against our community and repudiate Minister Farrakhan. Being a longtime supporter of the Nation of Islam and the work of The Honorable Elijah Muhammad, I told Ray that I had no intention of being a part of a repudiation of Farrakhan. The position of several members was that we'd repudiate the branch for misrepresenting the interests of its members, before we'd repudiate the minister and violate his first amendment civil rights.

In the meantime, the Jewish lobby kicked up the ante. About

a week before the event, they called for Mayor Tom Bradley to repudiate Minister Farrakhan before he spoke, in order to dissuade the public's growing interest in Farrakhan's appearance. Bradley, also a candidate for governor in 1986, knew that Jewish support was key to financing his candidacy. This wasn't an issue he could avoid. The Jewish community shrewdly put Bradley in the middle of a Black-Jewish head-on collision.

For six days straight, the Farrakhan issue was front page news in the *L.A. Times*, known to have a very heavy Jewish influence. Bradley's staff was lobbying very heavily for a repudiation based upon *The Times'* very biased reporting of alleged public sentiment. Of course, that sentiment didn't include very many Blacks.

Kerman Maddox, one of the mayor's community aides, convinced Bradley to at least solicit the opinion of the Black leadership before making a decision. Bradley summoned the civil rights leaders and a few Black clergy. It wasn't until then, that Bradley really understood two things: the community's hostility toward the Jewish demands, and the depth of the grassroots support for Louis Farrakhan, both of which his staff greatly underestimated. It was unconscionable to think that a Black man could fill the Forum -just speaking. Jesse Jackson, in the midst of a Presidential election a year prior, didn't fill the Shrine Auditorium in Los Angeles, which holds less than 4,000.

The Jewish community finally let out all stops. They threatened Jerry Buss with the loss of advertising, if he didn't find a way out of this event. The best Buss could do was to assure that no future events of this type would be held. Since that time, Buss changed the Forum lease policy to restrict the Forum's use to sporting and entertainment events, until he sold the venue to a church, in late 2000. Then, they approached every Black business and civic leader to ascertain their position on Farrakhan. Farrakhan became the litmus test for any future individual or collective Black-Jewish relationship, business or otherwise.

The so-called middle class or "successful" Blacks were running scared, playing the part of chameleon by trying to support Farrakhan, without being seen by Jewish influences that would affect their jobs and livelihoods. Friends for the Benefit of Economic Unity, a co-sponsoring organization of the event, had a dinner on the evening before the event. Bourgeoisie Blacks in Los Angeles, who never met a dinner they didn't like, went totally undercover for this event.

I facilitated the purchase of a table for my employer, at the time. The protocol was that I invite bank management, bank employees, and then use the tickets for business development. In a town where a free ticket is sniffed out quicker than you can say "free," there were no takers for this event. Management was conveniently unavailable, all twenty or so senior management. One employee agreed to go. I ended up with five vacant seats at the table.

Over 300 people attended the dinner. Some celebrities and elected officials attended. However, everybody was real low key, ducking cameras and avoiding the press.

On the day before the event, Bradley had decided to withhold judgment of Minister Farrakhan, until after the event. The branch, of course, was now the central focus of the Jewish lobby, because Ray had maintained his neutrality, up to that point. That afternoon, while watching on the branch office TV, the Jewish influence of the media just took over, by reverting to a misinformation campaign (like ones often used by the government), in which the facts are manipulated and the public misinformed. Several stations were announcing that the Farrakhan event was canceled, although it was not the case. While the branch officers and a few key Executive Committee members gathered in the branch office, Ray polled us by asking what should he do on the Farrakhan issue. Since no one else had spoken up to this point, I thought I'd have to fight to come out with a favorable position on this one. To Ray's and my surprise, those present overwhelmingly supported that the branch remain silent on the Farrakhan issue.

That didn't present much of a conflict for Ray, since the mayor was doing the same. Basically, the branch backed into a position, and though contingent on some very shaky influences, it worked in favor of the branch, the community and the upholding of a speaker's first amendment rights. If nothing else, it was perceived as Blacks having redefined their relationship with the Jewish community in Los Angeles. More importantly, how they interface with us on issues in our community.

The Farrakhan appearance was one of the most impressive demonstrations of Black unity in Los Angeles history, since the '60s. In spite of the Jewish Defense League's President Irv Rubin's threat of violence if Farrakhan spoke, 19,000 plus people stood in line for two hours or more without incident, to witness the most powerful Black man in America, then and now. Any man that could get Blacks to come in great numbers under duress and threat of danger, is truly God-inspired. No other Black politician, theologian, or civil rights leader could achieve such a task. And this was ten full years before the history-making (two) "Million Man March." Minister Farrakhan's support base was evident then, and ran deeper than whites (and most negroes) could ever imagine.

Bradley succumbed to the pressure, and repudiated Farrakhan the day after the event, claiming that although he had only heard excerpts from the speech, he felt that Farrakhan's statement could be interpreted as anti-Semitic. Apparently, Bradley heard something that 19,000 people hadn't. The Jewish community admonished Bradley for doing what they called "too little, too late." Anything short of a cancellation would have been "too little," and anything short of a pre-judged condemnation before that event would have been "too late." Like a child being punished for ignoring his parents, Bradley would suffer greatly during his second gubernatorial run. He may have lost the respect of many Jews, but for a moment, at least until the repudiation, Bradley had captured the admiration of the masses of his people again, something he hadn't witnessed since earlier campaigns.

In April 1986, four Korean merchants were killed in South Central Los Angeles. The killings centered around the abusive treatment of Black consumers who patronized Korean businesses. This would be the first issue that I would go out front on for the branch. Ray didn't see the need for any real involvement in the issue. Basically, the press was looking for a response to what appeared to be racially motivated killings.

Any time something happens in the Black community, and the press is looking for the "Black point of view," they call the NAACP. Half the time, the issues aren't even relevant to civil rights. Ray said, "How the hell are we supposed to know why Koreans are being killed?" That's when he assigned me to deal with it.

My research indicated that the conflicts between Blacks and Koreans had become more frequent and confrontational. Many in the community were absolutely outraged about their treatment by Korean merchants. This was the first wave of Koreans who had come into the country and established a significant presence in the Black communities. There was a great degree of hostility and cultural ignorance demonstrated by both races. Blacks complained about the way Koreans merchants "threw" their merchandise at them, without any kind of appreciation for their patronage. Not even a "Thank You," or a "Please come again." Koreans merchants said Blacks were rude, abusive and inconsiderate of Koreans' goods, mishandling them, until they were not fit to be purchased. Before long, the continuous bantering had reached a boiling point. Adversarial attitudes bred confrontational disputes. The killings were the results of those disputes.

Since there was no evidence to prove such allegations, the position of the organization, as well as, the Police Department, was that the killings were not racially motivated. This was to defuse tensions between the two communities. It was a manipulation of the people's perception. That's how our communities are handled. The message is: "You really didn't see what you just saw, and it's not for the reason you may think you saw it." Denial of fact and denial of truth run rampant in the Black community. Yet, denial is the singular most obvious sign to recognizing there might be a problem.

Even though I was charged with representing an opinion for the branch, it was obvious that the problem was much deeper than was being acknowledged. I was inundated with calls from our community after they saw me on television, stating some of the problems between Blacks and Koreans.

Blacks were harboring some extremely deep-rooted resentments toward Koreans. Unlike the Jews and Arabs before them, Koreans merchants were a lot less sensitive to the eccentricities of Black culture. Coming from a depressed and oppressive situation in Korea, most Koreans were uneducated about Blacks. Their only insights about Blacks was through television, in many instances. As extreme as it sounds, many Koreans' perceptions of Blacks, some thought, were 35 years old. Many came from stereotypes created out of disdain for Black men's engagement in the Korean War. The more I researched historical interfaces of Blacks and Koreans, the more I recognized an attitude among many Korean merchants that lacked an understanding of certain American protocols, period. Particularly, that of American enterprise was overlooked. Practices like, "The customer comes first" and "A happy customer is a faithful customer," were nonexistent, as far as, they were concerned.

Blacks in the city of Los Angeles, who have long been the victims of outsiders doing business in their community and historical (and well documented) victims of economic discrimination and redlining from financial institutions, were frustrated with the turnover of yet another economic immigration passing through their community. Their frustration was exacerbated by the apparent lack of appreciation by Korean merchants of the patronage and loyalty that Blacks consumers traditionally give to local business. Some Black consumers were beginning to feel helpless about how Korean merchants were treating them.

Several community and business interests began meeting on the issue, before any more deadly encounters occurred. I was asked to come in as the NAACP representative. After two weeks of discussion, it was decided that a yearlong selective buying campaign would be implemented to raise the level of consumer consciousness of the Black community. When businesses didn't respect the Black consumer dollars, money wouldn't be spent with that business. The campaign would also examine how the community could build greater consumer loyalty for Black businesses. We agreed that there would not be a picket against Korean businesses, just a promotion of Black businesses. I was elected chair of the group. The name chosen for the group, by former SCLC executive director, Marnesba Tackett, was the "Buy Liberty" campaign. It became an immediate hit with the community, and was now the focus of a proactive movement to get Blacks to support its community-based economy. The campaign was ultimately supported by almost 200 businesses and community organizations.

Meanwhile, the city's Human Relations Commission developed a Black-Korean task force that would allow for an ongoing dialogue between some Blacks and some Koreans.

The NAACP, from a branch perspective, didn't really involve itself in a strategy to address this conflict, after the initial press conference. Larry Aubry, a member of the NAACP Executive Committee, was involved as a representative from the County Human Relations Commission.

Because of the sensitivity of a selective buying campaign, the NAACP, while lending its name in support of such a strategy, took a position not to be directly involved. Even though I was the branch official originally assigned to respond to the issue, I was chairing the selective buying campaign as an individual. This precluded the branch from having any extended involvement in the conflict, other than in a peripheral capacity. It did allow me to get my feet wet in the advocacy arena. While becoming a pawn in the branch's leadership power struggle, my appetite to openly address the problems of Blacks was nurturing, and grew commensurate with my increased involvement. The more involved I got, the more I saw, and the more disgusted I became over the continued manipulations I saw working against my people's progress. Many of the manipulations were being facilitated by Blackfaces, Black people without a sense of conscious toward the state of their own people. The disappointing thing about it was that it was like nobody saw what was going on, or just outright refused to acknowledge it. The emperor, the body politic of mainstream Black leadership, was butt naked in the streets of Los Angeles, and everybody was complimenting his choice of fashion.

Ray's inflexible work schedule allowed me to represent the branch at more and more meetings. Whereas, before my involvement, Ray would just as soon send no representation, than send Melanie. The branch was now beginning to have consistent involvement in key community meetings. As I began to be exposed to many of the "behind-the-scenes" plots, which unfolded community scenarios and affected the lives of Blacks and other disadvantaged constituencies, I also saw the deal-making and collusion that exploited the Black community, and further entrenched us in a climate of dependency and confusion. It troubled me to see all the "head-turning" and "back-rubbing" going on, particularly by some of the politicians and church leaders that allowed the community's interests to be compromised, while some developer, consultant or corporation was enriched.

When I discussed these meetings with Ray, and disclosed some of my findings, his response was often that "we need to leave that alone," or "there's nothing we can do about that." When I'd inquire about how that can be, he'd state the political realities of the situation, which often meant to close your eyes, ears and mouth if you want to play with "the big boys" in this city. So while the people get screwed, we play a game of "see no evil, hear no evil, speak no evil."

Ray and I would get in long discussions about this. His position was that anything that didn't surface publicly wasn't our concern, so why make waves? My position was that if we knew and didn't address it, we were as guilty as those doing the evil. I was particularly sensitive to this twisted hide-and-seek game that the leadership was playing with the masses.

This was a fundamental difference between Ray and me that brought the intents of our involvements in branch issues to opposite extremes, and caused us to look at almost everything differently. It became well known in the community that Ray and I didn't exactly see things the same. Many times they would consult both of us to get a fix on the branch's involvement on an issue, not because of any pluralistic structure that was in place, but because I often represented a community-based perspective. While they had to show deference to Ray, because he was the President, I was a lot more accessible and responsive to community concerns, and more aggressive in formulating action-oriented resolutions. Even when the elected officials and special interest movers would try to work around me, usually a community-based player or some insider would put me "on notice," where I could approach Ray, and solicit his thinking on a project. This forced Ray to deal with the issue. Boxing in Ray helped flush out the issue. Either he would deal with the issue, or I would, by his failure to deal with it.

While Ray and I were trying to establish a working format suitable to our different ideologies, the dinosaur was slowly dying. Ray, in his lust for control, was becoming more distrustful of those around him. He abruptly, and without notice or an explanation, fired Joanne Robertson, the branch office manager. The Executive Committee said nothing at all about this very inconsiderate action. Ray considered Joanne too loyal to John, and not loyal to him. As a replacement, he hired an ex-school teacher with no clerical skills, little office skills, and no management skills.

A woman named Ernestine Peters was hired, under a veterans employment program, where her VA benefits would pay for half her salary for six months. It would soon become obvious why she was hired. It was perceived my many of the board member as a highly suspect move. Board members, who had just about enough of this petty behavior, started resigning in bunches. Productive, resource rich board members began turning their volunteer interests and resource dollars elsewhere. Carolyn Webb-DeMacias left, and immediately became President of the Martin Luther King Legacy Association, the sister organization to the SCLC-West, whose fundraising efforts went through the roof with her involvement. Colin Mitchell, a partner with Coopers and Lybrand, left to go on the national board of the American Heart Association. Joan Whiteside Green left to become President of the city's chapter of Jack and Jill. Ophelia McFadden left to become a lead official with one of the state's largest labor unions. From a resource perspective, this was a very costly exodus for the branch.

It was obvious that the "civil rights pups" were losing their bite, at least in the second resurrection of the aging dinosaur -- NAACP. Frustrated with the process, the politics, and the personality of its new leader, key players on the L.A. Executive Committee were seeing its effort to regenerate the organization as a waste of time. They effectively stepped out of the NAACP, and finally resigned themselves to what many of us began to see--that the public awareness of the internal bickering and compromised effectiveness, associated with the NAACP, wasn't exactly a privilege. As young professionals, many felt that they had paid their obligation to their ancestors, by trying to continue the legacy of the NAACP. However, it had become clear to many that the NAACP was fighting itself, more than the enemy, and it was doing more damage to itself, than to its enemy. As a new player at the table, it became very apparent that my fight was not only in the streets and board rooms, but in the stagnated attitudes and insecurities of those in the organization.

As I saw highly respected players forced from the table or exasperated until they left, I began to wonder how my own involvement would conclude. Most people I knew had long given up on the NAACP. Only my own naiveté and social commitment would allow me to remain, as others walked away. I was positioned to "test the system." I could either make a lie out of the NAACP, or out of those who had given up on the NAACP.

Refining a dinosaur is more than a notion, but it had to be tried. Not many had the heart to try, but many did, and are still trying. Our victory was not in succeeding, but in trying. There was no other way for me to find that out. In the process, we helped many people. John proved the tool could work with a little adjustment, but for how long? The Los Angeles experience was and is the basis for the NAACP survival test. Many perceived the L.A. NAACP as a dinosaur still out of step with the issues of the day. Many of us were mocked for even making an effort to try to fix it. We did try. The sincerity of many of the pups John left behind, to ride the dinosaur without him, proved to be acts of futility.

* * *

3

SLURPEE SLAVES

"It is a fool whose own tomatoes are sold to him."
- Akan Proverb

The prospect of economic reciprocity was supposed to be the reward for three decades of social equality engagement, where Blacks finally "pulled even" with whites to own businesses, even franchises in their attainment of the "American dream." But along the track of attaining the dream, came many pitfalls. One such pitfall was an exercise called the American "convenience" store. The irony of this concept is there is little "convenient" about it. It represented the advent of the "middle class" America "sweat shop."

One franchise, in particular, represented this. The next time you hear, "Oh thank heaven for 7-11!" think of other enslaving clichés like "Wait until you die to get your reward in the By n' By," "I'll get mine when I get to heaven" or "I like, pickin' cotton, cause pickin' cotton's all right with me."

Imagine working all your life to save $40,000 to $50,000, or being an immigrant, and bringing your life savings to the U.S. to start a business. Then imagine a partner telling you that, for $50,000, he can put you in a store and set up your business, but you can never own it; just lease it from your partner, over a period of time. If you fail to run it as agreed, he can take the store back, at any time. At the end of the lease period, no matter how successful you have made the store, "your partner" has the only option of renewing your lease, and continuing your business arrangement. Oh, and by the way, your partner will show you how to run the store, but they will never work in the store. Every month you will pay the partner 52 percent of the gross receipts from the store. He will pay the rent and the lights, which amounts to 15 percent of the expenses, you pay the other 85 percent of the expenses out of your 48 percent of the gross receipts. If you fall short, you have to make up the cash shortage in three days, or your partner can take over the store. Then you have to keep the store open 365 days a year, or you are in violation of your partnership agreement. You cannot pay yourself a decent hourly wage (only a draw), cannot hire any help without approval from your partner and cannot have any other business or employment interest. Can you imagine working two and a half times the hours you work now for somebody else, and receiving a third of the pay? Can you imagine your partner looking over your shoulder the whole time, harassing you while you struggle, and, in many cases, aiding your failure purposely, so he can resell your store at a higher price, after he either took it from you, or gave you what he thought your interest was worth? And it would be less than what you paid for it, after you increased the sales of the store.

You say you can't even imagine someone crazy enough to propose that to somebody, much less for someone to accept it. Well, let me introduce you to what was the wonderful world of slurpees, the all-American convenience store. It's a modern day sharecropping situation for anyone sharing space on 7-11 land. The name of the plantation's owner was called the Southland Corporation. The sharecropper is any hardworking person with a dream and cash to burn, all under the guise of having one's own store. That's what owning a 7-11 convenience store was like in the mid to late 1980s, and in some instances, well into the 1990s. It was the first national issue I headed, and it played out as follows:

* * *

In March 1987, I was contacted by a Mrs. Patti Tibbs, a strong Black woman, who owned two convenience stores. One was a 7-11, and one wasn't. She said she was told to talk to me, and not anyone else at the NAACP. It was a recurring theme that had become purposeful for several reasons, most having to do with the level of competency the community had come to associate with the branch. When people had a problem, they avoided contacting the branch and called my business office directly. Most of the messages received, at the branch, never got to whom they were supposed to get to, or the numbers were written down wrong. The insistence upon letting volunteers answer the phones often promoted a lesser accountability in even the most basic office protocols. It was perceived that the branch wasn't responsive to cold calls.

Patti said she was having a problem with the Southland Corporation, the parent company of the 7-11 convenience store chain. She said that she had been trying to sell her store for over five months. Every time she brought them a buyer, they would be disqualified for some strange reason or another. She could never get an answer as to why, or get any guidelines on what the qualifications were. I told her to save the details, and that it sounded like something the branch could look into. I told her I would have to contact our Branch President and set up a meeting with her and her husband, Jerry. Patti continued to inform me that there were seven other store owners who were in similar predicaments. I said we probably would meet with all of them at once, to best utilize everybody's time.

I called Ray at home that night, and told him about my conversation with Patti. Ray's first reaction was that there's probably nothing to it, and it would take some time. My position was that it couldn't hurt to meet with them and do our own questioning. If they had a weak case, we'd pass on it. Ray finally relented. The meeting was set for 7 p.m. at LaFiette's Restaurant on LaCienega Boulevard. We all arrived at 7 p.m. Ray got there at 7:20, appearing cavalier and impatient. We took a table in the back of the restaurant, which seated eight. There were five store owners present. Patti Tibbs wasn't present, but her husband, Jerry, attended.

After introductions, I asked each owner to tell us what his particular problem was, what the status was, and how they felt that we could help them. The store owners began to tell their stories. Their problems centered around issues of what appeared to be that of holding Black store owners to standards of performance that weren't consistently applied across the board, particularly, in the areas of cash management, inventory auditing and franchise marketing support. The owners felt that the actions directed toward them were racially motivated by their district manager who, according to them, seemed bent on driving all of them out of business. Store owners couldn't handle their own employees, which caused conflict amongst them. They wanted to patronize Black vendors, yet Southland wouldn't approve any for their use. Those were the lightweight problems. Their biggest claim was that via a redlining process, Southland was relegating Black store owners to low volume stores, which required a greater effort and greater cash reserves. Most of the stores were in South Central Los Angeles. Placement of the stores was also a concern. In some instances, Southland had put their stores directly across the street from a supermarket, which cut into that store's volume (revenue capacity). Many of the owners wanted to sell their stores, but Southland wouldn't offer them a fair market price. They wanted them to either walk away from their stores or take $5,000 to just walk away.

Many of those owners invested their life savings into their stores. They weren't about to walk away. If an owner had substantial profits and substantial equity interest coming, Southland would audit the stores, and come up with large differences in the inventory (shrinkage as Southland calls it), to reduce the amount of the owner's proceeds after the sale. Two of the operators, the Tibbses, who received national awards for store management was currently suffering $20,000 and $30,000 shrinkages. One store owner had a $60,000 shrinkage. To "shrink" $60,000 in inventory from one audit to the next, he claimed, "you'd have to load a truck up to the store and haul off three-fourths of the store's inventory." This was all part of a numbers manipulation, so they wouldn't have to return any significant dollars to the store owners. If the store wasn't for sale, the store owner had seven days to put cash in for the shrinkage, or Southland would take over the store.

To make matters worse, the Black store owners had reliable reason to believe that Southland was steering buyers away from them. When buyers inquired about the stores, 7-11 representatives would tell them, "You don't want that store, it's a dump" or "It's had some problems." Most of those stores had been on the market for five to seven months, and those guys were bringing buyers to Southland. In addition, Southland was known to have a waiting list of potential buyers for stores. By the time the owners sold their stores, they had been stretched out so long that they had no money coming, when the store sold under market, because Southland took out the alleged inventory shortages. Then, there was an issue of equity requirement. All stores were required to maintain at least $30,000 equity cushion. For what purpose, the owners could never really explain. When the store suffered a loss for the month, the store equity would drop below the $30,000. Even if they had a profit from a prior month that exceeded $30,000, it didn't matter. The only thing that counted was "the equity line." The owners would then be sent a three-day notice that the store would be taken over, if they didn't adhere to the demand. The store owners alleged that this demand was selectively applied, that many white store owners had never heard of such a demand letter, and didn't have that problem when they fell short on their equity. That was probably the most controversial clause in the franchise agreement. The store owners would be given absurd amounts to come up with in three days, in addition to the money they put up to buy the store.

Lastly, they expressed concerns over the unfairness of the partnership split. In an overwhelming number of cases, Southland took 52 percent of the receipts through wire transfer, and paid the rent and lights. The owner paid for everything else, with the 48 percent remaining-- inventory, labor, security, taxes, even franchise advertisement, which is supposed to be one of the benefits of buying a franchised store. It was highway robbery, and virtually impossible to make a living under this agreement, particularly in a low-volume store. On top of that, Southland manipulated the audit numbers, and told the store owners to find the discrepancy, or pay the money in seven days. Those were some legitimate concerns, but Jerry and Patti Tibbs, while having many of the same problems, had some unique ones also. Ones that proved most damaging to Southland in the end.

Jerry and Patti Tibbs were two of Southland's most innovative operators. They were also part of a select group of multi-store operators. They owned two stores: one in the largely white Westside area on Venice and Overland, and one in the View Park area on LaCienega Boulevard, with a majority of Black residents. The two stores were well run, and quite profitable, prior to an addendum to the franchise agreement that Southland forced on most of the store owners after February 1986. The addendum significantly changed how Southland computed expenses and profit splits. The Tibbses were high-profile operators for Southland. Southland even used them in national advertisements in Ebony Magazine to recruit minority franchise operators. They were even sophisticated enough to open an independent mini market in the Ladera Heights section of L.A., and sell food products and sandwiches to other franchisees. They were doing quite well financially, because of their ambition and experience in convenience store management.

After the addendum was signed and enforced, the performance of their LaCienega store fell off a bit, as did most of the stores whose owners signed the addendum. Many store owners later admitted to us that they were pressured by Southland to sign the addendum. They were told that if they didn't sign it, their franchise agreement wouldn't be renewed when it expired. Many didn't sign and were forced to sell within one year. However, Southland officials chose to blame the fall-off of the LaCienega store on the Tibbses' outside interest, namely their mini market and their sandwich business. Furthermore, Southland made blind and unfounded allegations that the Tibbses may have been using Southland inventory as part of the Ladera Heights Market. A Southland official even walked into their market and pulled the cash register out of the store, claiming it was Southland's equipment. The Tibbses proved the purchase of the register, and had to go to Anaheim to recover the register. Southland never admitted any wrongdoing, nor did they apologize for the inconvenience. Southland then aggressively suggested that the Tibbses sell one of their stores. After months of harassment, they relented and made a decision to sell the less profitable store on LaCienega. Southland dismissed that decision, and ordered them to sell their very profitable West Los Angeles store. Their options were to sell the store, or give up both stores based on violating their franchise agreement. The violation was that they were operating a competing business to their convenience stores. The Tibbses questioned the violation, because they personally knew of several operators who owned 7-11 stores and liquor stores. One franchisee named Herb Dominico, not only owned two 7-11 stores but five liquor stores, according to the Tibbses. Ironically, it was through Mr. Dominico that they found out that their West L.A. store had been selected to be sold, even before Southland told them. Dominico had called to make an offer for the store.

When the Tibbses started making a case for keeping their most profitable store, Southland started manipulating their audits. Suddenly, the West Los Angeles store started having big inventory shrinkages and high equity shortages. There was one thing after another, and because of their continuing conflicts, the time it took to deal with Southland took time away from their other operations. In time, the profits fell off, which Southland used to justify their demand. Subsequently, the Tibbses were forced to sell their West Los Angeles store. They gave Southland a list of potential buyers, whom they knew could easily qualify under the most stringent conditions. Most were Black and there were a few East Indians. Southland rejected every one of them, over a three-month period. They asked Southland to provide a qualified buyer. Southland said they could not find one (even though they had a list of potential buyers on a waiting list). Finally, Southland presented a buyer, Herb Dominico and the Tibbses protested. They said Herb was in the same position as they were. He was a multi-store owner with equity problems (even though Southland worked with Herb and never sent him a three-day notice by his own account), and owned outside businesses. Southland rejected the protest, saying they had nothing to say about whom they sold their stores to. To add insult to injury, Southland forced them to sell under what they felt their store was worth, and lessened that amount by a high inventory shrinkage that Southland came up with at the store closeout. It was estimated, at that time, that Southland had beaten the Tibbses out of almost $150,000 in equity and inventory. Soon Southland started playing those same games with the Tibbses' LaCienega store. At that point, they lost confidence in Southland, and decided to get out of the system. Nine months and some thirty or so declined buyers later, the Tibbses were still trying to sell their store. Meanwhile, Southland was conducting quarterly audits, and was coming up with larger and larger shrinkages. The intent was clear: to bury the Tibbses, as Patti and Jerry saw it. They had served them with a three-day notice for equity deficiency. They became convinced that Southland was trying to take the store before they could sell it, or was hoping that they would get tired of being manipulated and just walk away from it, cutting their losses. They weren't about to do either. In trying to find buyers, the Tibbses got a hold of an available store listing from one of the other store owners. They discovered that their store wasn't even on the list, and that in fact, Southland was steering interested buyers, who found out the store was for sale through other sources, away from the store. Southland was telling folks the store was sold, when it wasn't. That's when the Tibbses went public and contacted us.

While listening to the franchisees' claims, Ray, who I was watching all along, was acting very patronizing and uninterested the whole time. He ordered a shrimp cocktail appetizer and a drink, and was watching the door as if he was expecting someone.

I asked him what he thought. He looked at the men around the table and said, "Gentlemen, Southland is a very big company. This is going to take a lot of work. The NAACP has a lot of projects, but if you want our branch to handle this issue, particularly in court, you're gonna have to be prepared to spend some money." The store owners asked how much. Ray said about $2,500 each. I knew that Ray was asking each owner to buy a business or corporate membership. It was not a condition of handling the case; it just sounded that way.

Suddenly and unexpectedly, before any further conversation could ensue, Ray said, "Gentlemen, I'm sorry but I have an 8:30 appointment. Anthony will brief me with any further details and, of course, I'll have him get back to you on what we decide to do with this issue. Good night." Just that quick, he was outta there. It was about 8:10 p.m. Ray left the appetizer bill on the table. The franchisees looked highly perturbed. I talked to them for another 10 minutes, basically telling them that their claims had plenty of merit, to stop by the branch the following day, pick up complaint forms and get them back to me. I also told them to be as detailed as possible with their written complaints. We all exchanged numbers, and as I headed for the door, the waiter wanted to know who was paying the tab. All the owners had left. I pulled out a fifty-dollar bill, and just shook my head. There was no end to advocacy indoctrination.

* * *

I waited until the owners returned their complaint forms and statements. About a week later, I met with Ray. He was still weak on the idea. He didn't think there was enough there. I told him to allow me to do some homework and to let the owners get much information to me, as they could. Also, we could try to find more franchisees and get some surveys. Ray agreed. Finally, I told Ray that if we don't find anything else, the Tibbses' case seemed strong, even as an isolated case of discrimination. He agreed that their case seemed a lot more than coincidental. It was mid-April. In the meantime, Patti Tibbs was calling me every day with names of ex-franchisees and ex-employees we could talk to. I asked her to prepare a chronology of events as they had occurred. She was all too happy to do this. She just wanted assurance that we were going to do something soon. I told her I felt good about it, and if she'd just help me make a case, I'd run with it.

I began to talk to people about what they knew about Southland. Almost everyone I talked to held them in very low regard. Vendors I talked to claimed that Southland put all kinds of unnecessary restrictions on new vendors, including excessive insurance requirements, that prohibited them from doing business with the stores. I talked to four ex-employees, one was a franchisee, who told me absolute horror stories about how Southland reps talked about Black store operators at headquarters, often in the presence of Black employees. They made statements like, "You tell that fucking jungle bunny to get his equity up, or we're snatching his store," or "Whose store can we padlock today; let's look in South Central," (where most of the Black store owners were). I asked this particular employee if he was sure it was race-related. He said, "I guarantee it." He stated that they used to track the equity levels of the Black store owners just to send them three-day notices. The company had carried some of the white store owners with deficient equity, for as long as a year. He said they used to have a saying that when a Black owner had an equity problem, the Southland officials would call other franchisees saying, "We have a NBL (nigger below the line). Are you interested in buying the store before we put it on the 'For Sale' notification list?" This tied directly into what the Tibbses ascertained as to how Dominico had prior knowledge of their situation. He most likely received it from an inside source. The other ex- employees verified that this type of breach of confidentiality went on often, and not just to Blacks, but to other franchisees who fell out of favor with the corporate office. They also wanted to snatch their stores. However, they all maintained that Blacks were abused much more frequently, overall.

Our further investigation revealed Southland's extremely abusive mishandling of Black employees. They spoke with a vengeance, often restricted by anonymity, as if they had been, or were being seriously wronged. They maintained that Southland had no Equal Employment Opportunity (EEO) policy, had no minority advancement policy and had no Blacks in middle or upper management in the California region. Many of the Black reps were forced to mistreat Black franchisees, and if they didn't, they were written up, passed over for promotions or laid off. One sister, who, at the time, lived out of state, said she was forced to leave Southland, due to a conflict over her lack of promotions. She maintained that she was one of Southland's highest performing reps, and was consistently passed over until she spoke up. She was written up because she raised the race issue, and the other Blacks (mostly males) didn't back her up even though they knew the truth (as we discovered later). She said if they weren't going to stand up for themselves, she wasn't going to stand up for them, so she left the company. She was the first to say, "Southland is a wicked company."

Our dialogue with ex-employees produced another discovery: Southland had signed a trade agreement with Operation PUSH and a Hispanic organization called League of United Latin American

Citizens (LULAC). Southland fronted off both organizations cold-bloodedly, inasmuch as, they signed an agreement to promote minorities in the company, and in franchise opportunities, but had done little of either. It never amounted to much because neither organization monitored the progress of their agreement. In fact, we understood from our sources that they had less Blacks and Hispanics in franchises then (1987), than when the agreement was signed. Things were actually going backward.

Our investigation also discovered that Southland was very political. They had to buy a lot of support for felony tax fraud convictions that the government caught them in the year before (1986). It seemed Southland had been caught concealing income, and failing to report all of its sources of income. One of the support organizations they got on their payroll early on was one we knew in advance would be a tough wall to scale. We knew if we were to take this issue all the way, a confrontation was inevitable, and unless we had a lot going for us, it was one we couldn't win. At least, we knew what we would be facing in advance, and I wondered how this would affect Ray's decision to pursue it. Hell, we would at least make them address the issue forthright. The organization that we inevitably ran up against was our own national NAACP headquarters.

With the information I had gathered, I felt we were ready to charge Southland. All I had to do was convince Ray that we were ready. It had been about five weeks since we had first met with the store owners. Their respective conditions had only worsened. One store owner was being charged with arson for allegedly burning down his store. I heard the other store owners talking informally about the situation. None of them seemed to be extending any sympathy to Southland, nor were they casting any aspersions on the store owner. The owners seemed to feel that if the brother did do it, Southland certainly pushed him over the edge. The story was that Southland had padlocked his store the day before, and he had just completely lost out. All of his savings were gone. The sentiments of the other store owners were, given the same circumstances, they may have done the same thing. The sentiment inferred was, "Hell, I'd burn mine down too, before I'd see Southland with it." Their reasoning was "nothing from nothing leaves nothing." Southland had those people pumped up. Some of them were beginning to think that the NAACP wasn't going to do anything with the case. I told them the process takes time. We couldn't just jump out on a blind allegation.

Ray and I met on May 4, 1987. He seemed to feel comfortable with the discoveries and felt we had a stronger case. I told him about national's acceptance of contributions from Southland. He asked how much.

I said, "According to ex-employees we've talked to, mid-five figures. Maybe as high as six figures."

Ray became contemplative. He said, "that means national will be in this, before we're ready for them to be. They may even try to step in on Southland's behalf."

A very prophetic insight, combined with the fact that it could be perceived that we were attacking the agreement of another organization, our involvement might hasten national's reaction. My response was that those people needed our help. Apparently, Operation PUSH didn't respond to their letter. We advised them of what was happening. Maybe they were interested, and maybe they weren't. We would cross that bridge, when we came to it.

Ray said, "And what about national?"

I said, "Let's not let Southland tell on us. Let's go to national first, invite them to address the Southland chairman directly, and we won't bring up the guilt money unless we have to. With what we got, we can convince national to let us deal with this for a minute."

We didn't see it as jeopardizing Southland's support. I surmised that Southland would probably increase the support to national as we turned up the pressure. Maybe national would see what Southland was up to, and help us turn them around. Ray nodded.

The strategy turned to how we would initiate our attack. Ray sent a mail-a-gram to Southland's CEO, Jere Thompson and regional manager, Donald Tucker, asking them to respond in 48 hours to allegations of racial discrimination by five of their Black franchisees. Ray's thinking was that he expected Ben Hooks to be in the middle of this before long. He was looking to cover his ass. The branch scheduled a press conference for May 7, at 9 a.m. We asked all five store owners (six including the Tibbses) to prepare statements. As of 5 p.m. on May 6, Southland hadn't responded. Instead, we picked up on the news wire that Southland had scheduled a noon press conference for the next day. The battle lines had been drawn, and the fight was on.

* * *

The press conference was very well attended. Only three of the store owners showed up. We decided to allow the Tibbses to speak on behalf of the store owners. In the statement the branch read, we charged Southland with racial discrimination against Black franchisees, particularly in the policy manipulation of Black operators and the limiting of opportunities to Blacks geographically. That was big news, and the press went after it. Southland's press conference was at noon. While we didn't note it, we were sure that Southland had someone attend our press conference. We watched Southland's press conference on the 6 p.m. news. They had prepared responses to our charges, and had lined up a Black franchisee, Larry Williams, to defend the company. The brother got on television and stated that he had never had any problems with Southland, and that it was a very progressive company to work with. However, we knew that wasn't true. We had talked to Larry Williams early in our investigation. He was having some of the same problems that the other franchisees were having. He refused to involve himself in the joint complaint, because he was trying to get a second store. Any involvement with perceived "renegade operators" would jeopardize his chances. I was told that he was a pretty good operator, too. We verified later from inside sources, that even after helping the company with his comments, they never intended to give him a second store. He just never knew it. Needless to say, he never got the second store. Again, this was just an example of how Blacks are played against Blacks, and they still get screwed over.

Yet, the fact was that he had publicly supported Southland. We had to prove that the complaints were not just individual cases of operator conflicts, as Southland alleged, but problems that were racially systematic. All of that took care of itself. Once our case hit the news wire, we received calls from operators in Northern California, Washington D.C., Baltimore, Texas and several more from Los Angeles who contacted us over the next few days, and began to give us similar stories. Even white franchisees, who had it out for Southland, told us how reps went from store to store, telling them who was in trouble and about to lose their stores. There was no shortage of information.

This inundation of data also helped stifle what Southland had hoped to be a major strategy in snuffing out this conflict. Regional officials had represented to Dallas (Southland headquarters), that this was no big deal, just a local problem that could be handled by local players. We knew from dealing with other national franchisers (McDonald's, Coors, K-Mart) that the faster we got the snowball rolling, the harder it was for them to stop. If they're allowed to centralize the problem, and categorize it as a "local" problem, the higher executives don't have to make it a priority to resolve the problem. Thus, minimum impact would be made toward the desired objectives, because lower level executives would always have to take it to their bosses anyway, for a decision and a commitment.

We set the terms of the initial meeting. Sure enough, Southland came with that "we can resolve this amongst us" stuff. We calmly asked them about their problems in Washington, D.C., Northern California and other places. They tried to tell us that other areas were handling their own problems. We said we had no information to support that. We drew the line. This was a system-wide problem that would be dealt with from the top. We told them to advise Jere Thompson that he should give this his immediate attention, or we would have no other choice but to presume Southland had no intentions of dealing in good faith, and would communicate such to our national officials. We followed up this position with a letter to Thompson directly. A meeting was set up within two weeks. Southland stated the following conditions: 1) that we discuss the Los Angeles situation only, and 2) that only the NAACP and Southland officials would be involved in the meetings. No store operators, no press or press statements. We agreed to those conditions and prepared for our initial encounter with the Slurpee Kings.

* * *

We notified the store owners of the meeting. However, when we mentioned that they couldn't be a part of it, they were extremely disappointed. We assured them that we would pursue a meeting with the store owners at a later time. Overall, they seemed satisfied that progress was being made... for the moment. We met with them twice before meeting with the Southland officials. The store operators really briefed us on all of the tricks we could expect, based on their past dealings with Southland. One thing they brought to our attention was that no matter what they tell you, Southland president and CEO, Jere Thompson, would not be there. They said they doubt if he would make one meeting in the future. We maintained that after one or two meetings if he didn't show, we'd change our strategy. The operators agreed, "Might as well go to Plan B. We'll bet our stores that Jere won't show."

About a week before the meeting with Southland, some real strange things began to happen. Patti Tibbs and another operator, Glen Moore, really began to get harassed by Southland reps. That was perceived as punishment for going public. Both suddenly had equity shortages of $7,000 and $15,000 respectively, and were being pressured to bring in the cash. Furthermore, another buyer for Jerry and Patti's store had just been declined. It was an East Indian buyer who had plenty of money, and a history of operating markets. Southland came up with the excuse that they had determined that the buyer's wife didn't speak English well enough to support her husband in the store. I asked to meet the woman. Mr. Tibbs, the buyer and his wife came to my office. In talking to the woman, I couldn't imagine what Southland had in mind. The woman had an accent, but she talked better English than her husband. She certainly talked better English than many of the Koreans and middle easterners who were in many of the 7-11 stores around the city. We determined that those actions were retaliation for the store operators coming to us. We immediately sent a letter to Southland's regional office telling them that we were aware of their actions, and to cease any further harassment of those operators until our meeting. Any further actions would be perceived as retaliation and would receive a similar response.

When the day of the meeting finally arrived, Southland came in full force. They sent their legal counsel, Lon Williams, a guy named Charlie Barajas their equivalent to the minority affairs officer (they really didn't have one), and a special projects officer (who was really their bulldog), J.H. Snow, all from Dallas. Guess what? The operators were right. No Jere Thompson. Also in attendance was their Los Angeles operations manager, Donald Tucker, and two brothers (you knew they'd bring some), one of whom we already knew, Owen McKay. Owen was pretty well accepted and somewhat respected in the community circles as the "7-11" man. Our side of the table included Ray, Ellen DeShazer and me. Ellen was an attorney on our Executive Committee who replaced George Mallory as the branch's fair share committee chairman (formerly held by Melanie Lomax). Ellen normally took part in corporate franchise disputes. George was still peeved, and refused to work with me, because earlier in the year, I had exposed his Frank Sinatra dinner.

Ray opened up the meeting expressing his deepest disappointment that Jere Thompson wasn't there. Barajas claimed he had an emergency meeting and had to cancel. He assured us that the company's fullest attention was being given to the matter, and that's why the legal counsel was present. Ray said, "I understand you have a senior Vice President in charge of franchise operations. Where is he?" Barajas responded that he was in the same meeting as Thompson.

Ray looked at me and I shook my head. "Well, our normal process is for our president to meet with your president. And since your president isn't here, I'm going to excuse myself," Ray said. "I will, however, stay long enough to read the allegations to you." As Ray read the allegations, they were trying to answer them. We told them to bring them to the next meeting. They also were trying to find out where we received our information. We stated that we weren't going to outright divulge our sources. They pretty much knew who they were, so we didn't want to play any games. They sat silently until Ray finished reading the allegations. "I am going to leave now," Ray said. "If you have any questions or comments, you can address them to Mr. Essex." Ray got up and left.

The balance of the meeting was used to set up a future meeting. Southland wanted to get into some of the specifics, and address circumstances surrounding conflicts with some of the Black operators. I suggested that they respond to the allegations in writing, then we could discuss those items they refuted. Once we all knew their policies, we could address the allegations in relation to which policies were broken, discriminatory, or just exceptional circumstances. I also stated that whatever they refute, they should be able to prove otherwise. Most of what we were alleging, we had more than enough evidence to prove, or at least raise significant inconsistencies in their policies.

We agreed on a follow-up meeting within the next two weeks. I reinforced the importance of Jere Thompson's attendance, so that policy decisions could be made and commitments could be given to ensure an expedient resolution of the conflict. We all agreed that it would be the best way to end the conflict. The meeting ended with handshaking and well wishes. While the Southland officials were walking to their cars, I couldn't help but overhear how upset the Dallas people were over having to send four people here to resolve this "mess." Barajas told the local officials, "I'd try to get a hold on most of this stuff by the next meeting if I were you." I could sense a level of resentment from some of the local Southland managers in the way Barajas had already indicted them. We knew this local foolishness had gotten out of control, like it had all over the country. They seemed somewhat shocked at our allegations, and somehow felt that the whole story had not been shared with them. How accurate was that assessment.

Within a week of our first meeting with Southland, a miraculous coincidence happened. The Tibbses found a buyer for their store.

After 11 months and 31 buyers, Southland qualified someone. We couldn't help but wonder if our pending meeting had anything to do with it. Probably so. Southland was planning to eliminate any and everything that we could point to as support for our allegations, but it was too late. Plus, this was only the first hurdle the Tibbses had to jump before getting out of the store. Southland really started playing games with them on the sale price of the store. A store is worth whatever the market will bear. If a buyer is willing to pay what the seller asks, then what is the problem? The problem was that Southland didn't expect the Tibbses to come out with hardly anything, but found out they would come out with a nice piece of change--money. Southland didn't want to pay out.

Then Southland decided to get morally conscious, claiming they couldn't possibly ask a poor new buyer to pay such a price for "that store." They proceeded to try and adjust the sale price downward. The Tibbs went nuts. They called me and told me what had happened. I called Tucker and asked them what they were trying to do, by reducing the sale price on the Tibbses' store. He claimed he didn't know anything about that, and would have to get back to me. When he called me back, he said the problem had been taken care of, and that he wanted the Tibbses out of the system, as badly as they wanted to get out. He also said that it would just take a minute, and it would be all over. While this guy seemed somewhat sincere, it appeared that his subordinates had a way of handling operators, that really jeopardized the company's position against any claims of discrimination, particularly a district manager by the name of Mark Miller.

Miller just said and did anything he wanted. The company defended his actions by turning their heads away from his despicable behavior. Some ex-employees told us their position often was that if Blacks were doing what they were supposed to do, Miller wouldn't have to treat them this way. What way? Like slaves. That's just how he treated them. He would come into the operator's stores saying, "You work for me, so you do what I tell you, or this store is mine." He just antagonized and infuriated the operators most of the time. And operators paid Southland to take that shit! Usually, on a job it's the other way around. They pay you to take their shit. It was purely a case of the tail "wagging the dog."

There were no more problems that came to our attention before the second meeting. At the second meeting, Southland brought in their second in command, senior Vice President of franchise operations, Dick Dole. Still no Jere Thompson. Ray did participate in the meeting, however. We asked Southland if they had any responses to our allegations. They said yes, and proceeded to deny almost every allegation. They explained to us what their policy was in each case, and what they were doing to enforce the policies. I refuted their denials with some specific examples that we had investigated. Some of them they were prepared to respond to, and some they weren't prepared. Of course, the cases that they did respond to were not violations, but exceptions caused by extenuating circumstances brought on by the operators. So I gave them about five or six other examples and asked, "Are these exceptions, too?" I concluded that their exceptions all seemed to have similar traits, and would be viewed as "racially motivated." What they were doing was inferring that they had no intentions of correcting the problem. By challenging us to expose them, we would also be raising a possible conflict with our national office. In the time between the first meeting and the second meeting, Southland had agreed to become one of the national sponsors of the organization's national convention in New York. Inside employees communicated to us that the officials in Anaheim were running around the office saying they had the NAACP in their pocket, and this L.A. problem would be squashed momentarily. We were told that Southland wrote a $50,000 check to national, and picked up other expenses, as well. When we told Southland that we would submit a report to national at the convention recommending a timeline for taking direct action against Southland, they kind of chuckled. The second meeting ended with a recommendation to meet at the convention, and take a future course of action based on discussions that ensued thereof.

I prepared a 15-page report on our allegations, Southland's responses and our findings. We pointed out the discrepancy between their responses and our findings. Then we requested that it be a high priority item for economic direct action. I submitted the report to Ray. He forwarded a copy to Hooks and Fred Rasheed, the national director of economic development, asking for a meeting to discuss the issue at the convention. We received no response from Hooks. Fred Rasheed was receptive to meeting, but he wanted more details. Charlie Barajas had already called him, and had given his side of the story. It was time for the truth to come out. Southland had a few more tricks up its sleeve.

* * *

All during the Southland investigation, we had up-to-the-minute information on policies, management movements, and defense strategies that Southland was preparing to use in its counterattack on our investigation. Southland presumed that the Black employees were passing on inside conversations from internal management meetings and handing us internal memorandums; but that wasn't the case. In truth, the Black employees were scared to death to be seen alone with us. In fact, when we tried to get a couple to talk to us about their own situations, they missed appointments, and whispered when we were on the phone. A couple of employees on disability leave, David Allen and Rodney Wooten, both of whom I got to be good friends with after they left the company, were the only ones brave enough to talk to us. The rest were under so much pressure, that they felt they would lose their jobs by even mentioning the NAACP in the presence of white folk. We got more information in the form of anonymous phone calls from "concerned" Southland employees (most of whom were white) than we did from franchise operators. Some, I'm sure, were intentional to throw us off track. Most were legitimate coming from good, seemingly sincere white folk, trying to do right by the store owners.

Southland was a gossip house where someone from the inside would tell an operator and, a day later, the information would be circulated through the whole system. Southland tried to discourage operators from talking to each other, especially the Black operators who openly admitted that Southland actually pitted them against each other to keep them from helping one another. But Southland was running so many games on the operators, that if Southland told an operator it was daytime, the operator would call another one to verify it. Southland's credibility with the operators was very low. However, Southland in its own little in-house paranoia, began to really watch and follow one brother, Owen McKay. Owen's closeness to the community was being used to call his loyalties into question, and for that reason they may have been using this dispute with the Black operators to play him out of pocket. Owen was probably the most loyal and forthright person we met over at Southland. When he talked to us, he maintained the company's position, but offered solutions that both the company and the NAACP could buy into. Conversely, we would call him or approach him first, when we addressed an issue, because our level of comfort was higher with him. His superiors began to resent that. Eventually, they excluded him from the process and ultimately, he lost his job. Southland's loss of confidence in Owen really manifested itself in New York at the NAACP 1987 national convention.

We got there a day early, and so did Owen. Most of our conversation was light and conciliatory, but eventually it turned to the investigation. While Owen didn't give any clues, we knew Southland was planning to have a major hand in this convention. Yet, Owen still held the company's position. Then a funny thing happened that gave us an indication of exactly how much they trusted Owen. Owen, Ray and I were going up an escalator in the convention's headquarters hotel, the New York Hilton. We saw Charlie Barajas on the down. escalator. He saw Owen with us, and asked where we were going. We said, "Uhhh, to get something to eat." Charlie ran to the bottom of his down escalator and ran up the "Up" escalator to catch up with us. From that point, Owen had nothing else to say. Not even non-related small talk. Charlie answered everything, and Owen sat silently. Charlie kept trying to find out what we talked about before he got there. We kept telling him "slurpees." He didn't think that was very funny. Eventually, he got off that subject. However, it seemed like Owen could never be in the right place, at the right time, from that moment on. Every time we saw Owen, if it was for just a second, another Southland official passed us. Every time they turned over a NAACP rock, Owen was under it. Soon they had the poor brother scared to come out of his room. They made him leave the convention a day early, because of too much fraternizing with the enemy. Wasn't that what he was supposed to be doing? But, of course, he had to be in collusion with the enemy. A really ironic racist move on their part. It appeared obviously more discriminating from our perspective.

During the first day of the convention, I was in the hotel's convenience shop. What do I see on the front page of *USA Today* and the *Wall Street Journal*, "Southland Sells to Thompson Brothers in L.B.O.(leveraged buyout)." It all clicked. Southland was trying to avoid any major publicity during the leverage buyout negotiations, because its financing wasn't assured, and they didn't want to scare off the possible financiers with negative exposure of our discrimination claims. Southland sold off a good portion of its assets to make the deal work, and had a very ambitious repayment plan contingent upon almost a 50 percent increase in performance from 7-11 stores throughout the system. Who would pay for that? The operators. They pay for everything Southland does, including trying to buy off the nation's largest civil right's organization.

When I picked up my convention registration packet, what was on the bottom of the packet portfolio? "Sponsored by Southland

Corporation" with its 7-11 logo. I made my way over to the exhibit hall. Upon entering the hall, what did I see? -The Southland Corporation, right in the front door, with an exhibit twice the size of all the other exhibits. You couldn't miss it if you tried. And almost every person that walked into the exhibit area received a handshake from a Southland official. They didn't wait for you to come to their exhibit. They came to you. I heard little old ladies saying, "Oh, what a nice man. How nice it is for your company to co-sponsor our convention."

Southland was not only making a presence but also lobbying the members and letting each attendee know personally that they were here to support the work of the NAACP as a "co-sponsor of this convention." I've never seen anything like it before, or since. It was a lesson in damage control and reputation management that those little ole' civil rights groups were obviously not acquainted with. The mission was very obvious, and the intent was very clear: show Los Angeles how much juice Southland had in the national organization, and show us how very difficult a direct action campaign would be. Southland wasn't through yet. They had their own lobbyist, who was also a member of the national NAACP's Special Contribution's Board, and could pull aside the top echelon of the organization's officers and board members at any time, for anything. His name was Herm Willie. We nicknamed him "Worm Willie." If you ever saw this guy, you'd know why. He was a very unassuming, eavesdropping type of guy who could convince you of anything. Every time you looked around, he was staring at you, probably lip reading your conversation. Real "spy" kind of stuff. Our sources told us this was the guy who told Southland who could be bought and for how much. In return, Willie convinced Hooks and several other key board members that Southland was the best thing to happen to them since the Little Rock Nine. Southland was very well positioned for this confrontation. They were very visible to the members, and they were lobbying the delegates. It was also as if they were saying, "Come on L.A., make my day."

This high-profile strategy had not gone unnoticed by Ray, either. Charlie Barajas had arranged to take us all to dinner on Southland to just informally talk about the convention in general. I declined. Ray, to my surprise, declined also. I'm sure Charlie was trying to get us to back off of bringing up the investigation at the convention. We managed to stay out of his way, until we met with national.

I had first met Fred Rasheed in 1985, at a Black Dollar Days promotion, in Los Angeles. He's a very quiet and composed man, until he gets to the bargaining table. Then, he's a serious, uncompromising and persuasive individual. Fred could negotiate you out of your final position, and you'd thank him for letting you give away the ship. I got to work with him again in New York, as one of the branch representatives present at the signing of the McDonald's Fair Share Agreement. Ray, Melanie Lomax and I, as the newly elected Fourth Vice President, attended. Fred was extremely impressive and clearly in charge as the final details were hammered out, before the signing. Everything went according to terms. Fred, as director of the organization's economic development program, would be a key ally in the Southland battle. His was one of the few NAACP programs (other than the ACT-SO program) that had any real credibility left. Fred had done wonders in helping the organization. The nation understood that economic empowerment was every bit as important, as social and political empowerment, a key transition in the organization's post civil rights era involvement.

The program was designed to emphasize the vast and powerful, yet devalued, purchasing and resource capabilities of Blacks and their dollars. Particularly to companies that received significant consumer patronage from Blacks and had a social responsibility to give back in terms of supporting Blacks in management, business and Black community interests. The program also advocated retaliatory penalties to companies that refused to adhere to any sense of social consciousness or reason. The penalties were economic boycotts. "Don't spend your money with those who don't spend their money with you, or don't treat you fairly," was the motto of the economic development charge.

At the time, over 40 companies had been convinced to sign "Fair Share Agreements," promising to give Blacks a fair share of the economic pie. Many of the companies included Coors, McDonald's, Pacific Bell, General Motors, Ford, Chrysler and others who chose to put their commitment to Black economic empowerment in writing. While most of those companies had significant problems, none of them (except Coors) had the problems that Southland had. Southland was an ideal company for a fair share agreement. However, they were in the midst of a trade agreement with, which they were failing at miserably, and had absolutely no interest in signing another. PUSH and the NAACP (basically Ben Hooks and Fred) had an informal agreement to stay away from each other's projects, as a matter of courtesy. This also came up later, but it was good that we knew about it. Our investigation of Southland's discriminatory practices had been delegated to Fred, by Hooks, who was busy, respectfully so, for most of the convention. Fred had many meetings of his own, but he was always courteous, and tried to figure out when he could meet with us. We wanted to meet with him before the meeting with Southland. The meeting was finally set for 7:30 a.m., on the third day of the convention.

I met Fred at 7:40 a.m., as he was wrapping up a 7 a.m. meeting with another group. We talked about the convention and other activities planned for later in the day. We were trying to wait on Ray because Fred had an 8:30 a.m. meeting. So at 7:55 we rolled. I first started the meeting with a straight shot "outta the box" regarding some of the rumors we had heard about Ben Hooks and national being in Southland's pocket, and how evident that appeared to be based on what we'd seen to that point. Fred gave me a real hard look and said, "Well, I don't know if they've bought Ben, but they can't buy me."

I said, "Cool, then we can deal." My biggest fear was that we'd be giving all of our concerns and strategies to a "sellout," who would try to jam the issue or squash it, before they got a chance to be heard. Fred was nobody's sellout, and he was certainly the strongest national player I'd met in the NAACP.

The meeting with Fred couldn't have gone better. It turned out he knew of many problems that Southland was having with the Baltimore and D.C. Black franchise operators. Rasheed was shocked at how far the company had gone with the Los Angeles operators. He felt we had an excellent basis for investigating their actions, and felt that Southland must be forced to openly address those issues. Furthermore, Fred was of the opinion that Southland just had an unconscionable agreement that didn't just discriminate solely against Black owners, but all owners. The Black store owner situations were just further aggravated, by having the less profitable stores, where the disadvantages in the franchise agreement surfaced quicker and became more obvious, when operators got in difficult situations.

He conclusively felt that a meeting with Southland was appropriate, and that a national task force should be formed to address the issues across the board. He said he would apprise Hooks of what was going on, particularly of the rumors relative to Southland's intention to promote its "national relationship." I was very satisfied with Fred's assurances, and felt confident that for once the branch was working with the national office. As the meeting came to a close, who walked up, but Mr. Barajas. He looked at me like "I thought we were supposed to meet Fred together." I looked back as if to say, "Bad assumption." He said, "What's up, Fred?" Fred acknowledged that he was getting briefed on the branch's position of the investigation against Southland. Barajas wanted to know if we were going to meet about it. Fred said, "I think we should." The meeting was set for the next day at lunch. "Perfect," Charlie said. Then he was back to his B.S. rap. Something about flying us to Dallas to see a Cowboy's football game in Southland's luxury box. After nodding in disbelief, both Fred and I excused ourselves. Barajas knew we were together on the issue. It was time for something new.

* * *

Herm Willie, not knowing that we knew he was Southland's undercover man, came up and introduced himself to me in the middle of the ACT-SO award presentations. He said he had heard a lot about me, and was looking forward to working with me. I told him it depended on what he heard and whom he heard it from. This guy had a very strange feel about him.

Fred, Barajas, Willie, a guy named Jim Nortarnicola, Ray and I were at the luncheon meeting. Barajas didn't seem very comfortable with Willie's presence, nor with Nortarnicola's, for that matter. This appeared to be Southland's new "A" team. Willie was very quiet, as if he was taking notes on how the other two represented the company's position, and reporting back to somebody else. Barajas hadn't been that straight in all the times we'd seen him. It was kind of funny. As Fred elaborated on the concerns of the branch and resolution consideration, it appeared that Southland had concluded prior to the meeting that they weren't going to get the results they had hoped for.

Southland wanted to localize the issue. They wanted our local people to work with their local people, while the corporate headquarters continued to bankroll the pet projects of the national office. Fred pointed out that with problems in other parts of the country, that was an illogical proposal. Southland proposed a second alternative: two task forces, one on the East Coast, and one on the West Coast. Rasheed stated that he wouldn't oppose that if Southland's senior executives honored both task forces, were present at them and didn't dictate who represented the NAACP on either task force. Southland initially agreed to that. Fred would submit a list of representatives to Southland, and they would do the same. The first task force would meet within 30 days. Southland was less than happy with the arrangement, but they were in it for the long haul, and Herm Willie had just begun to work.

When the lists were submitted, Southland's list again excluded Jere Thompson. That caused a big delay. Thompson wrote a letter to Fred stating that he was still tied up with the leverage buyout, but his second in command would be at every meeting of both task forces, and would have the power to make decisions for the company. He assured it. Also, Barajas was no longer involved. He was leaving the company, and Nortarnicola was replacing him. That figured. Charlie probably knew that move was coming. In addition, the western regional executives were all changing. None of the people who initially sat down with us were involved anymore. Ray, DeShazer and I were submitted along with Fred and another East Coast Branch President. Fred initially stated that we would be the representatives of both task forces. Southland opposed that. They wanted more East Coast players for the East Coast task force. More than likely, they wanted to localize the West Coast players, who to had been more aggressive, strategically armed (with information) and organizationally prepared. The East Coast NAACP players would have to be brought up to speed to deal with Southland, who would've already had the advantage of hashing the issues out with us on the West Coast. Our team on the East Coast would be at a disadvantage, because Southland would know where the bodies were buried. The only common member of both task forces would be Fred Rasheed. I think it was also a cost issue with Southland, since the company would pick up the tab for the task forces. They didn't want to fly us back and forth. So the task forces ended up being regionalized, on the basis of personnel. Whatever policy recommendations that were to be adopted, in each task force, would become a system wide policy. Upon our return to Los Angeles, a press statement was released jointly, by the branch and Southland, announcing that task forces were formed to address the issues raised in the NAACP investigation into discriminatory allegations of Southland's 7-11 franchises.

Two of the major issues Southland was asked to address were EEO and minority procurement policies. We asked Southland to hire a consultant mutually agreed upon by both parties, to look into the company's current policies, to see if any existed, to make acceptable recommendations, or assist them in writing new ones. Our first recommendation was Earl "Skip" Cooper of ECII and Associates. Skip was probably the foremost minority business advocate in the city, who had served many years as president of the Black Business Association, and had been involved in helping several major corporations structure Minority Procurement Programs. Southland knew this was coming and flat out rejected Skip's firm from consideration. Skip was also a Vice President of the branch, which Southland used as a possible conflict of interest scenario that they wanted to avoid. The same reasoning was given to the second choice, Elvin Moon, who was a member of the branch's Executive Committee. Southland said they would prefer to use someone totally unaffiliated with the branch. In the ensuing weeks, several names came up. However, the task force eventually settled on two: One was perfect for the job; the other was a farce. What followed made a joke out of the whole process.

The one who really fit the role for the consultant was Rene Anderson of RCA and Associates. She had a full background of doing EEO and minority employment relations work for the state of California during former Governor Jerry Brown's administration. She was very well respected in state and local government circles, and had even offered advice to Ray early on, when the investigation first broke. I didn't know her at the time, but in talking to several people while trying to gather names, hers came up several times. I finally got to meet her at the Congressional Black Caucus later that year. She informed me that she had been in constant dialogue with Ray, and had hoped to receive some consideration on the consulting spot when it became available. I told her it was available, and asked if she had heard from Ray. She said she hadn't. I told her to call Ray, as soon as she got back to L.A., and if she didn't reach him, get her packet to me.

Within a week, Rene contacted me saying that her attempts to reach Ray had been futile. I told her to meet me over lunch and bring her marketing packet. I eventually submitted her name to the task force. Ray never returned her call. It soon became very obvious why Ray hadn't returned her calls. Fred Rasheed called me at 7 a.m. one morning to tell me he had received calls from Ray, George Mallory, and a Bill Elkins from Mayor Tom Bradley's office, on behalf of the consultant position to the task force. He wanted to know who this "Larry Irvin" was. I almost dropped the phone on the floor. I sat up and began to explain to Fred who this guy was.

Larry Irvin headed the Irvin-Hampton Company, a public affairs group out of Los Angeles, that specialized in facilitating or mediating issues of public concern. It was obvious that this was the type of consultant Southland was looking for, but one inconsistent with the objectives laid out in the charge, which was an emphasis on minority employment practices and procurement policies. Irvin had a history of facilitating issues perceived as detrimental to the interest of the people. His company was hired on projects by government agencies or special interest groups to lobby the support of the people, in order to gain acceptance of their projects. Straight out, many perceived that Larry used his race (Black face) on some issues, to front for white interest outside of our community, or politicians who had special interest in mind. Oftentimes, elected officials had a hard time convincing the community that what he was representing was good for the people.

Let's discuss, for a moment, how low this person was perceived by some in the community. In the early 1980s, the city of Los Angeles was trying to build a large incinerator to burn garbage when the landfills were almost full. The project was called Lancer. The city and the developer misrepresented the environmental impact of the incinerator to the people where the plant was to be built. It was to be built in South Central Los Angeles. They tried to convince the community that the plant was totally safe, that the emissions from the plant were non-toxic, and that it was within the air quality standards. However, they had no documented evidence that this was the case. For all intents and purposes, the city was saying that burning garbage was more important than the health of our people. You know you couldn't stand around a small incinerator that burned once a week, much less a big one that burned every day. Guess who was out there selling death to the people, by trying to convince residents to support Lancer? Larry Irvin.

At the same time the investigation was going on, the city was building a mall, which will be discussed later. The mall required a community-based consultant to protect the interest of the people. The developer and the city hired Larry Irvin and the project is still a failure. The city even hired Irvin to kick the homeless out of stairwells across the street from City Hall, on TV, when they were trying to clean up downtown. No job was too low for this guy. He always claimed to want to help the disadvantaged, but usually ended up exploiting them with the hands of the advantaged. The perception level of Irvin's sensitivity was that Larry would kick a one-legged man's only leg from under him, if it was tied to a contract. While it was clear to some that Irvin's firm specialized in managing projects that called for advancing special interest positions (even if they were positions of compromise), to others; Irvin was perceived as a sellout of the highest caliber. Coincidentally, he was a best friend of perceived Sinatra dinner sellout, George Mallory. They were high school chums. Now Mallory was in the loop, calling all around the country for his high school football teammate. Ray was jammed up to support Irvin, even though Ray had used Rene, and admitted to several people that she was a better candidate. Larry even had the audacity to try to lobby me for support.

I can never hide my disdain for one who is a betrayer of the people. He had me meet him for lunch at LaFiettes. Our lunch was very cold and short. He waited until he ordered to begin to talk about the subject of our lunch. He spent the first half hour trying to stroke me, telling me what a wonderful job I was doing with the branch, and how the community was impressed. Knowing who sent him and of whom he flocks with, I sat thinking, "I can't believe what an ass-kisser this guy is," knowing he really didn't mean it. I just listened and nodded a lot. He finally got around to asking me what I thought the Southland project needed to be effectively resolved. Knowing that he would be interviewing with Southland in a few days, I wasn't about to give him an edge. I started to tell him a consultant with balls, but instead I said, "You tell me." He went into some rhetoric, and I interrupted him, "Larry, tell me about your experience in minority procurement and minority employment policies."

He said, "Well, Anthony, you know that's not my expertise, but I feel overall that I can offer so much more." I nodded. After we finished eating, saying nothing in between, Larry said, "Anthony, I really could use your support on this." I told him to send me a packet on his firm, and I'd consider it. I'm sure he knew that if I had to choose between Mickey Mouse or him, based on what I already knew, the mouse would get my vote. Not to devalue Rene and her capabilities, I would never vote for people who I don't believe have our interest at heart. I hate sellouts. Larry excused himself after picking up the check, saying he had to call his office. That just meant they had to press Ray more, and they did.

* * *

The third meeting of the task force had a whole new look. The western Vice President was Don Burnside. The new regional manager was Mitch Telson. Terry Blocher had been installed as area manager. None of the original Southland people were involved. Elvin Moon was added to the task force from our side. Fred Rasheed had a conflict and wasn't able to make the meeting. We wanted to have an earlier meeting to discuss our strategy, but Ray's schedule wouldn't allow it. Southland had interviewed Larry Irvin and Rene Anderson. They were leaning toward Irvin, because Terry Blocher claimed that they hit it off a little better than he and Rene did. They also felt he was a little more politically connected, since Larry had the Mayor call on his behalf. At that point, it was obvious what they were trying to do, which just reinforced my decision to go with RCA & Associates. Elvin Moon and I were for Rene, because we knew she'd be thorough and unbiased, and she best fit the parameters the group had initially set. Ellen DeShazer said she really didn't know either one of them, but would go with our consensus. We already had a majority, but certainly had to give Ray's opinion some consideration. He was the president, but he certainly hadn't given us any indication that he would not support our choice. After all, we had done the work. How wrong could we be? Very wrong it turned out. Ray was late.

In the meeting we decided that the agenda would be setting a monthly meeting schedule, and the selection of a consultant to facilitate the process and record the task force meetings. We had set up the meeting schedule, and were getting ready to proceed to the selection of a consultant. I asked if we could take a five-minute break so that I could bring Ray up-to-date. I told him about the meeting schedule, which he didn't have a problem with, and where Moon and I were on the selection of the consultant. He wanted to know where Ellen was. I told him she was with whomever we selected. He said OK, and left it at that. Moon and I were under the impression that we had a consensus on Rene Anderson. Ellen had perceived the same.

When we got back into the meeting, Blocher started telling us how it was important for Southland to have a consultant who was easy to work with and could provide a variety of services, since they were paying for it. Blocher favored Larry Irvin, because he appeared to be more at ease with the whole situation. No, he wasn't as strong as Rene in the areas of EEO and minority procurement policies, which were the qualifications laid out in the guidelines for selection. However, he thought there were other factors to consider in making this choice. We asked what those factors were. He said he couldn't disclose them specifically, but they were related to possible future work for the company. We asked what that had to do with the work we were trying to get done. "If you want to have Irvin later, you can hire him later, but don't compromise what we're trying to do here," I said.

Blocher asked Ray who the branch was in favor of hiring. Ray leaned back and said, "I don't see any problem in your hiring Irvin-Hampton."

I said, "Wait a minute, Ray. That's not who we discussed."

"We didn't discuss anybody, Ray replied. "I never said I was in favor of one or the other, plus we were split on our selection."

"We weren't split," I said. "We agreed on Anderson, and DeShazer said she'd go with the consensus. Since there was no consensus, we always go with the majority in branch committees. Ellen's vote then became an abstention. If she didn't know one from the other before, she still doesn't know one from another, Isn't that right Ellen?"

Ellen kind of shrugged her shoulders and looked off, as if she couldn't believe we didn't resolve this in advance, and were sitting there arguing in front of white folk. None of us could believe that Ray would even try to pull this, since he was always talking about being unified on issues before the public.

Clearly, Ray had been jammed to support Irvin, but he didn't have the balls to ever try to alert his committee, much less persuade us to see his point of view. While we were trying to resolve this conflict, the Southland officials were looking at each other and smirking, like they had discovered something. And they had. Our division on this issue really ran deeper than two consultants and a matter of conflicting opinions. Southland had been trying to peep a weakness they could exploit since this process started. They found one. Southland, during the whole investigation, had found that I was a lot more persistent than Ray. Ray also loved to be schmoozed, wined and dined, as well as, to have his authority reinforced. Southland played to that and would say shit like, "Well, who's the president, you or Anthony? Usually, it was a non-issue, because we'd Mutt n' Jeff 'em most of the time anyway. We'd take turns playing "Good Cop, Bad Cop." But on the Irvin issue, Ray seemed to be listening to Southland. Larry had the benefit of Mallory whispering in Ray's ear. Ray was usually a stickler for qualifications, and Larry came up short there, too. And most inexcusably, Ray knew of Larry's track record in the community. People still remembered him from Lancer. This was a bad choice right behind the Sinatra dinner fiasco.

Many were convinced that the branch really didn't have the community at heart, when it came to representing the people and their interests. This was another example of that sentiment being played out.

Southland knew this was going to be an issue, because of the division on the branch's selection. They knew their problems could be hashed and rehashed publicly, in trying to decide which consultant would serve the objective best. To avoid being pulled into a public fight over branch compromise, they decided to hire both consultants. Irvin would handle the task force work, and Anderson would handle the more specialized work of developing the minority employment and procurement policies that would be derived from the task force work. That pacified everybody for the moment. A scope of work would be drawn up for each consultant, and they would be compensated accordingly. Of course, the main purpose for Southland hiring a consultant, however, was to facilitate the entire investigation impartially. They would make sure Irvin got that work. And it significantly compromised our intent, which was to address many of the issues from a minority business enterprise/equal employment side. Southland recognized it and dodged a bullet, only because the branch didn't come in united in their choice. The integrity of the task force's dealings took a significant compromise turn. We took an unnecessary stroke, and Southland got the break they needed, not because of anything they did, but because of the L.A. Branch President's departure from team protocol. That was a major fumble.

* * *

There were still major issues to be addressed on the franchise side. The Tibbses were out of the system, but Southland managed to tie up a good portion of their proceeds, in the closing audit. All the other franchisees managed to get out, except one. Even a new operator, a married couple named Emmanuel and Juanita Lewis, who had only been in their store ninety days, rescinded their option to become franchisees, not necessarily due to some of the nightmares that the others encountered, but because Southland put them in a store with no signs, no advertisement, and gave them virtually no support from their field representatives. Then Southland started charging losses against their store, and sending them notices about equity shortages. Those people weren't about to have their store taken, before they started. Southland tried to convince them to stay and give the system a chance, but the Lewises recognized that if Southland pushed them past the rescission period, they could kiss their $40,000 goodbye. They just casually mentioned that they had been in touch with us, and Southland promptly closed them out, with no problem.

The real problem was with the one renegade operator who hadn't sold yet. Glen Moore basically came in on the coattails of the Tibbses. But his was a different situation altogether. Moore owed Southland for inventory shortages he could never rectify. It was never determined if his employees were stealing from him, or if he was just losing money at his location. It appeared that he did owe Southland some money. Southland may have exaggerated the losses, and Moore refused to reconcile what he thought were ridiculous losses. Southland certainly didn't make the situation any better in their handling of Moore. Moore was convinced that Southland was out to destroy him. They went back and forth, back and forth. When Southland wouldn't return his calls, Moore withheld daily deposits.

In the meantime, Southland was starting to jam some of their Black field reps. Rodney Wooten and David Allen, as I mentioned earlier, were two of Southland's best performing field representatives. Rodney hurt himself in a company softball game, and filed for Workers' Compensation. Southland refused to pay, and made Rodney go back to work with an injured back. During that period, Rodney was asked to supervise a store audit. He was asked to do some heavy lifting of inventory, and hurt his back even worse. The company staff who assisted Rodney in the audit, both white, refused to stand behind his statements of the injury. Southland ended up trying to fire him.

David Allen had a similar story. David handled many of the stores in Los Angeles. While in the office, David began to witness firsthand the manipulation of many franchisees, Blacks and whites. David began to try to correct a lot of the mishandling of his stores. He recognized operators as hardworking people, who were running their stores properly and needed support from the company. Whenever an operator loss money, or had an adverse store condition, Southland immediately alleged store mismanagement. David didn't automatically assume such was the case. There were very few situations where the operators' claims were supported by the company field rep. Instead of Southland supporting their man in the field and giving assistance to the operator, Southland turned against the rep, saying that if the rep can't work out the store owners problems on his own, then he must not be able to handle the job, and maybe that area needs a new rep. David knew the company was the cause of many of the operators' problems, particularly those that had racial implications. And, during the initial stages of the investigation, he never betrayed the company's trust, even though he could have easily confirmed many of our allegations. But when they came after him, due to the decreasing performance of his stores, Southland's internal harassment caused some very damaging health problems for David.

David tried to resolve his conflicts with his superiors, but he ran into further difficulty. They accused him of talking to the NAACP and causing problems for the company. In David's defense, he never talked to us while he worked for the company; we talked extensively after he left, but never during the investigation. Not until after they forced him to go on disability for ulcers, and then tried to fire him, did David break ranks.

During that time, we were holding task force talks with Southland on their minority upward mobility program and their weaknesses in the franchise system. We informed them that we knew they were still playing games, not only with the operators, but also with their Black employees. Southland denied that they were harassing Black employees, calling the charges "isolated incidents" but we knew better. They also were beginning to make us look really dumb in the community by buying up all the friends they could find. Donations were going to every community kit and caboodle. To make matters worse, they'd taken on a fundraising campaign for Sickle Cell, and co-sponsored a voter registration campaign with our national office. We'd have to tighten the screws if we expected to regain any respect out of this thing. Believe me, people were reminding us every day of what Southland was doing in the community, but with the operators, it was still business as usual.

* * *

After displaying our lack of unity in the third task force meeting, we hit the fourth meeting head on. Southland came in ready to either refute our allegations, or announce adjustments to current operation. They came in with a map of all their stores to refute the redlining allegations. They were going to show, of course, that all of the Black operators were not in the Black areas (which we already knew). But eighty percent of the Black operators were. Our issue was not only of geographic redlining, but an economic redline. The branch alleged that Blacks received the stores with the lowest volumes. So we asked to see the top 20 grossing stores, the median average gross of all stores, and the gross incomes of the Black stores for the past twelve months. There were 33 Black store owners, 26 were in a Black area, two were in the top 20, 23 were below the median average gross, and most of them were losing money. So we were right.

Southland said they would offer the Black operators support to try to get their volumes up. We countered with a reduction in the franchise split. Southland said they would consider that. Southland announced they were going to suspend the equity requirements of all stores. That was a major victory. Southland said they would put more money in the community, which we thought was good. Then we dealt with the issue of Black employee relations, and Southland's minority procurement record. Both were extremely poor. Southland promised they'd bring back recommendations to correct the situation at the next meeting.

They wanted some assurances that we would not let the Glen Moore situation get in the way of our negotiations. We said if Southland could prove that the Moore situation was based solely on the fact that he owed the money, and not based on retaliatory and discriminatory actions, then we wouldn't. Otherwise, we were behind Glen.

Again, as was always the case, Southland had relegated this meeting to their local players. We said that should be the last time this would happen. Southland said they would make sure of it. I'm sure after the last meeting, the Dallas officials felt that with the dissension they saw, the issue could effectively be localized. We knew eventually they would try to localize the issue. Southland knew we were serious about that, so they put a plan in place to deal with it. Southland made an attempt to go around us. They called in their boy, Herm Willie, who set up an elaborate dinner meeting at the Century Plaza Hotel. Southland had just completed its organizational restructuring that came out of the leveraged buyout. Herm Willie insisted that the new regional Vice President (Telson), Terry Blocher and himself meet with Ray and me. However, they also invited the California NAACP State President Jose DeSosa. The purpose of inviting Jose was to convince us through Jose, that Mitch had the juice to handle all the problems, and that we didn't need Dallas involved. Jose is probably one of the best NAACP strategists I've met. He is very serious and straightforward, but a team player. Herm Willie was the host and facilitator. It was time for the cat to chase the mouse.

Jose had asked Ray and I to meet him at 7 p.m., to brief him on the Southland situation. I got there about 7:10. Ray called him and told him he wasn't going to be able to make it. I gave Jose a packet and gave him a chronology of events that had occurred, including how I felt national played in this. I apprised him of who Herm Willie was and his relationships to the national NAACP's Special Contributions Board, as well as to Southland. Jose was on top of it and ready to roll. We went up about 7:40. Our hosts were waiting. Herm ordered a couple rounds of drinks, and we just shot the bull until dinner was ordered.

That was about 8 p.m. At about 11:15, we were still arguing the merits and demerits of a localized task force. Mitch had not been able to convince Jose, nor myself, that Southland, was sincere in their efforts to maintain a national priority in their commitment to modify company policy. Secondly, that if Southland was so sold about Mitch's capabilities, then why wasn't he at the last task force meeting, as well as prior ones. Southland was really just fast talking us, trying to convince us that on the basis of what they had committed to thus far, they could handle the rest of the issues in a similar fashion. Jose said we needed to conclude. His position was that whatever issues were resolved on the West Coast, Dallas would need to apply those issues on the East Coast, and should be involved in knowing what the issues were.

Southland maintained the position that the East Coast had different problems. That was the biggest lie they had told to date, and we later proved it, when we met with the Washington franchise operators, at the 1988 convention, later that year. We left that meeting with an agreement that Mitch Telson would bring a letter signed by Jere Thompson, that he had the full authority to address and commit on all issues. We knew he wouldn't, but we decided to play it their way just to prove it. Our strategy worked.

A week before the fifth (and last) task force meeting to be held, several major incidents happened: First, we found out that during Southland's restructuring, they had created three new Vice President positions and seventeen new division manager positions. And guess what? Not one was given to a Black, not one. Here we had been in the midst of this investigation almost ten months, and one of the most crucial issues other than franchisee discrimination-- Black employee relations and development-- was seriously violated. And Southland passed over several qualified Blacks. We were all shocked. Second, that Ray and I made a conference call to Ben Hooks to update him on the lack of progress on the Southland issue, and our new revelations.

Hooks said he was concerned that Southland had a trade agreement with PUSH, and his information sources told him that many of our issues were being dealt with on that end. He said we needed to clarify that, and if it was the case then we should leave Southland to them. Ray and I looked at each other, then Ray said OK, and he'd get back to Hooks within the week. We called Rev. Willie Barrows, then-executive director of PUSH, and updated her on our investigation. She said she had been reading about the issues and felt that we were on target. We asked her if we waged a direct action campaign based on what had come out of our investigation, would she support it. Rev. Barrows said if Hooks felt it was needed to push Southland to address those issues, some of which were in the trade agreement, then, she would be for it.

I asked her if she was in dialogue with Southland at that time. She said that she hadn't discussed anything with Southland representatives on issues relevant to the trade agreement nor our discrimination claims. We asked if Jesse Jackson, Sr. was in dialogue with Southland. She stated that Jesse was in the midst of a presidential campaign, and wasn't handling any PUSH issues. We concluded the conversation by agreeing to follow up our dialogue in writing, and she would do so in kind. She was a very nice lady. It appeared by our conversation that Hooks was being misled and misinformed. We sent the letter and waited for her response.

The last incident entailed the last operator, Glen Moore, who had finally become desperate and despondent over not being able to get out of his store. Southland was stretching him out and he was basically a caretaker for their store. He couldn't pay himself more than a small draw, and Southland had long quit any meaningful dialogue, until they had resolved the issue of the audit shortages. Glen got fed up, and just disappeared with about two weeks worth of receipts. Southland was distraught. They were calling us. Glen was calling us. Terry Blocher called me, "Anthony, you've got to help us. Glen won't talk to us at the store and, we can't reach him at home. We have a store there that's running itself, and his employees are not cooperating."

I asked Terry, "You want me to use my influence with the operator to get Glen to talk to you."

"Yes, I do," Terry replied. I called Moore.

Moore claimed that he called Blocher every day for the past month and had been given the run around. "Know anything about that, Terry?" I asked. He claimed he specifically never got a message from Glen, and that the rep just made him aware of it. I said, "Terry, you've been sending a Brink's truck to the store for two weeks. They haven't picked up anything? You want me to believe that you wouldn't know anything about that? Give me a break with that shit, Terry." I finally told him I didn't appreciate him trying to bullshit me, and use me at the same time. He had to do what he had to do. It was his problem, not mine.

The next day, Glen called, "These lying sons of bitches, I don't trust them further than I can see them. Now they want to meet with me. There's no way in hell I'm going to meet with them alone."

"Glen, go with your attorney," I said. Then, he went off on a tangent about his attorney, calling him everything he could think of. He finally admitted that he didn't have any money. "What do you mean you don't have any money? You got two weeks worth of receipts," I told him.

"Oh, yeah," he said. Then he went back to, "Well, I'm still not going to meet with them alone."

I told Moore that it was not my responsibility to resolve Southland's franchise disputes, and that he should meet with them and close the store out. He said he would never meet with Southland alone, and asked for names of some attorneys he could call. I had my secretary give him some names, and he hung up. He called back two days later, twelve times, almost every fifteen minutes, until I took the call. He was calling my office, not the branch. Finally, I returned his call and Glen started again. "I will not meet with Southland alone," or "Why can't you meet with me."

I continually told him, "Glen, it's not a part of the investigation. I can't represent your personal interest."

Then he'd start with, "Oh, so the NAACP is gonna sell me out now," or "Southland has paid you guys off, like I heard they did."

He just made statement after statement, until finally I said, "Glen, you had the weakest case of them all. I have a client, I gotta go."

J.H. Snow, from Southland Dallas called. "Glen says he won't meet with us alone. He wants you there."

"I can't be there as a representative of the NAACP," I told J.H.

"We have to get Moore out of that store now," J.H. stated. Anthony, only harm is going to come to him, if he keeps this up. Eventually, we'll have to call in the police and claim it a theft. We have the executed franchise agreement calling for him to make the daily funds transfers to the agent of our choice. He's in clear violation of this. Anthony, what if we had you there as a mediating third party, just to bring both sides together? You wouldn't represent Glen or Southland or the NAACP. Just sit and mediate. Glen should go for that, right?"

"J.H., he should, but as far apart as you and Glen are, that could take all day. I'm already behind on my work. I don't really have the time to deal with this," I said.

J. H. replied, "I know this may spark some ethical questions of conflict of interest, but what if we paid you for your time?" I asked him what he meant. He stated he'd buy my time to mediate this meeting.

He stated, "You are a financial consultant, right?"

"Yeah."

"What does your time cost?"

"$75 per hour," I said.

"So what's the problem?" he asked.

"I have a liability here, I said. "You're not buying my services, you're trying to buy my influence."

J.H. maintained that if Glen wanted me, and they wanted me, and I didn't give any advice, but just made sure the dealings were fair and above board, so Glen couldn't say that he was railroaded or forced into an unfair resolution, where was the liability? "You're just a witness of our negotiations," J.H. stated. "I'd rather pay you a few hundred bucks and move this issue, than have thousands of dollars at risk, minute by minute," he continued.

"And you can't get anybody else to do this?" I asked.

"Glen wants you, and we want to resolve the issue," J.H. sighed.

"Let me call you back on that in a few minutes," I said. I called a couple of attorney friends of mine, explained the situation, and solicited their opinions. They both said Southland was scandalous, and to get the request for services in writing. As long as everybody understood that I was just there to mediate, at both their requests, I should be all right. I phoned J. H. and told him to set up the time with Glen, and have him call me. I told Glen that I was only there as a witness and a mediator, that he'd have to cut his own deal, and that I couldn't advise him on anything. I asked him if he still wanted me present. He said he did. We met at Southland's airport office.

Glen Moore, Terry Blocher, J.H. Snow and I were at the meeting,. Southland's corporate headquarters in Dallas had sent J.H. to close the deal, and to close Moore out of that store, or whatever it took. Glen started out very bitter and short. Southland opened their investigation.

Snow: "Where you been, Glen?"

Moore: "It doesn't matter. I'm here now."

Snow: "Where are the deposits?"

Moore: "I have the deposits."

Snow: "How can we be sure?"

Moore: "I guess you'll have to trust me, won't you?"

Snow: "We want to buy your store, today!"

Moore: "Good! I want to sell it, so I can use every cent suing you motherfuckers."

Snow: "Is that what you plan to do?"

Moore: "Count on it. For what you've done to me, you gonna have to pay."

Snow: "Well, let's get down to it. What will it take to get you out of the store?"

Moore: "Make me an offer."

Snow: "What do you think that the store is worth?"

Moore: "Are you going to give me what's it's worth?"

Snow: "We might, if it's reasonable."

Moore: "I want $300,000."

Snow: "You call that reasonable?"

That just set Glen right off. "You motherfuckers haven't been reasonable since you forced that damn amendment on the owners. I went from a three bedroom house in the Marina, to a one bedroom shack, and I'm supposed to be reasonable? My store has been for sale a year and a half, while you motherfuckers played games with my family and me. Have you been reasonable?" Glen said. J.H. and Blocher sat dead silent, probably thinking they should have searched Glen before they came in. Literally. Glen continued, "I've been trying to be businesslike in calling for three weeks, while you ditched my calls, and continued to send me notices. But I'm supposed to be reasonable. Don't give me that shit about what's reasonable, OK? You motherfuckers pushed the wrong person this time. A week ago, you would have taken your life in your hands talking this shit, so don't even think I'm going to be reasonable." Glen was yelling at the top of his voice.

J.H. said, "Let's take a break."

Glen and I stepped out. He was still fuming. The shit was funny to me, but I held a straight face. It was typical of how some whites have treated us historically, and just expected us to forget everything when master said, "Come on in the house and talk about it." Sometimes you really wonder if they ever will take Black folk seriously. Well, they were damn sure taking Glen seriously today, if for no more than a minute.

When the meeting reconvened, Southland was ready to get down to business. I saw an exhausted look in Terry Blocher's face. While outside, we could hear J.H. and Terry arguing, apparently over what they would settle with Glen. Dallas had given instructions to get the deal done. This was the time, because they knew Glen wasn't coming back, and they didn't know if the cost to get him would be prohibitive, in terms of what he might do in the future. J.H., who was clearly in charge, resumed his questioning.

Snow: "OK, Glen. Now make us a reasonable offer for the store, and we'll talk money."

Moore: "I gave you my offer."

Snow: "Well, make us another offer."

That's when I interceded, "He made his offer. Why does he have to bid against himself? Why don't you just counteroffer, so he'll have an idea of what you're willing to pay."

J.H. looked at Blocher and said, "Counter the offer." Blocher looked down, then he looked up with a pained expression. The conversation went as follows:

Blocher: "OK, $80,000."

Moore: "What do I look like to you? The last audit shortage you claimed was over $70,000."

Essex: "That's his price, Glen. Your turn."

Moore: "My price is $300,000. That's my price."

Snow: "The purpose here, Glen, is to eventually settle on some mutual figure between $80,000 and $300,000. If you're going to hold at 300, then we are wasting our time. We're not going to offer you $300,000, Glen."

Moore: "And you know I'm not going to take $80,000, so why don't we cut the bullshit."

Then Southland decided to throw some more shit in the game, figuring to leverage Glen and put something else on his mind.

Snow: "Glen, are you aware that the IRS has been in touch with us regarding the sell of your store, and that we've been instructed to notify them when the store has been sold?"

Moore: "You know I am. You people were the ones that caused the problem in the first place. If I had been allowed to borrow against the profits I put back in the store three years ago, I would have been able to pay them. Instead, I went to you, and you told me you weren't a bank, and you wouldn't give me my money. You screwed me all the way around. Now I owe penalties on top of penalties."

Snow: (looking at Blocher) "Is that what happened?"

Blocher: "I don't know. I just got here."

Snow: "Well, maybe we can work out something with the IRS, so that you can get your money, and resolve that issue with them. That's between you and them. Maybe we'll tell them we took the store back. You know Southland and the IRS aren't the best of friends any-way (referring to Southland's own felony tax fraud convictions of

1984)."

Essex: "Why'd you bring that up, J.H.?"

Snow: "I just thought we'd let Glen know that in spite of his mounting problems, we'll support him if he'll work with us."

Essex: "And if he doesn't, you'll put the taxman on him?"

Snow: "I didn't say that."

Essex: "Um-Hummmm, let's get back to the sale price negotiations. Glen, are you going to hold at $300,000."

Moore: "My store is worth what it's worth. I'll go to $275,000. Otherwise, we can go."

Blocher: "$85,000."

Moore: "Is he serious?"

I shrugged and looked away.

Moore: "$274,000."

Blocher: "$86,000."

Moore: "$273,000."

Blocher: "$87,000."

Moore: "$272,000."

Blocher: "$88,000."

Moore: "$271,000."

Blocher: "$89,000."

Moore: "$270,000."

Blocher: "$90,000."

Moore: "OK, I don't have time for this shit. We've been bidding 15 minutes and you've only gone up $10,000. I'm out of here. You can play this game by yourself."

Glen got up to leave. J.H. said, "Wait, we need another break."

Moore and I left. You could hear Snow and Blocher really yelling at each other. Glen and I were shaking our heads. It was obvious that J.H. was becoming a little impatient with Blocher's tactic. After nearly fifteen minutes of hollering and screaming, they finally called us back in. Blocher was obviously flustered. His hair was all over his head, and he was sweating profusely. Snow was really "sweatin'" Blocher's ass (as we say on the street). I remember thinking, "Damn, he was acting like this was his money he was holding." The shit was really funny. I guess we were blowing his slurpee budget out of pocket.

J.H. said, " Anthony, how much time do you have?" We had already been messing around about an hour and a half. I told them I had about another hour. Blocher then came out with his big offer, "I'll offer you $100,000," he said.

Moore looked at him and said, "Is that what we went out of the room for?" Glen told him he'd take $250,000. You could truly see where this was heading.

"Glen, will you take $125,000," J.H. asked.

"No," Glen replied.

J. H. said, "Make me what will be your lowest offer. We have other things to deal with. If we can't match it, I won't waste your time anymore."

Glen looked at them. With a quiver in his voice, he said "$200,000." J.H. leaned over to Blocher, who was wringing wet, and whispered in his ear. Blocher damn near jumped out of his seat. I mean the guy was agonizing over the whole process.

Blocher said, "OK, but you turn over the keys today and turn in the receipts."

Glen said calmly, "No, I'm not going to do that. I want a guarantee that you people will do what you say. You're the biggest liars I've ever met. We will close the store out together. You can have the receipts, when I get the money."

"Well, Glen we can't give you all of the money, until we clear up what you owe us." J.H. said. "Now, we will allow you to hire your own accountant to reconcile your records, but you will have to pay us."

"Well I know what you're going to do. You'll get me out of the store, and then tie up my money," Glen responded. "I'll have no money and no way to make a living. You'll have to give me some money for living expenses going out. I'm not a fool."

Blocher asked, "How much will you need?"

Glen said, "About $25,000. Then, you put the rest of the money in an escrow account to be released upon my satisfying the prestated conditions in our agreement. Then I don't have to deal with them, when you go home." (meaning the local Southland management).

J.H. countered, "You owe us $65,000 on the last audit. We'll hold that out until it's resolved. We'll put $120,000 in escrow. We'll give you $15,000 to live on, until we settle this over the next few days. You select an escrow company, and we'll be there tomorrow at 11 a.m., with your cash-out check and the balance to be deposited in escrow. Then tomorrow in the afternoon, we will do the store closeout."

"No, we won't," said Glen. "I'll give you the key tomorrow, and then I'll select an accountant, who will go through the closing with us. Plus, I'm not going to let you rush me now. There's more to life than news, weather and 7-11."

J.H. looked at me. I just laughed. I couldn't believe he said that either.

With an exasperated look J.H. said, "Can we agree on a date in the next five days?"

Glen said that next Tuesday was fine. Glen asked if his agreement could be typed up right away? He wanted to leave with an agreement in principle, so come tomorrow the terms wouldn't change. They said that was fine. I asked if they needed me anymore. We thanked each other. I left. Southland got a run for its money that day.

* * *

The fifth and last task force meeting was virtually a war. Jose DeSosa was on the task force. Mitch Telson brought in a letter from Jere Thompson, claiming that he was authorized to represent the company in that forum. With what we were getting ready to bring up, he wished he had left that to Thompson. Ray, disgusted that neither Thompson, Dick Dole nor Don Burnside showed up, jumped dead off in Mitch's ass with both feet. "OK Mitch, since you're the man, tell me about the 20 new positions that were created, where not one Black or Hispanic was given any of those slots. Mitch, can you explain this to me? Since you're the man, Mitch." Ray said in an intense, rapid-fire line of questioning.

Telson turned beet red. He didn't expect us to even have that information. He was shocked. He was going to try and play us, because he had hired some brother in San Diego and another young brother in Anaheim, that he brought to the meeting. Do you know what he said? While it was not his decision, the company did not have any competent Blacks in the management pipeline who were ready at the time of reorganization. It was a slap in the face to every Black Southland employee. The three Black employees in the room couldn't even look us in the eye. Owen McKay sat there dumbfounded.

After about two minutes of silence, Telson finally said, "Hey, Ray, give me something I can control. I didn't make that decision. I'm hiring Blacks. We will have qualified Blacks ready in the future."

"You have qualified Blacks in the company now," I said. "When do you think that the company is going to go through another reorganization again," (if ever) "where this much of an opportunity will open up? Have you ever seen this many positions open up before?" Telson shook his head no. "Weren't most of these decisions made in the last year, during this investigation?"

Telson said, "Probably."

"And of all your Black employees, which are how many, Mitch, two, three hundred, you didn't have one that you would have given at least a temporary shot? Or was there a Black you could bring in from another company, just to show us that you were at least making an effort to conform to what we've discussed," I said.

Telson, Blocher, Irvin or nobody else was ready for us that day. Southland had straight-up counterfeited the whole process with that move.

Ray said, "This is contemptuous, as far as, I'm concerned. I don't think we have anything else to talk about, unless you change this situation here and now, Mitch?"

"Ray, you know I can't, Mitch said. "Give me something I can control."

"Mitch, you said you were in control," Ray torted.

"Well, just let us present some of the other ideas we plan to implement very soon. We're sure you will be pleased," Mitch responded.

The rest of the meeting was anti-climatic. Southland talked about putting more money in the community. They proposed using their stores for certain projects, possibly shifting some of its expenses to stores that required higher security needs, and even shifting a point in the split.

I asked, "Where is the EEO policy, minority business procurement plan, and the revised franchise agreement we were promised."

"Dallas is still working on all of these items," Mitch claimed.

"Well, it looks like we're really on hold here," said Ray. "Those issues you could have impacted, you didn't, and the others are still being considered. But, locally, you did make a few changes to pacify us. And of course, you're the man, Mitch. Maybe this task force shouldn't meet again, until the major issues can be fully addressed-- the franchise agreement, the EEO policy, the Minority Employee Career Development Plan, the Minority Procurement Plan. These are in addition to the discontinuation of the harassment of Black franchisees and Black employees. Otherwise, we quickly need to help you bring these issues to reality."

The Southland crew just sat disillusioned around the table, as we all got up and left. That was the last time the task force met, but it was also the signal for the compromise to go into full effect. Two days after the meeting, we called Ben Hooks again, to update him on what had transpired with PUSH and with the task force meeting. The purpose of the call was also to feel Hooks out on the possibility of a national boycott against Southland. Hooks seemed very uninterested in what we were saying. When we finally got around to asking his opinion, Hooks emphatically stated, "I think you should leave Southland alone. I'll talk with them and try to find out what's going on. I don't think we should engage in a boycott at this time." We even tried to tell him to talk to Rasheed, if he didn't think we had enough to go on. Hooks said, "No, I don't have to do that." He said we could continue to try to remedy the local situation, but he didn't want the task force to meet until he gave us the go ahead. We knew at that time that Herm Willie had gotten to Hooks. Southland was able to break up the national focus and silently reduce our involvement to a local dialogue, with no recourse, after all.

A week later, Terry Blocher called Ray to tell him that he'd like to continue to try to work on some of the issues, even though we couldn't come to the table. Who told him we couldn't come to the table? At the last meeting, we left it open to our discretion as to when we would meet again. Obviously, Blocher knew what Hooks had told us. Either Hooks called Dallas, and informed them of his decision to put the task force on hold, or Herm Willie received an assurance in advance. Either way, we never heard from Hooks again on the Southland issue. While our efforts were being compromised internally, Southland was working externally to undermine any efforts of a possible boycott. Southland began using Larry Irvin as a public relations consultant. Larry introduced Blocher to the Urban League, SCLC and United Negro College Fund (UNCF) Chapters. Southland kicked up the ante and really started throwing money around to those groups like candy. The best way to make friends in L.A. is to give them some money. Southland was being perceived as a real progressive corporation. A primary case of "when a lie becomes the truth."

In the meantime, the Black operators were outraged that the task force talks had been broken off. They were publicly saying that the NAACP had sold them out. The Tibbses, though out of the system, were still trying to settle their closing shortage dispute with Southland. And Southland was really dogging them, since they thought we were out of the picture. Glen Moore couldn't get the balance of his money out of escrow, because Southland was still claiming he owed an enormous sum of money that couldn't be refuted by Moore or his accountant. Furthermore, Southland did put the IRS on Moore, and told the IRS about the money that was in escrow so the IRS put a hold on the escrow.

I just didn't want to deal with Moore anymore. I had done Glen his favor. If he was still having problems with Southland, he would have to get legal assistance. It was no longer a discriminatory issue. It may have started that way, but it had become widely known by the other operators and by the Black employees, that any mistreatment Glen Moore got wasn't necessarily because he was Black, but because he was Glen Moore. Their relationship had become personal. So why try to drag us in the middle of that.

Ironically, while we were in Washington, D. C. for the 1988 National Convention meeting with the D.C. franchisees (Fred Rasheed, Jose DeSosa and myself), Glen Moore and the Tibbses were on the radio (then KGFJ-AM which has since been sold) talking about the boycott they were forced to wage against Southland, because the NAACP had sold them out. Many people who heard the show, said they (not so much the Tibbses, as Glen Moore) talked about me like a dog.

Upon my return, I contacted the station to rebut. But Bill Shearer, President of the station, who had always been pretty supportive of me said not to worry about it, that it was just bullshit, and that it was more or less Moore's opinion. "An opinion is like an asshole, everybody has one," Bill said. I let it go.

Moore never did get his money from Southland. Moore's misdirected rage had more to do with his final audit and the IRS taking all his money, than the NAACP abandoning him. Had it not been for the NAACP, particularly myself, Southland would have taken Moore's store and jailed him, without a second thought. We backed Southland off, and forced them to deal with Moore civilly, but now we were to blame. I don't think so. Still, it was a no-win situation for us, because our hands were tied.

In the meantime, a second group of Black franchisees was formed, headed up by Tony Nicholas and Larry Williams (yes, the same one who appeared on TV the year before, telling the public what a good master Southland was). They were now having difficulties with Southland. This group was just coming in, as the other group was fighting to get out (except Williams), and was told to stay clear of the Tibbses, Moore and some of the others because, they were only troublemakers. Does this sound familiar?

They were demanding a meeting with us, but because of the bad press that the first operators received, they said they only wanted to meet with us, (the branch) if a member from national was present. They had contacted Fred Rasheed, who had agreed to meet with them. When Rasheed came to town, he and I met with the five new operators at my business office. Larry Williams tried to front us (the branch and me) off, by insinuating that we were all talk, hadn't done any work, and had sold out the other franchisees. Fred informed him that he knew that was not the truth, because of the reports he received, as well as, the meeting he'd been a part of. I told Fred that this was the operator that refused to join us earlier, got on TV and supported Southland, because he was up for a second store. (Or so he thought.) The store never came through. Then I pulled out three big legal files, stacked it about two feet high and said, "Here's the work that was done on Southland. Care to review it?" Williams' eyeballs almost dropped on the floor. As he was looking through the files, both Fred and I could see that he was shocked over the preponderance, depth and detail of the information we had compiled, particularly our inside information. Information not even he had seen before. In layman's terms, "He didn't know what the fuck he was talking about." I think we recovered a little of our credibility with Larry and the rest of the new group that day. But we were never able to put the same intensity back into the effort, because we never got the "go" from Hooks.

How did Southland get out of all this? Well, what do you do, when a major corporation continually displays contempt for minority operators? Or, what do you do, when corporate management continues to harass minority vendors who want to put quality products in your store, or continue to implement the same practices on a second group of operators, that you claimed you discontinued? What do you do with a company like this? You reward them, right? You put them on the Urban League board. You make them the Grand Marshall of the Martin Luther King Day Parade. Lastly, how about the dinner chairman of the Sickle Cell dinner? You think I'm kidding, right? All three happened within six months of each other. While Southland was virtually pissing in the faces of its Black operators in L.A. and all over the country, they were also pissing in the pockets of other community groups to disengage any possibility that the NAACP could reorganize against them. This is the perfect example of how our community groups will take money, no matter what snake is on the other end of it.

The perfect damage control campaign had been implemented against the biggest of the so-called "civil rights watchdogs," and the community bought into it -lock, stock and barrel.

Larry Irvin, who was then Secretary of the Urban League Board, took Terry Blocher right over to the Urban League, where he bought himself a seat. I guess I can't blame any of those groups. I guess they said if the NAACP national organization was in Southland's pocket, why not us. Which, I'm sure Southland didn't hesitate to tell them. This is why the condition of our community goes unchanged. We're the only group of people who can take a smile and a handshake, while getting kicked square off in our collective ass.

* * *

While Southland thought they got away, and the NAACP was telling operators that Southland was the "best thing that could have happened to them" (through my successor), and Larry was getting his friends in the NAACP service contracts for legal work, the problems kept coming. A third group of operators went public on Southland again. Suddenly, the Urban League and other community groups, who had taken Southland's money, acted like they were concerned. Blocher tried to explain it off as "old news." But, Southland was still buying all the friends they needed. In the long run, the NAACP could be held responsible for compromising the interests of Blacks in this situation.

The NAACP position was a correct one, and it had Southland dead to rights. Southland was in a very delicate position. Their proposed leveraged buyout, weak from the start, was an ambitious plan that eventually failed. They sold it to a group of Japanese investors to keep from going under. Had the NAACP pressed the issue, Southland would have had no choice but to conform, or be destroyed. A national boycott would have complicated the sensitive negotiations of the LBO, and Southland's banks would have probably pulled out of the deal.

Southland knew that, and was prepared to spare no expense in trying to save this leveraged buyout. It meant too much to the Thompson brothers, to let a bunch of so-called "nigger operators" sink their dream of regaining the majority control of Southland. So they went out and bought every so-called "niggah of influence" they could find, and pitted them against each other.

They started in the NAACP. With the assistance of Black

franchisees, the NAACP went from damn near controlling the destiny of current and future franchisees, in their ability to make a decent living, to being, once again, compromised on the plantation. Sharecropping little of their own harvest, on our own land controlled by a master of their fate.

The major victory in all of this was that the Tibbses sued Southland in court, and was awarded $750,000 in damages and legal costs. I was told by David Allen, the ex-employee who testified in the case, that much of the information used in the trial, was derived from the reports we'd put together in the branch investigation. One of the partner's of the law firm that represented the Tibbses (Foster and Ripley, James Foster), was also a member of the L.A. branch's Executive Committee. The court found that the Tibbses were unfairly discriminated against, and were forced to sell their store for racially motivated reasons. Good for them. Glen Moore lost his case. I'm not one to say, "told you so," but we all knew Moore's case was part fact and part full of shit. He blew his case early in the game with some of his freewheeling antics, and his case wasn't as well documented as the Tibbses. The Tibbses were just one case, in over one hundred fifty past and current franchisees, who, if they had documented their claims properly, would have had a successful case against Southland, of discrimination or unfair business practices.

Many of them have lost their life savings, will lose their money, or barely salvage some of their initial investment, after many hard years of labor and aggravation. But many of them will stay in the system, and continue to be harassed and manipulated, by a company that represents itself as the "All-American Convenience Store." Southland will continue to buy off Black leadership, while it has its hands deep in the pockets of poor franchise owners and the community.

Yes, "Oh, thank heaven for 7-11," and please don't forget to pray for the poor operators, who live their lives out of the bottom of a slurpee cup, working their own businesses harder than slaves worked the cotton fields. That's just what they were. Slurpee Slaves. Slaves to "the Slurpee kings."

* * *

4

Police Abuse in the 1980s:

The Father of Rampart

"The doctrine that submission to violence is the best cure for violence, did not hold good as between slaves and overseers. He was whipped oftener who was whipped easiest."

-Frederick Douglass

Many of the civil right compromises that Blacks experienced throughout the 1980s were centered in the abuse and repressive conduct on the part of law enforcement agencies, and a passive attitude on behalf of Black leadership, to criticize such behavior. This blatant failure to uphold and protect the rights of Blacks, in addition to the aggressive handling (or mishandling) of many law enforcement encounters with Black and brown populations, undermined the notion of equal and full protection under the law. This was never more prevalent than in Los Angeles where an implied criminality sought to justify suppression tactics in urban-based policing methods.

In most Black communities, it's estimated that ninety-six or ninety-seven percent of the people (depending on your source) are, for the most part, law-abiding. Meaning, they don't go out looking to get involved in criminal activity. They usually resist the temptation to do something dishonest, and seek to consistently comply with the law. It is estimated that three and a half percent of the population may have done something legally incriminating in their lives and gotten caught. They are not career criminals who involve themselves in non-death threatening incidents, like auto theft and robberies, etc. Less than one-half of one percent of the Black population is of a dangerous element to the public at large. They may be armed robbers, rapists and murderers or whatever menace society chooses to label them. Still, their criminal activity is not even proportionate to crime levels of the larger society. Yet, Blacks were (and still are) represented in the public eye, (particularly electronic and print media) as criminally suspect, and their prosecution and incarceration rates are highly disproportionate to others within the society. Blacks are stopped more frequently (without probable cause), charged more frequently and prosecuted five to eight times (according to various sources) more than their white counterparts. Central to higher levels of prosecution and incarceration is societal indictment of people of color, that casts aspersions of suspicion upon any unknowing and unsuspecting person, who finds him or herself in environments considered reserved for whites. Even so-called "upper class" Blacks, those of advanced education and/or income means comparable to their white counterparts, are not exempt from this "profiling," associated with the racial underclass. Thousands of "isolated incidents" have now been recognized as system-wide, or institution-wide problems, known as "racial profiling." But long before it became a catchword, it was reality practiced by law enforcement agencies around the country.

Many law enforcement agencies allow distorted and stereotypic portrayals to affect how Blacks are handled and treated in their custody. Blacks, in this country, basically pay taxes for these agencies, to act as agents of repression; to disrespect, fail to protect and, in many instances, abuse decent citizens. Many citizens are forced to choose between receiving compromised services, or no services at all. Most urban citizens (particularly the elderly) are pro-police. They often advocate for money to support creative programs to sensitize law enforcement to community perceptions, only to see that money go in suppression (more guns, more tanks, more men). Many fear reprisal if they complain about quality of services in the community, when in fact, they already suffer from a lack of services

Police deployment is the focus of every urban community. In most urban communities, the number of police per capita is significantly less than their suburban or exclusive area counterparts. For example, if a mostly white area has a police officer per capita rate of one for every 1,000 residents, the Black community is most likely to have one for every 2,500 residents. Furthermore, most agencies deploy where they chose to, not where the greatest need is, and not where those who suffer the most are. Deployment favors those who are the most politically and socially affluent. Some immigrant communities receive fairer police deployment, than many Black communities. Blacks remain unprotected more than they deserve to be, and they also suffer greater abuse. Police misconduct became a principle focus of my advocacy, because no city was more disparate in its abuses of equal and just protection under the law, than Los Angeles, in the mid-1980s. Law enforcement mentality in the 1980s was reprehensible.

Los Angeles' predominant law enforcement agencies, the Los Angeles Police Department and Los Angeles County Sheriff's Department, both had a history of being among the most repressive in the country. With a history of unnecessary fatal shootings and unethical conduct, dating back to the '40s and '50s (and in some cases, as early as the turn of the century), both agencies had national reputations for abuse. In the 1980s, those departments maintained a "what we don't see, can't hurt us" policy, which gave street officers the green light to abuse their authority, under the guise that the department would back them up. And many times, it did. The department's (former) chief of police, Daryl Gates, commonly referred to the men as "the family," in a Mafioso context, communicating to the public at large, that the police will "go to the wall for the family." That attitude would eventually be the downfall of Gates, and the burndown of Los Angeles, for the second time in 27 years.

Both the Los Angeles Police and Sheriff's Departments had become very sophisticated in their approach to hide their oppressive behavior and "above the law" attitude, with community outreach and relations divisions that are designed to massage the concerns of the masses, while taking a "business as usual" posture. This has allowed for disharmony and disagreement to persist among the "so- called" leaders of our communities, with respect to their attitude toward these departments. It also made applying any unified pressure on these departments virtually impossible, except in the most outrageous and extreme cases of misconduct. A half a movement is really no movement at all in the civil rights game. The police know this and, many times, played to the needs of the certain "so-called" leaders' desire to be recognized, and those same leaders, in turn, looked away from many of the department's real problems. In L.A.'s case, it was a pervasive misconduct that was being ignored. Some key politicians came out of law enforcement, such as Tom Bradley (an L.A. police officer, before going into politics), who bought and defended the departments' justifications for inferior service.

For Blacks in the city of Los Angeles, it was a continuous compromise of dignity and respect. Every day of a Black man's life in L.A. was a crap shoot, when engaged in a routine traffic stop by LAPD. A cop's authority allows them to take the two things a person values most, their liberty and their life. A bad cop's will to reinforce this authority could end up killing a person over minimal offenses, like a failure to obey a simple command. This combined with personified machoism, "escalated attacks on Black men. This was the order of the day in Los Angeles law enforcement during the 1980s. The world witnessed the attack on Rodney King, in March of 1991, and the misconduct scandal that came to be known as Rampart, in 1999 (the biggest in the department's history) all came out of a corrupt culture fashioned in the1920s, practiced in the 1940s, institutionalized in the 1960s and perfected as unwritten policy in the 1980s.

* * *

In Los Angeles, the notion of equal protection under the law, by police has long been a major question for the poor and disadvantaged. Most of the time these questions are discredited as rash assertions, dismissed by law enforcement agencies. Yet questions that centered around the fair deployment of officers, the subjective treatment of minorities, the excessive use of force, and police misconduct always seemed to get lost "in the spin." The Los Angeles Police and County Sheriff's Departments became public relations "gurus" in the 1980s, countering obvious contradictions in policies, and covering up actions of its officers with generic statements of denial, or endless internal investigations. However, when not tracked, these abusive violations seemed to continue, and become more serious with each occurrence. When follow-up inquiries were made, both departments would claim that they were on it. Every now and then, something would happen that would totally discredit the police's rebuttal that everything was in check. When one had to ask the question: "Who's policing the police?" The answer they got was "nobody."

Several things happened during 1987 and 1988 that gave rise

to major concerns of both the LAPD/LACSD's treatment of Blacks in Los Angeles. During early 1987, the branch had received many complaints over the indiscriminate stopping of Blacks, by L.A. police or deputy sheriffs, on the basis of where they lived, and what they were wearing. If anyone, but particularly a Black male, were driving through parts of South Central Los Angeles after 10 p.m. wearing dark clothing, they were stopped without justifiable cause. Then they were told to get out of the car, lie on the ground face down, or kneel with their hands behind their heads. When we received some of the initial calls, we made inquiries about them. We were told that they were probably a few gang-bangers who were upset over being stopped and searched. L.A.P.D., in particular, had no other explanation other than it was the officer's judgment call to stop the car.

However, a few days later, we got a few more calls, including one at my home from someone I knew. A doctor and his wife, returning from an exercise spa--both wearing sweat suits, were stopped, and forced to lie face down, on the busiest boulevard in South Los Angeles (Crenshaw), for 30 minutes. He was livid. In his hysterical state, he described their treatment as "Gestapo" type tactics, because of the verbal abuse he and his wife suffered. This occurred, even though they tried to cooperate.

Much of the public, including the Black middle and upper class, think they are far removed from such treatment. Many L.A. Blacks in the mid-1980s felt that they had transcended race issues until they were forced to face the realities of the masses: a rude, impatient police officer telling you to "shut the fuck up" when you ask him why he stopped you (which is your right).

As a sidebar, these situations exemplified the compromise Blacks were in, because many thought that their educational or professional accomplishment had somehow changed their social status, in the eyes of an oppressive, racist system. These Blacks wanted to hold themselves to a higher standard of treatment, because they had achieved a higher economic standard. Conversely, in trying to portray higher standards for themselves economically, they confusingly felt they should be held to the same social standard as whites. Some went to extremes, where they subliminally communicated to whites that "I'm one of you," forgetting that almost every issue in a Black/white encounter comes down to the determining factor of race, directly, indirectly, subconsciously or whatever. Many whites, particularly in law enforcement, see "Black" before they see anything else, and harbor hostile views towards Blacks of any social status, before they even get to know. Even when they do, it does not change much. Still, in the face of frequent racist encounters, many Blacks chase "racial equality," and so, forget that they will never become--socially accepted. Many have to be shocked back to reality. There is no shock like a racist law enforcement encounter. Experiences like these reinforce America's race reality, and should cause such Blacks to reexamine race. But at that moment, those Blacks, doctor or not, understood their social status was meaningless.

As the branch investigated more closely, we found that Mexican residents were also being unfairly treated. We confronted each department about their officers stopping citizens on the basis of race and clothing, which were violations of a person's civil rights. Both departments claimed they issued a policy addressing this issue, but complaints kept coming. So, we went undercover on them.

Former Hawthorne (CA) police sergeant and police abuse activist, Don Jackson, the branch's Police Abuse Committee chair, designed a strategy for several of us to catch misconduct in action. We dressed in dark clothing, drove older cars, rode two to three deep, and carried tape recorders and video cameras. The L.A. Police and Sheriff's Departments made a few stops, but recognized us and let us go without responding to why we were stopped. From that time, they would track our movement, and warned other officers, in the area, that we were out to "entrap" them.

Later in the year, Don would implement a similar strategy in the outlying cities, to monitor the misconduct of some of the smaller departments, including Long Beach, California. Their department's abuse made the NBC national news, when Don took a camera crew undercover, and was stopped in a dramatic fashion. A situation unfolded when Don questioned the officer, as he surrendered. The officer responded by pushing Don's head through a plate glass window. Don became a national hero, but his actions made one thing undeniably clear: The treatment of Blacks was clearly adversarial in nature, and representative of the treatment of the whole. Many departments claimed that you can't judge the actions of all, by the actions of one. That is true. It can also be surmised that just because you haven't been caught on tape, doesn't mean that it doesn't happen.

The ones with the biggest smirk on their faces in Los Angeles, the Police and Sheriff's Departments, would be caught at a later time, not necessarily on tape but by their own evidence. In February 1988, another action demonstrated the lack of respect for the Black community, where equal protection under the law was concerned. For many years, there had been allegations, by the Black community, that the Police and Sheriff's Department had less regard for the lives of Blacks versus other ethnicities.

In the midst of a gang war, where daily killings occurred, there were concerns of unfair deployment of police, because of lengthy or unanswered response calls in South Central. Police drove by distressed citizens flagging them down for help, while other areas of the city were being well-policed and well-protected. No matter how much the residents of South Central Los Angeles called for re-deployment, the police and (some) politicians maintained that they were doing the best they could to maintain a balanced deployment throughout the city.

Then it happened. An Asian woman was shot down in Westwood (near U.C.L.A.), allegedly a gang-related drive-by shooting. The largely white and Jewish "westside" communities were up in arms that such a thing could happen. They demanded immediate assurance that this would not reoccur. Our suspicions became quite clear.

The next day, 300 officers were re-deployed, in West Los Angeles, at the demand of Zev Yaroslavsky, then the district's councilman. Plus, a special task force was set up to investigate the killing, and a large reward for information leading to the arrest of the killer went into effect. The Black community was stunned and shocked. In South Central Los Angeles, where there are five killings a week - many being innocent bystanders - officers were never re-deployed expeditiously. The residents of South Central could only ask one question: Was the value of life on the Westside of town (predominantly white) worth more than the value of life in South Central (predominantly Black and Hispanic)?

Of course, this type of blatant, unequal treatment forced Black (and Negro) leaders to respond. Some did so in their usual shuffling manner, and some came out strong. Ray was very indifferent to it and, of course, since the mayor was in it, he relented to a "wait and see" posture. Meanwhile, I received tons of calls at my office asking, "What are you guys going to do?" I decided to participate in several rallies that were being planned, to at least give the branch presence. We should have taken a leading role, however.

Assemblywoman Maxine Waters (now Congresswoman) held a rally at First AME Church, which was attended by over 300 people including the press. Over 30 organizations were represented, and made statements, as did I. When my statements were aired on the 6 p.m. news, Ray thought he might want to take the lead on this project (to no one's surprise, since Ray was perceived as a media hog). The running joke around the community was that he would call a press conference to say "hi" to his mother. Other than a couple of staged media patrols around Westwood, he never did anything with it. He always wanted to be in the media, but rarely had anything of substance to say. There were also picketers at the Los Angeles Police Commission meeting. There were several organizations meeting suddenly on the police deployment practices and the quality of life issues. Many were searching for answers to questions few had the answers to. There are only so many police in Los Angeles. White folk were showing that they weren't about to give up their protection in a city gone mad.

The question then became: How do we get more police, specifically in South Central Los Angeles? In what many believed was a sincere effort to remedy the problem, became what could have been one of the most damaging precedents in the history of this country: a police tax on the residents of South Central Los Angeles. The proposition allowed for 300 new officers to be hired, specifically to patrol South Central Los Angeles. There were several major flaws with that proposal, which would be implemented in the form of a ballot initiative: 1) There would be no guarantee that the residents of South Central would receive the 300 officers, since the Police Department would still be responsible for deployment. The residents of South Central, possibly those with the lowest incomes in the city, could be paying for additional protection in the San Fernando Valley (citizens who had significantly higher incomes). 2) What would then happen if another community wanted protection, and was willing to pay for it? At some point in time, those who could afford to pay the most, would buy all the police protection, while those who pay less taxes would still be bound to an irreversible tax. 3) What about people who couldn't afford to pay any tax at all? Would there not be priority police protection for those at the bottom? given little or no assistance or protection?

* * *

Keith Krause is a good brother. He's a hardworking Black man, who is college educated, and was a supervising engineer with an aerospace company. He had no police record, was clean as they come, and didn't do drugs. He was a social drinker, a beer or wine, when engaged is his favorite past-time, dining gorgeous women. He didn't really hang in the streets. He chose to entertain at home. Keith is quiet, with a somewhat gregarious personality. He lived in the area patrolled by L.A. County Sheriff's, Lennox Station. They were known on the streets as a "gang in beige (their uniform colors) or "thugs in cop uniforms." This department's station was known to have abusive behaviors amongst their officers. This station had one of the highest numbers of questionable shootings and complaints in the country. Many of their officers were repeat offenders of "bad shootings," and had file histories of abuse. Some of these cops also had questionable integrity. The word on the street was that they allegedly (and with very reliable support) staged shootings, and engaged in other forms of setups, that ended in highly disputed claims of misconduct.

On July 4, 1988, I received a call from Keith, who I knew from my fraternal affiliation (Phi Beta Sigma), but I hadn't seen him in over five years. I had been President of the branch for more than a month. He had called a mentor of mine, Oscar Morgan, in distress over what had happened the night before. Oscar told him he should talk to me. Keith had just been beaten to within an inch of his life, when some nineteen Lennox deputy sheriffs came in his home and attacked him. Because I didn't know the nature of the call, I had planned to call him the next day after the long weekend. Keith called my home again, and left an urgent message. I had just gotten home from church, when I spoke with him. I couldn't believe what I heard. I sat down and told him to give me the whole story.

He was sitting in his home entertaining a lady friend, when there was a knock on the door. When he answered, there was his estranged wife (with whom he was in divorce proceedings), standing at his door with two Lennox deputy sheriffs. They said that they were called by his wife, because she wanted to get her things out of the house, and was not getting his cooperation. One deputy stated that they were there to assist her. Keith then stated to the deputies that not only had she not called him earlier, but she had gotten all of her possessions from the home on the date prescribed by the divorce court. Also, she had been ordered by the court to stay away from the house, since, on several occasions, she had come to the house to cause or continue their marital disputes. According to the deputies, Mrs. Krause had represented that she had interest in the house, and should be allowed access. Just as Keith asked the deputies if he could get the deed to prove she had no interest in the property, one of the deputies interrupted him and stated that he didn't need to see the deed, that he believed her (meaning his spouse), and to let her get her stuff. Keith again reiterated that she had nothing in the house. She had no right to be there, and if he could just show them his papers, this would be resolved.

As Keith turned to go back into the house, a deputy told him to "freeze." His wife said, "Don't let him go into the house; he has a gun in there." A deputy told Keith to exit the house, and allow his wife to enter. Keith said he'll come out, but she can't come in his house. The sheriffs pulled their batons and stated that she would enter, if they say so, and proceeded to physically try to remove Keith from his own home. As the deputies tried to place Keith in a choke hold, he was able to slip the hold, and was now standing outside his doorway on his front porch. Keith asked the deputies why they were doing this, and why don't they let him show the papers. His voice was slightly raised in the earshot of neighbors, who were now witnessing. Just then the deputies tried to grab him to handcuff him. Keith took a full spin to balance himself, and as he did this, his wife further heightened the tension of the situation by saying, "Watch out! He knows karate." At that time, one deputy ordered the other to call for backup. Within two minutes, neighbors whom we talked to said they saw between 12 to 15 sheriff cars lined up on the street.

Our investigation found that the deputy making the call created a climate for Keith's potential murder that night, when witnesses heard him say, "Deputies in need of assistance to subdue martial arts suspect. Suspect is also armed." One neighbor counted 19 deputy sheriffs. Another neighbor videotaped it. There were so many deputies moving back and forth, it was hard to ascertain the number on tape. Seven of the deputies bum-rushed Keith off his porch. Every neighbor Keith and I spoke to later, said they heard Keith say, "OK I'm down, I'm down. Stop hitting me." From that time, it was estimated that at least 10 deputies simultaneously beat Keith with batons for three to five minutes, and took turns beating him, while some stood by laughing.

Keith's guest, who had remained silent and out of sight up to this point, ran out of the house, screamed and ran toward Keith. The deputies looked up and stopped. She probably saved his life. Two deputies ran in the house, and one female deputy was overheard saying, "Where is the gun? What the hell are you guys doing here?"

Keith was beaten beyond recognition over an unsubstantiated allegation by his estranged wife. He was totally within his rights to defend entry into his home. We later found out that the initial call for the deputies to go to Keith's house was never placed. The department had no record of the first call, only the subsequent call for assistance. It was suspected that one, or a number of the deputies may have been associates of Krause's estranged wife. It appeared to be a setup stemming out of their marital dispute. Only, she had law enforcement do her dirty work, after the courts didn't support her contentions. It smacked of extreme misconduct and abuse of authority. After Keith was hospitalized, they even had the nerve to charge him with assault on a police officer and resisting arrest.

I sat stunned on the phone, as Keith tried emotionally to get through the recount of this nightmare. I told him to meet me at the Lennox Station at 1 p.m. Upon my arrival, Keith and his lady friend were already waiting. As we approached the doors to the station, Keith began to direct my attention to the deputies he had seen at his house that night. They appeared very surprised to see us, particularly Keith. After the condition they left him in, they probably thought he'd be hospitalized for a while. As we walked, one of the deputies shouted, "Hey, Keith. How's it going?" Keith responded casually. The nerve of these thugs, I thought. After bum-rushing him and damn near killing him, this cop ran up to him like it's "old home week."

I looked at this excuse for a cop and said, "I'm Anthony Essex from the NAACP. We're here to file a complaint. Is the captain in?"

Just then, the command watch sergeant walked by. "Hello, Mr. Essex, I know why you're here. I've seen you on television."

I looked at Keith, and asked the sergeant, "Why am I here?"

He said, "I presume you are here to discuss the charges against Mr. Krause."

I responded with a degree of sarcasm, "Not quite. But if it happens to come up in the conversation, I'd be glad to hear about 'em."

After taking us back to his office, he tried to explain how he had heard about the events that night. I asked if a report had been filed. He told me the captain was reviewing the incident. I asked him why. He couldn't answer. He proceeded to tell me that he is Ukrainian and had suffered discrimination before, and he felt as sorry as we did. We asked for the complaint forms and left. Keith showed me some pictures he had taken the night of the event, after he came home. There were bruises everywhere: back, legs, arms, chest, face; you name it.

The following Tuesday, we placed a conference call to deplore the actions of the Los Angeles County Sheriff's Department. We called for an immediate response to misconduct charges, and announced that a civil complaint would be filed. I referred Keith to Johnnie Cochran, the city's most famous criminal trial lawyer, who had agreed to handle the case. Johnnie was famous in Los Angeles, long before Michael Jackson and O.J. Simpson became his clients. Cochran was known as a police abuse specialist, who had received several major judgments against law enforcement agencies for misconduct and abuse. A few days later, the Sheriff's Department claimed to be holding their own internal investigation. However, they refused to drop the charges against Keith. The community responded very kindly to Keith, who had suffered a grave embarrassment, not to mention, he couldn't work for three weeks. The Sheriff's Department treated this as just another case, where the suspect was the aggressor, and they did what they had to do to defend themselves -their standard posture, damage control.

In their investigation, they went around to all of the neighbors and intimidated them, while taking their statements. They also manipulated the witnesses' versions of the event. The neighbor who videotaped the occurrence had told Keith of the video, for his defense and use. No one else knew the tape existed except for Keith's family and me. They found out from one of the neighbors that someone might have taped it. The neighbor who taped it never mentioned, in his conversation with the investigators, that he had a tape. At the end of the interview, the investigators stated, "We need to get the tape you got for evidence."

The man asked, "What tape? I don't have a tape," and shut his door. They never got the tape.

Keith went to court and won a large settlement for his pain and damages. But more than that, Keith exposed one of the nation's most corrupt law enforcement agencies, who for a long time, had intimidated a community by compromising their dignity and respect through its continuous acts of misconduct. But countless others had been injured, and even killed through such acts, as was the case with Oliver X Beasley, two and a half years later (discussed later in this book).

* * *

In the Los Angeles Police Department's efforts to deter gang violence, it had ventured on several expeditions, some which bordered fanatical, and most which were clearly unconstitutional. Certainly, it gave me insight to the type of mindset and brain trust (or lack of it) that ran the department. It was perceived that former L.A. Police Chief Daryl Gates had such a low regard for the Black community, that anything that happened in our community, short of anarchy, could be dealt with in anyway his officers saw fit. Many of whom demonstrated such a hostility toward the community, that they might as well have worn their white sheets to work.

Gates didn't even respect the mayor, to whom he reported. Projects Gates implemented in the Black community posed more of a legal (and criminal) liability, than additional safety to the public. Most cities would have prevented these projects, because of their controversy and high risk to the citizens. Gates took an "anything is better than nothing" approach to justify his civil rights infringements. His demonstrative projects, such as the battering ram, a domesticated modification of an armored tank (where he would ride out front like General MacArthur) and gang sweeps, gave us reason to have great concern for his demented view of law enforcement. For instance, his battering ram knocked down "alleged" rock houses to stop the sell of drugs. The first time it was used, it knocked down a house that had no drugs, but just a woman and her baby. He sat on the tank with this shit-eating grin on his face, while the TV cameras filmed this staged attack. Then the community wondered why the department was so haphazard in its dispatch of justice? Because, the police chief was the same way.

This was never more evident, than after, what was called "one of the biggest fiascoes in the department's history." It became known as the "39th and Dalton" incident, where the Police Department demonstrated the same haphazard mentality that the community had come to associate with its police chief.

One evening, in late June 1988, it staged what was purported to be a routine drug raid of an apartment on Dalton Street, where a young teen-ager alleged to have gang and drug ties, lived with his mother. However, when the police stormed the unit, they didn't find any drugs. Certainly, they couldn't have made a mistake? The drugs had to be there somewhere. So they busted out all the walls, tore the stuffing out of the couches and chairs, tore up all the books, turned over the refrigerator and stove after pulling all the parts out and dumping the contents on the floor, dumped the food out of the cabinets, pored out all the food that was opened and unopened, broke the mirrors and all windows throughout the house, broke the face bowls and toilets in all the bathrooms, dumped and destroyed all mattresses, drawers and clothes in the bedrooms and knocked out the tubes in all the televisions. They even went outside and tore apart the dog house. They found nothing. Infuriated by this, they went upstairs and did the same thing. They went from one apartment to the next. In total, the police ransacked and totally destroyed five apartment units rendering them totally inhabitable. Now guess what? Not a single ounce of drugs of any kind turned up in any of these units. This was just the start of this ape show.

Totally embarrassed in front of all these neighbors, they started pulling every person they could find off the street, and handcuffed and arrested them. Fifty people that they pulled off the street (including the residents of the five inhabitable units) were charged with various offenses. But guess what? With five units and 50 people arrested, they didn't find any drugs. They claimed they found one rock on one of the teen-agers they pulled from off the street, but several witnesses suspect that one of the cops planted it. Does this Animal House story end yet? Not hardly. The treatment of the people was inhuman. They left a pregnant woman with her hands cuffed behind her, lying face down on her stomach for an hour and a half. Only when she started crying in pain and the community shouted "let her up" to the police, did they offer her any relief. Furthermore, when the police van came to take all of the arrested to the station, the people (about 35 of them) were packed face down into the van, (which only held 12 to 15 persons). People were crying that they couldn't breathe, that they were cramped, with their limbs bent in distorted positions, and to the disdain of everyone there, the police laughed about the whole time.

This was the scenario recounted by the people, whom I interviewed personally, and who were forced to participate in this abuse. Once they got to the station house, the misconduct of the police worsened. They made many of the young men, according to their own testimony, dive face first out of the van onto the cement sidewalk. When the young men did it, and it wasn't to the officer's satisfaction, they were made to do it again. Then when the officer got tired of this game, they made the arrested people whistle the theme to The Andy Griffith Show. Those who refused were hit with batons until they did. Then they were made to run through the center of two columns of police, while they took swings at them. The behavior of the officers was totally inexcusable. The department had a problem on its hand this time.

Most of the elected officials and community leaders walked through the units in the few days to follow. A fund was set up, because the American Red Cross did not consider this forced displacement of five families an emergency. But you know, the one person who showed no remorse whatsoever during this whole period, didn't even walk through the scene. Yep, you guessed it. The one who probably made these officers feel that their conduct was appropriate, and that the department would stand behind them. In fact, they were probably trying to emulate their highest example in their misconduct, Police Chief Daryl Gates.

Instead of offering an explanation that was sensitive to the apparent abuse used in this case, coupled with what appeared to be a no-win situation for the police, Gates' department countered this latest controversy, with a fabricated alibi to support their ridiculous denial claiming. They claimed that after the police legally searched the homes in question, they abandoned the search when, no drugs were found. The story went on to say that when the police left, hoods from the neighborhood went into the homes, and trashed the units, causing excessive damage. The police returned to the scene, after receiving calls of vandalism going on in the area. However, we could not get any corroboration on this story. Witnesses said the police never left when they got there, and they had most everybody in the area under arrest. Who was on the street? Residents who lived in the area couldn't even get into the area.

Even though Gates had his deputy chief, Bill Rathburn, walk through damaged units, it was obvious to most, that the Police Department was less than sincere in its efforts to gather the facts. Nothing short of a full investigation would be necessary to defuse the cover-up that was now in full effect. Mayor Tom Bradley ordered a full investigation of this case, and promised disciplinary action for those officers guilty of wrongdoing. This halted community anger for the moment. In the meantime, the families were still displaced, and had a very difficult time relocating.

A few months later, the Police Department announced that 15 of the officers involved in the Dalton Street incident would be disciplined. Three of the officers were suspended. In May 1990, 50 residents who filed a class action civil suit against the city of Los Angeles, settled the suit for $3 million. The police's arrogant misconduct was finally beginning to come to light. But they still insulted our intelligence and sense of fairness, by forcing the victims to sue to receive damages for actions that they knew were obviously in the wrong, from the beginning. Still, they just tried to tell us anything, and expected us to go for it.

In August 1988, the branch received a letter from some inmates in the Los Angeles County jail, stating that they were being discriminated against while being held for trial. Twenty-three inmates signed the letter. The unique angle about this letter was that it was sent by a most unwanted segment of the Los Angeles society, widely publicized as the most vicious and dangerous gang in the nation - the Crips. I asked the branch's executive director, Harold Webb, to investigate the letter, and get back to me. Meanwhile, I tried to find out from members on the street what was happening at the county jail. I knew I couldn't bring this to the attention of the Executive Committee, because most wouldn't understand why we were trying to defend the rights of "alleged law breakers," as gang members were purported to be. Still, it was a civil rights issue, and the Constitution guarantees rights, even to the "accused." I felt it was an opportunity to look deeper into the L.A. Criminal Justice System. A deeper look than even I could have imagined.

Going to the aid of gang members was, in fact, a very controversial proposition in the 1980s. They were being represented as the scourge of society, and not without just cause (at least on its face). At that time, Los Angeles was in the midst of a gang war, unlike any other city had ever seen. The city was considered the "gang capital of the world." What more likely target for police to practice their excessive tactics than gang members. The public outcry would be such that most people, including Blacks, positioned themselves to resist response, because of the distorted media campaign being waged against these youths. That position was that these "gangs," as they labeled them, were such a public menace, that they should all be handled, by any means necessary, to make the streets safe again.

While Black gangs, at the time, represented only 37 percent of the street gang activity, they represented almost 90 percent of the police department and the media's attention. Almost every time you saw a television news account in the mid-1980s, you saw Black youth lying on the ground, sitting on curbs or kneeling with their hands behind their heads. The misperception that Blacks made up the bulk of gang activity caused Blacks, in general, to be further ostracized by the larger society. Conversely, they are more closely monitored when integrating with the larger society, and often distrusted, without just cause.

This had been effectively demonstrated by the police department's chief antagonist, former Police Chief Daryl Gates, through the implementation of controversial "gang sweeps." It was just a matter of time before this practice would be challenged as unconstitutional. The policy allowed police to stop anyone on the streets, on any given night (they generally selected Fridays and Saturdays), question them about their activity, at the moment, tag them (a process that puts one's name into a computer for future reference, whether they are gang members or just high-risk youths), and arrest them, if they were found in violation of any laws. This was to encourage youth to take a lower profile, or even stay off the streets on weekends, and to discourage any gatherings that would draw attention to violent acts, such as drive-by shootings.

It appeared sensible enough at face value. However, implementing this process was a violation of a person's civil rights. It broadened police officers' discretion to stop an individual without just (or even probable) cause, because they happened to drive through a sweep area (where they might live), had more than two people in a car, or were wearing dark, blue or red clothing. Black citizens, in many cases, were unethically and illegally singled out. Furthermore, it entrapped law-abiding citizens, approached by biased officers. Many worked this detail, for overtime pay, thinking these were the Blacks they were supposed to "keep in check." Their attitude, according to several insiders, was that they were "kicking ass," and making money for it. Law-abiding citizens didn't understand this antagonistic attitude executed by the officers, who responded in an adversarial manner, which would justify an adverse reaction. The citizen would end up getting dragged to jail, on minor bullshit, or roughed up by the police.

Most every Monday, during that period, you would see grand pronouncements in the papers: "Police Arrest 350 in Gang Sweeps," or "625 Swept During the Holidays." By reading the headlines, the public was misled into believing that 350 or 625 gang members were arrested. However, the small print would say that of the 350 people arrested Friday night, 180 were "alleged gang members," or "known to have gang affiliations." This meant that 170 people were just caught in the trap. Almost half of those arrested were people who were stopped without probable cause, and for whatever reason, were arrested by police. Whether these persons had warrants, were disrespectful, or were driving over the legal alcohol limit was not the issue. The issue was: Did the police have a legal and legitimate reason to stop these people? The answer we found in most of these cases was, no. Citizens were stopped because of the area they were in, and the time of night. A time that the officers felt law biding citizens had no business being out on the street. The "stop 'em" identifiers were always the same; more than one person was in the car, and wearing dark or reddish colors. So, in fact, what you saw was an unofficial curfew (a form of marshal law), which was placed on a group of citizens easily identified by race, clothes and geographical location. And, to add insult to injury, most of the whole city was going along with it. Capetown (apartheid South Africa) was alive and well in America.

During the four months that we monitored the activity of the gang sweeps, over 7,000 persons were arrested. Over 3,300 (45 percent) were law-abiding citizens. The gang crisis made many citizens willing to relinquish some of their civil liberties and civil rights, if it could prove to end the gang war. What it proved was that the police really didn't differentiate gang members from the law-abiding citizenry. All were treated the same-- like criminals. The sweeps opened the eyes of many people who were accosted by the police during this period.

The program could have been called a "Black sweep," since 85 percent of the arrested were Black, or a sweep on law abiders, since they represented half of the pickups anyway. What was called then "gang sweeps" was Daryl Gates' effective plan to tag Blacks, jam Blacks and control Blacks. I called them "youth sweeps," and "race sweeps," because that's exactly what they were. With picking up so-called gang members as the premise, and the police department as "the witness," detainees at the county jail (run under the auspices of the L.A. County Sheriff's Department) were now victims of their own circumstances (Black and gang-affiliated). The facts were that public opinion supported keeping these troublemakers off the streets. Whatever happened to them while they were in jail, they deserved it. "Hey, who cares?" was the public sentiment.

The Sheriff's Department, knowing that there was not a lot of sentiment for these young men, conducted a regular three-ring circus-- much of it for their own entertainment-- while holding the inmates for trial dates. They were treating the detainees in a cruel and inhuman manner. The area where this behavior was most prevalent was the unit called the "Crips" module, where the handling of Crips was savage. The sheriffs claimed they had to be treated this way, because the Crips were more violent than other gangs. The sheriffs would come into the young men's cells, toss it up, call them vulgar names on the loud speaker, and involve the inmates in other acts of perversity. Certainly, nobody cared about what they did to these people. Right? They were the city's outcast. Whom could they call? Who would come? It was no small wonder that Black males were so vicious, when they came back on the streets. If you slap a pup every time you see him, you'll make him mean. This generation of Black men are warriors. Many were so mean, because of the mistreatment they were forced to endure in so-called correctional facilities.

In talking to these youths on the outside, they gave us some of the most damaging information against law enforcement, and a true indictment to the level of corruption in Los Angeles law enforcement, particularly with respect to the police being implicated in drug dealing and gun running. Gang members were the first to incriminate "the police" in the drug trade. We'd later find out, eight years later (in 1996), that the involvement ran higher than local police, but also included the federal government (several agencies including the CIA, the DEA, the FBI and ATF, all who have denied their involvement).

We do know that fifteen Sheriff deputies went to jail for skimming drug money in the early 1990s and several stated in their trial that the government "knew" and "was involved" in bringing drugs, through gangs, into the country. These deputies knew what was going on, because they weren't jammin' (arresting) the drug dealers. They were jammin' the gang-bangers. Still, at that time, there was no way of knowing this. At first, their allegations seemed absurd and unbelievable. Certainly, these guys weren't the most credible guys we could put on the stand. But they assured us, if we went inside, we would corroborate the stories, not only by inmates, but by Black officers.

The first story they told us was that the Los Angeles Police Department fueled the gang war. They did so by telling different gangs that one member from a rival gang did or said something that "offended" his homies, to get them to retaliate. They would also talk to members within the same gang, to cause leadership disputes in those sets. These rumors would cause conflicts, which resulted in overthrow attempts and gang splits. We heard this story no less than 10 times, most of the time, at some of the summits and at Old Gangster (O.G.) meetings, held at Nickerson Gardens, a Watts housing project. Police would further exacerbate the problem by picking up some of these guys, and dropping them off in rival territories. The police knew, as the youths did, that they had little or no chance of getting out of a rival area with their lives, particularly when the police would alarm the locals with shit like, "Ain't this supposed to be Crip territory?" When the youths would respond, "Yes," the police would tell them about the youths they just let out of the car and say something like, "Well, how come I saw a slob (a Crip name for a Blood) a couple blocks back?"

Then as the youths say when it's time to rumble, "It's on, it's on." And they're out looking to smoke (kill) another youth.

The youths were trying to stop but every time they tried, something would just happen, and another shooting would occur, which would fuel a retaliation. This happened until they started talking to each other, and found that the police were playing sides against the middle. Whittling a stick at both ends leaves you nothing but sawdust when you get to the middle. Brothers were fast becoming sawdust in the 1980s. They were dropping like flies, because they didn't know. That's one thing (beyond peace treaties) you can credit those late 1980s gang summits for bringing to public light; finding out how dirty the police were.

The second revelation was the degree of police brutality, and its cause. We had heard that white supremacists had been joining Los Angeles law enforcement, and some of the smaller agencies on the city's outskirts. The gangs detailed how, on many occasions, white officers would shout obscenities at them, and tell them that they were members of the KKK, and how they were there to save Los Angeles from terrorist niggers. Any chance they had to physically abuse them, they did. They even told them that they were supporters of the then Apartheid South African government, and would readily go there in a race war. The Los Angeles Police Department's automobiles had been seen on several occasions with bumper stickers that read: "Property of the South African Government." The department claimed they were looking for the person(s) responsible for this, but every time one was removed, it would reappear a few days later. This was the first time we had heard that cross-burnings were going on in the county jail. As far-fetched as both of these stories seemed, the former seemed a little more realistic than the second one. We would find out it was the other way around.

Our plan was to file a federal civil rights lawsuit against the Los Angeles Police Department and L.A. County Sheriff's Department, as soon as, we had enough data to support the case. The initial step was to go into the jails and either witness the treatment ourselves, or gather firsthand accounts of abusive and misconduct situations.

It took us almost three months to get into the county jail. Many of the inmates who signed the letter had left to go to the state penitentiary, or had been released. The Sheriff's Department officials acted like they didn't know what the hell we were talking about, when we inquired about discrimination allegations. They claimed that every inmate is treated equally, and that no one is treated as criminals until they have been tried in court. They also claimed that everyone's innocent until proven guilty, and that this is just a holding center for those awaiting trial. They gave us the whole spiel. They wanted to know where we got our information, because we wanted to interview certain inmates. Of the 23 inmates who contacted us, 11 were still at County jail. We set up interviews with them, in December of 1988. We first met with the jail administrators, who were really giving us the song and dance. The NAACP Western Regional Director Jim Martin, who accompanied Harold Webb and myself,carried on small talk with them, as long as they wanted. (Jim loved to talk) but they knew why we were there. Tired of exchanging insincere pleasantries, I asked to start the interview process. A watch commander, who seemed pissed that he had to be there in the first place, tried to tell us how much more violent the Crips were than the Bloods, or how they fight and sodomize each other, and that's why they had to be handled differently. I asked him what is "differently." He seemed irritated that I would ask that question and said, "Look, I don't know what you're looking for." At that time, the assistant jail administrator interrupted to take us to the inmates. I knew we were on to something, at that point.

When the interviews began, they brought in the inmates. They were locked down with chains on their hands and feet. We asked the brothers lightweight stuff like their names, if they were affiliated with a gang, what they did to get arrested, and how long they had been in the county jail. We saw each interviewee one at a time and asked each person most of the same questions. The most important question we asked them was why had they tried to contact us, and how they thought we could help them. They stated in detail that they had heard about my work to try to stop gang violence. They also heard, according to them, that I was also down on the police (which I was), that I had grown up in Los Angeles, and was from the streets (a sobering reality that meant credibility to them). They said they didn't want to talk to any bourgeois Negroes who thought they knew "what was good for us, but didn't know us," or "didn't have any love for us." They stated that this was the third letter they had sent. The first two they tried to pass through the regular mail process by giving them to the guards to mail. They assumed the mail never got to us, when they heard no response. The third one was smuggled out of the jail.

The first letter was sent in June, the last at the end of August. They felt we could help them get back on track as brothers. We asked if we helped them, would they tell the brothers on the streets to stop the drive-bys. They said it would be difficult, because "the police was in the middle of the gang war." They said they would, however. We said, "let's roll."

They kept their word. Most of the violence that occurred in the ensuing 12 months was from Latinos gangs. Only the press never relented on their intent to make the gang problem a "Black gang" problem. Back to the lecture at hand.

The first thing they brought to our attention was how specific officers treated them. They said some of the Black officers treated them like brothers, let them listen to the radio, and tried to treat them with a little love. But when they were with white officers, the officers were different and colder. They said they were treated the worse when there was no Black officer present. They said the white officers were almost always verbally abusive, and many cajoled some of the inmates into confrontations that turned physical. They would turn up cells for no reason, tear up their letters and sometimes their pictures. They said they knew they had "nothing coming" with white officers. One officer was even reprimanded for calling the inmates "niggers" over the speaker system. About six of the inmates reinforced this theme.

Next was the distribution of cold food. While the administrator claimed that this was a resolved issue, the inmates hadn't seen any difference. Many of them had been penalized for cooking in their cells, which was against jail policy. Then they told us of some of the degrading games they played with the inmates, from time to time. One that all the interviewees recalled was where the sheriff cell officers made the whole module strip down to their underwear, put on feet shackles and handcuffs and run through the shower. Then they made them stand there dripping wet and hum. One of the officers shouted, "You niggers look like you came straight off a slave ship." This activity went on for about an hour.

Then came the one we were waiting for. In June 1988, two crosses were burned on separate occasions in the Crip module. The inmates said that there were at least eight officers present, all of whom were white. One officer, in particular, bragged regularly that he was a Klansman. Others had stated so at various times, but weren't as open as the first. We asked these inmates if they were absolutely, positively sure about this. They said yes, and that a Black officer found the burnt wood. We let the inmates know that we would return to talk to them again. We gave them our cards and told them if they received any threats or retaliatory actions from the officers, to call us.

We then took a tour of the rest of the facility. We asked the administrator about some of the things that we asked the inmates. They addressed them all casually, until we got to the question of the cross-burnings. There was silence, then denial. I told them that we had a problem, and that they should check it out. I received several anonymous calls from several sheriff s deputies, who told us about other discriminating acts. A week later, we went public.

The Sheriff's Department had no comment, but later admitted that the incidents did occur, which was a change in their story. However, future attempts to access the county jail or other county sights were met with great resistance. We couldn't get any future appointments to interview any more inmates, largely due to the inability to get phone calls returned. L.A. County Sheriff's deputies claimed they were conducting their own internal investigation, and would prefer to complete it before the interviews continued. When we inquired as to how long this would take, we were told "an indefinite period of time," which meant to us "after we find all the bodies and bury them." We never heard from the Sheriff's Department again, although six months later (after my presidency ended), some officers were disciplined for the cross-burning incident.

* * *

The Black community was beginning to see what was happening here (those who wanted to see). The city's police department had virtually gone crazy. The sheriff's department, too. Could they really be trusted to protect the interest of Blacks, when they seemed to be such a willing accomplice in the conspiracy to destroy Black males and, ultimately, the community itself? What about brothers and sisters who worked in those departments? Some of them had completely betrayed the race by being involved in some of these atrocities.

White officers were white first and police officers second. Although some are fair-minded, a bias exists with respect to the way they police Black communities. They conform to the "police culture." Some Black officers seemed to take on the culture totally, and were oftentimes worse than white officers in their handling of Black people. There were plenty of good brothers in the ranks, but those who showed any empathy with the department's treatment of Blacks are purged from the fast track, when they demonstrate such sensitivities.

On occasion, we appealed to Black officers to make these agencies come clean. It was their responsibility to prohibit this abuse and misconduct from being perpetuated against their people. However, we also knew the discrimination they faced on the inside-- the ape pictures being taped to their lockers, and the "nigger" applications passed around their divisions at roll call. This should have been an indication to Black officers of how their peers felt about them. It should have made many Black officers (if not all of them) wonder, when "they" (law enforcement), as a system, are through with their current mission to destroy our people, what is "the department" going to do with them?

Many already knew. The question was why don't they tell their people the plans many law enforcement agencies have for the compromised services, which lead to the destruction of our communities. In the past (as during the 1980s "decade of police abuse"), their silence made them an accomplice to their own peoples' murder and social compromise. We knew, in 1989, that the future of law enforcement was highly suspect in Los Angeles. We knew it was a matter of time before the Rafael Perez and David Macks (Black police officers convicted for corrupt acts in the line of duty in the 1999 Rampart Corruption scandal), eventually surfaced. We knew, and some Black officers knew too, that the culture was breeding offspring throughout the department. Many Black officers have since found out, in our communities, police make their own rules -rules that ended up becoming a department-wide scandal called Rampart. The acts of the 1980s must claim ownership as Rampart's forerunner. Rampart's daddy was the internal cover-up of 1980s police misconduct.

* * *

Souls (and Awards) for Sale

"Nobody has a right to put another under such difficulty that he must either hurt the person by telling the truth or hurt himself by telling what is not true."

- Samuel Johnson

Prior to my involvement in civil rights advocacy, I had a perception that recognition for trail blazing, altruistic, sacrificing service to disadvantaged people was the basis for award recognition. Second generation advocates thrive for such recognition, as the ultimate confirmation of being accepted into the historical civil rights legacy. 1987 was a landmark year in my maturation as a civil rights advocate. It was also a time when my naiveté was eclipsed by the realities of the struggle in which I was involved. The NAACP was no longer in a struggle for equality. It was in a struggle for survival. People often ignore the economic realities of being "defenders of the socially disadvantaged." Facing payroll tax problems that threaten to have the branch doors padlocked, the L.A. NAACP's pride was at stake. The economic realities of advocacy had made the Los Angeles NAACP "hustle" for money. When you're struggling to survive, you "do what you have to," as they say on the street. When you're not too proud to beg, you'll compromise principles, values and even your integrity.

By 1987, the Los Angeles NAACP was "fronting" as an advocacy organization. Some of us were in it for real, others (including most of the leadership) were in it for "show" and notoriety. Some didn't know the difference. Consequently, the notoriety they sought, they got, in the form of the biggest advocacy compromise I've ever witnessed, the Los Angeles branch's annual fundraising dinner of 1987. It was also the dinner that pretty much solidified the Los Angeles branch as the organization of compromise, in the "City of the Angels."

The NAACP, the oldest and largest civil rights organization, not only has a rich tradition in civil rights activities, but also in recognizing those who have made great contributions in their particular areas of endeavors. Awards given by the NAACP, on any level, do not come easy. People would give their right arm, or pay to list an NAACP award on their resume, because it not only meant extended service, but social responsibility.

The national organization's Spingarn Medal is considered one of the most prestigious awards given to any African-American, by any organization, period. Named after NAACP co-founder and former President Joseph Spingarn, the award recognizes the negro who has made the greatest impact on American society, in the past year. The recipients of this award are truly a who's-who in American history: Martin Luther King Jr., Daisy Bates and the Little Rock Nine, Jackie Robinson and others. Of course, some of the award's luster has been lost, since it was discovered, a few years ago, that Joseph Spingarn used the NAACP to spy for the government, on key Negro leaders. Still, the national organization has set standards and criteria for the branches and regions to uphold, in order for its award to hold similar prestige and honor, for the hardworking and deserving recipients who are chosen to receive these awards on regional and local levels.

The Los Angeles Branch NAACP had tried to establish its own form of recognition, by having an award (or several) presented in conjunction with its fundraising dinner. The purpose of the dinner was to raise money to support the operations of the branch. The highlight of the dinner was recognizing those individuals who had made substantial contributions (not monetarily) to benefit mankind, those who have never compromised the dignity of Blacks by participating in an event that didn't accord Blacks full rights as human beings, and those who have continued the fight for equality, in every way they know how.

Even the name of the awards held the highest prestige. The Roy Wilkins Award was named after one of the organization's most revered and dedicated leaders. The decision to select the prime honoree for the 1987 Roy Wilkins dinner came on the heels of the 1986

Roy Wilkins dinner. Prior to 1986, branch dinners were not largely successful at all, because of planning difficulties, resulting from everything from personality problems with event consultants, to prior extravaganzas that just lost money. A desperate branch Executive Committee decided to allow the branch's dinner Committee to work in conjunction with a "shell corporation" that the branch created, called the Crenshaw Economic Development Corporation (CEDC). This will be discussed in detail later. In order to eliminate the debt, the branch would be able to keep more of the money by passing it through this "dummy" corporation. The National NAACP has this old outdated requirement that branches must forward 50 percent of all fundraising proceeds to the national organization. This makes it barely possible to run a branch, and makes it damn near impossible to run a branch the size of Los Angeles that has rented office space and paid staff. By holding the dinner in conjunction with the CEDC, the branch could retain 75 percent of the proceeds, simply by splitting the proceeds with the CEDC 50/50. In this way, the branch would only be required to send the 50 percent of its 50 percent share of the proceeds to the National office.

In 1986 the Roy Wilkins Awards dinner made over $100,000 for the first time. Kenny Rogers was the Humanitarian Award honoree for his work on the "Hands Across America" project. However, the highlight of the evening was the initiation of the Life Achievement Award, named after local civil rights pioneer and co-founder of the Los Angeles branch, Dr. H. Claude Hudson. An even more fitting tribute was that he would also be the initial recipient of the award. It was a final tribute to the man everyone called "Mr. NAACP." Dr. Hudson was a man of high moral standards and deep compassion for his people. He showed it daily for over 75 years. A 10-minute standing ovation was given to Dr. Hudson, as the near 100-year living legend stood at his table, with his walker, to receive his award. An award that would go to only the highest achievers-- men and women without compromise, men and women of the highest dignity and dedicated to the progress of African-Americans, and that would bear his name forever.

After that night, most people associated with the NAACP would never see him again. With the exception of a few more public appearances, he would spend the rest of his life in semi-seclusion, seeing only family and old friends. But now certainly the standard had been set. It was a standard for future generations to strive for recognition that would truly say that one's stripes had been earned, and that justice and equality were more than just words. They must be lived every day with the vigor, vitality and commitment that its namesake, Dr. H. Hudson, represented for so many years. Or, so we thought.

In the wrap-up meeting, we were going over some of the final details of the 1986 dinner, and commenting on its success. The Committee had hired an outside consultant to do the 1987 dinner. Many of us on the Executive Committee were skeptical, for several reasons, based on the branch's past experiences with dinner consultants. Much of the scuttlebutt had to do with her race. The McMillion Group, headed by Liz McMillion, a white woman, was retained at the last minute, because we were in litigation with the prior planner of our 1985 Roy Wilkins dinner. There were lack of performance issues, which caused the final payment installment to be held up. Because of this, she bad-mouthed us all over town, so nobody would touch us. Those who might have been interested, because of the short planning time (four months), wanted large retainers up front, before agreeing to provide their services.

We didn't have any money, so we were in a dilemma, until Liz popped up. I really don't know how she was referred to us, but she agreed to do the 1986 dinner on short notice, with a minimal retainer, and the balance to be paid on net proceeds. She had done a dinner for Nancy Reagan and a couple other celebrity charities. Many members of the Executive Committee objected to us not hiring "a Black firm." Others, including myself, didn't have a problem with her race, per se, as long as, she was competent. She was right for our situation. When it became clear that we couldn't afford the others, and we didn't have a lot of options open to us, the Executive Committee approved her contract.

During the wrap-up meeting, Liz's assistant mentioned how they were looking to do something with Frank. A couple of us asked, "Frank who?" "Frank Sinatra," he replied. "We've been looking to do something for Frank, and we think he may be receptive to being honored by the NAACP." "For what?" I asked. The assistant responded, "It'll be a hit, a sellout." The Executive Committee members glanced at each other, and the conversation changed to another subject. We all realized that he had just told us something that he shouldn't have. Something to which we had not been privy. It was sort of like testing the water for a response, so they'd know how much selling they would have to do. It turned out that Ray Johnson, Jim McBeth and George Mallory had already agreed to the award in principle, if Liz could get

Frank (and she knew, for some reason, she could). If all things worked out, he would be our 1987 awardee. Mind you, this is still July 1986. But the compromise was already in motion.

The Executive Committee was pleased with the results of the dinner, offered praises to the Committee, and motioned that the same Committee be retained to plan the 1987 dinner. The motion was unanimously passed and accepted. The 1986 Roy Wilkins dinner Committee was composed of Ruth Anderson, Norma Johnson, Elvin Moon and myself representing the branch, plus Jim McBeth and George Mallory, who were also on the Executive Committee, but were representing the Crenshaw Economic Development Corporation. Jim and George were also the co-chairs for 1986, and would be so for 1987. However, the Committee would go through a tremendous metamorphosis, in that one year.

Even though none of us resigned from the Committee, and all of us expressed a desire to work on the 1987 dinner, all of us were eliminated from the 1987 dinner planning efforts. The reason was to facilitate and expedite planning of the 1987 dinner. We don't want or need anybody in the way," McBeth would state. McBeth and Mallory claimed that except for Ray, George and himself, no one else sold any significant number of tables, so they didn't deserve to work on the next dinner. That was all bullshit, of course.

The purpose of eliminating key members from the Committee was to eliminate the serious debate that would ensue, over the selection of such a controversial honoree. In a Committee format, they would have been in the minority, and wouldn't have gotten the selection out of the Committee. They later added Elvin back to the Committee, after the decision to honor Sinatra was finalized. Their claim of being the Committee's workhorses was totally untrue. In fact, they delegated the real work.

The 1986 dinner Committee had no money to retain the consultant or the hotel, because we still owed them money from the previous year's dinner. I approached Carolyn Webb-DeMacias, then a manager with Pacific Bell, and asked her to help us with $5,000. Carolyn, who is one of the nicest and most committed sisters you'd ever want to meet, resigned from our Executive Committee, because of irreconcilable differences with Ray Johnson. She felt he dogged her dinner consultant, Betty Bankhead, the prior year, for no other reason than his own personal insecurities. Carolyn had been our largest corporate contributor, and was on the Executive Committee for the past three years (prior to 1986), contributing up to $10,000 per year. When she got tired of Ray's "bullshit," she resigned, saying that she didn't have any time to deal with an insecure man. She was immediately gobbled up by the SCLC-West, who elected her President of the Martin Luther King Legacy Association. The big bucks shifted from our coffers to theirs. I was one of the few players on the Colored People's board, who did not cower around Ray during their fallouts. Carolyn and I have remained friends, to this day, because of it. Because of the funky way they handled Carolyn, Ray and his corporation cronies knew they couldn't say anything to her, without getting cussed out. But the fact is, as Carolyn told me, when we met, "I'll always be there for the branch." NAACP money was still in her budget. He would have to ask for it, alluding to the fact that whether he was being either too stubborn or too stupid, Ray hadn't asked for his contribution.

I told her we needed the money immediately and that we would have a request letter to her office in the morning. I also told her because of the support Pac Bell had given us in the past, they were being selected as the first recipient of the John T. McDonald III Corporate Award. She thanked me, because of the significance it had given her friendship with John, but she didn't want to be tied to it in any way. Carolyn sent us our first check that year. Many other checks came as a result of Executive Committee members soliciting from a list that McMillion had. Elvin Moon brought in about eight tables himself through his own solicitation efforts. Ruth and Norma spent many days distributing invitations and picking up checks. George, Jim and Ray would approach corporations that had given in the past from Liz's list, while the rest of us were given non-contributors to cold call two weeks before the dinner. So, of course, their level of response was going to be greater than the rest of us. Yet, this was their justification for eliminating the rest of us from the committee. However, the way the process worked was any member can serve on a committee with approval from the Executive Committee. The President only appointed the Chairpersons. At no time, did the revised committee come up for approval. We were for it.

By the time we even suspected that the committee was meeting, I saw a "save the date" letter, with "Tribute to Frank" across the top of the stationary, signed by comedian, Bill Cosby. The letters were in the branch office being prepared for mailing. I asked if there was a dinner committee meeting recently. Ernestine claimed she had no knowledge of one. We later found out that they were paying Ernestine under the table to handle administrative functions during her normal working hours, "double dipping on the branch's payroll. When I asked Ray about it, he said that they were inquiring into Frank's availability, but it would come to the Executive Committee, before a decision was made. Meanwhile, different corporate people, who I would see from time to time on other projects, began to inquire more frequently about the rumor that the "L.A. NAACP" was about to honor Frank Sinatra. At that point, all I could do was deny it, because it had yet to come to the Executive Committee, and the dinner committee was meeting secretly, so that the issue could not be raised, before they were ready to deal with it. However, to an inquisitive community, I was an unknowing party to the cover-up.

The branch was now in a peculiar situation-- how to justify to the members and to the public the selection of Frank Sinatra as its (get this) 1987 H. Claude Hudson Life Achievement recipient. It was a joke, and everybody knew it. Yet the dinner brain trust consisting of Ray, Mallory and McBeth were prepared to go through with it. The position advanced was how could the branch turn their backs on this kind of money? To them it was worth the try, and what they perceived as the temporary backlash.

What had Frank done to merit the Life Achievement Award by a civil rights organization? He had participated in a demonstration to desegregate a public swimming pool in the 1940s. He paid for Joe Louis' medical bills during his serious illness in 1974. OK, well that might have gotten him some consideration for humanitarian recognition. But his lifetime achievement in the area of civil rights isn't exactly what one would call trailblazing. In fact, it was considered dismal at best. It was certainly nothing to be compared to H. Claude Hudson, who served 80 out of his 100 years of life fighting racism on a daily basis. So Frank helped to integrate a swimming pool in the '40s, but Dr. Hudson integrated Los Angeles beaches 30 years earlier. Sinatra was late as far as most of us were concerned. Even Dr. Hudson's humanitarianism seemingly exceeded Frank's. Yeah, Frank helped ole' Joe, but did he help the average Black on a consistent basis? Many whites don't see Blacks like Sammy and Joe Louis as "niggers," as Spike Lee would later point out in his 1989 movie, "Do the Right Thing." They were "different," meaning that they had risen above the common everyday racist treatment that Blacks were subjected to, because of (money-making) gifts they were blessed with, that would have long been recognized, had they been white. Frank felt compelled to help "good ole' Joe," who was a credit to his race, by winning every fight. It was hardly justifiable to try and make a case for Sinatra's selection as a civil rights achiever.

The one thing that Frank Sinatra did do that would disqualify him as a conscientious human rights advocate, meritorious of any lifetime recognition, was to be the first major superstar entertainer to play the apartheid supported South African vacation resort, Sun City. He lent the credibility the resort needed to attract other big name entertainers, for the big paydays that were being offered. The government of South Africa was trying to attract tourism in a major way; however, they were not pumping Peoria or Botswana, where the world could be a firsthand witness to their brutal apartheid regime of oppression, racism and baby-killing. No, they would get tourists to come to a first-rate, world-class resort, where corporate investment was booming, and slick propaganda would dramatically distort to tourists and the world what was really happening.

Most of the world knew this and, as a result, artists, athletes and entertainers were asked not to perform in Sun City, making a conscious political statement to the government of South Africa. Their cover-up of human indignities would not be ignored by the rest of the world. As a result of this effort, a Blacklist was created of artists who deliberately ignored this request. So, while most of the world knew of this significant human rights effort, Frank would claim he didn't know of South Africa's apartheid policies when he performed there. Well, Dr. Martin Luther King Jr. brought forth the issue of South African apartheid policies, in comparison to our own civil rights injustices, as early as, 1960. If Frank was such a committed civil rights advocate, surely he would have had some level of knowledge or sensitivity to this issue before 1987. Apparently, Frank was in a vacuum, or Sun City officials offered him so much money, he didn't care.

Now, the L.A. chapter of the NAACP wanted to make him a lifetime standard bearer for his civil rights achievements, in the likeness of Dr. H. Claude Hudson. It would have been funny, if it wasn't such an obviously shameful compromise. The whole community knew it too, and they weren't buying any of the branch's bullshit propaganda of how deserving Frank Sinatra was.

Frank Sinatra going to South Africa, was like Pete Rose betting on baseball. He was his game's greatest hitter, and there was no excuse to justify it. Now a NAACP Lifetime Achievement Award was equivalent to a Hall of Fame election (at least in the civil rights arena). That trip to Sun City should have cost him permanently. Do you think the

Anti-Defamation League, or the Simon Weisenthal Center would give its highest award to anyone who supported Nazi Germany during the holocaust years, or befriended the Palestinians in the pre-peace talk days? Some Jews make you pay for life, and for any and everything that you ever said or did that was not perceived to be in the best interest of Jews. The Jesse Jackson saga is the best example of this. Jesse has apologized 100 times, and Jews still dislike him with a passion, 17 years after his "Hymietown" statement. Giving Jesse a lifetime achievement award would be out of the question. Then again, Blacks are too forgiving when it comes to making people pay for betraying their trust or common interest. Sinatra would have paid had the branch's selection process been followed. When the curtain went up, those dinner committee Negroes started tap dancing their ass off. Their initial strategy was to come with a power-packed honoree rostrum, stacked with people who maintained a high level of respect, popularity or sensitivity in the Black community, from outside the organization, and from within, to bury Sinatra awards in the midst of the honors.

Their honoree slate was pinned as follows:

(Then) California Assemblywoman Maxine Waters

The Humanitarian of the Year Award

(A very worthy choice and deserving of the honor).

Danny J. Bakewell

Business Achiever of the Year

Head of the Brotherhood Crusade/Black United Fund in Los Angeles, who was one of the first African Americans recently hired as President of a Wall Street securities firm

Frank Sinatra -

The Lifetime Achievement Award

The objective was to have a triple-billing, whereby community outrage would be muted, under the pretext of Maxine and Danny buying into the program. The community would support the dinner, out of the respect they have for these two legitimate and worthy freedom fighters, while Frank pulled in the money as he had promised (he would admit later). The other honorees were just as political.

The Community Service Award would go to "Sweet Alice" Harris and Maude Clark, founders and directors of Parents of Watts, a community-based, self-help program for problem, at-risk youths. Alice started out of her home, and it has expanded into a model program. Another deserving choice.

The organization's Volunteer of the Year Award would go to Mrs. Vivian McDonald, the mother of the branch's late President John McDonald, who had continued to work with the branch even after John passed. What a noble feat, given that many had left the branch after John passed, because it was still too emotional, because of disdain for the dramatic change in leadership styles, or because they were just personally loyal to John.

The last award was one created that year for those who had distinguished themselves in the area of law (either legal practitioner, judiciary, legislative law or law enforcement) - the Judge Thomas L. Griffith Award. California, and particularly Los Angeles, has a laundry list of longtime outstanding achievers in this area. Tom Bradley, Gus Hawkins, Bernard Jefferson, Assistant Police Chief Jesse Brewer, whose selection would be pushed off until next year, Johnnie Cochran, Merv Dymally, Speaker Willie Brown, Diane Watson, Gwen Moore and many, many more. The person selected to become the first recipient of the Judge Thomas L. Griffith Award was a local attorney, Joseph Duff.

Duff re-filed the Los Angeles Unified School District's desegregation case in 1981, and had not done much with it since. The case was unceremoniously settled, in September 1988. Many education advocates, including the organization's general counsel and assistant general counsel, privately blamed Duff for mishandling the case, as a major reason for having to settle it. Joe later became the master puppet in my effort to retain the presidency I inherited from Ray, which will be discussed later. Joe's selection was based on the fact that they needed to get Joe out of the loop, when this thing came to the Executive Committee. As unimpressive and uninvolved as Duff had been for the last couple years (as he would continue to be until October 1988 when he announced himself as a candidate for branch President), he and Henry Dotson (another hypocrite to be discussed later), could always be counted on to be sticklers of process and procedure except, when it was convenient for them. Then with the exception of Aldra Henry, old man (William) Dailey and myself, everybody else would sleep on any circumvention of procedure. In the case of the Sinatra dinner, Henry was compromised early, because he sat on the board of the illegal corporation the branch had formed, which was co-sponsoring this dinner, and pushing this Sinatra thing. I would bring this up later in the meeting, and Henry would later take a seven-month sabbatical from branch activities, because of the reality that hit him cold. He had been bought and sold on something that would eventually hurt the branch. Giving

Joe his award would eliminate him from rocking the boat. Then they would just have to deal with me, which they were prepared to do. Just then, their little plan started falling apart.

Maxine Waters and Danny Bakewell weren't buying into the program. Neither was going to be anywhere close, when this Sinatra bomb blew up. Both sent strong letters of condemnation on Frank Sinatra, and his appearance in Sun City, regretting that the branch chose to honor him, and declining their awards on the basis of not wanting their legitimate accomplishments tainted, by having to share the stage with such a questionable and controversial selection (Bakewell would accept his award nine years later in 1996). To make matters worse, virtually every major Black newspaper in the country had now heard about the selection, and were criticizing profusely the proposed award to Sinatra.

By the time this issue reached the Executive Committee, Jim and George had their tap dance ready, while Ray was ready to manipulate the process from the chair. They had put together packets for the Executive Committee containing an article that appeared in the October 13, 1986 edition of *Jet Magazine*, entitled "Relationships of Sinatra with Blacks." This article contained information that a recent book, His Way: The Unauthorized Biography of Frank Sinatra, did not talk about. The packet also included a list of other proposed honorees. I guess these simple Negroes felt that they could pass on the age-old supposition that "if it appeared in *Jet*, it must be true," because Black folk swear by this magazine. The way these three clowns played it, George would be the mouthpiece, and stand up there, scratching his balls (metaphorically speaking), and stroking the committee at the same time. George would tell us how well the dinner was coming together, and who the committee was "looking at" honoring, implying that the Committee had yet to make a decision. A few of us had information that Sinatra had received an offer to be honored from the branch, as early as, October 1986, and had confirmed by December, when a "save the date" letter was sent out. This was February 1987.

In the meantime, all decisions were made when the committee had met earlier in the month. Why had not Elvin Moon, Norma King, Ruth Anderson and I been notified? George played ignorant, claiming that he didn't know who was on the committee, but stated that the committee had not met to his knowledge. McBeth then stood up and said that most of the work was being handled by the Co-chairs and the President, because time was of the essence, and they didn't want to get "bogged down." What he meant was they didn't want any opposition. When asked how he could get bogged down, McBeth stated that they only wanted the workers involved, and not the talkers. I stood up and asked what he meant by that.

He asked, "How many tables did you sell last year?"

"First of all," I explained, "are you saying that only those who sold tables last year can participate? Everyone on the committee sold tables. Now whether they sold as many as you, we on the committee know how that worked, so don't even try to play us like that."

Elvin Moon stood up and said, "I sold as many tables as anyone else. How come I wasn't notified?"

"Plus, there were many other responsibilities on the committee, other than selling tables. Still, how can you, Jim, determine who would be on the committee, when this Executive Committee voted to retain the same committee as last year?" asked Norma King, the branch secretary.

McBeth tried to say that the dinner Committee didn't do that, but Executive Committee member William Dailey, who made the motion (and remembers every motion he ever made), reiterated that fact. Ray cut the discussion short by saying that the committee would meet soon to discuss the dinner's progress.

I asked, "Will these proposed honorees be discussed at that meeting also?" Ray acknowledged that they would be. There was never any dinner committee meeting held, and later it would become public that the Los Angeles branch had agreed to honor Frank Sinatra, amid loud community outcry.

What Ray, Jim and George may have perceived as being a quiet shuffle soon turned to hysteria, as well, it should have. After looking the Executive Committee in the face, just a few weeks earlier, and after claiming that no decision had been made on honorees, these Negroes had set the branch up to be ridiculed by not only the Los Angeles community, but the international human rights community, as well. Several national Black newspapers wrote stinging articles criticizing this move. Branch members were getting bombarded from all sides. Ron Wilkins, Boycott Task Force chairman of a group called the Unity in Action Coalition, an anti-apartheid organization in the Los Angeles community, were waging a brutal attack on the Los Angeles NAACP. Many of the branch's board members were jammed up by much of the local civil rights community, and all most of us could say was, "We didn't know," which was partially true.

Jim, George and Ray had been prepping the Committee with articles and all this "Frank is great" talk, so we knew it would come up at some point. We also knew it was our option to accept or reject the Committee's recommendation, which we never got the chance to do. Those Negroes had committed us to honoring Sinatra, and circumvented the branch's authority check, in the process. They greatly underestimated the negative response that ensued.

Those of us who were regularly in community coalitions, amongst grassroots people, many of whom we had joined hands with on several South African anti-apartheid demonstrations, were trying to defend (unsuccessfully, I might add) this foolish selection. The irony of this farce was that just two years earlier, the branch honored Bishop Desmond M. Tutu, South Africa's most renowned freedom fighter and 1984 Nobel Peace Prize winner, with The Humanitarian Award (only because the Life Achievement Award wasn't established, until the following year). It also pledged to support Tutu in his continued fight for civil rights, and against racial injustice. Now the same branch was rewarding, by his very appearance, a supporter of the same system that had perpetuated those very injustices. I'm sure Tutu headed straight for the nearest round file with his award. I would have.

While it was obvious to all that Frank Sinatra didn't merit The Life Achievement Award, many people were trying to make a case to have his award switched to The Humanitarian Award, given his lack of civil rights credentials. And given the award's precedence set by Bishop Tutu, ole' Frankie still would have had trouble measuring up to the achievement of the award's previous honoree, even if a case could be made for suggesting an award switch. Either way, a vote for Sinatra had Ray's ball in a vice.

The Sinatra choice was proving to be a very ill-advised selection-- a snowball on the roll. In addition to having to explain to the branch why his cronies outright lied to the Executive Committee, Ray also had to explain why, if Sinatra was such a great choice, two major (highly respected) community leaders were rejecting their awards. The rejection letters, that weren't brought to the attention of the Executive Committee, were being circulated by the anti-apartheid groups, who were questioning Danny and Maxine about their involvement in this NAACP fiasco. Danny Bakewell, whose rejection letter eventually ended up in the hands of the *Los Angeles Times*, stated: "To honor Frank Sinatra is to dishonor the Black community ... I must reject the acceptance of your award, on the same platform with Frank Sinatra." Maxine

Waters refused her award, on the basis of her support for U.S. divestiture in South Africa, and that sharing a stage with Sinatra "provided a serious conflict."

Ray was forced to call an emergency Executive Committee meeting to try and stem the tide of concern that was surrounding the community. Again, Ray had Mallory get up and do his tap dance. This time Mallory fessed up and admitted that they had committed the branch to the award without their approval, because "they had to move expeditiously to get Frank," as he stated. Mallory never answered the question, as to why they didn't tell the committee at the last meeting, about this decision, as opposed to having to hear the news in the street. Mallory proceeded to put it on the President, Ray, who made the decision to withhold the information from the committee, saying it was up to the President to decide how they would present this information. A real chickenshit way of getting out of the situation. But then that was Mallory, who proceeded to ask the Committee what they wanted to do about the award, while conveniently interjecting that the dinner was already a sellout, and all the sponsors were in place contingent upon, of course, Frank's involvement. The branch wasn't in a position to rescind the award, as far as, most of the Executive Committee was concerned. To rescind the award would kill the dinner, not to mention totally alienate the corporate community. The branch would have been a hero in the Black community, but in the final analysis, the branch needed the money, and would have to just bend over and take this swift kick in the behind.

To try to save face, the Committee instructed Ray, Jim, and George to get a letter of apology from Sinatra for appearing in South Africa, and a commitment that he would never appear there again. I guess this was a way of trying to soothe the pain and embarrassment of extending an award that should have never been extended. That's not how America works, for Blacks at least. For entertainers like Paul Robeson and Josephine Baker, who were extremely outspoken on the issue of racial discrimination, America was never forgiving enough to allow them to return to their birthplace to practice their trades, even after "separate but equal" was abolished. Both died in exile, by choice, as victims of a country that was adamant in its discrimination against Blacks, and has yet to apologize for it. Yet, Blacks are supposed to just forgive and forget those who make unconscionable decisions that affect the plight of Blacks, and frequently fail to recognize that many racial reoccurrences throughout history are a direct result of key figures failing to condemn wrong, at the proper time and place. There is no way in hell that a Nazi war criminal can expect to receive a top award from a major Jewish organization by issuing an apology and a condemnation. Not in five, 10, 40 or 100 years. Jews are just that adamant in the rejection of their former oppressors, as Blacks should be. You can accept their apology, you can acknowledge their repentance, but you will always have to question their character of not standing up for right, at the time wrong is committed.

Martin Luther King Jr. said "a measure of a man is not where he stands in times of comfort and convenience, but where he stands in times of challenge and controversy." I am inclined to believe that the majority of whites in America are not overt racists. I do believe, however, that the vast majority of whites are indifferent to those who do commit acts of racism, and to the social and economic conditions of Blacks caused by racism. The overt racists are relatively few in comparison to the overall population, but are strategically placed to influence the opinions of the masses. Whenever racists are able to effectuate change through discriminating actions, many Whites, and even some Blacks exude an indifference that allows those actions to persist. These are the ones who will never do a day in jail or be publicly denounced, but spend their lives committing immoral crimes by remaining silent on the question of race (wrong vs. right), social protocol and ethical correctness. Are these persons any less of a law-breaker or a criminal?

It's a question America refuses to hear, even today. History will bear out the fact that racism was allowed to exist, in both America and a pre-independent South Africa. Whites, who may have opposed racism theoretically and even morally, never allowed their sense of right to exceed their levels of social comfort. They were never prepared to challenge their comfort or convenience. In that sense, Martin Luther King, Jr.'s position remains correct to this day. To this day, our communities and much of our leadership lack true integrity. It's not because they did something criminally wrong, but because they won't call out the public injustices that everybody sees, and because they lack the integrity to call out the backroom compromises that ultimately cause social compromise to be advanced into the front room, and then out into the community.

The Sinatra dinner was a classic example of this. The branch was compromised in the back room, and before long, the compromise deal to honor one individual (for pay) was now an issue for a whole community. The branch didn't have the courage to step out of the deal, and we were honoring someone who had dishonored himself, by becoming comfortable with our brothers' social discomfort, (in South Africa) having to live in an oppressive society. This is where Frank Sinatra failed the "integrity test."

Whether Frank Sinatra ever admitted it before he died (probably not--never having a reason to since apartheid was eventually dismantled), his appearance in Sun City gave the resort enormous credibility. It validated the resort's existence for lesser performers who may have questioned the country's apartheid there. Other entertainers felt that "the situation," as they liked to refer to it, wasn't all that bad, and that Frank wouldn't risk his reputation by appearing there. Frank Sinatra built Sun City by legitimizing it as an international resort. His level of comfort was sufficient enough for him to ignore the most pressing human rights boycott in the world, at that time. Apparently, Sun City had made it so convenient for Sinatra, that he felt he could "overlook" the "situation" up the road in Botswana or Johannesburg. Sinatra was comfortable enough to perform in a racially suppressive police state, while the whole world condemned South Africa's deplorable behavior. Yes, he did it "his way." In the opinion of many nationwide, Frank Sinatra forfeited his right to qualify as a symbol for civil rights advocacy.

In America, if you're convicted of a felony and serve your time, you're still an ex-felon. You may have paid your debt to society, and you have even been forgiven, but you still forfeit certain rights. You're forgiven, but not forgotten... still labeled (in most cases) for life. In a similar context, there is no bigger felony in the world's civil rights community, than to show any sympathy for an oppressive regime that shows no sympathy for oppressed people in its country. Sinatra's appearance in Sun City demonstrated sympathy toward South Africa, at a time, when most entertainers, particularly those of, or even near the caliber of a Sinatra, refused to appear. Furthermore, it blatantly disrespected Blacks worldwide, thereby disqualifying him as a conscientious objector to racism. If Frank Sinatra can look past the oppressive conditions of South Africa's racist apartheid, and feel comfortable enough not to refuse performing there, then he could, in the opinion of some, look past anything. Yet the L. A. NAACP, who was prepared to ignore Sinatra's serious indiscretion, was compromising the integrity of a whole community.

Blacks are always expected to forgive and even forget. It wasn't unreasonable to request an apology. Nor were we unjustified in making a public condemnation five and a half years later. Sinatra received an enormous sum of money. Sun City was up and thriving. The Executive Committee took the position that we wanted to see the apology in writing, and Sinatra's assurances that he would not appear in South Africa, again.

Now that their asses were in a sling, Ray wanted to open up the committee. Other than Elvin Moon, he got no volunteers. Many of the members of the Executive Committee were still extremely despondent over this turn of events. They felt, as they should have, totally betrayed and compromised by the backroom dealings of Ray Johnson, George Mallory and Jim McBeth.

* * *

As the event approached, it became evident that they were not going to get an apology out of Frank Sinatra. Here was a man who prided himself on, not only doing it his way, but did not apologize in the process. Many of his showbiz "friends" have attested to Sinatra's stubbornness, particularly in this case. As far as, he was concerned, as he would later state, the NAACP approached him. He didn't seek them out. They had a deal. The branch needed money, and he could get it. Frank wanted some recognition, and the branch could give it to him. Hell, Frank wanted to know what the problem was. Sinatra's attorneys were coming up with all kinds of technicalities to try to justify his appearance. In letters to Mallory, their case was that Botswana was an "independent republic or homeland" that had the right to bring in entertainment, and not be associated with South Africa's apartheid policies. However, Botswana had segregation laws, though they were more relaxed, than the rest of South Africa. Botswana was a resort land that did all it could to defuse its South African heritage, but the fact was that Botswana discriminated against Blacks. Whatever technicality Sinatra used to justify his appearance was apparently enough of an excuse for Ray, Jim and George (who were doing most of the negotiating). But an apology was out of the question, as far as, Frank was concerned.

In order to comply with the branch's mandate, via the Executive Committee, this sellout trio now concentrated on getting Frank to condemn apartheid and his pledge not to return to South Africa. Drafting a pledge statement, within the time constraints imposed by the Executive Committee, was more difficult than they anticipated. Negotiations for the proper wording acceptable to the branch stipulations, were delayed on account of Sinatra's people maintaining that Sinatra should have been allowed to appear again, in "independent homelands," in South African territories that have "relaxed" apartheid policies. Relaxed policies, inasmuch as, those homelands are not as aggressive in enforcing racial separation. Of course, Sun City is considered such a homeland.

The whole intent of the pledge was to eliminate any such sympathy to any country, territory or homeland that practices any form of racial discrimination. Focus on such technical interpretations gave rise to much opposition by many anti-apartheid activists, as well as, many of us in the branch, who opposed this fiasco. Sinatra had an obvious reluctance to committing to not appear in South Africa again, and therefore, was leaving the door open to reappearing, in the future.

There had been documented evidence that Sinatra may have had a bigger role in the development of South Africa venues, than just as a performer. This surrounded questions regarding his apparent involvement in the promotion of South African venues, as well as, an active role in luring other performers. Still, the purpose of this pledge was to understand, with clarity, where Frank was on this South African performance issue.

It appeared that instead of trying to clarify Sinatra's position on future appearances, the pledge negotiations uncovered issues that only clouded his position even more. Each side was consulting with activists and South African pro-development experts, who supposedly knew the "real" conditions of the so-called independent republics. While the evidence greatly tilted in favor of the anti-apartheid activities, the NAACP representation (Ray and George), seemed to be looking for any information that supported Sinatra's right to return, to at least the independent homelands. Even, if it meant a softer pledge. As long as, they had some type of pledge that addressed the branch's concern, they could move on with their dinner. Whether it was specifically addressed, the issue of Sinatra's future non-appearance was another story.

When it came time for the Committee to hear what George had resolved, the report was dismal. First, Sinatra offered no apology. Second, a statement was produced that Sinatra had no intentions to perform in South Africa anytime, in the near future. However, nowhere did it say he would not perform there again. It just said he had no intentions to perform there, which to many meant that he could perform there, if he wished. This, in no way, could be interpreted as a pledge not to perform there. All of this report was with George's side commentary of how "Frank never apologized to anybody;" "how we couldn't be totally unreasonable;" "how he felt that Frank was sincere in his dealings with the branch;" and, of course, "how this dinner was a guaranteed sellout of $300,000 that the branch needed." Surely, in this case, it was very easy to assess that "it takes a sellout, to know one." But all it really did was misdirect the committee's focus, on whether their requests were complied with. They were not. George provided the committee with the condemnation statement that Sinatra had issued. Sinatra condemned South Africa for its apartheid policies, and made a statement on how all man should be treated equally regardless of race, creed or color.

It was a pretty simple statement. The Executive Committee sat in silence looking at Ray and George, then looking at one another for direction. Certainly, they (Ray and his cronies) weren't going to provide any direction. This was typical of how things went with this branch. If points of order weren't brought up, then it was ignored. They usually weren't brought up, because the Executive Committee usually lacked either the background, or evolving details to adequately address the subject. Conversely, they relied heavily on the reports they heard (very few were in writing), whether the reports were incomplete, ambiguous, conjecture or outright misrepresentations. This report was definitely in the misrepresentation category. The Executive Committee was being given the impression that its request had been complied with, to the degree that it could be, and that what had been achieved, to that point, was sufficient and not worth risking the $300,000 the dinner had pre-sold.

The public objections and award refusals were all monkey wrenches in Ray's plan to railroad this highly questionable nominee past the branch. Still, all of these red flags were not signals enough to raise the committee's objections, above the few who really understood what was happening. Much of the Executive Committee's reluctance to reject Sinatra's involvement centered around the timing of the event, and the committee's sensitivities toward inter-organizational conflict. It was now willing to just let the chips fall where they may, on this one. However, they picked one of the worst possible times to decide to show support for this President. Any concern they may have had about the abuse of the process, the non-compliance of their requests, the national uproar, was lost in the Committee's silence. "All in favor show by the sign of Yea." About six out of 30 people voiced their vote. "Those opposed show by the sign of Nay." Three of us voiced our vote. Motion passes. The dinner is on. The room is silent. The compromise has won.

* * *

Within weeks of the dinner, the community was buzzing that the "Sinatra" dinner would be picketed. Several members of the branch would be involved. Some of the officers were asked to either join the line, not cross it, or to stay away from the dinner. I was one of them. I had agreed to join the demonstration. Because of my other involvements within the branch, I had developed a significant following in the press. Of course, the press is always prepared to play up differences amongst Blacks. It got out to the press that the branch was divided on this Sinatra award. The more discussion was held on the dinner, the bigger the division got. Several Executive Committee members wanted the dinner canceled, if the award wasn't rescinded. Ray's position was that we couldn't cancel the dinner, because the branch stood to lose its credibility, by doing so. Hell, in the eyes of many, they had already lost it. Eight members resigned over Ray's refusal to reconsider. Everybody was finally realizing that this was bigger than we thought. It was too late to debate the issue. The committee had slept the issue, when they had the chance to kill it. Ray wasn't about to let it be re-opened for discussion.

The national news was covering the issue very closely. Our national organization was outright rejecting the selection. Ray then contacted Ben Hooks, and explained to him how much money was involved. The tone of the national branch's responses softened to statements like, "The branch has the right to honor who it chooses, but we make a clear distinction that this is not a national award." It was clear to all that the national office was stepping, as far away from this situation, as they possibly could, without destroying the event. National was never a big supporter of the Los Angeles branch, and they weren't about to become one.

In the meantime, the planning was going forward. Ray, Jim and George continued to restrict branch level participation, including only the branch staff, Ernestine Peters and Elvin Moon. I continued to implore Ray's reconsideration on the dinner. Ray, unwilling to discuss the matter, kept referring me to George, who wasn't returning my calls. Then, Ray stopped returning my calls. Finally, I decided that I would join the demonstration, and told the organizers that I would be with them. When word got out on the street and in the press that I would be picketing, guess who finally called me back?

"Anthony, this is Ray. I hear you're considering picketing the dinner?"

"That's right, Ray."

"Why?"

"Because I don't believe that we're doing the right thing, and because of the way this thing was railroaded through."

"Anthony, the Committee voted to move forth."

"You gave them very little choice. You committed us prior to approval and you didn't get everything they asked for. You made them think the branch would fall apart if we didn't get this money. You heard the vote. Damn near the whole Executive Committee abstained. What kind of shit is this, Ray?"

"Anthony, what we're arguing about is water under the bridge now. I just called to say, we have to be united on this. You have to go with the majority. You are expected to as an officer of this branch."

"Look, Ray, it's mighty strange that I had to go to this extreme, to even get a call from your ass, to discuss this thing forthrightly. You know that this Sinatra thing circumvented the process. You guys haven't been square on this shit from the jump. You've misled the branch and the community into thinking that Sinatra is worthy of something, that the whole world sees that he's not. I don't have to buy into shit."

"You guys got Sinatra wrong on this ..."

"Ray, save that bullshit for the press. I was sitting at the table last year, when Liz McMillion brought this Sinatra shit up. This award has nothing to do with honors, it's about the money, Ray. She told us at the table that 'she,' not 'we' wanted to do something for 'Frank,' and that if 'we' could 'put together something nice,' it would be a guaranteed sellout. Did you forget about that, Ray?"

There was silence on the phone.

"What do you want me to do about it now, Anthony?"

"I would like for us to reconsider this Life Achievement Award. I know it may be too late to rescind the award, but give him a Humanitarian Award, or give him your award (The President's Award). But why fuck up the award that potentially has the greatest weight, when you just got it off the ground? You know how sentimental everyone is about Dr. Hudson?"

"Anthony, call George and run the idea by him. That doesn't sound too unreasonable."

It was about 11:45 p.m. I asked Ray, "Is he up?" Ray said, "Yeah, I just got off the phone with him." After hanging up with Ray, I immediately called Mallory. He sounded asleep. "Ray, said you were up. I called to talk about the dinner." "Uh-Huh," "I discussed with Ray the possibility of changing the Frank Sinatra award..." "Anthony, could we talk about this some other time?" "Well, George, I've tried to call several times, and you guys have been avoiding my calls." "Well, I can't do anything for you tonight." "Well George, we can at least talk about it, and I think we need to discuss this intelligently." "Look, I don't give a fuck what you think. I'm sleep and I don't want to talk about it." Then he hung up. I called Ray back. His answering machine came on. I didn't leave a message. I just hung up.

I called Mark Ridley-Thomas, then executive director of the SCLC, who was a late-nighter. We talked frequently about issues in the community and our personal lives, and had become pretty close associates, even friends at this point.

"Mark. Anthony."

"Hey doctor. What's up?"

"This Sinatra thing. It's really bothering me."

"Hear you gonna picket?"

"That's the plan. Ray called me tonight to talk me out of it."

"So what happened?"

"We went in circles about the process being end-arounded, we talked about changing the award, but he pushed me off on George, who wouldn't talk to me, and he hung up on me like a puss."

"Tough situation doctor. Dealing with the NAACP is more than a notion."

"I can't support this dinner, Mark. It's totally against what I am about. It's a total sellout."

"You've got to go with your gut. The city's buzzin' about it. I just hope Ray knows that the city sees this for what it is. He really doesn't seem to care though."

"Yeah. He's in hook, line and sinker," I said, as we concluded the discussion. After I hung up with Mark, I just sat thinking: Is it really this easy to manipulate Black folk? What are they getting out of this, to buy in so strongly? This branch would make money without Frank. Maybe not as much, but a nice piece of change. And we'd maintain the integrity of the event. McMillion played us like a fiddle. She knew where the money was all right. Who would she bring us next, Peter Botha? Tom Metzger? Ronald the Ray-gun? I fell asleep thinking about how cheaply we'd been played. How did something so meaningful turn into something so meaningless? The dinner was a sellout, in more ways than one.

* * *

The day of the dinner, every major news channel was previewing the awards dinner. This dinner was getting national coverage, which was highly unusual for a local award. The media has a way of picking up the ironies of Black conflict, and projecting them to the world, probably more or less for their own entertainment. If there was consensus on the Sinatra selection, it would have been just another award Sinatra was receiving. But because of the strong outcry over this highly suspicious selection, a second-year award, by a local chapter, was being treated like the Springarn. It was definitely misleading. There was a sense that in the air that something special was happening, but more of a "believe it, or not," or "what niggahs will do for money" type of news potpourri. A newscaster would stick a microphone in Ray's face and ask, "Why are you giving Frank Sinatra this award?" And while Ray was giving his answer, the reporter would have this "as if I didn't know" sarcastic smirk on his face. Then, he would announce that the dinner expected to be picketed.

The national office gave statements from "this is a local award," to "no comment," when asked if they supported the local branch's selection. The Los Angeles branch had gone from a local mockery, to a national one overnight. This certainly wasn't any of Sinatra's doing. He is what he is, and was what he was. If some group wants to capitalize off his notoriety, in spite of his past baggage, more power to 'em. It's not every day that you have a major civil rights award dropped in your lap. Why not go with the flow, regardless of the reason?

Sinatra was comfortable with his place in showbiz history, and the NAACP certainly was comfortable with its civil rights legacy. One questionable award would not deflate Sinatra in the eyes of his fans and admirers. However, the NAACP couldn't afford this hit. They can't just "crossover" to stroke others, at will. In the eyes of the public, particularly Blacks, they must be perceived as representing the interest of the oppressed and disadvantaged. The NAACP can be attacked over issues of truth, but never over issues of compromise. This was a hit that neither the branch, nor the organization had to take. Because of a few silly niggahs' inability to see past the dollars involved, this whole scenario of hypocrisy was being played out on a world stage.

I had long resolved to not participate in the dinner. I most certainly would not give any money to this fiasco. The Executive Committee was so split on this dinner, that less than a dozen members had confirmed to attend, even after they (Ray, Jim and George) had reduced the Committee's tickets to $100. I was planning to picket some time around 6:30 p.m., as most of the guests were arriving. Ray had heard that I was confirmed to participate in the picket, and called me several times that day. I purposely didn't return his calls. I felt that since he hadn't sought me out before then, there was no need for discussion at this point. I got home from the office at around 3 p.m.

While preparing to picket the dinner, the phone rang. It was Raymond. He asked me if I was going to the dinner. I told him that I wasn't.

"Why, Anthony? I need you to be there," was his response.

I said, "Oh, I will be there. Don't worry."

I heard you were picketing the dinner."

"That's right."

There was a long silence on the phone. "Anthony, I know this dinner hasn't gone fairly, but the branch needed the money."

"Just because you are willing to prostitute yourself, doesn't mean I'm willing to do so. Plus, Ray, you didn't need me when you were willing to go this route," I shouted.

"Anthony, the branch is divided enough without you doing this. You know the press is going to pick this up. We need to be together on this. Please, don't do this," he said.

"Ray, I tried to reason with you on this issue for the last few months. You ducked me. You never even started returning my calls, until you heard I was picketing. Don't put the guilt trip on me by saying that I'm dividing the branch. You divided the branch, when you and your ass-kissing cronies tried to slip this past the branch," I said.

"Well, Anthony, I wish you would reconsider. You are the first Vice President of the branch. You can be upset; that is understandable. But we need to be united in public..." he said, as I interrupted him.

"So what do you want from me, Ray? I'm not paying no $100 to go to this thing. I don't even have a ticket. Plus, I thought this thing was sold out."

Noticing a change in my attitude, Ray interjected, "I'll give you a seat at my table."

"We'll see, Ray. I need to think about it," I responded.

"Just promise me you won't picket the dinner, Anthony. I need to know where you are on that," Ray pleaded once again.

"Why is it so important to you that I be involved in this farce? Are you trying to compromise me, too?" I asked.

"No, I'm trying to show some semblance of solidarity amongst the officers of this branch. I'm sure you'll be in this position one day," he said.

"Are you saying I'm the only officer not attending this dinner?"

"Yes, I am. Everyone else will be in attendance."

"How many Executive Committee members will be attending?"

"I really don't know."

"All right, Ray."

"So you'll be there, right?"

"I'll be there, Ray."

"Your ticket will be at the door. Thanks, Anthony. I really appreciate your being there for me and the branch. See you later."

"Right, Ray."

As we hung up, my wife said, "You gonna go?" I reluctantly admitted that I was considering it. Ray had made some good points. The branch really didn't need to be embarrassed any further. Hell, the compromise was already national news. My opposition to the dinner was well-documented, and my point had been made. Did I have a responsibility to the branch to attend this function? I guess an argument could be made for it. A refusal to attend now could seem like I was being childish and stubborn, supporting only what I agreed with, as well as, being insensitive to whatever branch responsibility that could be associated with this event. It also could mean an adherence to a principled position. After going back and forth, I decided that I did have a responsibility to the branch, even though I didn't agree with its position on the dinner. With that thought in mind, I pulled my tux out of the closet and concluded that I would be in attendance.

As I walked into the Century Plaza Hotel, I felt very awkward entering the private cocktail reception. Security was very high. Everyone had to have credentials. I just walked past the security, almost daring them to ask me anything. My first spotted Ray standing next to Jim, George and Frank Sinatra, posing for the press corps, looking like he had died and gone to heaven. "Glad to see you decided to come," Ray said.

I gave him a less-than-appreciative look. "Yeah, right. I'm here." I couldn't help but think about the people in the picket line. I'm sure that they knew I wasn't coming by now. Everybody was inside. I wonder if they knew that I was one of them. I had parked at the ABC Entertainment Center across the street, and took the underground tunnel to the hotel. I didn't want to see the picketers, or was it that I didn't want them to see me.

After picking up my dinner ticket, I went to my seat at Ray's complimentary table. As I looked around the room, the table, and the program, something hit me. Where was the NAACP logo that is usually the backdrop at all the major branch dinners? And the freebies on the table, the glasses, the matchbooks-- they all said: "Congratulations, Frank," with no mention of the date, time, place or event, and no mention of the NAACP anywhere. The program, which usually had the late great Roy Wilkins on the cover, had Frank Sinatra on the cover. There was no mention of the Roy Wilkins dinner, or the NAACP anywhere, except on three pages containing the program and the branch officers (which we had to make McMillion put in). Otherwise, all other advertisements reflected acknowledgments to Frank Sinatra. I sat there wondering if the public even knew who was giving this dinner.

The NAACP had been completely whitewashed. McMillion wanted to do a dinner for Frank, and that's what she did. The NAACP was along for the ride. But then most of the people in the room wouldn't complain about riding on the coattails of Sinatra. Except this wasn't what the dinner was supposed to be about.

Just as I was drowning in the amazement of this event, Ruth Anderson, the branch's director of publicity, furiously came over to me and said, "Anthony, Sinatra's security is telling the Black press that the dinner floor is closed to photographers. Look around." As I looked around the room, there were news photographers taking pictures everywhere. When I went to the back of the room and looked into the foyer, there were about 20 Black photographers standing outside, looking like children ,with their noses pressed against a candy store's plate glass window.

I asked Ruth, "Does Ray know about this?"

She said, "Yeah, but he won't deal with it." I immediately went to the door and waved them in.

A big Italian fellow in a tuxedo stepped up and said, "Excuse me, sir, but the banquet hall is closed to photographers."

I presumed he was one of Sinatra's security people. I said, "Oh! Well what is that?" and pointed to several photographers taking pictures of Sinatra at his seat. He proceeded to tell me that the dinner was about to start.

I said, "Not without these photographers being allowed the same opportunity, as the others."

"Who are you, sir?" He asked.

"The first Vice President of the branch, and I'm about to turn this dinner out."

"That won't be necessary, sir." He turned to the photographers and said, "Please ladies and gentlemen, come right in."

As I walked to Ray near the stage, I walked past Sinatra at his table. He had a very cold, glassy look. I asked Ray if he was aware of what was happening. He half-smiled, trying to look pleasant, and stated: "Well, there's nothing we can do about it now, but try to get through it." As I looked around, I saw then-Motown chairman, Berry Gordy, instructing Stevie Wonder on some dialogue he was to give on the program. The planners hadn't missed a beat in trying to create the illusion that support for this thing was greater, than it actually was. You couldn't tell that by the crowd mix. There were very few Blacks or community people there. While the price was often prohibitive, usually there are some seats that are given, or discounted for our people who cannot afford to pay for the high-end tickets. Turning my attention to the back of the room, I saw where they had seated the Executive Committee members (and their guests) who attended -all nine of them. There were roughly two tables. This was very low participation, considering the branch had almost forty-five Executive Committee members. Ray had created the assumption that the Committee was together on this. If this lack of attendance didn't give rise to division, I don't know what would.

On the way back to my seat, a young man named Bill Upton introduced himself to me. He would later play a key role in my betrayal, but for the moment, he was concerned about feeding the production crew he had brought to tape the event. Apparently, Ray didn't tell the planner to feed this group. He was being pretty inaccessible. I called the head-waiter over, and instructed him to feed them.

The program started with a few pleasantries. Ray was given three minutes to make his President's remarks. It was the first time that evening that the NAACP was mentioned in a direct and significant manner. All other pronouncements were: "Welcome to The Roy

Wilkins dinner," or "We all know why we're here-- to honor a man..." But all who got an invitation just saw: "Join us to honor," and respond to the McMillion Group, etc. There was no mention of the NAACP from the start.

After dinner was served, the audience was treated to an appearance by Sammy Davis Jr., truly the highlight of the evening. I've always respected Sammy's hands-on involvement in the struggle for Black rights, before, during and after the civil rights struggle. Hell, we should've recognized him. A lot of people had criticized him for "not being Black enough," for not speaking Black enough, and for fraternizing with the enemy, when he hugged Richard Nixon. But the bottom line was that, when the going was tough for our people, Sammy Davis, Jr. could be counted on. Given his accomplishments, standard of living, extended measure of success, and frequency upon which he was called to help, this was more than you could say for most people, much less celebrities, including Frank Sinatra. Even though I knew Sammy was there that night to support Frank, more than to support us, I appreciated seeing the top entertainer of our last two generations make an appearance, in spite of the controversy of the occasion. Sammy's three-song performance was prefaced with a monologue that addressed the controversy, by innuendo. He stated the need for us to come together as partners in the struggle, and stop finding reasons to separate ourselves. He concluded by saying to Frank that "it was about time" that he was recognized for his contributions.

Sammy had an undying loyalty to Frank Sinatra, because of what Frank had done for him. If Sammy had understood the very comments he was making, which, given his proven commitment, I'm sure he did, he also had to know that Frank had made a very crucial mistake.

While we were trying to come together in America, South Africans, were still separated on the basis of race. While laws that justified racial separation were no longer on the books, in the United States, the South African government still fostered, with great illegitimacy, reasons to continue apartheid. As an entertainer, Sammy knew the importance of the imposed protest by performers to support the anti-apartheid movement. Yet, he never made the mistake of performing over there, even when his career had the highs and lows that made him vulnerable to the type for lucrative offers that seduced Frank. Sammy's own suffering, here in the states, and his personal witness to the struggle of his people, sensitized him to the plight of Black South Africans and their struggle for liberation.

Frank either was not sensitized by the Black experience in America, or thought the world would turn its head to his appearances. Either way, I'm sure Sammy was embarrassed for his friend's social shortsightedness, but was compelled to stand with him through it.

After Sammy finished, the program continued with awards to other honorees. Joe Duff picked up his award, as did Ms. Vivian McDonald. However, particular attention was given to "Sweet Alice" Harris and Maude Clark, founders of Parents of Watts; not because of noteworthy accomplishments of the program, but because they had to call them twice. In an attempt to cater to Sinatra and other politics that would ensure that the dinner came off, Ray and his planners completely forgot about the only community honorees on the ticket.

Generally, there is a dais or a table where the honorees are seated close to the podium. "Sweet Alice," as she is affectionately called, and Ms. Clark, were seated in the back of the 1,500 seat ballroom. Most people would have complained or left altogether. But Alice and Maude stepped high and proud, with their chins up. They had a different type of eloquence, than those in this ballroom had come to see. It was great to me, but I could see the stage director blush behind her script. A major "diss."

The time had come to bring on, what had been billed as, the evening's "featured recipient." Several speakers came up to remind the audience of the social significance and accomplishments of the honoree. Included in these statements were those delivered by Stevie Wonder, a man whose respect crosses creed, color, social class and status. Stevie's comments focused on the need for forgiveness, and how we all had to have a forgiving heart, just as Jesus forgave those who came against him. Stevie implored to those who felt that Frank wasn't meritorious of this recognition to reconsider, and to be forgiving of his past mistakes. It was a very deep request. Deeper still was that the request was coming from one who is arguably the foremost social commentator (musically anyway) of his time.

Finally, Sinatra came up, of course, to nothing but wild applause. Reading from a piece of paper, Frank immediately got to the short strokes of how people want to protest about something he has acknowledged was a mistake, and wouldn't do again. Yet when they need money, they call him to bring it in. He talked about how he has always stood up for right and would continue to do so, in his own way, and those who don't like it "can kiss it." It was a speech that was insulting to the integrity of those in the apartheid struggle, and to the intelligence of those who were forced to acquiesce. He belittled his South Africa appearance, and the legitimacy that followed, in the eyes of the entertainment world. Then he made it seem like the honor was secondary, and that we ought to feel honored that he consented to be honored by us.

That's what I got out of Frank Sinatra's Life Achievement Award acceptance speech. The dinner ran a tight two hours and was over by 9:30 p.m. In passing members of the Executive Committee on the way to the valet parking, we all just looked at each other in sheer amazement of what we had just experienced. Ray, McBeth and Mallory were on their way up to the hospitality, suite in the Century Plaza. Ray invited me up. I declined. I had enough compromise for one night. I certainly didn't want to feel any more a part of this, than my presence had already signified.

I knew I wouldn't be able to separate myself from the branch on this issue. Philosophies aside, regardless of why I was there, the fact remained, I was there. In the eyes of others, my attendance implied support of the award. Ray did what he had to do to keep me from embarrassing him, but now I was more embarrassed than he could ever be, for having been party to this fiasco. I now knew what it was like to be part of a sellout, and to be sold out (neither having to do with seating occupancy at a dinner). All happening at the same time, in the same night.

I looked down at the program and saw Frank Sinatra's face, where Roy Wilkin's face should have been. My naiveté about an "independent civil rights struggle" went out the window that night. We were all bought and sold, on this occasion; first and second generation advocates alike. It may have been "the civil rights" way.

* * *

6

Perpetuating Stereotypes

"America calling, Negroes, can you dance? play foot/baseball? nanny? cook? needed now. Negroes, who can entertain ONLY. Others not wanted (and are considered extremely dangerous.)"

- Haki Madhubuti (formerly Don L. Lee),
Introduction: "Think Black"

The refusal of the mainstream to accept Black people, en mass, as equals in this society is a major contributor to this country's continuing racial problems. A second contributor is their refusal to acknowledge that there is a race problem. Claims of racism are thought to be either infrequent "isolated instances" or gross generalizations. They are actually neither; it is a pervasive mindset that plays itself out at the most inopportune time. This reluctance to acknowledge Black equality, often gives rise to the perpetuation of negative stereotypes about Blacks, which create distorted perceptions of the race.

Compounding the equality problems for Blacks is American society's insincerity in conforming to the tenants of civil rights and equal justice. Because of the bloodshed and violence that the civil rights struggle produced, as well as, whites recognition that the eyes of the world were witnessing their cruel and brutal treatment of Blacks, America tried to change its face almost overnight. It went from being hood-wearing, tobacco-spitting, drawl-speaking segregationists, who couldn't stand the sight of a nigger one day, to peace-loving, cheek-turning, desegregationists the next. Make no mistake about it, most white folk have never been supporters of integration. They desegregated because they were made to, but they never integrated in mind and heart. Suburbia (otherwise known as white flight) was the mass reaction to integration.

Blacks, in their eagerness to receive this newfound acceptance by whites, misread the degree of sincerity, upon which this new bond was established. While it became "en vogue' to have a Black on your arm, a Black on your block, a Black at your table; Blacks mistakenly allowed themselves to be disconnected from the realities of the past. Many Blacks met this treatment with a great deal of cynicism. The majority of the Black mainstream wanted so badly to believe this flip-flop as legitimate, they encouraged all to come on board or be severely criticized for refusing to accept the hand of reciprocity. Many confused the hand of reciprocity and the hand of equality as one and the same.

The cynics, however, hypothecated that white America's effort to extend opportunities to Blacks had nothing to do with being equal. When the reciprocity ran out, would Blacks be anymore equal or socially accepted than when this hugfest began? Black cynicism inferred that whites were doing this more to relieve the racial pressure from themselves, than to help raise the quality of life for masses of Blacks. For those who jumped at the bait, it has been and continues to be a convoluted misrepresentation of how some Blacks' equate singular benefits for massive missed opportunity. Blacks' vulnerability to this posture exemplifies the widespread illusions of social change and progress.

Time has revealed that the commitments to racial parity have been suspect, at best. There have been continuing instances, where individuals not normally thought of as racists, have made statements that suggest that America's commitment to equality has, in many cases, been less than sincere. Some of those charged with moving forth the equality agenda have expressed distorted views of how Blacks are generally perceived. America's public face has been radically different from its private face. This position has been maintained, for a while, in many undocumented instances. Disparate views over the notion of Black parity have become increasingly incipient. As America's continuing commitment to social parity and economic reciprocity for all "people" has been called into question, so has the sincerity of eliminating the inequities of racism. The frequent occurrences of racial indiscretion offer little solace to the notion that "all men were created equal. The question of equal opportunity has yet to be answered. As the question becomes more pressing and time becomes more nostalgic, "Americans" become more willing to exhort their true opinions. These are the same opinions they were once forced to camouflage as a result of having to conform to the 1970s equality masquerade.

There were three major occurrences during my involvement with the Colored People's Association where conflicting racial perspectives became public. Each occurrence was made in confidentiality, supposedly "off the record." Two of the instances involved an informal atmosphere where alcohol was a factor, giving some credence to the old adage, "A drunk ass always speaks a sober mind." Two involved Blacks in athletics. All involved indictments on Black intelligentsia. All involved the media; all were considered experts in their fields of expertise with the ability to influence the thought and actions of their industry, as well as the general public. Each reflected stunning realities that demonstrated after all these years, many so-called Americans (and American institutions), have yet to come clean, with the African-American, in their belief that all men are created equal.

* * *

Monday, April 7, 1987, was a pretty uneventful day in the world of power politics. However, there was a side issue of some social significance to Blacks. On that particular day, 40 years prior, the sport that is known as "America's game" decided to open its field of dreams, its national pastime-- baseball -- to all Americans.

What made this anniversary so special was the recognition of the man chosen to break the color line. One who dispelled the stereotypes that America had used to prevent Blacks' involvement in baseball and, to a larger extent, society. Lack of ability, lack of intelligence, lack of fan appeal (no one would come watch niggers play), lack of personality, lack of social decorum, were few of the many reason whites came up with. Jackie Robinson, with eyes of every American centered on him, defended and vindicated the integrity of the Black American.

Robinson certainly proved that Blacks had the ability to play baseball, but in the process he proved that Blacks had a humanity. Robinson's humanity that enriched the game of baseball and made America realize how foolish it had been in its felonious assertions. This realization exposed the fallacies of race superiority in a way that the arrogance of Jack Johnson or the bumbling humility of Joe Louis couldn't. Where Johnson and Louis excelled in an individual sport, the concept of a white relying on a Black in a team sport, was just unthinkable. Changing the inbred bias of a premiere sport, much less a country, made Jackie Robinson, with the possible exception of Joe Louis, the first post-Reconstruction American hero. Robinson was not just a sports hero, but a hero that contributed to the upliftment of American society, Black or white. Jackie Robinson's accomplishments in American society, superseded his athletic contribution. His participation in major league baseball removed a barrier of racial antipathy that was the beginning of America's human rights maturation. Or so we thought.

The 40th anniversary of Jackie Robinson becoming the first Black to play professional baseball was intended to be a time for reflection of the significance of Robinson's contribution, an opportunity to assess the progress (or non- progress) that has been made, and a forum for discussion of what the future held for Blacks in professional sports. ABC television's national late night news commentary *Nightline* had scheduled an interview with Robinson's former Brooklyn Dodger teammate Don Newcombe for some personal reflections. Sportswriter Roger Kahn was to give an addition assessment. Newcombe was in transit and wasn't able to make the show.

ABC had just nationally televised a Monday night game between the Los Angeles Dodgers and the Houston Astros. As a replacement for Newcombe, the network selected then Dodger general manager, Al Campanis. Campanis, was a teammate of Robinson's, who could provide insights into the hiring patterns of baseball's executive levels where the absence of Blacks had become very apparent. What should have been a very memorable tribute, in terms of the importance of baseball promoting future progress, turned out to be "a throwback in time, place and racial retrospect." Americans would witness one of the most spontaneously insensitive and irresponsible race commentaries in 25 years. I say innocent because the statement did not appear to be premeditated or mean-spirited but contained a perversely "matter of fact" sincerity that couldn't be anticipated or denied.

Ted Koppel, the host of *Nightline*, started the show with a tribute to Jackie Robinson, then moved on to interviews with Campanis and Kahn. Campanis, still at the ballpark in Houston, appeared to have been a little disoriented (red-nosed and all). The more he talked about the occasion, the more you could tell he had been drinking. Then Ted asked the question: "Why aren't there more Blacks in the front office in baseball?" Campanis responded that "many people in baseball feel that Blacks do not have the experience nor were they willing to pay their dues in the farm systems and, therefore, didn't have the necessities to hold field management positions in baseball."

A shocked Ted Koppel tried to give Campanis every conceivable out to clean up his statements, suggesting that Campanis' indictment on Blacks could be interpreted at best as stereotyping and at worse, as racist. Campanis, instead of recanting his statements, tried to justify his perception and substantiate it with another stereotype that "Blacks weren't good swimmers because they lacked buoyancy." An exasperated Ted Koppel had no other choice but to go to a commercial and leave the country in contemplation of Campanis' racial infamy. When they returned from the commercial break, Koppel stayed away from Campanis until closing remarks. The damage had been done. Al Campanis, a baseball "lifer," in one statement, jolted the myth that Blacks had become an integral part of the game. In another statement, he reduced Blacks to commodities to be exploited, traded and sold, but were unable to manage or have ownership in the game they helped make successful. Moreover, Campanis' brutal "matter of fact" analogy gave rise to a mindset that was long perceived as abandoned. Campanis exposed the game in a way that violated the rules of those in power, not only in baseball but any other industry nationwide.

While Blacks in this country all along had maintained that nothing had changed, most whites in power had adopted a "get along" philosophy to eliminate overt racism but to continue covert racism. The unsaid, unseen and undocumented are only open to conjecture but can't be immediately proven. While the absence of Blacks makes a particular organization suspect to claims of racism, they often represent it as circumstantial and therefore invalid. Whites had (then, as now) a multitude of reasons to justify why Blacks were not a representative part of the systemic brain trust of institutions that run this country.

Short of a documented admission of racial prejudice or what could be perceived as race insensitivity, Blacks are hard pressed to claim racial discrimination. Whites will often dismiss such claims, attributing impatience or obstinacy to those who persist in that vein. This leaves Blacks to deal with racism, while trying to dissuade a perceived lunacy. Conversely, many qualified, responsible Blacks spend their lives trying to convince the world that the Black reality of exclusion is not a figment of our imagination. Author Ellis Cose would eloquently articulate and document this frustration in his book, “Rage of a Privileged Class.”

All Al Campanis did was break the "new" secret rule of "do evil, but speak not of it," which carries a penalty of banishment for life. White folks learned that lesson in the 1960s when their race politic put them on the world stage. They now had too much going on, launching the "new world order" global economy to have to give any significant time to their domestic race question. The politics and global competitiveness of capitalism doesn't allow for one to be perceived as an open racist, as it once did. However, being a closet bigot, at that time and even today, never went out of style. You can practice racism, just keep it amongst the boys (and girls), don't talk to the press, don't put it in writing or on tape, and everything's cool.

America has a growing ethnic population (including a segment of fair-minded whites) that rejects overt racism. Those in power understand that and act in a manner that's hidden but effective, lest they open the country up to anarchy and lose control, as has been the case in East Germany, Russia and other oppressive countries. Al Campanis had lost his place in time.

Upon hearing Campanis' statement, Dodgers owner Peter O'Malley initially maintained that Campanis would not be fired. Campanis immediately apologized. The press gave plenty of testimony to Campanis' character and benevolence. However, many of the Black ballplayers, past and present, were appalled at the statements but attested to their validity. Even Black Dodgers players broke the usual "no comment" protocol on highly controversial issues and expressed their disdain over Campanis' comments. Within 24 hours, O'Malley changed his mind and fired Campanis.

The community was obviously outraged. Ray called a press conference and called for an investigation by then-Major League Baseball Commissioner Peter Ueberroth into the hiring of Blacks in baseball. The branch requested that the Dodgers facilitate the investigation. The national organization called a meeting for branches in professional sports cities, from Los Angeles to New York, to develop strategies to address this issue. I attended the meeting as the representative for the L.A. branch.

The LA branch had already implemented many of the recommendations derived from this meeting, but our proactive movement became the brunt of Ben Hooks' jokes. When addressing how the branches were to keep national involved, he used the analogy: "Don't be like Los Angeles and go out on your own." Everybody seemed to get a kick out of national's continuing bantering about the Los Angeles branch.

Los Angeles, at that time, had seven major sports teams. Of the seven, clearly the Dodgers, the Angels and the Rams had obvious race problems. The Angels and Rams were in Orange County. We forwarded letters to them but since the Orange County branches were closer, we opted to hold off meeting with those teams until we had discussed it with those branches. After analyzing the teams in the area, on the basis of their minority hiring policies, Ray decided that the Dodgers would be our primary focus.

The Los Angeles Clippers, at that time, had a Black general manager (Elgin Baylor) and a Black head coach, named Don Chaney. The Los Angeles Raiders was perceived as one of the most progressive employers of Blacks in professional sports. Even though no football team had a Black head coach or general manager at the time, the Raiders had several assistant coaches with head coach potential. Many felt if any team would hire a Black head coach anytime in the near future, it would be the Raiders. Sure enough, a few years later, this proved to be accurate when the Raiders' hired Art Shell as their head coach.

The Los Angeles Lakers had no Blacks in its front office, nor any Blacks on its coaching staff. A few ex-players were very critical of the Lakers' treatment of its Black former players. I had a phone interview with Happy Hairston, a member of the 1972 Championship team, who disclosed several issues of racial disparity. Hairston supported his contention by pointing out that the Lakers could never find a place, in its organization, for its first Los Angeles superstar, Elgin Baylor. Baylor, who a year prior to our public condemnation of professional sports teams' minority hiring practices, had been hired as general manager of the Los Angeles Clippers but was out of work for years while the Lakers had several front office positions turn over. They even created a few, in Hairston's opinion, but never one for Baylor. Hairston even disclosed that celebrities could get Lakers playoff tickets easier than members of its first championship team, stating that he himself had been denied several requests for passes.

However, the Lakers were now sacred cows in Los Angeles. With a cast of seven rotating players (six of whom were Black, and after Kurt Rambis left, all seven were Black), the Lakers was the prototype for 21st century basketball. They were the league's best team, the city's winningest team in years, and on their way to winning the first of back to back championships in 17 in years (the first team to do it since Bill Russell's Boston Celtics in the late 1960s). With an almost cult-like following called "Showtime," it would have seemed very ill-timed to attack the Lakers in the midst of a championship run. The Lakers were a speeding bus that nobody was willing to take on (including myself, being an avid Lakers fan). The Dodgers were the logical choice because the team was in a high profile market and was vulnerable, because of the recent occurrence of events. The Dodgers had lived 40 years on the "Jackie Robinson" stigma. They had created the illusion that their sensitivities to Blacks were greater than everybody else's, because they were the first (in modern league history) to put a Black on the field.

This couldn't have been further from the truth. The Dodgers had several players through the years that were perceived as excellent managerial prospects, including Maury Wills and Frank Robinson. Both were former players who were hired as managers (two of only four Blacks ever hired, at the time). But their most notable prospect was Jim "Junior" Gilliam.

By most accounts, Gilliam was one of the most brilliant baseball minds to ever play or coach baseball. Gilliam was a catalyst for the Dodgers winning three world championships (in 1959, 1963, 1965) in their first seven years in Los Angeles. Gilliam served, with distinction, as a coach for almost ten years after his retirement as a player. However, one of the major issues raised during Gilliam's tenure was that he never was able to get out of the first base coaching box, to the so-called "thinking coach's box" on the third base line. Many attribute this failure to baseball's stereotypic perception of Blacks, which allegedly the Dodgers have subscribed to; that Blacks didn't have the necessities to manage. Because of the stability of the Dodgers ownership and success of its franchise, in terms of profit and management, it was perceived that the league owners usually followed the lead of the Dodgers. In the early '80s, this was never more evident, than when it was disclosed that the Dodgers were one of the lead organizations accused of engaging in collusion against free agent players, to hold down the price of large contract signings. The Dodgers treatment of Gilliam certainly was consistent with statements disclosed by Campanis. Jim Gilliam died in 1978, as the first base coach of the Dodgers. Yet, the Dodgers will forever be known as the team that gave Blacks a break in baseball. A private face different from a public one.

The branch formed a negotiating team comprised of Ray, former major league pitcher Jim "Mudcat" Grant and myself. Dodgers President Peter O'Malley agreed to meet with us. It was in the team's best interest to meet with us, if for no other reason than for damage control. To not to meet with us, would have given the branch a reason to blast the Dodgers as insensitive and uncooperative. That was not good, in light of the Campanis statements. O'Malley didn't earn the reputation as one of the shrewdest players in baseball from selling hot dogs.

The first meeting, on May 17, was a catered lunch in O'Malley's Dodgers Stadium office. There we had the opportunity to interface with one of professional sports' real bluebloods-- the O'Malleys of major league baseball. O'Malley's family tradition with the Dodgers is historic. His father Walter O'Malley was heralded as bringing baseball to the West Coast. Dodger Stadium was the prototype for the state-of- the-art sports facility, and after 35 years, is still a class stadium. Peter O'Malley, as his father's successor, earned the respect of his peers by running a winning and profitable organization. In the 1970s and 1980s, the Dodgers had regularly led the league in attendance and ran a very fiscal-minded payroll. Other than the New York Yankees and maybe the Dallas Cowboys (at that time), there wasn't a more valuable sports franchise than the Los Angeles Dodgers.

Peter O'Malley was a very polite and cordial man, with no apparent racial hostilities. He appeared sincere in his apologies for his organization's impropriety, and his willingness to move past this point. Ray started the meeting by raising concern about Campanis' replacement. The Dodgers had appointed Fred Claire as interim general manager. O'Malley stated that they were interviewing candidates, and would be most happy to entertain any recommendations the branch would make.

I gave Mr. O'Malley the questionnaire that the national NAACP asked that each organization complete. Some goals and timelines were set, and we left each other to discuss our encounter. Our overall impression was that the Dodgers were receptive, but very noncommittal, to any specific personnel or policy moves. Our objective was to get O'Malley to be a little more responsive.

In the second meeting, on June 17, O'Malley informed us that he was working with the commissioner's office to develop a minority hiring policy, but he refused to allow us to see it. O'Malley disclosed that he had met with other community leaders. He specifically mentioned meetings with Jesse Jackson, Rachel Robinson, Golden State Mutual Insurance CEO Ivan Houston and (L.A. Black Business Association President) Skip Cooper. They had hired John Roseboro as a minor league manager of one of their farm teams. They had interviewed Curt Flood Jr. for the general manager position. He had not completed our questionnaire. We also discussed the organization's procurement policy, which was the proverbial "old boy system" (doing business with people they had done business with for years). O'Malley admitted that he hadn't given much thought to the issue of using minorities for products and services, but he said that he would. Again, there were no specific timelines.

Frustrated with O'Malley's deliberate, generic negotiating posture, Ray informed O'Malley of the June 1 deadline imposed by the national organization for the teams to announce a strategy to employ Blacks in management. One owner, Edward Bennett Williams (Baltimore Orioles), had already hired a Black man in the front office. O'Malley expressed his concern over the ultimatum, and felt teams should be given more time. Ray pressed on, saying that the Dodgers had sufficient time, and that the L.A. branch was now concerned about the team's credibility. Ray asked O'Malley to come to the NAACP's national convention in New York, to discuss the Dodgers plans and to show good faith. O'Malley rejected that suggestion. Ray told O'Malley that he was leaving him with little choice but to go public on the Dodgers lack of action. O'Malley who refused to be pressured, told Ray that he understood his position and stated: "You gotta do what you gotta do, Ray."

That was the last meeting we had with the Dodgers. While I was disappointed in the Dodgers' lack of action, I really respected O'Malley for his position. I don't believe we gave the Dodgers sufficient time. O'Malley is what Blacks used to call "good white folk." Not racist or mean-spirited, they just need to have their conscience pricked from time to time, but they invariably try to do what's right. O'Malley proved that with his firing of Campanis. However, O'Malley was isolated by a mindset that he wasn't (or may have been) part of a bigger problem and negotiated from that position. In doing so, it made him a party to the greater racial insensitivity that plagued his whole industry. He didn't have to succumb to the pressure of meeting with Blacks. Blacks by and large represented less than 3 percent of his attendance. So a boycott didn't frighten him. He just needed time to address the issue in a manner where he didn't feel pushed or extorted.

In a progressive negotiation, the NAACP usually allows for that adjustment period. This whole culmination of events basically evolved over a two and a half month period. Hell, it usually takes more than two months to get a response from many organizations involved in racial conflict disputes. Ray, in an attempt to pre-empt the national organization and bring captives to the convention, short circuited the negotiation process and thereby compromised the overall goal of facilitating the movement of Blacks in management position with the Dodgers. Under the right circumstances, the influence of Peter O'Malley could have allowed for the branch to have a greater input into the policy that the league was trying to develop. The Dodgers eventually hired Fred Claire, a white male, as their permanent replacement for Campanis. They did, however, hire ex-Lakers star Tommy Hawkins as their first Black Vice President in a non-community relations capacity. Another twenty-six minorities were hired that season, in a band-aid approach to a scathing open wound. Did baseball get smart overnight, or was it about damage control? History has demonstrated that baseball's response that season was suspect, at best. 1997 celebrated the 50th anniversary of Jackie Robinson's breaking baseball's "color line." The underlying discussions, all season, was the lack of Blacks in front office management; the very same discussion that took place ten years earlier, -only without the public side-commentary of Al Campanis. Baseball is still every bit American as the flag, hot dogs, apple pie and racism.

* * *

Less than a year after the Campanis incident, another sports figure made an equally absurd public statement about the anatomical development of Blacks. Bookie turned sports commentator Jimmy "The Greek" Snyder was being interviewed about the performance of athletes in sports. It was apparent that he had been drinking prior to, or during the interview. Supposedly, the discussion continued after the interview had concluded and was "off the record" when Snyder gave his assessment of why Blacks are better athletes than whites. This was his assessment:

"Blacks are better athletes because during slavery, the slave master bred the slaves for productivity. Conversely, he mated the biggest and strongest men with the biggest mama slaves to produce physical specimens bred to lift, move, run and jump. It is in the genes of Blacks to be able to outperform whites physically and, therefore, making them superior athletes."

Of course, this caused another furor. In a matter of days, The Greek was "history." CBS Sports announced that "Jimmy the Greek" would not be returning to its NFL pre-game show, nor would he be affiliated with the network in any other capacity. Since this incident was caused by a communication medium, then Beverly Hills-Hollywood branch President Willis Edwards called for CBS Sports and the other networks to hire more Blacks in the sportscasting industry.

Because of my experience in handling issues, Willis asked me to work with him on this matter. This was the second project Willis and I had worked on together. Willis had previously invited me to work on a task force to investigate discrimination allegations at Hughes Aircraft Company. This initially caused problems for Ray because he saw the Hollywood branch as competition. Really, with 12 other branches in the area, how could Hollywood be singled out. All branches in close proximity fight for attention and members, and they all compete for solicitation of contributions. Many from the same companies. Inter-branch collaboration didn't bother me one way or the other. To resolve the matter with Willis and Ray, I just gave Willis $10 and became a member of his branch, while also holding office in the L.A. branch. There was nothing that prohibited my involvement in two branches. Plus, I really didn't care about Ray's insecurity. The sportscasting industry was an issue I wanted to explore.

Willis and I went to New York three days later to meet with CBS Sports management. Working with Willis was a different kind of experience. Upon arriving at CBS headquarters to meet with then CBS Sports President, Neil Pilson, the receptionist announced that Mr. Pilson was awaiting our arrival and asked, "Will Dr. Hooks be joining you?" Willis promptly responded "We expect him any moment, I think his plane was delayed." Fifteen minutes later Willis asked to use the phone and called Hooks. Willis told him that we were in New York getting ready to go into a meeting with CBS Sports management and asked if was he coming. Hooks stated that he would not be able to make the meeting. Willis advised Pilson that we would proceed with the meeting without Dr. Hooks, per his instructions. I somehow suspect that while Hooks knew of Willis' intentions, he had not committed to this meeting. Willis basically facilitated the meeting using Hooks' name, which added incentive for CBS Sports to meet. Influence-peddling at its best, though Willis would never admit it. Still the objective was to get CBS Sports management to respond quickly and agree to meet. Willis clearly met the objective, in a tongue-in-cheek sort of way.

In the meeting, CBS was forthright and direct in expressing its decision to fire "The Greek." Pilson espoused that they paid Snyder for his professional commentator expertise, not his anatomical opinions. He stated the station felt it had no other choice but to denounce Snyder's statements as racist and that they did not reflect the opinions of the station, nor its shareholders and management. Pilson said that Jimmy was a very popular personality for its pre-game show and that the station had received quite a few calls in support of Snyder. However, they felt they had done the right thing. Apparently, CBS was well rehearsed in their public response to the Snyder situation.

While they were feeling so sanctimonious, we decided to take the discussion in a different direction, and focus on the sports network's fair employment of Blacks over the past five years. What we discovered was disappointing. Other than Irv Cross, CBS Sports had no other Blacks in any of its sportscasting employees or commentator positions. These people represented some thirty employees. Of their behind-the-scenes technical support crews, (some 200 or more employees responsible for getting CBS sporting events on the air), there was only one Black employee, former UCLA basketball star, Roy Hamilton. He was the only Black on the executive track that management could identify. These representations were diametric to the commitments to fairness and parity that CBS management intimated earlier in our discussion. Certainly, CBS wasn't doing the right thing when it came to hiring Blacks. Clearly, CBS had demonstrated that its commitment to minorities was less than proactive, that the network's position on Snyder was more of a reactive posture to control public perception of the station rather than to reinforce a commitment to racial parity. CBS' shortage of Black employees and its justification for it was every bit as ridiculous as Snyder's explanation for athletic superiority. While CBS chose to give a public perception that it was sensitive to race in its social context, our survey proved that the network was irresponsible and insensitive to the involvement of Blacks in the network's dispatch of services. CBS was representing one frame of thought, and practicing something totally different. It was saying that we don't condone racism in any form or context. Yet, it was allowing Blacks to be continually excluded from having equal employment assess to network jobs. A public position clearly different from its private practice.

We received a commitment from CBS to begin to identify Blacks for on camera and high-level (behind the camera) technical assignments. Willis made a commitment to forward a list of qualified industry personnel for the network to choose from. We also requested their annual report, shareholders information and an organizational chart of the network's hierarchy. While the CBS meeting proved cordial, you couldn't help but think what were the real perceptions of Blacks held by those we were meeting with. If we could have solicited their personal thoughts, what would we have heard? Any reaffirmation in a belief in racial parity would have provided an even greater contrast in public persona, based on our discoveries.

Yet for them to straight out tell us "they can't stand niggahs," would appall us and everybody else who disdains, not so much racism, but2 any break with social protocol. Like burping at the dinner table, overt racism has become more like manners to be minded. Still we know, like they know, that many of them could care less about Blacks. Blacks lack of presence in their work environment, very often, reflects this. Our absence in their circles of influence are indicative of that. However, the continuous denial of their private views lessens the credibility of the deniers, and creates a pretentious condition that is illegitimate, and makes suckers of those who seek a sincere solution to the question of parity. It has become another mockery, creating hypocrisy on the question of racial equality. Our recognition of this will bring into reality how gullible and naive Blacks are when addressing the sincerity of whites and their references to brutal nomenclatures like diversity, inclusiveness, equality, fairness and opportunity. For none of them really exit. They know, we know it, everybody knows it. We all just wear the masks that grins and lies...

* * *

A particularly disturbing occurrence perpetuating Black stereotypes made the news in late August of 1988. Los Angeles was gearing up for its first really competitive mayoral race in years. Mayor Tom Bradley, who was vying for an unprecedented fifth term in office, finally appeared vulnerable, in light of several controversial issues. His most formidable challenger was considered to be a fairly popular city councilman from the city's Westside. Zev Yaroslavsky, who is Jewish, had long been groomed as a potential heir apparent for mayor. Yaroslavsky had set up an exploratory committee to examine his chances for mayor.

At the same time, Yaroslavsky was also backing a major ballot initiative for opponents against oil drilling in Pacific Palisades. The oil-drilling initiative was being managed by the political consulting group of Carl D'Agostino and Michael Berman, who is the brother of U.S. Congressman Howard Berman. Michael Berman was also the lead strategist for Yaroslavsky's exploratory committee. During this period, Berman was analyzing the political temperament of the city and advising Yaroslavsky on how he could benefit from issues facing the city. The controversy was raised when in one confidential memo to Yaroslavsky, Berman stated that "Yaroslavsky could win the election if he outdebated Bradley on the issues." Berman went on to say that Yaroslavsky had 50 I.Q. points on Bradley and could outsmart the mayor in the upcoming election. Now Yaroslavsky is not exactly one to make anybody forget Einstein. He is known for his political aggressiveness and inquiring (even pushy) tenacity, but not particularly for his intelligence. Yet, in an effort to pump up Yaroslavsky, Berman and his company insulted the L.A. Black community by implying that race stereotypes regarding Black intelligentsia had some credence as it applied to Tom Bradley.

It was common knowledge that the city's Black constituency was becoming increasingly disenchanted with Tom Bradley. Yaroslavsky's strategy included trying to court Blacks who weren't inclined to support Bradley the next time around. If anyone had a right to get stereotypical, it would've been Blacks in their assessment that Jews position themselves by exploiting Black community weaknesses (once again). By courting the anti-Bradley Black constituency, Yaroslavsky would take advantage of a Black versus Black conflict. Certainly, it would be a smart move on anybody's behalf. Yet, it just seemed ironic that a Jew, who is stereotypically represented as smart, would be waiting in the cut to exploit "a dumb Black constituency" and beat what his managers perceive as "a dumb Black mayor."

As ludicrous as it sounded, it looked even more ludicrous in print. Berman and D'Agostino tried to underplay the statements as "humorous" and "private communications reflective of the real world where political battles are won and lost." Certainly, there was nothing funny about what they were implying. However, they did bring home one perspective that was perfectly clear: that, again, in private forums the private perceptions of Blacks and other minorities are different than those perceptions whites represent in public. Furthermore, when there are stakes on the table and they are forced to see the reality of a situation, whites hold fast to their opinions about minorities, whether they're true or not. They go back to what they know the real world to be, stereotypes included. Yet, they maintain a consistent state of denial about this, which allows Blacks and others to only suspect that their representations about race are honest and just. This, in most cases, couldn't be further from the truth but it couldn't be proved until now. Very few mainstream bigots put their bigotry in writing.

In what was to be one of my issues while serving as President of the branch, I was contacted by the press, to respond to the comments by Berman and D'Agostino. I told them that we would respond in a press conference the next day. I had already received copies of the statement from Mike Davis, the branch's governmental affairs chairman. Davis, also an aide for then Assemblywoman Maxine Waters, had acquired the entire memo. He felt that the statements were outrageous and merited a response. It was obvious to all who read the memo that it was a sincere and deliberate attempt to exploit some Black voters' lack of sophistication, where Zev could benefit from their indecision on Bradley. That strategy was clear. The editorial comments only gave a racial slant to Yaroslavsky's perceived objective.

Once the memo became a major topic in the press and in the community, Yaroslavsky reacted quickly by releasing a statement saying that he didn't share Berman and D'Agostino's opinions and that he would not be using them for his mayoral campaign. A smart move but not quite enough. While Yaroslavsky's mayoral campaign was still exploratory, the anti-oil drilling initiative was on the ballot. The campaign for the no-drill supporters was still being managed by, guess who? Berman and D'Agostino. Yaroslavsky was the co-sponsor of the initiative (along with Los Angeles City Councilman Marvin Braude), and certainly had some power to influence a decision on how the ballot measure campaign would continue to be managed. Armand Hammer, Chairman of Occidental Petroleum, was courting the Black community very heavily to support a counterinitiative favoring drilling. The Blacks would be a key constituency to lobby and lock up. It would be very difficult to look past the Berman and D'Agostino relationship, if they continued to be involved in the drilling campaign.

The branch called a press conference to request that Yaroslavsky and his anti-drilling supporters drop Berman and D'Agostino from the campaign's management. The branch was being heavily lobbied, as was other community interest charged with delivering the Black vote. At the press conference, I called out several concerns about how these consultants had the ability to mold public opinion through their candidates. How could any sector of the public feel comfortable knowing that these types of stereotypic analogies were harbored by those entrusted to guide political candidates and issues, -particularly someone who was running for mayor.

We took the position that the Berman and D'Agostino memo was very damaging to the efforts Yaroslavsky was making to build a support base in the Black community. It was an open attack on Blacks not to be taken lightly. We wanted to see what was more important to Mr. Yaroslavsky, the success of the initiative, or his relationship with the Black community. If he dismissed the bad consultants, it would jeopardize the anti-drilling initiative. Of course, if he continued to retain them, it would jeopardize his chance to pull significant Black support in a mayoral race. "In fact," I stated, "unless Yaroslavsky moves to mend fences with the Black community, he'll have to see whether we have enough I.Q. points to remember to vote (for the anti-drilling measure) in November." The press conference received significant coverage, emanating immediate responses from both Yaroslavsky and the mayor's office. The mayor's office used the opportunity to address other issues in the memos that implied that Yaroslavsky was planning to solicit from the list of charitable organizations, which was an illegal act. Yaroslavsky responded that, in spite of the memo controversy, they would continue to retain Berman and D'Agostino.

Yaroslavsky was able to determine just that quickly where his loyalties were. He was willing to bet on the short memory of Blacks, versus the wrath (and money) of the Pacific Palisades anti-drilling supporters. This was clearly another instance when doing the right thing went the way of compromise. In the process of advancing or protecting other people's interest, Black interest as well as the integrity of Blacks was compromised. Ironically enough, where the anti-drilling initiative went on to win, Yaroslavsky opted not to run for mayor. Yaroslavsky, however, is now a Los Angeles County Supervisor, which in some capacities, is even more powerful than being a mayor.

These hidden attitudes provide some serious dilemmas for those in the mainstream society who must begin to declare their position for those interests that diametrically oppose Black progress. It will become more evident as time goes by that racial equality is not going to be conceded by those in control. That is not to say that all whites and divergent cultures think this way. Some really try to discern stereotypic myths from cultural realities. Many in power represent those negative plights publicly, and try to make them apply to everyone in the culture. Therefore, many whites and immigrants in this country perceive Blacks and their culture from a state of ignorance. Yet, as ignorant as they may be about some things, certainly, some common sense should prevail about others. Still the society would rather, by its silence or non-rebuttal, imply that the stereotype is the truth. While many of them publicly exercise some sense of intelligence and discretion regarding their views, they still harbor, and privately perpetuate, the stereotypes and racial myths that prevent the masses of Blacks from achieving widespread acceptance in the social and economic mainstreams.

Blacks would like to think times are changing, but they must take a closer look at those whites and others that they interface with, and reserve judgment as to how they are perceived. Some are fair, but many are not. And just as whites distrust Blacks, until they feel comfortable around them, Blacks have to learn to do the same (as opposed to trusting them first, as we've been socialized, and getting disappointed later). Blacks must be on guard to make sure that the philosophy, interaction, and final results add up. It's not always what they say in public, but what they do, in place, that discerns their level of sincerity. If they are sincere, their private views will eventually show. If they are not, Blacks need to be able to recognize such insincerity. Otherwise, Blacks will continue to fall victim to the public posturing of closet bigotry and societal racial ignorance.

* * *

7

Redevelopment Compromise:

Municipal Gifts and Community Plantations

"Real tragedy is never resolved. It goes on hopelessly forever."
- Chinua Achebe

The notion of economic development has been a misrepresented issue to a largely unsophisticated Black electorate. Over the past 30 years, during a period in the late '60s and early '70s, social and political gains were expected to bring about better quality of life to the Black masses. A good number of Black politicians were soon exposed to the realities of wealth sharing, when urban redevelopment projects were found to be the key to improving communities and removing urban blight. Elected officials thought they finally had a vehicle through municipal bonds, commercial tax bases and community development block grants to train youths, build businesses, create jobs, create commerce and create beautification, all in one full swoop. Moreover, community redevelopment projects were designed to put economically deprived communities to work and make them industrious, allowing residents and businesses to share in the growth and renewed prosperity of their own environment. The concept of merging politics and economics, establishing true "political economies" proved to be the cornerstone of urban restoration strategies in cities like Cleveland, Baltimore and Atlanta.

Los Angeles, conversely, had been a city that had experienced tremendous growth and industrialization, over the twenty years coinciding with the Tom Bradley era (1973-1993). This era brought significant economic growth particularly in the downtown and Westside of the city, where commercial development brought about regional commerce expansion that turned Los Angeles into the "Ellis Island" of the U.S. Much of it was private development courted by the city. Others included public/private partnerships as well as federal and state subsidized projects. Los Angeles became a regional hub for the Pacific rim under Bradley-- a Black man-- perceived (and who prided himself) as a mayor of "all the people." However, as much as Los Angeles appeared to be the model city for regional and global trade-- growing in economic prosperity and commercial development, the Black and Hispanic communities of East and South Central Los Angeles remained largely neglected. As a result of the lack of commercial development, business and commerce deserted these areas. White flight probably can be attributed as a secondary factor. Commerce just followed the money to the suburbs. An unintended (or maybe, intended) consequence of the politics of separation.

As an incentive to keep business in the inner city, the Los Angeles Community Redevelopment Agency (CRA) became a proprietary department, with an open checkbook, during the 1980s. Its charge was to establish commercial enterprise zones designed to promote business growth or relocation and to target certain areas for commercial redevelopment. Under such programs, retail shopping centers were built with the help of private enterprise in the Watts, Wilmington and Vermont/Slauson areas of Los Angeles. Some of those developments were creatively structured to allow the community to benefit through community development corporations. Vermont/Slauson had one such project.

The guidelines of such CRA developments usually required the area to be largely a community dependent on housing, public services and consumer conveniences. Usually, the residents of such an area would have lower to middle incomes, were more likely to rent than own, and depend on public transportation. The higher income areas were usually developed by commercial business (private industry). If the area didn't fit certain parameters, the area wouldn't qualify for public money. The other side of the coin was, if the area was considered "too blighted," private industry refused to come in.

This was the unique position of one of the nation's most

affluent Black communities, the Crenshaw/Baldwin Hills District. The Crenshaw/Baldwin Hills area encompasses several small districts, which include Ladera Heights, View Park, Windsor Hills, Baldwin Hills and Leimert Park. The area includes over 15,000 homes that, at the time, were valued between $175,000 and $500,000. Its residents had a median annual income that exceeded $40,000. A significant portion of those household incomes, however, far exceed that amount. Prior to 1965 (when L.A. burned the first time), this area was 90 percent white. As late as the mid-70s, it was still 50 percent white. In the mid-1950s, this community was the recipient of the nation's first community shopping mall. Once one of the finest shopping facilities around, it had become a victim of urban blight. Many of the anchor tenants like May Company (now Robinson-May) and The Broadway department stores were considering pulling out of the area. While the shopping center was decaying, the affluent community around it shopped elsewhere. Beverly Hills, the Beverly Center, South Bay malls, (Del Amo & Old Towne) and Fox Hills Mall (at that time, the most profitable mall in the country for a mall of its size)--were receiving significant Black consumer dollars, largely due to the inferior products and services the once great "Crenshaw" shopping center was now providing. However, no private developer was interested in coming to in the heart of one of the richest Black communities in the country to refurbish this shopping center. And, technically, the area didn't qualify for public development funds. So what would be done to save Crenshaw?

What initially started out as an exciting opportunity for Black economic empowerment and self-determination ended up being, at best, a questionable manipulation of public funds. Or in the worst case, it was an exposé in political cronyism, public deception and unabashed greed, that would economically enslave the community for some time to come. The project became known as the Baldwin Hills/Crenshaw Shopping Plaza. It started out innocently enough, as a restoration project for the Crenshaw Shopping Center. The forces behind it were former councilwoman Pat Russell, then President of the Los Angeles City Council, David Cunningham, 10th District councilman and Mayor Tom Bradley. The shopping center site was on the line between the 6th District, represented by Russell, and the 10th District, represented by Cunningham. (formerly represented by Bradley) Financing for the project initially had included federal grants, city funds and a proposed private money infusion that would form one of the first private-public joint ventures the Black community had known. In order to justify the city's CRA funds, usually reserved for economically disadvantaged communities, the boundaries of the CRA expansion area, which ran east and north of the site, had to be gerrymandered (moved for political convenience or expediency) to include the shopping center area. Otherwise, the site didn't qualify under the development guidelines. There was no opposition to this boundary shift since there was a consensus on the shopping center's need for restoration. In the selection of a joint venture partner, it was publicly represented that the appropriate bids were held, and that Alexander Haagen, a longtime Bradley supporter and developer in the Black community, had been given the contract to develop the restoration project.

Alexander Haagen had a long and somewhat controversial history with the Bradley administration. Haagen was the former chair of the Coliseum Commission. He had represented to Al Davis, President and general partner of the Los Angeles Raiders football team, that the Coliseum Commission had no intention of honoring the commitment they had made to him to improve the Coliseum. Stadium boxes and other amenities, worth millions of dollars, were offered as incentives to attract the Raiders to Los Angeles. Al Davis in turn told him and the Commission to kiss his "you know what" and proceeded to look to take his team elsewhere. The Commission stated that they never supported Haagen on such a statement, and removed him as chairman. Los Angeles ended up having to bid five times what it would have cost them initially to keep the Raiders in L.A. for another few years.

Once the developer was in place, the city had to convince the disgruntled anchor tenants to stay. This was a very long and highly sensitive process. The major issue was how to get the customers back to the Crenshaw shopping center. How would the developer address issues like quality of stores, public safety and the loss of revenue? The city or developer really didn't have that worked out. They just knew the renovation would be first class, and no expense would be spared in the solicitation of community support.

However, several events occurred that broke up the consensus base of support: First, councilman Dave Cunningham was forced to resign over alleged ethics improprieties with a developer who did business with the city. The developer was later indicted and convicted on these same allegations. This took the community's focus (and City Hall's) off the mall for a while to concentrate on a succession. It was the first open seat to come up in the council (in what was considered a Black seat) in over 12 years. It was a real free-for-all. Everybody had a candidate. All the "Negro powers that be" had a candidate. It was also seen as an opportunity for "the up and coming" players (second generation of the post civil rights era politics) to step on stage. Many felt it was "their turn," a chance for new leadership to show what they could do. This would be a battle that would affect Black leadership and community unity for the next few years to come. It certainly held up the mall discussion for a minute.

While that free-for-all was climbing to a fever pitch, the mall's political architect and biggest supporter, (as well as the mayor's) City Council President Pat Russell, was coming under increasing attacks by different factions of her constituency. The Westchester area was concerned about Russell's pro-growth posture, and the Venice Beach area was concerned about Russell's apparent inattentiveness to environmental issues. Also, she had been long criticized for what the Crenshaw area felt was insensitive and inadequate services and low-priority representation. She was about to lose her seat, unless she made some drastic changes. She lost to a liberal environmental activist, whose chances were greatly enhanced when she was attacked in her home in Venice. She survived and captured the sympathy vote that put her over the top, in spite of being out-manned, outspent and out-endorsed. Russell had Tom Bradley personally campaigning for her and still lost. That wasn't the only beating Bradley took in that election. His hand-picked candidate, Homer Broom, was beat by a career politician named Nate Holden. It was important for Bradley to have great success with the Crenshaw Plaza since it was the first real significant project he had done in his former district. He had just lost his two biggest allies on the council, the councilpersons of those districts from which the mall would draw its clientele. As big of an upset as these two losses were, it wasn't about as bad as the beating he was getting ready to take on Crenshaw Mall project.

The Crenshaw Plaza (Baldwin Hills/Crenshaw Shopping Plaza) was being represented by both the city and the developer as the quintessential public/private sector joint venture. It was an opportunity for a community to directly participate in every phase of the project's development-- ownership, construction, professional services (advertising, accounting, technical assistance) tenant leasing stores, management and employment. The Community Redevelopment Agency's policies require active participation of community residents and businesses where the development is being built. Furthermore, the contracts on such a project had to reflect the ethnicity of the community where the project was being constructed. The first phase of the project was estimated at $50 million. The community was excited about that facet of the project.

The second strategy that mustered community support was that a Black individual, or consortium of Blacks would retain ownership in the mall. The community again was thrilled at the possibility that some of our money would stay in our community. Alexander Haagen offered up 25 percent of the mall (50 percent of his 50 percent) to Black investors. Many people thought that this was a generous offer on Haagen's part. It was quite the contrary. Haagen was trying to lessen his exposure to the mall in the preliminary phases by using an "OPM" strategy (Other people's money). He put up his balance sheet and everybody else put up the cash. The $50 million construction bond he acquired with First Interstate Bank was to guarantee completion of the mall, but financing hadn't been secured until all of the proposed anchor tenants had signed. If any of them fell through, then Haagen was out of there. If they came through, however, Haagen would be sitting pretty with no money up front, 25 percent of the project, and the management contract (i.e. control) for the mall. Still, there were some people who were very interested in the proposition.

With these factors working, the community began to inquire about the mall. However, when people in the community called, they never seemed to be able to get the information they were seeking. The ownership issue was already in serious negotiation. Two entrepreneurs, a local husband and wife team named Harold and Patsy Brown, had stepped up to the plate to hold Haagen to his public promise. The Browns, who owned several businesses; most notably a scrap iron company and a grocery store, backed their son Patrick's bid to buy into the mall. Haagen's requirement was that the individual(s) involved be able to cover half the bond, which meant they had to have a net worth of at least $5 million. It appeared initially that this would not be a problem for the Browns. There were big announcements (headlines) in the local community press (*Wave* and the *L.A. Sentinel*) and a bunch of groundbreaking and picture-taking. The community was under the impression that the ownership issue was handled. It wasn't, however.

There were many business people who wanted to know how they could get information on leasing a store, bidding on contracts for the construction phases and offering professional services. No responses were forthcoming. With serious grumblings beginning to surface, Haagen hired the Los Angeles Urban League-- as a clearinghouse-- to handle inquiries and disseminate information to the public. The Urban League would take the appropriate requests and either forward them to the Haagen Company for leasing information, or to Bayley Construction Company, which was the prime contractor for the mall's construction. When the people heard nothing, they began to call the Haagen Company directly. The Haagen Company put a screening process in place that was highly unethical, illegal, in fact. Many of the prospective lessees were told that if they didn't have $100,000 in the bank, they need not even apply. The concerns were: (1) Why did it cost $100,000 to get into the mall? (2) If they had $100,000, why would they give it to Alexander Haagen? So many people thought they were being "gamed on." Then another nasty rumor hit (that at least two city insiders confirmed later) that Haagen was going heavily after Korean money. It was rumored that Koreans were standing in line to get into the mall. That's when Blacks began to get vocal, feeling that they were possibly being discriminated against, by a white developer, in favor of Koreans merchants. This was a very dangerous and explosive mix. Several individuals then approached me. I had handled the Black-Korean conflict for the branch the year before, and came out with a very strong statement on how Korean merchants were handling Black consumers. I was even elected chair of a community-based, year-long selective buying campaign called "Buy Liberty"`Campaign to address the issue of Black consumerism.

The very thought that Koreans would be in that mall before Blacks, spelled death for that mall. The city went to work quickly to address this latest crisis, a "cultural conflict" between Blacks and Koreans. The best strategy would be to hold community hearings where people could address all interests in the mall, the city, the CRA and the developer. The public could then find out how they could get involved and get responses to the many rumors that surrounded the project.

* * *

Talking to citizens concerned about Crenshaw Plaza, several issues began to surface. Of course, the primary issue was that of Korean participation. I phoned a couple of people I knew who assisted Korean immigrants in setting up businesses. One Black businessman, named Lee Rubin, who made his living buying liquor licenses and community businesses for Korean businessmen, told me outright that Korean business owners were planning on being heavily involved in the mall. When working with him on the Black-Korean conflict, he said to me on one occasion, "Anthony, for the last year that I know of, there were 300 Korean businessmen that came to Los Angeles every day, with $100,000 cash in a suitcase. That's $30 million a day, $200 million a week, and almost a billion dollars a month. I'm having problems now trying to find something for them (Koreans) to buy." He did confirm that, "Yes, at least 20 businessmen, that I know of, want to get into the mall." Having verified that the demand was there, the key issue was, how did they get in the mix?

CRA laws require the project to be representative of the ethnic mix of the resident community. The demographic study, which the city had done, showed that within a five-mile radius of the proposed development, the population was 82 percent Black, and within a 10-mile radius it dropped to 63 percent Black. However, in the assurances that Blacks would be included, the term "minority" would always be used. "The community can be assured that 'minority' participation in this project will be substantial," the mayor said.

Now that the community was sensing some insensitivity from Alexander Haagen, other issues began to pop up. Discussion surfaced that Haagen had been handed the project on a silver platter by Tom Bradley, purportedly as a payoff for his developing the Watts (Kenneth Hahn) Shopping Center and Vermont/Slauson Shopping Center where, according to Haagen himself, he (presumably) didn't make any money on those deals. There hadn't been a bid process held for the construction contract on the Mall, as previously represented. In researching the issue, no legitimate bids could be found other than Haagen's. The city's explanation was that Haagen was the only one to bid. City Hall insiders told us that the bid was never advertised, and no one else even had time to prepare a package on the project. Conversely, the deal that Haagen cut gave him total control over the project, even though city funds were involved. Haagen could accept or reject, which he later would do on numerous occasions, any supplement proposal to the plan; whether it made sense or not. While the horse was now out of the barn, this would be the beginning of the exposure of cronyism in City Hall politics.

The last, and greatest, area of concern was the issue of the 40 plus small businesses in the Crenshaw Shopping Center, and the Santa Barbara Plaza (across the street), who would be effectively put out of business, if not included in the new mall. These businesses had served the Crenshaw community for over 20 years (many of them), but would receive virtually no consideration as to what would happen to their businesses. Of course, two-thirds of the businesses were Black. The Haagens had made it known that this was to be a first-class regional mall; no Mom and Pop shops. Only franchises and first- class shops. Implying that a Mom and Pop can't be first class. This was a slap in the face to longtime residents who worked and lived in the community. The time had now come for the politicians, bureaucrats and their cronies to pay the piper (the people).

The city held its first community meeting, in early May 1987. It was a very basic meeting, giving many of the particulars that were already circulated around the community i.e., the cost of the project, the concept of a regional mall, the jobs the mall would provide, and how to get involved with the mall. I didn't attend that meeting, but by the personal accounts of those who attended, the meeting wasn't publicized very well. The meeting was facilitated by city staff and representatives of the developer. When the mayor heard of the turnout, he was extremely disappointed. He immediately wanted another community forum held, and he wanted it properly publicized. The second meeting would be held on June 1, 1987. This would be the meeting where the Indians would get to Custer. I attended that one.

In the three weeks leading up to the meeting, the community's concerns would be enlarged by the continuing manipulation of the developer's selective screening process. Further frustration would be added by the fact that the demolition phase of the construction had begun and not one Black face was seen on the construction site, not even to move dirt! Subcontractors were being told to submit bids to the Urban League, who would in turn submit the ones they considered qualified to the contractor. Not one of their recommendations was accepted. Everybody was basically doing what they wanted to do, and using whomever they wanted to use. And they were not using Blacks. Haagen was in control, which was everybody's initial assessment. To bring matters to a fever pitch, Haagen had rejected the Browns' offer to buy the 25% interest he'd publicly offered. Haagen claimed the Browns weren't financially qualified. The Browns claimed that was a lie. They also claimed that after reviewing the shopping center's financial proformas, that Haagen skimmed funds off the project, in terms of excessive management fees that included sliding percentages of the lessee's receipts. Secondly, on the takeout of the construction loan, the Browns alleged that Haagen would get a significant portion of his front money (what little he put in) back immediately, while the Browns' front money would be stuck in the project for 15 years (according to Haagen). Lastly, there was something significantly wrong with Haagen's financial projections. Based on the rental scales in the projections and all assumptions being real, the mall should start making money in the eighth year, not the fifteenth. It appeared that either all expenses weren't being shown, or Haagen would be pulling out money at the end of the seventh year, while his joint venture partner would be required to wait, until the fifteenth year. A sucker's deal if there ever was one. Nobody in their right mind would've accepted a deal like that, and they didn't. Nobody wanted to be part of a regional mall that bad. This deal made no business sense, for all the hoopla that was being made about it.

Many around him felt that Bradley just didn't know the structure of this unconscionable deal he put together "for the community." And Haagen had the community over a barrel. The more Bradley got into the deal, the more unconscionable he found out the deal was, and there wasn't a damn thing he could do about it. The Browns asked Haagen to adjust the terms on some of the projections. Haagen arrogantly rejected the request. His position was: "Do you want in, or don't you?" The Browns, according to Patrick's recall, told Haagen, "I don't know what kind of Negroes you are used to dealing with, but we ain't them kind of brothas. So you need to have Bradley bring you the kind of suckers you're looking for." They walked out of the deal. Patrick Brown, who was the lead negotiator for his mother and father, said that they had made several attempts to reconcile with Haagen and save the deal, but to no avail. Haagen, in Patrick's opinion, was being extremely unreasonable and now was even being vindictive. Just because the Browns had the audacity to challenge the integrity (and validity) of the offer, they felt Haagen would surely stick to his position by trying to stick it to the Browns. Even in the one meeting that the Browns asked Bradley to mediate, Patrick said that Bradley sat there like a zombie the whole time, and barely said ten words, while Haagen continued to be insulting and adamant about his right to keep his original proposal. Haagen stated that it was really the only reason he agreed to do the deal in the first place. Patrick said confidentially, "Shit, if I was offered the plum that Haagen was, I wouldn't get off of it either." Brown felt that both Bradley and Haagen knew the kind of deal Haagen had was a "gimme." But like most backroom deals, they felt the public would sleep it and everybody would get paid. Bradley was only interested in having his mall and his constituent's votes.

This was truly perceived, by many, as a white collar "dope deal, gone bad" (a street comparison to an illegal deal made with no knowledge by others, no trace, or a handshake, with of course, no recourse). With the community meeting less than a week away, several business persons from the Santa Barbara Plaza called me to ask if the NAACP was aware of what was happening with the mall. I told them that I had been following it and had talked to some people, but the branch hadn't discussed it yet. They asked if I would bring it to Ray's attention and consider taking it as an issue. I told them I would and to get back to me. When I approached Ray about it initially, he said he would get back to me on it after he did some research for himself. A couple days later (about two days before the meeting), I caught him at the branch after trying to reach him all afternoon. He hadn't returned my phone calls. He said he would rather not get involved in the Crenshaw Plaza issue because it would look like we were coming out against Mayor Bradley. I said, "How would it look like we were coming out against Bradley if he is trying to do the right thing. And should we be in support of Bradley if he is the cause of this problem?" I continued. Ray just sat silently, while I hammered home my point, "then Mayor Bradley needs to be taken on if he is behind all this. How could we lose if we're standing for right?" Ray's position was that he didn't want to fall out of Bradley's favor (not that he ever was in Bradley's favor). To know and understand Ray's reluctance, you'd have to know the history of the relationship. City Hall insiders expressed that the mayor really never held a real high regard for Ray as a community leader. One reason was his orchestrated ouster of Melanie Lomax.

I told Ray that I thought he was missing the point on this, and thought he may want to keep his eyes open. We left the conversation at that. The case was as clear as Black and white. It was a dirty deal all over. I then decided to go to the meeting as NAACP representative whether Ray was in or not.

* * *

As the second meeting started, Mayor Bradley got the turnout that he wanted-- almost 300 people. They weren't there for what he thought they were there for. He came through and did his little song and dance. He told the people that this was their mall for their good and anything they wanted to know about the mall they should come to him before they asked anybody else. Then he did his early exit number. I got there just as he was wrapping up. A community optometrist named Karim Answar and a community advocate named Vicki Phillips came up to me and briefed me on what was happening. Wil Marshall of the Mayor's Office of Small Business facilitated the meeting. Project manager Richard Benbow was representing the CRA. He got up there and told the people that this was their mall (the underlining, reoccurring theme), and the CRA was going to ensure that there would be minority participation (there's that word again) in every phase of the mall's development. Then he talked about how the certification process worked, gave out his number and sat down. They asked the audience to hold all questions until the end. Then the developer's representative got up. I'll never forget this as long as I live. It was the most patronizing presentation I'd ever seen. It was like a kindergarten teacher talking to little children. It was like he was trying to pump us up for play time or something. He stood up there as if to say, "I'm excited; you should be excited. We're gonna learn something today. Are you ready to learn today, boys and girls? You're gonna love what you're gonna learn." Then he'd tell us what we already knew. It was real insulting. I'll never forget this guy's name-- Andrew Natker.

Natker started off with his excitement spiel. Then he began naming the stores and the other amenities that would be in the mall. He proceeded to tell us how proud we should be to have this mall, how committed the developer was to the success of this mall, how great the new mall would be for the community, and how many new jobs it would create. That's when I had enough, and I knew I wasn't the only one that felt this way. People were mumbling, meeting in groups, walkin' out and shit. When I walked to the aisle, Vicki said, "Get 'em Anthony." I said, "Excuse me. But all you've done for the last fifteen minutes is talk about how glad we should be for you to be here. You have yet to tell us anything of significance other than you can get us a job. Most of these people here don't want to hear about a job. They want to know how they can get involved in owning a piece of the mall, leasing a shop, getting a contract. They want to know how to stop getting the runaround." The audience broke out in applause. I continued with, "We don't need no white boy coming here insulting our intelligence with some stuff about jobs. We want to know how this community will get a piece of that $50 million you got to build the mall. If you can't tell us that, then maybe we won't use your mall. Maybe we'll go to the city and tell them to give us $50 million to build our own mall." Standing ovation...tore up the meeting...the crowd was on their feet.

Then Richard Benbow (who I really found to be a good brother, once I got to know him), stood up to contribute to the discussion. I perceived this more as a Negro standing up to defend his white counterpart, so I laid into him. Benbow started talking about how the city was looking out for the people, and that they had contracted some "minorities" to be involved in this project. I challenged him to go across the street and tell me how many Blacks he saw, not minorities, but Blacks!!! "You won't see one. Not one," I said. "So don't stand there and talk that stuff about how you're looking out for us. The city has never looked out for Blacks economically. What makes you think they'll start now?" More applause and witnessing.

At that point, Wil Marshall grabbed the mike and said, "OK, OK, brother. We know what the agenda is; we see what it is. Why don't you just let us get back to the program, and we can address all of these concerns at the proper time."

"This is pure bureaucratic rhetoric," I said. "I don't think you can address the concerns that these people have and that I have with the rest of your program." I suggested that they allow the people to address the issues that they wish to address. Marshall and the others agreed to that.

A woman who asked, "Why did it require $100,000 to get a business in the mall before I could submit an application?" Andy Natker then returned to the mike only to put his foot back in his mouth. He told the woman that she must be a little confused and that no one would tell her something like that. Forty-five other people (including actor Taurean Blaque) stood up and shouted that they were told the same thing. Natker tried to justify an apparently irrefutable claim with the excuse that it would be expensive to put a store in the mall because the lessee would be responsible for building out his/her space, (which wasn't always true), and that the developer wanted to make sure that applicants had the financial wherewithal to do so. One man stood up and said, "Well, what does that have to do with anything? I could go to my bank and borrow the money, just like Haagen did. I don't have to use or even show my money." Natker, who was on a toe-choking roll by now, cut his own throat with this next statement. Natker said, "Well, if you knew the type of mall you were going to have, you would really appreciate his position. This is going to be a first- class mall. There will be no Mom and Pop shops in this mall."

Of course, he was saying this to 300 Mom and Pop shop owners. What he was telling them is your small business, whether it's quality or not, is of no interest to us. So we are going to generalize across the board, and exclude you all by imposing this ridiculous $100,000 cash requirement. But what also came out of this was that this $100,000 cash thing was not a requirement to get into the mall. So, where did it come from? Natker said the right thing: "You'd have to address that to the developer," who, of course, wasn't there.

The next controversial discussion was the issue of Korean participation. One man asked if the developer was trying to keep Blacks out, to get Koreans in the mall because they had the money they were asking for. Natker denied any knowledge of trying to keep Blacks out of the mall. He did say that the mall would be open to all "minorities," which set off another furor. The crowd began to get territorial at that point. "Why are you so concerned about other minorities?" one person said. "We don't get jobs or contracts in their communities," another said. And they were right. This kind of thing only happened in the Black community, which put Benbow back on front street when a contractor stood up and said that he had been trying to get contract bid information on the mall for four months. The contractor (Bayley Construction) stated that the job had been let, but he found out through a secondary source that the job was still open. Benbow seemed a bit taken aback that this had occurred and said that he would check into it for the gentleman. Others said that they had similar experiences. Misinformation was running rampant.

After about an hour of this, the facilitator, Marshall, had decided to close down the meeting (the ole' "running overtime" ploy). Two things were clear: they had lost control of this meeting, and the people were being misled, wholesale. The people recognized it, and started exchanging numbers and setting up meetings. The city and developer now knew that they had a lot of work to do to restore the community's confidence in the mall (something they would never really get). They also had another problem to deal with: how they would now deal with the community's newly drafted spokesman (as unintentional as it was)--me. The mayor's chief aide, Bill Elkins (who would have a key role in misleading the mayor to the community's sensitivity in the matter), immediately wanted to know who I was. Once he found out I was "part of the NAACP," Elkins said something about having Ray deal with me. That's how the mayor's office was. They tried to punish you for speaking without "their" permission. This wasn't the type of fight the city or the developer needed. But, it was well on the way, and it would be great for Blacks in L.A. who were demanding some accountability.

When news of the meeting got back to Bradley, I was told he was livid. He immediately made an urgent call to Ray at the branch. Ray probably was pissing on himself, when he finally returned the mayor's call. The mayor wanted to know what happened at the meeting. Ray said he had heard that the community was upset about the mall. The mayor said, "Yeah, after your Vice President instigated the issue." Ray told the mayor that I was not speaking for the NAACP. The mayor then wanted to know what was the branch's position on the mall. Ray told him that the branch hadn't taken one yet. Ray invited the mayor to speak at the general membership meeting.

The mayor said he'd get back to Ray on that. That was the end of the conversation. Ray called me later that night. We talked for about an hour. He wanted to know if I was there representing the NAACP. I told him that I was invited as a member of the community and as a businessman who had a business in Santa Barbara Plaza that would be affected by this mall. When I spoke, I never said I was from the NAACP. I spoke as a community member, insulted by the way the developer's representative attempted to "front off" the community. Everybody else knew I was with the NAACP, except Bill Elkins. If I had mentioned NAACP, then he would have known whom I was. Ray then went into how the mayor wasn't very happy about how things turned out, and how he felt that my statements were causing unnecessary panic among the people. I told Ray that the people were in a panic when they got there. The only reason they didn't jump on Bradley's ass was because he left. What came out of this meeting was the frustration of the people. "Everybody's not stupid, Ray, just those around the Mayor," I said.

This was the latest example of what people were saying-- that Bradley had long lost touch with the people. A lot of that had to do with his advisers. Many people in the community had long lost faith in Bill Elkins as an effective adviser to the mayor. Some felt that Elkins' arrogant manner had caused the Mayor irreparable harm in the Black community and that Mayor Bradley would have been elected Governor of California if he had not allowed Elkins to misrepresent the importance of the Black vote in the Mayor's first gubernatorial run. Many felt that Elkins allowed the Mayor to dismiss his core constituency, Black support. Bradley ended up losing a statewide election by 48,000 votes, most of which were right in his own backyard. Many attributed this outcome to Bill Elkins. Now, he had Bradley thinking how one man could cause all of these problems for him on this project. I concluded my conversation with Ray saying that we should be involved in monitoring the project. Ray said he would bring it up at the Executive Committee meeting, and we would decide then. We hung up.

About a week later at the Executive Committee meeting, Ray stated that we had been monitoring the Crenshaw Plaza, an outright lie, and stated that Mayor Bradley would be at our next general membership meeting to address any concerns the branch may have relative to the mall. Of course, the committee felt he had been part of some type of coup. But what was happening here was that Ray was setting me up to be hammered by the Mayor. Even though I knew Ray had invited him to address the general membership meeting, he never told me. I learned it from the branch staff assistant, Ernestine Peters; a first rate gossip, who stated that Ray used to beg Bradley to speak at the meetings. When he declined, Ray would leave the door open for him to change his mind. Despite five or six invitations, he never did. Now Bradley was finally coming, and Ray was tickled pink. Ray had confided to a couple of the board members that Bradley was coming to straighten out Anthony. One of the members called to warn me. I hardly thought Bradley would be prepared for what he was about to run up against.

The day of the meeting had arrived. Ray had changed the meeting time to accommodate Bradley. It was at 10 a.m. on Saturday, at Bryant Temple AME. There were nearly 100 members in attendance. (Everybody comes out when they think somebody's going to be there, or something's going to happen.) We went through our normal meeting process, taking care of branch business first. Then the central focus of the meeting came up. The air was thick with anticipation. Bradley finally arrived at about 10:50. He was dressed casually, because he was on his way to a parade. The crowd received him well, and Ray gave him his propers. Then Bradley started off slowly, first talking about the good work of the NAACP, and then he got into the history of the Crenshaw Plaza; how it all came about, how it overcame several hurdles, and how it was a paradise of opportunity. Finally, he got to the rumors that the community had been waiting for and stated: "No matter what anybody says, I'm telling you it's not true. And if you have any concerns, you come directly to me."

I sat in the front pew of the church that day directly in front of the pulpit, a departure from where I usually sat--next to the branch President. A couple of the businesspersons were whispering in my ear from the pew behind me to get up. I kept saying, "Not yet, not yet." Bradley was still in the middle of his rhetoric, telling the audience what he intended to do to ensure "minority participation."

After allowing the Mayor about 15 minutes to get his strokes in, I finally stood up and said, "Mr. Mayor, are you aware that right now there are no Black contractors involved in the mall, no Black laborers, no Black (confirmed) tenants and no Black ownership? How can you stand here and tell us that this is 'our shopping mall' when our people are nowhere to be found? The developer that you chose has done nothing but run Blacks around, set up improper screening qualifications that we recently found out were not the truth, and prepared to substitute Koreans for Blacks as the minority. You're talking about it's our mall, but the community thinks you're not being told the truth about the mall."

The crowd got real quiet. Mayor Bradley asked for some specifics. I gave him about eight specific incidents of Blacks being excluded from the involvement process and that the Urban League could back up my story. Bradley then tried to find out how I knew this and asked, "Did the person speak with you, or was this something you heard?" I refused to even be baited and respond to questions about how I knew, what I knew. I told him if he did his homework, he'd find out that we were correct. It was apparent that the Mayor was relying greatly on what Haagen and Bill Elkins had told him. This was not the most opportune time to find out that their assessment of the situation wasn't quite accurate. I was tearing Bradley a new butthole on his pet project. By the time I had finished, Mayor Bradley was responding to almost every question with "I'll look into that, and have an answer for you later." One question that the crowd wouldn't accept that day was asked by Vicki Phillips, who was videotaping this whole event. She told the Mayor that the community where the mall was being built was 82 percent Black and that really we should be asking for 82 percent of the contracts, the tenant leases and the jobs. Vicki reasoned, as unrealistic as that was, could Blacks expect a reasonable portion (at least 25 percent) of the money to be spent on that mall. Mayor Bradley began to regurgitate his spiel about how he was committed to ensuring minority participation. I stood up and asked what percentage of that will be Black. Bradley continued with, "You can be sure that minority participation will be significant." Several people stood up and shouted, "Which minority?" Bradley was visibly uncomfortable with that question, and fell into a stutter and said, "Er, I, can't, I can't, say what..."

Vicki interrupted his answer. "Mayor Bradley, you know this development should represent the racial ethnicity of the area where it's being built. So what's the problem? Why can't you say that Blacks will be given such and such instead of coming with this minority stuff? We'll look up and the minorities you're talking about won't be us." The audience applauded Vicki's comment.

Bradley then reared his head back and said, "Is what you want me to say is that Blacks will be involved significantly in this project?"

The crowd shouted, "Yes!" as if to say, "Damn, is the Mayor that dense?"

He started stuttering again. "OK... I, I don't have any problem with saying that the participation in the mall will be Black. There, I said it," he chuckled.

The most painful part of this whole scenario was to see a Black man so far removed from his race that it was like he was referring to another race of people. We probably could have gotten a white or Hispanic politician to make a quicker commitment to Black involvement than it took Bradley to say that he would take up for his own for once. It would have been a non-issue with almost any other community or a politician of another ethnic group.

Many Black politicians are often so committed to other interests, that it seems like they have a built-in defense against trying to show any degree of partiality to Black constituencies. Most of them overcompensate to hedge against a perceived partiality. In an effort to show the mainstream that they are fair to all persons, Blacks are even discriminated against by their own politicians; many who want to avoid even the appearance of possible allegations of favoritism toward Blacks. Self-preservation is the first law of nature, but it was an anomaly for Black politicians in non-Black cities to powershare with Black communities. That's why there is little synergy in Black community political economies. Black economics are separate and distinct from its politics and policy making. This project was an example of how difficult it was in exacting economic benefit from Black politicians in non-Black cities.

Tom Bradley had constructed his whole political career on the premise of being the Mayor for all of Los Angeles. He regionalized Los Angeles in a way that every ethnicity from Tokyo to Korea, from Canada to South America, from Europe to Russia established roots in the "new headquarters of the Pacific Rim." Ethnic communities prospered and received great economic benefit under Tom Bradley. Several

Blacks got profiled through appointments, received access and experienced individual success, through some contract opportunities under the Bradley administration. He had done more for almost every ethnic group in the city then he had done for Blacks. West Los Angeles (highly Jewish) is highly developed. San Fernando Valley and Westchester (highly white) are highly developed. Chinatown (highly Asian) is highly developed. And Koreatown (highly Korean) is highly developed (in the last five years). Even parts of East Los Angeles (highly Hispanic) has had a greater development rate than the Mayor's own backyard, South Central Los Angeles (highly Black). For many years, Tom Bradley was a sacred cow who Black Angelenos wouldn't criticize publicly. Most Blacks could see what was going on around them. Tom Bradley concentrated so heavily on avoiding the label of being a "Black" Mayor or being partial to Black interests, that he soon was considered by many Blacks as a Mayor who just happened to be "Black."

Fifteen years after Blacks elected Tom Bradley to office, he stood before an NAACP membership, in a Black church, in the middle of a Black community, shaking in his boots and nervous. In a barely audible voice (like somebody was going to go tell white folk), he whispered that he didn't have a problem saying that the minority participation in the mall would be Black. It was evident that Tom Bradley had forgotten who he was, and it was probably just as embarrassing for us as it was for him. It was embarrassing for us to even have to take him through this, because in his pride, he refused to admit to his debauchery involving this mall. He was just beginning to fight the truth on this and we were just fortunate to catch him short on this day. He was unprepared for the attack he received by some of us, and we (community advocates) didn't succumb to the intimidation of challenging his power seat. From here on out, no aides would handle Crenshaw. It would be handled by Bradley personally, and the opposition (particularly me) would have the benefit (or the detriment) of his full attention. Since Ray was still maintaining that I wasn't talking for the NAACP, and the NAACP hadn't taken a position on the mall, I stood again and told Mayor Bradley that I had been chosen as a spokesperson for the merchants, and that I had been formulating a list of concerns that had been expressed to me.

I asked if I could communicate that to him in a report in the next week or so, so that he might become more acquainted with the major issues surrounding the mall. Mayor Bradley said he would like that. He asked me to call him personally to discuss it with him upon forwarding the report. I acknowledged that I would do so. Bradley then asked if there were any questions. There were none, and he proceeded to excuse himself for another appointment. The audience stood and gave him his customary applause as he exited, but the moment he hit the door several of us pointed at each other and shook our fist with the unspoken exuberance of just having knocked out the heavyweight champion.

Ray was seated at the pulpit with 'shit all over his face,' apparently because the meeting didn't turn out as he had expected. He promptly took up a collection for the branch and dismissed the meeting. As several of us huddled in front of the church, many Executive Committee members came up to me stating that my presentation was excellent, and that they had never seen the Mayor put on the defensive like that before. Ray, overhearing this, came over and gave some obligatory compliments like, "You seemed to be really prepared" or "I couldn't believe that you were the same person." "The same in comparison to what?," I thought seeing that he tried to set me up. But I just said, "Thanks," and continued talking to the others. However, one thing I did notice was that even though several members came up to Ray to ask, "How was the branch going to pursue this issue?" Ray never responded in the affirmative, or even expressed an interest in pursuing the issue. Ray was hardly thinking about pursuing any further confrontation with the Mayor.

In the meantime, Bradley was wasted no time in waging a full-fledged war on the troublemakers, who were beginning to get the community's ear. His intention was to cloud the issue by putting the Bradley stamp of approval (his credibility) on the project, and tell the people not to concern themselves with what they were hearing. Again, another attempt to summarily dismiss us as "loose cannons" trying to stall the mall's development for reasons that were insubstantial and lacking merit. Mind you, there were some loose cannons in the group, but for the most part, we were all sensible, rational thinkers, who were open to sincerity and reason. We were very straightforward and nonsensical, and weren't easily intimidated. One thing that they never gave us credit for from beginning to the end, (but would realize in the end that we were right) was that we knew what the hell we were talking about, and had the data to prove it.

Bradley knew we'd have a hard time pitting our word against his, and that Ray was trying to distance the NAACP from the conflict. He tried to isolate me as some political gadfly or attention-seeking community activist. This would make it easier to discredit our position, because most sensible people would think that if the mall was such a discriminating and corrupt deal, then why wouldn't the NAACP stand behind one of their own in his attacks on the mall. That is the correct way to think, if the so-called community advocate is unbossed and unbought. However, this wasn't the case with LA/NAACP, and the more that would come out of this, the less insane I would look. The branch would be viewed in the community as remaining consistent with the compromising posture of pitting common individuals against the "credible institution" of the great Tom Bradley.

The very next day, Bradley hit the church circuit. That's when he'd drop by five or six of the city's largest Black churches, and the preachers would interrupt the service for him. It was so rare for them to see him during a non-election year period. He spoke to the congregations of those churches for about 10 minutes each, but he reached some 8,000 or 9,000 people in one morning, which was more than he would reach in some of the Black newspapers (depending on the issue), or at a community meeting. We were told he spoke at West Angeles Church of God in Christ, Trinity Baptist, First AME and St. Bridgettes Catholic Church.

I caught him at the 8 a.m. service at First AME. Bradley, who was always received well at First AME (because it's his home church), was more animated and energetic than many had seen him in years. He went through his speech and gave the history of the mall, the historical significance of its restoration, the city's financial commitment, the high-end stores and "Black" participation. The whole spiel. Then he went into this fever-pitched scenario on how he's been our Mayor for the last 15 years, and whenever he's made a promise to this community, he has never broken it. He went on to say how he's built a reputable career as a public servant based on his word, and that if he says the mall is for the community, and the community is to be involved, they can damn sure bank on it. "No matter what anybody else tells you, forget the rumors, and forget about what a few troublemakers want to take issue with. I, Tom Bradley, am telling you that the Crenshaw Plaza is worthy of your support. I don't care what anybody says. If you have any concerns, you come and see me. I put the deal together; I should know the best."

It was the most impassioned, non-election year speech I ever heard Bradley give. As he was wrapping up his plea for support he was staring right at me in my pew aisle seat, some six or seven rows from the pulpit. I could see the whites of his eyes, sort of speak, and the intensity in his face. As he carried his message to the other churches, a couple of people came up to me after alter call and said, "You're through in this town." I said, "Thank's for the support." Clearly, it was obvious that I would be the focus of Bradley's counterattack in defense of his "baby."

* * *

After a couple of weeks of trying to find out where Ray was (he still maintained that the branch was not involved in the mall issue), I began to meet with merchants and contractors, who had been calling ever since the last community meeting. The NAACP had not taken a position on the mall, and I couldn't answer why. I told merchants, "I am interested in helping you protect your interest as a businessman in this area." I was asked to bring to the next meeting a plan of attack to address this issue, which I agreed to do. Meanwhile, I ran into Mayor Bradley at another reception a couple days later. He came up to me and stated that he was awaiting my report and that he had been checking the mail for it daily. I told him that it was almost complete and that I was waiting for a couple of the merchants to bring me some information I wanted to include. I told him that I would have it to him within 10 days.

The Los Angeles Sentinel and *The Southwest Wave* gave the issue front page coverage. While it was Bradley's intention to stem the tide, he was standing in front of a rolling snowball that was picking up speed. Betty Pleasant, then editor of the *Sentinel* (and a very strong, good sister), was attending our meetings and keeping the issue hot. The SCLC called for a community forum on the mall at West Angeles Church of God in Christ. Mark Ridley-Thomas, then executive director, called me to say it was imperative for me to be on the panel. They would set up another direct confrontation with Bradley, and this time Alexander Haagen. I told him that the branch wasn't in this issue yet and how was he willing to represent me. He said he didn't have a problem with me representing myself from my company, Liberty Financial Network. I said fine. I would do that, and that's the way it went off. While the community forum was coming together, Haagen was adding fuel to the fire. In the original plan, the Haagen Company had hired the Los Angeles Urban League as the community component, to make it look like there was some semblance of community inclusion in this project. The appearance that the Urban League would be the facilitator for "qualified" (whatever that meant) Black participation threw the dogs off the fox's tracks momentarily, while the developer and the prime contractor let contracts in the demolition and excavation phases of the project. The people were barking at the Urban League's door where they were put through some motions that just prolonged their eventual decline. Then when the applicant would ask the Urban League, they would tell them that the developer or the contractor declined them because they didn't qualify. The applicant would say, "Well, I thought you pre-screened us for qualification?" The Urban League would say, "Well, the process was to package those firms that best fit the profile for possible qualification, which was to be determined by the contractor or the developer." The applicant would ask the Urban League, "Why was I declined?" The Urban League would respond that they didn't know. The applicant would ask them, "Well, what do you know?" The Urban League would respond, "We don't know anything," which would then infuriate the applicants who couldn't get anything from the Urban League. If the applicants attempted to go around the Urban League, they would be sent back to them. It didn't take long for the community to realize that it was being jerked off, and as any bad marriage, the one being abused is always the last to know.

The Urban League had become more than just "spooks who sat by the door" with the mall project. They had become the developer's whore, taking money for prearranged services by keeping the people off their backs while the developer moved ahead. The Urban League thought they were facilitating minority involvement, but after they recommended over 35 applicants for contracts to hire, not one was hired. The Urban League was just sitting by the door, holding the bag for applications Haagan had no intention to use. Haagen left the Urban League with the dirty hands making it appear that they weren't bringing them any qualified applicants. So it wasn't their (the developer's) fault if there were no Blacks on the site. The Urban League was 90 to 120 days into that process, and still didn't know the developer's guidelines for a qualified applicant. That's because there were none. They made them up as they went along. Finally, John Mack, President of the Urban League (L.A.), realized that they were being played for suckers and pulled out of the contract, but not before letting the community know that the Urban League was not responsible for the misleading actions of the developer. The project now had another strike against it.

Bradley, in the meantime, was instructing his people not to say anything about the mall without his approval. He also stated that all documentation on the mall would remain confidential until they were ready to release it (after they had doctored the numbers), and that all meetings were to remain confidential. Hell, it was a little too late for that. I was receiving blind copies of almost all city and CRA-related correspondence regarding the mall: the demographics study (two actually) that the developer prepared for the city, the contractor's bid list, almost everything. While everybody involved knew how sensitive this project's situation was, they knew this was the one chance to clean the project up before a massive cover-up took place. There were a whole lot of people rooting for us on the inside but couldn't even say that they knew me, or even talked to me, or they'd jeopardize their jobs. I'd get packages in the mail with no cover letter with information highlighted and circled. I'd get anonymous phone calls about selected community meetings on the mall at City Hall, the CRA or the Urban League, indicating the time and place and then I would get a hang-up. Bradley or his representatives (usually Bill Elkins) would almost shit when they saw me. It got so that whenever I showed up to a meeting within 10 minutes, one of the Mayor's staff (either Bill Elkins, then Deputy Mayor, Mike Gage or Mayor Communications Director, Fred McFarland), would show up to sit in on the meeting. This happened about eight times. There's nothing stranger than for a meeting to be in full process and you walk in, and everybody stops talking. First they wonder how you found out about the meeting, then they wonder how they are going to get their strategy around you.

Pretty soon, they just started sending me the information themselves. They just put me on the mailing list. The fact that they did so was an acknowledgment of my presence, but they were also conceding to the pressure I was imposing; for full disclosure of the facts that pertained to the issues in question. The compilation of this data just solidified the issues. We could now boldly charge Bradley and Haagen with malfeasance on this project and use their own numbers against them. In many instances, their own written documentation directly conflicted with their public denials. You've never seen paperwork travel so fast around a community. In the upcoming community forum, all parties would now be equally armed.

* * *

The SCLC's community forum on the Baldwin Hills/Crenshaw Shopping Plaza development had finally arrived. Ridley-Thomas had done his usual meticulously detailed arrangement, which included the press (en masse), a forum moderator (one of his board members, Denise Fairchild, a sharp, young sister who should have received the support of Bradley in the 1987 10th District city council race), and five panel members who were major focuses in various capacities. There was also Patrick Brown, who was there to give direct insight on the collapse of his mall ownership proposal. There was Richard Benbow of the CRA. Then there were two surprises: Alexander Haagen, who had agreed to participate but was a no-show, and didn't send a representative. Tom Bradley was also a no-show, but he sent his aide, Bill Elkins. I represented the community interest perspective. I was extremely disappointed, as was the almost 400 people who attended the forum, that Bradley and the developer didn't show. These were purportedly the two most accountable individuals in the project. All issues raised were conjecture without them there. Elkins can only say what he "thought" the Mayor supported, and the CRA can only suggest what the developer would do on the project. Between Patrick and myself, there would have been enough questions raised, that Haagen had blamed the city for or that the city had blamed Haagen for, to have either a straight out fight. Or for the community to see some firsthand, old- fashioned, "Little Rascals," "Three Stooges," "Laurel and Hardy" type of slap-stick foolishness. Somebody was gonna be made a fool of that night. It appeared that the odds on bets were going to be absent. It sure as hell wasn't going to be me.

Still the show went on. Fairchild opened with a very strong commentary and admonition of the city's apparently gross dereliction of duty to the people of the Crenshaw district. Everyone was allowed to give five-minute opening remarks relative to their position with and perception of the development. The CRA's Benbow opened with a very straightforward position of commitment to Black involvement in the project. He told Crenshaw residents that wherever they were able to influence or demand Black participation, they would. Those statements were received with a great deal of cynicism. Next up was Patrick Brown, who proceeded to explain how the developer had manipulated their legitimate offer to share in the project, including profits and liabilities, into a position of disproportionately assumed risk, with remote possibilities of ever seeing their investment double much less make a profit. Brown represented it as a virtual handover to cover Haagen's risk position, (which was already covered by the city).

Brown's impassioned presentation really got to the audience. This would surely put the squeeze on the city to explain how they could allow this to happen to the Browns, and also try to anticipate what I would say coming up behind them. I'm sure Bill Elkins wondered what in the hell Tom Bradley had gotten him into. Too bad Tom had to miss this. When Elkins got up, of course, he tried to act like Brown's statements were news to him, and that as far as he knew, the deal was still alive. The city had every intention of making the developer hold to the commitment made to the Browns. Then he got defensive, talking about how he couldn't understand what all the hullabaloo was about, just because some "Johnny come lately" (what he meant was "Anthony come lately") makes some claims about the lack of minority participation in this project. "This is your project. Why would the Mayor not protect your interest?" (That's the same question the community was asking.) Visibly irritated, Elkins tried to communicate the city's same position-- that they were sustaining all efforts to increase Black involvement in the mall, enumerating several "new" attempts to reassure the community that their efforts were, in fact, valid. However, the preponderance of evidence coming to light, straight from the horse's (Brown's) mouth, combined with what I had yet to say, didn't really give a whole lot of credence to Elkins' position. Let's just say there weren't a whole lot of people crying for Elkins.

When I came up, it was virtually easy pickins! I started out by saying that what we were witnessing was an extreme contrast in perceptions-- the community witnessing one thing, and our "supposed" representatives seeing something else. I continued saying that the deal the city cut was a bad deal from the start. The best way and first step to correcting a problem is to admit that there is one. The city needs to own up to the fact that some errors have been made, then we can move on with correcting this problem. The audience broke out in applause, and I started dropping bombs from that point on. Sister Denise was kind enough to let me go a little over my five minutes after working up the crowd. But from that point, the city never stood a chance and Elkins knew it.

After opening remarks, there were a series of questions posed by the facilitator relative to what corrective actions that the community should take. It was mostly Patrick and I from there on. We were pretty consistent in our opinions, except on the issue of boycotting the mall. Patrick felt that the community would lose if we chose not to participate, and that the best way to effectuate the change was to allow this phase to be built (in his words, "since the horse was already out of the barn"), and jam them on the next phase or the next project. This was too benevolent of a position for me. If the Mayor's office and the developer hadn't been so blatant in their disregard for both the city's redevelopment law and the community's interest, you could probably look past this, and take a softer, more corroborative position.

For the Black community its always, I repeat, always "Next time, we won't do it this way." "Next time, we'll consider a Black for this position." "Next time, I assure you that Black representation will be adequate." "We'll include Blacks on the next go 'round." "Next time." "Next one." "Next trip." "Next, Next, Next." When does tomorrow ever come for Blacks? Never. It's been 440 years of "Next Times" for Blacks in this country. Tomorrow never comes. Lifetimes have expired waiting for "next times." Tomorrows never come for the Black masses because every time tomorrow gets here, the faces have changed. This was Tom's promise. Tom's promise is not the next Mayor's promise. "I didn't know anything about it," would be the next Mayor's line. The game changes, the community changes. In many of the Crenshaw resident's lifetimes, this would be the last community redevelopment effort we would see.

Urban renewal efforts usually take place every 20 to 30 years. It wasn't like they were going to put up another mall next year, or even in five years. And they're certainly not going to spend the type of money that was spent on this project. Only 35 percent of the total contracts had been let on the project's construction, and only some 15 out of a projected 120 stores had been leased to date. It was time for the Black community to press their point. Twenty-five percent of the overall project was still up for sale (if the Brown deal wasn't solidified), and the management of the mall hadn't been decided. If they felt it was too late to get in on the deal, they wouldn't have been there that night. Oh, no, the city and the developer had to know that if they didn't make some radical changes quick, this would be the biggest public funds spectacle in the country. It would be definitely boycotted. The crowd was really with me, in theory and in sentiment.

In closing comments, I postured the community for a fight to ensure our participation. I cautioned the audience. "In everything we protest against, our opposition waits us out. After our cries have subsided, everything is treated as if nothing has happened. The game is going to happen in this project, if we are not careful." As the forum closed, the community was astoundingly appreciative of what came out of the forum. Neither the city, nor the CRA could refute anything that Brown or I said. It became obvious by the business supporters in the audience that it was certainly more than a one man show. In the midst of receiving congratulations from observers, Elkins came up to me and said, "The Mayor is still waiting on your report."

"It will be in his hands this week," I said. He just nodded and left. The report was critically important to what would happen in the future phases of the mall. With three straight victories under our belt (community hearing, the NAACP meeting and tonight), we knew we had the developer and the city on the ropes. But this would also be a lesson in "old style" politics, where they shoot the messenger after they receive his message. The messenger becomes the martyr and the undeserved becomes the beneficiaries.

* * *

After several meetings with the Santa Barbara Plaza merchants and key community leaders, the report for the Mayor was finally ready. It was a very comprehensive report addressing the community concerns and making several recommendations. In making the recommendations, the community had become very distrustful of the city and its agents who "supposedly" represented their interests.

The community had rallied around me as a hardworking and capable spokesperson, in spite of my conflict with the NAACP and its inability (Ray's inability) to oppose the mall, in spite of, the current developments. Several merchants were of the opinion that it was absolutely necessary to have a community-based consultant to raise issues in the interest of those who wished to participate in the mall, and monitor the compliance of community input. Several of the merchants recommended to the group that I be the community-based consultant. The group was all for it. I was kind of cool on the idea because I didn't want the integrity of the project to be compromised by claims that I was only involved in the project for money. Yet, I had clearly become the focus of the community's campaign for participation. I had contractors calling me every day when Haagen or Bayley didn't respond to them. I talked to no less than twenty merchants who wanted to lease space in the mall, but were afraid to go direct, because they felt they wouldn't get a fair shake. Many offered to pay me to handle their application package, which I declined. Even established players had problem getting their deals done. Jim Jones, a very successful entrepreneur who owned two Sizzlers restaurants, called me when his negotiations stalled on the Marie Callenders restaurant he was bidding for. There were plenty of opportunities to make money, but I never accepted any money offers because I was always suspicious of a setup to discredit me during this project. The L.A. NAACP had not committed to get involved other than holding a meeting on the issue. It had not taken a position on the mall. It had not taken any charges under investigation. With the business acumen to analyze and interpret this project, it certainly qualified me to be considered as a community-based consultant, and be compensated for my involvement.

Having cleared these conflicts in my mind, I agreed to submit my firm for consideration, should Bradley accept the idea. I then forwarded the report to Bradley, which was compiled and prepared by my firm. I sent the report on my company's stationary, in which I did ask Mr. Bradley to consider me as a possible candidate for the community-based consultant. That was it. No heavy lobbying, no phone calls, no backroom deals. Just a cover letter and a report to the Mayor that I volunteered to do (which he would have paid for if he had Arthur Andersen or some major issues management group assess the situation). And in return, I asked to continue helping on the project. That was it. So I thought.

It turned out that the Mayor now wanted to use the letter (and did) to compromise my whole involvement in the mall project. His inference was that I was using my position with the NAACP to jam the mall project, in order to receive a contract for personal gain. This couldn't be further from the truth. However, those who perceived my only affiliation as being with the NAACP wouldn't know any better. Bradley then had his flunky aide, Bill Elkins, call Ray, John Mack and Mark Ridley-Thomas to notify them of the solicitation he had just received and tried to imply that my involvement was self-serving and less than sincere. Mark, who was a friend of mine at the time, notified me immediately of the newest scheme by the Mayor. He said while it didn't seem to be a big deal to him because he knew the relationship, it could be seriously misrepresented in the press. Mark recommended that I squash the issue immediately by withdrawing my firm from consideration. I told him that I would draft a letter and have it delivered to Bradley's office the next day. He also suggested that I copy Ray,

Mack and himself for backup, just in case, they ever tried to refute that I did withdraw. Elkins also sent copies of the report and letter to the same three.

Ray never mentioned anything about this to me. As always, Ernestine did. She told me that Ray had received a hand-delivered copy of my letter and report, and that he made some statement about how the letter "would come in handy one day." I couldn't relate to that then, however; a year later I would know what he meant. Ray did try to say something to me about why I sent the report on my company's letterhead. I responded, "Whose letterhead was I going to send it on?" He tried to say the branch's, and I quickly reminded him that the branch wasn't involved in this.

He then stated, "Yeah, but I authorized you to do the report."

"How the hell are you going to authorize me to do anything, when you're too fucking afraid to take a stand? I yelled. "What you tried to do was set me up; I got the tip before the meeting. But when you saw me kick Bradley off in his ass, after you kissed all over it, you didn't have shit to say to me about the mall. I volunteered to do the report, and since I couldn't represent the branch publicly on this issue, I wasn't about to do it in writing." As always, he sat there with this dumb shit-eating look on his face.

It was now obvious to me what extent the Mayor was willing to go on this. By trying to spread around the community that I wanted something for myself out of this, it just made me more obsessed with taking his ass to the floor. Now that my company was out of the running, I would make sure Bradley knew that the fight was on. It was very ironic that Bradley and his cronies would make such an allegation about me on Crenshaw.

A year later, while Bradley was running for a fifth term, it would come out that Bradley used his position as Mayor to influence city deposits to be directed to two banks, which he was a paid member of these banks' board of directors. He would receive over $100,000 in director's fees, some of which he gave back, after he was busted. The snowball rolled downhill from there when it was discovered that the Mayor had not disclosed all of his financial holdings on forms he had prepared himself, and that the Mayor may have benefited from some insider trading information aided by his relationship with the white collar criminal of the 20th century, Michael Milken. Many of his cronies were showing up on contracts, commissions and loans for work that was never performed, buildings not personally owned by the parties in question, and a federal investigation over his finances and relationship to many of the parties in question. These actions only confirmed what I had been saying all along-- that Crenshaw was a sweetheart deal given to cronies for past political favors. For most of the time that Bradley had been Mayor, he had been a fantastic abuser of cronyism. The talk had been circulating that way for years. Yes, Tom Bradley was a victim of a conspiracy against Black leaders, to a degree, because of the way the *Los Angeles Times* came after him for such an extended period. But Bradley definitely betrayed the public's trust, and put some of his cronies interest before the city, which is what he tried to accuse me of. The people should wonder about the deals that were made that will never come to light. Believe me, there were many. So, the fact that he would try to compromise me by implying something that he'd been doing all the time was hypocrisy on the highest order, even after I withdrew the offer. Still, the perception in the city was that I was in it for gain.

I was determined then that I would go after Bradley and Haagen with a fever pitch. If we were working together, a resolution would shape up quicker, than the adversarial road the Mayor had chosen. I had made up my mind that the NAACP was going to be involved with this. Since I tried to go the other way, and still got accused of influence-peddling, why should I allow Ray to keep the NAACP out of a legitimate case of discrimination, public fraud and deception, just because he didn't want to be perceived as going against Bradley? Hell, the NAACP was supposed to be for right, and I was right on this one. Bradley was caught dirty with his pants around his ankles. He'd have to just suffer through this one. The NAACP was not going to lay in the cut any longer.

The Los Angeles Times was putting together a piece on the mall. They had been directed to me as the center of the community's dispute. As we interviewed, I walked them around the mall construction site to validate my case. After about 40 minutes of discussion, I told the reporter that the bottom line was that more Black folk were going to have to be involved in this mall or we'd boycott this white elephant until every tenant pulls out of it. I pointed several things out to *The Times* photographers who took pictures. Finally, the reporter asked me whom I was representing for the article. I had been very careful not to say anything about the NAACP. I was either a spokesman for the merchants, or representing my business. Today, all that changed. I stated that I represented the Santa Barbara Plaza merchants, as First Vice

President of the Los Angeles NAACP. The fight was now in full effect.

The article hit the next day's front page of the *Metro Section*. I got a call from Ray at 7:15 a.m. I had already gotten about four calls, so I knew what was up. He wanted to know who authorized me to involve the branch. I played like I was crazy. "Didn't you? You said in our last conversation that you authorized me to write a report, so I certainly felt that I was authorized to talk about it." Ray got real quiet on the phone. He was seething. I knew he was trying to figure out how he was going to calm Mayor Bradley. Ray said that he wanted to talk to me later, and that he'd get back with me. I said OK. It was almost a week before I heard from him again.

In the meantime, the mall was having some more problems of its own. The African Collective, a community advocacy group, had filed a lawsuit and lien against the mall property on behalf of the community. This really complicated matters because now the project's financial backing was concerned about the project's future. Would this action stall the development? It would. And it would cause some very serious legal problems for the city in court about the CRA violations in the project, the controversial bid process allegedly held for the developer, the absence of participation representative of the community's ethnicity and the absence of ownership. Oh, the collective had 'em going.

Bradley, meanwhile, was still going about his damage control campaign trying to make the people believe that all was well. In many of his speaking engagements, he would make mockery of some of the recommendations the community was making. The one he used most to make it seem like opponents of the mall were insane, was the issue of lease incentives or discounted rent options. Bradley was going around to churches and other constituencies saying that opponents were looking for a free rent situation. Then in mockery he would say: "This is a business proposition, not a give-a-way program." For Bradley to say something like that really showed either how ignorant he was, or how exploitative he was prepared to be about community people's lack of knowledge. Historically and categorically, Blacks and their communities are always presented singular or fewer options in business propositions. In examining Black business opportunities, propositions are oftentimes represented as the "only option" available, which is oftentimes the best option for the proposer. The Baldwin Hills/Crenshaw Plaza is a perfect example of this type of unjust manipulation.

Anybody who knew anything about commercial developments, which certainly a Mayor should, knew that the primary objective of the development was to make more money, but through the most sensibly feasible strategy. The most sensible strategy in a commercial development is to reach maximum leasing capacity at the earliest possible point in the development. In almost every new commercial development you see today, lessee incentives are the first strategies implemented, even in residential developments like new condos, townhouses and tract homes. "No money down." "Ninety days free space." "We build out (prepare the space)." "No payment for six months." There were several commercial developments, at the time, offering one-year free rent on a seven-year lease, particularly the downtown high-rises where there was an excess of commercial space. The same was the case, in the westside Wilshire district, and even in the newly developed Corporate Pointe in Culver City, CA. The development would rather have 90 percent or 100 percent occupancy, and little or no cash up front, than 40 percent to 60 percent occupancy with ridiculous buy-ins up front.

Black merchants of the Crenshaw district had been in business for ten and twenty years, and made a comfortable living. They were now being told to forfeit two or three years' profit (for some of them), for the sake of a developer's lack of confidence in the longevity of this project. And here was this Negro Mayor propagating this foolishness like a puppet on strings, never admitting to the people that the option being represented was not suitable for most communities, much less this community. It's very hard to surmise that Bradley didn't know any better. I wasn't even prepared to give him the benefit of the doubt, given the resources he had at his disposal to find out what was real and what was not. To add insult to the injury, he was confusing the issue by making mockery of probably one of the best options for survival of the mall. The lease options were just beyond comprehension.

The pitiful reality of the situation was that people, somewhat intelligent people even, were sucking this nonsense up. The truth was that it wasn't that the developer couldn't consider free rent, but didn't want to. It wasn't that the merchants were asking for an option that was out of reason, it was just that the developer didn't see a reason (in his mind) to consider another option. While in the real world our proposition would have been viable, in Haagen's world, it wasn't an option on the table. And why? He had no real money up front. The money he had up front, he got back when the city kicked in. The city was assuming most of the risk. It was being built for the benefit of "the people." What was the problem? The developer's greed was inflexible and so was his financial scenario for this mall. The point wasn't that the community was trying to get something for free, but that we were trying to suggest more flexible economic options that were conspicuously absent from this proposal.

There were also these community stakeholder "divides" that put stress on the community input piece. A big debate ensued with the developer and the city to either try to convince Vons to stay, or bring in somebody else other than Boys Market or Alpha Beta. My position was, "Why not lobby for Papa's Grocers (who went out of business in early 1997, two years after the death of its owner, Patsy Brown), or some Black grocer?" Some community residents publicly stated, "We want Vons." Seeing it as a bait issue I told the residents I wouldn't lobby for anything other than a Black grocer and that their fight wasn't my fight. We needed to expand the stores we owned, where it would get to a point where one of our own could buy a major food chain (like Hispanic businessmen eventually did with Vons during the early 1990s).

After all these years, everybody's ice is still colder than ours. But this was the type of foolishness we were forced to contend with on this mall-- issues that were really irrelevant to the overall issue of community self-determination. It was just another diversion from the real issue-- having Blacks splitting hairs on someone else's head. I just wondered how they, the residents, were convinced that naming a grocery was their victory. How did they win in an agreement on Vons over Lucky? Vons has fresher lettuce. Lucky has fresher meat. I mean... give me a break. There was $120 million at stake to be earned and controlled by Black folk if we lobbied right, and this was the shit we preoccupied ourselves with.

In the months to follow, there would be significant improvement in the construction phase of the mall. "Black" participation would go from virtually zero to 20 percent. It was a start. Much of the credit was to be given to Benbow and his CRA support, who wouldn't acquiesce to the prime contractor's claim that they couldn't find any "qualified" subs (subcontractors). When a job was up for bid, and it didn't include a Black subcontractor, they extended the deadline. In one meeting, there was a bid that CRA couldn't find a qualified Black subcontractor (so they said) to participate. I suggested that for as long as there were no qualified Blacks in this area of expertise, there would be no opportunities for Blacks to participate on this project or future projects, which would continue to perpetuate the problem. Mentoring programs were started. Several subs got jobs that way amounting to over $2 million. The CRA was really trying to do its share. The city and the developer were another story. 10 years later, mentoring is now a very popular "access" concept for many minority businesses. Particularly for (white) woman owned firms.

Tom was still doing a lot of stylin' and profilin' but to no avail. In early 1988, he made this big announcement about the city's commitment to do business with minorities and that all city departments would be asked to meet a 28 percent procurement goal. (A gutsy call and progressive, if it was sincere). I was impressed for a minute. But what did that have to do with the mall? Bradley still had yet to reconcile Haagen and the Browns on the ownership issue. Haagen had publicly said that Brown's deal was dead. While other prospective investors slid deals under Bradley's nose, Bradley asked then highly touted Beatrice chairman and entrepreneur, the late Reggie Lewis, to look at buying into the mall. Insiders communicated to us that Mr. Lewis gave Bradley his first real indication of what kind of deal Haagen was putting his proposed joint ventures into. The word we got was that the mall deal absolutely sucked. "It was a fool's deal," which Lewis purportedly called it and respectfully declined. While the conversation was between Bradley and Lewis, our information was being relayed through a third party as Bradley dejectedly relayed this information to his insiders. It confirmed almost everything that the Browns had objected to in their negotiations. Bradley finally realized what a sweetheart deal he had given Haagen. The same sweetheart that now had him and the community handcuffed.

Faced with the likelihood that no halfway sophisticated investor would go for such a chump deal, Bradley devised such a far-fetched scheme for Black ownership, that even his people had to smirk. They just didn't do it in front of him.

Bradley announced that the city would sell shares of the Crenshaw mall to anybody who wanted to buy in. He stated that he hoped that the Black community would take advantage of such a "great opportunity." They had no other details about how the shares would be sold, how many would be issued, what would be the cost, and what they potentially would be worth. Nothing other than, "You want in; boy have I got a deal for you."

The announcement was made on the construction site at a press conference. Of course, I wasn't invited, but I knew about it from numerous sources, right after Bradley scheduled it. When I got there, Fred McFarland, then Bradley's press aide, while handing me a copy of the release stated sarcastically, "I hope you brought your checkbook." I just looked at him and shook my head. Bradley was there with the councilwoman that replaced his former ally (Pat Russell) Ruth Galanter, the developer Al Haagen, and various community groups standing behind him. Then one of L.A.'s most respected preachers, E.V. Hill, got up and gave a stirring speech on how important it was for us to invest in our own community, etc. It was a great speech. Preachers have a knack for raising money in a pinch, but this was ridiculous. While it was an appropriate issue, it was the wrong project.

Again, this was another tactic to divert the community's attention away from the real issue of the developer's unscrupulous and unyielding control of a community project, by creating false impressions of culpability with such a far-fetched unconventional concept. Can you imagine the hysteria that would be created, if Black folk actually gave their hard-earned money to Alexander Haagen for some stocks or bonds to be paid on later? What would be the worth of the bonds? What would prevent the developer from pulling all the profit out of the project through management fees, or leveraging out the project where little or no equity would be available at the time of cash in? Haagen would just have seven, ten or fifteen years to play with the people's money. Worst yet, where would Haagen or Bradley be in fifteen years, after this game played out? It was insane, but that was how far Bradley had been beat on this project.

Blacks weren't faring very well in the tenancy department either. Many of the merchants were still being ignored. Of the forty or so tenants who had either signed leases or were negotiating leases with Mrs. Haagen, only three were Black. Andrew Natker, the project's manager, claimed that they were still having problems finding "qualified" Black merchants. What we found out was that Haagen was giving preferential treatment to larger white franchises who directly competed with many of the more respected and established Black merchants.

Two of the best examples were the issues with Baldwin Hills/Crenshaw Stationers and Cookies by Connie. Both merchants were Black. Alexander Haagen had promised that the first merchant to be in the mall would be a Black couple, Joe and Roberta Howard who, at that time, owned a small stationary store called Baldwin Hills/Crenshaw Stationers. They were two of the nicest people you'd ever want to meet who had served the community faithfully, working their store 60 to 80 hours a week for the seven years prior to the proposed mall development. The construction of the mall virtually killed their shop with sales dropping off almost 70 percent. Many of their patrons almost expected them to be in the mall. The initial offer Haagen made to them was $3.50 a square foot and a location at the end of the mall. When the Howards, of course, tried to negotiate a better deal for themselves, Haagen gave them an ultimatum to take it or leave it.

Haagen had managed to successfully price them out of the deal. His defense, of course, was he gave them an offer, they couldn't meet it, so he moved on. However, we later found out that they had been negotiating with Hallmark Card Stores, who was being given a lower rate and a better location. When confronted, Natker claimed that as a national chain, Hallmark had a wider selection of products and a greater ability to withstand the mall's initial growth period. Now this was where rent incentives would have helped a Black business. Instead, they got played out of pocket.

In the case of a Black businesswoman named Connie Bass, it was a totally contemptuous situation on Haagen's part. Connie is probably the most sincere and conscientious person you'd ever want to meet. She loved her people and would do anything to promote Black self- determination. On top of that, she had the best cookies in the whole world. I repeat... she had the best cookies in the whole world. Her cookies made you so happy, you'd want to slap somebody. To get slap happy in Los Angeles could be pretty dangerous these days, so it's best to eat her cookies when you're alone. Connie and her daughters, Susan, Jayne and Margaret set up shop in the middle of Watts because they wanted to serve their people. The Haagens knew Connie because she was a tenant in his Watts mall. People were begging for Connie's cookies to come into the mall because many of them were afraid to go to Watts. Cookies by Connie was fast becoming a fixture in the Watts community. They would give cookies to all the kids in the neighborhood if they went to school or got good grades. If some kids came to buy some cookies and one kid didn't have any money, she'd slip 'em a cookie anyway and tell the kids to pay her when they could.

Can you imagine giving poor kids cookies on credit, and the kids would actually come back and pay her? It was that type of motherly love and trust that made the community embrace her. She didn't have the most favorable location in that shopping center either. She was at the end of the center, right by the massive (and incomplete) Century freeway construction. The Watts center was only two-thirds occupied and all the empty shops were at her end of the mall. In spite of all of his promises, Haagen never made good on his commitment to get quality stores around Connie to increase traffic around her shop. Still she struggled over three years in that location.

The Crenshaw Plaza was an opportunity for Haagen to bring a well-respected businesswoman with a quality product into the mall, and make up for past amends, as far as Connie was concerned. Instead, Haagen openly chose to court Mrs. Fields' Cookies to come into the mall. The community was incensed, and, of course, Connie was insulted (and she should have been). Here was a woman, who had given her life and livelihood to the Black community, had an excellent commodity and a following, and she still wasn't good enough to get the first option to come in massa' Haagen's Crenshaw plantation. Then to add further insult to injury, the community had put so much pressure on Haagen this time, that he was forced to relent and allow Connie to come in. However, Connie would be forced to compete against Mrs. Fields because there would be two cookie vendors in the mall. The community said no problem, Mrs. Fields has never done anything for the community and there was no contest about whose cookies tasted the best. Mrs. Fields was getting ready to get her ass kicked (as they were saying on the street). Then Haagen threw some more shit in the game. Even after giving Mrs. Fields a more select location in the mall, Mrs. Fields' people were still very uncomfortable with Connie's presence. They told Haagen that they had not anticipated any competition and that they were not coming in the mall unless they were the only cookie vendor. Haagen then raised the leasing rates on Connie making it unfeasible for her to afford the space. The biggest insult of all was that Haagen suggested that Connie sell out to Mrs. Fields. Connie, of course, rejected that idea (not before adding a few expletives to Haagen's vocabulary.) Haagen then signed Mrs. Fields as the mall's cookie vendor. Mrs. Fields later elected not to come to Crenshaw for reasons unbeknownst to us. Haagen tried to go back to Connie, and was summarily cussed out again.

The overall point of these examples was that two legitimate business opportunities owned by Blacks were compromised and subordinated for even less legitimate non-Black offers. How could the developer continually maintain that he had a commitment to the Black community when he was refusing to give our community businesses a chance to compete? New ventures were getting even less of a chance to compete. He had convinced the city that Black businesses lacked the retail marketing capabilities to effectively compete in a regional shopping mall, particularly if they've never been in one. He suggested that the city provide some supportive services to assist in this area, and maybe Black tenancy would increase. Ironically, that's the same thing we suggested in our report to the community-based consultant. While it appeared that the Mayor was going to take on the recommendation, his choice had a lot to be desired.

Known as Mr. Lancer, Mr. Southland, Mr. Anti-homeless (and any other project that sided against the disadvantaged), the project's new consultant was now Mr. Crenshaw. Los Angeles resident sellout, Larry Irvin of the Irvin Hampton Company. I was sick. It is absolutely ridiculous how brothers and sisters labor, risk opportunity, reputation and even their safety to go up against the status quo. People raise issue and questions of integrity to create opportunities for Blacks, only to have those who have allowed this situation to persist by saying nothing, to lay in the cut and surface conveniently in the midst of the discussion like, "I'm here .... we know what you've been talking about, you need me! Opportunistic bastards who really don't give a damn about our people or the issue. Just a chance to make a buck, punk us out and sell us out at the same time. What could we expect next-- a white overseer to manage the mall, right? This was like the script from hell.

* * *

This issue of who would manage the mall had always been a highly touchy subject. The issue was raised early in the game to the city, the developer and the CRA. "Who is going to manage the mall?" We were emphatic about hiring a Black mall manager. We even wanted to submit a short list. Haagen claimed he had to hold a "national search" to find the most "qualified" person, since this wasn't just any kind of mall. It was a regional mall. What Haagen was saying was "he'd be damned if he hired anybody we suggested." So he took his time to find this "so-called" right person. What it eventually produced was a brother named Louis George, who had managed several malls including one property the size of the Crenshaw Plaza. They had a little press conference and made an announcement in the papers. Irvin was now handling the public relations for the mall to try to boost the community's confidence. This appointment was supposed to be a step in that direction.

In the meantime, Bradley, Haagen and the CRA were determined to open this mall in September 1988, even though the mall was only 40 percent occupied, with many tenants caught up in meticulous lease negotiations. No other community would be forced to come to a grand opening for a half full mall. But I guess this wasn't just any other community, right? Plus, the Mayor promised that this mall would be open for Christmas. From our point of view, a half full mall would only reinforce our position-- that the city and developer weren't concerned about providing what the people wanted, only what they wanted. More rumors on the mall were coming out every day-- that Nordstrom wasn't coming, that several franchises weren't coming because Haagen's leasing structure was too high and out of line with similar malls like the Glendale Galleria and Old Towne, and that they were going to put the biggest Sears in captivity in the mall. So much for the high-end stores. All of Ladera and Baldwin Hills shop at Sears, right?

The Baldwin Hills community knew that this wasn't just their mall, that the demographic five-mile radius had just reached significantly to the east, and that people would catch the bus to go to Sears (just as their numbers bear out). Bradley and Haagen couldn't win for losing, and the mall's occupancy showed it. As a prelude to opening the mall, they had an opening of the Sears store. About 60 people showed up. I'm sure all the Windsor Hills, Ladera Heights and Baldwin Hills socialites just probably forgot to calendar the opening of their newest high-end store. Merely an oversight. I'm sure that's the way Bradley and the others explained it. Hell, the whole mall was on the verge of becoming an oversight.

With the first phase of the mall almost complete, part of the new P.R. strategy to increase the mall's support was to take the community on guided tours through the construction site. The first tour consisted of politicians and business and community leaders. I was now President of the branch so they had no other choice but to invite me. The tour usually started off with an introduction of the developer and other players in the joint venture (the city and the CRA), then they had the new "Black" manager say a few words. Then after a light lunch, the tour would proceed. They drove us out to the site in vans, and we wore our little hard hats. Then they broke us up into small groups. On that day, Andrew Natker was our tour guide. When he saw me get in his van, he had this look on his face like, "Just fricking great! Why do I always have to take the ass whipping?" He knew that's exactly what was going to happen. But surprisingly enough, not from me. I basically went to objectively observe so that I could report back to the branch and be able to discuss the benefit of a branch tour.

Apparently, the fight hadn't been in vain. Natker was taking us around the portion still being completed, where we were able to observe the composition of the labor force working on this particular day. Natker made the statement of how the construction labor force was 30 percent Black. Now for all of us that can't count, this means approximately for every two non-Blacks you see you should see one Black. Charles Stewart, an aide from then state Senator Diane Watson's office, kindly and intelligently said, "Excuse me, Andy ...., but it doesn't appear to be that many Blacks on the labor force today." Natker couldn't leave it alone, and proceeded to say that on any given day Blacks make up 30 percent of the construction contracts and work force. All the community people looked at each other and simultaneously started counting. There were 83 people working in the area we were in. We counted seven Black males and two Black females. This was about 9 percent of the labor force. When we got outside, we saw about 15 more workers and one Black male. We all concluded that they must be counting the security guards in which there were about 12 of them. But still out of 110 construction site employees (of which the security shouldn't be included, because they make nowhere near what construction workers make), Blacks on this day only made up 18 percent of the work force, and only 11 percent of the construction workers. From that point, Natker's credibility went out of the window. Everybody wanted to know on what day the 30 percent of the Black workers worked. Crenshaw never had a 30 percent labor force that could be verified by anybody other than those involved. Anybody should have been able to show up on any day and count, and reach 30 percent. I was very glad to see community representatives finally realizing what we (the merchants) knew was happening all along. Natker was pretty exasperated after the tour, and he should have been. Trying to defend a political lie was more than a notion. He had to do this every day, four times a day, five days a week until they had reached enough of the community to justify to themselves (certainly not to the community) that they had done a sufficient job of informing the community about the mall. Now it was time to move forward with the opening.

The opening of the mall would be consistent with every other event associated with this project. A rhapsody in deception. There were balloons, food, music, politicians, celebrities, proclamations and commendations. The gang was all there: Bradley, Haagen, Galanter, Mack, and everybody associated with the mall. And, there were other people there, too. However, Bradley's projection of 35,000 people in the first three hours was absolutely insane. An outright lie. There were maybe 3,000 to 5,000 at best, our counters estimated. The purpose of this misrepresentation was to entice our people to come to this fiasco. Many people I talked to who went were extremely disappointed in what they saw. "There was nothing over there," or "I don't even know why they opened, when most of the shops were closed," were the recurring themes. Stubbornness is why they opened, if you sought an answer to the question. Haagen was determined to show the mall's opposition that no matter what they said or tried to do, this mall was going to open. It was going to open with or without the community's support, and it was going to open on time. Whether there were 100 shops or 30-something shops (which is what it was), I believe Haagen would have been sick enough to open it with 10 shops. And as crazy as it sounds, Bradley would have been out there proclaiming it a success. I didn't attend the opening (although I was invited) because of a business scheduling conflict. In the over 30 accounts of the event, the most consistent observation was how sad it was to see so-called community leaders participating in this charade that was the ultimate embarrassment to everyone involved. And for sure, they weren't even through. Of the 30 shops, only three were Black. Blacks were having an extremely difficult time getting any kind of sensible deal for space. The city had announced a loan assistance program, which nobody could qualify for. The preferred space in the mall was being held for franchise stores that would almost never come, and the merchants in the Santa Barbara Plaza were dropping off like flies. Yet, it was heralded as a significant day in the history of the Black community! Yeah, to say the least.

* * *

The last move that would cement the Baldwin Hills/Crenshaw Plaza to a hypocrite's graveyard forever was a move Haagen pulled five months after the mall had opened. In January 1989 Haagen would fire the mall's manager, Louis George, for what he called an inability to run a mall of this magnitude. What would bring a fervor to the community was that Haagen would replace this brother with a totally unqualified political appointment. Haagen would appoint Janice Hahn, the daughter of then county supervisor (and political godfather to Black folk in Los Angeles), Kenneth Hahn.

Hahn had a loyalty amongst Blacks that was also sacred. For anybody to oppose Kenny Hahn, for any reason, was sacrilegious. Haagen figured no one would raise a peep over the firing of George, if he followed it with the appointment of Janice. He was almost right. Everybody was extremely cautious and guarded with their statements. People were saying things like, "It's unfortunate that things didn't work out, but we're very happy to have another Hahn serving the community," or "We think Haagen's firing may have been premature; however, we are satisfied with the new appointment." Ridley-Thomas of the SCLC and Mack of the Urban League, did intimate that they didn't think that this was the smartest idea, given the controversial circumstances that have surrounded the mall heretofore. Also they both had nothing to say about the appointment of Hahn's daughter. I, however, came out swinging with both barrels loaded. I stated: "After Haagen claimed that he had to search nationwide for a qualified mall manager, how does he come up with a white woman who is an ex-housewife with no mall management experience? I suggest Mr. Haagen rethink this one immediately or he will have problems in the very near future." Everybody in town knew I was not bullshitting either. I never said it publicly, but I had already made the call to state President, Jose DeSosa, for permission to boycott. I mean we were planning to knock Haagen's ass out the box on this one. We had just brought the Carson Mall management to its knees one month earlier, and made national news over the Black Santa Claus issue (Chapter 12). As far as, we were concerned, it was a test run for what we would one day do to Haagen. Now the wheel was in motion sooner than we all expected.

Our City Hall sources told us that Bradley was shouting at Haagen at the top of his voice saying, "What the hell are you doing, Al? I don't give a shit what you do but you better not give Essex a reason to boycott this mall." The Mayor knew we were working, and he knew that Haagen had placed himself in a position where he didn't have a lot of time. One thing was for sure: Janice couldn't stay in that spot. An announcement would have to be made very soon to jam whatever we were planning to do. One week would have been too late. Haagen made the decision to remove Janice three days later. But Haagen, in his own stubborn manner, spitefully replaced Hahn with an equally unqualified choice, one of his own in-house operatives. Leo Ray. And he was perceived, by some (including myself), as one of the biggest Toms you'd ever want to meet. Haagen was acting just like a repugnant slave master who just refused to admit any form of defeat in a slave revolt that he initiated. His actions reflected the attitude that "If they want a nigger, I'll give 'em a nigger."

The last Black we expected him to choose was Ray. Even Ray was shocked that the job fell in his lap. Ray wasn't even on the short list when the national search was in effect. He wasn't even in the running, period. Haagen would have probably fired him if he had dreamed of asking for the job and didn't wake up and apologize. That's how long a shot Leo Ray was. If there was ever an instance where Blacks were being punished for standing for right, this was it. Janice Hahn could do more in her sleep than three Leo Rays. However, she was thrown in the middle of a game where issues of racial self- determination were at stake, and she was the wrong player for this game. But this didn't mean that because we wanted a Black manager that we rejected his white manager, and that any Black face, qualified or unqualified, would do. Haagen, again, in his attempt to stifle us, purposely compromised the integrity and intent of the whole justification of wanting a Black manager. A simple announcement that the search would be re-opened would have sufficed. Haagen wickedly knew what he was doing, and again the undeserving received the benefits out of the labor of the deserving.

The moment he got the position, the press and the other community leaders called to inform me. After two days later, Larry Irvin had the nerve to call me saying, "We got a replacement for Janice."

I told him, "We ain't got shit," and I changed the subject on him. "What's this you're telling Southland that they don't have to worry about me, because I'm through as President of the branch."

He just stuttered. I hung up the phone. "Silly Tom," I said to myself.

I saw Leo Ray at the 1989 SCLC King dinner. He was sitting with Andy Natker and Larry Irvin. A sorry sight to see. I looked at Ray and said, "There is such a thing as miracles," and walked off. He, to this day, still believes that he got that position on his own volition. Another silly Tom.

In the meantime, Janice Hahn called me to set up a meeting just to talk about her perception of the whole situation. The first conversation was brief. She said she wanted to meet me. I asked why. She said that she was curious to find out why I never gave her a chance on the mall, and to gain some insight about me as a leader and a person. I told her the issue wasn't about her and I'm sure she's heard more than enough about me, not to mention what Haagen's people would have to say. Janice, in a humorous tone, said: "I really can't tell. Every time I mention your name everybody starts to move so fast. Where is he? What did he say?" We both laughed. I told her I'd like to meet her some time soon and that I'd get back to her. A week later she called to set a specific date about two weeks later. It turned out to be the day of the funeral of Los Angeles' most noted civil rights activist, Dr. H. Claude Hudson. Janice called me the morning of the funeral to ask me if I'd be in attendance. I told her I would. She asked if we could still have lunch after the service. I told her that I would see her there, and depending on how things went, we'd decide there. Before we got off the phone, she proceeded to tell me how I was the topic of her family's dinner conversation with her father and her brother, Jimmy Hahn, the city attorney for L.A. I said, "Oh."

She responded, "Yeah, they were just a little concerned about me. I told them you seemed to be a very nice young man. Much different than what we had read in the papers. My dad said he'd be interested in sitting with you one day to discuss your position on some issues."

I was like, "Yeah, I look forward to it." (It never happened.) We said our farewells, until after the service.

The service was an elegant parting tribute to a real pioneer. Over 1,500 people attended. It was more of a celebration of life, than a mourning of death. Dr. Hudson was 100 years old. After the service, I was standing out front giving my condolences to the family, when Janice walked up. I told her I had a few more condolences to extend, and I'd get with her. I finally located her in the huge crowd of people still mingling outside Holoman Methodist Church. She was standing there with Brad Pye, her father's chief deputy, and her brother, Jimmy, who was the City Attorney for Los Angeles. There were several plain clothes police standing around them. Both Brad and Jim were in this whispering match with Janice, and they had these worried looks on their faces. They were talking to Janice like, "You're really going to go through with this?" And (as I later found out) they tried to convince her to let someone else go with us. She brushed them off saying she'd be fine. As I walked up, Janice said, "Anthony, you know my brother Jim, and Brad?" I nodded to both.

Brad asked Janice, "Where are you going to eat?" She said she didn't know and she'll call them later. Brad Pye stood there looking at me like he was getting ready to piss on himself. He probably thought that if anything happened to Janice, that would be his ass and, of course, mine also. So there I was, L.A.'s rebel without a pause, going to lunch with Kenny Hahn's free-minded and spirited princess, in front of 1,500 people wondering who was this white woman I was walking off with. We joked on the way to the car. I asked if she had half of the L.A.P.D. tracking her whereabouts.

She said, "You know, brothers will be brothers. Do you think we'll be back by 3 p.m.?" (implying, of course, that that would be about the time they'd come looking for her). We both busted up laughing.

It was really a very pleasant lunch. We went to Aunt Kizzy's in Marina Del Rey. Janice Hahn is really a remarkably, nice young woman. I had nothing but positive things to say about her. She was honest, straightforward, witty and funny. We talked about a variety of subjects. When the conversation finally turned to the mall, she turned extremely serious. She pointed at me and said, "Anthony, I could have done so many things for the mall and community, not because I am Kenny Hahn's daughter, but because I have commitment and desire. Now, I'll only be known as the white woman who was a former housewife with no mall experience. That's not very fair, is it?" As I looked at her, I saw the hurt in her eyes and the pain on her face. I proceeded to tell her that her disappointment was no greater than that of Black people who have been effectually dismissed from positions of responsibility for less than legitimate reasons or for no reason at all. Or of qualified Blacks who never get an opportunity at all to receive a position like the one handed to her. Janice seemed to be hostile to the claim that the job was handed to her, stating that she asked for that job because she wanted to help the community. My position was so did a lot of other people; however, I admonished her not to be so naive to think that she wasn't chosen because of who she was and what she represented. I continued to demonstrate to her that Haagen knew that she (as a white woman) was not the most politically conscious choice in the midst of this issue, but chose to throw her in this fire anyway. As self-sacrificing as she was, the issue was never about her, Janice Hahn, the person. It was the act of Haagen's insistent defiance to accommodate the will and needs of the community.

The community wanted to see a role model, a Black in a position of responsibility in this mall's management position. If Ronald Reagan had been hired, he would have been jammed as a "white man and a former actor who served as President and governor, but had no mall experience." This whole issue was about allowing Blacks to help their community by holding positions of this caliber. As many as were available. And when Haagen reneged, we had to fire on him. She was a victim of the circumstance who was caught innocently in the crossfire. She had Haagen to thank for that. She began to define Haagen as a kind and generous man who had given her an opportunity to expand her career. She stated that she felt that Haagen was being misrepresented in this whole matter, and she committed to get Haagen and I together to talk about our differing perspectives. I told her that while I knew she was a superwoman, Haagen had never accepted any of my invitations to talk so why would he now. She said she couldn't speak for him but said, "I promise you, if I don't do anything else, this little former housewife is going to get you two highly respected individuals together." I told her that was a bold challenge. We toasted to former housewives. (In 2001, Janice Hahn was elected to the Los Angeles City Council, 15th District, in the same election that her brother James Hahn was elected as Mayor of Los Angeles).

* * *

After almost 15 months of haggling with this project, in February 1989, I finally had the opportunity to meet one-on-one with the elusive Alexander "The Hagg (as I had begun to call him)." True to her word, Janice Hahn facilitated the meeting promptly, and without the usual restrictions that I heard was the norm for meeting Haagen. Mainly, Haagen doesn't meet anyone without the presence of his wife, particularly where the mall was concerned. It was well known that she called the shots pretty heavily on Crenshaw. The former housewife scored a coup. Hats off to former housewives, and second-generation power brokers (in her own right).

The Haagen meeting was really anticlimactic, in terms of its significance to address the many problems that existed and continued to persist in the mall project. The community's alienation was too great to make amends without significant concessions to African-American interests. Concessions that even I knew Haagen had no intentions of making given the placement of Leo Ray and the absence of an aggressive solicitation of Black merchants in a mall that was still 50 percent vacant. While certainly I would put these issues to Haagen, his temperament, as was mine, was not conducive to the placation and small talk this meeting was arranged for. I think he was as curious about me as I was about him, and Janice reached his soft spot. However, if I got too heavy for him on the substantive issues meritorious of extensive discussion, I expected no less than for Haagen to discontinue the meeting because there were no advance parameters set for this meeting (as a result of Janice's persistence for us to meet).

There was a period of ice-breaking and a feeling out period. Haagen sat at the end of a long walnut conference table. I sat at the other end of the table. Apparently, he wanted to make sure I knew he was aware and that nothing was wrong with his eyes. He complimented me on my necktie (by designer) and my taste in jewelry by virtue of a gold opal ring I wore that day. He then began to recite Shakespeare and talk about how he looked forward to the simple things in life--playing with his grandchildren, etc. Finally, he broke out a book about when he, as developer, was involved in the planning of a seemingly impossible project-- the Vermont/Slauson development. He said how he got no money for it, and that he did it to help "poor people." I could see a pattern forming here. Then he proceeded to tell me about how he built the Kenneth Hahn Plaza on Wilmington and again carried the burden of the expense for "poor people." Finally, we got to Crenshaw, a project he claimed he had no intention of getting involved in. Haagen stated that Bradley called him to get involved with it and he rejected it twice. He said the city made fantastic promises to him for support and for financing, much of which (he claimed) never came through. I'm sitting there thinking, "Damn, you could have done better than what you already had?" Haagen further claimed that many of the community sensitivities that were raised during this project were not unexpected, nor was it his intention to appear cavalier in the interest of the people. Haagen insisted that Bradley and the city officials assured him that nothing would come of community dissatisfaction, that it would be squashed and that the only thing he (Haagen) needed to worry about was completing the mall according to schedule.

Haagen said the ownership concept was his idea. He said he wanted the Black community to own something for themselves, but when other demands and issues were raised, he was told not to worry. Given that Bradley and the others didn't appear to be too concerned when he was approached, more and more he began to respond as he was advised by the city to "let them handle things." Afterall, he did have a deal, and the city said they would handle the heat surrounding the project. But as certain issues failed to be addressed, he felt other entities in the project, namely the CRA, began to blame him for some of the problems when he was moving forth as instructed. Then the CRA, who was apparently unaware of Bradley's back- room support of Haagen, began holding up money until certain demands were made, which Bradley was forced to acquiesce to at the risk of divulging his role in the deal. Haagen looked out the window the whole time he relayed this story and then turned and looked at me and said, "Didn't it ever occur to you that Bradley never requested or demanded a response from me? Everybody else did. Bradley was protecting our deal, but then you and the CRA forced his hand, and he was forced to take the lead on your demands." But now Haagen was the scapegoat.

Haagen resented that inasmuch as, he didn't feel Bradley was honest with him when the shit hit the fan in the first place. Haagen felt he probably could have made more changes in the project had he been allowed to in the earlier stages-- changes that would have benefited Blacks with no problem. But as discussed earlier, Bradley's tendency to dismiss a few concerns snowballed into an issue of significant social and economic proportions, and Haagen realized that the sweetheart deal that he and Bradley had agreed upon would have to be adjusted to accommodate the community's demands. Bradley resisted that and in Haagen's words: "He began to take your assault on the mall personally, and greatly underestimated your ability to rally interest in what you were protesting. Haagen (as he called himself) was taking a beating all the while, and he became the demagogue for a lost cause that he hoped he could save."

I found it very interesting how Haagen was quick to lay blame elsewhere when many of the problems with the mall were by his agents or decisions that he (or his wife) had made directly. Decisions like tenant selection, federal monies that he had received to assist Black businesses and Black subcontractors, many of whom never saw the money, and his handling of certain merchants who had been loyal to Haagen's projects like Connie Bass and Joe Howard, only to be played out of pocket. Some of this he had brought on himself, an arrogance well known in political circles. Yet, here he was trying to convince me that he was the man with the golden heart. Give me a break. Some people just try to talk to you any kinda' way. The pitiful side to this is that we often let 'em.

I let Haagen know that I believed some of the issues he raised might be accurate, but that I also knew some were not. I told him that I would like such detailed issues to be the subject of a future meeting so that I could have my information to support refuted claims. Haagen said he saw no problem with that. He called his chief assistant in and let him know that our dialogue would be continuing and that we should get to know each other, which we did. We then exchanged pleasantries. Janice came back in to take me to lunch. Haagen begged off saying he had a follow-up meeting and couldn't make it. My meeting with the fabled Alexander Haagen was over. That was the last time we would talk, due to the fact that my NAACP affiliation would end the following month. But that was hardly the end of the problems with the Baldwin Hills/Crenshaw Plaza.

* * *

In retrospect, the Baldwin Hills/Crenshaw Shopping Plaza confrontation, where a city was made to include Black participation at the risk of jeopardizing the project itself, was the first of its kind involving public money. A similar strategy was implemented in Chicago six months later, on a highway construction that had similar problems.

The issues raised during the Crenshaw Plaza project demonstrated still how unsophisticated we (the Black community) are, when it comes to public developments and their financing. Elected officials shouldn't continue to perpetuate false ideas about the Black community's abilities to bring to fruition complex projects in acts of self-determination. Black elected officials shouldn't allow non-Black interests to come in the community and feel that they have to baby-sit urban projects for the sake of the poor. It's an insult to the community, and an indictment on their integrity, when these officials play an active role in the misinformation, disengagement, and outright placation of Blacks. It's sick to see how easily projects are given away in the Black community when there were dozens of qualified constructors who could have handled this project. Maybe none of them had the track record of handling a project of this size. But if they can't start in their own community with public funds (a part of which they pay), then where can they start? Black firms aren't given a fair shot outside their community on projects where minority participation is not required, and they're not given a break in their own community. This is only part of the story.

The way the Black community is misinformed and manipulated by Black (and white) politicians is outrageous. I grew up figuratively worshipping Tom Bradley. It hurt my heart to have to openly challenge our political icon. But not only did Tom Bradley cut a bad deal on the Crenshaw Plaza project, he lied about how the deal went down and never admitted to his own people that he made an error in judgment on this project. All the time, he tried to make it seem like opponents of the mall were crazy, and that I was insane for challenging the Mayor (of all people). Yet the more we uncovered about the mall, the more truth came out of our advocacy. But that didn't stop the city authorities from continuing to attack my credibility, even though I was right. It didn't keep them from using community groups who have the interest and influence of the people, to represent inaccurate positions and to further confuse the issue was reprehensible. One of my last acts as President of the branch was to arrange for the Executive Committee to take a tour of the mall. By that time, however, the branch was so embroiled in the electoral politics of the branch, that my opposition was supporting the mall, just because I was opposed to it. Larry Irvin had convinced Bradley and Haagen that the NAACP could eventually be reeled in. By then, it really didn't matter to me, because I knew everything we had raised issue with had come true. It would just be a matter of time before these truths came out. Still, many in the community knowingly (and some unknowingly) compromised the overall objectives of self-reliance, by allowing themselves to be used, either by intimidation, extortion, blackmail or seduction. And for what? A lie, a failure, an opportunity for everyone to benefit, except those for whom the development was intended.

In February 1990, two and a half years after the mall opened, the mall was still only 50 percent occupied. Not until the civil revolt of 1992, would the mall reach 70 percent occupancy. Ironically, several major tenants moved in after the riot. The mall was the biggest benefactor of the riot in South Central. This tragedy benefited in its illegitimacy. Some injustices just go on forever. Before the riots, many of the stores were refusing to come in, because of the ridiculous rent scale. There were only seven Black tenants, out of almost 70 stores, and all of them were failing, because of broken promises, bad locations and lack of supportive services, etc. The mall's investment program whereby shares in the mall could be purchased, was never heard of again. The Negro manager who Haagen appointed was telling an associate that the state of the mall was due to "that damn Anthony Essex." The associate calmly told him that if it wasn't for me, he wouldn't have his job. He still was a silly Negro. *The Los Angeles Times* did an article about the mall and its progress two years later. The same people who were pulling for the mall's completion were now talking about how inferior the quality of goods were and how poor the selection was. In 1994, it was reported that the city of Los Angeles' interest in the mall had been lost after Haagen sold part of the mall (including the city's interest) to a company he owned. Real tragedy is never resolved, it goes on hopelessly forever.

The mall had turned out to be exactly what it was intended to be: a magnet for Black consumers, with no return on their investment. The project compromised the community's economic equity and future efforts of collective self-determination.

The Crenshaw mall project, because of the hypocrisy that surrounded its redevelopment, is now a historical landmark for a new generation of Blacks. It's a constant reminder of a compromised community's disregard for their apathetic state, and how easily it can be supplanted by disingenuous community leadership. Furthermore, it will forever serve as an example of how misinformation campaigns can effectively orchestrate the collective community misdirection. They can so paralyze the truth, that honest, decent people and well-meaning organizations can be manipulated to play surrogate roles, as disciples for less well-meaning, and sometimes wicked interests, outside of the community. Misinformation was propagated by prevaricators in Black faces, who destroyed (and continue to destroy) the integrity of a community's self-determination effort for a few crumbs from the proverbial "rich man's table." A little persistence and unity would have gotten the Crenshaw community the whole loaf. Unfortunately, these are often the same people whom the community very heavily relies on, to help us out of powerless conditions, through their respective training and expertise. It's a recurring example of how ethnic loyalty and collective wealth play secondary priority to greed and personal benefit. And for as long as, Blacks fail to call a spade, a spade, and sit silently while the rape takes place (as the NAACP tended to do), Crenshaw and many other acts like Crenshaw will continue to occur. Blacks will continue to have much at stake, but no claims to another man's gift, which only ends up as a plantation, advanced under the guise of municipal redevelopment.

8

A Synonym for "Niggah Shit"

"Great Spirits have always encountered violent opposition from mediocre minds."

- Albert Einstein

It was the summer of 1987, and it had become pretty obvious that the Los Angeles branch had been running without a clear sense of direction. After the Frank Sinatra fiasco, more Executive Committee members resigned. The practice of prostituting the organization for money had become so blatant, and distasteful, that many committee members could not justify the branch's recognitions, nor their own affiliation. The participation in branch affairs was dropping like Mercury on a winter night. Hardly any money was coming into the branch from memberships.

Ray was oblivious to anything going on in the community. He was still high on the Sinatra piece. The convention was coming up in New York, and he intended to play the role. The branch picked up a two-bedroom suite and paid for two branch staffers to go to the convention (supposedly to work). One staffer had only been on the job for one week. The branch hosted a reception at its own expense, costing almost $10,000. Ray's airfare was almost $600, even though everybody else's was approximately $297. We later found out in a finance committee meeting that the ticket included a stopover in Birmingham, Alabama (where Ray's wife was from), and we adjusted the price to cover just the trip to the conference. In total, the branch spent almost $17,000 at that convention.

The branch took another $20,000 in delinquent membership dues, from local members who had forwarded money to the branch, but the branch had spent the money instead of forwarding it to the national headquarters. This is why the first question members asked was: "Why haven't I received my membership card?"

The branch also gave a freedom fund contribution of $35,000, a negotiated settlement of what was considered "national's share" of the Sinatra dinner. That was, of course, after the branch hid half of the net in a dummy corporation set up by the branch. More about that later. Truth be told, a branch that was broke two months earlier dropped over $72,000 at the national convention in New York. It's not hard to figure out that not long after, the branch was in financial straits again.

This put the branch in the very precarious position of having to go to "the corporation" (as the Executive Committee called it) for money. It was the same corporation that the branch set up to keep from giving the national office its required share of fundraising profits. And the same corporation that the branch intended to use to circumvent national policy regarding branches owning real estate to buy a branch headquarters. Though the branch strategically included the Crenshaw Economic Development Corporation (CEDC) as a joint sponsor of its freedom fund dinner to divert funds from the branch, the money raised was in the name of the NAACP, not the Crenshaw Economic Development Corporation. Yet, the branch was forced to borrow its own money from its own dummy entity. Its board members were officers of the branch and members of the Executive Committee. A less than arms reach arrangement.

Way before the dinner and even before the last election, it was known that Ray was now looking for a way out of the organization. It had been long rumored that Ray was going to leave the branch. Many felt he was ill-suited for the position and shouldn't run for re-election.

The Sinatra dinner was the coup de grace for Ray's administration. A most appropriate out; this fiasco would be all she wrote for Ray's presidency. Raymond Johnson, Jr. ran for re-election to protect the commitment he made to the Sinatra dinner. After several discussions about a possible challenge, Ray gave his assurances that I would be the next President of the Los Angeles branch. When I queried him as to how he could be so sure, he only reiterated that I would be. That led me to believe that Ray had no intentions of completing a second term.

Upon our return from the national convention, there was virtually no activity at the branch level. With no meeting due until September, people had plenty of time to contemplate their future involvement in the branch. Because of my staunch opposition to the Sinatra dinner, as well as my extended involvement in the Southland investigation and the Baldwin Hills/Crenshaw Shopping Plaza dispute, I had become the most visible of the branch's Vice Presidents. I was the most logical choice to succeed Ray. When Melanie Lomax and Richard Jones became inactive during Ray's first term, and when Melanie didn't surface to challenge Ray in the succeeding branch election, Ray virtually relented his control on many branch projects. That was, unless he felt there was high visibility in advance. This was very hard to predict. Ray was now concentrating his efforts on trying to translate his NAACP visibility into a professional benefit.

In the midst of trying to do so, on one occasion, Ray became entangled in one of the Los Angeles judicial courts' biggest controversies of 1987. In August of that year, Ray in one of his monthly "the NAACP is shocked and appalled" press conferences, called for the immediate removal of a Glendale Municipal Court commissioner, who had used the term "nigger," while presiding over a case involving a Black assault victim. Reportedly, the statement was made while Commissioner Daniel Calabro was set to hear a case, where an 18-year-old white male attacked a 32-year-old Black man who was waiting at a Glendale bus stop. Allegedly, the white boy confronted the Black man saying, "Your kind is not welcome here, nigger." Then he and three other white youths beat the brother.

That case was followed by another case days later where similar terms were stated. According to the transcript, Commissioner Calabro supposedly said, "Another nigger case? Another one where this nigger business came up. We're not past that yet?" The fact that Calabro used "nigger" on the bench was the center of public outcry in the Black community. Other community groups and leaders followed suit in their condemnation of Calabro, charging that the commissioner may have biased tendencies if he could be so easily solicited to use a defamatory term. Ray was quick to call for his removal, as were other community leaders. And the Black community's political godfather, Kenny Hahn, also called for the district attorney to step in on this issue. As a result, Calabro was suspended from hearing any criminal cases, unless both plaintiff and defense attorneys agreed.

In the meantime, it was circulating throughout the Black community that Ray was about to accept a job in Kenny Hahn's office. Office administrative assistant Ernestine Peters confided in me that I may have to take on an even bigger part of the branch's responsibilities, because Ray would be going to Hahn's office. She further stated that it was all but a done deal. This wouldn't have been a problem to any significant degree, except that Ray's alleged future boss leveraged his authority to cause him to take a position adverse to the community's position.

A few days later, Hahn called together a small prayer breakfast of about 50 people to have Calabro apologize to the community. Ironically enough, it was supposed to be a gathering of preachers and civil rights leaders. Ray represented the only major civil rights organization. Hahn called Ray and Calabro to the podium after Calabro had apologized. Hahn told Ray, "Go 'head accept his apology." Like a puppet on cue Ray, before everyone gathered and the press assembled, accepted his apology. However, Ray took it one step further.

Like a kid who can't make a decision without the consensus of his friends, he included the whole community in "his" acceptance. He stated, "I accept your regrets. I believe the Black community does as well."

Big mistake. The Black community exploded over seeing Ray sheepishly follow suit in allowing Hahn to posture a community sentiment from one individual. Damn near everyone reacted to the 5 p.m. news report that afternoon. It wasn't even about what they had heard Ray had said. It was what they saw him say, with their own eyes, combined with the rumor that Ray was on his way to Hahn's office. This added fuel to the fire.

The Urban League's John Mack, SCLC's Mark Ridley-Thomas, and then Langston Bar Association President, Charles Dickerson, called an immediate press conference to refute Ray's position that "the community" accepted Calabro's apology. They stopped short of naming Ray as the impetus for their having to call the press conference in the first place. Ray later tried to clean up the situation by doing follow-up articles in *The Sentinel* and *The Wave*, claiming that the NAACP's stance on Calabro was a "mistake." This just wasn't the case. Ray had overstepped his boundaries and allowed his influence to be peddled by the relationship he was trying to initiate with Hahn.

In the midst of this embarrassment, Ray searched high and low to find how it leaked out that he was going to Hahn's office. Ray called the officers of the branch together to find the source of the leak. He asked me over and over "Where'd you hear that?" I told him that I'd heard from Mark Ridley-Thomas, over at the SCLC, which I did because Ray had called him first. Mark then called me to find out if Ray was trying to sweat him for information because Ray knew that Mark and I talked frequently. Mark played him off. Later that day, we had this "leak interrogation" meeting. Still, I'd heard it first from Ray's aide, Ernestine Peters. Had Mark not called me, then Ray may have figured that Ernestine was the only person I could have gotten it from. Ernestine was basically protected in her disloyalty to Ray, by others refusal to "give up their source, including myself. It was necessary to keep an open direct line to Ray, given his undecided future.

The rest of the year would be spent in a personal psychological battle between Ray and myself. He was trying to cover up his growing disinterest in the branch, while trying to publicly remain the center of the branch's leadership focus. On the other hand, I was trying to focus on the integrity of community issues without obviously overstepping Ray's role as President of the branch. The effort often became the brunt of Ray's jokes, but it really was a legitimate effort on my part to cover down in what had become Ray's constant absences at community affairs. This happened because Ray would insist on representing the branch, at meetings that he knew he wouldn't be able to make, and he refused to delegate the appointments. Soon people began to go around Ray, and asked me to come to the meetings. They didn't really care about the politics or protocol of the branch. They just wanted the most responsive delegation of community leaders, particularly the civil rights delegation, when meeting with corporate heads or government leaders.

NAACP presence, particularly in the eyes of most white folk who knew very few Black organizations, added legitimacy to those meetings. When the NAACP is not there, they often feel that they're meeting with some surrogate or second-line leadership. They didn't want to disappoint their bosses by not having NAACP representation present. So when Ray didn't show, I'd get a call about why the NAACP missed this meeting or that one. Finally, I started going regardless of what he would tell me. At times we'd both show up. However, most of the time I'd be the only one there. People would ask me where Ray was and I'd reply, "He's not available" or "He couldn't make it." Ray would later joke that I would purposely not tell him about meetings so that I could represent the branch. It really wasn't true. I really resented him saying that when it was actually the other way around. Most people knew that I was covering for Ray, who couldn't (and sometimes wouldn't) attend any meetings during the day. Ray had to joke to masquerade the lack of performance he was hiding from the members.

Representing the branch, in Ray's absence, posed another significant contrast. Ray's politics of compromise and accommodation were significantly different from my politics of confrontation and expedition. Ray would accommodate people on issues we would protest. Conversely, the ultimate aim would be compromised, at some point in time, as part of the accommodations that would have to be conceded to reach an agreement. I would confront the issue and seek the most expeditious resolution of the conflict. They would hold their breath, either glad as hell to see Ray, or glad to see me. When I showed up at a meeting that was presumably set for accommodations, it proved to be an exercise in frustration. Conversely, when Ray showed up at a meeting set for confrontation or a strong personality, that meant the conveners were in for the painstaking experience of placation and disengagement.

Conversely, collaborative efforts to include the NAACP often required planners to take into consideration which one of us would be involved. One meeting that comes to mind was a strategy meeting that Brotherhood Crusade President Danny Bakewell, then also a securities firm executive, had called at the Cranston Securities offices. He wanted to address concerns over the perceived misinformation and perpetuation of negative news that the *Los Angeles Times* was running on issues in our community. When discussing courses of action to be pursued, the discussion of boycotting the paper came up as a secondary option. Of course, being no big fan of *The Times* or the *Herald Examiner* (which has since folded), I was in favor of it as were many in the meeting. However, Danny looked at me and said, "Now Anthony, can we count on the NAACP? We know that you and Ray don't exactly share the same line of thinking." I assured him that I felt we could support the group's position and that Ray would be convinced to buy in. Still, the community now knew the difference in philosophies that existed in the branch's leadership. Because of the increasing rumors of Ray resigning from office, most felt comfortable in allowing me to represent and speak for the branch whether they agreed with my politics or not.

1988 began with the whimper, the same way the prior year had ended. Membership meetings were now down to about 25 people in attendance. Branch membership dropped below 2,000 members, for the first time since the McDonald era. The branch was broke again, and we were being forced to go to the dummy corporation, CEDC, to borrow money that the branch had raised. Ray's relationship with the members of the corporation had become very tenuous, inasmuch as the branch had developed a dependency on borrowing from this group. They were now concerned over the rumors of Ray's resignation for more than a few reasons. One, the understanding that the CEDC had with Ray was that the money the branch was borrowing would be repaid at some point in time. If Ray resigned, then they would have to deal with me. My position was that the CEDC was a support vehicle for the branch. Why should the branch have to borrow and repay its own money? I wasn't inclined to repay any money the branch had received from the CEDC. They knew this and weren't prepared to accept that position. Two, they also were in discussions over the planning of the 1988 Roy Wilkins dinner and were undecided at that point if CEDC would have a role in that event. Either way, the branch would owe them money either from outstanding money that they had previously borrowed or the proportionate share of this year's dinner proceeds.

Resentments were still running strong from the prior year's Sinatra fiasco to where Mallory, McBeth and Dotson were now planning to oppose my presidency, be it in December or sooner. The position they put to Ray was that they would not chair the dinner, but they would work with the dinner committee and expect the CEDC to be compensated. When it became apparent that Ray may not be present for the dinner, they threatened to withdraw their involvement altogether unless Ray committed to staying on until the dinner had been completed. Furthermore, they had to be assured that I was not going to be involved in planning the dinner.

Ray acquiesced to all of their demands. Ray appointed Johnson to chair the dinner. Jarone was a former director of Founders Savings, who was ousted when the feds took over the savings and loan, due to mismanagement. When I left the bank, I sued him, the management and directors of the bank for wrongful termination. Jarone basically came on the board to jam my continued involvement in the branch and to appropriately position himself prior to elections to supplement whatever opposition was forming to go against me.

It was January 1988, and the dinner was planned for May 31, 1988. Rumor had it that Ray was due to leave in March. Between January and March, the dinner committee had pretty much excluded my involvement. Toward the end of February, Ray stopped denying that he would resign. It was just a matter of time when he would leave. It now became evident that I would be President before the next NAACP convention, which was in July. The community began to call more about directing my involvement, versus Ray's.

Still, there was the issue of the branch's finances. Debt was accumulating, much of it very questionable. Ray wanted to pay these bills before he left, and many couldn't wait until the dinner. Some of the debt was being paid from the portion of dues that were supposed to be sent to the national office. Members would not receive their dues cards or their Crisis magazine until this money was paid. However, the total elimination of the debt would require borrowing money from the CEDC.

At the end of February 1988, Ray had a conference call with the board of the CEDC: George Mallory, Jim McBeth, Henry Dotson and Skip Cooper. Everybody clicked in except Skip, whose answering machine picked up. When the message unit cleared, Mallory left a message and clicked out, so he thought. Skip's recorder went on to detail the remainder of the meeting. The meeting continued with the four of them discussing how much money Ray thought he needed to clear the branch debt. Ray responded, "About 30" (meaning $30,000). Mallory asked how much he thought he needed right away. Ray said, "12 or 14" (meaning $12,000 or $14,000). Then Mallory asked Ray point blank, "When are you leaving, Ray?" Ray only responded with, "Very soon." Mallory was trying to get a fix on the time involved and asked, "30 days, 60 days?" Ray said, "About that or sooner." Mallory then expressed his concern over the money being repaid. He stated that he knew that I wasn't supportive of the corporation and he wasn't inclined to leave the decision of repayment to someone who is not in support of the corporation. Then he asked Ray, "How would Anthony feel about repaying the money?" Ray stated that they would have to ask me. Mallory stated that it didn't appear that they would be able to "get me" before Ray left, and they would have to get me in December. He interrupted his thought to ask Dotson, "How's that coming anyway, Henry?" Dotson only responded, "We're working on it." Mallory continued, "Well, it looks like we're going to have to deal with him for a minute. Can you set up the meeting, Ray?" Ray acknowledged that he would. The call ended with the agreement that the CEDC would hold off lending the branch money until after they meet with me. The same day this call was made, Skip called me and played me the tape. Immediately, it presented me with a preponderance of issues to deal with.

First, I was preparing to inherit a financially troubled, politically undermining branch within the next 60 days. I was not prepared to be President right then. I was anticipating that move for next year, and I was just beginning to stabilize my business from a partnership split. And, I was in the midst of trying to resolve or terminate some marital issues. Now was not the time for this. Still I had to take into consideration all of the time I had invested and the commitment that still needed to be addressed. I felt that I was up to that. Second, I was aware that Ray was part of the plot against me, and I specifically knew who the enemy was. I felt comfortable enough to know that I had done the work, and had earned the right to go forward, serving as Fourth Vice President for two years and First Vice President for a year. I thought I was prepared for anything they could throw at me. Third, I had to deal with how this meeting would go down, and how I would handle it. It was also apparent to me that anything coming from these guys had little or no integrity behind it. Should I even meet with them? Should I force Ray to handle it? Should I have them bring it to the branch and take myself out of it? There certainly was little time for hurt and sensitivity over what I had heard. I could begin to prepare myself to juggle my business and the branch responsibility until I could decide how I would proceed for the full term.

Ray called a day later. He said, quickly and to the point, "The corporation would like to meet with you sometime this week."

I had no intention of giving him any indication of what I knew and responded accordingly. "For what, Ray?" He said the corporation just wanted to see how the membership drive was going, and if we would be in a position to repay a loan that he was requesting from them. Now, remember, he still hasn't told me that he is intending to resign, but I played his game anyway. "Well, Ray, why would they want to meet with me when they know how I feel about the corporation? Plus, you know I don't like these guys and they don't like me, so what's up?" This gave him an opportunity to give me the real deal. Still, he refused, maintaining that he needed some backup dealing with these guys and he'd appreciate it if I met with them. After sweatin' him a little longer to see if he would give up anything, I reluctantly agreed to meet with him and his boys later that week.

The meeting turned out to be what can only be described as "Three Stooges" kind of bullshit. All of the members of the CEDC were present: George Mallory, Jim McBeth, Henry Dotson, Skip Cooper and Ray Johnson. I was the only member in attendance who wasn't a member of the corporation. Held in the branch's conference room, Mallory sat at one end of the conference table, I sat at the opposite end, and everybody else was scattered in between.

Mallory started the meeting by stating its purpose and intent, which was to get my position on the corporation lending the branch money and having it repaid, given the possibility that I may become President, during the time which the money was outstanding. I stated that I didn't know anything about that, given that this was the first public acknowledgment that Ray might resign. I turned to Ray and asked if that was true. He stated that it was, and that he was still undecided about resigning. The others seemed a little disturbed that Ray was still playing this charade, particularly in light of what they were trying to accomplish. Still, I played it out saying that I hadn't changed my position on the corporation, and since I'm not President, nor did I know if or when I would become President, that I wasn't particularly inclined to participate in hypothetics. Since they all were trying to bullshit me, I threw some shit in the game stating, "And, furthermore, it appears to me that the corporation has a hostage situation going on here, that I'm sure the Executive Committee would be very interested in."

Seeing that this wasn't going anywhere, Mallory told Ray that he wasn't comfortable with my response and unless he had assurances that the corporation would be repaid, they weren't giving up any money. The only way Ray could assure them would be if he stayed until the branch's fundraising dinner was over. He wasn't prepared to commit to that. Ray then went off. He went through how he didn't feel that the corporation was representing the branch's best interest and how self-serving the members appeared to be. He reprimanded Henry Dotson, who considered himself the branch's "watchdog" for participating in this hostage situation while the branch's doors were on the verge of being closed. Dotson, Ray and Skip would have provided a majority vote. Then Mallory and McBeth attacked Ray for trying to go back on "their deal" (to allow the corporation to keep their money and work independent of the branch) and accused him of "fucking off" the branch's money, not managing the branch's resources and not planning other events that would raise money. I sat there as if I was watching a ping-pong game with my head going back and forth, while they hollered at each other.

Finally, Ray got up and said, "Look, it's the branch's money. We need the money and I trust you gentlemen will work it out. Good night." Then he walked out of the room. There was a moment of silence as they looked at each other and I bit my lip to keep from laughing my ass off. Mallory regained his composure and felt the need to correct Ray's last statement saying, "Contrary to what Ray had just stated, it's not the branch's money." Then he looked at me and asked, "What do you want to do?" My response was, "I'm not the President and my position hasn't changed. The branch shouldn't have to borrow its own money." With that everybody concluded that there was nothing else to talk about and the meeting ended.

However, Ray was back to square one. The branch was still broke, the corporation still had branch money, and the branch still had bills to pay. More critically, Ray had some bills that he would prefer be paid before he left. After he left, the bills would come under major scrutiny. His boys had now provided a major hurdle for him. They were no longer on the same team. They perceived Ray as being less than honest with them, even being "played" to a lesser degree. Now they were playing him to that same degree. The same monster that he had set up to save the branch, and hold the branch's skimmed proceeds, now had him by the leg. They were not about to relent until there was an assurance that "they" would be repaid. Ray could have done that very easily, by remaining until after the Roy Wilkins dinner, and then paying all the bills that were of priority (his, of course), the day after the dinner. Then he could resign. That would have taken the decision to pay the corporation out of my realm of authority. But because he wasn't willing to do this, he gave everyone the indication that he wasn't as flexible in his plans as he represented, and that his leaving was both scheduled and unrelated to anything with the branch or its current state of activity. So now all bets were off as far as the corporation, Ray and the branch were concerned.

* * *

For all intents and purposes, Ray had left the branch in early March 1988 though he didn't give his notice of resignation until the last week of April. His official date of resignation was May 31, 1988.

Ray went on a trip to Israel at the invitation of some Los Angeles Jewish religious leaders trying to develop a relationship with Black community leaders. Ray was the only one of the major local civil rights leaders to go. Rumors were now running wild that Ray had abdicated the presidency and had no intention of coming back. Many of those rumors were perpetuated by Ernestine Peters, who was in regular communication with Ray's wife, Tamara, who was in Birmingham. She chose to put out bits and pieces of what she and Tamara had discussed in confidence. Peters was trying to get others in the branch to address the increasing indebtedness, to avoid missing some paydays.

Ernestine would call me to try and address the more important issues that Ray didn't want me to know about. She would also express her dissatisfaction with the whole situation. When Ray had pissed her off she would turn informant and let out some information that she felt was inappropriate behavior on Ray's part. She did on numerous occasions. One case that was especially damaging was bank statements that she showed me that were purported to be a hidden account that Ray had established to take NAACP contributions for his own use. This account was used to take a donation from a USC law professor who assisted the branch in the Los Angeles City Council redistricting case. When the federal case was won in favor of the plaintiffs, they also were awarded legal fees of about $34,000 per attorney. Ray got the branch involved by presenting its own version of a redistricting plan. The branch never received any money for their involvement nor from the donated contribution.

The second case was that Ernestine implied that Ray had allegedly received a computer purchased with branch money. The branch had authorized close to $10,000 for a personal AT computer, a printer, and a modem, all of which would have cost a maximum of $6,000 according to an estimate I had received a few months after I became President. Yet, the branch was invoiced for much more. Peters would put these things out and I would not make comment. However, I did note what she was doing. She was breaching Ray's trust to save her job, and to endear herself to those whom she perceived would inherit the branch's leadership. However, to me, this was a very bad sign. For as the saying goes: "A dog that would bring a bone will carry one." Bones were pretty transit about this time. Enough to fill a closet or two. Still it allowed me to gain access to information that I had not been previously privy to under the guise of trying to cover down, until Ray made his announcement official.

Another key effort that was going on at that time was the planning of the Roy Wilkins dinner. As previously stated, Ray had appointed Jarone Johnson to chair the event, when Mallory and McBeth claimed they didn't want to do anymore events for the branch. Jarone had an agenda of his own. What made him attractive to Ray was the unlikelihood that we'd get close enough to have any substantive dialogue about anything, particularly a dinner in which he was honoring himself. He wanted to send himself out right, in light of his resignation. However, after Ray's trip to Israel, he began transitioning for his permanent move to Birmingham. The last four months of planning basically fell on Jarone. When it appeared that the dinner might not come off, Ray convinced Jim and George to help Johnson by calling their committee together from the previous year, which was about six Executive Committee members. Jim and George only extended themselves to the degree that they referred Johnson back to the event planner Liz McMillion, the same planner that put on the Sinatra event. While she felt in no way obligated to the branch, McMillion made it clear that she was deeply indebted to Jim and George, and was doing it only because they asked. Still, I wasn't asked to be involved, until Ray had officially announced his intention to resign, thirty days before the dinner.

With all of these side issues in play, it became very obvious that the transition would not be smooth. There were no transition meetings with Ray to bring me up to speed on issues he had been involved with. Ray knew of meetings that he had no intention of attending--mainly because he was out of the city--yet he kept them from me. This would infuriate the faction of the community that anticipated NAACP participation, making them hostile toward any future branch involvement. Of course, dozens of phone calls were going unanswered daily because they were for Ray and he gave no instructions on forwarding the calls. As it became apparent that I was about to inherit this mess, I began soliciting the opinions of those I considered my friends and cohorts at that time. There was a vast array of opinions expressed. Very few had any idea of what was waiting in the cut with the bills piling, a do-nothing Executive Committee and, of course, an ambush in the planning. Still, there were those who felt the NAACP was a hopeless case. There were also those who felt that the right leadership would revive the branch again. Then there were those who really understood what was up and what was about to happen. They couldn't have predicted that it would happen as nasty as it did. But they had dialogue with Mallory and past branch President, Henry Dotson, who made it no secret that they did not support my leadership and gave some indication of the extent that they would be prepared to go if I decided to run for a full term as President. And, sincerely, they questioned why I would want to put myself and my family through that.

The most profound discussion I had was with my SCLC counterpart, Mark Ridley-Thomas, whom I considered a good friend at the time. Mark's civil rights advocacy started at the NAACP as the youth and college division adviser. Mark usually stayed up on NAACP issues, from a competitive perspective and because he had a better understanding of most of the inner workings of the organization. When I asked Mark if I should accept the presidency, he expressed great reservation. He quite flatly warned me that there are inherent problems in the NAACP that prohibits and restricts progressive leadership. When I tried to downplay the problems and intimated that the "niggah shit" could be resolved, Mark sternly remarked, "Anthony, the NAACP is a synonym for it. Pure madness. Every administration, Celes King's, Paul Hudson's, Dotson's, McClendon's, John's (all past Presidents of the branch) and Ray's were all plagued with bickering and dissension. Yours is not likely to be any different. I come from the NAACP. I know." As much as I wanted to refute Mark's analogy, he was correct.

Philosophical, procedural and structural problems are at the core of the branch's current existence. Not just the L.A. branch, but every branch. The NAACP branch structure is dysfunctional, to say the least. The Los Angeles branch in particular, was to understand the pettiness and bickering that submerged any residual benefit that would be generated in the community. In addition, NAACP policy is extremely prohibitive when it comes to endowing the financial interest of the branches. Conversely, there is never the capacity to amass tangible assets. The national NAACP prohibits branches owning buildings, and accumulating wealth without its approval, which you never get (at least in Los Angeles). Therefore, branches are bogged down with housing expenses with no capacity to build any equity nor any hope of reducing its rental debt service. This is very costly over time with nothing to show for it in the end.

An example of how out of step the NAACP was with this position is clearly demonstrated in Los Angeles. The Los Angeles NAACP was (at least) twice as old as any other civil rights or community organization in Los Angeles. The Urban League, SCLC, the Brotherhood Crusade, the National Council of Negro Women for instance, all own the buildings that house their organizations. With the exception of the Urban League, the Los Angeles NAACP, at one time, had a greater fundraising capacity than all the other organizations. Yet it has less to show for its fund raising, than all of the other organizations. A residual benefit submerged in antiquity.

As cumbersome as these issues are, there is nothing as ridiculous as the internal fundraising competition within the organization. There is competition for money between branches and national, between the branches and neighboring branches, between branches and the state conferences, the regional office, ACT-SO, the fair share program, and it goes on and on.

Where there was only one Urban League in Los Angeles County or one SCLC office on the West Coast, there were eleven NAACP branches in Los Angeles County, not counting Pomona and West Covina. There's a branch in Los Angeles, Watts, Compton, Beverly Hills/Hollywood, Santa Monica, Inglewood, Carson-Torrance, Pasadena, Altadena, San Fernando and Long Beach. Maybe four of those branches, Los Angeles, San Fernando Valley, Beverly Hills and Pasadena were necessary to service the required advocacy needs of Los Angeles County. The Los Angeles branch really could serve the whole area, yet all of these branches have events that competed with one another. The competition also spilled over for media attention. The bottom line is that all of the branches end up being shorted by their own organization. To try and address some of these problems is to be forced to deal with the schizophrenic-like personalities that continue to reinforce the NAACP's obsolescence.

This and a number of other factors gave Ridley-Thomas' analogy substantive credence. Mark's major point was the present mix of the Executive Committee wasn't conducive to success. It was clearly segmented with various interests and agendas, no loyalties to branch leadership, no respect for the leadership structure or direction. Clearly this was a train out of control that can only be directed at a standstill.

Still, there are those who are in it for the adrenaline rush. Subsequently, that was the difference between Mark and me. I was willing to try a system known for confusion and disarray, even though it was out of control. He felt it would be better served to try somewhere else and succeed. Why waste time and risk jeopardizing one's reputation on tested failure unwilling to change.

I appreciated Mark's position and, ultimately (as history proved), he was correct. It was foolish to maintain that there was no basis for his argument, because there was. Still, this was certainly no "win-win" situation with the L.A. NAACP. Not with the hand I was holding. It was either win-lose or lose-lose. I could win the election and some personal recognition on a few key issues, but I would still have many of the same players to hamper and even sabotage my program for change and productivity. Or, I could lose the election and lose some credibility in the fight to change what most perceived as unchangeable. Not a particularly unappealing idea.

A very remote possibility was a win-win, but I'd have to be dealt an entirely different hand to play with. I could try to eliminate some of the stagnation, bring in new players, win the election and implement a more progressive program for the NAACP branch. That wasn't so far-fetched, so I thought. Turns out--it was impossible.

While not totally dismissing the consequences of the downside of lose-lose, I played to win-win. The reality was win-lose, because it appeared that I had at least a full term in the cards. My opposition had not found anyone to run against me. What I didn't acknowledge was the extent to which my opposition would go to get me, and the type of campaign they would run to do so. In my mind, I felt they would have to throw the "baby out with the bathwater" so to speak, meaning they'd have to discredit the NAACP, the community and themselves in order to get me. In a time game of "Dare," it just didn't appear that the stakes were that high, particularly since this bunch cared so much about what they thought "white folk" would think.

Still, it was a very prophetic discussion Mark and I had, because he called it as he saw it. And I saw it, as he saw it. We just had different views about how to deal with it. Certainly we both saw very distinct outcomes to this "no-win" situation. Neither of us, however, could anticipate that my ascension to President would initiate what would be termed by many as one of Los Angeles' most public personifications of the term "niggah shit," in this Black communities' history.

* * *

9

Presiding Over Pretenders

"Most Blacks are consumed in a vacuum of non-commitment that we like to refer to as 'doing our own thing,' which most times translates to 'doing nothing, but pretend that it is something.' We've become a race of pretenders. You have to call out the hypocrite, before they make a hypocrite out of you."

- Anthony Essex
Reception Speech, June 1988

June 1, 1988, is the day I took over the presidency of the branch. Inheriting the branch leadership felt more like a beast of burden than a blessing. Instead of looking at how the branch needed to evolve, I was looking at over $30,000 in branch debt, a year's membership dues that hadn't been turned into the national office, a postponed dinner, five months of unanswered mail and messages, virtually inactive Executive and branch committees, and an impending plot to have me seceded as President in the December branch elections. Not to mention that both my business and personal life were showing signs of deterioration, largely due to lack of attention, because of my extensive NAACP involvement as first Vice President. Now, as President, I would carry twice as much responsibility and the personalities that go along with it.

Given this predicament, I made two decisions that I would carry through, come hell or high water: The first decision was to bring in some new faces with energy and expertise. This would allow the branch committees to become activated and take productive roles in branch projects. Out of the standing and ad hoc committees of the branch, only three (Education, Women's Auxiliary and the Dinner Committee) were active. The Political Action Committee was partially active. The others were dead committees, meaning they either had no members, or just had the committee chair. This inactivity could be attributed to a number of reasons, but were largely due to two factors: age and incompetence. This meant that either the members did not have the inclination to carry out the work, or they didn't know how to carry out the work. This was not exclusive to age. However, that was the way my opposition would eventually represent this move.

The Los Angeles branch had too much dead weight. Many of them were seniors who either could not, or would not do the work. This was not to say that all of the seniors were not productive. In fact, our most productive members were two senior citizens, Kathryn Anderson and Cash Black. Ms. Anderson was a member of Second Baptist Church, who had controlled the L.A. NAACP for over four decades and had routinely brought in 500 memberships or more a year. Mr. Black was a member of another local Baptist church and brought in about 250 members a year. They were the thrust of any membership activity the branch had. The committee had no chairperson. However, they were only two of forty, half of whom were seniors who came to meetings and dozed. It sounds hard but it was true.

Executive Committee meetings were more teaching sessions than planning sessions. Hardly anyone wanted to do any work, other than for high profile stuff, where they could get a free ticket, by being on the committee. Real work was limited to a few. Many NAACPers were just good common folk, either looking to just "be involved" (heightened their community profile) or were selected by their church to be involved with the branch; largely because of the membership the churches hold in the branch or due to the relationship the branch has with the church pastor. Many of the churches hold their best expertise for themselves (internal development) and their church programs, or they allow involvement based on the fact that the person's been doing it forever.

The branch had too many critical activities not to have sharp and directed analysis, irrespective of age, in its operational ranks. My strategy was to approach the seniors first; assess their interest level and skill capabilities, then, do the same thing with the non-productive younger members. The same strategies many major corporations use to streamline its operations through attrition of its senior workers; often offering an incentive to voluntarily step aside. The incentive here was branch productivity. I knew I couldn't do it all myself.

The second decision I was staunchly committed to was hiring a paid executive director for the branch. This had been part of a discussion that every President has had since I'd been with the branch. It is absolutely crazy for the NAACP's larger branches not to have a paid "lead" executive. It allows for more accountability, a greater focus for programs, a greater continuity in change of administrations, a greater follow-through capability, a greater fundraising capacity, and on and on. It is impossible to even think that a volunteer NAACP branch President, even with a small administrative stipend, can compete with full-time paid executives from the Urban League, SCLC, Brotherhood Crusade, ACLU, NAACP Legal Defense Fund, and any other community groups smart enough to recognize the most effective management for community-based non-profits are fully trained, highly educated full-time, paid staff.

The greatest task for a NAACP branch President is to be everywhere at one time. Whether it is at community functions, hearings, handling crises, or in policy meetings with public-and private-sector organizations, it requires extended blocks of time, administrative follow-up, hours of reading, inter organizational briefings and strategy meetings, and expenditure of funds to get where you need to be or take somebody to eat (or drink). No matter how organized you think you are, there's not enough hours in the day to handle a full-time advocacy organization and make a living, too.

There is a perception that public service positions are glamorous and powerful. They can be at times, but for that five-second sound bite, or that picture in the paper, you put in hours and hours of work, running from one issue to the next, being at meetings and receptions, trying not to slight supporters or potential supporters. You also take the brunt of criticisms from the ranks. All the time you are trying to be everything to everybody when it is just not possible.

As much as, a John Mack of the Urban League, Mark Ridley-Thomas, then of the SCLC, Danny Bakewell of the Brotherhood Crusade and even Ben Hooks, the Executive Director (now the President/CEO) of the National NAACP may love our people and love advocacy work, they were in it, because they were paid to do it. They were paid to attend meetings, paid to organize, paid to advocate, paid to fund raise and paid to produce results. The advocacy is their primary livelihood, meaning everything else they do comes after their work. And none of them advocate for free. I repeat. None of them do this work strictly for the love of it, or for the rightness of it. Some might say they would do it for free, but actions speak louder than words. When it comes down to it, one's interest is where his paycheck is.

Everybody recognizes this except the NAACP, who expects their branch Presidents to advocate on a full time basis, for free. I was committed to bringing this "paid advocate" point of view to the L.A. branch, the last organization in this community yet to realize this. If the NAACP was to succeed in Los Angeles, it had to be competitive. The only way for the branch to be competitive was for it to have a solid brain trust and a full-time executive to carry out the plan. I sincerely felt that I needed new talent. I lacked the team to carry it off. With the opposition that I faced and without a program and the loyalties of the people charged to run it, success in my tenure would never come off.

In my first Executive Committee meeting as President, I discussed in my report how I perceived the status of the branch, and many of the members concurred. I then asked for permission to hire an executive director to manage the day-to-day operations of the branch and facilitate key cases. This person would also fund raise to pay for his salary. Henry Dotson, a past branch President who had been absent most of the year, was now back in the fold to "watch Anthony." He raised issue with hiring a director and felt I should do the work. I flatly told him that it was unreasonable for him or anyone else to even expect me to do it. Dotson's position was that everyone else had done it. My response was that no one that I remember had done it successfully, pointing out the condition of the branch for the past five or six years. I intimated that maybe this was part of the problem and that the branch or its President would never be successful, as long as it relied on volunteers for full-time advocacy work.

My position was quite clear. I was not going to do this work without a paid executive. Simple as that. The case I made was strong enough for the committee to approve the hiring of an executive, only if I could raise the money to hire one.

I then introduced my plan to have a "Stop the Madness (violence)" concert at the Los Angeles Memorial Coliseum. Dotson again jumped to ask whether the branch could pull off such an event, what the liability would be, how would the branch be paid off, and who else would be paid. Basically, he was trying to do more to confuse the issue than clarify it. I told them I would bring a written outline to the next meeting. Then I asked for the resignation of every branch standing and ad-hoc committee chairperson. It was my intent to re- appoint those who were functioning, and those who were not, and replace them with new players. I explained to them that it was the only way I could reactivate the committee system.

Later, the constitutionality of such a move would be questioned, but not challenged. I had the right to ask them to resign. Whether I had the right to replace them without Executive Committee approval was another story. Still the committee, not knowing what I had in mind, reluctantly approved. Finally, the last issue discussed was the postponed dinner. Jarone Johnson had been left holding the bag on the dinner. He was cussing Jim and George left and right, and as much as he hated to, Jarone knew he had to work directly with me as the new President to even pull this off. The dinner was pushed back because of a lack of ticket sales. Ray tried to run it from Alabama, and told Jarone not to inform me about anything. So I knew it was postponed two days before they decided to do it, a week before the actual dinner. Some of the Executive Committee never knew it was canceled until they heard it at this meeting.

Two issues had to be dealt with: One, the dinner needed to be supported by having members sell tickets and make cold calls from lists provided by the event planner. The dinner was rescheduled for June 15, which was less than three weeks away. Two, we had to seek money from the corporation, because the branch was strapped for cash. Ray left without even resolving the branch's $30,000 in delinquent debts. Most was due at the time he initially requested money from the CEDC three months earlier. On two occasions prior to my becoming President, the Executive Committee instructed Jim McBeth to "get with the President" and come to some agreement on money.

After the meeting that Ray walked out on, much of the CEDC's reluctance was centered on what they perceived as my refusal to acknowledge the branch's obligation to any funds the corporation would lend the branch. Conversely, they chose to play a stall game that made it seem like we "just couldn't get together" when, in fact, there was little or no effort to get together. The request was initially made to provide a gap loan or an interim capital until the dinner. As a result, the CEDC was able to successfully delay disbursing any money.

Now with the dinner postponed, and the debts (payroll, taxes and rent) threatening to close the branch, the corporation issue had now come to a head. McBeth stated that they did not intend to lend to the branch, without a written agreement signed to repay CEDC. The committee agreed to sign an agreement and, as the President, instructed me to comply. The Executive Committee also instructed to get it done after the meeting, so as to avoid any further delays.

With all the major business completed, the meeting was adjourned. McBeth said he had to get with the rest of the board members at a convenient time to discuss this "loan" as he termed it. We met a few days later with Dotson, McBeth, Mallory and the branch's treasurer, Dr. Arista Chaney. Although McBeth was supposed to be the chairman, it always appeared that he gave his brains to Mallory. When McBeth talked, Mallory's mouth moved. Mallory, who was now CEDC's mouthpiece, wanted to see all bills to decide which ones would be paid and which ones would not. Dotson chimed in that they felt this was the most responsible way to look after the corporation's money. Dr. Chaney lit into him and said, "Look Dotson, don't put us through this. Don't tell me about being responsible when you let $89,000 sit up in an interest-free account for over a year. Was that responsible, Henry? I've never seen a niggah so dumb in my life."

What Dr. Chaney was referring to was a report that McBeth gave earlier in the year, when it was discovered that the account that the CEDC had set up was "supposedly" non-interest bearing. I say supposedly, because the account was set up in an escrow trust account -- a holding account. Dr. Chaney, who was also a sharp real estate professional, knew that interest is paid on many trust accounts, not to the account but to individuals who control the accounts as incentives to keep the accounts at a particular bank. The interest never showed up on the accounts or bank statements.

When the Executive Committee heard this report they were literally in shock. The room was that quiet. McBeth had, heretofore, been so secretive about the CEDC records and did not want to produce reports. He told us to go to the CPA's office, if we had questions. This eliminated collective discussion and scrutiny of CEDC's activities. On one occasion, McBeth brought "the CPA" to the meeting specifically at the request of the members who were tired of getting the runaround on questions about the money. Now it appeared awfully strange that an attorney (two attorneys if you included Ray), a contractor, a CPA, and Dotson, who always queried the branch on fiscal accountability, would forfeit over $7,000 in interest on a non-profit, fundraising account. It made no sense at all, yet that's what we were being told.

So, after Dr. Chaney recalled that discussion, Dotson had nothing else to say for the rest of the meeting. While Dr. Chaney was pulling up records, Mallory, McBeth, Dotson and I met in the President's office to discuss the terms of this so-called loan. During the course of the discussion, Mallory felt it necessary to give me, in his own little punk way, his perspective on how Jews work together, even though they hate each other, and how we allow little things to prevent us from doing things. Then he told me how this little thing between us was now getting personal, and how he didn't want to wake up in the morning thinking about me, which he was now doing. He backed up right there to let me know it wouldn't be on the level of a physical fight, but something much more permanent. I immediately perceived this as a threat. I looked at him and told him that he was responsible for the very thing he was just preaching about and that if he wasn't such a hypocrite, in trying to force the dinner down our throats the way he did, we wouldn't be having this discussion. I also told him it could be dangerous for him to threaten me, which he immediately denied.

I perceived this as his way of letting me know that they had something in store for me. While I already knew about his plot and had it on tape, his comments were making this situation very explosive. By this time, Dr. Chaney had come in with the bills, which were outrageous. They included a $1,000 three-month old portable phone bill for Ray's car phone, where he made frequent calls to Birmingham, Alabama, a copier machine contract Ray had signed authorizing a $700 a month payment for three years, and hundreds of dollars in bills to a secretarial service for presumably branch correspondence. The branch already had three employees that could send out letters. Yet, it was spent under the President's administrative budget. These were just a few of the bills that were left for us to deal with. We ended up agreeing on the payroll, the back taxes, the rent and the in-house phones, which totaled $15,000. Now all that was left was for them to cut the check. McBeth said the agreement would be ready in a few days.

When the agreement was dropped off at the branch it had some clauses relating to the time of repayment, which were not supposed to be in it. They also snuck a clause in to try to make me personally liable for repayment of the loan. I crossed out all of the inappropriate wording, signed the agreement and had Ernestine call them to pick it up. They, of course, did not agree with my changes, which left the issue of getting a loan from CEDC unresolved until the agreement's wording could be resolved. This required another meeting, of course, and they didn't know when they would be available again. Chump games being played by a bunch of punk lames.

We were in the second week of June. The dinner was in another week and a half. I also had other planned events in the works. I began to concentrate on the dinner. By this time, Jarone Johnson was looking for a friend anywhere he could find one.

The honorees for the 1989 Roy Wilkins Dinner were Ed McMahon, Lou Rawls and Marilyn McCoo for the Life Achievement Award, Los Angeles Councilman Gilbert Lindsay for the W.E.B. DuBois Humanitarian Award, Los Angeles Assistant Police Chief Jess Brewer for the Judge Thomas L. Griffith Legal Award and Mrs. (Thomas) Jannetta Kilgore for the Volunteer Award. Roy Wilkins was back on the cover of the program (unlike the year before). The J.T. McDonald Corporate Award went to NBC (a tie-in to Ed McMahon), 100 Black Men of Los Angeles and Father Paul Banet of St. Bridget Catholic Church received the Community Achievement Awards. Usually, the branch had given an award at the President's discretion called, "The President's Award." This year, it was the best kept secret of the dinner. Why? Because Ray had decided to give his President's Award to himself, and prior to the dinner's postponement, he expected to receive it in his grand finale exit.

After two weeks of feverish soliciting and follow-up, we managed to get a decent turnout. The dinner went off with a few hitches, but we all managed to be cordial to each other for a night. The dinner netted over $60,000, enough to pay most of the back debt. But it was nowhere near enough to cover the year's upcoming operations, national's portion of memberships for the last nine months, and to hire a paid executive director. I felt confident that we had the ability to raise more money with the person I was looking to hire as executive director.

Harold Webb was a former President of the Pomona NAACP, and had been very active in the Pomona area. He had waged a discrimination fight against the California State University system and won. Webb was a 20- year NAACPer in his late 40s, a visionary when it came to advocacy. We hit it off real well. He understood the organization and was pretty well liked throughout the region. Webb understood the need to revitalize the organization. Moreover, he was a NAACP President before, and recognized that volunteering was a compromised advocacy practiced the way the NAACP branch is forced to deal with it. However, if you take the advocacy seriously, then you don't have time to do anything else, which meant your livelihood suffered. Webb had been on the other side of that fence, and had made the choice to become a full-time paid advocate, versus a part-time (or full-time) volunteer. He was a consultant to the branch during the dinner. I told him that we would hire him after we returned from the convention. It was my intent to get national to wait on some of its money, and hire Harold with a fundraising clause in his contract that would allow him to raise his salary. He agreed to that, and we had a deal. Webb even agreed to come on a month earlier to help organize the branch office. Organizing wasn't the issue, restructuring was. The office currently had three staff: one office manager, a clerical staff and an administrative assistant. However, other than answering phones and opening mail, it was real hard to discern what else the staff did.

In trying to send out correspondence to muster support for the branch, I gave Ernestine three letters to send out immediately. It took five days to get the final drafts back. Now I knew why Ray had a secretarial service. So what did Ernestine do all day? Did she supervise staff or attend meetings? This troubled me. None of the staff was computer literate, except the administrative assistant, Ms. Pigler, but only to the extent that she could input memberships. In terms of clerical skills, the newest staff person, Wanda Hines, was most efficient. However, they only let her answer phones and stuff envelopes. Clearly, the branch wasn't getting the maximum use out of its staff. I asked Harold to assess the situation for me and give me his opinion.

After about two weeks he basically told me, "She talks on the phone all day, leaves the office from time to time, comes back and gets back on the phone. I can't really see anything that she does that the clerical staff can't do." I asked him how he got along with her and he said fine. I said, "Good, because when you come on staff, she is your problem. You'll be accountable for her performance and she'll have to be accountable to you." Webb didn't have a problem with that. He felt he could bring Ernestine around, or so he thought. Ernestine resented him being there much less having to report to him. She didn't make it very easy for Harold.

In the meantime, I was filling committee vacancies. One of the first that I filled was the personnel committee chair, with a sister named Janice Carter, an executive from California First Bank (now Union Bank). I immediately asked her to develop job descriptions and scopes of work responsibility for all positions in the branch. I asked her to please have them by our August Executive Committee meeting (that was the third week in June). I told Harold to keep an eye on things, and we'd deal with them after the convention.

I was still trying to muster community support for the branch. That was extremely difficult and expensive. Los Angeles is a funny place. Advocacy, in many regards, is non-existent. People rarely step out front to change things. They only react to things, and not in a very aggressive manner. In particular, mainstream Negroes don't want to do anything until they know others are participating. As I took people to lunch to ask for branch support, they always asked: "Who else you got?" "What are they doing?" The time and money it took to get around to a few people made me realize that I'd have to get them all in one room or it wouldn't work. I touched bases with a couple of my corporate friends, and asked them if they'd be interested in underwriting a reception to re-introduce the branch and the goals of this administration. One of them, a longtime supporter of the branch stated they'd be happy to do it. We immediately moved to start planning the reception for 350 people, at the Wilshire Hyatt. We sent out 500 invitations. Dr. Chaney cut the check, at my request, based on my commitment from the sponsor.

A week before the reception, the sponsor called me back and said that they wanted to shift the money to host a reception at the national convention. I told her no problem; we'd work it out. Since we just had the dinner, we could cover the check. But now it posed another problem. Because the reception was supposed to be underwritten, advancing the money was not a real issue. However, now the branch was paying for it, and I hadn't sought the finance committee's approval or branch policy for expending funds. I couldn't plead ignorance, as my two predecessors did on many occasions, because it was I who formulated the policy. I had been the foremost advocate about fiscal compliance. I can't say what John (McDonald) did, because we only found his debt after he died. Ray had this real slick way of bringing report requests for expenditure after the money had been spent. Even in finance committee meetings bills would be presented for payment that had no prior approval, but the expenditure was already made. The branch never had proper accounting of its money.

With the help of another executive member, Mr. Daley, and Henry Dotson, and the assistant treasurer, who never knew what the hell was going on until the Executive Committee meetings, we put a budget and invoice process together. It restricted all expenditures to what was in the budget, with a limit of $300. All requests had to be requisitioned and approved. Ray still found a way to work around it in some instances, but for the most part, the system proved effective. Now I was in a "catch 22" with the system I helped create. However, it would be perceived that I didn't see it as a major problem as long as the money was replenished immediately. Moreover, I saw this effort as critical to making the branch credible again in the eyes of the community. The reception was for the benefit of the branch, period.

One of the things that had become evident to me, in this transition, was that I was being watched very closely. I was being watched by those who expected me to take an aggressive leadership posture that would take the branch out of a mindset filled with uncertainty and indecision, as well as, those seeking to help me fail. I knew this, but I wasn't going to be a sittin' duck for my enemies. Not that I intended to try and circumvent NAACP procedure, but if something happened that prohibited procedure from being followed to the letter of the law, I wasn't going to sweat it. I felt I had no other choice, but to change the image of the branch and reach out for new blood. The situation wasn't going to change by itself.

* * *

In the meantime, my opposition in the branch was at work looking for people to challenge me for the presidency. As is the case in many organizations, rumors fly like wildfire when a challenge is evident. One thing Dotson, Mallory and McBeth let me and everyone else they came in contact with know for sure, was that I would not run unopposed. So who they would run became the big question. In talking to people they were trying to recruit to support their power move, they hadn't identified anybody to run. With less than five months left before the election, it was real obvious that they weren't getting the bites they had hoped. However, several names were being mentioned.

The first name thrown around was Margerite Archie-Hudson, a very brilliant sister who was very pro-Black and was recently defeated in her effort to be re-elected to the Los Angeles Community College Board of Trustees. Ms. Archie-Hudson, who since has become President of Talledega College, had the exposure and experience, and had demonstrated herself as a skillful issues activist, debater and negotiator, as a participant on a local public affairs show. However, it was said she didn't have an interest in jumping in the middle of what she perceived to be a family fight. Plus, she had some other options that she was pursuing, including a possible run for state office (she was elected to the state assembly and served two successful terms). It was "no-go" as far as she was concerned. The other name most frequently mentioned was Melanie Lomax. As the story was being relayed to me, we couldn't help but chuckle. The same group that ran Melanie out of the organization was now so desperate that they considered asking her to return. Who would they send to ask her? Mallory, the person who urged Ray to replace her on the Fair Share committee? Dotson? The person probably most critical of Melanie (behind Ray), while she was in the branch, and who was used to co-sign every policy move Ray made to censor her. Not only did they not have the right person to approach her, but she would have been a tough sell to the same Executive Committee, after the job they did on her a couple years back. Approaching her certainly posed a very interesting dilemma.

There was talk of Mallory running, or Dotson coming back to run against me. Neither gave me any reason for concern, because neither had been very active in local issues. Dotson had been out of the fold for most of the year, and both were part of the Sinatra compromise and the corporation that was used to hide part of the proceeds.

Mallory was a behind-the-scenes operator with a liking to hidden hand acts. He didn't have the balls to come up front in such an obvious manner. Plus, it would have brought his premeditated opposition of my candidacy into the light. Too easy a hit. I would have welcomed an opportunity to discuss the NAACP obsolescence. Those were the only candidates being discussed at the time.

While they tried to figure it out, I began to move ahead with plans to implement some of the other projects to bring the branch greater notoriety. I felt it needed widespread attention, and left the political speculation to those who wanted to deal in conjecture. New faces in the branch was priority number one.

Over 400 people attended the reception. Two hundred and ten of them renewed or purchased memberships at $25 or more. We collected over $4,800, which was more than enough to pay for the reception. More importantly, there was a spirit of unity in the people who attended. We invited a select group of ministers, corporate and business leaders, heads of organizations and community leaders. Some members of the Executive Committee were ecstatic about the reception the branch had received. Many known skeptics of the NAACP were in the room, not so much to see what had changed, but to see what support this new President could pull in. Dotson and some of the other opposers of my presidency stood in the back of the room, chagrined at the show of support. As I walked around the room thanking people for showing up, I overheard a couple of them actually taking credit for the event. "Yeah, we're trying to do some things, change our public perception, bring in some new blood." I just shook my head and moved on. When it came time to start the program, a few dignitaries said a few words. Celes King, a former President, and now the state chairman of CORE, said some very complimentary things. A few of the elected officials sent letters and commendations of congratulations.

When the time came for me to give comments, I didn't waste the opportunity. With prepared remarks, I spoke about 35 minutes about the stark realities about life in Los Angeles: police harassment, the economic disparities of Blacks receiving contracts and business opportunities in their community, Blacks losing jobs to the Hispanic population parity factor, gang violence and a host of other issues. Then I dealt with the purpose of my calling them all together: our own self-betrayal. I talked about how Blacks in Los Angeles had allowed themselves to be effectively removed from determining their own agendas, by subjugating their right to advocate. "Black advocacy," I said, "was outdated in philosophy and strategy, and Black folk, by and large, had abdicated any responsibility for advancing quality of life issues in a visibly determinative manner." I illustrated several examples of how Blacks had become "low key" or "invisible" in their advocacy, largely under the guise of doing their own thing.

Oftentimes, advocacy meant writing a check to the NAACP, UNCF or giving at the office to the United Way, when the United Way rarely gives to us. I know most in the room knew what I was talking about, because over half of the room started witnessing, while the other half were clearing their throats. I talked about the Blacks who have achieved or made money because of the advocacy, but couldn't find time to support the advocacy.

That about covered everybody else in the room. I concluded with thoughts on how we, as a people, no longer paved our way, so we could no longer pave the way for others, or talk about what others have done or are doing to us because of our own hypocrisy. We could no longer afford to pretend that we were on post, when we were really asleep at the switch. I stated that we had every responsibility to fulfill an active commitment to our advancement as our forefathers had in their advancement. I asked them forthrightly why should we expect to do anything less for our children, than our grandfathers and fathers did for us. Then I brought the hook and asked them who would give the NAACP a second chance. A chance to give yourselves, our community, and children another chance to have opportunities that we now enjoy, but are disappearing fast. Finally, I asked who would be willing to help with TIME and/or MONEY, to give the old ship some new life. By the time I finished, the branch had some very influential converted supporters. We received over fifty new volunteers for committee work, 12 commitments for major sponsorship for next year's dinner, and five heavy players for the convention to be held in Los Angeles the next summer.

The only thing that spread faster than the spirit in the room was the way the spirit had spread to the streets. People began to hear all over how there was "a new day in the NAACP." Most met the news with skepticism, saying that they'd wait and see if what they perceived was the new day taking effect. Then again, that's Black folk. We never met a bandwagon we didn't like, or couldn't catch. From the Black bourgeois to the Black grassroots, we had the full spectrum of the Black social stratosphere involved with getting back in the branch's advocacy. The motivations varied from "doing the socially responsible thing" to "if they're Black enough to let the Blackest brother we know lead, then I'm with it." Most let me know that I was what the NAACP and the community needed at that time. A true "new day" advocate in our oldest, most obsolete advocacy organization.

That was major buying power for everybody, and the least common denominator for so many groups of diverse interests and agendas. Within the first 90 days of my presidency, over 3,000 members would join or rejoin. The membership, which was down under 2,000, would top 5,000 for the first time since John died (four years earlier). Before my term would end, membership would top 8,000 (2,200 brought in from the election process). Much of this activity was due to the fact that I held a reception to encourage the Los Angeles community to give the NAACP another look. And they did. I left for the national convention on a real high. I felt that there was little that could stop us, once we had the appropriate infrastructure in place. I went to this convention committee to achieve one goal: secure authorization for a paid executive director to manage this transition and growth.

* * *

The 1988 convention was in Washington, D.C. I had decided that I would make a mini vacation of it and go down to Atlanta afterward, for the Democratic Convention. Dotson and the bunch made sure I paid for the Atlanta leg of the ticket, after the objections I had raised on Ray the year before.

If you've never been to a NAACP convention, you have to attend one to know the experience. It's unlike anything you'll ever see. I had attended ones in Dallas and New York and thought I'd be kind of used to the various elements. Not so. If I'd try to describe one, I'd describe it as part church revival, part protest rally, part shopping exhibit, part chippie chase (with the parties and receptions every night) and part seminar. There are meetings, caucuses, receptions and convention events all convening at the same time. Half are exclusive to most of the many board members and dignitaries attending the conference. If you don't know someone to get you in, a delegate can very easily spend the week sitting in the lobby or walking the exhibit hall.

What is most peculiar about a NAACP convention is how the organization chooses to represent itself as the choice of the common person, while its hierarchy spends the week trying to separate themselves from the common NAACPer. First, there are many badges or buttons that identify you as someone everybody else should know. This entitles you preferred seating at all events, preferred entry to exclusive receptions and other forms of recognition. Then there are the decadent receptions. Thousands of dollars are spent on food and liquor that could be put into the organization or into branch communities. Most of these dollars were specifically intended to profile "socially responsible" corporations.

Of course, these conventions are where the tobacco and liquor companies are king. The idea is to get your product out there, which they do. With free booze and cigarettes flowing from everywhere including the exhibit hall, maintaining sobriety is a real achievement. These are some of the more obvious experiences one sees at an NAACP convention.

However, once one gets past the glitz, glamour and perpetual confusion, the more powerful and long-lasting impressions of the conference take over. The impressions I'm talking about are the who's who from every walk of life who return "home" to pay homage to this country's greatest civil rights legacy. It's a pilgrimage, of sorts, that everyone should experience at least once, where Black elected officials, judges, lawyers, educators, entertainers, athletes and other Black achievers, by their mere presence, acknowledge that many of their opportunities to achieve came largely from the work of the NAACP. Regardless of how relevant or obsolete one perceives the NAACP to be now, its historical accomplishments can never be denied, nor diminished. The emotional impact of one who is forced to reflect what Black life may have been like, if not for the NAACP, is very dramatic. For that reason, and that reason alone, no Black ever gets "too big" to make "the homecoming" when called or inclined to do so. To a large extent, this is why many of the NAACP's other nuances may be largely overlooked. Just an opportunity to interface with history and legacies of the past and present, in most cases, is worth the trip.

Usually, opening night of the convention is when then executive director Ben Hooks would give his "State of the NAACP" address. Press from all over the world cover the speech. The public is usually invited to increase attendance for the evening. Not that they really need it, with 15,000 delegates from over 2,200 branches. After the first day's opening program (Hooks' speech), they have what is called a membership laydown. It's a spinoff from church laydowns, where branches throughout the nation come up to the podium and present checks to Hooks for memberships sold prior to the convention. Los Angeles has always done well in the membership laydown having won it twice in three years prior to 1988. We would win it again in 1988. I took almost $35,000 to Washington, D.C. and delivered $25,000 in membership fees (a portion of them back dated from memberships sold in the first six months of the year, but never sent in). The other $10,000 was the portion of the Roy Wilkins dinner the branch had agreed to give to national, as the fundraising tax.

The director of branch services, William Penn, was awaiting my arrival. With Los Angeles not being one of his favorite branches, he had threatened to take action against the branch for failure to remit membership fees, including not allowing us to participate in the conference. Prior to coming to the NAACP, Penn was a career military person. His demeanor comes off as brash and cold as a fish, although it initially appeared unintentional. Over time you realize he just had a no nonsense approach about things. It turned out that Penn had a long history with the Los Angeles branch, which predated my involvement. During the John McDonald administration, Penn had ordered an audit of the branch because of news releases that stated that Los Angeles had 15,000 members, when the national office never had record of more than 10,000. At that time he called out organizational improprieties which included: Los Angeles issuing its own membership cards, its expenditure process, its solicitation of corporate accounts committed to national, not reporting in-kind contributions, and not advancing national its proportionate share of in-kind contributions. Then there was national's perception that the Los Angeles branch was flamboyant "showboats." National felt that L.A.'s showboating nature often contributed to its inability to pay its national money on time, whether it was the membership money or the fundraising tax. It had come down to many of the national's staff having contempt for L.A. If you were from Los Angeles, you were categorized as "off centered" and viewed with suspicion. Suspicion was drawn from the East, South and Midwest members that Los Angeles was in it more for the "show," rather than for the advocacy. And if it wasn't entertainment-related, L.A. wasn't to be taken seriously. It wasn't so much a California thing. Even the San Francisco branch was viewed in an entirely different light than L.A. The "Bay Area" branch was viewed as proactive and engaging as far as the advocacy went. It was an "L.A." thing, when it came to the "showboat" label. In fact, the general perception was, as one national staff person once put it, "All them niggahs from L.A. are crazy." Not understanding most of this bias before, I went prepared to meet Penn with a different objectivity. Anytime Penn could "put it to" L.A., he would. And did.

When I met Penn, his attitude was hostile, almost sarcastic, like he expected some type of excuse or "line" about not having the money, because of some major catastrophe. Once I demonstrated that I did have the money, he became less cynical. He even inquired about the status of the branch, in light of Ray's resignation. This was the opportunity when I advanced the subject of an executive director for the branch. Penn told me only four branches in the country had a director, and that the process had to be approved by his office. I proceeded to give him an analysis of the branch's activities and its need to have continuity on advocacy issues that the branch was dealing with. I told him who we had in mind for the position, and the agreement that the Executive Committee made. I also referred to the director having six months to raise his or her salary, and my finding the money to hire him or her. Penn then asked me if I had found the money. I told him, "Well, yes and no." I told Penn that the branch had forwarded a payment on the national fundraising tax for the dinner we had. We really needed the money to hire a director. At that point, I showed him the check for $10,000. I could tell by Penn's face that this was totally unexpected -the additional money and the request. Penn asked, "Is the branch in debt now?" I told him that most of the pressing debt had been cleared. He said, "I can't make a decision on a paid executive without a request. Go back, make the request in writing and put in all the specifics regarding salaries, job description, etc. I'll make a decision as soon as I receive it."

I asked him, "What about the money?"

"Put in a request that you want to use part of the fundraising tax to pay for this executive. We'll also make a decision on both at that time. For now, you can hold the check," Penn stated.

I breathed a sigh of relief. This Penn guy wasn't so unreasonable, I thought at the time. I thought we had even established "a little rapport" with each other. This whole scenario would later be misrepresented. I actually felt that national was trying to help L.A. get back on track. Surprisingly enough, as I left the meeting, who would I see standing in the hotel lobby, but our immediate past branch President, Ray Johnson. We spoke and he asked me what was going on in the branch, as if he didn't already know. He probably could care less. I started to tell him it was hard to tell from under all the shit he left me. But I said, "Everything's moving."

He said, "Good," as if he knew what I was really thinking. He went on to explain that he was there to discuss something with Hooks and would only be there for a couple of days. I nodded. This would be the last conversation I would have with Ray Johnson Jr.

I spent the rest of the convention trying to become better acquainted with some of my Executive Committee members who made the trip. One of the national board members from our branch spent an evening trying to teach me the different quality levels of liquor. The branch sponsored a very nice reception in a local D.C. club that was well attended. During the period in which we were putting lists together, I noticed Ernestine Peters and Ray Johnson huddling with one of our Executive Committee members named Joe Duff. I really didn't pay much attention to them, other than the fact that they all stopped talking as I passed, and Ray had this shit-eating look on his face. It was deja vu for me. Three and a half years earlier, Ray told me that he would never let Melanie be President. When Melanie walked by, he looked like he saw a ghost and damned near swallowed his tongue. As I walked by I recognized that same look. But given the way Ray left me out of the loop, knowing he was leaving, I knew he really wasn't with me. Still I really didn't tie Joe into their plan, at that time. I went on about my business and interfaced with other attendees.

The rest of the week was somewhat uneventful, except for the greatest memory I'll ever have of an NAACP convention. It had to do with the 1988 democratic nominee Michael Dukakis' selection of Vice Presidential candidate during the convention. Dukakis, on the day prior to making an appearance at the convention, selected Texas Senator Lloyd Bentsen as his running mate. This was after Jesse Jackson had garnered the second most votes in the democratic primaries, and registered more voters than all the other democratic candidates combined. His performance had surprised everybody. Jackson earned the right to be on the ticket. Yet, it appeared to be a bigger slap in the face to reject Jesse just prior to speaking to the largest civil rights group in the country. Many delegates felt it was an insult, and felt that Dukakis should not be invited to the convention. I was one. There wasn't anything Dukakis could say to me that would change my perspective of Jesse deserving to be on his ticket and, to a greater extent, Blacks being disrespected again by the Democrats.

Still, Dukakis was allowed to come, and he brought Bentsen with him. Prior to Dukakis' arrival, every time his name was mentioned, he was booed. Hooks tried to head off this disdain by saying that we should be hospitable to our guest and not mistreat one invited to our home. Black folk didn't want to hear any of that. Hell, we were hurt. We'd been screwed again. They made Jesse jump through every hoop they could think of, and a few we probably didn't see.

The excuse was Jesse wasn't a team player. Jesse became the commensurate team Democrat. They said Jesse only had a Black following. Jesse developed a multiracial coalition of disenfranchised who came together on a "common ground" theme, expanding the party's appeal. They said Jesse couldn't bring anything to the table. Jesse registered over a million new voters. Jesse brought more to the table than everybody else in the race. Then they said Jesse wasn't "qualified" to be Vice President. A throw back to the old subjective tests that prohibited Blacks from advancing.

How qualified do you have to be to be Vice President? They immediately pointed to Jesse's lack of experience in public office. Jesse countered with the fact that he had more foreign affairs experience, more domestic affairs experience, and more race-relations experience, than anybody in the race.

What was most apparent to Blacks was that it never appeared that the party intended to do right by Jesse. We, as a politically naive race of people, just assumed America had moved past the overt "double cross." Yet, this was as blatant a slight as Blacks had seen in awhile. This was an opportunity to voice our hurt and disapproval on a national stage, and Hooks wanted us to be polite. Could you imagine this same request being made of the rank-and-file UAW delegates, or a disgruntled shareholders meeting of General Motors? I don't think so.

When Dukakis appeared, he received a very cold reception. Halfway through his speech, some of the delegates started to boo. Hooks stood up and implied that the audience was planted with agents who were trying to embarrass the NAACP. Hell, there wasn't anybody else in the room but NAACPers? Why did we have to be agents for expressing our displeasure? The NAACP embarrassed itself when it let Dukakis try to rationalize the biggest insult, Black people had experienced, since Reagan offered tax incentives to colleges who eliminated affirmative action based admission. But then Reagan was Reagan. Dukakis professed to be a Democrat, who often represent themselves as the party of fairness and compassion.

Now that he showed that he, nor the Democratic Party were what they said they were, he needed to be booed out of the convention. If our leaders couldn't understand the frustrations of the rank-and-file, then something was seriously wrong. But to label your rank-and-file as "agents," speaks directly to how out of step the national sentiment is with the field sentiment. I'll never forget this experience, or the feeling of members being reprimanded for a very heartfelt expression of disappointment. I still booed my ass off. The next night Jesse Jackson appeared before the convention. He received a hero's welcome.

Regardless of what you want to say about Jesse, he had put America's political system to the test, and had exposed its insincerity. It was one of the most emotional civil rights gatherings since the movement's heyday. Jesse cried that night, while giving his address, and there were tears throughout the audience. We all cried a little bit that night (inside and outwardly). The sense of betrayal filled the auditorium. Jesse's theme was: "Was he qualified." I was never so proud of Jesse Jackson, or to be Black in America, than I was that night. But most of all, I had a great appreciation for the movement and the history that was made over the past few months. There was no place else for a civil rights advocate to be. It was only fitting that the NAACP be the national stage in which this piece of history would be played out.

I left Washington D.C. for the Democratic Convention in Atlanta and had a very exciting, eventful week. At every turn,

Jackson delegates were passing out buttons that stated: "WE WILL NOT BE TAKEN FOR GRANTED," creating a sense of confrontation, be it real or imagined. My kind of advocacy.

The Atlanta convention was interesting for a variety of reasons. The discussion among many conventioneers was the fact that the Democratic Party, just 24 years earlier, had refused to seat Fanny Lou Hamer and Black delegates at their 1964 convention in Atlantic City (because of the staunch opposition of the Southern "dixiecrats.") With over 1,200 Black delegates, the Atlanta convention seated the largest number of Black delegates in the party's history. The convention was being held in a Southern city, regarded by many as one of the most racially progressive cities in the nation, under the leadership of successive mayors, Maynard Jackson and Andrew Young. For many Blacks, Atlanta was truly a panacea in the 1980s. A true bastion of Black empowerment.

For a convention known to have minimal Black participation, though not as bad as their Republican counterparts, they truly were now a "Rainbow Coalition." Conceptually, at least, Jesse's platform would later become the foundation upon which party solidarity would be built. The delegates and party officials who were clearly divided over the treatment of Jesse, negotiated feverishly for concession points that would placate the Dukakis and Jackson camp. Meanwhile, people from all over the country came to Atlanta to witness and support our cause for fairness and equity in a political process that, once again, was trying to short change Black folk. There was quite a large delegation from Los Angeles. Black Los Angelenos take plenty of pride being wherever the action is, be it business, glitz or glamour. This was a little of all of that. I ended up spending a lot of time "party hopping" in a group of six people headed by California super delegate State Senator Diane Watson (now Congresswoman) and former television anchorman Larry Carroll. Super delegates are delegate status given to key party officials. All other delegates are elected by the people. Our group had an opportunity to discuss the politics of the convention, and convey to our people what was going on.

I tried to relax, when not caught up in the activities of the convention. I spent time with my brother Donald, then a sophomore at Morehouse College. He and his roommates were very excited about the convention being in town, but felt removed because they had no tickets for the convention. We instead went to hear Minister Farrakhan at a local church, where many of the Black delegates were also in attendance. It gave them a chance to be part of the convention and hear the minister's message to the Democratic Convention. In spite of all that was going on in Atlanta, Minister Farrakhan was the headline news. Most perceived this as a way to diminish Jesse's chances for Vice President, promoting the Jackson-Farrakhan connection of four years prior. The minister was splendid in his analysis of Jesse's political quandary, and appeared to be very supportive in his comments, urging the audience to help Jesse stand strong. My brother and his roommates had never seen Minister Farrakhan in person. We stayed up all night talking about their perceptions of the Nation of Islam, Blacks in American politics and other issues raised during the lecture.

The convention's moment of truth had finally come. A week of backroom negotiations proved to be nothing more than a stall to preempt any disruption of the convention by Jackson and his delegates. It became obvious that Jesse wouldn't be selected as Vice President on the ticket, nor was Michael Dukakis offering anything that would be perceived as capitulating to the demands of Jesse. Other than integrating the Democratic National Committee, Jackson walked away with a pocket full of "atta-boys." Still, his head up high, Jesse knew he deserved to play but wouldn't get a chance. Dukakis was nominated on the first ballot, 2,876 to Jesse's 1,218. In a turn of events, Jesse left the convention stigmatized, stating how the Dukakis ticket was still expecting him to "pick" votes (as in pick cotton) for the party, even though he had picked (registered) more voters, in the last two election years ('84 and '88), than any Presidential candidate since slavery. This was Jackson's way of letting the world know that he knew he was being used to deliver votes without a commitment to play a significant role in the party.

* * *

Upon my return from two historical back to back conventions, I was inspired to bring back advocacy in a serious way. My goals were to get the membership numbers up, to lead a national boycott against 7-11, to put on a "Stop the Violence" concert and to expose the growing misconduct in the police department. The ultimate goal of our police misconduct involvement was to file a class action federal civil rights lawsuit against the Los Angeles Police and Sheriff's Departments. However, there were some internal issues that also had to be resolved, most notably, branch staffing and Executive Committee participation.

Prior to the convention, my biggest concern had been the Executive Committee's inactivity in branch affairs. Only two standing committees, the education and political action, were functioning. Of the elected Executive Committee, only six members were active. Everybody else attended meetings and complained. In asking all standing and ad-hoc chairs to resign their seats, I was able to bring 16 new and energetic faces to the table. It was now time to decide who was going to play and who wasn't. My opposition now had a point person to serve as my competition in December's election. It was Joe Duff, my first Vice President. Duff had a name with the old-timers, because of his involvement with the L.A.U.S.D. school desegregation case. Imagine a mix between Homer Simpson and the Pillsbury dough boy, and you get a semblance of Joe Duff. His campaign was never about issues, but about stopping me from being elected.

In determining who would play, I had to determine was who was eligible to play. The branch had 61 names of people serving either on the Executive Committee as elected members, standing committee chair appointees or ad-hoc committee appointees. Of those people considered the leaders of the branch, 34 of the 61 people (56 percent) weren't current in their memberships. This wasn't really indicative of the level of hypocrisy we were dealing with. When you backed out most of the new appointees, that figure jumped to 70 percent, meaning almost three-fourths of the old Executive Committee weren't financial.

Some hadn't paid their membership since before John died, in 1984. And as is most always the case, the ones talking the most shit had the least right to do so. The branch secretary Norm King, unfinancial since 1985. Executive Committee member Elaine Crocker, unfinancial since 1985. Dinner chair Jarone Johnson, unfinancial. CEDC mouthpiece George Mallory, unfinancial. And the list went on and on. Those running the branch were part of our problem. Ernestine Peters had actually alerted some members that the list was being compiled. A few wrote checks before I could report on it. The bottom line was how could I ask them to serve if they weren't financial. Or, how could we ask others to be financial if the leaders weren't themselves. This was one of the saddest commentaries to the level of commitment I'd seen since my involvement, and I told the committee so.

Meanwhile, members of the committee were trying to block the newer members from becoming involved. "Anthony's trying to stack the board," several members were saying, which wasn't true. I was just filling vacancies of standing and ad-hoc committees that had been created by prior administrations, but hadn't been functioning. There were about fourteen, and only two of the existing committee chairs were being replaced. Still a hysteria was being promoted that I was "replacing all the old people." This was one issue my opposition already had pegged to create dissension.

While I suspected others were in opposition to my candidacy, I had George Mallory on tape. He was the only one of the CEDC board members who wasn't an elected member of the Executive Committee. He'd served as economic development committee chair, since John's administration, and I had no intention of appointing someone I knew was plotting against me. The other seat was the Roy Wilkins dinner chair, Jarone Johnson, whom I had gotten wind was compiling an investigation report on me (through a private investigator). I had already asked, then KGFJ Radio owner and Family Savings board chairman, Bill Shearer, to serve in that capacity. Shearer, a longtime community leader, was once chair of the Urban League board and was an integral part of them getting their building. He had agreed to try to do the same for us, once we got rid of "all the bullshit in the branch," as he put it. Those were the only two changes I was prepared to make.

In an effort to save George, both in his capacity on the Executive Committee and on the CEDC board (as the controlling vote), they had to run him for one of the two elected vacancy seats. There was an officer seat for assistant secretary that had never been filled, after former secretary, Pat Westmoreland, had resigned (requesting her name be taken off a hidden account that only she and Ray signed on). There was the Fourth Vice President position, which became available after Ray resigned, and all the Vice Presidents ascended one slot. Aldra Henry, a hardworking sister who had chaired the political action committee for years, and was the youth and college division adviser, had made it known that she wanted to be fourth Vice President. She was also an elected Executive Committee member. Aldra had a very loyal following among the women of the board, who perceived her as being the branch's first female President one day. She appeared to have lined up her votes and came ready to be elected by the Executive Committee.

When time came to vote, Henry Dotson and Norm King called into question a voting eligibility of the ad-hoc committee chairs. I responded that ad-hoc members had been voting since I'd been involved with the Executive Committee the last four and a half years, so what was the problem now? Dotson, a past President, who always tried to serve as parliamentarian, historian, interpreter and anything else, when it served his interest, decided that we hadn't been doing things right, in the past, and might as well start now. With this pronouncement, he had Norma call the roll according to the branch constitution, seven officers, 24 elected members at large, and the 14 standing committees as outlined in Article IV, Section 1 of the national constitution and bylaws for NAACP branches. The total number not to exceed 45 members. All the new appointees were sitting there taking this all in, more amused than alienated.

Recognizing what was happening relative to purging the eligible vote, I asked if financial membership status was criteria for voting. You could hear a rat piss on cotton, as my uncle Leonard used to say. I pulled out my list, knowing they already had a copy. Joe Duff, obviously now a branch candidate for President, asserted himself as the spokesperson for the opposition, questioned the validity of the list. After determining that the list was prepared by branch staff, and not by me, the Executive Committee pardoned itself, taking the position that membership status of the Executive Committee must be certified by the branch secretary. After a discussion ensued regarding the role of staff in maintaining membership, the discussion then turned to whether or not staff could be sure that Executive Committee members hadn't paid their membership dues for the current year. Now their reasoning was, "just because there was no record of it, doesn't mean it wasn't paid." Of course, nobody was saying whether or not they had paid, and Joe was the only one challenging the list, choosing to enact his best Perry Mason imitation. He thoroughly confused the issue by throwing a bunch of "legalese" in the game. Lawyers argue the law, when the law's on their side, or in absence of the law, argue the facts that weigh in their favor.

I called Aldra outside of the meeting, and asked her how she wanted to handle Mallory not being financial. Aldra was still weighing her options for the elections in December, and hadn't made up her mind about where she wanted to play. Not wanting to alienate one side or the other, plus thinking she had the votes, she chose not to challenge Mallory's eligibility. We proceeded with the vote and she lost. Several members who had promised to vote for her flipped when she went to them. They told her it wasn't about her, but about losing Mallory. Clearly, the members were now choosing up sides.

This was the signature meeting where my opposition let me know that they had no intention of supporting my administration.

Without the new appointees being able to vote, the original Executive Committee had a clear majority, which was greatly influenced by those most vocally opposed to my presidency. And they had no intention of supporting me in anything I brought to the table. My first two actions were infrastructure development issues: first a paid executive director, secondly, an increase in memberships. It didn't make sense to oppose either, because the branch was in such dire need of both. The charge became how to effectively change the results in a way that would be detrimental to me.

The strategy for membership was simple. If he wants members, let him bring 'em in. I had announced upon taking office that I proposed to increase membership to 25,000 up from the 1,500 or so members the branch had fallen to under Ray's leadership. The L.A. branch had developed a strategy that encouraged memberships to come through the branch by printing envelopes of their own, instead of using ones provided by national. The philosophy being it was best to have national wait for us to pay them, than for the branch to have to wait for national to pay us. The Executive Committee, in the past, had authorized payment for the printing of branch membership envelopes. It got back to me that they weren't going to do it now, and I'd have to use the envelopes national provided. With the branch owing national money from memberships collected from early in the year (the check I took to the national convention was for 1987 memberships), it wasn't likely we'd get our portion of the dues anytime soon. So even if my administration brought in members, the branch wouldn't have the benefit of the money.

The benefit of having new resources on the Executive Committee immediately kicked in. Berlinda Jamerson, a Southern California Gas Company executive, had accepted the appointment as chair of the corporate solicitation committee (one of those vacant ad-hoc committees the Executive Committee so vehemently opposed). Berlinda was one of the sharpest sisters in the corporate environment I'd met since Carolyn Webb-DeMacias at Pac Bell, and had a similar commitment. She immediately got 40,000 branch envelopes printed at no cost to the branch. We began bringing in 500 new members, on the average, per month. After a few months, seeing what could potentially happen at election time, my opposition joined in, and the number jumped to about 700 new members per month. The renewed interest was showing in the general membership meetings where the attendance numbers went from about 25 to 50 attendees per meeting (including the Executive Committee) to between 300 and 500 attendees per meeting (excluding the committee).

With the Executive Director decision, the manipulation was a little different. Once the Executive Director was in place, it would be his responsibility to manage the branch staff, which, had no job description, no scope of work, no workflow strategies and very little accountability. Harold Webb was hired as executive director. The Executive Committee's personnel chair was assigned the responsibility of meeting with all staff and developing proposed job descriptions. Until those descriptions were developed, the staff was instructed to report to Webb, who was accountable to the Executive Committee and to me.

Ernestine Peters, the administrative assistant, who had functioned independent of supervision, opposed being supervised by Webb. Webb discovered that Peters was computer illiterate, at that time. Furthermore, she refused to meet with him to develop her job description. As opposed to siding with the executive director's efforts to bring efficiency and accountability to branch operations, much of the Executive Committee supported by a core group of women, chose to ignore Ernestine's resistance to conform to an organized staffing plan.

It all came to a head when several assignments given to Ernestine went uncompleted. Webb, admitted he couldn't do anything with her. I set up a meeting with Ernestine to discuss her work accountability. Included in the meeting was Harold Webb and Jan Carter, the branch's personnel committee chair. Ernestine appeared very hostile from the start of the meeting. I opened the meeting with the concern over her hesitancy to sit with Harold to develop her job description. She had no response for that. I asked her what she thought her scope of work was or should be.

She answered sarcastically, "Answer phones, help Harold, I suppose." On the third question about the status or assignments Harold had given her, she went off. "I don't have to put up with this. I quit," she proclaimed, and stormed out of the room.

We all looked at each other and sat silently for a minute. I thanked Jan for coming and told Harold, "Don't let her take anything out of the office. I don't think she's going anywhere. We haven't heard the last of this. It's just more shit to throw in the game. Get ready for it."

Sure enough, a day later, two executive members, Norm King and Jessica Smith called an emergency meeting of the Executive

Committee. The subject: the firing of Ernestine Peters.

Once in the meeting, it turned out Ernestine had represented to the Executive Committee that she had been fired. She had called two-thirds of the committee, who came to the meeting under the supposition of "getting Ernestine's job back." Ironically enough, three years earlier, the Executive Committee sat silently when Ray did fire Joanne Robertson, a sister who should've been defended. In this instance, Ernestine walked off her job to avoid being held accountable, and lied to create hysteria over the notion that I had fired her.

Even though Webb and Carter stated differently, the hysteria continued. Ernestine provided direct access to all the inner workings of the branch for my opposition, including Ray, who was still in regular communication with her from Alabama. Secondly, she began to convince members that the move to hire Webb was a premeditated move to replace her (though she, at the time, lacked the skills to be executive director). So when she quit, it was perceived as a fulfillment of a prediction and retaliation for her continuous breaches of trust and confidentiality.

Executive Committee member, Elaine Crocker, took the lead on the attack solely on the premise that Peters had been fired, and questioned who had the authority to do it. The discussion went downhill from that point. Peters was reinstated and all staff would report to the Executive Committee until job descriptions were submitted and approved. However, Ernestine's little act clearly divided the ranks on the Executive Committee, and made her a definite enemy. From that point, there wouldn't be any information that the whole committee couldn't access. Press conferences began to look like Executive Committee meetings, because Ernestine would notify the whole committee that I was addressing an issue in public. And any action that I intended on bringing before the Executive Committee was stalled, which brings up the third project.

As mentioned earlier, we had been active in mediating gang truces through the efforts of Chilton Alphones and J. G. Guiness, both appointed as co-chairs of the branch's Gang Awareness ad-hoc committee. We had basically set the stage for a "Stop the Madness" concert to be held at the Los Angeles Coliseum. This had been done through meetings I had with, then Senior Vice President of MCA, Jheryl Busby, who lobbied branch support on behalf of the Spector Management Group, a private management company (and a subsidiary of MCA), up for consideration of the Coliseum Management contract.

Jheryl had sought me out through an associate of his named Lisa Collins. Collins had expressed interest in working with the branch after hearing about some of my advocacy efforts. I ended up appointing her to the Executive Committee in one of the elected vacancy slots, at which time, she disclosed her relationship with Busby and his willingness to want to do something for the branch.

The privatization of the Coliseum management contract was pretty much a done deal, but some last-minute rumblings required MCA (the Spector Groups parent company) to do some last-minute community based lobbying. When Busby asked if the branch could support Spector, my immediate response was, "What does the community get out of it?"

"What does the community want out of it," Jheryl asked.

"A few days of free community use of the Coliseum wouldn't be asking too much would it?" I replied.

Jheryl said he didn't see where it would be, and would certainly put that option on the table. From that point on, I had every intention of ensuring that there would be some community benefit by planning an event to exercise that option. In our initial discussions with Spector Management, it appeared that Busby had made good on the community use of the Coliseum when we approached them on the idea of a "Stop the Madness" concert. Offering a significantly reduced rate (but not a free use rate), Coliseum officials expressed tremendous interest in the project. One official, who had been involved with the "Live Aid" concert in Philadelphia a few years earlier, felt we had more than a good chance to succeed. Busby appeared as committed on ensuring our success, by preparing to allow his three hottest acts, which at the time were New Edition, Bobby Brown and Al B. Sure, to headline the ticket.

A top industry management attorney named Larkin Arnold, whom I had breakfast with, while in Chicago, helped us by referring us to a large stadium concert promoter named David Lombard (who would later manage the fresh new female group phenomena En Vogue). Through their association, we brought on actress-turned-event-coordinator Sheila Frazier to assemble and coordinate other talent we were looking to pull in. With the branch public relations director Ruth Anderson working with a community affairs consultant named Judy Johnson to act as branch/event liaison, we had a definite "A" team in place. Three major sponsors, a beer company, a public utility company and a bank were prepared to commit $25,000 or more each, with several lesser sponsors looking to make up the difference. No one wanted to be identified, until the project was a sure go.

We were initially looking at an early spring date in 1989. Then something happened to kick up the incentives. The 1989 NAACP national convention was coming to Los Angeles. National board member and branch Executive Committee member John Mance was appointed as local coordinator. He was charged to raise $75,000 for the convention. He had no idea how to raise the money. He approached me to help him. Here was a man who really never had two words to say to me before I became President, now laying his burden at my feet, like if he doesn't raise the money "L.A." would look bad in the eyes of national (as if it already didn't). Still, I agreed to help by moving the event during the convention, if he'd help get the concert through the Executive Committee. The notion of the "Stop the Madness" concert being held during the national convention was a win-win for everybody.

The concert became a major political "wedge" issue. I tried to distance myself in the committee meeting, by having Ruth make the presentation, but she didn't have enough information about key negotiations, and I would have to jump in. Then Dotson, Duff, Mallory or some other plant (but always these three) would motion to bring back another six or seven conditions to satisfy them before they would consider passing it, liability assurances, guarantees that the branch wouldn't lose money and contractual agreements from the promoter and talent. I understood then that the games had begun, knowing that if these two had to sign off to get the concert passed, hell would freeze over first. This went on for about three meetings. It was getting pretty cold, because we had gotten just about everything they'd asked for, plus I picked up some extra votes on the Executive Committee, due to Mance's involvement in the project. My opposition then made its move to seize the leadership.

* * *

The branches of the NAACP are guided by a constitution and bylaws dictated by the national organization ironically called, "The White Book." The White Book is the bible by which the organization's old-timers swear. If it ain't in the White Book, it ain't legit. Branches can supplement its bylaws with national approval, but the basis for all branch structure and procedure was all in the book. Buried deep in the

39-page pamphlet on page 31 is a little known, seldom used clause called Article X (Roman numeral, ten). Article X was entitled Expulsion, Suspension or Removal of Officers and Members and pertains to the processes involved with removing officers from office. Section 2 stated that "upon satisfactory evidence that an officer or member of the Association or of a subsidiary unit (a branch) of the Association is guilty of conduct not in accord with the principles, aims and purposes of the National Association ...." It continues by saying in that same section "or is guilty of conduct inimical to the best interest of the National Association for the Advancement of Colored People, it may order suspension, expulsion or other disciplinary action against such officer or member, after full hearing in accord with the provisions of this Constitution.

Irrespective of how one perceives conduct not consistent with NAACP aims and purpose or its best interest, given the consequence of such an article, action to trigger such a clause shouldn't be taken lightly. The trigger clause was Article X Section 3 that states a complaint for removal of office can be initiated by any three members. While it may have served as a recall clause for small branches of 50 members or less, at one time, for branches with more than 1,000 members, it was obsolete. Chances are, if you had ten Black people in a room, three are going to disagree with you, just for the hell of it. The clause was now being used as a political loophole for opposition cliques. The fact that all you have to gather is three signatures in a branch of then 5,000 (and growing) was outrageous. Yet if the public didn't know any better, they'd think there was major disruption in the ranks of the branch. It also causes indecision among the membership in choosing to follow an officer who was up on charges. In creating confusion around the present leadership, it allows opportunity for new leadership to make entry into the picture.

It was becoming more apparent to my opposition that the longer we were able to concentrate on issues and programs, the more difficult it would be to unseat me in a December election. While we didn't have a full team in place, we had a functioning team, compiled of the twenty or so new faces we had brought on. We had a functioning Executive Director, Harold Webb, who was lining up key dollars, not only to raise his salary, but to endow the branch. We were very visible and vocal on several key local fronts: police misconduct, gang violence, economic development (on several projects) and employment discrimination. The membership interest was also growing, now drawing over 300 attendees to the monthly general membership meeting for four months running. Up from the 50 (or less) that attended prior to my administration. Anything less than a major scandal, virtually ensured a continuation of the progress. In the absence of major news, you create some. A motto the LA/NAACP has long lived by. That's exactly what was about to happen.

An informal meeting was held at the branch to discuss my leadership. Eight to 10 people were in attendance, according to Harold Webb. Even though they were trying to groom Joe Duff, there wasn't consensus on his candidacy. Most in the meeting felt Joe couldn't beat me. The discussion turned to possible ways to get Essex out of office. A guy named William Upton suggested that they use an Article X complaint to charge me with malfeasance in office. He explained how he had caused one to be filed against Willis Edwards in the Hollywood branch, and how it was quite effective in getting attention in the press. Upton represented himself as a TV producer, and wanted to use branch funds to produce a branch television show. I saw him as a "wanna-be" trying to hustle the branch. When I told him that he'd have to raise the money himself, he became alienated. Now he had buried the seed of his alienation.

The plan was to first ask me to resign over my failure to get Executive Committee approval for the community reception we had in June, and for a briefcase that I purchased out of the branch President's administrative budget. Then there was the "Ernestine thing." If I refused to resign and did not expressedly state that I wouldn't run again, the complaint would be filed.

While the Article X clause was to be a last recourse, Upton made it seem like the final recourse. Firsthand account of his words were, "There's no way he can win in an Article X." I knew about the meeting less than 30 minutes after it was over. Later, I received a call from John Mance, and met with three respected, senior members of the branch. When Mance called, he was his usual jovial self. Mance and I developed a little lightweight rapport.

Mance, as a national board member elected by the members, had once been unseated. The year John McDonald ran unopposed, Mance didn't ask for branch support and was left off the slate, so he lost. His replacement was a young brother named Peter Cohn, who quickly fell from grace when he brought new and progressive issues to the national board. Peter is best remembered for mounting opposition to a key floor vote at the 1985 NAACP National Convention in

Dallas. He fell out of favor with Hooks, eventually resigned from the national board, at which time Mance recovered his seat. He stayed close to branch leadership ever since.

While I liked Mance as a person, I perceived him as a classic NAACP dinosaur. This perception was reinforced when Mance, Jose DeSosa, Jim Martin (who was representing Mallory) and I attended the annual Pacific Bell Fair Share agreement monitoring committee meeting in San Francisco. Headed by Fred Rasheed, this monitoring meeting was an active barometer of how this company lived up to its commitment to promote minorities, do business with minorities and complement other forms of parity in the workplace.

Pac Bell had gone through great lengths in putting its annual presentation in place, to convince us that they had met and exceeded its voluntary diversity objectives. However, we had heard prior to coming that several mid-level managers were being set up to have their positions eliminated. Our plan was to have this discussion and charge Pac Bell with undermining the integrity of the agreement. Pac Bell's plan was to never let it come up, by refuting such a charge through its selected progress presentations. After a bunch of fringe presentations and posturing, the time finally came to make the company's management diversity progress report. To make this critical presentation, Pac Bell put up Chuck Smith, the company's Black superstar. Chuck was a guy who had the confidences of senior management, and later became President of a Pacific Bell subsidiary. Smith had developed a good rapport with Fred Rasheed, as a corporate brother trying to do the right thing. Pac Bell probably felt we wouldn't be as hard on ole' Chuck. When Smith got into his presentation, his personal, lighthearted, yet concise delivery was very effective, inasmuch as you were more into what Chuck was doing, than the information he was presenting. Chuck got to rapping and dancing and prancing through his presentation, flinging his transparencies on the floor, and basically entertaining the group. I had never seen a brother tap dance this fast, probably much to the delight of his white supervisors. The Black Pac Bell employees in the meeting didn't appear entertained at all.

Halfway through the presentation, our opening came. Smith put up a chart that measured Pac Bell's diversity growth over a five-year period, roughly the time they had been in the Fair Share agreement. The number of "minorities" in middle management had grown some astronomical number, like 700 percent, but in the breakdown of the numbers, Blacks had increased less than 10 percent. Most of the growth was in the area of white women, who were included in the minority numbers. Fred and I immediately caught it, making eye contact. And as quick as the chart went up, it went down on the floor. I looked around the table to see who else may have caught it, and saw Jim reading the manual handout (which didn't include the chart). DeSosa was staring at Mance, who had fallen asleep. At the conclusion of the presentation, I asked Smith about the chart. He responded that he didn't think he saw that, but if I wanted to sift through his transparencies on the floor and find it, we could discuss it. I made up my mind, while looking for the chart, that I was going to tear ole' Chuck a new asshole.

When I found it, it clearly represented how Pac Bell had used the Fair Share program to promote white women. I asked how that could happen, when white women represented less of the labor force, than Blacks did, when the program started. There was dead silence on the Pac Bell side of the table, including Chuck and the three white women and two white males in the meeting. The two other Black Pac Bell employees had to restrain themselves to keep from shouting and jumping out of their seats. They commented afterward that they thought the NAACP was going to sleep the real issue ("like they always do," according to them). It was the first time they felt the NAACP had someone competent (from the California group) at the table. They were right.

The NAACP side of the table would have slept the chart, had I not brought it up. We often put people at the table ill-prepared to deal with complex issues. Racism was now so sophisticated, that many of the old-timers were out of their league, when dealing with high-tech racism. This was how I perceived Mance, and is why I called some old timers like Mance, classic dinosaurs. We had developed a tolerance of each other, that allowed us, to at least talk.

Mance finally got to the point: "Anthony, we need to meet with you about some concerns in the branch."

"Who is we, John?" I asked.

"A couple of Executive Committee members," he replied.

"Come on over," I told him. When they got there, Henry Dotson and Kathryn Anderson were with Mance. We went back in my office where they sat on the couch, and I pulled a chair across from them. I saw legitimate concern on the face of Mrs. Anderson, a mother of the branch and top membership recruiter. It was a good move to bring her along to ensure they wouldn't be thrown out, or cussed out.

Dotson had his usual look--the look of a total hypocrite, his eyes rolling back in his head. He was not able to look me in the eye during the whole meeting, the first sign that it was a set-up. He still had no clue that I knew he was only playing out his hand, as part of their clique's plot (Mallory, McBeth and himself), of which the other two probably knew nothing about. As for Mance, he looked a little nervous, because they now had him in a box. Serving as the lead inspector for this little inquisition, Mance was charged with validating their allegations, while knowing he needed me to help pull off the concert that would help him raise his money. He knew if he allowed this hand to be played out too far, he could forget any assistance from me. I could see him battling with that in his head. After looking at each other, Mance led in, "Anthony, the Executive Committee is concerned about some of the moves you've made in your short term as President. Particularly your infusion of new players and decisions that appear unilateral in nature. Some think you may not be the person to bring members together."

"Be specific, John," I said.

"They're saying you're replacing all the older members of the committee," Mance continued.

"Who's saying that John?" I asked.

"I can't tell you that Anthony. Is it true?" he responded.

"No, it's not, John. There are several members that I've appointed from the Prince Hall Masons who are older members. I had also appointed several community people who are older, so that's ridiculous. I'm looking for people who want to work, regardless of age. Is that a problem?" I said.

"No," Mance responded.

Mrs. Anderson chimed in, "It appears son, that some of the members don't respect your leadership. I feel we may need someone that can bring the members together."

"Does that include new members?" I asked. No one said anything. I continued, "What we have here are members who are doing nothing, but resisting someone who wants to do something. What am I supposed to do, wait and allow my opposition to label me as a do nothing? You are correct in your observation that some members don't respect my leadership Mrs. Anderson." Looking at Dotson I said, "No matter what I do, opposition to my becoming President was already in place. That's why there is such opposition to anything I do." I said. "So, what are we really talking about here? What's the purpose of this meeting, John?" I asked.

Finally, he came clean. "There is discussion about filing a complaint to national about you. After three straight incidents, they think you are too much of a one-man show--taking action without Executive Committee approval," John said.

"What three incidents, John?" I asked.

"Well, there was the reception, the purchasing of the phone system, and the firing of Ernestine. Can you explain such autonomous action?" Mance asked.

"The reception was underwritten and the sponsor backed out. There wasn't supposed to be any branch money involved. Still, the reception promoted the branch and made money from new memberships. The phone system went out. There was one working phone in the whole branch. What was I supposed to do? Go three weeks without phones and maybe, the Executive Committee would approve the expenditure? I don't have time for those kinds of games. Ernestine quit her job and lied about it, which is what I think all of this is really about. I did make a decision to make all paid staff accountable for their work. How is that an autonomous action? I don't believe I'm being given a chance to bring this branch up to snuff. There is nothing I can do to get some people's support. Right, Henry?" I asked as I finished my rebuttal. Dotson crossed his legs and looked away.

Mance then asked me, "Are you going to run in December?"

I responded, "I intend to. Do you intend to support me?"

Henry shook his head and stated, "No, I don't intend to

support you. In fact, we came here to ask you not to run." Mrs. Anderson looked down and Mance looked away.

Knowing what Henry's agenda was from jump street, I took off the kid gloves. "Henry, you and your boys have done more to discredit the branch than I could ever do. It's pretty bold for you to come up in here representing fifty people, and make a demand that I not run. I'll take my chances with the general membership, not with Ray's Executive Committee," I said.

Mance and Mrs. Anderson looked a little bewildered like, "What are they talking about?" Henry, of course, knew exactly what I was talking about. Everybody looked at each other like, "Well, I guess that's it."

"Anything else," I asked, as we all stood to end the meeting.

John said, "Yeah, what about this briefcase?"

"What about it?" I asked.

"Well, is it true you bought it with branch money?"

"Yes, out of my administrative budget. I think I've been extremely conservative with the branch's money. No secretarial services, no portable phones, or any of the other stuff the prior Presidents expended," I responded.

"May I see it?" John asked. I showed the bag to him, full of branch documents. He just looked at it and shook his head.

I received a letter from the Director of branch services, William Penn, that an Article X compliant had been filed against me by eight members of the branch. All were Executive Committee members except, Sandra Pigler, an ex-branch staffer, who once complained to me, alleging that she thought she was being sexually harassed by Henry Dotson. Now she was signing a complaint with him. Dotson, Mance, Johnson and Norm King, declared opponents to my candidacy were now leading the way on the Article X. The center of their compliant was spending branch funds without authorization on a reception, a branch phone system and a briefcase. They also tagged me with making several unilateral decisions like not participating in the national radiothon. Penn gave me thirty days to respond to the charges. I responded in a 28-page document that described the complaint as retaliatory and inconsistent with standards, by which the branch had been allowed to operate in the past. Penn called an emergency meeting of the Executive Committee, at which time he would investigate all of the allegations. While we all tried to carry on business as usual, we all knew this filing came at a time, when the members were starting to prepare for branch elections. But instead of preparing for the elections, I now had to prepare for some orchestrated kangaroo court, to be held at the whim of a handful of members, and put the branch in the middle of a public fight. In the process, the character of everyone would be on trial, and the integrity of true advocacy would take a backseat to compromise strategies seeking to drive change away from the branch.

* * *

10

AIN'T NO SUCH THING AS A "BLACK" SANTA CLAUS

"The basic tenent of Black consciousness is that the Black man must reject all value systems that seek to make him a foreigner in the country of his birth and reduce his basic human dignity."

-Steven Biko

In late fall, 1988, in the midst of the confusion caused by my opposition's subversive attack on my leadership and personal character, an issue arose that embodied the total essence of racial lunacy in this country. I was already involved in our investigation into the treatment of Blacks in county jails, and wasn't particularly interested in adding another issue to my already overcrowded schedule. I was in my office on the Friday after Thanksgiving, trying to catch up on some work, and listening to the 5 o'clock news. One of the topics addressed a man who had been laid off from his construction job, and went to an agency that trained people for the seasonal position of Santa Claus. This gentlemen, Rodney Newton, was seeking to provide a means for his family during the holiday season, and in spite of his unemployed condition, he wanted to bring some happiness to children.

The job had a dual purpose, I suppose. The agency dispatched Newton and his wife (also unemployed, but training as Santa's helper) to the Carson Shopping mall, in Carson, California (an incorporated suburb in Los Angeles County). When Newton arrived at his job assignment, the mall manager, pulled him to the side and asked who he was. When Newton responded that he was the Santa Claus that the agency sent, the manager allegedly replied, "You're the Santa Claus?" "Just a minute." The manager then instructed another employee to call the agency, because surely there must have been a mistake. Newton and his wife overheard her telling an employee "Who ever heard of a Black Santa Claus?" There ain't no such thing as a Black Santa Claus." After about 15 minutes the mall management sent Newton and his wife home. This was the account that Newton gave the news media. I just shook my head and went back to work.

My thoughts kept reverting back to Newton's words. "Ain't no such thing as a Black Santa Claus." I'm was sitting there thinking, "Damn, ain't no such thing as Santa Claus. Period. We can't be a part of their social reality, nor even a part of their children's fiction."

This whole statement, in and of itself, is a serious indictment on our society. It's bad enough that the period recognized as the birth of Christ has been exploited into a frenzied commercialization for merchandisers. Christmas as this society knows it, is the exact antithesis of the period's intent, particularly in America, and specifically as it relates to their relationship with the Black man and woman. The whole concept of "Christmas cheer and goodwill toward all" ranks second in hypocrisy to the Pledge of Allegiance.

Blacks have always been made to feel that our participation in holidays like Christmas and the Fourth of July were prerequisites to our fulfilling our citizenship acceptance in this country. Our "spirituality" and "patriotism" has always been highly suspect with whites in this country. Particularly, if Blacks failed to buy into these celebrated demonstrations of the "goodness of man" and our "right to freedom, equality and the pursuit of happiness," even though Blacks know and recognize neither is representative of American thought, as it relates to our treatment. Still, Black America often feels compelled to become involved in pseudo-celebration, recognizing a sub-existence that really doesn't include them. It's tantamount to looking through a fishbowl, a distorted perception of their reality, and a refusal to acknowledge our own reality. Christmas and the Fourth of July, as well as, other holidays, are like attending parties without an invitation. You can feel the fun, taste the food, and someone may even recognize your presence. But you and they know that they didn't invite you, and you question your presence. Still, everyone goes on enjoying the party. Blacks, in America, use these holidays as periods of eternal hope that whites will somehow honor unfulfilled promises, instead of celebrating their significant meanings. They hold little meaning in our day-to-day interactions, in terms of rising above the subordinated status allotted for Blacks in this society.

The concept of Santa Claus only further exacerbates this goodwill posturing, with the image of a jovial old "fat man" with flying reindeer, sliding down chimneys, and giving gifts to those who have been nice. America has never given Blacks anything, but a hard way to go. Eleven months out of the year, the mean-spiritedness of America is a prevailing state of existence for Blacks. Yet, when December hits, the country goes into this benevolent state, ambivalent to its feelings of racial hostility, unless provoked under the guise of Christian love and goodwill. Then these feelings are supposed to provoke feelings of giving, because society has taught that it is better to give than to receive. Yet, during the other eleven months, this society is capitalistic, opportunistic and indifferent to social and economic disparities of race. Another philosophical conflict for America.

This conflict goes even deeper for Black America. Blacks, as a collective group, are the ones that have the least (wealth, standard of living) in this country. Yet, they are the ones that spend the most. The pressure on Black parents to buy into Christmas is tremendous. All they see is this white man giving gifts, and none coming their way. So it must be all right to be white. The illusions that are created of Santa Claus are similar to the subliminal images that were once the society's perspective of Jesus. Santa Claus with very few exceptions has been represented as a white male. In the media (T.V.), advertisements of merchandisers and in public appearances, he is almost always represented as a white male. You almost took exception when you saw an ethnic Santa. Ethnicity in Santa Claus began to become more common in the mid-70's and early 80's, when Blacks became more culturally mature and economically sophisticated, regarding giving credit to this old fat white man.

Still this ethnicity issue posed problems for Black youths who had come to know this jolly old fat man as white. It wasn't an uncommon site to see little Black children challenge their parents in shopping center environments over the ethnicity of Santa Claus. You'd hear the child say, "Mommie, this ain't the real Santa Claus, cause Santa Claus ain't Black." This is an innocent, yet revealing statement as to how this mythical fallacy affects the minds of Black children, to the extent that they subliminally reject their own skin color as legitimate or equal. This was an updated confirmation of the old "white doll/Black doll" tests given to segregated children, in the early 1950's, to prove the damaging affects of racial separation. Those test confirmed a rejection of self, as less than best. While it took some time, Blacks, to a large degree, were able to arrest their children's anxieties over the complex question of the race of a mythical character, in spite of, the overwhelming media portrayal of Santa Claus, as a white man.

However, in the late 1980's, Black Santas had become commonplace in Black communities, and were making their way into some ethnically-diverse communities, as well. While Black Santas had not made it to any of the "big time" Christmas parades, certainly the very idea of a Black Santa would not appear to be sacrilegious to most free thinking white folk. Carson, California is an incorporated suburb of Los Angeles with a highly diverse ethnic population. In the late 70s, Blacks began to move there in large numbers and now represented more than a one-third of the city's residents. The City, however, borders communities like Wilmington, Torrance, Gardena, and Harbor City that have largely white populations. The Carson Shopping mall was the closest mall to many of these communities, but had a very high identification with Black shoppers.

The mall had retained a promotional marketing firm to advise the mall on the changing demographics and shopping trends of the area. The company, Serci and Associates, in recognizing the high Black patronage that the mall received, thought that providing a Black Santa Clause would give the mall a greater appearance to Black shoppers, which was a correct assessment. Until then, the mall had never employed a Black Santa. Now appeared to be the right time to make such a move. The agency sent Rodney Newton to the Carson mall, after he had completed his Santa Claus training. Upon announcing his arrival for the position, Connie Wilson, one of the officials for the mall management, immediately replied that there must be some mistake. After confirming with the agency that Newton was in fact the Santa, Wilson made her infamous statement, and had Rodney wait in another room, while a white replacement took his seat on the sled. After 45 minutes of confusion, where Wilson insisted that Newton would not be used, the mall's general manager, Cynthia Cinchek, supported her employee's ridiculous assertion, and asked Newton to leave.

On the following Monday, I received a call at my office from the branch receptionist, Wanda. Wanda was recently hired and, in spite of all the trivial politics that were happening in the branch, she remained highly professional and impartial. She had been instructed by my opposition to give all of my messages to Ernestine Peters, who would relay them to me. This was normal protocol.

However, Ernestine was clearly opposed to my leadership due to my criticism of her work. She was serving as the internal watch dog for my opposition. When I realized that for over two months, I hadn't been receiving my messages, I tried to change the process by which my messages were received. The executive committee objected saying that Ernestine was the office manager, and she should be allowed to carry out her duties.

Wanda did what she was told, until she witnessed Ernestine trashing my messages one day, when she thought Wanda had left the room. From that point on, Wanda tried to beat Ernestine to the phone, write the messages on a duplicate message pad and give Ernestine the original. Then she would call me with the message from the duplicate pad. Wanda called to tell me that a Rodney Newton had called three times, asking for "the brother that looked like Malcolm X," because he didn't know my name. Several friends and relatives had told him to seek me out over the weekend, and told him not to talk to anyone else. When he called the first time, Ernestine took the call. Because he didn't ask for me by name, she didn't acknowledge the call. Wanda overheard the second and third calls, copied Newton's phone number, and told me that the "Black Santa Claus victim" was looking for me.

In the meantime, the Carson-Torrance branch had announced that it was investigating the matter. The President of the Carson branch was Reverend Robert Wilson, a very polite soft-spoken gentleman, who also owned a Christian bookstore. I called Rev. Wilson and told him that the victim in the Black Santa Claus dispute was trying to reach me, and asked how he wanted me to handle that. With all that was going on in the L.A. branch, I certainly didn't need an allegation that we (or I) were infringing on another branch's territory. NAACP branches are highly territorial and competitive, when it comes to high profile issues. They usually state that they can handle the case, whether they can or not. That was certainly the response I had anticipated from Carson. What I got was completely the opposite, and it was quite refreshing. Rev. Wilson said that the media response had been quite overwhelming, that the negotiation may require a little more than what they are accustomed to, and that he would welcome the experience and talent of the L.A branch. I damn near dropped the phone. I was so tired of the senseless competition between branches, and welcomed the opportunity to work with them. We agreed to meet at his bookstore, and that I would return Rodney Newton's call.

I then called Rodney and set up a meeting for the next day. I called Wanda and asked her to send some discrimination complaint forms over to my business office. I intentionally agreed to meet Newton at my office to eliminate any of the branch's backstabbing politics from potentially interfering with this discovery meeting.

At the time, my opposition was trying to limit my exposure before the branch election, so it passed a motion that no press conferences were to be held without executive committee approval. I could make press statements, however. So whenever it seemed like I was putting something together at the branch, Ernestine would make a call, and Duff, Henry Dotson or Norma would drop by and sit in "to see what they could contribute." Usually they just prolonged discussion. They were just making sure I wasn't going to get any publicity out of it, not without them being there. In this particular case, discussion would have most likely been centered around whether we should have been involved in the dispute at all, regardless if Newton filed the complaint with us or not. This would have snuffed any possibility of branch (or individual) publicity that the dispute might generate. I wasn't going to waste my time or Newton's time, by getting his legitimate complaint caught up in a bunch of frivolous bullshit. If Newton wanted my involvement, then I was in. We met that Tuesday after Thanksgiving.

My meeting with Carson's branch President, Rev. Wilson, proved to be very fruitful. We outlined clear responsibilities that each of us was to take on, and the timeliness in which we expected to accomplish tasks. We agreed that he would be the lead interface with the Carson community, and that I would interface with Newton. We would both co-chair negotiations and press conferences. We would keep each other abreast of all changes. He would handle mall management, and I would handle the complainants. We would also touch base with each other before agreeing to anything. I asked him what they wanted out of this. Rev. Wilson stated compensation or re-hiring for Newton, and a "Fair Share" agreement with the mall. I asked what were they prepared to do if they didn't receive these things. He stated the "Fair Share agreement" was kind of a best case scenario, however, if justice wasn't given to Newton he would be prepared to close the mall. I want "Justice for Rodney."

Those were very prophetic words. They would become the battle cry for urban insurrection three years later for another Rodney case. Still, the fact that they were prepared to go to the wall for this Rodney, the "first" Rodney the country would hear about within a three-year period. It was talk I wanted to hear.

Apparently, the Carson community felt the same way. A community of about 40 percent Black, I had never witnessed a total community (of Blacks) come together, as quickly as, this one did. The weekend after Thanksgiving is usually the biggest shopping day of the year, and Black consumers tend to always use it as an opportunity to give our money away. Yet on this weekend the Carson mall was a virtual mausoleum. The news cameras had been out there all weekend, since Newton's allegation, showing the emptiness of the mall. If Carson residents were spending money that weekend, it wasn't there. This was great leveraging power. Usually when something happens that's offensive in our communities, we continue the level of spending patterns with the same people, and the offenders ride the controversy out. Not this time. What made our leverage even that much greater was that most mall profits are made in the last two months of the year, where up to 40 percent or more of the year's sales come in. Everyday this controversy went unresolved, the more money the mall potentially lost, at some point. A sense of urgency came over the mall's management, which meant we were in the driver's seat in the short-run. In this case, the short-run was all that counted.

Rodney Newton, a tall thin man and who was an out of work building contractor, and his wife appeared at my business office 15 minutes early. We exchanged pleasantries and moved right into the business at hand. Mrs. Newton did most of the talking. She said press had been calling every hour, on the hour and that mall management had called both of them back to work. I asked them how they felt about that. Mr. Newton interrupted his wife and stated, "This whole situation has taken me out of the spirit of being Santa Claus." "This was supposed to be something good." Even though I didn't have no job, I was trying to make Christmas nice for the kids, mine and other people's. "Why should it matter that I'm Black? Why does color always have to come in the middle of everything?"

Of course, I didn't have an answer for him, but what I was hearing was the testament of a very frustrated man. Apparently, this was not the first incident where race had impacted his livelihood. I asked Mr. and Mrs. Newton to chronologically recount the whole set of events to me, as I took notes. When Mr. Newton had been laid off from his construction job in late October, his wife suggested that they respond for a 30-day training program for Santa Claus characters after which time you would be placed as a Santa. The job was full time during the holidays paying minimum wage. It seemed pretty easy, so they agreed to go for it. After their training was completed, Mr. and Mrs. Newton were sent to the Carson mall. Carson was their first choice, because it was closest to their home. Their first day of work was the Friday after Thanksgiving. They were told to report at 8 a.m. Mr. Newton's first assignment was to perform for a magic show given to some community kids, to premiere the mall's first shopping day of Christmas. At the end of the show, Santa, (to be played by Newton) was to pop out of a transport box, pass out gifts and take his seat at the center of the mall. Yet, Newton was asked to wait in a back office, until they "were ready for him."

After about 30-45 minutes, Newton noticed that the show had started and that someone else was in the Santa suit. When he started to inquire about the delay, he overheard a discussion taking place between mall official, Connie Wilson, and marketing specialist, Donna Guidry. Guidry was in charge of the mall's Christmas promotion for Serci & Associates and responsible for hiring Rodney. She was inquiring about who the person was in the Santa suit. Wilson was telling her that she had replaced the Santa, because the "Black guy" appeared "too big" to fit into the box. Guidry asked her if she had Newton step into the box and she responded, "No." Then she said, according to Newton, "You never told me the guy was Black. Whoever heard of a Black Santa Claus? There's no such thing as a Black Santa Claus. We can't use him." Rodney said he and his wife looked at each other and went back to their waiting room. Moments later, the mall manager named Cynthia Cinchek, had apparently interceded in Wilson's and Guidry's conversation. She came to the Newtons and stated that a mistake had been made, that they already had a Santa Claus, and that agency would be calling them later. When the Newtons got home they received a call from Guidry, who told Rodney that she didn't understand what happened, that the Carson mall claimed that he was too big for the box they wanted him to pop out of, and needed a smaller person. Newton said there was a long pause on the phone. Then Guidry said "Rodney, I don't want to cause any trouble. I'm just trying to do my job. However, I think they didn't want you, because you are Black." She continued saying that she thought she could get them an assignment in Long Beach, with no problem. It would be just a matter of days. The Newtons, however, chose to break the story to the press.

I asked Rodney if he thought the comment was mean-spirited, or was it in jest. Both Rodney and his wife seemed to think that the woman was very serious when she said it. It was as if she really "deep down" believed that Santa wasn't Black. When I asked Rodney why he wanted me involved in his case and why he didn't just sue them, his response was interesting. He stated he didn't have the money or the time to sue, and that this was bigger than himself. Newton continued that "when things happen to Black folk, there's a little rumbling, and then they just seem to go away, until it happens again to somebody else. I was told that this doesn't happen with you. You bring things to a head and get them resolved to where they don't happen again. I want to get this resolved for me."

I thanked him for his confidence and informed him of the arrangement that the Carson branch and myself had formed. I told him it was our intent to resolve this before Christmas or there wouldn't be any Christmas-- not for the Carson mall owners. I told him to complete the discrimination complaint form and sign it. I made three copies. I gave one to him, told him to drop one by the branch and ask for Ernestine, and I kept the original and a copy. I instructed him not to talk to anyone, not press, not mall representatives, not lawyers, and to refer them to me.

As he was leaving, he asked me if I thought anything would come out of this. I told him to wait and see. When it comes to money white folk will believe in ghosts, flying saucers and anything else you want them to believe in, including Black Santas. I told him to give me three days, and I'd get back to him.

The next few days were spent trying to get the facts straight. The Carson community had turned out en mass to hear several different versions of the incident in meetings with mall officials. The first strategy was for mall representatives to go into a "denial" mode, to say that the incident never happened, and that Rodney and his wife were mistaken. At that point, they figured it was their white word against two poor Blacks. How many times had we seen this scenario played out? We ridiculed any attempt at that. They never once brought up that a third party, Donna Guidry, had witnessed the discussion. Guidry, who confided to the Newtons, figuring it would go no further, refused to make any comment at first. She felt that she was putting her job at jeopardy by talking against her employer. We later found out that she was instructed to comment no further. They even denied that they had talked to her about commenting on the incident. The community was adamant about talking to Guidry. The first meeting ended with the agreement that we would not meet, until Guidry appeared.

The second meeting began with a different strategy. Guidry appeared and gave a very general recollection of a "discussion" about Rodney. She "slightly" recalled something about Santa being Black, but that was the extent of it. It was clear that Guidry had been talked to, and was walking a very fine line. You could see it in her face and hear it in her voice. Also, the mall's general manager, Cynthia Cinchek, stated that she knew absolutely none of this, when she told Newton she couldn't use him. She thought they just had one Santa Claus too many.

We asked Guidry to leave the room. Rev. Wilson, after huddling with us, stated that he felt that Guidry was under duress and couldn't say what she wanted to say. Rev. Wilson requested to speak with her separately, and wanted mall officials to assure her that no retaliation would come to her, as a result of her cooperation. Mall officials were reluctant to commit to that, thereby, making Guidry reluctant to talk to us. They were beginning to isolate Connie Wilson as acting alone, with the mall accepting no responsibility for the mistake of an employee. The community wasn't about to let them off that easy. We felt that the mall officials weren't dealing straight with us. We made a deadline of Wednesday, at noon, to resolve the issue to the community's satisfaction.

The state NAACP President, Jose DeSosa was monitoring the activities of this incident. Of all the West Coast players in the NAACP, I have the most respect for Jose. He's serious and sincere about the advocacy. When discussing a possible boycott, Jose stated he was prepared to request permission as soon as needed. Until that time, we would encourage the public to stay away from the mall. And they did, which was beginning to bring pressure from another angle, the mall's major tenants, Sears and JC Penney. Also the Merchants Association was beginning to feel the pinch. The management had to do something, so they tried the next best thing. Divide and conquer. Translation: Get to Rodney.

When I returned to my office, I had received a call from Rodney, Joe Duff and also from a guy named Harold Becks. Though, I'd seen Harold around the Los Angeles political circles, I really didn't know him. He and his partner, Ron Wilson, had been hired to represent John Winthorpe, the owner of the mall. They had called Rodney first, and Rodney referred them to me. Rodney told me that they said they were interested in getting the issue resolved and wanted to know what he wanted. I told Rodney what had happened earlier in the day, and the deadlines that had been set. I told him I felt he'd know what he was worth by the middle of next week.

I called Duff, who was concerned about the visibility I was getting in this case. He inquired as to why the Los Angeles branch was involved in a Carson matter. I told him that Rodney Newton requested I handle it and the Carson branch welcomed our involvement. Duff's position was that I should have referred the complaint to Carson and stayed out of it. My position was, if Carson didn't have a problem with it, why should you? He couldn't respond to that, and promised to bring "glory seeking" up to the executive committee. I said "fine" and hung up without a second thought. I then called Becks, who identified himself as "a brother trying to do `what's right' on this Santa Claus thing." He let me know he represented the mall owners and sought to resolve the issue, as soon as possible. We agreed to meet that evening at the Boulevard Cafe restaurant to discuss our respective positions.

I was preparing myself to be a little dogmatic and confrontational with the brother, for no other reason, than what I perceived he represented. White folk always go out and hire Blacks to go against Blacks on issues of conflict resolution. So-called "brother" sits at the table and "talks" that "brother" shit, while representing people who impose injustices on his own people. They use Blacks to diffuse conflict and stretch out resolution, while their clients re-strategize and retool to come back the same way. The Blackface is most often a diversion to get past the Black/white thing, as the center of hostility. Still, when it comes to the issue on the table, the Black serves as the agent of compromise, trying to convince us that these "good" white folk are doing all they can to change the situation. It couldn't be further from the truth. Blacks end up with much less than they should, and the Black face gets paid. For this reason, I was not prepared to let the Carson mall throw a Blackface in the game, just to eliminate the pressure they were under. Conversely, I'm sure they anticipated a "different" type of NAACP official. One whose attention you could usually divert quite easily, throw 'em a bone and run off with the plate. I'm sure we were both a little surprised. After meeting with Harold Becks and his law partner, Ron Wilson for an hour, I was convinced they understood what they were in for, but I didn't view them as "sellout" kind of brothers either. We all hit it off right away. We didn't placate each other, nor did we attack each other. I was totally disarmed with their approach, inasmuch as they both expressed concern over such statements and the need to keep it from happening again, which meant clarifying what was at stake. We talked about separating the issues, the employee who said it, a position from the mall and compensating Rodney. For once I could say, like in no other complaint that I'd handled, there were no end runs. All issues will be resolved before a settlement is reached. It is very rare that we not only hold all the cards, but we also play the hand correctly.

If anyone knows anything about "Bid Whist," we were holding a "Boston" on this one. As long as we had Rodney willing to wait on this one, no resolution could come without coming through us. And the Carson community was playing their part like a gem. If the mall owners thought that this would blow over, and the people would just come back, like we do most of the time, they had another thing coming. All they had to do was to look at that empty mall everyday to realize "these niggahs ain't playin this time." And the clock was tickin'. Harold, Ron and I agreed to stay in touch, and that they would inform the owner of the seriousness of our position.

As I was walking back to my car, I left with an appreciation for Harold and Ron. Finally, I met some brothers representing white folk with some cultural integrity. It could have been a con, but I didn't sense that. I had a good feeling about Blacks playing mainstream roles without losing the cultural perspective. I know playing that role is tough, because whites are cautious about hiring Blacks that are "too Black" in mind, and in commitment to the Black community. That's the ultimate realization of a Black professional. Mainstream by day, come home to culture at night. That can be hard to do. When we do, it'll be the first step toward our community really turning around.

* * *

The following Monday morning, we were in a meeting with the mall's owner, John Winthorpe. It had been a long weekend for the merchants. Sales were down dramatically for a Christmas season, and the mall tenants were complaining to the management to resolve this matter fast. The story had changed again over the weekend, when Winthorpe got the first-hand account from his general manager, Cinchek, who now acknowledged that she knew what had occurred, and felt she had to support her staff's position. This was a departure from her denial of the previous week, where she stated that she knew nothing. This now put her in the same light as Connie Wilson, inasmuch as she co-signed this ridiculous assertion to be perpetrated. It also meant that he had to take on some of the liability. Wilson still maintained her statements were misquoted. She felt Donna Guidry was responsible for "blowing this whole thing out of proportion." There appeared to be no repentance on her part. In spite of what Cinchek's and Wilson's twisted philosophies implied, there was now a Black Santa in the mall's lobby. What a revelation.

Winthorpe appeared to be sincere in trying to understand the community's hurt and in trying to demonstrate his efforts to resolve this issue. The community was serious about carrying through on their promise. Once we had gotten the story straight, it was time to discuss what the community was willing to accept for the insults it had encountered. The sentence was stiff. Connie Wilson and Cynthia Cinchek were to be fired. Donna Guidry was to suffer no retaliation for coming forward. Rodney Newton would be compensated for this inconvenience and public embarrassment. The community would be allowed to give input as to what they wished to see in the mall. Lastly, but most importantly, the mall would issue a public apology to Newton and the Carson community for the insensitivity of Wilson and Cinchek in making such an outrageous statement.

Winthorpe said he needed to think about these "requests," even though they were more like demands. Then the discussion turned to how long Winthorpe had to work all this out. I couldn't have been more proud of the Carson community representatives. Mall representatives pulled out the stops to convince them that they were negotiating in good faith, but the community wasn't hearing any of it. The mall even had some handkerchief head Negro from the Carson City Council come in and make a plea to the community to "be reasonable" in their expectations of this situation being resolved in a matter of days. The deadline for resolving the issue was still Wednesday, at noon.

The very idea of his mall being boycotted at Christmas time, when 40 percent of his merchants were looking to pull even or make a profit was Winthorpe's worse nightmare. With millions of dollars at stake, there was no way for him to play any stall games, which cause many substantive issues to be compromised or lost. And there was no one to be bought off, in an effort to turn it around. The Carson community probably didn't recognize the significance of their position in this. Blacks are rarely ever in such a position to dictate what white folk will do, and when they will do it. Blacks are never, or hardly ever, able to control the destiny of whites by solely imposing their will, lest we ever demonstrate that we can affect the lives of whites and their corporations. In general, before whites will allow Blacks to impose any form of power or control on them, they'll tie them in litigation, create some other diversion to sustain the affect of the power, or straight out defy the authority or law empowering Blacks. It's just an antithetical concept to them. Black power. The power to keep people away. The power to decide if they'll shop somewhere. The power to have someone hired and someone else fired. Black folk rarely see "power plays" that are imposed on whites. Blacks in power (elected officials and government officials) who exercise it, don't keep it, particularly if they use it to favor Blacks. With few exceptions, this analogy can be applied to every faction of Black/white social interface.

It's one thing to give the illusion of power, but it's another thing to have it, and be able to use it at will. Now, in this instance, all that was left to be seen was whether or not the community would use its power, and how it would use the power. The leverage for the community was the fact that the mall was in its peak season, and there was much money to be lost. However, the community did not have the money or the legal resources to get into an extended fight. If the mall's management was allowed to negotiate past the deadline and invariably past the holidays, it would not only totally eliminate strategies that would impact the mall, but it would affect how much it would impact the mall. It would also cause the sense of urgency to be removed from the situation and force the community and Rodney to prove the malicious intent allegations charged to the mall's employees. Anything could happen, once the urgency was relieved. Clearly, it was in the community's best interest to resolve this issue in the short-run.

On the Tuesday before the deadline, I got a call from Rev. Wilson that the mall owners were ready to propose a response to our requests. They wanted to meet at 9 p.m. that evening and hoped to be able to announce a settlement at the press conference scheduled for noon the next day. Of course, the original purpose was to announce what the community's decision would be with respect to a proposed boycott.

Jose DeSosa had received clearance from national to proceed, if necessary. Getting approval for a direct action (the organization's term for boycott) campaign was very difficult, particularly for a quick turnaround. This is where the NAACP has been perceived as becoming weak in their "perceived" unwillingness to boycott when necessary. Many equivocate this hesitancy to a police officer pursuing a suspect in the midst of committing a crime on the street and then looking the other way. Some have gone, as far as, to say that the NAACP will pull its "justice and equality" gun, and then freeze when it's time to pull the trigger. When you freeze, at the moment of truth, you'll either get shot, or the suspect gets away. Before long you become a danger to your counterparts and the public, while developing a reputation for "choking" under pressure. Either you're not likely to be assigned to the high-pressure situations, or people take the gun out of your hand so you won't endanger yourself or anybody else. This is the jacket the NAACP was wearing. Why they don't pull the trigger is an array of other issues, but implicate the NAACP with, "officer on the take'" issues. Some of which, we have already discussed. The fact that DeSosa was able to get national to react in a timely manner, and then get a commitment was an accomplishment. The NAACP could have suffered some very, very bad press had they not been able to deliver on a boycott. The issue was in the National press and warranted a quick and immediate action. DeSosa got that to his credit.

The moment for real conflict resolution had arrived. The community came in with eight people, including five NAACP-ers. Reverend Wilson would speak for us and also facilitate the meeting. Winthorpe came in with just his attorneys, Harold and Ron. I seem to remember someone else from mall management coming in later, but Winthorpe handled negotiations himself. The meeting started with Rev. Wilson opening in prayer. Rev. Wilson then requested Winthorpe to respond to the position the community had taken in the dispute. Winthorpe allowed Harold Becks to respond on behalf of the mall. Becks proposed that Connie Wilson be disciplined for her actions, that Cinchek be reprimanded, that the mall apologize to the community and receive a seat on the Merchants Association council. Rev. Wilson asked, "And what about Rodney?" Becks responded that Rodney would receive a letter of apology and a small (four figure) settlement for his troubles. We all looked at each other. I told Rev. Wilson we needed a few minutes to discuss amongst ourselves. The Winthorpe contingent left the room.

I took the lead, stating that they hadn't met any of our major requests, and that we should reject the offer. The group was in agreement with that. Rev. Wilson asked if we needed to give a reason "why" we rejected the offer. I told him, "No. They know what they have to do. They're trying to feel you out to see what you're willing to accept. We'll get past all of this in a minute."

When they came back in the room, Rev. Wilson very calmly and quietly stated, "We reject your recommendation on Ms. Wilson, Ms. Cinchek and we reject your recommendation for Mr. Newton." Winthorpe turned beet red. You could tell he had yet to take us seriously. Becks wanted to know what we had in mind. Rev. Wilson responded, "A more serious offer to our specific requests." They huddled, whispered, then came back with a counter proposal. Becks proposed having Ms. Wilson suspended for 30 days and having Ms. Cinchek transferred to another mall. They would give Mr. Newton a mid-four figure settlement. We told them we had to talk about it.

This time we took about 45 minutes. Two of the community members felt we should take the offer, or at least amend our position. I asked them why. Their position was that they didn't think that Winthorpe would fire two white women, and give up money. They felt that we should take what they were offering and run. I asked, "Why are we in such a rush to bid against ourselves?" What seemed to be coming out was that old inherent socialization that we should take whatever white folk offer, because we're so used to getting nothing, that we jump at a little something. If it means being bought for cheap, some of the more insincere whites know that a little money can always soothe the hurt of those who don't have it. Even when we're holding all the cards with money on the table, we forget about the whole damn deal. In this case, Winthorpe's ace was his money, which he had showing. We knew what our hand was, but still a few of us were willing to try to hedge the bet and throw away our hand. We'd come too far to throw away the hand now. Surely not for chump change. Knowing most of them hadn't been in any fierce negotiations, I took the lead.

I asked, "What's the worse that can happen to us in this situation?" After silence I stated, "The worse that can happen is that we don't come to an agreement, and we move to boycott. Isn't that right?" Everybody concurred. "Now if we boycott, what's the worse that can happen to us? We lose time, maybe some shopping convenience. But what does he lose? Money. And in the end, he'll still call us back to the table. Now knowing his worse case scenario is a boycott, extended negative press that can cost him dearly way past the holidays, threat to his major tenants, and a close-down of his mall, do you think he's gonna leave here without an agreement?" Everybody sat looking like they had just discovered something. I continued, "To him it's not a matter of `if' he's going to pay, it's `how much'. His best case scenario is to get outta here cheap, and without firing anybody. Believe me, right now he's a lot closer to his best case, than our worse case. Much less his worse case. And believe me, he's gonna find out, before you leave, if you're serious about pulling the trigger." The opposition had quieted down, and it was time to proceed.

When they came back in the room, they seemed a little more confident that we were close to an agreement. Then with the same calm candor, Rev. Wilson stated, "We reject your recommendation on Ms. Wilson and Ms. Cinchek. We also reject your offer on Mr. Newton." This time Winthorpe looked like he was sweating bullets, and we hadn't even begun to turn the ringer yet. I think he was more afraid that we wouldn't come to an agreement than what he'd have to pay or do. But he knew then that those lightweight offers would not fly. Rev. Wilson pretty much let them know that the community would not accept anything less than the firing of Wilson and Cinchek, and a just and fair compensation for Rodney. Becks asked us how "just" is just. Rev. Wilson responded, "You tell us."

They left the room again for about 45 minutes. When they returned, Winthorpe looked as if he had been through the ringer. Sweat was running down his face. You could tell he was literally being sweated. Becks came in with this serious look on his face. He preceded his recommendation with, "This is my client's last and final offer." Rev. Wilson and I made eye contact. I winked at him.

Becks stated that Winthorpe would fire Ms. Wilson effective immediately. Ms. Cinchek would be suspended for 30 days, then transferred to another location. Rev. Wilson looked at me and I gave a real faint nod, indicating that was an acceptable offer. Becks continued that the mall would extend a letter of apology to Mr. Newton and the Carson community, that it would seek to remedy the situation by continuing to work with the community, and offering them a seat on the merchants council. Wilson and I connected and I gave a nod. Becks then stated that they were willing to offer Mr. Newton a high range figure to settle his concern of discrimination. The Rev. and I looked at each other. I shook it off, meaning not good enough. Rev. Wilson stated, "We accept your offer on Ms. Wilson, Ms. Cinchek, the letters and the community seat. However, we still must reject your offer on Mr. Newton."

Winthorpe, whose collar was now soaked and wet, blurted out, "Well, what do you think will settle this issue?" I blurted out a low five-figure number, which doubled the last offer. Everybody stopped and looked at Winthorpe, who had just taken a deep breath, and was sitting with his hands collapsed, wondering if he should accept or counter. I expected a counter. Others thought it was too much. I thought it was too low, but didn't know if the rest of them were willing to hold out for it. It wasn't a whole lot of money, in comparison to what he had to lose. I'm sure he knew that. Still he was acting like it was his kid's college fund the way he was carrying on. He asked if I was sure Rodney would accept that. I told him, Rodney was as close as a phone.

They excused me, while I made two phone calls. I first called an attorney associate of mine and asked how much Newton would expect in court, both in actual and punitive damages. He stated 10 times lost wages would be a good settlement. Then I called Rodney, and I told him what was on the table. He said call him back in ten minutes, he had to discuss it with his wife. When I called back, he said he'd take it. I returned to the room and stated that it was acceptable to Rodney. They huddled again. The figure was 15 times plus what Newton would have received for one month's work. When they broke huddle, Becks in a very calm manner said, "Well it is Christmas. My client has agreed "

At that point, my face broke out in a smile, and Harold noticed it. I wasn't trying to disrespect Becks or his client. It was just a perversity that came over me momentarily, that caused me to stubbornly oppose their reasonable offer. Not enough to break the deal, but enough to let him know that we could have been totally unreasonable, and we didn't appreciate him playing us light. So knowing I had the power, I pushed him just a little bit, just to let him know how it feels to be pushed. Blacks are pushed everyday and have to put up with it, because they are powerless to do anything about it. Blacks very rarely have the power to push white folk anywhere. If they have it, it's only for a moment and they don't use it. You know, "turn the other cheek," etc. Then when we lose it, we're back to being pushed around. Kinda like how white folk push the price up, when they know Blacks are trying to buy something, and have only just enough to pay what its worth. It's usually worth less than what they're asking. Kinda like the push we get on the job when we do more work for less pay, or get hired last and pushed out (fired or laid off) first. For once we had the whip in our hand, and the power to impose a few extra lashes for the hell of it. Now that I've felt it, I really believe this is why white folks really fear Black folk ever coming into power. They fear that we would indeed take pleasure in doing to them what they have taken pleasure in doing to us, for years. Human nature just took over all the retribution a people ever wanted-- a chance to get even with a smile and a chuckle. I guess subconsciously, I wanted to see how that felt. So I did. Now it was back to business. I straightened my face, while Becks finished his response to our offer. We had basically resolved every issue, except the issue of immunity for Donna Guidry. Winthorpe assured us that no retaliation would take place for Guidry coming forth. We agreed that the compensation to Newton would not be disclosed to the public. We all agreed that we would make a joint announcement later that day, since it was now 1:30 in the morning.

As we were leaving, Harold Becks commented on the community's resolve, and expressed his client's sincerity in trying to heal his mall's relationship with the community. We both joked that the guy (Haagen), over on Crenshaw, could take some lessons from this experience. I told him if the Crenshaw community had been as unified in its commitment to ensure community benefit, they could have probably written their own ticket. Still the Carson community did what Crenshaw hadn't been able to do, turn business insensitivity into cooperative economic benefit. Later, the Carson branch would even sign a Fair Share agreement.

We all benefitted from having to deal with inadvertent racism. The ability to deal forthrightly with an issue that none of us really had the time to address, but had the inclination on both sides to put such foolishness to death. Harold Becks and I would become good friends from this experience. A few of the community participants used the issue to launch themselves into public office. The issue brought together a community whose humanity had been challenged and leadership had been flawed. When it came time to defend the humanity of the people and the integrity of the issue, the flaw was exposed. Issues of integrity will always expose the integrity of leadership, mostly every time. Anyone that will stand up for something that's not right, and stand silent while people are being exploited, do not have enough integrity to lead people. This is the state of most urban communities.

There is much to be said for people who stand for right, as

opposed to those who stand for the sake of standing. Carson community activists understood some of this. Instead of just "accepting an apology" or maybe even some token hesitation, this group chose to flush out the whole issue of underlying racism. They chose not to allow themselves to be divided on superfluous issues that could have stalled or undermined that intent of the advocacy. Carson was everything that Crenshaw wasn't, and the results demonstrated that Carson's unity of purpose served as its biggest and most effective weapon.

For me, it was a wonderful diversion in the midst of a very chaotic period. It was also an escape from the hypocritical games being played out in the Los Angeles branch, which took the sense of purpose out of the advocacy, and the sense of satisfaction that comes with exposing wrong, and turning it in the right direction. And, at best, bringing out the rightness altogether. Even if it's the rightness of make believe. Yes, there ain't no such thing as Santa Claus. Nor the Good Tooth Fairy, the Easter Bunny, leprechauns or any of the other fictional characters our society perpetrates. But when we allow society to put a greater emphasis on race than on folklore, we have to destroy the folklore. It also gives us some insight as to how far gone we are in the reality of coming to grips with racism. A discussion always subjugated to mask feelings and perceptions that have never left. They have been buried or put up in a closet like Christmas decorations. They only come out for a reason. Unfortunately, racism now has more and more reason to be pulled off the shelf, but we still don't discuss it. We just ignore it until we bump into it, or it into us. Then we're forced to pick it up, to get it out of our way and back into the closet, so that it can spring out another day. But the saddest irony of all is that racism comes forward, in the most innocent of times. The arrogance of whiteness in America, and of white privilege, often promotes social ignorance and cradles insensitivity as some sort of "right" or statement of fact. It occurs when our hearts are open, our minds are clear, when we're caught off guard, oft times as we are trying to be sincere. We not only witness the ridiculousness of racism as the end product of a biased social construct, but how this society takes its racism from the ridiculous to the sublime.

* * *

11

The Day Change Was Compromised

"Compromise is never anything but an ignoble truce between the duty of man and the terror of a coward."
- Reginald Wright Kauffman

"What you seen, wasn't no dust of changes rising. It was the dust of sameness settling."
- Sterling Plumpp

The game finally began. The branch elections had been set for December 18, 1988 at Mount Moriah Baptist Church. Amid the Article X (ten) filing and public discussions about a split in the branch, I was getting some significant support from the community, and people were anxious to get involved. Joe Duff, a local attorney who had worked on the re-filing of the LAUSD school desegregation case, was now actively campaigning against me. Duff had not done any recent work in the branch, and his sloppy handling of the LAUSD case was a major reason for the case being settled, according to then General Counsel Grover Hankins. The case had been flat out mishandled, but now he was running for branch President.

This election was not going to be an Anthony Essex versus Joe Duff campaign, in terms of who can do what, or will do what. It was already set up to be an anti-Anthony Essex campaign. For it to work and be perceived as legitimate, they needed a living, breathing body, and Joe was it. With opposition, they could raise issues, relevant or not, under the guise of "the people need to know the best qualified candidate." It was a very short time before everyone (involved) knew what was up. Hampered with the lugs (Executive Committee) I inherited from Ray, I set out to bring new blood into the process. I began to put together names of people I knew were true advocates, not easily intimidated and hardworking.

The first name that came to mind was Kerman Maddox. Kerman was already serving as my political action chairman, and wanted to play a more significant role. He had a greater motivation. Kerman was building a track record for future public service ambitions. I didn't have the slightest problem with that, at all. I asked him to run for first Vice President. In the second Vice President slot, I asked Mark Whitlock to come back into the branch leadership. I considered Whitlock a friend then, and he was a major reason I stayed interested in the NAACP after John died. Mark always pumped me up as "the new leader in the NAACP," particularly after his fallout with Ray.

Moreover, I felt Mark would cover my back, stand firm in a storm of controversy, and keep his ear to the floor for me. This would not end up being the case, however, I felt we were close then. In hindsight, I was gravely naive about Mark's dedication to our friendship, but there was loyalty on my part. I felt Mark didn't have an ambition to be NAACP President or he would have been my first choice for first Vice President. He questioned me in church one Sunday about my choice of Kerman over him. My answer was simple: "Kerman wants to be President, you don't," I said.

Mark responded, "You're right. I don't really want to be President."

I felt the branch had to begin to consider future leadership and build for leadership succession.

I knew I'd only do another two years, at best, then I intended to move on. Sharing this insight would later be a point of public controversy. Kerman was right for the slot. Mark, I thought, was more loyal, but Kerman was more community focused. I brought other renegade advocates in the fold to allow them to continue their work in a collaborative effort. Brothers like police activist Don Jackson, gang activist Chilton Alphonse and Rev. Ralph Crabbe. Whether people liked them or not didn't matter to me; they were effective in what they did. They were not easily controlled, but they understood advocacy and the need to be strong. Police misconduct and economic discrimination were going to continue to be the concentration of my activity.

However, Chilton, Rev. Charles Mims, V.G. Guiness and others had increasingly involved me in the anti-gang violence dialogue. The more I understood how it impacted the commerce, economics and general social perceptions of our communities, the more I felt the so-called mainstream needed to intercede. There was a lot of dirty dealing behind the scenes of this gang activity. Much of it fueled by outside influences, mainly the police. Most of the sets were being played against each other by the police, and didn't know it, until we called for a treaty to dialogue.

About this same time, we were getting complaints from the county jail, which we set out to investigate. Don Jackson, chairman of the Police Practices Committee, was doing an excellent job bringing misconduct issues to the Executive Committee. The town hall meeting on police abuse that he and Kerman Maddox organized was really a highlight of my administration, only because it had the potential to rollover into something bigger down the line. Their ground work was well laid. Combined with the jail investigation, we knew local police would be cornered sooner or later. Too much dirty shit was going on and everybody knew it. Several other investigations were going on simultaneously. Advocacy was popping in the L.A. branch.

We were investigating discrimination claims against Brotman Hospital, because they were allegedly referring patients away from Black doctors. One heart doctor, Dr. Donald Ware, eventually filed suit, and won a multimillion dollar award that resulted from this activity. We had continuing investigations going on at both Hughes Aircraft and Southern California Edison, where Black employees were literally being spied on and harassed out of their jobs.

Our efforts to curtail gang violence was proving to be somewhat successful. Several gang sets had agreed to "stop the madness" (the name of our upcoming concert), sit down and dialogue. Out of that dialogue came the first "peace treaty," a truce between rival gangs that was seen as nothing short of a miracle. As a result of engaging in the dialogue, I was extremely criticized by mainstream so-called leaders and editorial writers ("What's the NAACP doing trying to stop gang violence?"- the late A.S. "Doc" Young). The young men discovered that they had a common enemy unbeknownst to either of them, the police or law enforcement operatives who would provide them guns and drugs to fuel gang warfare. But because they never got close enough to each other to inquire, neither set never thought about the fact that their conflict was being fueled and agitated by an outside force (eight years later this activity would be tied to the CIA). But now they knew it was "somebody," and were beginning to act in kind.

We were advocating on every level of the community for the youths, for the working men and women, for the entrepreneurs and their efforts to access corporate and governmental business and for Black professionals. The community was excited that they finally had, not just an advocate, but an activist in the NAACP again, and the people showed it by joining in droves. A branch membership that was under 1,500 when I took over (closer to 1,200) was now over 5,000, in a little over four months, and it was growing. We weren't through yet. In preparing for the branch election, our proposed slate brought in another 2,000 memberships. We just overwhelmed the opposition. They hadn't brought in 700 memberships between them for the whole period. We dropped 600 memberships on the last day of eligibility alone, 15 minutes before the agreed upon 6 p.m. deadline.

The Duff campaign came in with a little over 100 memberships, many after the deadline. When we tried to hold them to the agreement of no memberships after 6 p.m., everybody on their side got selective amnesia, claiming "we only decided on the date, but not the time." Cynthia Walker, who had coordinated our membership effort, was like a loose tiger saying, "Why is everybody running in here trying to beat 6 p.m., if we hadn't decided on a time. You guys are a bunch of liars." Nobody had ever really seen Cynthia go off, so they were really surprised to hear her come off like that.

Distrust was at its peak now. We decided to set those memberships aside, and get a ruling from national the next day. I decided to stay while Ernestine manually logged in the memberships. After about four hours, I just left knowing that we had logged our memberships and knew everyone that we had turned in. The next day, Bill Penn ruled in their favor, claiming the deadline was at the close of the branch's business day, and if the branch wanted to stay open to receive memberships, that was the branch's prerogative.

"Prerogative or not, it wasn't what we agreed to, Mr. Penn," I stated, "We pulled our people out of the field at 4 p.m. If we knew we had all evening, we would have brought another 500 memberships." I saw Joe's face cringe. He knew we were getting ready to run over him, and that we probably could have brought in the memberships.

Penn stated, "Well you just might get the chance to do that Mr. Essex."

At that moment, we got an indication of where Penn was leaning in his decision on the pending Article X complaint. The break that Joe and his crew needed, they were about to get. Time to bring a steamroller to a screeching halt.

* * *

Knowing that, they had to find some way to overcome 5,500 members we had influenced, from coming out to vote on December 18, the Duff campaign, engineered by George Mallory and Henry Dotson, began to increase their efforts to discredit me by trying to call my actions and character into question. At the November branch meeting, at Second Baptist Church, all candidates were to come before the membership and speak their position. When it came time for the candidates for branch President to speak, Joe launched into a full-fledged attack on my character. He didn't say one thing about what he would do in the branch. The membership was stunned that he would wage his character assassination campaign right out of the church pulpit.

I came behind him and talked about how my opposition had the nerve to talk about character and integrity when the only reason he was in this race was to crucify me. Then I talked about all we had done, and all we were doing to bring new blood into the branch. I received a standing ovation, while Joe sat in the pulpit with a shocked look on his face. At that moment, George Mallory, who had been sitting in the front row, next to one of my best friends, Floyd Frazier, began passing out Duff fliers containing this character assassination rhetoric and misinformation around the church. It was the absolute lowest act of personal integrity I had ever witnessed in a church, at that point in time (there was more to come, though). Many others felt the same way.

His flier contained a candid section that had in it several half-truths, and some outright lies. This data was derived from public record filings, as a part of a background investigation that the Duff camp paid for. They had complied a "So this man wants to be NAACP President" packet they were to send to key figures in the community. The federal government (the FBI and the Justice Department) would also end up with a copy in their hands. More on this later. Clearly, the lines for a character assassination campaign had been drawn. This had become evident a couple of weeks earlier, when at the branch's Executive Committee meeting, it was disclosed that Mount Moriah Baptist Church had changed its mind about hosting the branch election. One of the most vicious of the Duff supporters, a woman named Jessica Smith, who initially served on the Executive Committee, as the director of the Voices of Freedom (a choir initiated under John McDonald's administration), surfaced as a principle player in this effort to discredit me. I never really paid much attention to her, or these so-called Voices of Freedom. She, like William Upton and his NAACP television show, used the choir as an opportunity to inflate her fledgling music career. When I didn't give their projects the priority they felt they should have been given, both became vindictive in their activity to replace me. Jessica, who was now connected with Ernestine, in some personal way, took it upon herself (so Duff and Dotson claimed) to go around to every church and organization that would listen, and talk about me in the worst way imaginable. Because she was so indiscriminate in whom she talked to, a few times, I was called by the person, before she had even pulled out their driveway. She eventually got around to Rev. Wade, the pastor of Mount Moriah. Hearing Smith's version of what was going on in the branch, and reading between the lines, he chose to rescind his church's offer to host the election.

Duff's camp had overplayed its hand, and now the whole Executive Committee knew it. At the ensuing Executive Committee meeting, Duff, Dotson and John Mance had Jessica out in the hallway, jamming her on how she could be so stupid. Crying, she replied that she was only doing what she had been told to do. Not only had she made this little branch dispute a public fight, it also was costing the branch money. The branch had already printed 8,000 plus branch notifications about the elections being at Mount Moriah. They weren't mailed, but had to be reprinted. In trying to decide how the branch would select a new election place, a process took place that caused some very strange events to follow. After a very heated discussion, one of my appointees to the Executive Committee, Rev. Joe Hardwick, decided to act as self-appointed mediator. Hardwick would later turn out to be one of the most wickedly corrupt preachers in the city. He probably was then, but it was unbeknownst to me at the time, because he claimed to be a supporter and I perceived him as such.

The concern was not only when to hold the elections, but

where to hold the elections, and not give one candidate an advantage over the other. The churches with the largest NAACP memberships were First AME and Second Baptist. Second Baptist consistently maintained the largest single voting block in the branch anywhere, from 300 to 500 members annually. They not only bought membership, they voted in branch elections. We had garnered close to 800 of our 5,500 memberships out of First AME, in gearing up for this election. Clearly, FAME, as the church is known in the Los Angeles community, had the power to carry the election, if they could get their vote out. But whereas, Second Baptist had an older membership, who were civil rights stalwarts that marched and stood in lines to vote in the South and could be counted on in a branch election, FAME was known for its more secular, contemporary congregation, who might come to vote and might not, depending on what else was going on in L.A. at the time. Of course, if it was convenient, the FAME congregation was likely to vote, meaning if the branch elections were held there, as they had been in the past, the members would probably vote, as they left the church service. So when First AME came up as an alternative election site, Duff's opposition almost stood up in unison against having the election there. Of course, my committee supporters stood up against Second Baptist hosting the election.

In trying to determine the best neutral site, Hardwick said, "OK, Anthony, you're AME, so we can't have it at an AME church and Joe, you're what?" Joe paused, then started saying something like he had his own belief, to which Hardwick said, "OK, Joe is nothing (meaning he had no church affiliation) and so..." Everybody laughed and Joe got defensive, saying he didn't have a church home, at that point.

We had organizing meetings at FAME, putting in place our organizing strategy to solicit memberships, collecting memberships, setting up phone trees and getting out correspondence. Anywhere from 70 to 100 people were attending these meetings. It was clearly the most diverse group of Blacks meeting in L.A. We had Baptist, CME's, AME's, Muslims, Christians, Masons, Black nationalists, fraternity and sorority representatives, gang leaders and intervention counselors, city employees, Black firefighters, even Black policemen. We knew there were a couple of spies in our group from the Duff campaign. Elvin Moon, a member of the Executive Committee and a L.A. businessman, was one. He'd attend our meetings under the guise that he was with us, then we'd look up and he'd be on the other side. We didn't worry about it too much, because we had spies on their side, too. Our intelligence was telling us that their number one priority was finding Joe a church home. Their second priority was digging up more dirt on me.

One week after our little discussion on election sites, I got a call from Kerman Maddox. He wanted to meet with me A.S.A.P. When we met, he let me know that a church member had been hired to do the background investigation on me, and he had taken it to Chip, before turning it over to the Duff camp. The center of the discussion was the Founders countersuit, and its allegations of my personal impropriety. Kerman wanted to know if there was anything to it. I told him there wasn't, and explained to him that I filed against Founders, because they fired me due to my refusal to sign off on some improper transactions. When I sued them, they counter-sued me, claiming I lied about coming up with the down payment on my house.

"That's it?" Kerman said.

"That's it," I responded.

"Why haven't you told the rest of the group?" he asked.

"Because I didn't think it was necessary, Kerman."

Kerman then went into a long dissertation about how when you ask others to support you, you should get a FBI file on yourself, show it to the people and say, "This is me, do you want to support me or not? And let people decide if they want to."

I agreed with that, if it was a run for public office. "This is a branch election, not a run for public office," I stated.

Kerman responded, "But when people are being asked about your character, Anthony, they should be in a position to defend you. Clearly, we are not, and you need to do something about it, before you start losing support. I suggest you call Chip and have a meeting with him, and then call your group together, and tell them what's being put out there."

I agreed to do that. I met with Chip that same day. Chip didn't appear particularly distressed, at that point, but more annoyed that we had to be having this conversation. He just listened, then admonished me to "tie up some of these loose ends after the election." As I left his office, he told me to tell Kerman that "everything is the same" like some withdrawal of support was being taken under consideration.

The following Sunday, who do I see in the front row of the pulpit but Joe Duff. It wasn't until I spoke with Chip the following week that he told me that Duff had joined the church. "I'm still with you Anthony, we just have to do things a little differently now, so we don't split the church," Chip said.

What Chip may (or may not) have already known was that Duff and his camp had a plan to neutralize First AME, by splitting the church. Duff would join the church and try to split the FAME vote while Dotson and Mrs. Anderson would hold Second Baptist solidly for Joe. FAME had a large following in the legal community (lawyers who attended the church), which Duff and Mallory had inroads to. Many of the attorneys held key positions on the trustee and steward boards and had the capacity to reach some segments of the church population. So, unbeknownst to Chip, the church had already been put "in play." Now the play was to push the great Rev. Chip Murray to a position of neutrality by questioning his judgment in supporting a person with credibility issues in his past.

Chip relived this scenario ten years later with a person that had even worse credibility issues. This time affirming his support of FBI informant Julius "Julio" Butler--the man whose testimony was responsible for the 25 year imprisonment of Ex-Black Panther Geronimo Ji Jaga (Pratt). Chip backed Butler to the end (until Geronimo's release), but in 1988, Chip bit hook, line and sinker. By doing things "a little different," he meant taking a lower profile in his promotion of me. However, in the eyes of the public, it was perceived as neutrality. The philosophy of the opposition was clearly, "We don't care if you support him, just don't tell anybody."

I knew from then on that it was going to be a personal battle to save my relationship with Chip, as well as, maintain the integrity of this campaign in the process. In meeting with my campaign support group, there was virtually no fallout, at all. Nobody really batted an eye. Many of my supporter's position was that "this has nothing to do with the NAACP." Kerman didn't attend the meeting, choosing to stay away until this little controversy was resolved. Kerman, who had relationships on both sides, had the benefit of knowing what was coming down the pike, and was contemplating dropping off the slate. Both he and Mark were the primary targets of the opposition's effort to isolate me. By letting them know what was about to happen, the opposition was giving them a chance to steer clear of the "dirt bombs" that were about to be dropped. Even knowing this dirt was out there didn't deter our support from carrying a spirit of determination and change in the final leg prior to the elections. By then, I wanted to just get it over with. However, that wasn't about to happen.

*   *   *

The first week of December, less than two weeks before elections, a major bombshell was dropped. National decided to seize control of the branch. Elections would be postponed indefinitely. The day the branch was notified, everybody was scrambling to get their version of the truth in. The *Los Angeles Times*, who ran the story on the front page of the *Metro Section*, jumped at the opportunity to misrepresent the action by national. "NAACP Quarrel Leads to Takeover of Chapter in L.A." was the headline. William Penn, who had a long-standing feud with Los Angeles, couldn't wait to slam the branch, after receiving my response to the Article X charges. Instead of holding his inquiry, and then placing the branch in receivership, he chose the opposite. Penn, in his overreaction, wasn't really concerned about the Article X complaint. The committee on branches would deal with that issue. He was after the larger monies that had been diverted from the branch and put in "the corporation," CEDC.

Until the week before, most of the public didn't know the real reason behind the conflict in the branch. Betty Pleasant, who was the editor of the *Los Angeles Sentinel* had been approached by the Duff camp with all these criticisms of me and the Article X complaint. Trying to keep the drama at a minimum, I asked her if she had seen my response to the complaint. She said no. I had it delivered to her.

Betty read it and called me back. "This is pretty juicy stuff. Is this Jim McBeth married to Judge Veronica McBeth?" she asked.

I said, "Yes, why?"

All I heard was "Ahh-Ha!!! Well, Anthony, I'm not going to tell you much, other than it seems like they are trying to do to you, what they did to a friend of mine. They're even using similar language. I'll leave it at that. You'll have to read about the rest," she said.

Turns out Betty's friend was former presiding Municipal Court Judge Maxine Thomas, considered by many to be a brilliant young sister with "a state Supreme Court" kind of a future, until she ran into a conflict with her fellow jurists over assignments and her "high profile" persona. Judge Thomas was removed after a relatively brief tenure by a group of jurists, (the more vocal was allegedly Judge McBeth), over many allegations of juris prudence and expenditure of public funds, including an inaugural reception that came to be known as "Maxine's coronation." The similar language that was used in the information sent to the *Sentinel*, according to Betty, was referenced to the branch reception as "Anthony's coronation."

Next thing I knew, Betty ran a piece that gave probably the

most accurate account of what was going on in the branch and was perceived by most as a very positive piece for me. My opposition hated it, because not only did she not use much of the misinformation that they had given her, but she also got a dig in on Judge McBeth by associating Jim as "the husband of Judge Veronica McBeth." I didn't see any implication of the mention being tied to the branch activity. I had always viewed Veronica McBeth as a pretty fair sister, whose use of judicial discretion was creative and visionary. She was one of the first jurists to sentence slumlords to live in their own substandard housing tenements. At the time, I paid little attention to the mention. I was just glad to see a balanced article for a change. Unlike what the *Los Angeles Times* ran a week later, in breaking the takeover story. There was nothing positive or accurate about the *Times* whole story. McBeth (Jim) gave his side of the story, I gave my side, Penn gave national's position, but it was all tied together by one, who many considered a most unreliable source (and one who wasn't there from the outset of the conflict in 1987), a guy named Basil Kimbrew.

Kimbrew, who has called himself a political czar and gatherer of adverse information (dirt) on campaign opposition, had worked his way into my confidence, by supplying me some of the initial resource data on the Baldwin Hills/Crenshaw Mall Plaza project. After taking it as far as he could, he gave the information to a close friend of mine named Vicki Phillips, who in turn gave it to me. When people first saw Basil standing with me on the project against the mayor, they ran to me in droves saying, "Stay away from Basil. He's a big-time snake in the grass, at least, four people called him. So I watched him for a long time, before dealing with him, and didn't come to that conclusion (at least at that point). I tried (and still try) to deal with people based on my experience with them, and not others' biased perspectives. Ignoring all the snake warnings, I dealt with him for two years without getting bit. Well, all of that was about to change.

Basil bit me in the *Times* article, big time. Everybody knew it was coming, and when he did it, the calls came in. "He finally bit ya, huh?" There was nothing I could say.

Fred Rasheed once told me a story about "handlin' snakes." The story is about a man who found an injured snake lying at the side of the road, picked up the injured snake, took it home and healed it back to health. Only to have the snake bite him one day when he reached to pick it up again. The man said to the snake, "After all I've done for you, how could you bite me?" The snake replied, "You knew I was a snake when you picked me up." The is that one has to understand the nature of snakes and their disloyal behavior. There was nothing I could say to anybody about Basil. I picked him up when nobody would touch him, and now he had his fangs in me. All I could say, besides "Ouch!" was, "I knew he was a snake, when I picked him up."

Kimbrew first rehashed the Article X complaint focusing on the expenses, when there were several other issues raised of a non-financial nature. He stated that ten people had signed the complaint when it was actually only eight, all of whom were in opposition from the outset (which he knew but failed to say). He claimed the allegation of $65,000 being siphoned away from the branch was attributed to my 29-page response to the complaint, when nowhere in my response did I reference $65,000, nor did I imply that they siphoned off money. The Executive Committee knew where the money went, and it was supposed to be at the branch's disposal. The fact was that national was cheated out of its entitled share, (50 percent of it the branch raised) which was a major issue. No matter how it was cloaked, the money should've been controlled by the organization. This wasn't stated. It implied that I was trying to control CEDC. That wasn't true either, but I did demand a seat on the board, which every President before me had been allotted, and the Executive Committee had voted for me to have. It had yet been afforded to me. The article was a montage of unfounded assertions that did more to cloud the issues going on in the branch, than to clear them up. *The Times* had done its job in continuing to misrepresent issues in the Black community.

Basil didn't just stop there. He began "wining and dining" a sister on our slate named Bridgette Bellande. Bridgette was a very nice sister, very well-intentioned, but naive to the tricks of politics. As all is fair in love, war and politics, Bridgette never even saw the war and politics side of this sudden interest Basil was showing in her. She perceived Basil's overtures to her as a sincere personal interest. Pretty soon it was rumored they were engaged to be married. Basil even stood up in the church (at First AME) one day to join with her, hand in hand. It was the most despicable (and pitiful) trick I'd ever seen played on a Black woman. But it worked. Within a week of *The Times* article, Bridgette had dropped off the slate, and a major portion of our campaign strategy ended up in the hands of the Duff camp.

If *The Times* article didn't take the steam out of our battle, an indefinite postponement of the election did. It's tough to keep everybody's energy and spirits up for an undisclosed period of time. It was different for the opposition, because most of them were already involved in the branch. But for new people who really didn't understand what all of this was about, it was very difficult to explain, much less rationalize. Most of us who were involved didn't expect this, but now we had to deal with it. We met as an Executive Committee and for a minute, the politics took a back seat. For the first time, many on the Executive Committee heard the nature of the charges and my response. A lot of finger pointing was taking place. Mallory got up and made a statement of how I had put them in this predicament with my response, also stating that if his name was in the response, I'd be in trouble. I looked at him like, "Nigger, pleeease." I saw George Mallory as a bitch of the highest caliber, never man enough to do his dirty dealing out front; but always tried to represent himself as "proper" in front of the Executive Committee even though he was foul as hell. I had his ass on tape "plotting to undermine me" like a little mole, so I knew what he was up to and could give a damn about what he thought. This was just part of his hidden-handed act.

I responded to his comments by stating that I wasn't the one who filed the complaint to the National, and that it was their plot to play me out of pocket that had backfired. It was the first revelation that many innocent Executive Committee members were being used in their grudge match against me. The meeting degenerated from there. It proved how far gone we were as a unit. In a meeting that was called to deal with Penn coming to L.A., it was apparent that it was going to be me against them. Every man and woman for themselves.

* * *

William Penn, National Director of Branch Services, arrived on December 11 for a called Executive Committee meeting. With him was Jim Martin, the Western Regional Director and Jose DeSosa, the State Conference President. The meeting was explosive, to say the least. Penn stated out front that he wasn't there to deal with the complaint against me, but to investigate my counter-charges, and to audit the branch. At the conclusion of his investigation, he would make a recommendation to the national committee on branches.

The first thing he jammed was our hiring of Harold Webb, as Executive Secretary, who had been a dream to work with. Penn claimed he never gave the final sign-off on Webb's hire, and he couldn't remember giving back the $10,000, because it was not national's policy to turn away money. There was dead silence, and everybody looked at me for a response. I was so taken aback, I saw flashes of red. Penn was sitting to my right, and it took all the restraint I had to keep from cold-cocking his ass in the side of his head. I was furious. All I could say was, "That's not true, Mr. Penn, and you know it."

Before Penn and I could get into a shouting match, one of our old-timers, William Dailey, stood up and said, "Well Mr. Penn, if our President says he gave you the money, and you gave it back, we believe him. But we know that's not why you're here." Mr. Dailey will never know to this day how much that statement meant to me, at a time when it appeared everything was being turned around. This was a time of absolute madness and I was close to losing it. That little tinge of support was enough time for me to regain my composure and focus on Penn's response. Penn forthrightly stated that he was there to deal with the issue of this "corporation" that had been formed. He wanted to know where the money was, who controlled it, and to have it rightfully returned to the branch. Penn stated he would interview every member of the Executive Committee, over the next couple of days. He stated that Jim Martin would be the primary branch contact on press issues, and that no one would make comments to the press.

As the meeting adjourned, most of the committee hung around to kiss up to Penn, while the staff began pulling records Penn had requested. Still fuming, I looked Penn straight in the face and said, "Why would you say something like that, as many discussions as we've had? Is this going to be a fair evaluation, or is this your get-even move on L.A.?"

Penn just looked at me and said, "Time will tell, won't it?"

With nothing else to say, I left the branch. Mark Whitlock ran out behind me. "Anthony, why are you leaving?" he asked.

"What's there to stay for, Mark?"

"Well, if they were saying about me, what they are saying about you, I'd have been in there to defend myself," he said.

"Defend myself against what, Mark? A lie, a conspiracy? Is my presence going to stop them from collaborating against me, any more than they have over the past six months? I don't think so, Mark. I'm not going to run behind a bunch of liars to refute what we all know to be lies. The truth will come out."

"But what if it doesn't?" Mark said.

"Then I guess it would be a real sad commentary for what we say we stand for, wouldn't it?" I said, as I got in my car.

Clearly frustrated with my responses, Mark ran around to the passenger side of my car, and jumped in to finish our conversation. Not really knowing what to say, we both sat silently for a minute. Mark finally broke the silence. "Anthony, why are you letting them get away with this? You know, when you're dealing with pigs, you have to get down in the shit with them."

"What's that supposed to mean, Mark?"

"Maybe it's time for you to start throwing a little dirt, rather than being the recipient of all the dirt," he suggested. I had to agree with him. I certainly had received my share. Several others in my campaign also suggested that I play as they were playing. However, I was reluctant to go that way. I knew that once I reduced the game to that level, the hedge of protection that I felt was around me would be broken. I knew in my heart that all of this, in time, would be exposed. For God is the revealer of all things and truths. But I couldn't get many of my supporters to see that, so a few of them took the position that either I was weak, or that what the opposition was saying was true. It was neither. I wasn't falling for the trap that was being set. That's all. I could see what they didn't see and moved as God instructed me to move. But all I could tell Mark (who ironically now is a preacher, at First AME of Los Angeles, no less) was, "I can't go that route. This (branch involvement) is not worth it."

Mark's last comment was, "Is it worth it to them?"

"That's them, not me," I responded.

We said good night, and held our breath for what the next few days would bring. Penn went about his interviews, including one with me (in which I could tell he was just going through the motions). I had been warned by several inside sources that Penn wasn't with me, and that I should "get my facts exact and don't confide in him." I followed that advice. He returned to Baltimore to write his report, and the feud returned to normal.

December, 1988 was a month unlike any I had experienced in my life. Between concentrating on the county jail investigation, and the "Black Santa Claus" discrimination issue, I used the election postponement to fund raise and try to close out my business year on an upswing. I felt my life was moving at 200 miles per hour and I had no extra time for anything. The week after Penn left, our campaign group had a fund-raiser at football hall of famer, Jim Brown's home in the Hollywood Hills. Taurece had been on me all week to go Christmas shopping. Though I had been in the Carson Mall a half-dozen times, I didn't think to pick up one gift for my family. That Sunday, the day of the fund-raiser, Taurece and I spent the day shopping, which gave me some temporary peace at home. By the time we finished, I was late for the fund-raiser.

Speeding up LaCienega Boulevard in a Porsche is like holding up a flashing red sign that says: "Stop me, ticket me." As I crossed the Beverly Hills city limit at Pico Boulevard, I could see a cop car pull behind me. I slowed to 35 miles per hour. He followed me for three blocks before pulling me over. He came up to the window and asked me to step out of the car. I complied. "You have a taillight malfunction," the officer said. May I see your driver's license and registration?" I took it out and gave it to him. He ran a check. While he was waiting for the check to come back he noticed fliers on the back seat of the car. May I have one of these Mr. Essex? I appreciate the work you do for the NAACP," the officer said. Stunned that this was coming from a law enforcement officer, I nodded. A few minutes later, the officer came back. "I'm going to have to place you under arrest, Mr. Essex?"

"For what?"

"It seems you have three tickets that have turned into warrants," he said. I immediately went into furor.

"What do you mean I have warrants, I paid them over two months ago, when I registered the car."

In California, unpaid tickets are sent to the Department of Motor Vehicles and the local Municipal Courts, to ensure payment. You are not allowed to register a car if you don't pay the tickets. Even today, in Los Angeles, the city will boot your car, or you could be arrested after paying the tickets, because of a six-month lag time between the time the local municipality notifies DMV that a ticket has been cleared up. However, at the time, I just knew this was some kind of L.A.P.D. trick. I was in the middle of what proved to be a very embarrassing situation. The L.A.P.D. is known for its retaliatory measures.

The officer seemed sympathetic to my dilemma, but had already been instructed to arrest me. "Gee, I'm sorry, Mr. Essex, but there's nothing I can do," he said.

"Well, do what you have to do."

The officer remained calm and collected. It was straight out of the movie "Beverly Hills Cop." But this was no laughing matter. I requested that I be allowed to move my car to a side street, so I could have it picked up later. He agreed to let me do that. I asked that I not be handcuffed in public. He agreed to handcuff me in the car. Praise

God for small favors, if I had to be arrested.

Meanwhile, word had gotten up to Jim's house that I had been arrested. Several of the reception guests had seen me down on LaCienega, and put two and two together. There were already two messages at the station for me when I got there. "Call and tell us how much? Keep your chin up, Cynthia." Cynthia Walker had already taken charge of the situation, and was now ready to do what she had to do. She was one of the most "kick-ass and take charge" type of women I'd ever met. Within 90 minutes, she brought down the $620 needed to "bail me out." Never being one not to take advantage of a situation, I had to listen to "Big House" jokes all the way back up the hill. I got there in time to address some of the guests. Of course, Duff's camp had sent someone to the reception. The first message on my tape Monday morning was a woman's voice saying, "How'd you like jail?" It was a matter of time before everybody knew, or maybe it just seemed like everybody. Beverly Hills publishes everybody they arrest in the newspaper. There was nothing I could say. The tickets were paid. I got the money back, but I had been arrested, error or not. This little event just threw more shit in the game, and made my world spin faster.

Christmas, 1988. I have absolutely no recollection of what events took place on, or about that particular holiday. That's strange for me, because I can recall most experiences and events in quite vivid detail. It was a significant holiday period, because it was the last one I'd spend at home with the children, while married to Taurece. Moreover, it was the last time I'd celebrate Christmas at all. I remember, we got the girls bikes, and Tony a bunch of cars and a computer game that hooked to the television. But in terms of the warmth and the memories of gift opening and family coming together from that holiday, there are none. I just can't remember, and I know that this is attributed to all the confusion that was going on in the branch and the catch-up I was playing in my business.

The one thing I did remember was going to church. Christmas fell on a Sunday. I remember, because Taurece went to church with us. I would generally take the girls with me every other Sunday, but in the 14 years that Taurece and I were together, we went to church together less than a half dozen times. That Sunday she volunteered to go. I remember getting real emotional toward the end of the service. Tears came rolling down my face. It was the first time Taurece ever saw me cry. She knew I was deeply troubled. It all caught up with me on December 25, 1988.

I was working late on a business acquisition project for Datacom, a computer support business, owned by a brother named Michael Jamerson. He was in the process of trying to acquire an IBM "C" channel dealership, which allows a dealer to buy exclusively from IBM, at the lowest rate possible with guaranteed financing. At that time, those dealerships numbered less than a dozen nationwide, and were worth between $3 million and $5 million, on its designation alone. None of them were Black-owned. Mike's sister, Melanie, and I had been charged with performing the due diligence work that would establish a final valuation for the dealership purchase price. It had been raining earlier in the evening, and the roads were still very wet. On the way back into Los Angeles, Melanie and I were traveling on the Interstate 405 freeway in the number one (fast) lane, when my back left tire blew out. The car went into a spin across all four lanes and stopped on the edge of the freeway embankment that ran 40 feet downhill. We'd stopped two feet past the guard rail, so there was nothing to stop us from going down the side of the freeway, except the grace of God. Both of us, literally in shock, just stared into space, in wonderment that we got across four lanes, without being hit, and without ending up at the bottom of the embankment. I started up the car and rolled it down the closest off ramp. When I got out to look at my tire, I noticed that the blowout was from the side, almost like a partial slit, because there was no wear or tear around where the tire blew out. Melanie called Mike and Belinda to come and get us. That was the last time I saw my Porsche. I just walked off and left it.

I went two days later to pick it up, but it had been towed away. I had Katherine call every impound service in the Carson, Compton and Long Beach areas. Nobody had the car. Three weeks later I got a call from an L.A. County Deputy Sheriff, who had bought my car from an impound, and wanted my pink slip. "What do you mean you bought my car," I yelled. I never even got notification of where the car was, much less that it was being sold. It was sold by one of the impound centers Katherine had called. He had found one of my business cards in the car, so he said. I told him that my car had been sold illegally, and I wasn't giving him anything. I also told him I hope he hadn't participated in anything illegal.

He immediately got defensive. "I hope you're not threatening me."

"Call it what you want," I said. He hung up the phone. We called the impound and got placed on hold about six times. We did find out it was a Highway Patrol impound that sent the impound notifications to the wrong address, three times. Reversing the "6" and the "9" in the middle of my address. I found out that this was a frequent maneuver to stall an owner from retrieving popular cars that are often sold, for failure to claim them. In a time-sensitive play to quickly acquire these cars, many of these impound centers know that once the car is sold, it is almost impossible to get it back. Games that police play with public, but another fight I didn't need. I went out and bought a new Chevy Blazer the next day. While I missed the car, I didn't miss the significance that the accident had on my life.

Things were moving way too fast. Everything was happening, one right after the other. The faces and places of this period just meshed together like a montage of clips. I felt trapped in my involvement to an organization that at one time was a volunteer position, but now seemed like an obligation. The more I tried to bring about a change for the better, the more resistance I got. The more people we got involved, the more resentment I received from the older (in terms of time in the branch) players. The more time I gave to the advocacy, the more cases I got to do more advocacy. The more I tried to be at home, the more I was pulled away from home. It seemed like I wasn't making a dent in the problems facing our people, which made my decline in business and my separation from my family appear all the worse. The accident made me feel like a rubber band that had finally snapped. Spinning across four lanes of the freeway reminded me of how a rubber band snaps across the room after one end is let loose. Out of control, with no sense of purpose or direction. Surviving that spin was a very clear sign to me, SLOW DOWN, OR LET GO. Up until that point, I felt like I couldn't let go, and the more the branch bucked, the tighter I held on. My life was in a crisis, and I had to make up my mind about what I was going to do. Two events occurred back to back that helped me make up my mind.

The first Sunday of 1989, I felt like I needed a battery charge for my spirit. I knew that First AME wasn't going to do it that day. I needed something different. Plus, the likelihood of running into Duff at his new church home, and all the antics that would surround such a hypocritical encounter, would defeat the whole purpose. I had awakened determined to go get the spiritual enlightenment I needed, but it wouldn't be at FAME. I decided to go to West Angeles Church of God in Christ Annual New Year's services at the Shrine Auditorium. Bishop Charles Blake was considered one of the moral authorities of the city and one of the best spiritual lecturers (preachers) anywhere in the country. Bishop Blake could bring a lecture full circle in 25 minutes, with all the fire and emotion one would need to get through the week. He preached four services on Sunday, to a fast growing congregation in the city. Once a year, he called his whole congregation together as a family to worship in one service. And while everybody else was professing 5,000 or 6,000 members, Blake had a legitimate 5,000 and showed it on the first Sunday of the New Year.

A subtle but effective show of influence, Bishop Blake's sermon was on dealing with the challenges of life, saying in his sermon that people who can't stand the heat should get out of the kitchen. This parable was apparently directed at those who tend to criticize and talk about people who are trying to make some progress but do little, if anything, to help. He talked about how well-intentioned, good- hearted people are dissuaded by the mean-spirited who "cannot stand the heat," but want to stay in the kitchen and complain how hot it is. Bishop Blake went on to say how some people didn't even have any business in the kitchen and how too many cooks spoil the broth. It really was an appropriate message for what I was dealing with in the branch. By the time Bishop Blake finished with his sermon, 4,000 people were screaming at a fever pitch. It really was an impressive service. I left the service totally charged, and had all but made up my mind to continue with my candidacy in the branch.

Later in the week, an event helped me make up my mind for sure. At a reception to kick off the (Martin Luther) King week celebration, sponsored by the SCLC, Rev. Chip Murray and I happened to be standing next to each other in one of the casual conversation circles. Out of the clear blue sky, Chip said to me, while looking straight ahead, "Anthony, my son, why don't you let them have the branch, and drop out of the race. I'll bring you before the congregation and give you an award for your efforts." There was a long pause. I turned and just stared at Chip. As inappropriate as the moment was, I was waiting for his follow-up reasoning. He offered none.

Saying nothing, I walked away in disgust, never seeing Chip in the same light from that day on. I couldn't. Here was a man, who was like a father to me in many ways, telling me he'd give me a plaque to drop out of a situation, in which I was being attacked. I had over 100 plaques and awards. I didn't have any more space to put anymore awards. What did I need with another plaque? Another plaque didn't mean shit to me, and I damn sure wouldn't hang a plaque of compromise on my wall. Furthermore, he was asking me to receive a plaque of compromise in front of Duff and the whole church. How stupid did he think I was? I was thoroughly insulted by my own minister and hurt that he didn't have enough moral fortitude and courage to sit me down and explain to me why he felt I should not run and the potential damage he felt I would suffer. Chip was one who could have changed my mind about running, if the options and alternatives had been discussed and mediated in a fair and intelligent manner. I knew Chip didn't know all that was behind this, particularly what was behind Duff's candidacy. I did know he was in frequent communication with Joe, and was being convinced that I couldn't win, or would be removed from office, before I got the chance to run.

Neither was true, at that point, but I certainly would have expected Chip to share it with me, in a different manner than he did. To think I needed notoriety and recognition so badly, that I would trade the whole principle of progress in the NAACP for a plaque, was despicable. The plaque wouldn't represent honor. It would represent dishonor. There was nothing I could say at that moment that wouldn't denigrate both of us in public. The best thing for me was to walk away. But I walked away knowing I was going to run for branch President, come hell or high water. I wasn't going to concede Chip's support to Joe, neither was I going to let Chip off the hook for his support, but I knew I could no longer trust him. It was a very sad day for me.

The second week of January, the verdict was in. Penn had finished his report and was ready to discuss it with the branch's Executive Committee. The report was to include whatever recommendations for action he would make to the committee on branches, who would make a recommendation to the national board. As Penn read his own 15-page investigation report, the faces of my opposition on the Executive Committee went from smug smiles and winks to each other, to a nervous anxiety, to almost shock, by the time Penn finished. Penn first read a synopsis of what the eight members who had signed the Article X complaint had filed against me. Then he read a synopsis of what I had alleged against the committee and the prior administration. Penn stated that the report would not pass judgment on Mr. Essex, pointing out that the National Committee on Branches would deal with me, in February. Penn continued by saying that the Los Angeles branch's irresponsibility in handling funds for the past six years was a matter of historical documentation. Of the seven findings, his report produced, the first four were violations of past administrations that I inherited. They included paying an accountant for tasks the branch treasurer should have been doing, failure to pay payroll taxes, on several occasions over the past six years (the IRS threatened to close the branch, and did on one occasion), collecting memberships and not forwarding national's money within 15 days, noting that in some instances delays were nine months, and expending monies for beepers for the branch officers (we thought this one was petty). Penn then noted my authorization of a phone system for the branch that cost $1500 and was done without branch approval. The heaviest hit was Penn calling out the establishment of the Crenshaw Economic Development Corporation, and the branch's failure to compensate national for the 1986 and 1987 Roy Wilkins dinners. Penn called out the employment of the branch's Executive Secretary (also directed at me), without his (national office) approval. He was still maintaining that he never approved the hire. Lastly, he called out that national hadn't seen its proportionate share of last year's dinner, which he estimated at $50,000. Then he dropped the bomb. He supported my claim that the standing committees (except education and political action) hadn't been functioning in the past two years, and that most of the work was being performed through special committees. He mentioned that the women's auxiliary, personnel, police misconduct and fair employment practices committees (all headed by supporters of mine) were actively functioning. Then Penn listed 13 specific violations of the constitution and bylaws for branches of the NAACP. Only one had to do with action on my part (the hiring of the executive secretary), all of the others had to do with lack of action or inappropriate actions of other officers or the Executive Committee, not only for the past two years but the past six years. Penn was severely harsh in his condemnation of the branch's Executive Committee saying that they had failed to live up to its oath of office for the past six years, at least, and "had conspired and committed fraud, in order to deprive the national office from receiving its constitutional share of funds raised by the branch."

Penn then gave insight to the type of sanctions he was considering, including removing all of the officers and executive members, and not allowing them to run for re-election. There was dead silence. This whole little charade had backfired, but Penn wasn't through. Given that "such steps might be counterproductive, in that the turmoil created would be too disruptive, no such steps will be recommended," he read. Penn then said that because we had been parties to the widespread abuse of authority and responsibility, that he would recommend that no current member of the Executive Committee, nor anyone who had served on the Executive Committee in the past six years, be allowed to run for branch office (meaning any office other than Executive Committee member, including President), for an indefinite period. The net effect would be a need to reopen the nominations for the officer positions. Penn concluded his report by saying he would recommend that the branch stay in receivership for an indefinite period, that a repayment plan be set up, that a complete inventory be conducted of the branch's assets, and that a new date for elections be set up, as soon as the national board had acted on those recommendations. Penn stated that this was his report, and that he felt it was a fair and even-handed assessment of what had been going on in the branch, for the past six years.

Penn finally had L.A. where he wanted them. He was right. This had been going on for a long time. The problem hadn't just start with me, but it never was represented that way when the complaint was filed. For me, I felt Penn's report was excellent, even though he continued to misrepresent the situation regarding the hiring of Harold Webb. It was a small issue, in comparison to the larger issues that finally came out--that the Executive Committee had not been the guardian of the branch's interest. My objections had been on record for years so, although I was a member of those Executive Committees for the past six years, I knew I had fulfilled my responsibility to the branch. But I was as guilty as everybody else, in not being more vocal about CEDC, not until it became apparent that I was in line to become President, and would have to deal with my open opposition. I was willing to take my medicine, as long as, everybody else would be forced to take theirs, and accept responsibility for their actions. Penn asked us to discuss the report amongst ourselves, and left. He probably wasn't off the street before the finger pointing started. Mallory came to the front again with his madness, telling the group to look at the position I had put them in, but I wasn't having any of it. I called them all a bunch of hypocrites and walked out of the meeting.

The most exciting part of Penn's report was the notion of a total new leadership. This would be the change the branch so desperately needed. A new blood infusion. New ideas, new faces. That was an exciting proposition to me, even if I could not be a part of it. I didn't have to be "the actual change," but in sacrificing myself, I could be part of the change, the agent for change to come about. This was more important to me. The most important part of this whole process was that change would come about, a positive, progressive change for second-generation advocacy, and I didn't have to be the President for that to happen. With the numbers of members that we brought in, there was an excellent chance that a progressive agenda would hold up, regardless of who was at the helm, as long as, all the old players were out of the mix. If Penn had held to those recommendations, the branch would have benefited greatly. But he didn't.

Key members of the branch began writing letters imploring Penn to reconsider allowing current members to run for office. It even got down to what some would consider begging. Penn eventually relented and forwarded his report absent of the recommendation of excluding current members from running for office. Penn had effectively criticized the Executive Committee for gross malfeasance over the past six years, then opened the door for them all to come back and run the branch. All respect I had for Penn as being even-handed and fair vanished, right then and there. More than letting the real perpetrators of the branch's compromise off the hook, Penn had put me back on the hook. Had Penn done what he said he was going to do, and convinced the national board to enact his recommendations, the complaint against me would have become null and void. None of us would have been allowed to run. By backing off his position, he put the focus unfairly and squarely back on me. My opposition on the Executive Committee was ecstatic, because they had been told that no President who had misspent branch money had ever come out victorious in an Article X complaint. Penn, in fact, told me himself that he didn't know of a President that hadn't been removed for spending branch money without Executive Committee approval.

My opposition, reflecting Penn's insight, spread around the community like wildfire, that they had me over a barrel, and that if I didn't resign, I'd either be removed, or not allowed to run again. Kerman Maddox, even though he was no longer on the ticket, continued to try to help me. He called one day and told me to do an interview with a woman named Susan Seager, a reporter with the now defunct *Los Angeles Herald Examiner*. Kerman claimed that this woman was really interested in the NAACP's change agenda and that she had been following my work and wanted to do a feature profile, etc. I told Kerman my reservations about talking to the press. They never seem to get the facts, or the quotes quite right. Plus, we had a gag order on prohibiting us from talking to the press. "She knows that," Kerman said. "She'll write it in third party and only use what's already on record. I think this is a really great chance for you to clarify some things, Anthony."

"You do huh?" I responded.

"Yes, I do," he said. "Fine, set it up." I talked to Seager for two hours. We didn't talk about the current conflict just civil rights philosophy, the change agenda, the focus on police misconduct, gang violence and economic discrimination. She asked me if I intended to stay in the NAACP. I told her I didn't see myself as a career NAACPer, just as someone who was trying to do my part to keep the struggle alive. I told her as my forefathers had done their part to get us here, I was doing my time in the community, by giving back right now. That statement would be a real point of controversy later. She asked me about a life in politics. I responded by saying that I didn't like life in a fish bowl, but anything was possible. She promised she wouldn't run the story, until the gag order was over, or when a new election date was set. It was a pleasant interview. It seemed well-intentioned.

The National Board was due to meet in New York the second week of February. I called Penn to let him know I'd be coming to address the Committee on Branches in my own defense. Penn responded, "Why? This outcome is pretty predictable Mr. Essex. Article X cases are very straightforward, you either spent money, or you didn't. You spent money without authorization. Why waste your money and the committee's time?"

"It's my money, Mr. Penn," I said, not even wanting to dialogue further with him. "See you in New York," I said. That same night I got a call from attorney Chuck Dickerson. He had run into Mallory who, after doing his bad mouth number on me, told him I was as good as out and that national was going to remove me or not let me run. Chuck had a deeper concern for me though. He called to find out what was going on with me personally. He had heard from Mallory as well as another source that they (meaning the branch opposition) were out to destroy my life. Being very general, Chuck wanted to know if there was anything going on that they could send me to jail for. I told him nothing that I knew of (because that was the first I had heard of them trying to advance my Founders civil suit as a criminal issue). Chuck then warned me to be careful and stated that none of this was worth personal damage to me or my family. I agreed, and thanked him for his concern and advice. I began to hear more over the next few days about this pending indictment that was coming down in the next month or so. I denied it, of course, because it wasn't true. It was part of their strategy to continue the character assassination by misrepresenting the occurrence of events. The RTC had taken over Founders, and had made referrals of seven people to the Justice Department for investigation of any criminal impropriety. Because of the allegations in Founders' counter-suit, I was one of the ones being investigated, not indicted. I might as well had been indicted, because people were taking it as the truth. But I was being told by friends, who were in the legal circles, that calls were being made to both the RTC and the Justice Department to try and force down a criminal indictment before the election. I was advised that criminal investigations take a few months to a few years, and indictment discussions take even more time.

True or not, such a rumor was devastating to the confidence of people trying to support me in public. But, like the soldiers that they were, many of them put their heads down and pushed ahead. It was around this time that many people, who didn't know me, began to join the committee to help elect me. One was a real quiet sister from the church I had met at a wedding. She had a real professional polish, a very secure and confident demeanor, and a real humble spirit. Her name was Debra Ward. I didn't know at that time she would play a very significant role in my life, but I did appreciate that she and many others chose to come forward and advance my platform, even though they couldn't answer many of the questions being raised about my actions or my character. It made me all the more determined to fight.

The date of the national board meeting had arrived. I had caught the red-eye flight into Newark International Airport, and was on the shuttle bus that takes you into Manhattan, when I heard the bus driver say, "I don't have change for a 50." I looked up and saw Henry Dotson coming down the aisle asking people if they had change. He had no takers until he got to me. "Got change for a 50?" he asked. In a moment of personal debate, I couldn't think of anybody that I had more disdain for in the NAACP, with the definite exception of George Mallory, than Henry Dotson.

"Never know where you'll find a friend, huh Henry?" He just looked at me. I handed him $7 and told him to give it back to me later. After checking in the hotel, I took a short nap before getting up to survey the situation. The Committee on Branches didn't meet until early afternoon. Dotson, Joe Duff and Norma King were there from the branch. I saw several national players that wished me luck, including Fred, who invited me to sit at his table for dinner that night. I saw Willis Edwards, the Hollywood/Beverly Hills branch President, who was there to meet on the Image Awards. He let me know that everything wasn't as bad as it appeared.

"Everybody knows what's up in L.A.," he said.

"Everybody but Penn," I said.

Willis waved his hand, "Penn's full of shit. Just get in, and be yourself. You'll do all right." Willis made me feel good, but he wasn't on the committee. He did, however, have a good relationship with Rupert Richardson, a national board member who was then chair of the Committee on Branches, so I couldn't totally dismiss his advice. Willis had a way of getting the inside scoop, when everybody else was trying to figure "what's up."

Finally, the time to deal with this five-month charade had come. The Committee on Branches was in session. Being one of the national organization's most influential policy components, it was loaded with many of the national board heavyweights. People who could stand up and sway a majority of both the committee and the 64-member board, one way or another. The national President at the time, Hazel Dukes, was on the committee, as was Herbert Henderson, the late Earl Shinhoster, Nate Colley and Kelly Alexander, Jr. Also on the committee was John Mance, who had signed the complaint, which certainly gave my opposition an advantage, in terms of how the discussion could be influenced. There were two items ahead of the L.A. branch issue.

As we stood out in the hall, I was looking at the three of them, and they were smirking at me. I thought about how they had plotted and schemed to get me to this point and wondered what kind of act they would put on before the committee. Certainly, they had to have one. They weren't going to get up and tell the truth; that Henry was part of a group that had been planning against me since March of last year; that Norm turned against me, when I told her I couldn't support her for secretary; and that Joe was a mouthpiece candidate who hadn't been in the activity loop for some four years (since John had died), and was being propped up to attack me. The committee would never hear this, I thought.

Finally, they called us in. We sat at the end of four long tables placed in a rectangular form. I sat to the far left. Norm was at my immediate right, with Joe next to her and Dotson, on the far right. Ms. Richardson introduced herself as chair of the committee and had Penn read the charges. He was sitting to her immediate left after the charges were read. Ms. Richardson asked us to introduce ourselves. They went first. Dotson introduced himself as a past branch President, Duff introduced himself as First Vice President, and Norm introduced herself as branch Secretary and signer on the complaint. I introduced myself as branch President. Ms. Richardson surprised me by saying, "Oh yes, Mr. Essex, we're glad to have you present. Let's take these charges one at a time. Did you Mr. Essex spend the branch's money on a reception without Executive Committee approval?" she asked.

"Yes, ma'am, I did," I responded. Then I proceeded to explain the context in which the commitment to underwrite the reception was made, then withdrawn days before the reception, after the invitations went out. I explained that the branch was obligated at that point and would have had to pay for it whether we had it or not. I also explained to the committee the excellent response in terms of memberships received that far exceeded the cost of the reception. Ms. Richardson then asked the other branch members to respond. Dotson and Duff went into a discussion about how I was making arbitrary decisions for the branch, and how I illegally asked members of the Executive Committee to resign (it was actually standing committee chairs), and how this was the cause for filing the Article X. Norma got to bumbling about how she wasn't invited to the reception, and didn't know anything about it. After she said it twice, Ms. Richardson reminded her that she had said that already. She then opened the discussion to the committee members.

Influential committee member Herbert Henderson, who had to go to another committee meeting, stood up and said, "I'd like to say, that I'm for the President. In all of the hundreds of cases we've heard in branch complaints, this is the first time we've heard someone come here and admit they spent money, and give a somewhat reasonable justification. Anybody that has the courage to do this, I'm for `em." Then he left.

Hazel Dukes, who seemed to be preoccupied with another conflict taking place at the board level, went to the crux of the issue. "Mr. Dotson, is this the first time money has been spent in the L.A. branch without Executive Committee approval?"

Dotson, stunned by the question, stated, "Excuse me?"

Ms. Dukes, now getting perturbed, repeated the question in a much sterner tone, "Is this the first time a President has spent money without permission in the L.A. branch?" It was as if she already knew the answer.

Dotson gave a real faint, "No."

Ms. Dukes followed up the response, "Did you file an Article X complaint against any of them, Mr. Dotson?"

Again, Dotson sounding like someone had him by the throat, shrilled, "No."

"Then why are we here now, Mr. Dotson?"

There was no answer. Ms. Dukes then moved that the committee take up this issue later, and move on to other business. It was seconded and passed. None of the other issues got on the table in our presence. Ms. Richardson told us that the committee would take the complaint under submission and make a recommendation to the board. While Ms. Richardson was thanking us for coming, Dotson handed me the seven dollars I had lent him to catch the shuttle from the airport into the city, in front of the committee, as if he was giving me something. It appeared that he was trying to show some favor to his young protegee, now that the board had seen through their plot. What a hypocrite. I just shook my head, and thanked God.

I knew I wasn't out of the woods, but it was a great start. I found out later that the committee was actually more concerned about the money owed national, than what I had done. The committee would recommend to the board that I retain my seat until election, but I would have to repay the money and be admonished not to do it again. It was indeed a first (allowing a President to keep his seat), but the committee recognized that my expenditure was not willfully done, but the result of a circumstance beyond my control. After the vote, I was stopped by then Southern Regional Director Earl Shinhoster. He told me that the vote went the way it did, because of who I was and what I represented--a young warrior trying to bring change in L.A. He then told me to go out and prove them right. I told him I would.

The National Board was to meet the following day. I decided to relieve some stress by walking around downtown Manhattan, doing one of my favorite things, picking out neckties. Upon returning to the hotel, I saw Ms. Dukes in the lobby. Always on the run, I approached her and asked for a minute of her time. I told her I just wanted to thank her for addressing this issue the way she did, and for her support.

In her quick, stern way she responded, "Young man, I've seen some of your work. You're a good advocate, but you were wrong. Probably because you were taught wrong. We've been having problems out of Los Angeles for many, many years. It was unfair of them to bring you up on charges for something they had been doing for years, and could have handled at home, especially with an election coming up. Dotson and them knew better than to waste the committee's time like this. Hopefully, you've learned your lesson, and can go on about doing the business of the NAACP. Good luck, young man."

I thanked her again, and just like that, the National President was off into another conversation. I quietly dismissed myself, thinking that Hazel Dukes was all right. Many people had a problem with Ms. Dukes, because they felt she was controlling and domineering, much like some of the old-timers on the West Coast. I had heard discussions that young professionals, on the East Coast, were reluctant to join the organization, for many of the same reasons I was advocating, a lack of change. However, there may have never been a better time to see Ms. Dukes, in the light she displayed that day, demonstrating a fairness I hadn't see in most of the old- timers in Los Angeles.

With very few exceptions, in Los Angeles, it was about control, total control. And they weren't fair about their control either. If a young idealist wasn't about being controlled, then they were literally stepped on. While it may have been too little, too late, Ms. Dukes was fair enough to call out L.A.'s effort to step on me for something they'd always done but didn't have the integrity to call it out when others had done the same. Others may have had a problem with Ms. Dukes, but she shortstopped, for a moment, what could have been a bandwagon rolling downhill. And I'll always be grateful to her for that

The next day, the National Board voted to allow me to retain my seat and let the elections move forth. Again, I was told they spent more time on the branch diversion of funds than on my reception. People came out congratulating me and wishing me luck. Penn came out looking disgusted, clearly showing his partiality. "I will be in touch with you by mail. I must caution you again not to talk to the press," he said and walked off.

Later that evening at the board dinner, I saw Duff and Dotson in the foyer whispering to each other. Duff turned to me and said, "Make sure you represent the story right," inferring that I would talk to the press first.

"I'm more concerned about getting y'all's hypocritical asses out of the branch. How's that for a story?" I responded.

Dotson smiled and said, "You think you got away, but we're getting ready to show you what NAACP politics are all about."

I didn't respond, choosing to leave the discussion at that, but I knew what he was talking about. The dirt had just begun to fly.

Back in L.A., Duff's cronies couldn't believe it. I had "beat" (as they said it) an Article X. It was a major victory. Moreover, it restored some of the confidence in our campaign. The next major task was to draft a press release mutually acceptable to both parties. My opposition wanted to write a press release on my reprimand. They (the Executive Committee) had been more severely reprimanded, than I had. Penn sent letters to me and the Executive Committee, calling out the National Board's action against me and against them. Though Penn's letter had a lot of editorializing (from Mr. Penn himself), it stated that the board found that the reception was "for the purpose of promoting the branch," and the evidence was overwhelming to that effect. He also stated that the board concluded "that you (Anthony) probably had the authority to purchase the briefcase, since the Executive Committee has had a practice of allowing branch Presidents to spend up to $700 as administrative expenses, assuming that it was to remain the property of the branch. But given that I had put my initials on it, it was considered purchased for my personal use."

I was given 10 days to repay the branch for the briefcase and 30 days from the date of his letter (February 15) to recover $4,875.36. If I didn't repay the monies according to terms, I would "be declared ineligible to hold office, or run for office, in any unit of the Association, for the next four years." The last paragraph of the letter read: "You are reprimanded for your actions, and warned that should such occur again, you will be suspended immediately, and subject to other disciplinary actions." It was signed "Sincerely" William H. Penn, Sr.

The Executive Committee had similar admonishments, except they received a demand to pay $60,000 immediately, or be prohibited from running for branch office and would be sued for the money. Mallory was negotiating for the CEDC. Their position was that national was in no position to demand money that wasn't theirs, and that it would counter-sue the national NAACP, if it tried to take action against the members of CEDC. The compromise was that CEDC wouldn't turn over one cent, until after the elections. "If I was still President, national had a problem," which was the way it was put to Penn. If I wasn't, CEDC would negotiate a settlement. They all but inferred to Penn that if you want this money, you're going to have to help us get Anthony. Penn claimed that he didn't care about the branch's politics, he just wanted the money repaid. However, several events occurred that were to the contrary.

When it became apparent that we would not agree on the release of a press statement, Penn had everybody fax him a copy of their versions and stated that national would release a statement. When the statement was released, there was no doubt where Penn's biases fell. The statement almost entirely focused on my reprimand, with barely a mention of the Executive Committee's reprimand, instead saying that national was negotiating for the return of the money raised by the NAACP dinner. It also announced the date of the branch elections, set at March 12. The local papers ran with it like it was a war declaration. In a big, thick, bold type, the *Herald Examiner* ran "L.A. NAACP Chief Reprimanded." The same woman that promised to do such a positive story, wrote the most one- sided story I'd ever seen, quoting Penn and anonymous sources from the L.A. branch, who had leaked Penn's reprimand letter to me, but not his reprimand letter to the Executive Committee. I immediately called her, and asked her why she ran the story this way. She claimed Penn never made mention of a second reprimand letter, which I faxed to her. But it was too late. What was clearly a loss on their side of the table--a simple reprimand, instead of a removal from office (which they had sought)--had now been made to seem like a clear victory for them.

The *Herald Examiner* article generated a host of calls, including the *Los Angeles Times* who was also in the midst of doing a story. The center of all the questions dealt little about the branch itself, but on me personally, including issues surrounding the controversy involving my firing at Founders Saving. The *Los Angeles Sentinel* did a very balanced article of both reprimands, but they quoted me in the process. While sitting in the office with a business associate named Anthony George, my secretary Katherine interrupted the meeting. "Mr. Penn is on the line." I picked up.

"Mr. Essex, I understand that you were quoted in the paper today. You violated the gag order I put on the branch," he said.

I went off. "Look Penn, I'm not going to let these niggers destroy my life over this NAACP bullshit. I have a business and a reputation to protect, and I'm not going to let charges against me go unresponded to, while my opposition talks to the press anonymously. I'm going to defend myself." I was screaming at the top of my voice.

Penn responded, "Well, I have my secretary on the line, because I want a witness that you have been duly warned. If you make another statement to the press, you will be relieved of your office."

I went ballistic then. "Penn, I don't give a fuck what you think. Fuck this NAACP shit. Can't you see this is not about the NAACP? It's about me, and I'm not going to let them use the press to tear me down in public. So do whatever you have to do," damn near breaking the phone as I slammed it down. Sitting behind my desk almost hyperventilating, I tried to compose myself.

Anthony, not believing what he had just seen, ended the meeting by saying, "Maybe this isn't a good time to talk to you. But I do want to say, God bless you, brother, and stay strong."

I acknowledged his statement and walked him to the door. Storming back into my office and slamming the door behind me, I plopped down in my chair and just stared out the window. The intercom buzzed. "Mr. Penn's back on the line."

I just knew he was calling back to finish his mission. I took a deep breath and prepared to fight some more. I picked up the receiver and yelled, "WHAT NOW?"

"Mr. Essex, I just called to say that I've reconsidered my position on you talking to the press. My secretary agreed with you, that you should be allowed to defend yourself against allegations made against you in the papers. So, I'm allowing you to respond, as you need to." There was quiet on the line.

Giving a sigh of relief, I said, "Thank you for the consideration, Mr. Penn, and thank your secretary."

"You are welcome, Mr. Essex. Goodbye."

I later found out that Penn's reconsideration had less to do with allowing me to defend myself, and more to do with perceptions of the NAACP, if those one-sided leaks continued to take place. In relenting to me, he also relented to the Duff campaign, so now everybody was talking in the press. The gag order was effectually over. All the allegations and responses culminated a week later in an article the *L.A. Times* ran entitled, "Impolite Politics Divides NAACP Chapter."

In the article, Duff, Dotson and Norma King, the three who got slammed for bringing the complaint against me at the National Board meeting, discussed allegations of impropriety in my personal life, as the reason for their opposition to my candidacy. It was seen as the dirtiest article many could ever remember in a branch election. Dotson's justification was that I shouldn't be held to a different standard than an elected official. The public has a right to know. This was bullshit, of course, because I wasn't running for public office. This was an organizational election that did not involve the public. It was based on a membership, that represented a very, very small segment of the public. Now it was national news and everyone knew the difference. The following Monday, at the invitation of Bill Elkins of the mayor's office, I went to a breakfast of community leaders, in support of another "community friend" who was under attack. As we introduced ourselves, everyone knew what happened in the press over the weekend. Upon my introduction, I was given applause of support, but it hardly soothed the pain I was feeling. Finally, the community friend got up to speak of his impending prosecution. His name was Michael Milken.

At the very same time Duff was challenging my character publicly, he was showing his real character in the process. With the election date now set, each side had an opportunity to mail to the membership. The election rules allowed us to telephone members the week before election to solicit their support. I had received a call from a local attorney whom I had befriended in the Black Santa Claus case, Harold Becks. He, and a few other people, wanted to know when we were going to start calling for support. "I've gotten two calls from Duff's people already," he said.

Over the next few days over three of our people told us the same thing. These were people we solicited but didn't put our names on the outside of the envelope. We purposely didn't want anybody to know who solicited the membership. We felt the membership records were very vulnerable. Duff was the computer man of the branch. If the records were going to be violated, he was our prime suspect, given he had almost singular access to the membership database. We thought that the privacy of the records would be compromised at some point in time, and we were right. Duff had the membership list and was calling members at least two weeks prior to the date authorized. I immediately called Jim Martin, who flew down and met with Duff and myself. Joe, who supposedly was the only person to have access to the computer, didn't even deny he and his committee was straightout cheating (in contacting members before the timeline). I asked Jim what was he going to do about it.

He said, "Well, we'll give you the list, too."

"A full three days before I would get it anyway," I said.

"Three days is three days," Jim said.

"And two weeks is two weeks," I responded, while I watched Joe pull the membership roster off the branch's computer.

"What do you want, Anthony?"

"I want a written reprimand that Joe was found cheating, and a postponement of the election." Martin's face froze.

"We've already sent out the mailers, Anthony. It would cost the branch too much money," he said.

"What about the reprimand, Jim?" "Let me talk to Penn about

that, Anthony." The subject never came up again. When I asked about it, Martin would say that Penn was dealing with it. However, the closer it got to the election, it became obvious that Penn wasn't going to allow another charge of impropriety, particularly cheating, surface before the election. Even with a two-week head start, we were still confirming votes in our favor, almost two to one.

My campaign was almost beginning to dig up information on the Duff campaign. Led by an elder named Marion Hill, a former Executive Committee member, a list had been compiled on every member of their team with "something on each of them." They found that Dotson had been fired from his job for allegedly sexually harassing a white woman. They had info on how many times Mallory had supposedly taken (and failed) the bar, how Duff had gone from law practice to law practice, before eventually taking a job at Drew University, and how he "took payment" for working on the school desegregation suit. Still I refused to use the information. None of it (except maybe Henry's issue) was relevant to their ability to lead the NAACP. Hill and Mark Whitlock got pissed.

Finally, two weeks before elections, Mark Whitlock called me to drop off the slate. Mark claimed it wasn't in his best interest to stay involved, and claimed I hadn't been keeping him abreast. My response was that I was busy trying to convince people, who didn't know me, into supporting me and I didn't have time to babysit him. It wasn't the first time Mark had left me holding the bag, in the midst of public controversy. Three years prior in the midst of a Black community selective buying campaign (a strategic name for economic boycott), he dropped out, after it was made public that he had met with one of Tony Brown's "Buy Freedom" campaign people prior to the start-up of the "Buy Liberty" campaign.

Paul Brock, who was then Brown's representative, stormed a meeting of 150 supporters of ours claiming that Mark had stole his idea and brought it to us. He and I were publicly accused, by Betty Pleasant (whom I later befriended) of pirating Brown's idea. To defend ourselves, Mark got his wife, an attorney, to trademark our name. Then he wanted us to pay for it, after he dropped out of the campaign, saying the exact same thing. "It wasn't in his best interest to stay involved in the Buy Liberty campaign. Here we were, in a public fight with Tony Brown, which we needed, like we needed a hole in our heads. Tony was slamming us in every city, on TV and in the newspaper. And it wasn't in his interest to stay involved. He was the reason this whole controversy started in the first place. Now it was déjà vu, and ironically again, Mark was partially the reason I was in the fight. He was the very first person to approach me about running for President against Ray in 1987, and brought it up every chance he could, until I decided to do it. With a promise he'd help me, just like in the Buy Liberty campaign. I'd given Mark a second chance to betray my trust, and he did (and it gets worse, as will be discussed later).

Mark was now the third person to drop off the campaign, but probably the most key. A fixture in the First AME inner circles, many knowing that Mark and I were purportedly friends, it would be perceived as a lack of support in the church, and many people would question why they should support me, if my friends didn't. A relevant question. I really didn't know Bridgette very long, nor did I know what to expect of her. I knew Kerman was political and had no particular allegiance to me, meaning he would always do what he thought was best for his political ambitions first. So when the ground rattled a little bit and he bailed out, I couldn't say that it was totally unexpected. This was totally unexpected. Moreover, Mark knew me. Regardless of what people wanted to say, few (including Mark) could stand up to the type of scrutiny I was being forced to endure. It was part of their game plan. Mark knew this, and still buckled under the pressure.

Their isolation plan was working. The two others they went after, Cynthia and Steve Bradford, didn't budge, but the two they got, Kerman and Mark, were the most crucial, because they were two that were closest to me in the branch politics, and they were probably the two most widely known around the city. Explaining one departure was one thing, but explaining both of them, outside the implication of guilt, didn't make sense to anybody, including myself. The last week before election was very intense. The Duff campaign was working overtime calling members to communicate the latest slate departure. We still had close to 1,000 members confirmed to vote in our favor. Then a few more dirty tricks were engaged.

About five days from election, we started getting calls from our supporters asking, "Is the election on Sunday or Tuesday? We just got a call from somebody saying the election was on Tuesday." The Duff campaign was calling our confirmed voters trying to get them to miss the election. We had over 100 such inquiries, and had to recall everyone to confirm the date of voting. Then we had to deal with the members' increasing anxiety over the frequency of phone calls they were receiving. People were screaming and shouting, "This is the fourth call this week" or sometimes they would say, "Look, this is the third call tonight. What's going on?" Clearly, it was an obvious attempt to frustrate our support. Then two days before election, a bomb hit.

I got a call from my friend, Greg Brandon. "Es, have you seen this mail piece from the friends of Joe Duff?"

"No, what is it?"

"Man, it's the dirtiest campaign piece I've ever seen in my life. They've got your personal information in it, a letter you sent to Mayor Bradley asking for a contract, the *L.A. Times* 'Impolite Politics Divide NAACP Chapter' article, and a reprimand letter from the national office. They must have sent this to everybody. Five of the same letter came to my house today."

"Could you bring it over to me, Greg?"

"Sure man. See you in a minute."

Sure enough it was the coldest hit piece I'd ever seen. I immediately called around. Others had seen it too and had people they sold memberships to calling them. Everybody was saying they didn't like what they had received but as dirty as it was, they needed some explanation before they could vote for me. There was no time for an explanation. We immediately saw several points that were incorrect, even libelous, the way they had been taken out of context. I met with an attorney named Clifton Albright. We held a press conference announcing our intent to file a slander and libel suit against Joe Duff.

The *L.A. Times* and *Herald Examiner* were having a field day with this battle. Old against young, new civil rights agenda, against traditional civil rights agenda. Change versus the civil rights establishment. Everybody had something to say in the press. Melanie Lomax, who was now getting her long awaited shots at the branch, said in the *Herald* that the branch no longer had a sense of direction. Former branch President, Celes King, called it exactly what it was: "an attempt to keep the branch a social organization, instead of making changes to bring this ghetto back to life." Even Kerman Maddox was in the middle of the discussion, and was quoted in several articles, but was accurate in his analogies of the branch conflict. Surprisingly enough, in my favor. The papers were now accusing both sides of improprieties. The communities' comments were increasingly negative about the conflict, many saying they were glad to have the elections coming up soon. The public now knew what this was all about and the comments were increasingly in our favor. But the public weren't all members of the branch. And the members of the branch were in a total state of confusion. The day before election, we tried to confirm our vote count. It had dropped from almost 1,000 definite "yes" votes, to 450 "yes" votes, and another 200 "not sure" votes. But due to receiving the "hit piece" in the mail, we confirmed over 200 members had decided not to participate in the election at all. When asked why, they said because of the mail they had received. They felt they didn't know enough about either candidate to make an informed choice. One woman voiced a sentiment of many we talked to. She said, "Mr. Essex appears to be an excellent choice, but has some personal problems that he needs to resolve. But I'm not about to vote for someone who would send something like this out in the mail." This campaign was just too dirty for many people to get involved.

As dirty as it was, it was effective. A stay home vote was like a vote for Duff. Where we once had a two to one lead, the vote was not very close. We estimated Joe had about 500 sure votes, maximum. Half of them were out of Second Baptist Church, and I knew they were going to vote, big time. Cynthia came up with the strategy that we would all show up at Second Baptist Church for the first service, I would stay for the second service, while everybody else would head over to First AME for its 10 o'clock service. I knew Joe would be at First AME trying to split the vote there, since he had several people at Second Baptist, including Henry Dotson and Kathryn Anderson. My concern was that if I didn't show up at FAME, would Joe have an unfair advantage, should Chip introduce the candidates. The day before election, I called Chip Murray. We really hadn't talked since he offered me the plaque to drop out of the race. I had since heard that he had told several people I couldn't win.

He picked up the line. "Anthony, my son. How are you?"

"Fine, Reverend Murray, trying to put together an election day strategy. I was wondering if you will be introducing the candidates for President tomorrow? If so, when? I'd like to make sure I'm there."

Murray responded, "Probably not. Why?"

Against my better judgment, I told him (if you can't trust your pastor, who can you trust?) "We're expecting a large turnout from Second Baptist Church. I wanted to be there to do some last-minute campaigning."

"No, you do what you have to do. We'll make an announcement at both services to encourage our members to vote also," he said.

"I'd appreciate that Rev. Murray," still feeling that my support base there was greater than Joe's.

"Good luck, Anthony," he said. I thanked him.

March 12, 1989. Our whole campaign support, about 25 people, were out at Second Baptist bright and early. We met the people going and coming, at both services. The response was good. Many of the young people at Second Baptist said they were with us. The polls were due to open at noon. Jose DeSosa, the state conference President, was supervising the election. The L.A. branch staff was the primary support, but looking at most of the certifiers (the people checking registration and handing out ballots) were either supporters of Duff or associates of Ernestine Peters. I asked Jose how this happened. He said he didn't know. I appointed three poll watchers to ensure that the process had some integrity, but I knew they couldn't watch everybody.

I couldn't worry about it. It was time to hit the street. Members were already starting to line up at the polling area, which was set up in the community hall of Hamilton United Methodist Church. Pastor Emeritus of Second Baptist Church, Rev. Thomas Kilgore and about 20 Second Baptist members were at the head of the line. These were the civil rights warriors who had walked many miles and stood in line for days for the right to vote. You knew they were going to be there. I was hoping that it wasn't an omen. Right behind them were about 20 of my Prince Hall Masonic Brothers, headed by then L.A. Consistory (32nd and 33rd degree Masons) commander-in-chief, John A. Brasfield, Jr. While I didn't always agree with Brasfield, I felt a sense of great relief to see him and the brothers in the line. As I walked out to the front of the church, I saw many of the faces from my past and my present days--to support me. I gave each a look of acknowledgment to as many as I could, keeping my chin up and a determined look.

When I got out to the street, Cynthia was getting out of her car. She had a disgusted look on her face. That wasn't good. "Chip announced the election and asked the candidates to stand. Joe was there. You weren't. It looked real bad."

"Son of a bitch," I said under my breath. Fuckin' Chip said he wasn't going to do that."

Cynthia shook her head. "We can't worry about that now. We have an election to win," she said. Cynthia, always an optimist, but I am a realist. For the first time, doubt crept in my heart.

Just then Celes King came out of the polling area.
"Anthony, everything is going to be all right. You're going to win. Approach every member, supporters or not, 20 percent of all voters make up their minds in the booth," he said, as he drove off.

I took his advice. "I'm Anthony Essex, and I'd like your vote for President," was the constant line. After about three hours of this, I could tell the election was about fifty votes in the balance. The day had several altercations. Cynthia caught Dotson passing campaign material inside the polling place. Many of our supporters were being challenged (contested for voting rights), while Duff supporters barely had to show I.D. In the last hour of the election, there were several "last-minute" rushes of members into the polling booths. But all told, the turnout was far less than expected, and a low turnout favored Joe.

As the polls closed, I appointed Deborah Morrisetti, Henry F. Davis, Jr., Cynthia Walker and Vicki Phillips to go over and count the ballots. Around 9:30 p.m., we got the call. It was Deborah Morrisetti. Her voice was sad but as passionate as ever. In her usual direct manner she said, "It's over, babe. I wanted to turn the table over every time a Duff vote was counted. It was 494 votes for Duff, 307 votes for you. Really it was about 400 votes for you. They contested about 90 votes, which were mostly our supporters but it wasn't enough to make a difference. Anyway, it's been a long day for me. I'm going home. We all knew what happened today, Anthony, and it's not your fault. Change just died today." She had a quiver in her voice. I told her to thank Bro. Davis, Cynthia and Vicki and to walk out of there with her chin up. We hung up. Everybody had been listening to the conversation, but I repeated it anyway. I ended it just as Morrisetti had ended it with me.

"Thanks guys for your love and support. We did our best." Repeating what Morrisetti had said to me, "Change just died today."

* * *

12

Clinging To a Merry-Go-Round

(Out of Control)

"The credit belongs to the man who is actually in the arena, whose face is marred by dust and sweat and blood... Who at best knows in the end the triumph of high achievement, and who at the very worst, if he fails, at least fails while daring greatly."

- President Theodore Roosevelt

The last two weeks in March, 1989, following the election, I assessed the feelings that came out of this civil rights experience. Feelings of anger. Feelings of betrayal. Feelings of gratitude. Feelings of appreciation. Bewilderment. Relevance. Relief. Just feelings, period. I really didn't feel like talking to anybody about those feelings, but there were so many questions to be answered, and so many issues, professional and personal, to be cleared up. Then there was the issue of putting pride and ego aside, to heal a bruised and battered reputation. There were so many aspersions cast about my character, my intent and my integrity. Even people who really knew me, didn't know what to think. Most of them didn't know what was true, and what was false, what was real, and what was not. Many tried to defend me; they just didn't know what to defend. What was what? My personal and professional issues were very convoluted. It made for very interesting conversation for those who didn't bother to follow the maze of contextual circumstances, in which many of the allegations played out.

My advocacy was never an issue, yet it was never considered, except by those in whose issues I was involved. The fact was, I had been effectively mislabeled at best, and discredited at worst. At least, that's how I felt at that time. Instead of bouncing up immediately, I chose to lie there on the floor for a minute, and lick my wounds 'till the count of eight.' Even a champion fighter heals after a great fight. It's very hard to heal in the public eye. It's real difficult to pretend you're not hurt, when you are. Being in the presence of people whom you know stood silent, or even betrayed you, is a disheartening proposition. It was real hard not to take a swing at someone whom you knew to be perpetuating some of the untruths that came up in the branch campaign, while at the same time, smiling in your face and pretending to befriend. It's real hard to watch hypocrisy prevail. You know it for what it is, and it's not an easy pill to swallow. Moreover, everybody was now taking a rather cavalier position with what happened to me in the L.A. branch's "niggah shit." Several well-respected community players felt I should just forget about it, and concentrate on making some money, given my expertise in public finance and strategic planning. Others felt I should continue being an advocate for another organization. In fact, two NAACP branches invited me to come lead their branch. And another organization wanted to hire me as a "paid exec," similar to the role I advocated for at the NAACP. I chose a retrospective sideline role, while trying to bring some stability to my family and my business. A retrospect included working through what happened in my five-year NAACP advocacy experience.

The first two weeks were the most hectic, to say the least. I wasn't returning phone calls. My secretary, Katherine, took almost 200 messages the first week; many were press calls. I didn't have anything to say to the press. They were looking for more "sour grapes" statements. They had misrepresented me enough, so I thought. They had only just begun. Someone gave them my home phone number. One caught me on a call, and when I refused to talk to him, he wrote that I was still "obviously bitter" over my loss. No, I was obviously pissed about the press calling me at home. Call it what you want.

Many of the other calls were so-called "associates," "friends" and other acquaintances calling to express their shock that I had lost. Though a significant portion of my community support wasn't in the NAACP to begin with, my support base "appeared" to be broad. Supporters of my candidacy brought in over 5,000 memberships, during my nine months as President. I lost by 187 votes, with another 89 in protest, meaning another 102 votes wins the election. We had three times that number confirmed to vote that didn't. Over a hundred people called to apologize that they didn't get the opportunity to vote, for whatever the reasons. I really wasn't in the mood to listen to people's excuses. I would talk to my closest friends, who saw this or that person. The excuses they heard were: "I forgot about the election" or "I thought it was next week." There were also a few dozen calls for me to continue working on community advocacy projects. I would scream at Katherine on the intercom, "Tell them to call the NAACP; I don't do advocacy for free anymore." Katherine would only sigh and take a message. My clients were really good about sticking with me in the midst of this controversy. However, it did impact new business. It only meant I had to market some to get the business back up. That meant going back into the public, which by now, was a highly suspect proposition for me. Looking into the faces of hypocrites and compromisers wasn't exactly good for me. But I had to do it for the stabilization of my business and the sustainability of my family.

The home front was a completely different story. My wife at the time, as supportive as she tried to be, wasn't taking this well at all. She felt I had jeopardized too much for "the good of the community," while the community didn't give a shit about me, or anything else, other than selfish personal interest. And though speaking through a bit of hurt, she was right. She wasn't talking about the community inclusive, the state of the whole. She was talking about the community exclusive, those people who professed to have community interest at heart, but only seemed to come to the table when there was something in it for them. They were the ones who had competing agendas, or had no desire to create concern over issues of substance. These were many of the ones who supported me, supposedly. The ones who understood the game and knew the intent of my opposition's plan to discredit me, yet couldn't find time to vote for me on election day. But they could still find time to call me to do much of their confrontation bidding, even after a scathing election. I still had that much credibility. Yet, they all had the same excuse: "Well, I didn't think it would be that close." Taurece wasn't talking about people who didn't like me or support me. She was talking about those who claimed they did, but who were too trifling to follow through on their "so-called" convictions to support leadership, in their best interest, and let it get defeated to what she called "flake shit." And now they were calling the house trying to figure out how I lost. Since she was answering the phone, she would straight out ask them, "Did you vote?" Many told her that they got caught up somewhere else, because they just knew I had it in the bag. Taurece would then call me to the phone and say, "It's another so-called supporter," loud enough for them to hear, then she'd drop the phone on the table with a loud BANG!

T, as I called her since college, is a simple woman is a lot of ways, but she had some fundamental value about people representing themselves accurately. "Being real" was something she held at the forefront. She hated pretenders. Even in college, she had always said that most of the L.A. scene were a bunch of phonies. She couldn't stand to be around them. She hated going to the dinners, the receptions, the luncheons, and the socials--none of it. In her mind, none of them were real or sincere. This was not always the case. In this instance, I certainly couldn't argue with her, as I had tried to on many other occasions when soliciting her involvement. As far as she was concerned, she was doing her part by allowing me to be as involved as I was. She would say one of us has to stay rooted in "some sense of reality." When I'd ask what she meant, she'd only say, "The NAACP is not reality, nor is it real enough to deal with reality. If it is real, it would pay for what it is trying to represent, instead of taking anyone who would do it for nothing. Not many people are that benevolent. You'll see." And while she never discouraged my involvement, my wife could see the inconsistencies and would often say: "Something ain't right about the NAACP or the people in it."

In the end (as far as L.A. was concerned), she was right. She did her part by supporting me, taking phone calls at all times of the day and night, bathing, feeding and clothing three babies while I was getting death threats, and the house was constantly under watch. That was a lot of pressure. And she still had time to come and vote. Now, she couldn't understand all those so-called supporters calling with all their lame-ass excuses. Yeah, she was hurt for me, but she was hurt for her family. All that she was asked to give was everything, compared to what the community gave its leadership, and what they gave up in return. So while it became obvious to her that there was a lack of commitment and dedication on the part of those who professed to be like-minded, there was no real excuse for my losing. In spite of all the controversy, I was let down by those whom I had worked closely with and of whom I had a greater expectation. Because many of my "close" associates "forgot," "lost the election flyer," or “something,” the organization we all had worked so hard to change had basically been forfeited on her family's time, money and integrity. Yeah, she had plenty reason to be pissed, and she wasn't about to hide it.

It was obvious that I had allowed "this niggah shit" to not only hurt me, but my family, which caused me to get angry again. But it was time to become conciliatory, to prove that I was bigger than the loss. Most people in the community really didn't know what was involved in the loss, other than what was in the paper, which was a lot. Still the real viciousness was communicated to the membership for the most part. Many in the community still wanted me involved in an array of projects, most of which I declined.

As difficult as it was, I even agreed to appear at the branch's first activity after the election. At the urging of Chip Murray, who I now saw as the "hypocrite of life," I agreed to come to give the appearance of a unified front for the branch. Guess what the meeting was on? That's right. A rally against gang violence. The very same project Duff said we had no business being involved with during his sleazy campaign. Co-sponsored by the Brotherhood Crusade and the Community Youth and Arts Foundation, the branch was now a part of the "stop gang violence" discussion. What a revelation. The church was hosting the event. The branch and the church seemed to have formed a "hypocrisy marriage."

Chip opened up with this grand introduction of how it's time for us to come together to save our children, and how the NAACP must be in the forefront of such an effort. Chip introduced me and had me stand. He then went into a speech about how I had made my contribution to the organization and how I took it as far as I could but now it was time to support the new leadership, at which time he introduced Duff. Duff, in his stumbling, bumbling "white boy" mimic, thanked Chip for all he had done for him, and while looking out at me, stated that Chip made him a promise during the election, and kept to it, and he'll always be grateful for that. They then moved forward with the program. I tried to ease out without being noticed. On the way out, I ran into several individuals who got up to block my path to the door, creating a little bit of a stir. They wanted to let me know how displeased they were with the change of leadership. A few others praised my courage for being there again given the viciousness of the campaign. A couple more were still trying to involve me in activities I could care less about, at that point. I had done my part in this play, and it was time to go home.

On the way home, I couldn't help but think about what Chip had referred to as "having taken the organization as far as I could." That was more pure bullshit, straight outta the pulpit. A major sin, I suppose. The point being that I was never allowed to even get started, much less take the organization somewhere. And it was all calculatedly destroyed. Chip knew that. My major concern with this whole facade was not so much that I had lost to Joe but the way I lost and the affirmation he received for doing it as he did. It was like Duff won "fair and square." C'mon Anthony. Be a good sport. Chip and everybody else knew it was never about elevating Joe Duff, who at best was (and proved to be during his two- tenure) a very poor leader. Nor did he have the integrity he tried to display during the campaign. It seemed ironic to me that Chip would co-sign this process, while knowing and preaching on many a Sundays, on those who cast aspersions.

The church, as many friends and associates as I still have there, was now the basking place for the hypocrites who used it to mask their deceitfulness. Not that I had become holier than thou. But for all my faults, I never tried to assassinate Joe's character in the church, as Duff and his supports did when they brought fliers to the Second Baptist Church and handed them out. I also never used the church to manipulate (trick) the people, as Duff did when he joined First AME to convince churchgoers that he was an entrenched member. These were the activities that were not condemned by the church. In fact, it appeared as if the church even promoted this behavior.

Meanwhile, I wasn't running for God; I was running for NAACP branch President. And even though some of my personal affairs appeared to cast some questions on my integrity, they never translated into my branch leadership efforts. I never considered the reprimand a character issue, because it was something that had been done by every President since Celes King, and was the part of Duff and company's failed attempt to have me ousted from office--part of the coup. Still, if I had chosen to, some real negative character issues could have been raised publicly about each one of the individuals in Duff's camp, save a couple of the Second Baptist people. I believe that was the point most people had forgotten in this whole fiasco. I could have gotten very negative, but didn't, and it may have sealed my fate.

During the ride home I realized that I, too, was a hypocrite in more ways than one. For promoting this unified front, when it stood for everything I opposed. For allowing myself to be cast as "passing a leadership torch," when it had been knocked from my hand and trampled on, while implying that I had taken it as far as I could've. And for continuing to believe that my spiritual leadership had the moral integrity to call out this situation, when he had already become part and parcel to it.

The last Sunday of March, 1989, while watching the theatrics and feigned pandemonium at the 10 a.m. service with my mother, who had now become a member, I decided that I could no longer buy in to FAME's weekly stage show. My experience had exposed some personal weaknesses in me that required spiritual healing. As much as, I once respected Chip, I could no longer separate the man from the message. My healing required no promise to glory, just some timely counseling. Maybe I could have gotten that from Chip, if I could look past his personal faults. But it did require that I look into the word with a personal commitment and reasonable expectation, that if applied to all facets of my life, I would grow into the wholesomeness one expects from spiritual enrichment.

I strongly felt that this understanding must come from a direction I perceived to be one of righteousness, with the ability to publicly deal with real life moral questions. Not just speak to them from a pulpit in philosophical theology, but apply such a theology in real life situations. I felt that my spiritual leader must have the integrity to stand with "truth in error," even in defeat, rather than "treachery disguised as victory." The true believer must have the wherewithal to stand in the minority and stand alone, if necessary, rather than with a misled populous or a false prophet. Be it victory or defeat, misguidance can and must stand corrected, so that errors, be they moral, immoral, unintentional or unethical, will never be repeated. And if they are repeated, it wasn't because the spiritual authorities involved didn't publicly address it. In this case, the spiritual authority helped to brush moral and ethical issues aside, covering up the flaws in a shallow grave and giving them the ability to rise again (and in Chip's church they would rise again with the Julius Butler issue).

In my spiritual state, I needed to know that the one guiding me had a little more moral integrity than myself, and that he (or she) could address the higher moral questions that face our community. That was not apparent to me in this situation. Quite simply, I lost respect for Chip and his ability to provide moral guidance on issues of integrity. In his personal quest to be popular, he chose to "cover up" than to "play correct." Plainly put, I saw Chip Murray as nothing more than some street gamester, looking to get over--getting the largest church on the block--rather than to do what was right. No one benefits from cover-ups but the guilty whose actions prevailed, while the integrity of others are called into question. I'm sure my disappointment in him was no greater than his disappointment in me. However, he was supposed to be the wiser.

Then maybe I expected too much. Still, I knew that I needed a different form of guidance. The church had been good to me and for me. My mother and sister were now in the church, as were my children. I knew I'd have to maintain some contact with the church. But it was time for me to grow. So it was time for me to leave. I needed a greater understanding than I was getting at First AME Church. I looked elsewhere for spiritual growth and guidance.

* * *

About the time I began visiting other churches, I received a call from a brother I once knew as Chris Phillips. I had first met Chris during my college days at Cal State LA. I had worked with Chris on several community projects, while he was an aide to one of the elected officials. He had been very supportive of my leadership at the branch. Chris was now an assistant minister in the Nation of Islam at Muhammad's Mosque #27. I was still letting Katherine screen my calls for press and other types of Negro calls. Chris, who was now known as Brother Christopher X, was calling to give his regrets for my losing. We had a 10-minute discussion on some of the underlying issues that came out in the campaign. My discussion centered on my loss and how it was part of L.A.'s Negro politics. Chris, though acknowledging that some of my points were real, felt that the whole trip was part of a larger scheme to discredit Black leadership in general, and me in particular, being one of Los Angeles' few visible "pro-Black" leaders. He pointed to the press representations as an example. He certainly was right in this case. Still, we centered our discussion on the days ahead, and where Black people needed to focus their energies. He said that the (then) Western Regional Minister Wazir Muhammad wanted to meet with me, just to see how I was doing and to discuss a few things. I told him that was fine. Chris and Minister Wazir came over to my office later that afternoon.

Minister Abdul Wazir Muhammad was a distinguished looking, older gentleman with a calm demeanor about him and a very direct, penetrating stare. On occasion, when he found it permissible to smile, it was very lighthearted and refreshing. Minister Wazir, after allowing Chris to introduce him, sat down at one of the guest chairs in front of my desk. He let me know that I had been brought to his attention by then Western Regional Captain Wali Muhammad in July 1988, when I attended Minister Farrakhan's speech at the Democratic Convention in Atlanta. And again the following October when I attended Savior's Day in Chicago for the first dedication of the nation's reacquisition of Mosque Maryum and the NOI's national center. He also remembered that I had given $1,000 during the rally prior to the minister's speech, and that Minister Farrakhan made a point of personally thanking me at the rostrum. He continued to state that such faithful support of the minister hadn't gone unnoticed. I thanked him for his kind observations. I always tried to support the Nation during my frequent traveling. Whatever city I was in, if Minister Farrakhan, Khalid, or Dr. Alim were appearing somewhere, I'd try to make time to attend their lectures. Usually, either Brother Malik Farrakhan or Sister Claudette Muhammad (the minister's national protocol team) would recognize me and allow me to have dignitary seating along with my host. I had always appreciated the accommodations, given the highly security-sensitive environment of the Nation of Islam's leader.

Minister Wazir also commented that it was so unlike most NAACP officials, who still avoided association with the Nation, even after Minister Farrakhan broke tradition and called for his members to join. Even he became a life member in 1986. Over 50 members did, in fact, join the Los Angeles branch and supported my candidacy. We discussed how he, too, had been misled into believing that in spite of all the media attention, I would win easily. Minister Wazir said that had he known, a simple instruction could have made up the vote differential needed for my victory. However, with the Mosque preoccupied with the national center's drive, the whole situation kind of got away from him. I appreciated the notion of support.

He went on to ask how my family was taking this, and how it had impacted my business. I told him that both were in a tentative state, but could be mended with time (so I thought). Then he looked at me with a stare I'll never forget and said, "Brother, in your hurt and frustration, you probably don't realize what is happening to you. We have a tendency to underestimate who we are, but brother, white folk know who you are, and what you represent. You stepped into an organization controlled by the so-called Negro, but is greatly influenced by white folk. Your move to change it was met with great hostility, not because they wanted to do anything with it, but because they can't afford to have its own tool used against them. When the Negroes attacked you, you could see the hidden hand of cooperation, particularly in the press." I just nodded in agreement. Wazir continued, "Bottom line brother, you were never one of them. Your stand, your support of the apostle's (what many in the nation call Minister Farrakhan) work, these are not indicative of their leadership. You are of the people. You stand for the people and you stand with the people. You're young and they fear your mind. You're dedicated to the same work The Honorable Elijah Muhammad gave 40 years to. We need brothers who are born to lead." I nodded, and told him I appreciated his perspective. There were a couple of moments of silence where everyone kind of digested what was just said. "How are you spiritually, right now?" Minister Wazir asked.

I told him, "I dunno. I'm not sure where I am right now. I mean, I know God is God, and He's the creator of all things and controls all things. I'm not so sure where I practice is spiritually healthy for me at this time."

Minister Wazir defended Chip Murray, saying that he was probably the most sincere of the Christian preachers in the city. He always keeps his word to the Nation and whenever he has a chance to stand up, he stands up for the people.

"Yeah, I know," I said. "I'm not saying he's not a good brother, or that the church is not a good church. I still have a lot of support there. I just don't know if I can deal with the hypocrisy over there, Brother Wazir. I mean, I know hypocrisy is everywhere. I know nobody is perfect. Maybe I just know too much or have seen too much. But right now, I don't believe my spiritual well-being is at First AME. I'm not saying the spirit's not there. Apparently, my mother seems to think it is, and she'd been out of the church for over 25 years. Just where I know I need to go, spiritually, I don't know if FAME can take me there. I just dunno. I know I have to get past this, but it's real hard to look at some of these people in a spiritual light, sitting in church pews and not feel hostile. It defeats the purpose of going to church for spiritual cleansing. I'm not going to stop worshipping, so what do I do? My faith in FAME has definitely been shaken."

Wazir, very responsibly (considering I was very vulnerable spiritually) stated: "Brother, I'm not going to suggest what you should do. But the same vulnerability that caused this to happen to you is in the men of God also. We all stop short of the glory. And yes, hypocrisy will be most everywhere you turn, from tinge to total. You need to ask Almighty God Allah to guide you, and you need to submit your will to the will of Allah. If Allah wills you to stay at First, stay at First. In fact, I recommend your not leaving First, until you've had a chance to sort out your feelings completely. Maybe a change will come within you that will soften your heart toward those who did this to you. I'm not saying that you need forget what they did, or necessarily befriend them. But forgiveness will at least allow you to start to heal and grow spiritually. You don't need to think of doing anything, until you resolve some of your own personal and spiritual conflicts. Once you do this, Allah will guide you to greatness. I'm with you whatever you decide."

I didn't have the heart to tell him I had already decided to leave First AME. I just kind of stared at him, trying to read his face, for any game or insincerity. There was none. With that, Minister Wazir got up as did Brother Chris and said, "I know you're busy, brother. I'll be in touch to see how you're doing. May Allah bless you, protect you and keep you." We gave each other the salute and greetings, then I walked them to the door.

Just as Minister Wazir started to walk out he said, "Brother, remember what I said to you about knowing who you are. Stay in touch with Brother Chris. Travel alone, as little as possible. Stay with your family, as much as possible. If you need help, don't hesitate to call. Do you remember COINTEL pro, brother?"

"Yes," I said, "it was the FBI's program to infiltrate Black organizations and eliminate proactive Black leadership through conflict, and undermine the effectiveness of those organizations."

He said, "Right, except they destroy them outright. Do you know how they eliminate the leadership?" I looked at him as if to say how. Wazir continued, "Brother, the first step is to discredit you in the mainstream press and in the mainstream leadership. Brother you got more ink on this, than any Black leader in a long time, and they're not through by any means. White folk don't waste their space without a reason. You know the second step, brother?"

"No, what?" I asked.

"Isolation," he said. "Brother, the devil understands our people better than we understand ourselves. The same tricks he used to separate us in the past, he's using now. He knows our people believe much of what they read, and they run from controversy. It forces the one who stood up to be isolated. When they isolate you, brother, they can do anything they want, and blame it on known and unknown adversaries.

They can 'hit' you themselves and community sentiment will be low, because they figure you had it coming with all the press they created. Many people have come up missing on stuff like this, brother. This is classic COINTEL pro. Don't take it lightly, and be careful. As-Salaam Alakum."

"Wa-lakum Salaam," I replied.

I went back to my office, closed the door and reclined back in my chair. As I stared out at the window, I reflected back on my discussion with Minister Wazir. That was nice of him, I thought. I wonder if he really knew what was going on. I suspect Chris kept him pretty abreast. Regardless, whether he knew or not, this was the type of spiritual counseling I was in need of, and I appreciated him giving me that time. It also made me recognize that I wasn't getting any spiritual guidance from Chip.

Chip Murray did drop me a card telling me my blessings were on the way. "Oh really," I thought. The card said, "First the crucifixion, then the resurrection, and your blessings will come in abundance. You'll see." It was signed "Chip." I guess he didn't have to do that, but it did little to ease my hurt over his betrayal. I needed a little more than a card. I needed a spiritual renewal. But Islam? I hadn't really given it much thought. Even to the extent of having been called a "closet Muslim" on many occasions over the past 15 years.

I subscribed to many of the beliefs of Islam, but like so many Blacks born into Christianity, I was afraid to cut that slave religion's umbilical cord. So we drag on forever the ball and chain of illicit Christian practices taught to us by our slave master and our Negro predecessors, live a life of poverty and despair, and die looking to the sky for Jesus to save us. If Jesus walked up to most Black people today, he's liable to get "cussed out." Particularly if he showed up Black. "Niggah, get outta my face," most would say. Mainly because Blacks wouldn't be prepared for what they would see-- someone who looked like them. In my eight years as an AME, and a Baptist in my youth, this "reward in the hereafter" had always troubled me. The notion of heaven and hell, angels and devils, the color of Jesus--it all never added up.

As I grew older, I also researched some practices of certain Christian faiths that Blacks practice. I found many came right out of the slave teachings and into the modern church today. Lastly, if accepting Christ was the key to salvation, and if white folk were also worshipping the same Christ, why wasn't this Christian spirit of unity and kindness demonstrated in everyday practice? Hell, it wasn't even demonstrated in worship itself. Eleven o'clock a.m. on Sunday morning is still the most segregated hour in America and Christianity has always been used to reinforce racial superiority in this country. Notwithstanding the personal politics I encountered with my present church, I was still deeply searching for answers to questions of spiritual interpretation. I was searching for a level of enlightenment that didn't come in a bunch of music, whoopin' and hollerin' and holy ghostin'. Spiritual enlightenment and fulfillment of prophecy will be consecrated through man. I had always believed that. This belief is what made Islam so appealing to me.

I wasn't ready to make any major jump, but I did know FAME wasn't it anymore. I promised to expose myself to Islam with an open mind to heightening my spirituality. I couldn't afford to limit myself anymore to the spiritual confines and "comfort zones" of the American Negro. As I found out with the branch, the community and with the church, as well as with myself, nothing is as it appears.

Buzzz!!! "Anthony!" Katherine called on the intercom.

"Huh! Yeah."

"You busy?"

"Nope. Why?"

"There's a woman on line 61 and she'd like you to handle a discrimination issue for her."

"Have her call those niggahs over at the Colored People's Association."

"Where?"

"The NAACP, Katherine."

"Yes, sir!"

* * *

Beyond profiling an issue in the media, most people don't see the NAACP as relevant, in terms of being able to follow-up on and bring closure to issues. Relevancy is key, as far as the NAACP's preparedness and functional ability to address the changing scope of discrimination. Inasmuch as, the affects of this new racism are just beginning to surface in areas not traditionally identified under the realm of civil rights, what advocacy are the people to call? Who investigates economic discrimination or media discrimination or race-focused ballot initiatives with the kind of due diligence and tenacity necessary to stop it. Beyond simple mentions; nobody. The impact of racism on

Blacks in this present day society is as vicious as any of its predecessors. And it still includes areas of police misconduct, exacerbated gang violence, increased hostilities toward immigrant merchants, and impacts the economics and social fabrics of communities at large.

A casual review of the current public policy shift shows that bills being drafted for legislative action seeks to negate any move to promote full inclusion of ethnic minorities under the guise of "colorblindness." This represents a shift in the social construct brought on by a change in social attitudes. It's the same thing that was done after this country's first reconstruction period (1865-1877) when the courts and the legislature sought to reinforce the change in social attitudes. The shifts in "tactics" have allowed the agents of social and political repression in this country to be able to compromise the advocacy. De jure segregation policies were no longer necessary to affect the politics of social construct in this country when "interpretation" of race neutral policy can be just as effective. The NAACP and other civil rights organizations never adjusted to this change in strategy. School desegregation or busing are not relevant issues, when public policy allows other systemic processes to be manipulated, to the extent that the disadvantaged populations will suffer miserably from biased applications of civil liberties and public policy decisions.

Education is one example of how civil rights advocacy has been effectively compromised. Biased processes have prevented experienced teachers from being placed in inner-city schools to improve the quality of education where Black children live. Blacks, of course, know in hindsight that busing Black children didn't necessarily improve their education. The focus of the advocacy (the schools) was misguided, and its advocacy application (moving children instead of teachers or resources) was misplaced. This was just one example of the misapplications of the NAACP's irrelevant advocacy focus.

The other question of relevancy speaks to its willingness to use irrelevant tactics to facilitate advocacy action. The NAACP had gotten the reputation of being soft because of its outdated tactics. Yeah, some branches will march and picket for a day or a week, but do they have what it takes to engage in protracted negotiations? Will they go to court or call a boycott? Or will they even pressure discriminators to respond or comply once they've given notice?

These were the questions being raised during my involvement in the 1980s (that still persisted in the 1990s); that prevented a younger participation from understanding the real advocacy discussion.

It is a discussion that continued after my involvement subsided. I was able to extend that discussion for another two or three months of speaking engagements. In fact, many wanted to give me the opportunity to speak about what had happened, both out of fairness, and insight for the benefit of the future. It was during this period that I received a phone call from Brother Christopher X. I asked Katherine to put the call through.

"As-Salaam Alakum," as I picked up.

"Wa-lakum Salaam," he responded.

"How are you?"

"Fine, and you?"

"Fine. Beloved. I have a request of you from the regional minister."

"What is that, Brother Chris?"

"The leader will be speaking next at First AME. There will be two preliminary speakers: a sister and a brother. He'd like you to be the brother, who speaks on behalf of the Los Angeles community. Is that something you will be able to do?"

The leader he was speaking of, of course, was no other than the Nation of Islam's National Representative of Most Honorable Elijah Muhammad, and apostle of the people, The Honorable Minister Louis Farrakhan. This was indeed an honor and a distinguished privilege, reserved for ministers of the Nation, host ministers or high-profile community leaders, who had the utmost respect and trust for and of the leader. Well, Mosque #27 (the Los Angeles Mosque) certainly had the high profile part right. However, I was extremely pleased that the Nation viewed me as trustworthy enough to comment on the integrity of their mission, particularly since my opposition tried to make my integrity an issue. This made me question why I was selected, given some of the other noted supporters of the leader in the city.

I asked Brother Chris, "Why me?"

Chris responded, "Because we think you have something to say."

I told him, "I appreciate that. How long do I have to speak?"

"Five minutes," he replied.

"Five minutes, Chris?"

"Yes, sir. Ask Allah to guide you and you can say what you need to say within that period of time."

Brother Chris was being kind. What he didn't say was that the Minister will come out in the middle of your comments, if they're too lengthy. He doesn't wait long when he's in the house. He's usually in and up on stage. His point was well taken, and this was an opportunity I'd have taken if it was only one minute. I was elated with the offer. I thanked Brother Chris, and asked him to thank Minister Wazir for me. I committed myself to do him proud. He said he knew I would. Katherine came in after we hung up. "What are you going to talk about?"

"I don't know."

"I think you should talk about why we don't move forward as a people, because we compromise leadership."

"I only have five minutes." She smiled and walked out. I knew she was right.

The first week of April, about three weeks after the election, was my first local speaking appearance. The crowd was largely an invitation only crowd of business and community leaders and organizational representatives. Of course, once it got out that Minister Farrakhan was speaking, it was anybody who could get in. Over 2,000 packed First AME that night to hear the message. (Now Minister) Aishah Muhammad was the speaker selected to bring the message on behalf of the sisters. Sister Aishah always demonstrated the highest dignity and respect in communicating "the teachings." She encouraged the audience to "consider the time" we live in as a final calling to the righteous, and challenged them, their minds and their hearts to our reminder of this hour--The Honorable Louis Farrakhan. She was sharp, inquisitive, open and honest about why we were there that night.

As I took the rostrum, I could see many of the faces of L.A.'s changing politics as well as many who were part of the problem. My discussion was on the "hypocrisy of change" in Los Angeles. I talked about how many of us had to admit the problems that exists but for some reason didn't see ourselves as part of the problem. I urged L.A. to come out of its state of denial and diagnose the problem for what it is--a lack of strong leadership. I talked about the "established Negro" leadership, who continues to promulgate what we already know the problem to be, and could significantly influence solutions, but don't. I elaborated on how many of us are as guilty as they, because we continually refuse to take the personal initiative to get involved in Black productivity. I talked about Black folks' unpreparedness, and how we move through this community totally unaware of the type of climate that is in L.A. I talked about how the L.A.P.D. had been preparing for a riot as early as 1988. I talked about how L.A. was then the drug capital of the country and also the gang murder capital. I talked about how its law enforcement agencies led the nation in acts of police abuse misconduct, how Black student achievement was among the lowest in the nation, and how some gangs were responding out of social abandonment, not out of criminality. In closing, I stated why many were invited to hear a message of truth, courage and integrity. A message deserving of Los Angeles, known as the city of shakers and fakers who talk the talk, and front each other off. But when it comes time to walk the walk (as in a "Stop the Killing" march the prior Sunday that had a dismal turnout), you can't find them. Then I teed off on the NAACP for the first time publicly calling them the "Colored People's Association," because of its inability to address issues of the day, but instead choosing to pursue issues of token relevance. I stated that it was time to listen to relevant leadership, leadership prepared to take a stand and leadership with the people, and not leadership arguing over who is a leader. (Which was the case, when national leaders were questioning Farrakhan's right to be represented at the African-American summit in New Orleans later that month). I ended with asking the audience to support our brother in his work, to build a new Black nation.

The speech was well-received. Brother Chris was frequently simulating cutting his throat. I looked at the chronograph on my watch. Damn. Seven minutes and thirteen seconds. I had run over by two minutes. However, Minister Farrakhan was gracious enough to allow me to finish. Isidra Person Lynn, a public affairs talk show hostess, ran my speech in its entirety on her show the following Sunday, commenting that I was "on the way back."

After a musical selection, the minister came out, in all his usual splendor. Yet, there seemed to be something different about him on this occasion. The rumor was that there had been an assassination attempt on him a day earlier, during his appearance in San Francisco. The minister's level of awareness seemed to be highly charged. He seemed to look through each and every person on stage and on post -a look that sought to purge each and every person close to him for the slightest insincerity. No hypocrite would have withstood the pressure of his scrutiny that night, and the slightest misstep by anyone around him could have been fatal. His look communicated that message. His discussion on that evening was about "building a nation through the building of a new woman." As the minister spoke, I watched him very closely. I watched his eyes as he watched mine and everybody else's in the pulpit. I watched as he delivered a message of divine guidance to the women of the audience, and as he connected the divinity of Mary to the holiness of the prophet, Jesus. I watched as he told each and every woman she has the potential to birth Gods of her own. And as he delivered his message, there were no theatrics, none of the usual candor of the Farrakhan personality (the smile, the lightheartedness) and no devil talk. It was straight teachings from a man clearly in touch with his highest sense of spirituality. I was impressed.

I had always been a Farrakhan supporter, but clearly God was changing the minister before the eyes of the people. He clearly was not the Farrakhan I had met as a student at Cal State L.A. in 1977, or in 1985, during his highly publicized conflict with the Jewish community or even in Atlanta in 1988 just a year before. This was a man born to advance the struggle of Black people. The burden of rebuilding a nation's work had burned away most of the "perceived" imperfections that may have caused people not to come to the Nation. The fires of trial had molded this man into a divine teacher and guide, in the likeness of Christ himself. He certainly was walking in the footsteps of the Christ, as he was being publicly criticized for espousing the truths of the day. Minister Farrakhan was a living testament to the trials of the true believer and, in those trials, God was revealing truths to the minister that would cause us to be saved and redeemed from the fires of hell in North America. For the first time, I saw Minister Farrakhan in this new perspective, and he was someone I could spiritually follow.

After hearing the minister speak that night, I thanked Brother Chris, and asked him to give the minister my apologies for being a little long-winded. He told me that he appreciated what I had to say and to stay in touch. After speaking to a few friends, I drove out to Redondo Beach and walked the pier for two hours. My thoughts that night kept turning to Islam, particularly the Nation of Islam. Maybe my interest in the Nation had more to do with my own personal trials and spiritual growth, even though it was still very apparent to me that Minister Farrakhan's message was becoming more spiritual in nature. It was real obvious that Islam was making more sense to me than Christianity. Not that Christianity wasn't credible, it just was not what I perceived to be the answer for the uplifting of the masses. I had come to view Christianity as more "feel good" than "do good" ministry. More preach than practice. More into building bricks and mortar than human souls. The message gets lost in the music, and the intent of prophetic works are compromised. Not so much with my own

Christian experience, because First AME is one of the few Christian churches whose Christian outreach extended beyond the church walls, but with the Christian experience overall. I just didn't see evidence of "faith through work." This was clearly evident in the Nation. I'm not just talking about bricks and mortar, I'm talking about faith in a religion that turns around "Black men"--the hardest, most rebellious of young Black men and women. The religious indoctrination of the Nation of Islam works. There's something to be said for that.

As I watched the waves go in and out, I thought long and hard about the changes I was preparing to make in my life. Was I reacting to this tribulation in my life, or had I really come to a spiritual crossroad? Was I unreasonable in my personal expectations of the NAACP? Or the church, for that matter? Did I really see something that others did not see, or was I the one who needed to be reformed?

I concluded that it was, in fact, a little of both. Yes, I was correct in my assessment of the NAACP, and of First AME and of my community struggles. Yes, I needed some form of reformation to take me past that point in my life. Whether Islam was it, I hadn't quite determined, but I knew some change was inevitable. It was either change or self-destruct. I knew I couldn't keep fighting public and personal battles of principle and integrity, without a spiritual foundation. I also knew that with my faith in organized religion, shaken as it was, my personal life would also continue to be in disarray, if I didn't get a spiritual guide in my life. I didn't feel that I would perceive things the same anymore. I couldn't even begin to imagine how I would perceive things in a renewed spiritual enlightenment. Tonight was a sign to me. For the first time in months, my mind was clear. It was unjumbled from the madness of the past three years; conflict in almost every facet of my personal, professional and community experiences suddenly became clear. I liked this feeling. I just wondered how long it would last.

It was about midnight. I knew it was time to get back to reality. But before I drove in, I got the notion to drive past a street that was part of my childhood where I first committed to something in life. I drove by the old house on 47th and Main. The last house I ever lived in with both my parents in the home. There were a lot of pleasant memories on this street, some not so pleasant. As I drove by the house, I parked on the corner in front of the school grounds of the Holy Cross Convent and Middle School. As I looked at the old chain linked fence, I realized that the more things changed, the more they stayed the same. The same asphalt basketball court where I learned to play basketball. The same metal backboards. The same rim. The same old street light that dimly lit the court after dusk. We'd play until our mother called us in or one of the sisters in the convent would come out and confiscate the ball. They took about four balls of mine alone.

I got outta the car, went to my trunk and got my ball that I keep in the car for my "weekend wars" at the park. I threw the ball over the fence. I "hit" the fence in my two-piece, double-breasted suit, and got stuck at the top before I jumped off and almost slipped in my street shoes. Damn. It must've been 10 years since I hopped a fence. I took my jacket off, placed it on the bench by the fence, rolled up my sleeves and retrieved the ball. As I launched what was once a "jump shot," which is now more like a "hop/set" shot, from the top of the key, time rolled back. All at once it was the summer of '69. I took a few more shots off the metal backboard; the sound of the ball hitting the ground was like a major shout. BAM, ba-BAM, BAM!!! It echoed throughout the school ground. A light came on in the Convent. One sister peeked out of her second floor balcony window, just like in '69. Probably the same sister, I thought. It's probably been a while since they've come out at night, since the neighborhood was much more dangerous than it used to be. Still, I couldn't help thinking that they were probably trying to get some sleep and wanted to come out and take the ball. Let her come take this ball, I sarcastically joked with myself. I couldn't help chuckling out loud, thinking that with my luck, it would probably end up in the papers. I imagined the Herald Examiner or the L.A. Times headline, "Ex-NAACP PRESIDENT ATTACKS NUN IN THE MIDDLE OF THE NIGHT OVER A BASKETBALL." As crazy as it sounds, I wouldn't put it past 'em, knowing the onus of proof would be on me having to explain why I was out in the middle of the night playing basketball on private property. People wouldn't know nothing about this casual recollection--a momentary reflection of my youth. Only that Anthony had gone "all the way" crazy, attacking nuns in the middle of the night. I let the ball roll off and walked over to the bench and sat down. I realized the vulnerability of having the facts or pseudo facts twisted against me.

While leaning back against the fence and looking up at the sky, I realized that tears were rolling down my face. Tears from years of frustration and disappointment. Tears I didn't think existed anymore. I didn't know why they were falling. I wasn't trying to cry; they were just a momentary uncontrollable release of emotion. Maybe they were from disbelief that this was actually happening to me. Maybe they were from relief that it had happened. Maybe they were from real self-pity, outrage or just the sense of being unsure, brought on by years of working hard toward a goal, which started on this school ground. The goal of being somebody one day--a ball player, a news commentator, a congressman--anything successful. And having that goal momentarily toppled by misrepresentations, while trying to serve the community and the common good. It was gravely disappointing. I guess they were tears of reality setting in to this cruel irony I was now a part of. I looked at my watch; it was a quarter to two. It was a helluva night. The kind of emotional roller coaster that renewed the spirit and cleansed the soul. I jump back over the fence, jumped into my car and drove off. As I pulled into my garage, I thought of something. Damn. I forgot my basketball. The nuns got it anyway.

* * *

The next couple of months would be an adjustment period. It was the first time in almost eight years I could concentrate solely on family and business. Community involvement had always been such a large part of my adult life. Prior to my civil rights involvement, I maintained national fraternal involvements, which dated back to college and required extensive travel. Now I had the time to do what I have always wanted to do--write and lecture. But solidifying my business and family relationships were priority. Getting back into the straight "network" flow was a waste of time for a varied number of reasons: One, the L.A. reception circuit, which I called the new "chitlin' circuit," was the same people that showed up at all the same places and two, the "wannabe's" and "think they are's," continuously posture themselves as the city's Black movers and shakers, when they were actually tantamount to the city's foremost "fakers and flakers." I guess because of my preoccupation with the Colored People's Association, I had to be in those loops to expose the organization to people I perceived could help impact change in the community. Sure it gave me a certain amount of exposure but also I was doing the community's work. Now there just appeared to be a shallowness to many of these affairs that was more obvious to me. Most of the people there were either looking for someone to do something for them, or just there to be "seen" in order to consider themselves "in the mix" or "in the know." I often asked myself: "Why am I here?" "What necessitates my presence here?" "What is the benefit of my being here?" Oftentimes, I found no sensible response to any of these three questions, and concluded that I was there out of habit, a habit I had to break. Until then, however, I often found myself at "events" or "in circles" that seemed to have no meaningful purpose other than to oblige the invitation of a friend or an associate who I "felt" supported me. Or, I tried to stay on top of L.A.'s feverishly gossip rumor mill.

During that time, I felt like I was on a merry-go-round. The people, places and things associated with those events and times had all the characteristics of a merry-go-round. The dressed-up "posed" horses, the disjointedness of alternating up and down motions, and the staleness of menagerie music (conversation). And no matter how long you ride a merry-go-round or stare at its effects, you'll see the same faces on the horses going in the same motion to the same ole' song. There's one component to a merry-go-round: stay on and enjoy (or tolerate) the ride. You have to hold on, or at least have a willingness to, or you get dizzy and fall off. There was a dizziness to these circles, which required an intensely focused commitment, a tighter hold, so to speak. At the point where the dizziness began affecting me the most, I found myself less inclined to want to hold on to the ride. I wasn't ready to step off and I wasn't really enamored by the mirage or the shallow brightness the ride generated. L.A.'s "niggah" merry-go-round is perpetual; it never stops. I was clearly clinging to a ride that was going in circles. A ride not looking to stop. The quickest way to fatally hurt yourself is to jump in front of a moving vehicle. I clung from one horse (event) to another; it was clear that I was neither enjoying the ride or the people associated with it. I was just trying to get my balance long enough to jump off safely, before I fell off.

My temperament at most of these affairs was cordial, at best, and hostile silence, at worst. There were times when I would speak to everybody, even hypocrites I knew didn't care for me (and vice versa), or had been openly adversarial to my candidacy. There were other times when I spoke to nobody, other than who I came to see. Moreover, I would become annoyed with people who would try and "make me speak," which then required me to make a concerted effort to ignore them. I took it as a personal affront, to invade my personal space or privacy. But when you put yourself in a public place, things like that happen. Many times it was a sarcastic ploy by someone who opposed me to make me acknowledge their little momentary mental victory. Childish digs by many who had never done anything (in life) worth acknowledging, particularly when it came to helping our people but now wanted to let me know that they knew about my little "NAACP episode" by coming through and saying, "Hi, Anthony." More than a few got cussed out from playing this little game, giving both of us a little satisfaction from the exchange. It gave them the satisfaction of being able to tug my chain and get such a response. Yet, I knew that I was still "me," in letting people know I was not to be played with, and must be approached with the utmost caution and respect. My response kept others who witnessed this exchange from coming at me sideways in larger numbers.

It was one of those occasions when I attended a reception at the request of my friend Berlinda Jamerson, at Southern California Gas Company. I was still extremely loyal to those who had supported me, and tried to support them. That particular night, I wasn't in the mood to be sociable. I was just there to be supportive. As I moved through the crowd nodding in acknowledgment, I had nodded to a brother from one of the beer companies, who had been supportive of me while I was at the branch. He was talking to a young woman whose back was to me. As I walked past, suddenly I heard this, "Hello Anthony." I looked back; it was a sister named Janice Smallwood who was involved in the branch. She was one of those members who claimed to be impartial, although every time I looked up she was with the other side. Impartiality, at some times, became the same as opposition, as far as I was concerned. Standing for nothing was as bad as standing against me, and I began to treat them the same. Smallwood was also one of those people who tried to make you speak. I nodded to her and proceeded to leave, at which time she said, "Oh, you ain't gonna speak?"

I responded, "No. Do I have to?" implying that I had already acknowledged her, so what's up?

Janice took this opportunity to let me know that she knew what was up with my opposition's plan to discredit me and have me imprisoned. She said, "That's why your smart ass is going to jail in a minute."

I just looked at her and walked away. She had confirmed what others were telling me--that my opposition was still after me, even after I had lost the election.

Steve Bradford is a dynamic young brother who became a Gardena City Councilman, was a supporter who got elected, despite his support of me. He had overheard that the investigation packet they had put together on me had been "anonymously" forwarded to the L.A. division of the Justice Department, and the L.A. office of the FBI. At the first post-election board meeting, in the midst of their jubilation, they got a little loosed-tongue by stating, "Our boy's problems have only just begun. We were hoping for it earlier, but it doesn't matter." Meaning they had hoped for an indictment of some sort, or at least a public mention of me being investigated prior to the election. Joe had even begun to state that I would be indicted for my involvement at Founders. It was their strategy to justify coming at me personally the way they did. A criminal indictment could vindicate their underhandedness during the election, but it didn't come down in time. Up to that point, it had been largely hearsay, a vicious rumor put out by Joe and his boys. And to that extent, Janice was putting it back to me as fact, in front of others, no less.

My mind would roll from one scene to another, one conversation to the other. My bitterness would rise in the midst of my mind's endless debate of varied perspectives, pondering possible situations I had opened myself to. All not totally due to any willful unrighteousness on my behalf, as much as experiences exploited by those seeking to get to me. I was a moving target now. My sense of reasoning had outsmarted my street logic. Taking the high road to appeal to the so-called sophisticrats accomplished nothing.

I began to think more about what had happened. What was going to happen? How could I let this happen? Was I going to let this happen without retribution or revenge? In the end, who really gave a shit. My resolve to remain civil and not succumb to the pressures and pride of retribution by my own hand, was weakening. The more I thought about it, the weaker I became in my vulnerability to be guided toward "getting even," particularly in discussions with many who had observed the process from afar, and had come to the conclusion early on that this "NAACP thing" was a personal attack that had nothing to do with leadership changes, issues, platforms, or none of that. It was about "getting Anthony." One of my fraternity brothers, Floyd Frazier put it to me this way: "If we're at the park playing basketball, and somebody started shooting at you, which would you concern yourself with, the shooter or the game?"

"The shooter,"

He asked, "Why?"

I said, "Because life is more important than the game."

"Exactly, something you obviously forgot," he said. "For you, the game became more important than life. You never discerned the fact that while you were running a race for a branch office that ain't about shit, they were tripping you, shooting at you and everything else. You never stopped playing the game and they took you out."

I thought, damn, and they're still shooting at me and the game is over. Seeming to read my mind, Floyd responded, "Naw, good brother, the game ain't over, until you're out altogether. Now, what you gonna do about it?"

I pondered the same thing. Not so much from what had happened, but what was actually happening now. I wasn't about to let anything further happen that would jeopardize my health or well being. I had missed a few weeks at the park, where I played ball on the weekends as I was trying to deal with these hectic times. One of the guys had stopped by to let me know the "boys at the park" were with me. They had read some of what had happened and thought it was pretty chicken shit. He didn't even realize what I was going through, because I never showed it at the park. He stated at that time that he and some of the others "would handle this problem" any kind of way I wanted to handle it. In fact, several people made similar offers. I initially rebuffed his offer kindly, with a sincere appreciation that these brothers were prepared to come to my aid. I maintained that it wasn't necessary, at the time. Well, shit was "all the way street," now. They were back, this time at my request, for some reconsideration discussion. I told Katherine to let them in.

As I stepped out of my office, the brother's huge arms grabbed me as he hollered, "You know you my boy, right?"
Katherine jumped at her desk. Turning to his crew, two of whom I knew and two I didn't know. He continued, "This is my 'Mo'fo', Preach."

They called me "Preach," because they said I was all the time preaching to them about doing right. They told me six years ago that they didn't have time for that civil rights stuff, that do-gooders get done in. And now they had witnessed a brother they knew as a do-gooder get done in. Their street logic had come to pass. They didn't appreciate it, and I appreciated their support. We all shook hands and went into my office and closed the door. I looked back in time to see Katherine breathed a sigh of relief.

Once inside, we began to discuss the who's and what's of my recent election experience, why it happened and how it would be rectified. There was a coldness to the way we discussed these situations, which made it obvious that I had been pushed past the point of brotherhood, unity or even simple reason. I just wanted, at this point, to put this little witch hunt to sleep. Now was the time for me to get out of a civilized game with uncivilized people; to play as they had played and let the chips fall where they may. At that point, I didn't care anymore. I had basically relegated myself to become a street renegade again, reverting to another time and another place.

As we walked out of the office, my friend, Debra Ward was sitting by Katherine's desk. They both had very stoney looks on their faces. I looked at Katherine's phone and saw her intercom light on. She looked away. Debra looked straight through me. I walked my guests out without questioning either about what they had heard.

The meeting had lasted about 90 minutes. I was sure they caught the major portion of the discussion. Katherine knew that Debra had this very spiritual and calming personality that I referred to as "something strangely different," than I had felt with any other person, family, friend or otherwise. Her calming demeanor was very effective in getting her point across, which I had come to appreciate as forthright and sincere.

When I came back through to my office, I didn't say a word. I just closed my door. Debra came through the door, slamming it behind her. Staring at me as her eyes swelled up, she just blurted out, " S o , you gonna throw it all away?"

"It's already been thrown away," I snapped back.

"Anthony, that's bullshit..." and from there went into a role that I couldn't much remember, much less follow. I had never seen this side of the sister.

Debra was always very calm, analytical and deliberate in her approach. Now she was as intense and emotional as I had ever seen her. Still waters run deep, I thought. I reached to grab her by the hand. "Get your hands off me," she yelled. "Why in the hell am I wasting my time trying to talk you through this shit?" (*That tickled me, because Debra didn't usually cuss.*) "You are allowing them to pull you beneath their level. Have you lost your mind?" she yelled at the top of her voice.

"Maybe I have," I replied. There was silence in the room. I could tell Debra was back in her analytical mode, deciphering my responses for her own interpretation. After a few minutes passed, she said, quietly but firmly with a look that was piercing, "Maybe you need to take some time to find it."

I looked at her for about a minute and said, "What do you want from me? What am I supposed to do about this?"
She picked up her purse and walked toward the door. As she grabbed

the handle, Debra looked back and said, "I don't want anything from you except not to see you self-destruct. Your silly behind is playing right into the white man's hands. When you come to your right mind, you know how to reach me." She slammed the door behind her.

Half mad and half stunned, I sat in my office for another two hours. I didn't even hear Katherine leave. I thought about the events of the day, what my fellas had said, what Debra had said, and what I had said. Damn. How did it get to this? I was slipping and slipping fast. This niggah merry-go-round was now out of control. I could barely focus on a pitch, much less hit anything thrown my way. Debra was right, and I knew it. But I also knew what she didn't know about the continuing investigation and slandering that were going on. I knew I couldn't continue to be the sitting duck, but I also knew once I let go of the merry-go-round, I was gone.

Maybe she was right. Maybe what I needed now was some balance. I needed to get away. I called Janet. We really hadn't talked much after our partnership split. But now we were really estranged after the *L.A. Times* put her in the paper as the infamous friend I made a loan to that was now being called into question as improper. Still Janet was always more objective than I, and insisted that our friendship was bigger than the "niggah shit." In time she would prove it to be true. She had called me a month earlier to find out if I had wanted to go on her annual Memorial Day group package to Mazatlan, Mexico. I had always declined to go in the past, but someone always canceled at the last minute. Sure enough someone had canceled, and I ended up going.

Mazatlan was a change of pace. The group Janet had put together was a lively bunch of 30 people. although I was part of this group and a guest of Janet's and her friends, I was clearly on a different page. I spent a lot of time alone in the water, body surfing and looking for sea shells, just kinda wandering. I was playin' a little bid whist, doing a little hang-gliding, a little reading, and a lot of thinking. I was in a space to be tied to no one or nothing. I went with the crowd when I felt like it, and stayed alone when I felt like it. I would get into some real philosophical discussions about everything from war to women. Whether it was drinking tequila "shooters" on the beach, or dancing on the tables at Señor Frogs, I was clearly a solo player, much to everybody's surprise. I clearly wasn't my jovial self. I came just to get away.

Associations on this trip had caused distorted perceptions. Somehow my thoughts reflected back to my Founders experience--

being at the wrong place at the wrong time. I could very much become a victim of circumstances. This trip was a premonition as to how innocent actions can make you incriminatingly suspect to places, faces, spaces and cases. They all add up to alleged guilt larger than the actual culpability. The appearance of impropriety is just as bad as engaging in impropriety, if no one knows all the facts.

Once the facts become pseudo-facts, then mis-facts, then outright lies, how is one to differentiate which facts are real and which facts are not, particularly with our people? They don't have to know the whole truth. They'll take half the truth and run with it just fine. What had happened to me and was continuing to happen was becoming all too clear. Half-truths had created the distorted image of my life, my culpability and my credibility in the eyes of the public. I was fired from Founders. Regardless of the improperness or controversy surrounding the firing, it was a fact, but only half of the real truth. I was fired after I refused to cooperate with the bank President improper actions. I was sued for allegations on loans associated with me, but it was a counter-suit filed to get me to drop my lawsuit against Founders. I sued first but that was never stated. Their suit was found to be without merit, but that was never stated. Just the fact that they did sue me. It didn't matter to the public that it was partially true.

Another half-truth: I did spend money on a reception and a briefcase. Whether it was improper was still a question. Whether protocol was followed when the branch had no protocol or practice was still another question. The fact that three prior Presidents had similar practices wasn't a consideration. Only the fact that I did spend the money, and it did "appear" improper given the questions being raised. There were never any considerations given to the motives of those raising the questions either. The hidden hand of contrived conspiracy remained concealed. I did have "charges" filed on me during my tenure, even though they were eight members of 5,000, three of which were part of the undercover conspiracy. It was made to appear that there was major discontentment in the branch. The fact was the charges were filed. The branch was placed in receivership, because of the filing and the discoveries that came about as a result of the filing, most of which preceded my administration. Still, the fact was it happened during my administration. I was reprimanded by the national board for allowing the process to go on for as long as it did. They chose to allow me to remain in office when they had removed every other branch official for misusing branch funds--a vindication of sorts. A half-truth, solely focused on me when the activity of the branch was really the question before the committee on branches.

Each fact without a corresponding fact or clarification was made to look like I was just the "bad guy" or the wrongdoer, when if you looked beneath the facts or got the whole story in the proper contexts, motives would tie to intent and intent to resulted action. A clear review of all the facts would, in the worst case, minimize my involvement and in the best case, exonerate me. Yet, that wasn't the case and I was now in a position of imbalance, to the extent that one or two more "low blows" would take me right out of the game. The appearance of another impropriety, or being guilty by association would finish what my NAACP opposition started, which was a plot to discredit me. Of course, when happening one behind the other, it was very difficult to assess this. There's very little time to think in the midst of a bum-rush; there's just enough time to react. As the plane landed, and we all came through U.S. Customs, I could feel the same resignation settling in as before I had left. Almost a "back to the bullshit" type of anxiety. A change of scenery was nice, but it did little to change my perspective. I was still hostile toward my opposition and toward certain elements in the community that reinforced social compromise. I was impatient toward people who really meant me no harm, from what I could see, but was trying to understand what had happened. I just perceived that as "too little, too late." I probably ran a few good people away from me who were really trying to get to know me.

A client of mine, Quint Worthams, had contacted the Mayor's office to facilitate a property acquisition for a skilled nursing facility. The city had been eyeing the property for a police substation but decided against it. I had called the Mayor on the project and he had requested that we send him a packet. We hadn't heard anything in weeks, so when I saw the Mayor, at a reception for the reigning Miss America, Debbye Turner, I greeted him, and he nodded. As I asked my question, he walked past me to talk to somebody else, to my disbelief. I stood there for a moment, as I turned to walk away, the Mayor said without turning to look at me, "Anthony, I received your packet and referred it out to be handled. Call me if you don't hear anything within a week."

I turned around and said, "Thank you Mayor Bradley." He nodded and went back to his conversation. I appreciated the Mayor doing that the way he did. Though I was on his Task Force as a holdover from my NAACP presidency, I knew he wasn't a fan of mine, nor I of his. The Mayor had a reputation for keeping non-supporters out. When you were on the "outs" with the Mayor, you were on the "outs." Given our rocky relationship, he didn't have to respond at all, and had been known to ignore more than a few people in public. I appreciated the fact that he didn't ignore me on this particular occasion.

I began to decline all invitations I was still receiving to events that didn't have a real significance. I closed my public interfacing to clients and close friends. My perspective was changing. It was not necessarily changing for the better. Becoming a recluse wasn't necessarily the answer either. It would only allow my anger and frustration to be turned inward on my loved ones or myself. My marriage, which had been on very shaky terms over the previous three years, was certainly under serious strain. Where Taurece and I were once barely communicating, we were now not talking at all. By either talking through notes or the children, we managed to maintain some semblance of a family "for the sake of the children." However, children aren't crazy. When they see me sleeping downstairs and their mom upstairs, or everybody's watching the same thing on television in three different rooms, they feel the strain, too. My oldest daughter, Kellie, who was always the most sensitive of my children, would ask questions. "Daddy, why are you sleeping downstairs with your clothes on?" "How come mommy's not watching TV in here with us?" or "Don't you and mommy like each other anymore?" It became enough to make me stop and say "Whew!" I didn't know it had become that apparent.

I don't blame Taurece. While we had differences that nearly caused us to split a few years earlier, most of it was now on me. We both recognized how little we had in common other than the children, which we both always put first. We had little else. While we were a mismatch from the start (and we both knew it), our differences had become too great. I was extremely unhappy and there was nothing she could do to change that. We both knew that we couldn't go on living this way. Clearly, our lives were out of control. More my life than hers, but hers was tied to mine. I think Taurece knew I was losing control of my life. She knew me well and though she was use to seeing me maintain control, even in the eye of a storm, she could tell I was struggling now, grappling just to hold on. Moreover, I really didn't know how much longer I could hold on before I'd let go......of everything.

13

Rekindling the Spirit, Renewing of the Mind

"I beseech you therefore, brethren by the mercies of God, that ye present your bodies a living sacrifice, holy acceptable unto God, which is your reasonable service.

And be not conformed to this world: but be ye transformed by the renewing of your mind, that ye may prove what is good, and acceptable, and perfect will of God.

For I say, through the grace given unto me, to every man that is among you, not to think of himself more highly than he ought to think; but to think soberly, according as God hath dealt to every man the measure of faith.

-Romans 12:1-3, The Holy Bible, Red Letter Edition

"In the name of ALLAH, Most Gracious, Most Merciful.

1. *By the time,*
2. *Surely Man is in loss,*
3. *Except those who believe, and do good,*
   and exhort one another to Truth and exhort one another to Patience

-Al-'Asr (The Time)
Sura 103, *The Holy Qur'-n,*
-Muhammad Ali Edition

The next couple of weeks proved to be somewhat spiritually challenging. I really began to look inside myself to check my belief system. What did I believe in? Why did I believe in what I believed in? Why should I continue to believe in what I believed? Around the same time, events and actions were being revealed to me that made me further question my reasons for believing in "anything and everything." First starting with my belief in a supreme being. While my belief in something "bigger than myself" never wavered, how I worshipped was called into critical analysis. This Christianity thing. Why Christianity? Why were Black people largely Christians? Why were Black people permitted to be Christians? Was Christianity truly "the way" for Black people? Or was it "the way" to continue to control Black people? What did we believe in before white folk gave us Christianity? Why were Black people forbidden to worship anything other than Christianity for nearly 300 years? Why were other forms of worship labeled as subversive, radical or satanic in America when two-thirds of the rest of the world practiced religions other than Christianity? Where did the word "sect" come from, and why was it most commonly applied to alternative forms of worship? Why? Why?

In the meantime, the practitioners of Christianity weren't doing anything to help their causes. Community meetings were being held about trying to address the ever-increasing gang and drug activities in our community. Discussions were being held at the Brotherhood Crusade, largely because it was neutral to the church politics. This was similar to the problems I experienced at the NAACP, in trying to pull together a coalition of clergy for the "Stop the Madness" concert. Certain segments of the clergy were still divided over what amounted to be competitive jealousies, and couldn't meet at the Baptist churches, because the AME's and God in Christ preachers wouldn't come. We couldn't meet at the AME churches, because some Baptists wouldn't come. The CME's have friends on both sides and wouldn't show up, because they didn't want to alienate the other. They all pretty much stayed away from Muslims and other non-Christians, except in sparingly singular numbers, because of misconceptions about either their beliefs or leadership personalities.

This all translated into an inability to consolidate the power of the church, the biggest influence of Black people. Denominational factionalism is pervasive in the Los Angeles church community, and mostly over bullshit that men of God are supposed to be able to rise above. Jesus warned his disciples against disputing the teachings of God's law in the book of St. Luke 20:47, by saying their punishment will be worse for allowing the people to suffer, be robbed and misguided, while the teachers basked in hypocrisy. The Los Angeles Black community was in dire need of spiritual guidance, and nobody was big enough to "bury the sword" for the sake of unity.

During this period, I was extremely intense in my search for some spiritual clarity and was looking for every straw of truth I could grasp for growth and enlightenment. I sat and I listened, I read and I read, and I looked. It just wasn't happening. The lessons of the teachings of Christ were being buried in rhetorical shouts of praise to Christ. The message was being lost over the patronizing of the messenger. At least in name. In the name of Jesus! Thank you, Jesus! Jesus is with you! Jesus loves you. Jesus saves you. Jesus. Jesus. Jesus. Then all the ministers, associate ministers and student ministers would get up and try to "out Jesus" one another. Then the choir tries to out Jesus the minister. And then after 15 minutes of announcements and the passing of the trays, there's 15 minutes of some pseudo-message of the morning, that hardly ever comes full circle enough to reach the point of the lesson, and you're out of there. This is all within a two-hour service. I found this equivalent to having walked 100 miles for a gallon of water, only to be given a sip from a cup and sent on my way. Now maybe it was just my luck with Christian churches, but the other ten or so that I visited weren't much better. They can say what they want to about First AME, but at least Chip doesn't drag it out all day, and it's entertaining to say the least. You do leave the Christian church with one thing: knowing "the name" of Jesus. You may not know much else about the man or his message, or the God he serves, but you will be saying his name all the way home. "Jesus...Jesus....Jesus...Jesus!!"

In that sense, without trying to be blasphemous or sarcastic, Christian worship becomes an albatross on the spirituality of Blacks. We're told to believe, but we don't know why, or how to believe. We believe, because we have nothing else to believe in. We believe without really understanding what we're believing, and how it will affect our lives. And if the truth be told, we say we believe, but hardly demonstrate the faith or the deeds of a believer, in the ways and teachings of Christ. We use excessive music, theatrical preaching, and other gimmicks to get people out. Once the people are out, where is the message? It's buried in the gimmickry. It became increasingly difficult for me to sit through spiritual rhetoric. It was like sitting in the second grade for several years, no growth, or playing in a sand box as an adult.

In my search for a greater spirituality, I began to go to the mosque more. Many of their lectures, in my outsider opinion, at the time, were tantamount to what I call "devil-bashing." After you spent all your time talking about what "the devil" had done to you (which you already knew), there wasn't a whole lot left for you in terms of your own spiritual fulfillment.

I had been listening to Islam since 1974, when my sister "went to the truth." My sister left home at 16 to marry a man five years her senior. Both joined the Nation of Islam within six months of their marriage. My sister, Shawn, renamed Khaleeda Rasheed, was always a lot more street smart and a "cut to the chase" kind of person. When I came home from school, my mother was sitting at the dining room table looking depressed. "What's wrong, mama?" I asked.

She couldn't get it out fast enough. "Lord, that girl don't know what to do with herself. Your sister has become a Muslim." (The Christian equivalent to the "Boogie Man" at that time -as it is today.) My first inclination was to smile knowing my sister's independent streak. This was more than a task for her husband, given the Nation's former policy of women deferring to the authority of men. However, the "teaching" was very strong and it changed her life for the better. The tapes she left always began and ended with, "The Honorable Elijah Muhammad teaches us" or "Allah is the greatest, the beneficial and most merciful."

Islam, at least the Nation's teachings, always related prophecy to the "here and now" rather than the "hereafter." Being born into a Baptist family and hearing the "pie in the sky when you die" teachings, had never made any sense to me. Yes, I do believe in a hereafter and a greater glory after this life. But there's one major flaw in that teaching: Why would I have to wait to get all my blessings after I die, particularly the material ones? I wouldn't need them then. I can appreciate the Christian lessons of struggle and suffering, but for Blacks in America, this isn't suffering. It's outright degradation perpetuated by racism and Christian misinterpretation of scripture and prophecy. One of the first things my sister was able to sell me on, as far as Islam went, was that if it wasn't for the teaching of The Honorable Elijah Muhammad, Black folk would still be "looking in the sky" to get "theirs" in heaven. "The Messenger" of the Lost-Found Nation of Islam in the West told Blacks that "heaven and hell" are here on earth. And that the European white man has caused more deceit, doom and destruction to Black folk in America than any nation anywhere in the world. I don't care what religion you were, there wasn't a teaching that made more sense than that first-hand account of social suffering.

As the light of Islam came on in the minds of Blacks in America, Christian preachers were forced to come down "outta the clouds" and deal with the prophecy. Most then shifted their emphasis from "the hereafter" to the "suffering of Jesus" to justify our suffering condition. "Suffer as Jesus suffered," they preached. Well, I don't ever remember reading in any of the three dozen versions of the Bible that Jesus suffered at the hands of racists. Racism goes past a belief system or an honor system.

Racism is a humanity compromise, based on a violation of one's right to live freely, to express one's faith or test a society's integrity. A compromised humanity can't express beliefs independent of the master, much less an understanding of life. Blacks' historical interface in America has been to believe what they are told to believe, and they act as they are told to act. What kind of a belief can one have when one worships and acts contrary to what he knows is right? We know a fair, beneficent, merciful God couldn't believe in supporting the type of treatment and injustices Blacks in America have had to (and continue to) endure. And who would bless their wicked actions "in the name of God," and expect those same victims to pray to the God of their oppressor? Whose God is America worshipping? What God would condone the wickedness of slavery, the post-Reconstruction and the Civil Rights periods where the spirit of America was unveiled in all its racist glory and justified in the name of God. And what is the religion of America's God? Christianity, of course. The same Christianity that was forced on Blacks, in spite of the first amendment. For Blacks in America, it was (America's) God, or no God. The same God that America used to prop up his "Christian nation," to justify slavery and second class citizenry for Blacks. The same God that America used to placate Blacks by insisting that instead of coming to him for justice, they should pray to "Jesus," and he will provide for us in the "by and by," while receiving all his blessings now, at the expense of our humanity. No God could be so unjust. God said that the devil was as powerful as a God, but was not the God. As Blacks have worshipped the God of his master, the only God they were allowed to know, for all they knew, they may have been turned into "devil worshippers, "not worshipping for their own good or the good of all people. Whatever whites worshipped is what Blacks have worshipped, including immorality and materiality.

Just the fact that Islam gave Blacks a spiritual option to seek a form of self-knowledge that had been taken away by America in order to enslave us, gave me reason to explore it. Because of my personal understanding of this society's systemic racism, I wanted to be careful that I didn't become vulnerable to the "devil talk," and not receive what I was seeking, which was spiritual enlightenment and growth. As I began attending the mosque more and more, one assistant minister that had a very focused and delicate understanding of Islam and its relationship to the personal self-improvement and the upliftment of the community, versus concentrating on "the devil," was Brother Christopher X Phillips (now known as Minister Christopher Muhammad). On one occasion, Brother Christopher's "lecture" was on "The trials of Allah Bringing Spiritual Self-improvement." From the Holy Qur'~n, Sura 29, Section I entitled "The Spider," and subtitled "Trials Purify," and quoting from verses one through 15, Bro. Christopher, in a very smooth and methodical delivery, discussed how we, as believers, will say we believe but when our beliefs are tried, we are often found in disbelief. In referencing verses one through three, he reminded the attendees that "Allah is the best knower (Sura 29, Section I. Verse 1) and Allah through prophet Muhammad (peace be upon him) asked the question: "Do men think that they will be left alone on saying we believe, and will not be tried?" (Sura 29, Section I Verse 2). The lecturer went on to say that as Allah has tried others before us, we will also be tried. And Allah will know those who are true and those who are "the liars" because Allah is the best knower. The true believer's faith is tested with "a major trial," at least once a year, and that the true believer becomes purified by these trials and thus more healed in faith and his dedication to righteousness.

It was one of the most impressive lectures I'd heard outside Minister Farrakhan himself, the national staff or even some of the higher profiled mosque ministers. You expect lectures of this sort from Dr. Alim Muhammad, Bro. Jabril Muhammad, Sister Tynetta Muhammad, Sister Eva Muhammad, or even Dr. Khalid on certain days. But to hear a brother that came from where I came from, in more ways than one, give such an in-depth spiritual teaching, opened my eyes to the power of Islam. Chris grew up where I grew up. We had common friends. We ran in common circles. We were both college-trained and had common interest in public affairs: Chris, through his association with elected officials, and my associations in the community, civil rights and urban finance affairs. Chris was a professional who was able to position himself in the Nation's ranks. That was a real concern for me. There were allegations that professionals didn't fair well in the Nation, largely due to the time commitments being in conflict with their schedule and "rank-and-file" officers relegating professionals to responsibilities that "underutilized" their skills. There appeared to be little for the professional brother to do. (His was a clear contradiction to that claim, and in our discussions he arrested many of the concerns regarding this issue to my satisfaction.) In representing it as "a trial" for even the educated brother to find a way to use his God-given talents to uplift the Black nation, ignorance and insensitivity to one's background is something that the professional has to learn to overcome. Chris really hit home when he said that it's certainly "no less" than the resistance that the Black professional encounters every day, in trying to prove his worth to white folk.

We give our whole lives "trying to prove ourselves" and we're being underpaid, overworked, non-credited and discredited for doing so, if we stay around long enough. Yet we don't leave at the slightest bit of resistance we encounter. Chris stated finally that if all brothers weren't at least tested with some resistance in the ranks, we wouldn't know the believers from the disbelievers. This is really the root of the problem with Black people. Betrayal is so easy because every strategy or secret we have can be penetrated on its face. The Black face, that is, who penetrates any group or organization we have, with not as much as a question asked. Strange faces just show up and we haven't the slightest idea if they're "friend or foe," but we let them sit in anyway and we end up having our plans sabotaged. Having been in that situation, I could really appreciate Chris' explanation, and I really believe he, most of all, could appreciate where I came from and the "adjustment" difficulties I would encounter should I decide to "join the ranks." Now that I had heard Chris' insight on "the teachings" from a self-improvement perspective, I felt really enlightened about my personal strife in its context to my own spirituality and personal development.

* * *

That Monday, following Chris' lecture, I felt better than I had felt in a few months. I also did not feel any of the anger or anxiety of the past six months. I was just sort of on "cruise control" for a minute. Katherine buzzed in and said, "Debra Ward's here to see you." I hadn't heard from her in over three weeks, since the last time she ran out of my office. To be truthful, I had really missed her. Her smile, her calming demeanor, her unclouded insight and, of course, her no nonsense approach to things. I can't really say why I hadn't called her. Maybe I didn't want to hear what she had to say. Or maybe because I didn't want to admit that she was right.

My position had little to do with what was right, as much as it had to do with what was most conducive to resolving my personal anxiety over what had happened to me. Though I still felt I was wronged, I knew my advocacy was on point. Most pedestrians hit by cars are in the right, either by having the right of way or by being in the crosswalk. They end up dead, even though they are in the right. Why? Because of personal negligence, because of taking their eyes off the car and assuming it would stop, because of assuming the alertness and integrity of the driver and because of abandoning personal safety by assuming everyone is abiding by the same laws and rules. But they're still right. As right as Debra probably was in many of her assumptions, I had no intentions of being negligent or abandoning my personal safety by assuming that the NAACP election fiasco was over. The light had changed but the traffic hadn't stopped, in my opinion. She probably could never understand this, but then I didn't expect that she would. Still I appreciated her concern for me.

After about a minute passed, Katherine buzzed in again. "Did you hear me? Debra's here to see you."

"Send her in," I responded. Debra came in and sat in the chair in front of my desk. We just looked at each other for a minute. Then I spoke:

"Hi. How you been?"

"Fine. How have you been?"

"Fine."

"So did you go through with anything?"

"Nope. Not yet."

"Do you plan to?"

"I dunno. Depends."

"Depends on what?"

"Depends on what I see or hear coming at me. I can't keep lettin' people take shots at me."

"How do you know that it's not over?"

"Cause I know. People are dropping little things here and there."

"How you know they're just not doing it to mess with you, to keep you off balance?"

"I don't know that they're still plotting on me, but I do know that there will be some carryover from what they've already thrown out there."

"So you don't think that maybe this is just a little paranoia on your part? Or do you see this as real?"

I could see Debra analyzing me to see if she was dealing with some kind of nut, or if I really believed that I was in some imminent danger. She was trying to believe me and was asking questions to satisfy the correctness of her position. Emotions notwithstanding. I got a little defensive at her inference.

"No, this is definitely real. Is that what you think? That I'm paranoid? Shell- shocked?"

"Anthony, I don't know what to believe. I'm trying to believe in you. I've heard some of the rumors that they're still after you. I just wanted to know if you had any proof yet, that's all."

"Yes, I have seen the proof. Just a few people who've talked directly to the sources that did the investigation for my opposition. And to a couple people who heard firsthand accounts of where the packet they compiled would be sent. I got my ears to the floor, and they tell me that it's not over."

"So what do you want to do about it?"

"I'm gonna wait right now. Wait and watch. When the time is right, then I'll act."

"So you pretty much still feel like you did before?"

Fearing my response would set the stage for another argument, I didn't say anything. Debra threw a folder on my desk. It said: "Inter-Africa Tours" on the front. I opened the folder. It was an information packet and itinerary of the National Council of Negro Women's African-American Business Symposium, to be held in Cairo, Egypt in a couple of weeks. I had put a deposit down on the trip a couple of months earlier. On the right hand side was a plane ticket. I looked at Deb. She was looking through me.

"What's this for?" I asked.

"You need to get away," she said.

"I just got away. I went to Mazatlan for a change of pace. It really didn't help much."

"That's because you don't need a change of pace; you need a change of perspective, Anthony. Maybe going to Africa will bring that about and soften your heart in the process."

"How did you get my ticket?" I asked.

"How do you think I got it; I paid for it. You owe me $745."

As I took my checkbook out, Debra said, "No checks, cash."

I said, "Afraid of a paper trail?"

"No," she said sternly, "I don't need my monetary benevolence coming back to haunt me."

"You don't want your boyfriend to find out," I said smiling.

She smiled, but then turning dead serious she said, "Or your wife. I'm just doing this to help you save your life. Maybe you'll do the same for somebody else one day. People may not understand my actions, but you're a good brother and you don't need to self-destruct."

"People like who?" I asked only hearing the first part.

"Just pay me cash and let's be done with this. I was afraid you would let your deposit go to waste. You need this right now."

"We gotta go to the bank."

"Let's go."

As we drove to the bank, I couldn't help but appreciate Debra's sincere concern for me. The sister just had a different kind of spirit. I hadn't really thought about a change of perspective. Was my thinking so clouded that I really had a skewed perspective? Was I making this bigger than it was? And why did she care? Was it just about saving me? What else could it be. Our relationship had none of flirtation or promiscuity of the normal male-female interface. Nothing sexual. Nothing material. Just a strong mental connection tied to a spirituality, a peacefulness that was higher than anything I had dealt with heretofore. And though she barely knew me, she could read me like a book. She really had no reason to believe me, or even trust me, much less try to save me. Maybe she was one of those sisters who had a mother complex. You know, the kind that just has to have a project. Or maybe she was a godsend. Nobody else was bold enough to spend $745 of my money telling me I needed a change of perspective. She was right in one sense. I had become so consumed in my perception of being under attack, that I probably would have forfeited my deposit on the Egypt trip. I wasn't thinking about Egypt; I was thinking about "getting even." So now I was Debra's reclamation project. If this was the case, she certainly picked a helluva project this time I thought, as I smiled to myself. Debra noticed me smiling.

"What you smiling about?" she asked.

"I was just wondering if you wanted small, unmarked bills."

"Get out the car," she retorted.

* * *

On a bright June morning in 1989, I arrived at the Tom Bradley International terminal at LAX two hours early, as required for international travel. As I stood in line awaiting check-in, I recognized a good portion of the Los Angeles contingent: "Sweet Alice" Harris, Lillian Mobley and Audrey Quarles. These women are considered "the mothers of the Los Angeles Black community." I also saw Ken and Jennifer Thomas, publishers of the *Los Angeles Sentinel*, several of the Brotherhood Crusade employees and board members and other familiar faces in the community. As I got up to the counter and handed over my ticket and passport, I realized that I was actually looking forward to this "change of perspective" excursion to the "cradle of civilization." It was going to be my first trip to Africa, the soil of my native land. And I just wondered how Debra would know and understand the kind of impact this would have on me. Most of my travel had been in the Western Hemisphere and one trip to Hong Kong. None of those trips had an impact on my "perspective." However, I had a different expectation for this trip.

As I turned away from the counter, who was in line directly behind me? You got it, my godsend. Daydreaming in line, I hadn't even looked behind me.

"What are you doing here?" I asked.

"I'm taking a trip," Debra responded.

"Oh? Where would you happen to be going standing in this line? This is the line to Cairo."

"As in Egypt?"

"Yeah."

"Then that's where I'm going?"

"What a coincidence. When did you decide this?" Debra hadn't told me she was going to Egypt, though it was a pleasant surprise.

"Since I decided I needed a change of perspective also."

Debra had been contemplating several major moves. As pleasant and happy as she always appeared to be, she wasn't happy with several personal elements in her life. While she loved the organization she worked for, she felt stagnated in her present position. She was tired of Los Angeles and wanted a change of pace and place. Most critically, she was engaged to marry someone she didn't really love and didn't know how to break it off.

"So now I'm going to have to look after God's grounded angel for eight days in Egypt," I said. I called her that, because Debra was about as "straight an arrow" as you can get. I had often criticized her for the naive approaches she often took in life. Plus, things would happen to her that you'd have to say was more than fate. People approached her in an adversarial state and became completely disarmed. She's lost her purse twice, and had it returned to her with money, credit cards and everything still in it. There was a rape and attempted suicide at her office building where the rapist, a security guard, came in and talked with her for 15 minutes before deciding to rape another woman and jumped out a window, attempting to kill himself. Every time she seemed to lose something, she'd gain something else--almost immediately--as if she's being divinely guided. And she probably has the strongest sense of right and wrong of anyone I've ever met. One example that speaks to her sense of rightness, though only in a token sense, was when a group of us went to lunch one day. The parking lot was across the street from the restaurant. We all just naturally crossed the street. I believe "jay-walking" is the legal term for what we did. When we got across the street, somebody said, "Where's Debra?" We looked back and saw her walking up the block to the corner light. It was one of those long blocks, too. She got teased that day as being "the last good girl." I still call her that every now and then, because she was what she was--a naturally good person, very ethical and moral in her approach to life.

The week I was due to leave for Egypt, a significant event happened to me at the invitation of Debra and at the spur of the moment, which gave me some indication that my spirit was being uplifted and that Debra, in a sense, was a guide to that uplifting. She called out of the blue and asked if I wanted to go to Bible study. I immediately said, "Nope."

In her calm manner, she said, "Well, if you change your mind, I'd be real happy to see you there," which was her way of saying "be there."

I hadn't been to the church for a while and really wasn't interested in going. But I went. Late. Deb had saved a seat. I asked her, "How'd you know I'd come."

"I just knew," she said. My mom was there also. Mom was always glad to see me come back to the church. Bible study was uneventful. Didn't really move me one way, or the other. After mingling a bit, we started walking to the parking lot. As I said my goodbyes to Deb and my mom, I heard a voice from behind me.

"I knew you would be here," said a sister I had come to know as

Bridgette. Bridgette, you recall, was the first to defect from the NAACP slate and was, by and large, their "plug" into our strategy. Plainly put, she was used against us. She had tears in her eyes.

"Hi, Bridgette. What's up?" I said, ignoring her first statement about my being here.

"This is the first time I've been to Bible study in four months since the election. I've been wanting to call you, but I didn't have the courage to. God gave me strength to get up and come out tonight," she continued.

"Why?" I asked.

"Because I had something I had to get off my heart, and he told me you'd be here. I couldn't let you walk away without saying this to you."

"Say what, Bridgette?"

"Anthony, I never imagined this would turn out like this. I never imagined they would do what they did. And they were only allowed to do it because the people you had around you weren't really your friends."

"Like who?" I asked.

"Like me; like Elvin Moon and Mark Whitlock, who was supposed to be one of your best friends."

"What do you mean, Bridgette?"

"Mark sold you out. Basil offered to raise money for Mark (as the co-chair of FAME Family Day in 1989), if he dropped off your slate, but only if Mark did it that night. Mark called Basil back in 30 minutes saying, 'He was off the slate.' I was laying next to Basil in bed during the whole conversation."

"Who sent the hit piece?" I asked.

"The group paid for it. Basil put it together and mailed it," she responded.

"Why are you telling me this now?" I asked. Because you told me that Basil was only seeing me to get information on you. You were right. I did give them information to use against you. I thought you would still win the election. But I never thought they would carry it on past that. They wanted to see you in jail. Did you know that?"

"Yes, I know," I said.

"You're a good brother, Anthony. You stand up for Black people and you were the best thing that the Los Angeles NAACP ever had." She said she had to leave before she got too emotional, but hoped I didn't hate her for this.

I told her I didn't. We hugged and she left. I stood there stunned for a moment. I would have never known about Mark, if not for Bridgette's confession. I had always known Basil sent the "hit piece." Several people on their slate claimed they didn't agree with it and had tried to distance themselves from it by coming to me in advance. I thought Mark's backing out had to do with his lack of courage. As discussed earlier, Mark had a habit of conveniently getting out of the "line of fire." But a "quid pro quo," a deal? That was open betrayal. The next few days, I became extremely dissolute of the notion that a friend sold me out. I vowed this would never happen again. But it only made me isolate myself more against well- intentioned people trying to help me heal. No one was to be trusted. While in the midst of this little reflection, I was pondering Debra's response in the airport to my "grounded angel" comment.

"Anthony, there are no strings attached to you," Debra said. "You're free to do whatever you want to do. I'm not here to 'cramp your play' or 'blow your action.'" I'd tease her sometimes when I'd see her at different places and we'd talk for a moment. Then I'd tell her, "You can't stand here too long, you're blowin' my action. Move around." She'd usually shake her head and walk away smiling. Apparently, she remembered those little lines. "OK, you can hang with me for a minute, but when I give you the sign, you're outta here. No conversation." Debra looked at me like, "Niggah, please. Give me a break." The reality was that I was pleased to see her. She was good company, a great conversationalist, and she looked good, too. No man would complain about being seen in her company.

We walked up to the coffee shop and sat, while we waited for the boarding call. About that time, Debra saw a brother she had gone to school with, and called out to him. "Hi, Ali." When the brother saw Debra, he looked relieved. He came over with his very attractive wife, Jeanette Ali. Debra asked him if he was going to Cairo. Looking flustered and frustrated, he said no. He was there to drop off his wife, who was going. In carrying on a very innocent conversation, Debra asked him why he wasn't going. His wife kinda looked off in another direction. He responded that his wife's grandmother had bought the ticket and couldn't go, and gave it to Jeanette. He had been trying to convince Jeanette to sell it to a single person, reasoning that this is not the type of trip a married woman should take by herself, particularly since Jeanette didn't know anybody. Apparently, he wasn't very successful in convincing her of this, though he was making an effort of it up until boarding time.

It appeared that they were in an intense discussion when Debra called out to him. Apparently, resigned to the fact that Jeanette was going, he did the next best thing. He brought Jeanette over to Debra and said, "Hang with Debra (after making sure Debra was traveling alone). She'll help you stay out of trouble." I guess he was also aware of Debra's "good girl" reputation. Debra whispered, "I guess we got a real lonely heart's club goin' now."

After Ali kissed his wife, said goodbye to Debra and left, Jeanette came over and started talking like long lost friends at "old home week." "Girl, I'm outta here when I get back," implying that she intended to leave her husband, when she returned from this trip. "He's a nice guy, but he's not for me. We have little in common, and we never do anything. I like excitement. Isn't this trip exciting?" Deb and I looked at each other and kind of nodded. We both just listened to Jeanette talk to two people she barely knew, although, we knew almost her whole life, before the discussion was over.

The first leg of the 19-hour flight to Egypt was uneventful. I was separated from Debra and Jeanette, because we all checked in separately. When we got to New York, we couldn't deplane, because we'd already been checked through customs. So we sat on the plane during the entire two and a half hour layover.

Leaving New York, the plane filled up fast. In spite of a full plane, I was able to trade seats to get within a row of Debra. After about an hour of looking back over the seat, both our seat-mates were asked to trade seats, so we could sit together. For the balance of the 12-hour flight to Cairo, our discussion centered largely on the anticipation of spending five days in the cradle of civilization. During that time, I noticed how much we were alike. Neither of us particularly enjoyed small talk -- talking for the sake of talking. We almost sensed when one felt like talking and when the other one didn't. We made a lot of the same observations during the flight, from similar perspectives. There wasn't any pressure to make or fake conversation. It was just a real nice flow. Something to take notice of.

Once we landed in Cairo, Debra and I got separated. Air Egyptian representatives picked up our passports to check us through customs. I was pulled into a dignitary waiting room away from the other 300 or so passengers. There were several prominent business people included in the group: Mr. and Mrs. Comer Cottrell, owners of Pro-Line Products, Jesse Jackson and his family and several L.A. elected officials who had made the trip. All of these people were the special guests of Dr. Dorothy Height, the President of the National Council of Negro Women, who was received royally, as she deplaned. After an hour or so of refreshments and "hobnobbing," they gathered our luggage and shuttled us to the hotel. The host hotel was the Inter-Continental Seminaris. It was considered one of the five-star hotels of Cairo. It sat on the bank of the Nile River and was sort of a landmark for tourists, because you could always look up in the sky and see it. The bellmen took the dignitaries up to a VIP check-in window, where they told us that the travel agency, Inter-Africa, was handling our rooms. So much for VIP treatment. I had a couple of hours to wander around the hotel. Coming away from the front desk, I saw Debra and Jeanette standing with another brother from Los Angeles named Eric Chapman. I had met Eric on the layover in New York, when he came up to introduce himself by saying he had supported my work in the NAACP, and was sorry that I had lost in such a dirty campaign. I appreciated his comments, because it was good to know that many others, not necessarily connected to me, saw the election for what it was.

Debra noticed me and called out, "Where have you been? You just disappeared at the airport."

Not bothering to explain, I responded, "Yeah, I just caught my own camel and came right over." Debra and Jeanette just rolled their eyes like, "Oh, Brother, corny, corny, corny." Eric just shook his head. Sitting in the lobby of the Inter-Continental, we began to meet African-Americans from other cities.

At the front of the Inter-Continental hotel, you immediately saw the Nile River in all of its ancient glory. Walking up the street a little, it became apparent that Egypt was under some strife. There were men in military uniforms on almost every corner with machine guns, which made the group a little uncomfortable, though we tried not to show it. Soon we encountered the first lesson of Egyptian tourism, trying to decipher real papyrus paintings from fake papyrus paintings. The paintings were beautiful; however, they were many beautiful fakes. One merchant would show us his, another would show what he had, then each would try to discredit the other's product. Everything from the quality of the papyrus paper itself to paintings being printed. Then the bidding and bartering would begin. While the group stood in the middle of the sidewalk taking papyrus lessons, I ran up the street to find out what this big "cruise ship" decked in front of the hotel was. It was a dinner cruise ship that sailed the Nile River for two hours while they put on a dinner show. I thought that would be a great way to spend the first night in Egypt. Plus we'd beat the rush before the rest of the conference found out about it. I made reservations for a party of 10. The maitre'd agreed to hold the spots until 6:30 p.m. The cruise pulled out at 7 p.m. There was also a later cruise at 9 p.m. They both had to be paid by 6:30, or it was first come, first served.

The line for rooms was out the door and down the hall. It took about 45 minutes to get my room. It was a nice size room with a great view of the Nile River. My roommate wasn't due to arrive until the next day, so I had the room to myself for the first night. I unpacked my bags and called back to "the states" to let my family know that I had arrived safely. It was nine hours difference and mid- morning in Los Angeles. The kids were already at school, and Taurece at work. The answering machine came on. I left a message that I had arrived safely, where I was staying and to give my love to the kids. I didn't realize, until after I had hung up that I didn't say anything about loving my wife. I began to realize that maybe the time had come where I didn't love my wife anymore. Not if I didn't automatically think to say it. I began daydreaming, while lying across my bed and staring out the window. The more I thought about it, the more I knew I couldn't, and finally I realized what was missing. Some of it had to do with her and our incompatibility, but a lot of it had to do with me--my own ambition, my own selfishness, my priorities in putting community before family. I wasn't happy with what I had become. I knew she couldn't be happy with it. I finally acknowledged a love that was never really there. Now that I had to "be true to myself," I knew had to leave.

As I was lying there "kicking my own ass" mentally, the phone rang. "Bout time to go to dinner isn't it?" Debra asked. It was a quarter after six.

"I'll be right down," I said. When I got there, Eric was already there. Jeanette came a few minutes later. We started looking at the conference packet and noticed that there would be a briefing at 9 p.m.

"We probably need to be there," Debra said.

"Well, the cruise will be over by 9 p.m., because the second one pulls out at 9," I said. "We can come in, change clothes and be there by 9:30. They'll probably start late." We all agreed that both dinner and the briefing were doable, so we went for it.

On our way out of the hotel, a couple of sisters from Chicago joined us. The six of us boarded the boat and sat at tables on the outer deck. As we started to cruise down the Nile River, the group was pretty much involved in idle chatter. I went to stand alone against one of the side rails so I could watch the water and the Cairo skyline. All at once, I realized the beauty of being home and of our people being the reason for civilization as we knew it, and knowing it all started here. Any Black that came here could never be told that they were nothing ever again. I hadn't been here a day and I already felt the difference. A sense of self, unlike I have ever felt. Our current society would like to make you think that Egypt is not part of Africa, but in the "middle east." Middle east of where? It's Northern Africa. Once you get there, there no controverting that issue. Deep down in your heart, you just know.

Jeanette called over to me. "You didn't pull us on this cruise to stand over there by yourself."

I broke from my deep thought and rejoined the group. We "toasted" to the Motherland, took pictures, told jokes and just laughed until we were dizzy. Nobody had a trouble in the world on this night. We went into the ship's dining area, had dinner and watched the dinner show--a belly dancer. As the ship made its way back, we all went back out on the deck to let the warm, humid African breeze blow in our faces. We all were intoxicated with the very notion of being in the same place as our ancestors, outside the slave land, of course.

How many millennia had our people navigated the Nile River before our oppressors came and got us? Before they even had knowledge of themselves? The notion of having what we once knew as "free winds" blow in our faces was great. The connection to a legacy, of finding the center of one's soul, a sense of home. How many American Blacks ever get this feeling? Home for us is where the master leads us, or where they leave us when they're through using us. Home for Blacks in America is tantamount to coming home to an empty house every night for 440 years. Blacks know firsthand that a house is not necessarily a home, but just a place to lay their heads. It doesn't have the comfort, the warmth, the love, the security that comes with living in a home. In fact, there are very few places Blacks can feel safe in America, in large numbers. In small numbers, Blacks are safe as long as whites feel secure. When they become threatened, we become threatened. Then we're as safe as we are invisible or timid.

This little ole' dining car tourist cruise boat goes in and out twice a night, and is probably very indiscriminate in who it picks up. It doesn't know what type of problems its occupants may bring with them. But on this particular night, every problem I ever thought I had blew out on this Nile River. It was the type of mental cleansing that allows for clear thought and philosophical growth. The type of open-mindedness that fosters a renewed spirit and a healed heart. As the cruise ship docked, I was so high, I felt as if I was walking on air. I never imagined I'd come in feeling so good, not from a boat cruise. As we walked into the lobby of the Inter-Continental, our travel cohorts were looking bored, waiting for the briefing to start and wondering why we were so lighthearted and giggly. We told them about the cruise across the street and, of course, 25 people who we'd never seen before, all wanted to know why we didn't come and get them to go with us. Some things never change, in the follies of the American Negro. It didn't change my mood any. They'd have five days to catch the boat. I left them in the lobby, to go shower and change for the briefing.

The briefing was more of a presentation of Jesse Jackson Sr., and the usual Jesse comments. I wore a suit. Everyone else was casual. I stuck out like a sore thumb -a throw back from being on the merry-go-round so long. Introduced by Ms. Height, Jesse was short and brief. There was a little discussion about the symposium sessions and the public ceremony, which was to feature the first lady of Egypt, Suzanne Mubarak. The briefing lasted less than an hour.

Our young adult group, about eight of us now, went over to the night club in the hotel. It had indoor and outdoor seating. We went outdoors and stood on the balcony overlooking the hotel lobby. As we stood outside "kickin' it," Jesse Jackson Jr. and his associate came by. They were taken by Debra and Jeanette, and told Eric and I that we were the luckiest guys on the trip, twice, because our women were attractive. After we let them know that everybody there was "flying solo," we suddenly had two new friends. Before long, everybody was posing for pictures and making time to get back together. Debra was getting tired and wanted to go to her room. Eric walked her up.

Going back to my room, I reflected on my first day in Egypt. My heart hadn't been this light in years. The cruise on the Nile River was an all-time high. Upon entering my room, I pulled open the drapes and sat in front of the balcony window to watch the calm of the Nile and the Cairo night life. The surrounding building lights were reflecting off the river. It seemed the energy of the river was bouncing off me. I was so pumped up, I couldn't go to sleep. It was like the river kept calling me. I sat there for two hours at least, staring at the river. I had never believed in being dipped in water as a form of spiritual cleansing. Baptism, as Christians call it. I felt it was more symbolic than anything.

Yet the mystique of the Nile was calling me. I started talking to myself. I was really trippin', I told myself. Or was I? There seemed to be something bigger than me controlling me. It was hard for me to discern whether I was hallucinating, or if this was real. It was a quarter 'till three. I put on my shoes, ran downstairs and out of the hotel. I ran across the street next to the boat we had cruised on earlier. Looking around to see if anyone noticed me, I removed my shoes, and hung my feet into the water. The water was lukewarm. Then without another thought, I fell forward into the river.

All I saw were bubbles and darkness. I'm sure I was underwater less than a few seconds, but it seemed like an eternity. I tread back over to the embankment and pulled myself up. Dripping wet, I put my shoes back on and walked back across the street, through the lobby, up the elevator and to my room. People in the lobby and in the elevator just stared. For the first time in my life, I didn't care what people thought. Whatever I looked like, whatever they thought happened, whatever the situation appeared to seem like, I didn't care. I don't know what those people were thinking, but I did know that what I had done was good for me, spiritually, and I could care less what they thought. Back in my room, I wrapped myself in two towels: one around my waist and the other around my shoulders. I sat back in the chair and contemplated what had just happened to me. The conflict I had felt earlier, the river calling to me, all were gone. There was just calm in the room and in me. The last thing I remember about that night was lights reflecting off the Nile, in the shape of a smile. And I smiled back.

I woke up to the sound of a key turning in the door lock. I opened my eyes to the rising sun in the east. A beautiful site. I had slept in the chair all night. My clothes were damp and wrinkled. Coming in the door was my roommate. He had just got in from Washington, D.C. He spoke, trying to figure out why I had slept in the chair, and why my clothes were wet. "Long story," I told him. It was about 7:30 a.m. I felt very rested on four hours sleep, in spite of the chair. He immediately got into his bed to catch up on his sleep. The opening ceremony was at 9:30. I had time to shave, shower and have breakfast. I got downstairs about a quarter past eight. Deb and Eric were already in the lobby.

After breakfast, we headed toward the room where the opening ceremony was being held. Egyptian security was all over the place, due to the first lady's appearance. The invitations to attend the conference event were made on papyrus paper (real papyrus) with Egyptian paintings on them. For this particular event, consulates general and dignitaries from other African countries came dressed in their native attire, in their official capacities. Some even wore European suits, but somehow didn't look like European or act European, like many American Blacks do when they put on a shirt and tie. This was an interesting observation; a demonstration in cultural pride. In knowing who you are regardless of what you wear, or wearing your culture on your sleeve regardless of the suit. The way they moved and the way they articulated discussion was very impressive. They had a keen sense of cultural awareness and purpose of mission. Those are the two things most absent in American Blacks, for the most part-- purpose and mission. Without a purpose, there can be no mission, just aimless wandering.

While sitting there watching the crowd fill in, my thinking kept shifting back to the African-American's sense of purpose and our collective mission. I couldn't help but ask myself: "Are Black people in America a race of aimless wanderers, and if not, then what is our mission? Freedom? Equality? To be like white folk, have what white folk have, but with no sense of mission for community empowerment or collective economics or the ability to sustain ourselves in times of crisis or self-defense? Just cultural mutants existing, as long as it's some semblance of what American whites view as prosperity. As I keep looking at our African brothers and a few sisters, I thought about the individual materiality American Blacks call wealth, and the lifestyles they consider prosperous. And if you talk to people in our communities, they think "they have it goin' on." Yet, these native brothers and sisters, from underdeveloped countries and less prosperous by American standards, had something that the American Black never had, doesn't have today, and if he maintains his current state of mind and affairs, will never have -- his or her own country. An economic infrastructure; no matter how fragile, they have one. The American Negro has never run a nation. A nation the Negro can call his own that produces a measure of self-wealth, prosperity and pride whose value is unascertainable. American Blacks can claim to be African all they want, or disown it all they want ("I ain't goin' back to Africa"), but the bottom line is American Blacks ain't from nowhere. They're not from Africa and they're not from America. America may be their birthplace or residence, but the reality is that most Americans do not perceive us as Americans. It's like we were born on the plane. Once we landed, we were given temporary rights that they have to affirm through legislation every 25 or so years. They don't do that for any other Americans. You don't hear them talking about civil rights act extensions for themselves. Their civil rights act is perpetually valid. It's called the United States Constitution. Until they cut out this foolishness of having to grant to Blacks everything that comes, by right, to everybody else, we are not Americans. We're just from America. These thoughts came to me just as clear as if I was watching a movie plot unveil. The clarity was remarkable.

The program had started but I had hardly noticed. Dr. Height was now up introducing then the United States Ambassador to Egypt, Frank G. Wisner, who introduced the featured speaker of the morning, the first lady of Egypt, Mrs. Suzanne Mubarak. Egypt's first lady gave an outstanding presentation of her country's perspective of world affairs, its willingness to strike a partnership with the African-American woman, and its intent to measure the sincerity of America's politics by its treatment of Blacks. Mrs. Mubarak's comments brought to light the increasing awareness, worldwide, of the race politics in America. It demonstrated that many "nations of color" were beginning to pull off the hoodwink that the United States had put on the darker nations of the world, that racism had subsided when in fact, it hadn't. It was just disguised more effectively. She even committed to a Cairo chapter of the NCNW, as part of her country's intent to solidify ties with its American cultural counterpart. Mrs. Mubarak's comments were followed by remarks from Jesse Jackson Sr. Everybody was pretty pumped at the conclusion of the opening ceremonies. Mrs. Mubarak and the other dignitaries were rushed out, while the conference attendees discussed the events of the morning amongst themselves. Jet lag was beginning to catch up with me. I excused myself to take a nap, while the others wanted to go walking and shopping during the lunch break. I told Deb to call me if anything worth seeing happened during the afternoon session. About three hours later, my phone rang.

"You might want to come down and see this," Deb said on the other end of the line, referring to the afternoon session that had just started up.

"Why?" I asked.

"Because a lot of good information is being debated about our role in Egyptian history. Just come down and see for yourself," she said and hung up the phone.

When I got there, there was a real intense discussion going on. It was the question and answer portion of the first presentation, which was a symposium on the history of Egypt. The first speaker was a woman named Dr. Fayza Haikal. She was a professor of Egyptology at Cairo University, supposedly speaking on the topic, "Women in Ancient Egypt." Apparently, during the course of her presentation, Dr. Haikal implied that the current culture of Egypt is the oldest in the world without the influence of Europeans. She went on to comment how, in spite of what all the ancient artifacts of the country reflect, the current "look" of the Egyptian--the pointed nose, fair features, straight hair and square jaw--has always been the look of the native Egyptian.

What we were witnessing was the Europeanization of Egyptian history, as told by a European-trained Egyptian. During the Q&A, someone asked about the predominance of the Kemite and Nubian cultures prior to Persian, Greek and Roman invasions. Dr. Haikal responded that darker skinned cultures were mostly slaves brought into Egypt by European invasions. The second speaker, Dr. Asa Hilliard, Professor of Antiquities from Atlanta University, took exception to Dr. Haikal's explanation of dark people's role in Egypt. Dr. Hilliard brought to everyone's attention how Dr. Haikal's packet and the one from the Cairo Tourist Bureau in its presentation of Egyptian history, failed to even make mention of the Kemet culture, which lasted over 5,000 years. Furthermore, everything that referenced Egyptians prior to the European invasions, should be referenced as Kemet, Dr. Hilliard insisted. Lastly, Dr. Hilliard expressed grave disappointment that Dr. Haikal, as a fellow Egyptologist, would perpetuate and distort history that Black Africans weren't the indigenous people of Egypt, and never ruled their own civilization.

Dr. Haikal couldn't say anything but, "That's not true."

To which Dr. Hilliard said, "Oh, but it is true, and my presentation will speak to it." Dr. Hilliard's presentation entitled "Egypt's Contribution to the World" virtually discredited the prior presentation. With handouts and a slide presentation used on the history of Kemet, Dr. Hilliard lectured almost two hours on the specific dynasties of Kemet, in chronology, with histories of their rulers, all of native "Black African" royal descent. It even included a presentation of Cheikh Anta Diop's eleven categories of conveying evidence (in summary) that proved, according to scientific, physiological, historical, biblical and "osteological" evidence, that the ancient Kemites were native Black Africans. It was one of the most impressive presentations of history most of us had ever witnessed. But in a million years, we couldn't have imagined it being presented in direct rebuttal to another "so-called" expert's presentation of the same subject matter, which made it all the better.

You'd figure that two experts sharing a panel about something as well documented and matter of fact as historical accounts, would share some points in common. Not in this presentation. They were as different as night and day. You would have thought each speaker was talking about two different people and two different cultures. What was even bigger than the most accurate historical account of our history being displayed here, was how history had been and continues to be misrepresented. History, as in the manipulation of history and the facts leading us to historical events, is according to the storyteller. And as it is told, it is written. If one expert of a different mind and nature like Dr. Hilliard, had not attended this conference, most of us would have left Egypt with a totally different interpretation of Egyptian history. We have a totally distorted view of our own American history and the documentation of events that happen around us on a daily basis, based on similar individual (and not necessarily accurate) interpretations.

Documentation of events is the recording of history from one person's perspective. If it is written, without challenge or commentary, it will stand as written in the annals of time. History gets lost because there are singular sources with no rebuttal. And depending on who is ruling, all rebuttal is destroyed. Be they books, artifacts or other documents that may provide evidence to the contrary, history is molded to fit the needs of those in power to justify their legacy. Why else would Michelangelo paint over the images of dark-skinned people in historical accounts of portraits, or King James re-write the Bible and leave chapters referring to dark-skinned people out of his version all together. Dr. Hilliard's presentation had much more meaning in the face of an open contradiction because he knew this opposing version wasn't the truth and he knew how to keep history from being manipulated. Dr. Hilliard, now on a roll, was telling us how history is most exploited when told to those who know no different. He then proceeded to tell the conference what to look for when we went on our tours over the next few days. He showed us slides of some of the older artifacts in the Cairo Mukhtan Museum, that may have been hidden in the corners of the storerooms out of public view. "Look for them," he said. "They give a more accurate view of the culture of Kemet, because they are so much older. They may not look as nice, which is one of the reasons why they (the tourist bureau and museum curators) set them to the side, but they are more valuable in a historical context than most of the more popular exhibits." Now how would we have otherwise known this? With each slide, the science "just kept coming."

The session went one hour over time. The hotel was trying to kick us out of the room, but nobody moved until the session was over. While everyone was ecstatic over our newfound revelation of history, much of the group's discussion was about the conflict in the two presenters' versions of the history. Even in the face of overwhelming evidence, some of our group sided with Dr. Haikal. "She is Egyptian; she should know her history," a couple said. Of course, that took us into a discussion about knowing Black history, just because you're Black. We ended up kicking it in the hotel nightclub for most of the evening. It was a combination of live music and a deejay. Everybody was commenting on how the deejay was up on the latest music. But that wasn't the highlight of the evening. You haven't heard anything until you've heard an Egyptian vocalist sing Motown.

The next couple of days proved to be more than a notion for the Inter-Africa tour guides of 350 culturally reborn Black people. The first day of tours was to the museum. I heard it was an interesting tour. I got sick during the night after trying Egyptian pizza (with shrimp). I couldn't even stand up without running to the bathroom. I recovered after a visit to the hotel doctor and a few hours of rest, in time to go to a sound and light show at the pyramids.

The second day, we got to see more of the current Egyptian culture. We visited old Cairo where the women were covered up, including their faces, as they went through the daily rituals of Egyptian life: shopping, washing clothes and looking after the children. This, of course, raised a significant number of questions regarding women's roles in Egyptian culture, and the freedoms of women in European culture. Black women's beliefs and moral values are, by and large, a direct assimilation of America's predominant culture, that of Europe or the Western world. Freedoms like dress, work, being out in public and speaking in the presence of a congregation of men were not given to Egyptian women. At the time of our visit, Egyptian women were forbidden to go out in public with any part of the body exposed. It was forbidden for Egyptian women with young children to work outside of the home. In a meeting of men, Egyptian women couldn't speak, unless spoken to first. Egyptian women were not to be out in public alone after sunset. Egyptian women must look down when talking to men, unless permitted to do so otherwise. There were about six or seven other things Egyptian women were " forbidden" to do. What made it so emphatic was the way our tour guide would say, with conviction, "It is forbidden for a woman to..." then go on to make his point. The women on our tour bus were like, "Damn, what are women allowed to do?" Much of those prohibitions were part of everyday life for American women. The men kidded that most of the women on this trip would be stoned to death. Most of them were in agreement. It was classic culture shock.

As the tour continued, we visited the foundation of the Egyptian culture--its historical places of worship. We viewed the mosques of Ami-lon-as and Ibn Tulun, built in 642 A.D. and 878 A.D., which are respectively, the first and second oldest mosques in Cairo. We walked through the Sultan Hassan Mosque and University, built in 1356 by ruler Mameluk Sultan Hasan El-Nase, and is considered one of the finest existing examples of Arab-Egyptian architecture. Then we walked through the mosque of Egyptian ruler Mohammad Ali, located in the Citadel of Saladin. The most impressive features of the Mohammad Ali Mosque, built in 1857, is its great dome, which can be seen from almost any point in Cairo.

The serenity of the mosques in Cairo was impressive and demonstrated by the traditions of burning incense and the Adhan (call to prayer). The most impressive part of the Egyptian culture was its adherence to religion. The predominant religion in Egypt is Islam. Worshippers of Islam, (which means "submission and obedience" or "peace") are Muslims. The first duty of every Muslim is to declare his or her faith (Shahadah): I bear witness that there is no God but Allah, and I bear witness that Muhammad is his prophet. The second duty of every Muslim is prayer (Salah). The Muslim makes a minimum of five prayers a day. On this day, we were in time for Zuhr (the midday) prayer. Everybody stopped wherever they were to pray. On the street or in the mosques, people pulled over in their cars to make prayers. Then, just like that, everything went back to business as usual.

Clearly, the dedication to culture and to the sincerity of prayer on a daily basis seemed like cumbersome, restrictive exercises to us, particularly from the women's perspective. But then, as Blacks in America, it would be difficult for us to comprehend a commitment to culture when we only think about it during the month of February, or when it's en vogue and we "dress up" like some off-season Halloween ritual. Our religious practices tend to be just as suspect, given that we still practice religion in the way our former slave master taught us. Some estimates on Black religious practices claim a third of us pray only on Sunday, another third make an effort to pray publicly (attend church) twice a year (on Christmas and Easter), while another third (or greater) are not even in the church, or practice any form of religion. The point is that daily prayer for most American Christians is somewhat an anomaly, but some do pray every day. So, of course, praying five times a day or enforcing culture to maintain civility is foreign to us. But such a commitment to culture is not without its benefits or drawbacks, particularly in advancing a morally upright community.

One of the most frequent references by the tour guides is that Cairo has virtually a zero crime rate. If someone leaves a bag in the middle of the street, it is most likely to remain there unless someone is turning it in to the lost and found. If it appears that an Egyptian is stealing, they rarely call the authorities. The community punishes the thief, we were told, which the thief probably prefers. When the civil authorities are called in, if found guilty, the thief would have his hand cut off. If a woman goes out inappropriately dressed, the community sends her home to dress herself. A disrespecting woman, one who is perceived as trying to arouse men's passions, is not tolerated. It breaks down the moral fiber of the culture and the community. She is often warned about her actions, then punished severely if she persists. The same with a man who disrespects a woman. Rape in Cairo was also virtually nonexistent. A man risks serious injury by the community or castration by the civil authorities. Egyptians are not allowed to gamble, or involve themselves in games of chance. Later that evening, when we visited the casino, at the Hilton, we saw that Saudi Arabians were checked for I.D. to make sure they weren't Egyptians trying to gamble.

What seemed like cruel and unusual punishment by the civil authorities, made for a moral, self-correcting society. It also made a lot of sense to many people on the tour, as we pondered how such community action would work in the states. Could you imagine stopping a robbery, stepping in a dice game, or telling an American Black woman to cover her breasts, or pull her miniskirt down over her knees?

Alternative lifestyles have become a mainstay of American life. "Relative" values promote fast attitudes and perverse behaviors that push societal standards to new lows. Immorality has now become a claimed right in America. The moral majority is a cloak for right-winged race politics. The American community (collective) has few moral rights, because society has abdicated them under the guise of individual rights. You have to be in a moral society for a minute just to see how far we, as Americans, have gone. The prices you pay for morality are civility and freedom. This little cultural experience was just an attitudinal sampling of how we'd rather have unlimited immoral freedom, than limited moral freedoms, which also explains why American society has become increasingly less civil. And we, as Black Americans, have become parties to it. We have become a morally blind community. The more I saw, the more examples came to me of how my community turns its head to wrongdoing, including myself at times.

The women on our tour had just cause to call out some of the burdens placed on Egyptian women as "cruel" and "outdated." Some restrictions seemed cruel while others were clearly to maintain the integrity and high esteem of women. While the woman's role in this society's development was clearly understated and even obsolete, in many ways, her dress and demeanor were clearly her protection against being violated, socially and personally. Everybody was very contemplative after we got back to the hotel, even after we all went through the motions of doing the "night life in Cairo" thing. We clearly were going through our own little form of ethnic cleansing. Somehow nobody had the same perspective of our roles in American society. Our values were changing by the moment. We were like thirst craved transients, who had been given a taste of water and told to come back tomorrow for more. We couldn't wait.

As we boarded the bus for the next day's tour, the discussion was still buzzing from the previous day's tour. The running joke amongst the women on the bus was: "I wonder what women will be forbidden to do today?" Yet it was apparent that everybody was still pumped up over the cultural experience from the previous day. Today would be a different story. We were due to visit churches of other religions practiced in Egypt. Many came in the Greek and Roman periods succeeding the Kemetic rule. We visited a Catholic church (St. Guergis), and a Christian church called "the hanging church" (El Moallaka), because they hung people who refused to conform to the religious rule of that period, (which sounded too much like an American folk story). We couldn't get to Ben Ezrea Synagogue, the oldest Jewish Synagogue, before lunch, so the tour guide told us we'd get to that and a few other non-denominational churches after lunch.

After taking my daily nap, I met the group downstairs for the trip to the bazaar. We had a pretty lively group with us. Many were conference attendees who were on other tour buses. Everyone had a chance to exchange thoughts and compare notes about the tours over the past few days. Jeanette and Deb had been invited out on a date after the banquet later that evening. Eric and I teased them about playing behind our backs.

The banquet that evening featured a keynote by Jesse Jackson Sr. A surprise appearance by Sam Namoja, the leader of SWAPO, was the delight of the crowd. He was a candidate for President in Namibia's first free elections, to be held in October of 1989 (he was elected). It was great seeing a real life revolutionary. After dinner, Deb and Jeanette prepared to go on their date. I called it a night.

The next day was our final day in Egypt. The last leg of our tour package saved the best for last -- tours of the pyramids, the Sphinx, the Sahara, the Necropolis and Mastabens. At last, we were walking with the ancestors in the longest standing structures on the face of the earth, as we touched the surfaces and walls of the step pyramid of Zoser, built over 4,500 years ago. As we visited other sites along the tour route, it became obvious to me that there wasn't anything as important on this earth, as understanding where you came from. Learning about the cradle of civilization is one thing, seeing it is another, and a comparative analysis of what you see, and what you've been taught is something worth experiencing altogether. You begin to understand why European cultures wanted to hide the truth about the wonders of Kemet.

You begin to understand why European cultures make such an effort to disconnect Blacks enslaved and held captive in the Western world from this rich history. If you ever walked the streets of Kemet, now known as Egypt, and looked into the faces of the countless statues, pictures and artifacts, you'll see that they look like us, our mothers and fathers and grandfathers and grandmothers. There is no mistake what they are when you see the wideness of their eyes, the broadness of their noses and the thickness of their lips in statues we have never, ever seen before, because Europeans either tampered with the pictures, or took pictures of the later statues that reflected European influence. It is clear to understand how some of these pictures never made the world history books. They would have blown the whole cover, once we saw the look of a Black woman on the face of these statues. You know we know that "sista look." And sisters know that "brother look." We were all looking at statues, and then looking at each other. We all realized, at that point, that "we knew" they couldn't tell us anything different, ever again. About the third stop just before lunch, it finally clicked in everybody's mind that these were Black people. This was us. There was a silent emotion that came over everybody when we got off the bus for lunch at an outdoor Egyptian restaurant.

A group of Egyptian males hollered out, "Hey, American Nubians." Europeans always tried to represent Egyptians and Nubians as looking the same. In seeing some of the pictures, Kemites saw themselves as Nubians, who look distinctively different than Egyptians of today, who by and large have taken on European features. However, because even Egypt is in denial about its real history, it chooses to perpetuate the myth that Nubians were brought into Egypt as slaves and live there today as remnants of their slave past, like Blacks in America live today. We all said to ourselves about this little race thing going on in front of us: "Damn. Egyptian racism."

The afternoon portion of the tour was as powerful as any experience I've had in my life, prior to coming to Egypt and experiencing what I did the first night there. To ride up on the pyramids of Giza guarded by the Great Sphinx was the most impressive site. We piled in the bus like children running to a playground. Standing at the foot of the Khafre pyramid (the largest pyramid of Giza), you see the architectural magnificence that still leaves modern scientists in amazement. The pyramids of Khufu and Menkaure were just as magnificent. However, in this wonderment that is the last remains of the ancient seven wonders of the world, none of the pyramids had the mystique and architectural presence of the largest single mass stone carving known to the world as the Great Sphinx. Certainly, one of the pyramids without the Sphinx wouldn't pose as much a dynamic site. The Sphinx, called Her-Em-Akhet, represents Kemetic science and philosophy at its greatest. Its name means Hern of the horizon. Hern, after sun Netcher and Akhet, means "places" where the sun rises and sets.

At the front of Giza pyramids, the Sphinx, the first carving to represent the connection between man and animal (the head of man and the body of a lion), faces the rising sun. This is seen to have spiritual significance in more ways than one. First, the head of man represents a level of intelligence that must be achieved to elevate to a spiritual state. The body of the lion represents, according to historians, the royalty and power of the divine spirit in its lower physical form. Man seeks knowledge to achieve a level of intelligence necessary to become divine but only after conquering the beast within. The beast in man is ignorance, and divinity is achieved through enlightenment or knowledge of self in relation to the greater being -- God. Hern represents the conqueror of good over evil. Her-Em-Akhet, by facing the east, is the receiver of light at the dawn of every day, and thereby empowered daily in his eternal conquest to overthrow evil. The Sphinx has been seen as the guardian of the secrets to the pyramids and ancient Kemet. Many attribute the spiritual significance of the Sphinx, as named by the Greeks, as one of the reasons. The Giza pyramids and Her-Em-Akhet have maintained virtually all of its original form for over 4,000 years, and have withstood the assault of every dynasty that sought to destroy or deface them, with the hope of erasing any connection to its past Kemetic legacy. Without the testament of the pyramids and the Sphinx, it was very possible that the legacy of Kemet could have been lost forever. Of course, we got the tourist version of the history. Some fact, some fiction. We were all so excited, however, we missed it. Everybody jumped off the bus and ran toward the pyramids. After taking pictures and riding camels, we tried to climb the pyramids, (which was not only very dangerous, but against the law). We would then hear the familiar call of our tour guide, "Inter-AFRICA, please come down off the pyramids; it is time to go."

You should have heard us. "Time to go? Time to go? We spend five days in Egypt and only get one hour at the pyramids. That's cold, man." It was like trying to get your children to leave the playground before they're ready to leave. Once he got us all back in the bus, we found that we actually had another half-hour. The bus took us over to where Sphinx was. Although it looks in close proximity to pyramids, the Sphinx actually covers some significant ground. The walk may have been a little long for some of the seniors. After creating the same hysteria at the Sphinx that we did at the pyramids, the tour guide brought to our attention that souvenirs, though they were nice, probably wouldn't get past customs, and that we should leave them right here next to the bus. He was talking about the pieces of pyramid and sphinx rocks that everyone had filled their pockets with. I guess he must go through this on every tour he guides. Given the millions of people who visit Egypt each and every year, if they all left with a pocket full of rocks, there wouldn't be any left to hold up the monuments. So like kids, we all dropped our rocks as we stepped on the bus. There must have been a three-foot pile of rocks lying there as we pulled off. Everybody I saw kept at least one. I know I did. Despite the short the stay, it was a trip fulfilled. It was back to the hotel to pick luggage and make our flight.

* * *

The flight back seemed much shorter than the flight there. A virtual daydream. My mind, racing at 1,000 miles an hour when I left, was now slowed to a snail's pace. The issues that preoccupied my thoughts were no more than an afterthought. As concerned as I was about the possibility of a federal prosecution, my spirit had been rekindled to the extent that I was prepared to deal with it. I also left Egypt resolved to change my family life, one way or the other. I knew what that would probably mean, but heretofore, wasn't prepared to do what was needed. I was now prepared to eliminate all conflict out of my life. Included would be any conflict I had about my marriage, my community involvement and my spiritual beliefs. Especially, my spiritual beliefs. I had never felt as focused about what to believe. Any of the conflict associated with a spiritual belief system was eliminated. America's spiritual belief system was contradictory to its race politics. I knew from my experience in Cairo that I couldn't go back to worshipping God as I had. This feeling of peace was too great. It was as if I had released all confusion and conflict, much of which was associated with a shaken confidence in an already suspect method of worship. As we landed and waited to clear customs, I felt great gratitude for Debra, who foresaw this change of perspective as the remedy for bringing some clarity of thought. But she could have never anticipated the renewed impact this trip would have. Neither could I.

The next two weeks would prove to me that I was now in a renewed spirit and mind. I immediately began to rebuild the business, which, by and large, had been ignored most of the year. Within two weeks of my return, I picked up six clients. The Brotherhood Crusade organized a "Taking Back our Community" press conference. For a community "photo op," most of the so-called "players" were there. As I walked up to the group, the late Rev. Frank Higgins, then President of Baptist Minister's Conference, greeted me. "Hey, young fella.

How are you?"

"Fine," I told him.

"You know," he continued, "we really miss you in the NAACP. I haven't even heard anything from that other fella." Joe Duff was standing two feet away, and the head of the city's largest ministerial alliance didn't know him. It was the first time I could stand in Joe's presence, without wanting to take a swing at him -the benefit of a renewed mind. Joe has this thing of walking up to you and talking like "everything's cool." Overhearing our conversation, he came over and spoke. I nodded, not bothering to introduce him to Rev. Higgins. "Essex, what church are you a member of?" Rev. Higgins said, continuing our discussion.

"First AME," I said, recognizing this was not the time or place to disavow my membership.

Higgins said, "That's right. Everybody who gets his support gotta be a member of his church." I didn't know if that was a dig at me or at Chip, who was also standing a few feet away. (Everybody by then knew Chip didn't support me.) I chose to leave it alone. It was a good little test for me. I had not a twinge of anxiety over the whole discussion.

When Brotherhood Crusade President, Danny Bakewell, arrived everybody did their little "pose and shoot" thing, and gave their comments to the press. I didn't have anything to say. Danny approached me about administrating the project. I asked what the money was like. Danny said it was negotiable. I told him I had to get back to him. I had to discuss it with my family.

When I did bring up the issue, Taurece went off. "The NAACP didn't kick your ass enough? Now you want to take the whole community back from gang bangers and dope dealers. You must be some kinda of fool." When I tried to justify my involvement by saying the project would make our community a safer place to live, she held her hand up. "For about a month. Then they'll be back, or move to another part of the city. Give me a break. And then what? Save the homeless? A cure for AIDS? There's always a project with you. Always something or someone you gotta save. When is your family going to become 'a project'? When are you going to save your family?"

After a period of silence, I asked, "So what do you want me to do?"

She was crying now. "Anthony, I don't care what you do. Besides, you always do what you want to do anyway. But I'm not going to go through this again. I'm tired of people watching our house. I'm tired of the threatening calls. (I received several death threats during my NAACP tenure. There was even some undercover surveillance.) All I ever wanted was a family. I never wanted to be rich. I never wanted this big ass house. I never wanted to be Coretta Scott King, or second to some man's mission. I just wanted a family and a quiet home life. You can't give me that, can you?" When I didn't answer, she said, "That's what I thought," and left the room.

Taurece was right. The advocacy was now a part of me. It had always been since college. I'd never been the home-by-6 p.m., pipe-and-slippers, in-the-easy-chair kind of guy. I knew Taurece was hurt about a lot of things. The problem is that running away didn't stop crime, injustice or racism, all of which dramatically affect the survival of the family. Who would do that work? However, she was right on point with her question: "Does it always have to be me?" She was also right about my continued involvement. Even if I passed on this, at some point in time, I was going to take up another fight. She had clearly made her point, that it's not a life she wanted to be part of. And, clearly, no man should be involved in any cause without the support of his loved ones, particularly his woman. After that discussion, some serious decisions had to be made in my life. I left to attend my fraternity's convention, which was more of a nuisance trip at that point.

Upon my return, I secured an apartment and moved out. I turned down several opportunities to share homes in Ladera Heights and Baldwin Hills, and chose a two bedroom flat over a garage off Crenshaw Boulevard. I needed to become grounded in a sense of reality again. People were falling "outta the hills" left and right looking for roomies, because they were living above their means, "You can't live down there,' some said, "You're above that now." I didn't see it that way at all. I was looking to get my balance back; get back to the basics. Back to reality.

When I went to my office, I couldn't help but think how fortunate I was, in spite of my separation, to get a chance to start over. Or was I? In fingering through the prior week's messages, I pulled out three that were marked urgent. They were from the Federal Bureau of Investigation.

* * *

14

Can You Die For Telling a Lie?

"Runnin' 'round, thinkin' you so Black, boy,
You don't know how Black you is till you been tested;
Till you git in a smoke-filled room with white folks, and sometimes Negroes,
and they start offerin' you things you don't even know what to do with;
You don't know how much you worth, till somebody tries to buy you;
You don't know how "Black" you is, till you git a chance to be "white."

"Papa on Blackness"
- Listervelt Middleton, Fatback and Cavier

Within a day of returning their call, an FBI agent was sitting in my office. He was investigating a criminal referral from the Resolution Trust Corporation. The RTC, who was now the receiver for Founders Savings, was investigating not only the referral from the bank, but "other documents" they had received about allegations made about the loan on a home I purchased five years earlier in 1984. The home was occupied by my wife and children, ever since we were separated. The questions centered on how I purchased that property, and what assets I held at the time. The intent of questioning was to explore the validity of allegations made by Founders, in the counter-suit they filed against me four years earlier. Their counter-suit was in response to the civil suit I had filed against them for wrongful termination. Founders had called into question my down payment (two years after I left the bank) and my percentage of ownership in three properties I had owned, in partnership with Janet. The agent also inquired about an insurance policy that I had inadvertently put the face value of the policy in the space where the cash surrender should have gone, and vice versa. I had previously acknowledged that it was an error, and it wasn't a determinant in the approval of the loan. Really, neither was my ownership in other properties. A borrower is not required to have an abundance of assets to buy a house. Most first-time home buyers have literally no assets at all. The asset liability analysis basically determines stability and reliance on unsecured debt. Neither was a factor in my case. The down payment was an issue, however. It was very popular in the mid-80s to sell high-end properties to buyers, who would agree to buy the properties at discounted values, if the seller leaves money in the deal, showing it as a partial down payment. It was the quickest way to sell the properties in a slow market. It also saves the buyer from having to make a huge down payment. The issue from a lender's perspective was that the buyer had no investment in the property and could walk away from the property. Founders alleged that I did not make a down payment on the house. Of course, I asserted that I did, and the seller corroborated that position.

It became clear that the government was now reaching to make a case where none existed, especially since there was no conflict on the issue of a down payment. If the government had a case, it would be on this issue. The major question was, however, why was the government even pursuing this transaction since it was fully secured by collateral, and the loan hadn't defaulted? Even if it did default, there was no possibility of a loss on the loan. I put this question to the agent. He just shrugged his shoulders, while making notes on his pad. The whole meeting was less than one hour. I felt that if this was all the government had, they really didn't have anything. He let me know, in no uncertain terms, that he would be talking to me again.

I told him I'd look forward to it. I showed him the door. Katherine buzzed in and asked if I was OK. I told her I was. She let me know that Debra was on the line. I quietly said thanks.

She said, "Hold on." She came in my office and said, "You sure you're OK?"

I asked "Why?"

"Because your spirit seems to be down a little."

"Is it that obvious?" I asked.

"Yes," she said. "Don't let the devil shake your spirit, Anthony. This is the trial God prepared you for on your trip to Egypt. Now is the time to show it." I just shook my head and picked up the phone. "Sorry to leave you holding, Deb. We just had to run the devil up outta here," I said as I winked at Katherine. She smiled back and walked out.

"What are you talking about?" Deb asked.

"I'll explain it to you over lunch."

We met at Ja'net's Jerk Chicken Restaurant on Martin Luther King, Jr. Blvd. Deb looked rested and refreshed. We had talked on a couple of occasions, but we hadn't seen each other since the Egypt trip. Since then, we both had made some real critical decisions about the direction of our lives. I hadn't spoken to her since I moved out. She hadn't spoken to me since she decided to move to Sacramento to accept a Senate fellowship. I told her about my morning with the FBI. She told me about her decision to break off her engagement. For the first time since we'd met, we both were available. However, neither of us were prepared to even discuss any semblance of a commitment. Being each others confidant and sounding board for this transitional period in our lives was just fine.

After lunch, I decided to take the afternoon off. That day was the first realization that the indictment plot was no hoax. As confident as I was that it would amount to little, if anything at all, it was a very sobering moment, knowing that I had been served up to the government, on a platter, by so-called Black people. I wasn't completely blameless in this escapade. I just didn't know how I got from doing what "everybody did" five years ago in buying a house, to becoming an outspoken civil rights outlaw, to now becoming a prosecution suspect. I believe, to this day, that I made some mistakes as a young adult. We all do. But the level of scrutiny that now was coming upon me was totally unjustified. The allegations weren't that serious, given there were no losses. Also knowing what the government was capable of, in their ability to manufacture something out of nothing, I wasn't very comfortable with the thought that my fate was now up to the interpretation of my real enemy.

While pondering this state of affairs, the phone rang. The machine picked up. I heard Debra's voice. She was calling to let me know that she noticed my spirits were down and to keep my chin up. She invited me to come out to the church's overnight lock-in program that started around 5 p.m. The lock-in program was First AME's male mentoring program for teens. This time it was open to both males and females. Debra noted that they were short on male mentors, and could use my help. Plus she felt it would cheer me up. Dozing off, my thoughts were to pass on the lock-in. I was feeling like I wasn't in the mood to be bothered. After a couple hours of sleep, I felt a little better and changed my mind. Plus, what else did I have to do? It was about 4:30. I showered and went on over to the church.

Once I arrived, I did begin to enjoy working with the group I had been assigned to. About one hour later, Deb came in and waved. She let me know how much she appreciated that I came. I let her know that I didn't plan on spending the night, but I would stay as long as I could. During the course of the night, I saw a lot of people who I hadn't talk to in awhile. I also saw Mark Whitlock for the first time since Bridgette's "little sellout" revelation. I didn't let on what I knew; I just nodded. About 11 o'clock, I set out to leave, giving Deb and a few others some parting acknowledgments when my good friend Sharita Franks saw me. She was also leaving. We walked out together. Sharita was also greatly affected by the way the church and others stood by and let the unfairness in the branch campaign take place.

As we talked further into the night, we both concluded that few people stand for anything anymore, and that the only way to change it was to be directly involved. We talked about destiny that night. It was Sharita's way of letting me know that what God allowed us to see in that experience was a revelation, not another victimization. "You'll see," was her words to me. "I know it's been revealed to me what I must do with my life," she said.

"And what's that?" I asked.

"Give it to God because man has gone crazy," she said as we both busted up laughing. Sharita whispered, "I'm so glad to see you out tonight."

"I'm glad to be seen," I responded. I promised to stay in touch. We both got in our cars and drove off.

As I thought about the evening's events, I really did enjoy interfacing with the young people. I also appreciated my discussion with Sharita but I wondered about this destiny revelation. How was trial and tribulation tied to destiny? Certainly, if tribulation was a prerequisite for destiny, I had been given enough lessons to graduate. However, Sharita raised some interesting points: 1) that this wasn't just happening for the sake of happening, or it wouldn't have been made so public and in terms of rising from the ashes, 2) how I couldn't have been given a better script if God wrote it, and 3) he definitely was guiding me. Clearly, others could see that some guiding was taking place and they were rooting for me to play the hand out. We often fold our hands too early because it doesn't look good to us. We later found out that we had a better hand than we thought, which would have been good enough to win, had we played it out. Destiny unfulfilled. My charge was not to fold my hands, though it looked pretty dim from where I was sitting, and the next few rounds would only make it look worse. If not for a belief in destiny....

* * *

Founders Savings and Loan was a whorehouse. That's about the closest comparison I can make to an institution that was clearly misguided and mismanaged into a state of having to sell itself for profit. If you stay around a whorehouse too long, you either become one, or become the trick (user of the service) of those who work there. Simpler than that, my mother used to say, "If you lay around with dogs long enough, you'll eventually come up scratching fleas. Whatever it took to stay open, Founders Savings did it. Only I didn't know it when I was hired as its Vice President of loan administration. I was more elated to come back to the community, after working five years for white folk, where they had little or no respect for our people. While I had heard Founders was in financial trouble, I had no idea or inclination that the trouble was due to corruption, which I discovered only after I was employed there and in the middle of it. The President of Founders Savings was clearly a dinosaur in a changing industry, which really wasn't his worst fault. While there was a lot of incompetence in the institution, there were some highly competent players strategically placed to keep Founders afloat. But they were usually handicapped with support that had some relationship to the President, who regularly called on that relationship to undermine the authority of those they were charged to support. The President would regularly allow acts of insubordination to prevail, which kept the institution in chaos. Allowing management to be undermined wasn't the worst of the President's faults. His ability to continually manipulate his management, regulators and elected officials into positions of favor and compromise wasn't his worse fault. His worst fault was a perceived total lack of integrity that promoted greed and self-dealing, and didn't hesitate to involve and implicate others. The biggest challenge any employee of Founders Savings had was going home every day with their integrity in tact. You really don't know how important integrity is until someone tries to take it, or you lose it, and try to regain it. The challenge to maintain one's sense of ethics was a daily fight.

All of this was the case at Founders Savings. I learned a lot about integrity and ethics from my days at Founders Savings. In trying to defend the integrity of "his" bank, my integrity was challenged at best, and compromised, at worst. If there was a period in my life when I lost my perspective on who or what was right or wrong, it was while I was at Founders. While I never totally succumbed to the games I was asked to play, the misguided behavior of certain people at Founders rubbed off on me. Some of the key management and board principles set for some very bad examples that I, as a young (and impressionable professional) elected to follow. The pressure of earning the "stripes" of a "team player" can (and often does) alter one's judgment and ability to stand out of line with team leadership. Given the choice of being a player or a pawn, sometime you choose one not recognizing you're both. I saw how the pawns were treated, and chose to be a player; not knowing I'd made a deal with the devil, and was still a pawn in the end. The price? A challenge to my neophyte ethics. In trying to play with "the big boys," I allowed myself to be compromised in a game of "quid pro quo," with a man whom I later found to have no scruples and no sense of what was right or decent. Yet, he was a President of a bank, something I one day wanted to be, among other ambitions.

Ambition uncontrolled has a way of making us blind, and very presumptuous. I figured he did what he did and therefore got what he got by doing what he did, assuming (correctly) that this is how the game is played. But that didn't necessarily make the game fair or right or legal. Ambition misguided makes one vulnerable to compromise and unethical behavior. This is best how I can explain what happened to me at Founders. As a young 27-year-old financier, I really had an opportunity most don't get until later in their careers--some in their mid-or late 40s. My experience at Founders Savings from a technical perspective, was invaluable. While most of my counterparts or contemporaries were trying to figure out car and house loans, I was assisting the restructuring of a community institution. Most of our Black bankers, particularly those working for white institutions, spend their careers trying to "get in the game" with their banks, and are forced to play it from the ground up. Founders provided me the opportunity to learn "the whole game" from the top down. Not just to learn to run a minuscule function of the bank, but to run a bank, period. Irrespective of the underlying motives for my being there, to structure and administer a $200 million portfolio in my 20s, was an accomplishment. I learned more in 16 months at Founders about complex transactions, how institutions leverage, recycle and sell money, extend credit (to an institution) and regulate institutions than I'd learned in the prior six years in the industry. I brought lending expertise and a master's in public finance to the table, but there was no way I would have learned the type of wheeling and dealing that goes on in the major lending arenas (one million and above) had I not sat in the many closed door meetings and watched these deals be put together.

As a result of this technical experience, there wasn't a deal I couldn't put together, or take apart (as I was able to demonstrate on the Baldwin Hills/Crenshaw Plaza deal). But it seems as though what I gained in technical experience, cost me on the political side of this experience. Part of it can be attributed to what I call the arrogance of youth, and the other part to the vanity of power politics. I wasn't able to realize soon enough that I was positioned in the bank, not totally for my skills, but to serve as an object for the bank's President to stay a layer removed from his self-dealing, and not take on a direct hit (responsibility) for some of the deals that came to the bank. The price I paid for a little power and vanity (presented to the community in such a high-profile position) was to become a tool of compromise.

When I came to the association in July 1984, Founders Savings had become known as the institution of "last resort," meaning when no other bank or lending institution would touch a deal, you could bring it to Founders Savings and get "better than even" odds on approval consideration. Then there were the "relationship" deals. Everybody who came in knew the President of the bank, Peter Dauterive, and they let you know they knew "Peter". When a loan was declined, they'd come running in the bank, "Where's Peter?" In almost every case, the relationship prevailed and the loan was made. Then there were the "depositor" deals, which were extremely important since Founders always had problems maintaining its liquidity requirements. These were depositors who had money in the bank, and would threaten to pull it out, if you didn't approve their loan. Black people are famous for this. Most take the position that they're doing you a favor by having their money at "the colored bank," in the first place. I don't doubt that was probably true since it was always rumored that Founders was on the verge of collapse. It usually took all the public relations and outreach the bank had to stall a depositor run. Apparently, making loans to depositors was one of those "outreach strategies." Then lastly, it was the President's deals that usually accommodated an order to "get it done." This usually meant close it and get the paperwork later. When you finally got the paperwork, the deal didn't make sense and the challenge was to figure out how to justify it to the regulators.

Of course, being the new kid on the block, I wasn't aware of any of this until I was deep in the middle of the justifications. Initially, I was trying to acquaint myself with the operations and work capabilities of my staff, so I tended to have a greater reliance on others telling me how things were done. And certainly, one would assume (as I did) that when you receive direct instructions from the President of the association to do something involving a loan, it is going to be proper and in the association's best interest. The supposition is if there's not a sense of ethics anywhere else in the bank, there would be with the President. This is where young professionals came into management situations very naive. "On the job" is not a good place to have your first lessons in ethics.

My experience at Founders was a pure seduction, and the mistress was my ambition. I was in charge of the association's business development strategies, which included loans and deposits, restructuring the existing loan portfolio, auditing and review of all loans including underwriting. I supervised a staff of nine, five of whom were virtually unskilled when I got there, which meant they had to be trained. The personalities of the two departments I was in charge of were such that there was no spirit of cooperation or unity. The two most experienced people, my head underwriter and my senior processor, weren't even talking to each other. Everybody else was just there. Except one. My commercial loan officer, a Guyanian woman named Brenda Henry, was the most skilled and ethically focused person in the bank. Her straightforward approach, brash truthfulness and determination to uphold the integrity of her work kept her in constant conflict with the President. I had basically left the commercial lending to Brenda, because I knew she would do what was right.

It took me three months to assess the skills of the rest of my staff. That is when my first conflict in the bank came about. Everyone whom I assessed as having less than competent skills was put on a training program, to which they had a certain period to comply. Most of the staff made every effort to do so. However, one staff person refused any effort to be trained, and was very vocal in her restraint. Turns out, by her admission, that she had a relationship with the President outside the bank. Everybody in the bank knew it, except me, of course, which was why she ended up in my department. All the other officers and managers refused to work with her. Now that she was being asked to be accountable for her work, there was a problem. She and I had two conferences about it. First, with the processing supervisor, and then with the President. The result was her announcement in front of all the employees in the middle of the bank, that "this is one girl, you will never be able to fire." I wrote her up on it, to which she laughed and responded, "You know I'm going to get you for this." When the President waved it off, I knew there was a relationship. I isolated her, put her up front and out of the way of the department's work flow, and basically, tried to ignore her.

Within my first six months at Founders, I had turned the association loan production completely around, from under $2 million to over $5 million a month, in the lending off season. I brought in over a half million dollars in new deposits, not brokered deposits the bank had become dependent on. Broker deposits were where you pay brokers to move their clients' deposits to your bank. Not only do you pay over and above the normal deposit rate, but there is no loyalty with the deposit. When someone else offers to pay more, the deposit is gone. Founders almost closed a couple of times when brokers pulled out $200,000 - $300,000 at a moment's notice. I brought in community-based deposits that we paid 7 percent, not the 14 percent like we had to pay brokers. Deposits that came with a renewed sense of loyalty to rebuild a community institution. However, Founders Savings lost money that year, because of a discount that it took on loan sales and high operating overhead. Two weeks after I was hired, Founders took a $7 million loss on a bulk loan sale of non-conforming loans made in the early '80s. Non-conforming in the sense that they were loans with balloon payments, which meant their yield was limited and they possessed a higher risk due to the short call dates they had. Founders needed the money for liquidity and operating expenses, plus it was better to sell the loans than continue to try to collect them.

The high operating overhead was largely due to employees on the payroll for no justifiable reason. Those who had no accountability, had been counseled about their work ethic (or lack of one), but still had their jobs. Despite recommendations, they weren't let go. The biggest commonality of those employees was that they were all closely associated with the bank President. They were also all women. I recall one senior staff meeting where we were asked to submit a staffing plan for the following year, including recommendations for reduction in staff. Of course, everybody recommended the least productive person in the department to be laid off. Not one recommendation was approved. In fact, the employees that were laid off were some of the more productive and dedicated ones. It was tough looking sincere people in the face and telling them we had to cut back when they worked their butts off and could look across the way, only to see their co-worker polishing their nails on company time. This was the unethical and callous nature of the work environment politics at Founder Savings. Most of the non-productive confusion in the workplace was caused by some of the women at Founders, who, ironically, all called the President by his first name. All his senior managers called him by his last name. "Mr." was his first name to us. There were nine or ten of these "assistants" (for lack of a better word) in all, who increased Founders' operation expense over a quarter million a year (when you included benefits). Combine this cost with the cost of broker deposit fees, penalties for a higher cost of money, because of the association's poor credit rating, non-performing assets on the books and cost of keeping the system greased (political contributions, trips to Sacramento and Washington, etc., to keep regulators out of the bank), and you saw that Founders was carrying over a million a year in non-contributory operating expenses. This was the condition of the association when I got there and the first six months thereafter. However, the last quarter of 1984 would be the last time Founders would lose money while I was there. Customers were writing letters on my behalf and telling the President that I was the best person he ever had in the bank. With the help of several dedicated staff, I had even turned around the quality of loans we were receiving, in spite of the President still bringing us his deals. People were bringing us their deals first, instead of last. However, it would require such a change in the historical operation of the association, that by the second month of 1985, my honeymoon at Founders was clearly over.

In January 1985, a state regulator came and spoke to the officers and the board of directors. He said that Founders would not make it out of 1985, if it didn't change its operations and that the board and officers would be held legally liable for decisions they made. They were specifically concerned about loans Founders was making in construction and the commercial loan departments and specifically warned the officers of the loan administration that they would be held accountable for the loans they made. Both Brenda and I both knew what they were talking about. We thought it was pretty peculiar that it would be called out to that extent. Founders Savings, contrary to stated belief, did not have a lot of bad loans. The ratio of bad loans to performing loans was way within the 2 percent the state regulators allowed for bad debt. In fact, during my entire time at Founders, we made almost 500 loans and serviced another 600. Less than 20 actual loans (that I oversaw) went bad. I brought in only four of them, which were largely due to change in circumstance (loss of job, divorce, major illness, etc.).

What the regulators were talking about was the association's propensity to make large development-type loans that were poorly monitored, and were suspect to being closely held, meaning the bank, or someone in the bank had interest in the deal. Only a certain percentage of the loans can be made to an employee, and their interest must be stated in advance, to uphold the fiduciary responsibility they had to the institution. Founders had several large transactions that were being looked at, which were on the books prior to my being hired. Three were construction deals gone bad. One was a restaurant deal the bank was trying to save (or so I thought). The others were commercial loan deals made in 1984 and called into question, because of the suspected relationship with the President of the association. Brenda had also called some of those same loans into question and was overridden. Now they were being discussed by the regulators in a board meeting. Brenda submitted her resignation the following week. She was convinced to stay 30 days until a replacement could be found. But clearly the boundaries had been laid.

Most of the operating management had known of the association's problems. Brenda, who was always straight-up and professional, put together a little "going away" packet for me on her last day. She had assembled Founders' annual reports for the previous four years, and key memorandums from the state and federal home loans bank board. Founders had been on the closure list for three years (since 1981). The auditors reports in each annual report had called out deficiencies in Founders construction loan controls, its operating efficiency and, of course, its inability to maintain sufficient capital. She also left me a list of borrowers and loans I should be concerned about, due to their relationships with the President. Many of those transactions had caused much conflict between Brenda and the President, because they were made under duress, meaning Brenda was forced to make them. In most of those cases, however, he just refused to sign off on them. In notes attached to the list, she admonished me to be careful and refuse to sign any and everything I don't agree with. After the regulatory meeting and

Brenda's information packet. I began to suspect everything wasn't above board and that what had gone around was getting ready to come around, where I was concerned. The seduction of ambition had already taken effect with my taking an active role in Founders turnaround strategy. I was getting pretty full of myself and unbeknownst to me, the compromise was already in place.

The month before, I had an opportunity to buy a four-bedroom, approximately 3,000 square foot foreclosure house for $135,000. About 70% of the market value price, the house was estimated at about $200,000. The investor needed his money out of the house by the end of the year and was selling it for what he had in it. And he'd pay all the costs to close the deal. The only condition was that I would have to close it by the end of the year or there would be no deal.

The lender that I usually took my personal real estate loans through, Countrywide, told me they couldn't close it in time. It was already the fifth of December, and most lenders don't really push work around the holidays. They didn't want the liability of being perceived as having made an agreement to close the deal. So finally, I decided to take control of the deal myself. I brought the purchase to Founders, and took it to the President, and told him what I was trying to do.

I then declared my interest in the transaction, fulfilling my fiduciary responsibility to the bank. He asked me what I was going to do with my present home. I told him that I was selling it to my mother and my sister. Dauterive said it was fine and to just make sure everything was there so we could sell it. He called my underwriter, Derrick Payne, and told him the same thing: "Don't bring it up until it was ready for resale." We packaged and processed the loan in two weeks.

Just before Derrick took the deal to the loan committee, he informed me that he only had one year's tax return. Fannie Mae's secondary market guidelines required two years of tax returns. The 1983 tax return was missing. We had started packing for the move and I couldn't find my personal tax files. After two days of looking and the loan committee (the final one of the year) coming up the next day, I called someone I knew and had one made up. Not for extra money or anything. The amount was commensurate with what my wife and I had made the year before. Only I put my name on it, not to have to involve her, and delay the process. When it was brought over, I signed it and put it in the file.

My intent was not to deceive, only to comply. Since the bank knew how much I made, it wasn't an issue of financial qualifications. It was a matter of trying to protect the bank from regulator scrutiny of an employee loan. That simple. If we didn't need it, I wouldn't have done it. It was a common practice in the '80s to make up returns to qualify for loans. It was common knowledge throughout the real estate industry and the financial community, and it wasn't something you called somebody on unless the return was just outlandishly unreasonable. Most people just did it for the extra $200 - $300 a month they needed to get their debt ratios in line.

In hindsight, I really didn't have to do it but never, in my wildest dreams, figured it would come back to haunt me. I did not view this as a serious challenge to my ethics or my sense of what is proper and right. This again can be attributed to a naiveté to the potential damage that could be done to my career and family. If I had even the slightest clue of the potential ramifications, I would not have done it. But nobody had ever heard of anybody being prosecuted for what the whole banking community knew was commonplace. I exercised bad judgment and understood that it was definitely wrong. But I witnessed such a frequent lack of discretion taken with other deals that involved the bank's President. I took the same misguided, inappropriate discretion that I had so often fought against and applied it to my own loan, thinking if we (the bank) can do it for others, we can do it for me. I'd seen it done a hundred times during my finance experience in the '80s, even after I left the bank. We closed the loan on December 28.

It was about that time that some of the employees with some history (longer tenure) brought to my attention that the prior loan administrators, both women, had quit over getting pressure to sign off or recommend loans they weren't in agreement with. They just walked off the job. No notice, no nothing. Everybody was sure, now that Brenda was gone, that Dauterive and I would begin to clash more. That would be true, but not over loans initially. The association was mandated to put together a five-year strategic recovery plan, by June 1985, that had to be approved by the state and federal regulators. Each department head was supposed to write their goals and objectives and develop the short-and mid-range plans to achieve them. Because some of the other managers didn't have a clue as to what a plan was, I ended up having to write the plan for my department and three others (loan services, new accounts and branch development), with a short- handed staff. In the senior staff meetings, I let my feelings out about it. I felt any staff that couldn't plan a department, shouldn't run one. It didn't win me any friends in those departments, but at that point, I didn't care since I was the one staying until 10 p.m. to do the work. This "give it to Anthony" stuff didn't sit well with me at all.

My department required greater community outreach. It was at that point that I became fully involved with the community, more as a career enhancement move than anything else. I became an officer of the L.A. NAACP (as a Vice President) and a trustee of First AME Church. I joined the Los Angeles Black Business Association, Black MBA Group and the Urban Banker's Association, to give Founders a greater community presence. I tried to join the Los Angeles Chapter of 100 Black Men, but was too young at the time, causing them to set the application aside. (They accepted me three years later when I turned 30.) The point is that I was willing to join whatever civic organization was necessary to bring the association exposure and a broader clientele. It also meant that in order to maintain $5 million a month in loan volume, I would have to make a greater time commitment in the community which required a greater reliance on front-line staff supervision. This became impossible when, after giving our staffing plan recommendations, the employee that was supposed to be laid off in 60 days was given a 25 percent increase in pay, a week after the plan was submitted.

This was the same employee that I got stuck with, and tried to get rid of, after our little floor show. On top of getting the raise without my knowledge or input, she told everybody what she got. She was making as much as my processing supervisor and my head underwriter.

They both hit the ceiling. My processor immediately gave a 30-day notice to quit. My underwriter went into a shell, and refused to say or do anything (other than underwrite), until the situation was resolved. Whereas I could always depend on him to stay until 6 or 6:30 p.m., he now left at 5 p.m. Of course, that work fell on me. Finally, Dauterive agreed to give him a little more money, but that wasn't the issue. If he was going to pay somebody to do nothing in the workplace, let her stay at home. I'm sure he was picking up the benefit in some other form or fashion. Now, she knew she had the President's support, and was trying to run over everybody again. Once the lead processor left, nobody else could handle her. I had put my secretary (who also served as processor), Trish Payne, in the lead spot, until we could fill the vacancy, which took about three months. Meanwhile, true to prediction, Dauterive started bringing me his deals.

At first, he would send the applicants in by themselves. I would usually try to pre-qualify the deal. Once I was able to determine its feasibility, I'd inform the applicants whether we could help them. Most of the time, we couldn't. Then Dauterive would insist we put them on application to fully determine eligibility. After I would decline it, then we'd have discussions about how I must have missed something. No, I didn't miss anything, the deals didn't qualify. Then he'd try the psychological approach, by trying to appeal to my sense of reason, by taking a "whatever makes sense, we should do" approach. Once he even came in and gave me a one hour lecture on the need for a greater community sensitivity. His point was that as a community lending institution, we had to be less stringent, if we were to help our community. Dauterive said straight out that I was declining too many loans. We made an agreement, then and there, that I would provide an analysis of each loan to support my decisions. After about 30 days and no real change in the decisions on the clients that he was sending to me, he reverted to pure force, by telling me to "put the paperwork together on this and bring it to me." When I'd comply, he'd call back and say, "That deal you brought me, you didn't sign it."

I'd respond with, "I didn't know I was expected to since we didn't qualify it. You're the President, can't you sign it?"

He'd respond, "If I have to sign them, why do I need you?"

I'd put it back on him and say, "If you're going to circumvent the process, why do you need me? Why don't you let me do my job?" We'd go back and forth until he'd virtually order me to come up and sign off on the loans. There was about a dozen loans like that. I finally figured out what he was doing. He was passing the questionable deals through his subordinates. If and when they were called into question, he would be one level removed from the deal. As time went on, the deals became more and more questionable, until finally I stopped signing on commercial loans altogether, if they weren't qualified through the normal process.

At that point, he told me that I was being insubordinate and that he could fire me for it. For the first time in five years, Founders was making a profit-- largely due to my business development and the operational restructuring efforts of the bank's CFO, Art Meadows. Yet he was threatening to fire me over a handful of loan declines. At that moment, I knew there was more to these deals than he was letting on. Recognizing that I was doing my job, in spite of our disagreements, Dauterive's position then became more rigid toward allowing me to independently operate my department. First, he took the position that, since I was being so selective about which commercial loans I would sign, that I had abdicated that responsibility in its total scope, and therefore wouldn't have the responsibility to do without oversight, meaning I had no authority to sign alone. I would bring all deals to him. I would, however, be allowed to give my analysis and recommendations on whether or not to make it. I would also have to initial the submission sheet so he'd know I'd reviewed it. He would OK it and we'd fund it. I later found out, after having me bring the file to his office, that he was giving verbal OKs on the loans he wanted to make, but never signed off. So even though he'd authorize the credit, his initials still never appeared on the file. Only mine. That was another dozen or so commercial loans. Finally, I stopped putting my initials on files until he was there to initial right there in front of me.

Then the game became one of him not signing any deals until I signed off on the deals he preferred. Customers were now bringing quality loan applications to Founders, meaning virtually no non-conformities to the qualification. I'd send the files up for approval and he'd hold them for two or three days. Sometimes even a week before he'd respond to my inquiry. Then he'd comment on how he didn't see someone's application on credit request. When I'd tell him that the file wasn't ready yet, he'd tell me to bring it up when it was ready, and pick 'em all up, at the same time. Qualified files would be held, sometimes for as long as three weeks, while we processed someone he wanted to fund. Sometimes it went from the ridiculous to the sublime.

On one occasion, he wouldn't sign the files, until I initialed, and I wouldn't initial, until he initialed. So we agreed to initial at the same time. If I pulled back, he pulled back. If I faked like I was going to sign, he'd fake like he was going to sign. This was some real crazy stuff going on in a bank President's office that would have been hilarious, if it wasn't so unethical and deplorable. That was how the nation's largest Black-owned savings and loan (we went from number two to number one due to Family Savings' restructuring) was being operated. Still there were times when I didn't sign, and all the loans he had in his possession were declined, for no other reason, than my refusal to sign on one of his associate's request. Quality customers who came to the association in good faith would go away infuriated, particularly when I couldn't justify the decline, totally destroying any goodwill that prevailed, at the time.

In spite of all the games and conflicts, Founders had profitable back to back quarters, for the first time in over five years. Finally, the conflict came to a head in July 1985. Dauterive asked me to put together a deal for a corporation he had formed with the bank counsel, some Korean merchants and several others, to buy some gas stations. The newly formed corporation, according to Dauterive's request, was applying for $200,000. No guarantors. The merchants were to put $100,000 in the association, and we were to fund $200,000 to allow them to run the gas station. Nobody had any previous operating experience. There was no business plan or documented evidence that the operation would eventually profit. I flat out said it couldn't be justified, and I wouldn't sign on it. This discussion came one day after I had refused to sign on a car loan request by a Dauterive associate, who was seeking 100 percent financing on a seven year-old limousine.

The next day, Dauterive called me into a meeting with Art Meadow, and himself. He stated that I hadn't been doing my job, my employees had been unhappy with me, and maybe it was time for me to move on. At the time, loan volume was close to $7 million (summer is peak season in the loan business). The association was almost $3 million up for the year, largely due to my department's performance. Clearly, with Art managing the costs and savings side, Founders Savings' turnaround was in the making, and Dauterive wasn't a part of it. I told him that I'd done everything I'd been asked to do, and that this was not about my performance. My employee efficiency was up, because of a turnover that allowed me to hire Trish Payne, one of the most efficient and responsible support persons I'd ever worked with. She managed to audit, correct and properly track all those screwed up construction loans Founders had on the books (before I got there), plus handled my correspondence and reporting functions. And, most importantly, she was extremely loyal and kept an eye (and ear) on the renegade employee I couldn't get rid of. Everybody else had been cross-trained to support every critical function of the operation. Productivity was at an all-time high, in spite of not having a lead processor and this other woman that did damn near nothing. With all this on my side, plus my wife being eight months pregnant, I wasn't about to voluntarily resign. So with all the calm in the world, I looked at Art and said, "You gonna let this go down like this?"

Art looked down and said, "I'm sorry Anthony. It's Mr. Dauterive's bank." I told them to put their request for my resignation in writing, and we'd go from there. I got up and walked out of the meeting. I never got the request in writing, but after a few days, it became apparent what the strategy was next.....to make me quit.

The first thing Dauterive did was to restrict my business

development to one morning a week. He claimed I was out of the office too much, and needed to manage my staff better. Flexible business development hours are critical to high loan volume. Meeting realtors, loan brokers and business people in the community were key in developing business loyalty. As much competition as it was for loan business, brokers didn't have to come to anybody. If you wanted their business, you went and got it. If you expected it to come to you, you'd be waiting a long time. The reason Founders had no volume when I came, was because they had no presence in the community for developing loan sources. Now we were about to return to that. In addition, he hired a lead processor named Dee Ann Thomas, who was named as a strict regimented disciplinarian to "watch me, while she got the department together." Dee Ann and I soon became allies, once she had her first run-in with the same employee I'd been trying to fire, since I got there. She peeped the situation immediately.

Secondly, he began to play games with adjusting our loan rates. In the highly competitive area of mortgages, when rates move with the majors (Bank of America, Home Savings, Cal Federal, etc), the smaller institutions have to follow, if they want to remain competitive. The difference of a quarter of a percent means all the difference in the world, where brokers take their deals. When the rates move, you have about five days to move with them. Otherwise, brokers take their deals elsewhere. It also affects walk-in business for customers shopping for the best rate. The first time rates moved (after the resignation incident) a quarter percent lower. Founders didn't move at all. While the brokers squealed a little bit, volume barely fell off. About two weeks later, rates moved again, another quarter percent lower. Founders was a half percent above the market. Dauterive refused to lower the rates. Volume fell off a third of what we were doing. The loan committee and the board of directors questioned the drop in loan volume. Dauterive told them that I wasn't doing my job, and that I needed to be monitored. And if it didn't change that they may need to make a move.

Thirdly, in what was the "coup de grace," as far as, loan volume was concerned, Dauterive decided to put a cap on what brokers could charge on their deals. This wasn't uncommon in the industry. However, the industry's average was usually between one and one-half percent, and two percent of the amount of the loan. Founders imposed a one point (percent) cap. You can't kill loan business quicker than messing with a broker's money. Volume dropped to around $3 million, mostly deals nobody else would do (B and C paper), and therefore they couldn't argue rate. Founder's chairman of the board and loan committee chair, the late Frazier Moore, asked Derick Payne and myself what was going on in the loan department. I explained to him all that had been going on. He asked Derick if my explanation was accurate. Derick stated that it was. Dr. Moore said he thought so too and muttered, "My boy is at it again." He then told me directly what occurred at the last board meeting, and warned me to take steps to protect myself, because I was being made to look like "the fall guy" down there (meaning in the loan department).

By October, the projections in the first year of the plan were close to being blown out of the water. We were still about a half million dollars up after three quarters, but since Founders relied heavily on the fees generated from loan closing, the loss of volume was now beginning to take effect. In a senior staff meeting, Dauterive thought he would use this meeting to try and reinforce his position in trying to establish a basis for my firing, by pointing to the last three months loan volume, as the reason for not meeting the projected goals. He had some of the directors there including his lap dog of a general counsel, Attorney John Harris. Harris' primary purpose as house counsel, in the eyes of some, was to justify Dauterive's actions, legal, or illegal.

I sat there as he tried to berate my performance, then he made the mistake of letting me speak, by asking what was my assessment of the situation. He forgot that I wrote the plan, so I knew what the support contingencies were and exposed areas of responsibility that fell in his (and Art's) area of action. I went on to tell about the restrictions on business development, rates and points that were beyond my control. I also pointed out that the plan stated that any time loan volume dropped under $5 million in consecutive months, the contingency action would be to sell off loans (at a profit) to make up the difference in income lost, as a result of low loan volume. Since loan volume is seasonal, we had anticipated a drop off in the last quarter anyway. Dauterive's plan to get me only brought it (the drop in volume) on a few months earlier. The contingency plan to sell loans however, was never implemented. That was on Art and Dauterive. The room went dead silent. They knew I was right, and they knew I knew I was right. The meeting moved on, while Dauterive sat there beet red, fuming that I had turned the table on him.

Then the attack became all out. Dauterive and John Harris met the day after the staff meeting for two whole days. The subject of the meeting? How to legally fire me. During that time, he told everybody to stay out of my office. Any time anyone would come in my office, his girl up front would call him, and he'd come flying down the stairs to inquire why the person was in my office. If I shut my door, he'd come down and ask why my door was closed. If I left the bank, he'd be standing at the security guard station (by the bank's parking lot entrance) waiting for me, upon my return. Then he'd inquire where I'd been, why I'd have to go, etc. This went on for almost two weeks.

In the meantime, almost every cursory function of the bank got dropped on me, even when it wasn't a function of my department. Association staff would bring me a report or some customer service crisis to handle. I'd ask why they were bringing it to me, and they replied, "Mr. Dauterive said, let Anthony handle it." This was clearly part of the plan to frustrate me into quitting. In the meantime, much of the senior staff knew what was happening. Beth, the Vice President on the savings side would come take work piled on my desk, wink and say, "hang in there."

Derick Payne and Martha Jackson would do the same. If anything would be sent over from our Compton branch, the manager Roy'el Mengiste, would have me send it back. Employees outside of the management circle also rallied to my aid. I had an information source in every department of the association, a direct line as to what Dauterive was either doing, or about to do. Even Dauterive's secretary, Susan, began dropping me information, memos, and discussions she'd heard come right out of Dauterive's mouth. When he found out she was the leak in his office, he laid her off under the guise of staff reduction, though he had a new secretary the next week. Everybody recognized for the first time, since they'd been associated with Founders, that it was running like a financial institution was supposed to run, and running profitably. For once everybody was feeling a little security that the regulators weren't going to walk in and close the bank, even though Dauterive used to brag that the bank would never be closed, as long as Ronald Reagan was President of the United States (because of a long-standing Republican relationship). The feeling was that we could save Founders Savings in spite of an inept President and his rubber stamp board of directors. It was largely due to the commitment of the other senior managers and me, to do what we knew was best for the association's longevity. Now they saw it coming under attack with Dauterive's effort to dismiss me, and they knew it would only be a matter of time, before he disassembled the whole team. To keep control of the ship, he'd have to find some new puppets to play with, because the old ones now had an understanding of what his game was about.

We also knew that the Federal Home Loan Bank was investigating Dauterive's association with a restaurant loan that was unethical and improper at best, and illegal at worst. He'd taken gifts, made side loans and even taken an ownership interest in the restaurant. The day the deal went belly up (the owner of the restaurant filed bankruptcy), Dauterive's special assistant and Vice President of operations, the late Lynn Carratelli came in my office crying, "It is over, I don't know how he's going to get out of this one." She then explained what had happened, and how they were now working to save the deal.

My only response was, "I guess Founders is now in the restaurant business." However, the senior management knew the FHLB was involved, and that the best case situation would be that Dauterive would be forced to resign. Worst case, of course, was that they'd close the institution. We were confident that if they saw how the association had operated over the past nine months, they would recognize where the problem was, and remove Dauterive. Dauterive knew what was up too. He took the position that if he was going to be removed from his own institution, none of us would be there to see it. Definitely not me. This was one of the first discussions Susan had relayed to me. Now this period was like a race to a finish line we couldn't find.

What would happen first, my resignation or the regulators stepping in? It was getting pretty unbearable, because Dee Ann had gotten fed up and had given notice. Then Trish was unhappy, because Dauterive hadn't made good on a raise he'd promised. As long as I had the staff, I could last. Derick was telling me every day, "Don't quit, the regulators will be here any day." That still wasn't a guarantee that Dauterive wouldn't fire me first. It came to my attention that he was interviewing for my position, and that as soon as he found someone, he was going to do just that. It was on the street that Dauterive was looking for someone to replace me, purportedly, because he was unhappy with my performance. Then he tried to turn it around on me, accusing me of looking for another job.

The final blow up came the first week of October. Dee Ann was gone. We were short staffed. Trish came in with a letter of resignation. She gave her two weeks notice, and said she'd only reconsider if something "significant changed around here." I went to lunch and returned to find that Trish had been asked to leave. Lynn had told her there was no need for the two weeks, and paid her in lieu of notice. At the same time, Art Meadows had discovered that most of the adjustable mortgage loans had been input incorrectly, after the association's recent transfer to another computer system. As a result, the loans were not adjusting payments, when changes in the index called for payment adjustments. The association was losing thousands of dollars from this error. The loan service department was responsible for the error, and should have been responsible for correcting the problem. Dauterive called me into his office. It was the first time we'd talked about bank business in two weeks. He didn't say a word about letting Trish go. He went immediately into, "We have a problem in loan service. I need you to handle it."

I told him that we were two people short, I had no loan processors, and he let go of the most computer-literate person I had in the department. I asked, "Who am I going to get to re-input over 1,000 AML's."

He said, "You."

I said, "But that could take all month, maybe longer. What about the loan department?"

"Worry about that after you handle this," he said.

I asked if loan service was offering any support to this effort, since it was their error?

"Nope, just you." I told him fine and left his office. That was my last working day at Founders Savings and Loan Association. I went out on a temporary stress disability.

The disability was a 60-day first step relief treatment to determine whether the work environment was the cause of my stress. It also provided the opportunity for Dauterive to build his case for my termination. Upon my notification of taking a disability leave, two of my subordinates in the commercial loan department were ordered to put together an assessment of the loans in the department. Under the supervision of the President, they were to grade the merits of each file, whether they deemed the loans standard, substandard or poor, and whether a file warranted an extension. These two employees had no commercial loan experience. One had a year of auto loan experience. The other was a document processor. Both were hired by Dauterive, without my involvement. They were also ordered to pull selected documents out of certain files. They were ordered to pull out all of the file analysis and approval/decline recommendation reports that I had prepared on each file. This prevented anyone who was to look at the files to see that some two dozen loans were made despite my decline recommendations. The only thing they were allowed to leave in the file was the top sheet I initialed, to demonstrate to Dauterive that I had reviewed the file.

Marquita Bynoe, an employee that was doing the work, told me. She saw me coming out of church one Sunday, and just confessed what was going on. Filled "with the spirit," she told me that it was being made to look like I hadn't done my job, and made bad loans. "Dauterive," she said "was going to use John's report to try and fire you." "You're being set up," she said. John Washington was the other subordinate in charge of the project.

In a letter dated November 6, 1985, Founders Savings terminated my employment for allegedly missing a disbursement on a golf course project in Kentucky. Dauterive, who signed the letter, further justified this decision by mentioning that he had previously asked me to resign, due to the amount of substandard loans the department had made. That, of course, was untrue. There was never a discussion about the quality of loans, only the appropriateness of "his" loans. Now he was using my objections to his loan requests as the basis to fire me.

For the first time, this is the total account of the Founders Savings story, the whole story. Heretofore, those who knew weren't talking, and those who were talking didn't know. Many of those who knew and were talking were part of the Founders problem, and were trying to shift the blame. I was their out. So they thought.

I proceeded to make the necessary moves to open my own business, a mortgage company. Then I sued Founders and Dauterive for wrongful termination. The bank was served on Christmas Eve of 1985. Founders counter-sued in February 1986, and alleged that I had committed some improprieties on my loan, my mother's and my ex-business partner's. The feds also stepped in and removed Dauterive during that same month, two months into the Bush administration. Dauterive was right, though. He didn't go during Reagan's terms in office.

Of the 600 plus applications I reviewed or approved, the only ones Founders could claim as having an appearance of impropriety were those I identified as having a relationship with. All bank officers and directors are required to disclose any loan or relationship they have a stated interest in, directly or potentially, as a fiduciary responsibility to the bank. Since neither of my relationships had the same name as mine, there was no common tie. In each instance, I disclosed my relationships. Still they tried to insist there was something improper taking place.

The case was mediated in August 1989, with neither being

awarded any damages. The mediator determined that although it was very unconventional, Founders had a right to fire me over the missed disbursement, as "ticky tack" as it was (he actually said that). Since they could not identify any negligence and willful wrongdoing, I shouldn't be liable for specific damages on any loans made during my tenure at Founders.

Still my opposition used the pending suit to cast aspersions on my character. They were also successful in getting the government involved in an issue that under normal circumstances, they wouldn't have looked at twice. Now the government was involved and other issues were coming into play: the high profile of my NAACP involvement and dispute; my marital dispute; Founders failure; and, most importantly, a U.S. Justice Department coming under fire for not moving on failed S & L's fast enough.

The attention on S & L defaults had been clearly intensified, particularly, since Neil Bush, the son of the U.S. President, had been part of a $150 million loan that defaulted on its first payment at Silverado Savings in Texas. When the Justice Department called, I knew that this would be a very political discussion.

* * *

My first meeting with the Justice Department was in September 1989. I attended with Attorney Frank Sanes, who had represented me in the civil suit. I wasn't very happy with what he had done in the civil suit, but since they had contacted him, and he had a history on the case, I didn't oppose his coming. We met with assistant U.S. attorney, Terrie Bowers, and a special prosecutor by the name of Greg Schetina (pronounced Shit-teena). They wanted to talk about admissions they claimed I had made during the civil suit deposition. One was regarding an overstatement of assets on my application, specifically centered on five properties I owned at the time, as well as, the cash value of my insurance policy. The second admission was regarding the down payment on the house. In the deposition I had admitted that I had paid $13,900 outside escrow, which was returned at the close of escrow.

I was sitting there listening to Schetina and looking at Frank thinking, "Motherfucker, you let me answer something that would allow me to incriminate myself." I couldn't believe it. Still I sat there showing little emotion.

We were going nowhere with the discussion, when Bowers stated that they had sent the IRS a copy of my 1983 and 1984 tax returns. The 1984 returns came back OK. However, 1983's were not the same, as in my file.

"So what are you saying?" I asked.

"Either you submitted a false return, or you've evaded paying income tax? Which is it?" Bowers said. Schetina gave Sanes a draft of the five-count indictment the government was preparing.

Sanes then said, "Where's the damage? There's been no damage." Neither Justice Department official could respond with a justification of damage, other than I'd been late on my house payments, and my wife was behind, at the time of the discussion. Sanes pointed out that even if the loan defaulted, where was the damage. "There will be no loss, because you have the house," he continued.

Bowers mumbled something about it wasn't about the loss, as much as it was about the intent to defraud.

"You know, this is political isn't it?" Sanes demanded.

Bowers said, "What do you mean?"

Frank continued. "People default on loans every day, because circumstances change. This man has owned this house for five years, and made payments for five years...."

Schetina interrupted, "But they were late most of the time...."

"That doesn't make a difference," Frank continued. "The payments were made. Why the payments were late could be attributed to any number of reasons, including this man being unfairly terminated for doing his job, his spousal separation, and the negative effects the NAACP fight had on his business. The bottom line is the man bought the house for his family, lived in the house and made his payments, where is the intent to defraud?"

Bowers and Schetina just sat silently. After about 20 seconds, never answering Frank's questions, Bowers spoke up,

"So what do you want to do?"

"What do you mean 'what do I want to do?' I answered.

"Well, we have evidence that you submitted a false document to a federally insured institution. "How should we proceed?" Bowers asked.

"How would you suggest I proceed?" I asked.

"Plead guilty to bank fraud," Bowers said with a straight face.

"Let me get this straight." I replied. "Even though I was the one to clean up Founders, brought the regulators in, made them aware of the mismanagement and inside dealings, you want me to plead guilty to bank fraud, when there was no intent to defraud the bank, and no potential loss on the house?"

Schetina kicked in, "Well, the evidence is material."

Sanes, clearly having a good day, interrupted. "No. Materiality speaks to the level of influence the document submitted had on the loan decision. Since he was an employee,and they knew how much he made, what is the likelihood this loan would have been made, if the document hadn't been submitted?"

Schetina responded, "Probably that was very likely, but still a false document was submitted."

"An immaterial false document," Sanes responded.

"Well, the court will decide how immaterial it is," Schetina snapped back.

I told Schetina and Bowers that I'd take responsibility for what I did, but I wasn't pleading guilty to bank fraud. They could forget that. Sanes asked what could be done to resolve this.

"Not much," said Bowers, obviously acting as if he wasn't going to tell us anything that would change the politics of the case.

"What if they paid off the loan?" Frank asked.

"Then obviously we'd have to reconsider our action. It doesn't mean we still won't file, because what was done was done. We'll just have to see," Bowers said, and he left it at that. That was the end of our conversation. On the down elevator, Sanes recommended, "Your best bet is to pay off the house."

I agreed. Doing it was another story.

My now very estranged wife, Taurece had maintained all along that she wanted to keep the house. However, even with child support, she couldn't afford the house without a roommate. I had tried to get her to sell the house on a number of occasions. Her position was that she liked her house and wanted to keep it. Payments hadn't been made on the house since I left, and since she knew that the feds were watching the house, she had no intention of doing so. The pressure was clearly on me. In a sheer power move, Taurece, not being able to separate emotion from reason, played a shrewd game of dare. Chicken, we called it in our childhood. She was sitting on equity and had cooperation in selling the house. Still she refused to sell or make payments, to do anything, thinking that I'd either come back, or I'd lose the house. Of course, during the course of this battle, the discussion of what about the children, "keep the house for the children" came into play.

However, it was obvious to me that she wasn't prepared to do what was best, or at least most responsible for our children. She acted as if she had nothing to lose. The indictment was hanging over my head. All she had to do was play her hand right and sell the house. Sell the house, the indictment goes away. She could get another house with the sale proceeds. She chose to do nothing instead, and lost everything; her house, her equity and my respect for her parental judgment.

I believed the government was going to do whatever they were going to do. But even though they would lose nothing either way, they had less of a case with the house paid off, than with the house in their possession. The blame was really on me for not resolving the issue before I left, but I also knew 'T' would never sell the house, if I was still there. Neither of us was thinking straight, at the time, but our battle wasn't over possessions, it was over freedoms. Now we were trying to deal with the government in the middle of personal life issues. They were betting that our estrangement would become bitter, and that we'd turn against each other. My wife's bitterness caused her to lose me, the house and her equity. She didn't have to lose it all. She chose to. Our marriage was over, and there was no coming back. I was prepared to leave her everything and start from scratch (which I did anyway). Both of us didn't have to lose, but that's what happened. We do these things to injure ourselves sometimes. She knew I would be hurt worse with the government's help. Within a week of losing the house, the government went forward on an indictment recommendation to the federal grand jury.

* * *

On December 14, 1989, I got a call from an *L.A. Times* writer named Darrell Dawsey. He called to ask if I had any comment on the statement released by the U.S. Attorney, that on Friday the 15th, they would issue a five-count indictment against me for bank fraud. That was how I was notified of my impending indictment. I had no comment because, at that point, I knew nothing. Not that I would have commented had I known anything at all. I had developed a real contempt for the *L.A. Times*. The *L.A. Herald Examiner*, now out of business, was one rag I certainly didn't miss. Both had grossly misrepresented issues involving the branch conflicts, and I knew *The Times* was about to have a field day with this one. So would the *Herald Examiner*, if it was still around. But since I didn't know what I was being charged with, it was very easy to resist their "don't you want to tell your side of the story" baiting.

The story broke on the television evening news, and made the Saturday (and Sunday) *Metro*. The first call I got was from my friend, Colin Mitchell, who offered his support any way he could help. By the end of the weekend, I picked up over 40 messages between my home and office answering machines. Both tapes ran full. When I came in Monday, Katherine had another two dozen messages, including two from anonymous callers. One said, "Yeah, niggah, we got your ass this time." The other said, "Bon Voyage, troublemaker. Let us know how you like jail. Your friends from the branch." In rewinding the messages, the first call was a male, the second was female. My friend and then business partner, Daryl Sweeney, came in my office and didn't say a word. He didn't want to know if I did it, didn't do it, whatever. He just handed me a check for $500, and just sat there with me, until I was ready to talk. Daryl will never know how much I appreciated that. It's something I'll remember all my life. Colin and his wife, Charlotte, who were sharing space in my office, while the space for their accounting office was being built out, came in later.

For the whole day, I just sat looking at the wall and out of the windows. I took only two calls that day. One from Frank Sanes, calling to see if he could represent me. I told him, "Not this time, Frank. I need a trial specialist, or someone who can squash this." He was disappointed, but he said he understood. I wasn't in the mood to pacify anybody. The second call was from Debra, in Sacramento. She said it was the talk of the capitol. Nobody really knew our relationship, so the talk ranged from support to condemnation, depending on where the politics of my association fell. She was calling to see if I was OK. I told her to the extent that I could be OK. She asked how my mother was taking it. "Pretty hard," I told her. I relayed to Deb the events of the weekend, before and after the announcement. I told her mom had joined the church, and my feelings about it. I told her I thought mom was trying to save me by herself. I was still concerned about how the whole experience would affect her. I tried to warn her that it was coming on Thursday night. She made me promise to go see Chip on Friday, and I did. He didn't have a lot to say, since it was now public knowledge that I was processing in the Nation. Still, he took me down in the sanctuary, had me kneel with my hands on a large brass cross in front of the pulpit, and prayed for me. Afterward, he told me to stay strong, and he left. I stayed behind in the sanctuary another 20 minutes or so, reflecting about my own salvation. I was praying to the very Christian God of the hypocritical Christian nation now persecuting me, wondering how could we possibly, even remotely, have the same God.

Could the same God of the biggest defrauder of humanity in the history of the world, who now wanted to pass judgment on me, be my God, too? My thoughts continued in that vain, when my mother came by the following Sunday, and asked me to go to church with her. At church, 2,000 eyes seemed to look through me, as if I had murdered somebody. I watched as my mother prayed for me, and promised to give the rest of her life to "Jesus," if he spared my life. My mother, who had been a critic of hypocrisy in the church, and hadn't been affiliated with a church for over 25 years, sealed her promise to God, by coming forward when the preacher called for the converted to come.

I had very mixed emotions. I had feelings of gratitude that my mother would give her life and soul, to spare me the grief and anguish of this public persecution. I knew that if God was anywhere in that church, he heard my mother's prayers that day. And I knew my mother would find God in sincerity, not in hypocrisy. I also had feelings of cynicism that my mother's earnest prayers and commitment to spiritual healing was being made to a Christian God I could no longer buy.

I had no reason to believe in America's commitment to equality, its frayed system of fairness, nor its belief in a God. Everything America has ever given the Black man and woman has been a lie, including "one nation under God, indivisible with liberty and justice for all." If the God that guided this nation was the same God he gave to us to pray to, then I had to reject it. It is the God of the hypocrite. There was absolutely no reason for me, or any other Black to believe that this country would lie about everything else, and tell the truth about religion. In fact, it doesn't add up, when we can worship a Christian God in a so-called Christian nation, and not worship the same God, at the same time, in the same house. Their God is not our God, but our God is their God. I don't think so. One of us really wasn't worshipping God. Or, if we were following the lead of our hypocritical oppressor, then maybe neither of us were.

All I knew was what God had now allowed me to clearly see -- that when in trial and tribulation, you become a lot more spiritual. However, in persecution, you have nothing to influence your perspective but what you know as the truth. You reject everything else. I knew, in truth, I couldn't sit there and continue to believe that the God of the world's most hypocritical government, in terms of human and civil rights, was going to save me. But I knew my mother was doing what she knew best. It's very difficult to reject all that you've come to believe as true, and to say what you've believed in all your life is a lie. I know that wasn't where my mother's focus was. Her focus was on saving her son by the only way she'd been taught. Whether the deal had been sealed with the God of righteousness or the God of the devil was a bone of contention. I sensed she wouldn't have cared, as long as her prayers were heard.

Debra was silent on the phone. I asked her if she was all right. She said she was. She thought I might be right not to break my mother's spirit about Christianity, First AME or anything else that would cause her any mental strain, and interrupt her support for me. I agreed that I would go to church with her, as long as she wanted me to, and deal with everything else that cames with new found spirituality. The legislative session was due to end by the weekend. She said she'd be coming to L.A. for the holidays, and we'd get together then. Talking with Debra always brightened my spirits and gave me a clearer head to deal with things. It made doing what I had to do easier, in terms of talking to people who really wanted to support me, and ignoring the attitudes of people who were now shying away from me. The rest of the week was very telling, in that respect.

Within two weeks of the indictment, there was a white male sitting in front of my apartment. I had a communications specialist and an ex-FBI operator examine my phone lines. Not only were my business and home lines open, my mother's line was open, Debra's L.A. line was open, and my ex-business partner's lines were open. The most common reason for open lines is that the phone's off the hook. The second most common reason is that the phone line is being tapped. I could tell that everybody had their phone on the hook, when the line was tested and a code I was given was dialed into the phone. I developed a code system to talk to my family and friends. I didn't talk about anything crucial on the phone. Most nights, I stayed up writing and watching the person in the car watch me. A few times he fell asleep, only to have students walking to Crenshaw High bang on the car yelling, "Wake up, Cop!" He'd wake up and look at my place. I'd give him the thumb like, "Yeah, I'm still here," and then I'd flip him off. For those reasons, and many others, I moved very cautiously. Mainly, because I had yet to receive the formal summons to appear in court for arraignment.

I received the hard copy two full weeks after the *L.A. Times* first broke the story. There were five formal charges. The date had been left open as December 1989. This was highly improper. The analysis from my legal advisers was that the U.S. attorney was trying to get the indictment in under the five-year statute of limitations, generally guiding the length of time that one can be pursued for an alleged crime. We later found out that such a status had been suspended specifically, for pursuing so-called S & L bandits, but it appeared the U.S. attorney wasn't taking any chances either way on my case. The major count (count one) was for bank fraud [18 U.S.C. Sec. 1344], which is defined in the federal statute as the willful intent to defraud a federally insured institution, by way of a planned and deliberate action without the intent to restitute (pay back the money).

Counts two through five were false statement charges [18 U.S.C. Sec. 1014], which is, according to the federal statute, knowingly causing material false statements to be made to a federally insured financial institution. Knowingly and material are the key words here. Each count was for a different allegation made on facets of the loan application packet. The 1983 tax return was one count. The W-2 form was a second count. Both were knowingly submitted, but their materiality was highly questionable. A material false statement is a statement that would so influence one's decision to make the loan. Neither document was critical to the loan's decision, since it was a prior year's return. The likelihood is that the loan still would have been made without the document. The third false statement count was on the loan application, in which there were errors on my life insurance, and my real estate was inflated. This wasn't a material false statement and it wasn't done knowingly. The loan would have been made if I didn't have any life insurance or owned any additional real estate, and both were estimates of assets, as was the fourth false statement count, which called out the same information, on a schedule of real estate owned. Yes, I knew I didn't own 100 percent of all the properties I listed, but again, real estate owned was not material to the loan decision.

The bank's fraud count carried a five-year jail sentence and/or a $250,000 fine. The false statement charges carried a two-year sentence each, and $250,000 for each count. If I were convicted on all charges, I'd be looking at 13 years and $1.25 million in fines, for a maximum sentence. The case was being prosecuted by the major fraud section of the U.S. attorney's office. A section that investigates fraud claims of $250,000 and above. Generally the cases they choose to prosecute are in the millions. One million and above in hard (actual) dollar losses. My case was worth zero, because after the house was sold, they owed me money. That is why nobody, including the several attorneys reviewing my case, could figure out why the case was being pressed, and what it was based on.

Yes, my case was part of a criminal referral made by Founders to investigate the possibility of insider abuse, as were four other cases, including the President of the bank. None of the other cases were prosecuted. Two of which had much greater loss factors, along with a greater preponderance of evidence. One factor that my case had that the others didn't have was the notoriety factor. Because of my high profile involvement in the branch, I was considered a public figure. Prosecutors, as do reporters, make a name for themselves by taking down public figures. In my case, they chose to overcharge me to make a case.

It was very clear to many, that these were trumped up charges, especially the bank fraud charges. That was the major count, the one that grabbed the headlines, and the one that carried the most severe consequences, both criminally and professionally. A bank fraud count is virtually an exit pass out of the finance industry, which was my livelihood. The false statement charges, though partially factual, were tort charges, which means they usually coattail them to a more significant charge, to get them heard. Tort charges are not likely to stand on their own.

From the start, I was prepared to acknowledge and accept responsibility for submitting the tax return and W-2. I was prepared to plead it out, pay a fine or whatever. I had done what I had done. Bowers and Schetina maintained that I couldn't plead to the lesser charges, without pleading to the major count. I wasn't about to plead to bank fraud, so I didn't plead to anything. I saw this case as another example of unknown prosecutors trying to make a name for themselves, by overcharging a Black, and using a high-profile case to gain notoriety. I didn't intend to create any type of movement around, what was obviously, a very political prosecution. It wasn't about symbolism, or martyrism, or anything about guilt or innocence. It was about accepting responsibility for what I had done. Nothing more, nothing less.

The purpose was bigger for the government. Its purpose was to try this case in the media, and further tarnish my reputation by making it even more difficult for me to even step back into a leadership position. Guilt or innocence wasn't the sole objective for them, either. Just the appearance of guilt, enough to create doubt in the community, would be enough. Enough to create a question about my integrity, and discredit any status that I might have. It's the achieved price one pays for ambition gone astray. And sometimes our own make us pay forever. The government knows this, that's why it attacks integrity first.

I had one week to find an attorney. I placed a call to Johnnie Cochran, the Los Angeles community's best criminal attorney, in the opinion of many. Cochran responded the Monday following Christmas. We met on the issues for about one hour. Johnnie was familiar with some of the issues, having represented Founders Savings' President, Peter Dauterive in his negotiated resignation with the Federal regulators. A couple days later he referred me to an attorney named Cornell Price, due to a potential conflict of interest. Price, who had an active relationship with Joe Duff, as his appointee to the Century Freeway Affirmative Action Committee. He suggested his law partner, Robert Ramsey. After meeting with Ramsey, I waited a day or two to check his credentials, being highly suspect of lawyers at that point. I retained Ramsey for the purpose of making the January 2 appearance, to be formally charged and fingerprinted. I was to come back in three weeks to enter my pleas. Ramsey said he needed time to go over the box of information I brought to him. We agreed to meet a week later.

During this period, a lot of my friends did all they could to show confidence in me, and keep me in good spirits. Though my business fell off again, a dozen or so loyal clients called to give me assurance that they were with me regardless, which I appreciated very much. Regional Minister Wazir Muhammad and Regional Captain Wali Muhammad reinforced their commitment to me by appointing me the head of the community coordination effort for Minister Farrakhan's February appearance at the Los Angeles Sports Arena. Wazir was in touch with me daily just to make sure I was OK, as were my friends, Ron Carter and Floyd Frazier. Malik Farrakhan also called to check on me frequently, although he was traveling as security chief for the conscious rap group, Public Enemy. When in town, he would play ball at a West L.A. park during the noon hour, where a bunch of actors and entertainment types would exercise during their shooting breaks and lunch hours. It really gave me the opportunity to work out regularly, during this very high stress period. It allowed me to get into the best shape since my college playing days.

It also gave me a chance to spend more time with my son, who was having problems in school, largely due to my marital separation.

My not being in the home affected him so adversely, that his teachers at the Marcus Garvey School couldn't get him to do his school work. So he spent the day with me for a couple of weeks to try and work through his introversion. We often underestimate how adversity in our lives affects our children, until they say something out of the blue, or they shut down on us. In being around me during this time, Tony, though only 4 1/2 years old, seemed to know that something wasn't right with his dad. The public consensus of friends and foes alike, was that this was an "inside job." A prosecution being pushed inside for political reasons. The damage done just wasn't that great. One of my friends jokingly argued that we should go to trial, because they've already done everything but shoot you for telling a lie on a loan application five years ago.

Apparently my son had heard some of that discussion. The next day, on the way home from our noon workout, out of the clear blue sky, my son said, "Daddy, can you die for telling a lie?" I quickly turned around, only to see his eyes swelled with tears. I rubbed him on his head, turning back in time to stop for a red light.

I looked back at him and said, "Well, son, lies put you in a position to be hurt sometimes, as does telling the truth. How much you're hurt depends on the lie and, yes, sometimes, we pay for our mistakes with our lives. Not so much with actual dying, but a pain similar to dying, by having to live through the lie."

It occurred to me that I was rationalizing the answer more for myself than for him. My response was a little more complex than I had intended. Still he seemed to be with me. While not trying to underestimate him, I went straight to the point. "So the answer is yes, and no. Yes, you can die, and no, it doesn't have to be real death. There's physical death and spiritual death. Sometimes living through a difficult period is worse than dying. Do you understand, son?"

He shook his head, yes, unlocked his seat belt and grabbed me around the neck.. Cars were honking behind us. We had missed the green light. My son's hug was worth the wait.

* * *

15

Bork(ism) & Media Manipulation:

Trial by Pat Hand

"I could tell you, if I wanted to,
What makes me what I am.
But I don't really want to.....
And you don't give a damn."

"Impasse"
-The Panther and the Lash, - Langston Hughes

"Ex-NAACP Head Charged With Bank Fraud." I had never felt anything like it in my life. Reading the headlines sprawled across the front page of the *L.A. Times-Metro Section* of the paper, placed in a position where one would almost have to read it. Prosecutors love high-profile cases, and so does the media. For the prosecutors, it's a chance to break out of their little "cubby hole" cubicle and make a name for themselves. For the newspaper reporters, taking someone down is like an extra reference of some sort. Prosecutors and newspaper reporters are alike, in a lot of ways. A reporter will fabricate a scenario (or a case) to make a story. A prosecutor will fabricate a story to make a case. Neither has to have all the exact facts, close will do. Their sources are confidential. And contrary to popular opinion, the burden of proof is not on them, but on you to prove them wrong, which only makes both exaggerate charges and enlist a greater public discussion.

As long as they have much of the truth, they can fill in the blanks. Both have access to almost any kind of information, and neither ever has to reveal the source of that information. Once they put what they have out on you, they both have deep, deep pockets to back up their version of a story. True or not, they both can break you financially, before you get to court, and both can greatly manipulate the court proceedings. It was almost an indefensible position and I was resisting all the way, which only made it better for them and made it appear worse for me than it really was.

A real property default doesn't constitute a criminal act nor does it constitute loss. When you default, they come get the collateral which is the property. Simple as that. Not only was I being charged with a crime because of a change in personal circumstance, I was being severely overcharged. This issue of bringing forth an inappropriate case and excessive allegations is probably the biggest and most common similarity that prosecutors (be they local, state or federal) and the press share. A bias toward Blacks in the courts and in the press. Blacks are more apt to be prosecuted, overcharged and have their cases sensationalized in the media.

The government and the press have a pretty cozy relationship. They turn on each other from time to time, but both spend the majority of their time manipulating the people. They often work hand in hand. Media manipulation is routine for Blacks. No matter how small the offense, it's made to look bigger because of how the media plays it up. And it is very effective in the Black community. Blacks are highly gullible where the press is concerned. Most Black people believe what they read, in white-controlled media.

In preparing to defend myself against the charges filed against me, I quickly recognized the collaboration of the government and the press. The initial press release was virtually a public relations piece for the government. For a loan application of $121,500, over five years ago, the government claimed the indictment stemmed from a joint investigation by the "FBI and the IRS" into the failure of Founders. This was not true. Neither the FBI, nor the IRS investigates bank failures.

The FBI investigates leads on ongoing criminal activity with cause to believe that such activity poses a threat to the public. Sometimes, they're involved banks investigations, because of Justice

Department involvement in major fraud threats. My one home loan didn't represent such a threat. The prosecutor in the case, Gregory D. Schetina, was assigned to the Justice Department Bank Fraud Bureau, after President George Bush ordered a federal crackdown on S & L fraud. He had FBI support to aid his investigations. Many perceived this order as a diversion to take attention away from his own son, Neil Bush, who was accused of defrauding Silverado Thrift of $150 million.

Neil Bush allegedly steered a loan to Silverado, as a member of their board of directors. The loan was for a commercial development project and was owned by Bush and a business associate, whose name was on the loan. The directors approved the loan, purportedly at Bush's urging, and the loan defaulted almost immediately. None of the money was ever seen again. The President then ordered a federal crackdown, which this case was supposedly a part of, resulting in four criminal referrals by the RTC (Resolution Trust Corporation).

It was the opinion of several trust regulators and legal experts who conferred with me, that my case wasn't prosecuted, because of its loss value, but its notoriety value. My notoriety as an NAACP President meant much more to the Justice Department at that time. The Justice Department was coming under fire for the lousy job it was doing in prosecuting S & L crimes. While my case didn't net them any real dollars, it gave the public something to bite on, while they were figuring out what to do. Public Enemy has a lyric in their song Welcome to the Terrordome that says, "The bigger the Black, the more the Feds want a piece of that BOO-ty." There is more truth to that statement than most people realize. The press blows up on any news involving Blacks of notoriety.

The real purpose of the intensified effort was to stem the fall of the Savings and Loan industry, while insiders walked away with millions of hard dollars and assets, like multi-million dollar commercial developments, large housing projects, restaurant loans or some huge land deal that defaulted and caused the institution to fail. If there were some type of fraud alleged, usually it was over $1 million, though the Justice Dept. went as low as $250,000 (lower in cases of actual cash losses). There was a definite loss involved, and the one accused of fraud walked away with a substantial amount of cash.

In the case the government filed against me in the initial indictment, the dollar amount was substantially under $250,000. There was no cash ever stolen, or given to me (it was a home loan), and there was no loss anticipated on my loan. My single home loan did not contribute to the failure of the bank (the bank sold the house almost immediately, and MADE money over and above what was actually owed to them). The $11 million in losses ($4,370,817 in 1982 and 1983, plus a $7 million loss on loan sales in mid-1984, all prior to my employment), in addition to the continuing operational mismanagement (heavy payroll) of the President caused Founders to fail. The default on the Van Ness house property hurt no one, but me and my family. So with no loss to point to, no direct tie to the bank's failure and no personal benefit, why was the government prosecuting this case?

With the Founders case, in particular, there were criminal referrals made that fit the total bill, meaning there were losses over $1 million, cash was missing, there was significant benefit (to someone, somewhere) and there were several loans whose default directly contributed to Founders' failure. It didn't make any sense to prosecute me, when there were bigger fish in the tank. Other than the fact that I was, in my limited notoriety, a very timely example for the government to use. They often identify fall guys whom they (the government) hope they could shake up (and luck up on) some information to get the others. They could receive some "big time" press in the process of chasing "civil rights advocate" who also was a "small fry" in the Founders case. Founders needed a fall guy. President Bush's S & L shakeup needed a fallguy (other than his son, Neil). I had some culpability on my own home loan and the timing was right for the prosecution. I was served up for lunch.

The government, by prosecuting me, picked up a "high-profile stat" for their S & L damage control campaign, and discredited an independent-minded leader at the same time. What else was there for them to gain? Absolutely nothing. But in going through the motions, they played it up like it was a major break in the S & L scandal. And the government used every resource at their disposal including the FBI, the IRS and its influence with (or control over) the print media. The *Los Angeles Times*, in all its racist glory, manipulated the prosecution to the hilt. Usually, when a major story breaks, it runs in bold captions, occasionally with a photo. Major losses in the banking industry is generally something in the billions, much less millions to be press worthy. Losses in the thousands very rarely get any space, much less a picture. Follow-up stories get even less space, unless some major discovery takes place that requires additional attention. The *L.A. Times*, not only ran a large heading and photo when they broke the story, but in every follow-up story in each phase of the case, it did the same. Each article and photo was strategically placed in the paper, referring to me as an Ex-NAACP official to grab headlines and public attention. And it was effective, doing exactly what it was intended to do, to advance the government's case, and discredit me in the process.

* * *

Being in a public conflict with the government is like having a disease. Nobody in their right mind was going to stand with someone under direct attack from the government. People run on sight. The actual charge was a false statement on a loan application, and a false document in a loan package, both of which the community was very familiar with. A few of my friends recalled some of the conversation going around in the community. They were joking that half of Baldwin Hills and Ladera Heights (two relatively exclusive sections of the Los Angeles Black community) were as still as church mice. The implication was that many of them understood what they had to do to get their homes, and how vulnerable they were. The lending double standard in the Black community was (and still is) such that the slightest non-conformity prevented one from getting a loan.

So many had become frustrated over being declined by banks in the community, that many reverted to using loan brokers, because "loan brokers knew how to get the deals done." Getting the deal down often meant doing what the broker told you to do, if you wanted that house or that loan. If it meant putting down what they told you to put down or turning your head while they handled your tax documentation, the bottom line was "get me in the house." That was the way it was in the 1980s and we learned it from white folk, because those of us on the inside saw what they were doing to get "their deals" done, for much more money.

Credit is the biggest trick ever perpetuated against Blacks in the history of personal wealth development. Credit tries to objectively address the issue of one's character but is actually the most discriminating factor in an individual's economic enhancement. Furthermore, it is extremely selective, in terms of how a reviewer can interpret one's personal economic capacity, based on something happening in the present, or at some time in the past. Furthermore, it unreliably tries to predict one's economic capacity in the future. The biggest flaw in credit is that it does not take into consideration circumstances and it gives little credence to circumstantial justification. This is where racism and privilege separates the haves from the have-nots. Prior to credit checks (pre-1970s), Blacks rarely had any and if they did, they paid double for so-called "the risk," which was nothing more than the risk of being Black. That's how the check cashing, finance company and pawn shop industries were created and lucratively expanded in poor communities. It was an option for those excluded from the banking (and later S & L) industries. Blacks couldn't get loans and checking accounts from white-owned banks because of their racist perceptions that Blacks couldn't be trusted to handle their money or repay their debts. With the deregulation of the banking industry in the 1970s, competition variables forced the industry to reach out to Blacks. However, the trust factor was still an issue.

Anybody who has ever dealt with banks know that the banks want to see money. Yet when one files his taxes, the objective is to pay as little taxes as possible, so you show as little income as possible, either by taking deductions, claiming rental write-off or showing dependents, etc. Now, Blacks in the 1980s learned what some whites were doing all along, even though they had the benefit of selective judgment in their favor-- that if you're going to make money and deal with a bank, you're going to have to show cash flow and net income (not gross). Economic discrimination forced Black people's hand, in many cases. Mine wasn't one because I controlled the situation and didn't have to do it. But I did play the game the way the industry played the game, as unethical as it was. Wealth creation in America is a very unethical game. During that time, others who didn't control their situation, did what they had to do.

Tying it back to the discussion of Ladera and Baldwin Hills being as quiet as church mice, over 200 people that I saw personally during that time expressed surprise at the shallowness of these charges. Most of them said, "Is that all you did? Hell, my agent told me to do this or to submit that." Everybody knew that it was a common practice. I had several judges, police officers, attorneys, doctors, preachers, elected officials and businessmen tell me confidentially that they did the same thing. But nobody was saying anything publicly for fear of the government digging up their loan applications and putting them under scrutiny. It was a scary proposition for most people, to think that the government could go back past the standard five-year statute of limitations. It was suspended in my case, because of my tie into the S & L probe, (The governments position was that most of the abuses occurred in the early and mid-eighties).

But to pull my file and accuse me of lying, fraud, based on what they had--five years after it happened--was unconscionable. This was now a ploy by the government that could touch a lot of people in a very negative way. Many in the community had to stay clear of it.

The story broke in December 1989, around the time when all Christmas parties and receptions took place. In the Los Angeles Black community, very little work takes place the last two weeks of the year. The "talk" of this holiday season was the "Essex indictment." My friends and other people (basically acquaintances and business associates) who cared were calling me on a daily basis, to give me "the latest" on what I did. Everything from "robbing the bank" to "embezzling funds." Embezzlement, of course, is actual cash taken out of the bank. There was no cash given to me nor was any involved "bank cash" in my home loan. It was a home purchase. However, the "embezzlement story" made the discussion more interesting and, by most accounts, was the line being put out by my detractors. It was a rolling snowball. One friend called and said, "Well, today I heard you embezzled a million and a half dollars set up in a Swiss bank account and you're contemplating fleeing the country." On another occasion I took so much money the bank folded. These were some of the more extreme stories floating around, but they certainly contributed to the drama of the moment. However, I was also given more than three dozen accounts of discussions my supporters observed of people standing up for me, as well as those who spoke against me. There were many more positive than negative. But those who spoke negatively were those who were more apt to smile in my face when they saw me, or didn't know me at all.

On one occasion when a friend, Marie LaFargue, in a well-intentioned effort to keep my spirits up talked about me so bad, she literally "made" me go out with them to one of these holiday parties. I sat at a table with one of those "in the know" fakers. In spite of all the stares and people coming by patting me on the back, offering supporting comments, this so called "brotha" tried to make table conversation to impress the sistahs at the table. He started by saying, "What do you guys think about that EE-sex situation?" He couldn't even pronounce my name right. Everybody kind of looked at each other like, "Uh-oh."

Most at the table knew me ,except another woman who, of course, engaged him further by responding, "Uhmmm, that was something, wasn't it? I heard he took a million dollars, and didn't give the NAACP any of it."

The brotha continued. "Well, I know the brother, because I did a little work with the NAACP. I knew something wasn't quite right with him, when I met him."

I'd never seen this person in my whole life. Knowing my unpredictability and inclination to react, though I hadn't at that point, one of the women (a friend of Marie's) at the table thought she'd better try to shortstop the conversation, before it got too slanderous. "Uh, maybe we should all introduce ourselves. Get into some holiday spirit," she said, interrupting the conversation.

The sister to whom he was responding turned and said, "Well, that was rude!"

Marie's friend said, "Not as rude as it could get, if you keep talking." Then she said her name, to which everybody else followed suit. I was about the fifth or sixth person around.

When it got to me, I looked at the woman and said, "My name is Anthony, and it wasn't a million dollars. It wasn't any money at all. Then I looked at the brother and said, It's Essex, not EE-sex. I've never seen you in my life, and I hope I never do again.

The brother was one of those fair, "Rico Suave'" looking Black men. We used to call them "high yella" when we were trying to be mean-spirited. He turned flush red, and his eyes got round and beady. I just looked at him. The table was dead silent. All of a sudden everybody wanted to dance.

Marie said, "Anthony let's go dance." When we came back, both were gone. They got talked about the rest of the night by the others at the table, but it ruined my night. I went out very little during that holiday season.

Representation had now become a point of great consternation for me, because of my distrust for attorneys, and because my first choice, Johnnie Cochran, wasn't available.

Since the indictment came down, the overwhelming sentiment of my friends and family were, "You need to get you a white boy." Moreover, "a Jewish white boy." The thought of it made me cringe. I don't interface well with white males, because most of them underestimate the capacity of Black males to think for themselves. My experience with Jewish males has been even worse. They tend to be too damn confrontational (with me, not the opposition) and just too damn pushy on their point of view. I don't respond well being pushed into something. People were saying to me, "You still trust Blacks after they did this to you?" "Hell yes, all day. I would put my life in the hands of my people, before I went to white folk, who I didn't know, or couldn't discern if my interests were being represented. I somehow believed that as bad as our people are, they will never be as bad as the most liberal racist, disguised behind a smile, handshake and three-piece suit. There are many goodwill, fair-minded, socially and racially sincere white folk out there. But how do you quickly discern their sincerity? I didn't want to have to be wondering if some whiteface opportunist was sincerely trying to help me, or playing out the role the real enemy had called out, while trying to make a name for him (or her) self. I wasn't going to be part of some private club steam room compromise where some white boy tries to force some unacceptable plea bargain on me, by asking his college roommie or former law partner now in the Justice Department or on the bench, to be light on his "nigger."

Many tried to say that I misread Black sincerity with the NAACP conflict, and look what it got me. My rebuttal to that was that I never perceived my opposition in the NAACP as sincere. Never. Even before I heard Mallory's taped phone meeting calling out the plan for my pre-election compromise. Even before Ray decided to leave. I always knew the forces in and around the branch leadership who were insincere. What facilitated my downfall (including this prosecution) was the reckless way they came after me, including pulling the community down with it. It also included pulling the government and the press into it.

The branch situation was clearly a hostage situation where once they found something they could hold hostage, by way of their investigation, it was like a criminal had ambushed a policeman putting a gun to his head and telling him to drop his gun. If he drops his gun, he's dead for sure. He keeps his gun, he challenges the criminal's own sense of mortality. Is the criminal as willing to die, as he is to kill? The officer only knows if he holds to his gun. They both may die in the process, if the integrity of the question comes out in the process. My opposition was going to shoot me either way, but what they were really all about came out in the end, and we all died a little bit in the process. The point: I could more easily discern sincerity in us, than in whites.

It wasn't the time to drop my gun and become totally dependent on the benevolence of whites, many of whom I know don't like pro-Black leadership, and are just looking to take our money, while they take us out. I wasn't going to give this "Black scapegoating" position any credence that tries to justify that we must always turn to white folk to save us. And I damn sure wasn't going to give them the satisfaction of thinking that I believed such foolishness. If I went down, I would go down believing that Blacks could help each other in a qualified manner. While I may lose faith in some Blacks who act out of spite and ignorance, I'll never lose faith in my people as a whole and our capacity to rise to challenges, to grow in our understanding and to represent the best in ourselves. That's what others do, when the shoe is on the other foot. They believe in the best of themselves, for themselves. And so should we. No. I wasn't looking for a white boy to represent me (though I did talk to a few to make sure the brothers were competitive).

Robert Ramsey was a former federal prosecutor (along with his partner Price) who sort of "grew up" in the federal ranks with Terrie Bowers, the prosecutor who was then deputy U.S. Attorney supervising the case. I had taken a liking to Ramsey, who was in his late 40s and appeared to be a real intellectual, kind of book smart with perfect speaking diction. Plus he held similar views I held about the government's disproportionate prosecution of Blacks in the federal system. After a few conversations with him (and others), I agreed to let him represent me.

My first appearance to be arraigned by the federal magistrate was on January 2, 1990. Ramsey had concurred with most who had reviewed the case, that it was a chicken shit charge and forced under bullshit terms. It was also obvious to him that I was overcharged. Ramsey called Terrie Bowers, put him on the speaker phone and asked him what this was all about. He told him about the false tax return and W-2. Bob (as Ramsey preferred to be called) asked "Is that all you got?" Bowers said, "There were some misstatements on the application."

Ramsey then asked him point blank, "How did you get fraud outta this?" Is this a pressure move for testimony, or were you guys looking to build your stats." He meant statistics on the number of prosecutions in a certain area for year-end reports to the department. A *Los Angeles Times* article had reported earlier in the year that over 1,000 cases went un-prosecuted in the U.S. attorney's office. It was public knowledge that the Justice Department was under pressure to "improve its numbers."

Bowers denied that allegation claiming, "You know we're not in this for stats, Bob." Bowers went on to say that they were prosecuting bank tellers, for as little as $2,500. How could we let this get away?

Ramsey, who was really on it, responded, "That was an unsecured cash loss, Terrie. Where's the loss here?" There was dead silence on the other end of the phone for about 10 seconds. Bowers came back with some weak analogy on the government's part that the indictment is based on the amount I intended to defraud the bank out of, which was $121,000 (the actual amount of my mortgage). Ramsey then said, "Terrie, explain to me how there's fraud if nothing has been lost. You had the man's house for Christ sake. No money went in his pocket. His family lived in the house. He made payments for five years, until he separated from his wife. He stops making payments, you take the house back. His equity more than covers the debt. What are we talking about here?"

Bowers, clearly exacerbated at this point said, "Bob, I don't want to argue this case on the phone. He lied to get the house, and was in a position to influence the loan decision to his own self benefit."

Ramsey said, "OK, charge him with aiding and abetting. You've hit him with the false statement count a few times. This whole case stems on your major count. Just because a man's domestic circumstance changes, doesn't mean he intended to defraud the bank. Terrie, we can resolve this thing, if you drop the bank fraud charge."

Bowers told Ramsey the same thing he told Frank Sanes and me, prior to the indictment--that my plea bargain would have to include the major count. Ramsey ended the conversation with "I guess we'll see ya in court then." Bowers concurred and that was the end of the conversation. Ramsey surmised from this brief conversation that if this was all the government had to come with, we'd win on the bank fraud count, and argue the relevance of materiality on the false documents. At this point, we stood a good chance of coming up outta this thing. What we had to deal with next was the court appearance.

My appearance in court was a news item. I met Ramsey at his office. We drove over together. We rushed past the press gathered on the steps of the federal courthouse. In my appearance before a federal magistrate, I was formally charged and told that upon selection of my judge, I would be arraigned and allowed to submit a plea of guilty, or not guilty. Then my attorney, the prosecutor, Schetina, and I went to the U.S. clerk's office to participate in a process, that I'll never forget in all of my life--the selection of the federal judge that would hear my case.

* * *

While I was first vice President of the Los Angeles NAACP, I was one of the co-chairpersons for a regionwide coalition to reject the nomination of former federal Appellate Court Judge Robert Bork's nomination to the Supreme Court. The national move to reject the nomination of Bork was one of the most organized, inclusive efforts that I'd ever worked on in my life. This project demonstrated to me, firsthand, that Blacks, browns, Asians, whites, gays, handicapped and women can work together for the common good, when they have a common objective or a common cause. Any and everybody who had ever been considered disadvantaged or underprivileged, had good reason to fear the doctrine of Robert Bork. The interpretation of Bork's judicial philosophy on constitutional law went past race, creed and color. It went to the issue of classism in America. Even labor unions saw where a mindset like Bork's could take us. It was the only time I had ever witnessed a unilateral concern for rights and freedoms of all people of color. For a Supreme Court candidate to come forth and advance the rights of the privileged was outrageous. It was one of the most effective "people movements" in this country's history.

Robert Bork was considered the father of the theory called "Original Intent." The Original Intent theory was the interpretation of the United States Constitution reduced to its fundamental context, where law would be interpreted "as the framers of the constitution originally intended." American society, for the most part, had silently acknowledged the wrongs of racism (though there has never been a public apology and/or repentance) and it had pretty much recanted overt discrimination (covert discrimination never ceased, however). Now, someone was nominated for appointment to the Supreme Court whose philosophy was "forget what is right and just, enforce the wicked and unjust intent of the constitutional framers. The devil was getting ready to take a seat on this society's highest legal authority where judgment sets the law. This was serious.

This theory actually caused a movement throughout the country, spurned by President Ronald Reagan's wish to "return to yesterday, when things were simple, and life was peaceful and the American people ran the government." Reagan's move for less government bureaucracy promoted constitutional fundamentalism, and Robert Bork's theory of "Original Intent" played right into Reagan's push to return government to the people and return history to the activities of the past. Only they went way back into the past, all the way to the start of this country's governance. Now when you look at who was at the table when the Constitution was framed, the only ones there were white male aristocrats (land owners, slave owners, scholars, governors and military leaders). There were no poor whites, no women and no people of color. People were saying why would anybody want to return to a time when nobody, but rich white men had any rights. Rich white men reinforcing their position was what the Reagan-Bush administrations were all about. Some political pundits perceived that Reagan was now trying to institutionalize constitutional fundamentalism (in effect, racism) by politicizing the federal courts. He had already begun appointing judges that had conservative and ultraconservative mindsets consistent with his political leanings. But now, Reagan was going for the knockout. The move that would ensure a return to the customs, mores and values of yesterday's social culture. In nominating men who shared his social views, he could execute legislated law of the land, and then have his court appointments validate it, if challenged.

To hold favor with Reagan, jurists and potential jurists had to "get like" Bork, if they wanted the President's nod. Conversely, you suddenly saw a host of "baby Borks" getting nominated and confirmed into the federal court system. The organization and opposition created by the focus on Robert Bork was so effectively intense that he was rejected in the Senate confirmation process. However, the doctrine of Bork, the constitutional fundamentalism that "Original Intent" represented was effectively seeded throughout the federal court system at the lower levels. While Robert Bork didn't make it, many "sons and daughters of Bork" did (Reagan appointed 47% of all the sitting federal judges by the end of his term). And now the federal jurists deck was stacked with "Baby Borkers" who pop up like trump cards in a whist game, cutting every other card that tries to make a play for fairness and inclusion. In cases where one's criminal fate must be decided by constitutional fundamentalism, the class and color will come into play. Knowing their attitudes toward slaves and commoners, all you have to say to yourself is: "How would the framers of the Constitution try your case?

My experience with the politics and motivations behind the Bork nomination rejection gave me significant insight, into the adverse impact of the process in which I was about to partake. In the Black advocacy community, we often use metaphors to demonstrate how adversely racism has tilted the scales of justice and equity. We often choose to use a metaphoric analogy that "the deck was stacked against Blacks," in such an instance. Well, when you go to federal court to select a judge, it's no longer a metaphor to say "the deck is stacked." It's real, inasmuch as all the judges' names are placed in a stack of 3 x 5 index cards. In Los Angeles, at the time, there were 26 active federal judges. At the beginning of each day, the deck of cards are shuffled and bound. To determine a case assignment, the federal prosecutor and the defense attorney (sometimes with the defendant) go to the clerk's office, where he takes out the deck of cards, pulls the card on the top of the deck from underneath the binding that holds the cards. That's your judge in the case. The next case that comes up goes through the same process and so on, until all 26 judges have been assigned a case. Then the deck is reshuffled and the process starts over.

In the Los Angeles federal courthouse, there were no less than a dozen federal judges, who had been appointed during the Reagan-Bush administrations, a scary proposition in and of itself. However, out of that number were about five judges that, according to Ramsey, we did not want to get under any circumstance. These were the arch-Conservatives, and even many of the prosecutors and defense attorneys doubted their ability to be fair when it came to certain cases. Certain cases like immigration crimes, drug crimes and yes, crimes involving Black males, set some of these judges dead off.

No matter how big or small, these offenders had no business in their courtroom, as far as these jurists were concerned. They weren't around the table when the original framers sat down to draft this thing. So the mindset was that the law of fairness, equity and justice didn't apply to them. Yes, these were L.A.'s "baby Borkers," and they were in the deck like jokers waiting to pop up. Schetina knew this and was rubbing his hands together hoping for the luck of the draw.

The clerk pulled the card. "The Honorable William D. Keller," the clerk said. I saw Ramsey give a slight wince. Schetina damn near jumped for joy.

"We definitely must have got a joker," I thought to myself. The lawyers shook hands, and everybody left. "How'd we do?" I asked Ramsey.

"We could have done worse," Bob responded.

"How worse?" I asked.

"Well, of the three that we didn't want, we got one of 'em. But the other two are worse than him," Ramsey said. "Keller has a thing about drugs and guns, which don't apply to you, but he's also known to have racial tendencies."

"So, he's a racist?" I asked.

"Some people think so," Bob said.

"What do you think?" I asked. Ramsey shrugged his shoulders. I didn't take that to mean "no." Time would prove I was right.

While Ramsey started working on a defense for my case, I tried to add some normality back to my life with two things in mind: trying to explain my innocence (and guilt to an extent) and to raise money for my defense. To try a case in federal court (at least in Los Angeles), the retainer amount is $25,000, and it goes up from there. If you go to trial, it would be more like $60,000. I gave Ramsey $5,000 to start and $10,000 two weeks later. But he made it clear he'd need more than that, if we went to trial, or else he'd have to substitute off the case. Even though this was a very high-profile case that would bring him more publicity than he could buy, it was clearly about the money for him (and his partner). I could appreciate that given all the free services clients tried to get from me. Eventually, you gotta pay the bills, and that's how Ramsey saw it.

In the meantime, I was given my first community assignment in the Nation of Islam, as the project coordinator for the "Stop The Killing II" appearance of The Honorable Louis Farrakhan, in February. I had been in constant communication with Minister Wazir and Capt. Wali since my charges hit. They both said they know of the impending situation before it hit and understood why it had happened. They felt it was best that I "go to work," at that time, so as not to focus on some of the negativity surrounding my case. My charge was to head the mosque outreach organization. Friends for the Benefit of Economic Unity brought together an effective community coalition that would help sell out the 16,000-seat Los Angeles Sports Arena.

1990 started out as a very repressive year, in terms of the affairs in the community. It just appeared that so many things were going backward, with regards to advancing issues for the community. Tom Bradley was still under attack from a federal investigation on influence peddling, so activity out of the mayor's office was slow. None of the civil rights organizations were really talking about anything. The gang peace treaty that we had helped negotiate wasn't getting any support. And the police, both L.A.P.D. and L.A. County Sheriff's Department were damn near doing what they wanted to do. In fact, it was the misconduct of law enforcement that would wake up Los Angeles and its sleeping Negro leadership.

On the early morning of January 3, five members of the Fruit of Islam (FOI), the Nation of Islam's men's organization were out returning from their 5 a.m. karate training when they were stopped by the

L.A.P.D. The official reason for the stop was because of a broken taillight. However, after all the FOI members were out of the car, it became obvious that it was one of the L.A.P.D.'s harassment moves. The L.A.P.D. had this policy of making Blacks "get on their knees" with their hands behind their heads. If it wasn't this move, it was making you lie face down in the street. This was the most publicly humiliating process one could endure. The police didn't care who you were, and it was the biggest law enforcement complaint I received as an official of the NAACP. "I was made to lie face down in the street for a simple traffic violation." Doctors, lawyers, professors, women--the L.A.P.D. didn't care. It was either on your knees, or down on the ground.

That night, the L.A.P.D. gave the order, "Down on your knees." The FOI members responded, "No, sir,"

The police asked the men, "Are you resisting arrest?"

The FOI members, who are taught to obey the law, as long as it does not conflict with God's law, again responded, "No, sir."

The police then responded, "Well, we gave you an order. Get down on your knees."

One of the FOI responded, "I cannot do that, sir."

The officer responded, "Why?"

"Because it is not the law, sir," said the FOI member, who was correct in that response.

The officer's order was not the law. It was a selective procedure an officer could choose to use to enforce the law, if it was necessary. In this instance, it wasn't necessary. In fact, in most instances, in which they used it, it wasn't necessary, but a procedure that had become common abuse practice in the Black community, regardless of who you were. In Latino communities where gang conflicts were a problem, they were also victims of this practice. When it became obvious that the five FOI members were not going to obey the order, one of the officers pulled his baton to try to make them comply. The officer swung the baton and missed. One of the FOI members caught his arm and broke it. The other officer ran and called for backup. Within five minutes, there were no less than 12 police officers trying to subdue five FOI members. A fight ensued. When the fight was over, a half dozen officers had to be hospitalized and treated for injuries, including a couple broken arms, a broken leg, broken ribs and a busted lip. One of the FOI members suffered a broken limb from a baton blow. But when it was all said and done, it was a public relations nightmare for the L.A.P.D. Even the *L.A. Times*, as pro-police as they tend to write, couldn't clean this up. The L.A.P.D., by damn near every account, got their ass whipped that night. They were the laughing stock of the city and probably the law enforcement community, particularly the Sheriff's Department, who competes with the L.A.P.D. over who can be the most brutal. The community talk was that they were glad somebody finally stood up to the L.A.P.D. The Negro leadership was suspiciously quiet over the whole issue. Three weeks later, almost to the day, the Los Angeles County Sheriff's would engage in an ambush that would shock the city and be a significant turning point in the Nation of Islam.

On January 23, 1990, another encounter with law enforcement occurred, this time with the Los Angeles County Sheriff's. Some young FOI brothers were returning to the FOI house in the Athens area of Los Angeles. Athens is a little segment of the county, between L.A. and Inglewood patrolled by the Sheriff's Department. It had been discussed on several occasions that, because of the conflict with the L.A.P.D. three weeks earlier, sheriffs had been camping out around the corner from the house. The concern was that sheriffs were watching the "comings and goings" of the men too closely to be coincidental. The thought was that an ambush was in the making. Sure enough, that evening, the sheriffs pulled over some brothers, just as they pulled up to the house. The driver of the car was a young, 18-year-old FOI member named David Hartley, a processing brother. The sheriff claimed Hartley was speeding, and demanded the brothers out of the car. Upon witnessing the sheriffs stop Hartley, several FOI members came out of the house to observe the procedure. In Los Angeles, or any other city for that matter, it is not against the law (contrary to popular belief) to observe so-called peace officers carrying out the law. Some laws require you to stand 10 feet away, others 25 feet. If the scene is dangerous to the safety of the public or requires space for the officers to carry out their duty, they can barricade the scene so you don't interfere or stand so close that you put the officer or yourself in harm's way. However, in most cases, you can observe the law being enforced.

One FOI member, Oliver X Beasley, asked the officers what the problem was. The sheriffs, in the midst of jacking up Hartley against the car, ordered Beasley and the other FOI members to go back into the house, which was an inappropriate order. "Stand back!" would be the appropriate order in that situation. Hartley told the officer, "I cannot do that," according to witnesses, "he's one of our soldiers." At that time, again according to witnesses, the sheriff moved to draw his gun on Beasley. He was immediately disarmed and beat up. The other deputy also tried to pull his gun and was disarmed. He was taking an ass-whipping when he pulled a second gun while on the ground and fired shots into the crowd, hitting Hartley in the back. Meanwhile, Beasley had knocked the first deputy to the ground, picked up his gun and tried to hand it back to him. "All this isn't necessary; let's just keep this situation under control," he was heard to have said.

The first deputy, coming to the aid of his partner, approached Beasley from the rear. He saw him bending over his partner on the ground. As he ran up on Beasley, the deputy on the ground said, "He's got my gun, shoot him." Before Beasley could react, he was shot in the back of the head. It was virtually an execution-style killing of a man trying to defuse the situation. Of course, this wasn't the account that was reported in the papers.

There was a buzzing in the streets unlike any that had been seen since the confrontation that took place between Marquette Frye and the L.A.P.D. just prior to the Watts riots in 1965. It was as cold a killing by a law enforcement agency as the city had seen in awhile since Eula Love (the woman who was shot by the L.A.P.D. for wielding a knife at police officers after refusing to allow her gas to be shut off). There's a saying that "three strikes and you're out" (in fact, it would later become law in California). Well, during these period of social compromise in Los Angeles, Black leadership and law enforcement had been given five strikes. Outrageous social travesties of this sort (crimes) against the Los Angeles Black community would occur five times in a two-year period. Of the five strikes that the Black community in Los Angeles would suffer on its way to a second rebellion, the killing of Oliver X Beasley was the first. The others, in succession, being the Latasha Harlins killing, the probationary freeing of Soon Ja Du (Harlin's killer), the beating of Rodney King and the first verdicts that freed the cops that beat Rodney King. However, both law enforcement agencies (L.A.P.D. and County Sheriff's) and the Negro leadership thought the people would take to the streets on this one. Everybody was scurrying to meet with Mosque #27 officials. The community was expressing support and outrage and the police and Negro leadership were trying to defuse any response or retaliation. To add insult to injury, the district attorney's office had charged David Hartley with counts of resisting arrest and assault on a law enforcement officer.

This was a common practice of law enforcement in L.A. County, particularly when the LAPD or the L.A. County Sheriff's department were involved. When they were in the wrong, they would charge you. It was a leverage point to minimize liability against the department. Sort of a "we'll drop our charges if you drop yours" kinda thing. Only most of the time, the police didn't have a basis to charge and they didn't drop all of their charges. They just made 'em, then trumped 'em up. And it put the victim at a serious disadvantage. On top of that, the DA was holding Hartley and others without bail, which only made community sentiment more hostile. The temperament of the community was such that it was ready to respond in kind. The police, of course, was watching the movement of the Nation. Some in the community were trying to force the issue by seeking to provoke the situation even more. "What the Muslims gonna do?" "I know the Muslims ain't gon' take this," were the whispers in the streets.

It really proved to be a period of great restraint, not just for the Nation of Islam, but for the whole Muslim community. The Black community has no idea of the power of Islam, in terms of its ability to organize and protect its community. The total Islamic community responded to the killing of Oliver Beasley. In Los Angeles, there had been a deep and prolonged division in the ranks of the Muslim community between Warith Deen Muhammad's World Community of Islam in the West (*formerly the American Muslim Mission, formerly the Nation of Islam inherited from The Most Honorable Elijah Muhammad himself) and the reborn Lost-Found Nation of Islam in the West as taught by The Most Honorable Elijah Muhammad under the leadership and guidance of The Honorable Minister Louis Farrakhan. The division, along the lines of philosophical thought regarding orthodox Islamic teachings, had caused the two communities to operate pretty much separate from each other since the rebirth of the Nation of Islam in 1977. Since that rebirth took place in Los Angeles, there appeared to be some added hostility on the part of the world community believers. However, none of that hostility was apparent upon the news of Oliver Beasley's murder. There were two "call out" meetings held to address the issue of Beasley's death. On both occasions, the believers of World Community joined Muhammad Mosque #27 and believers (Muslims) of the surrounding Southern California area. Emotions were high and the spirit of love and unity were evident. It reminded one of a family feud being mended in crisis. No matter how big the fight, family--real family, come together in times of crisis.

The overwhelming sentiment on both occasions expressed by many of those in attendance was that they hadn't seen this many Muslims in Los Angeles since "prior to '75." 1975 was when The Most

Honorable Elijah Muhammad was last among us in physical form. After his departure, the Nation of Islam fell until Minister Farrakhan stood up to rebuild the work of the Honorable Elijah Muhammad in 1977. This crisis in 1990, however, was especially emotional for many of the "prior to '75" believers, many of whom were involved (or were around) on April 27, 1962. On this date, a day of infamy for the Nation of Islam, the Los Angeles Police Department attacked the Mosque (then called the Temple), shot several believers including William Muhammad, who is confined to a wheelchair and lives in Los Angeles. The most vicious casualty of this attack was the cold-blooded murder of Ronald T.X. Stokes. Stokes, according to all firsthand accounts (except those of the police and the papers), was shot and killed while his hands were raised. He didn't even have a weapon. Many of the older believers recall that day like it was yesterday and the comparisons to the murder of Beasley were startling. They also remember how the community rallied around the Muslim cause as a result of Stokes' death.

Within a year of Stokes' death, Black Los Angeles elected its three public officials in city and state government. Those elected would go on to change the politics of the city state and nation. Those officials were Mervyn Dymally, (to the California Assembly), Tom Bradley, (to the L.A. City Council), and Gil Lindsey, (to the L.A. City Council). Dymally would later become the first Black lieutenant governor and later congressman. Bradley became L.A.'s first Black (and longest serving) mayor. Lindsey became L.A.'s longest sitting councilman. All were thrust into public office by the power of Muhammad and a stand for righteousness. But for Blacks in L.A. to progress, somebody had to die and Muhammad's man, Ronald T.X. Stokes was that man. It also represented a turning point for the Nation, which grew in leaps and bounds from that point. The older believers remembered that and relived much of it on this occasion. With many of the Negro leadership now jumping to the front of the issue, it was like "history repeating itself." Many said, "But they also remembered what they said in '62-- that not another Muslim would ever be killed by the police again. Never." Many of them remembered that pledge and were out on this occasion to show solidarity for what we all now had in common, being Muslims under attack in America who were brought into the knowledge of self by the same divine leader, teacher and guide, The Most Honorable Elijah Muhammad. It was as moving a tribute as the messenger could ever hope for.

The community leadership called for a solidarity rally of its own, to publicly stand with the Nation of Islam. It was to be held at First AME (of course), which virtually assured that a segment of the ecumenical leadership would not show up. And they didn't, but it didn't matter much. Those who did attend represented a cross section of the community. Everybody wanted to know, "What was Farrakhan saying about this? What was Farrakhan going to do about this? Is Farrakhan even coming?" Minister Farrakhan sent his national assistant, Khalid Muhammad, to advance the NOI's position on the issue and to keynote the rally. There were over 1,000 persons in attendance. The lineup included most of the Black elected officials including newly elected Congresswoman Maxine Waters, and all of the major civil rights organizations and key grassroots and ecumenical organizations. Rev. Chip Murray and Brotherhood Crusade President Danny Bakewell facilitated the program. Danny introduced the speakers and Chip stood by the podium microphone to cue the speakers (when they spoke too long). Then the long litany of speakers came forth. Each more impassioned than the prior. After about 10 speakers, Danny brought up L.A. NAACP branch President Joe Duff, who was received by a very light applause. When I say light, I mean about five claps, then silence. Joe started speaking in his little "white boy" mimic and the crowd went dead. He tried to get impassioned with his presentation, publicly telling Gates and the L.A.P.D. that "if you keep going like you are, you're gonna go down, man." The crowd was dead silent. Some of the leaders behind him were looking at each other like "What the hell is he talking about?" Minister Wazir looked over at me, smiled and shook his head. I just shrugged my shoulders like I hadn't heard that since the '70s either. Joe winded down, got his five claps and got on off.

Danny introduced me as head of the Friends for the Benefit of Economic Unity, the sponsoring organization for the "Stop the Killing II" event. I received a respectable round of applause. I opened my speech for the first time ever with,

"IN THE NAME OF ALLAH, THE BENEFICENT, THE MOST MERCIFUL. I BEAR WITNESS THAT THERE IS NO GOD BUT ALLAH. AND I BEAR WITNESS THAT MUHAMMAD IS THE MESSENGER OF ALLAH."

At that point, my eyes fixed on Minister Charles X, the assistant minister of Muhammad Mosque #27. He thrust his fist in the air and shouted, "Allah Akbar (God is the Greatest)," knowing what I had just done. Chip, who was standing on my right holding the podium microphone (for speakers that got too longwinded) whispered to me out the side of his mouth, "Oh Anthony, my son." He also knew what I had just done. If there was any question (which there was) of where I was spiritually, it was clarified, at that moment, in front of the Los Angeles activist community, leaders and followers, supporters and hypocrites, believers and non-believers alike. I had just made my public Shahadah (declaration of faith). It was publicly official and the community heard it from my own mouth. I was now a member of the Nation of Islam. Casting an acknowledging glance in the direction of Chip, I ignored his comment and spoke on. I criticized the L.A.P.D. for historical acts of criminality against the Black community. I told the community that this day (the killing of Oliver X Beasley) would go down in L.A. history, as did April 27, 1962, as a day of infamy. The crowd rose to their feet. I told the crowd that the only way to stop the L.A.P.D. and the L.A. County Sheriff's Dept. is to stop and watch them, because anytime they stop somebody in our community it's not to protect us but to "serve us," meaning beat us. I asked how many people planned to attend the "Stop The Killing II" featuring the message of The Honorable Minister Louis Farrakhan. The whole house raised their hands. I then asked who didn't have their tickets. About 100 people raised their hands. The brothers (FOI) moved to get them their tickets. I closed out by asking the community to turn out in tribute to the life of Oliver X Beasley and the community's commitment to stop killing itself. As I left the podium to a strong round of applause, Congresswoman Maxine Waters winked at me and smiled. I winked back. Khalid hugged me and whispered in my ear, "Excellent presentation, Bro. Anthony. Welcome to the ranks."

Minister Wazir hugged me, and said, "It was like night and day, brother. You never can go back to being colored."

I said, "No, Sir. You're right." What Wazir was talking about was the obvious contrast between Joe and me, which was adequately demonstrated with us speaking one behind the other. The contrast was quite clear in a public forum (we later mused that Danny had done that on purpose) and became real plain to the community and the leadership. It was clear that the L.A. branch's best leadership wasn't in the President's seat right now. Nor was I in their Negro ranks any longer. I had been elevated to a higher rank, a more serious rank of community salvation, and I was proud of that.

Khalid closed out the rally with a fiery presentation that kept the people on their feet, promising that when Farrakhan comes to L.A., he would bring a message of hope and salvation for our people. A few days later, over 2,000 people attended the funeral of Oliver X Beasley. The Honorable Minister Louis Farrakhan made a last-minute decision to appear in Los Angeles, under very tight security, to deliver the eulogy. A week later, over 19,000 people packed the Los Angeles Memorial Sports Arena to witness Minister Farrakhan's scheduled appearance. With a 15 foot picture of Oliver X Beasley as a backdrop, the minister was very serene in his lecture. "Respect for Life." In a fitting tribute to Bro. Oliver, Minister Farrakhan acknowledged that Beasley was the first Muslim to lose his life in a war-like confrontation, in the second resurrection of the work of The Honorable Elijah Muhammad. He said that Beasley was a martyr, and a sign to the living that we must stop killing each other, lest we become easy prey for our enemy.

Almost lost in the occurrence of events surrounding Brother Oliver's death was the peaceful attendance of almost 2,000 Crips and Bloods (separated, at that time) at the event. This, at the time, was almost unheard of. Much of the impact was lost due to the emotional focus on police attacks on Muslims, twice in a period of a month. With both police abuse and gang violence at its zenith, Los Angeles was nothing but a ticking time bomb, and the Negro leadership didn't have a clue.

* * *

After the "Stop The Killing" event, I pretty much reverted to being a recluse in order to concentrate on my upcoming trial. Though I was somewhat "high profile" during the planning of the event, I rarely went out beyond personal friends or the Mosque. I went out four times during the entire months of January and February.

The trial preparation was going excellent. Ramsey felt good about the fact that there was nothing in the indictment to substantiate willful intent to defraud. This was backed up by the civil suit arbitration on the same claims raised by Founders in its counter-suit. Generally, criminal cases are even harder to prove than civil cases. Bob felt that the most a jury would find me guilty of was using poor judgment, but not of acting out of any sense of criminality, particularly since this was an isolated incident. This was the weakness in the prosecutor's case and we'd go to trial all day on this. However, Schetina was looking to go in with more, which confirmed our suspicion that his case was weak. Ramsey, as a former U.S. prosecutor, understood the mindset of the government. If his case was so solid, he'd go with what he had instead of trying to bring more charges a couple weeks before trial, Ramsey reasoned. Schetina had shifted the focus of his case for several reasons: one, he couldn't show criminal intent on my loan alone. He had to show more than a singular involvement to justify an intent to defraud, and two, he couldn't show a loss on a collateral loan. No loss, no fraud, regardless of what he wanted to say about some figurative loss and, thirdly, the government couldn't take a chance on going to trial and having the issue of selective prosecution being raised (which was the case and a proposed strategy in our defense) on such a weak case. The whole case could be thrown out then. On a high profile case, like the media had made this one, it would be a major embarrassment to the U.S. government. A case for involvement beyond my personal loan, now made all the difference in the world to the government. They were calling around to see who would "pop up," if they beat the bushes hard enough. They called "known associates" (as they put it) of mine, including my estranged wife, whom they had hoped to use against me. She didn't give them any satisfaction. I was proud of her, and will always respect her for that. But one friend I will love even more was the one they came after the hardest, my friend and ex-business partner, Janet Caldwell.

The whole banking and finance industry is about relationships. White folk make loans to their friends, to their family, to their associates, and whomever else they feel like making loans to. Sometimes they can pay them back, if they want to, and sometimes they don't, and that's fine, too. That's how they play the game, as demonstrated in the Neil Bush situation. He never even did a day in court, much less jail. Many of the privileged ever do. The government was trying to say that because Janet was a friend, she didn't merit the loan. This just wasn't true. The U.S. attorney was now trying to use that loan to prove "insider abuse" beyond my personal transaction. That was the real reason behind them pressing the Caldwell loan. My position on that was, and still is, given the chance to make Janet that loan 100 more times, I'd give it to her every time, without remorse. Particularly, since it qualified for CRA consideration, and given that most of the major banks were redlining the hell out of the Black community on business loans (as hindsight has revealed). And I'd make it not only for those reasons, but because it was what I wanted to do for a community businessperson who happened to be a friend, period.

In trying to pin me into the Caldwell loan, the government investigated the documents in her loan file. When they pulled up her tax return, the government noticed that she hadn't taken partial deductions for a couple of properties we owned jointly. We'd often take whole deductions on some of the properties because it made accounting easier. She actually claimed more money than she really received so they couldn't claim she evaded taxes. But because she didn't wholly own the property, the government claimed Janet had also filed a false tax return. They also noted that two digits in her social security number had been transposed. The bottom line was that the U.S. attorney was holding this information over Janet's head. In a Blackmail move, the government had one request, and based on how Janet responded to that request, would dictate the government's decision to prosecute her. The request was that Janet say that "Anthony Essex prepared her tax return." That's all she had to do and they'd forget about "the little errors" in her tax return.

Janet was a 50-year-old woman, accomplished in her trade, respected in her social circles, and at a very comfortable period in her life. The adverse publicity of having her name tied to my case was already an embarrassing disruption in her life. Now the government was threatening her with jail, if she didn't lie. There were some real stark realities to the predicament Janet was in, as well as what those realities meant for me. If Janet agreed and testified, she could walk free. In fact, her attorney advised that she do it. For me, it definitely meant a bank fraud count and the possibility of all the other charges snowballing. My chances went from the likelihood of an acquittal of misdemeanor charges, to a minimum of seven to 10 years in jail, when they finished this case. My friendship with Janet had already become strained over the resolution of our business affairs. The reality was she didn't owe me anything.

In those two weeks, the government turned up the heat on Janet. I discussed this issue with my closest friends, who were raising money for my legal defense. Nearly a dozen people said this decision didn't look good for me. In reality, most of them said that if they were in the same position, they would save themselves. And before I could get upset, most all of them said, "Anthony, what would you do if this wasn't you we were taking about?" At that point, I couldn't truly say what I would do including saving myself. We all can be "as Black as we want to be" and talk about what "we would do" and "what Blacks ought to do," but when the situation is placed on us, we all do what we "have to do." In that sense, Janet had a right to think of herself first and to do what she "had to do." I couldn't blame her for any decision she made, be it true or not to what actually happened. She wasn't coming forth on her own volition. The government was pressing her and, given what it had up its sleeve, it made all the difference.

However, for the second time in 12 months, the issue of friendship loyalties had come into play. If I learned anything of the past few years, it was how shallow friendships can be, and how most perceived friendships are just associations of success. If the success is called into question, so are the friendships. Friendships are tested in degrees (or at various levels). A little mudslinging in a branch election is one thing. A federal indictment was another. Then there were those who never were friends but envious of success and used both situations to justify their own forms of character assassination. In time, anyone suffering in the midst of a public controversy can, very quickly, understand the true meaning of friends. You also find out the differences between supporters, friends and acquaintances. It was during this time that I found out who my friends really were. While the government was working on Janet, we were preparing for trial. This meant more money, at least another $25,000. Floyd Frazier organized a legal defense fund to raise money on my behalf. He planned a fund-raiser three days before I was to go to trial. The three weeks of organizing this affair was probably the most personally painful of this whole experience. I thought I had pretty much purged my friendship box during the NAACP election. I wasn't even close.

While putting the committee together for the fund-raiser invitation, it was most difficult getting people to return Floyd's call. He requested that I get involved, which I was very hesitant to do. Many came forth once I talked to them. There were many others that were conveniently unavailable. I know how that could be, but I refused to think the worst. However, to my dismay, several people whom I considered close friends refused to allow me to put their names on the invitation. Only five elected officials came forth (the late Gil Lindsey, State Senator Diane Watson, former Councilman Bob Farrell, Inglewood Councilmen Danny Tabor and Garland Hardeman). A few of the major ecumenical leadership came forth, including Chip Murray. About the only reason Chip and I are able to talk today is because he did that for me. (He also gave me $1,000 through a church offering.) Even with our differences, I will always be grateful for his participation.

In all, 54 people came forth in time for the invitation printing. Another 12 came after we went to press. A respectable showing, but much less than I expected. However, the event was sparsely attended. Roughly 40 or so people were there at the peak of the event. Another two dozen or so "passed through," during the course of the day; all told, maybe 100 people came through. Many who came, came more out of curiosity rather than support, peeking around to see who was there and giving condolences as if they expected the worst. It occurred to me, at that moment, that I had lost the battle with the media.

It had won, in terms of what the perception and extent of my guilt and innocence was. It had effectively convicted me, before my fate could be determined at the trial. It was in the faces and voices of the people who were there. I sensed that some felt almost obligated to be there. I drew on the vibes of those who were there out of sincerity, and during the acknowledgment period I gave the speech of my life. I talked about what this was really all about, an attack that originated out of Black betrayal. I talked about how the government basically carried out what was sent to them and that systemic racism carried out the rest. I talked about the media manipulation, the judicial manipulation, the overcharges, the pending charges and that in spite of what was going on, I guaranteed them that I would never, ever plead guilty to bank fraud. Never.

My talk went over very well. Afterward, we raised almost $30,000 in donations and pledges (of which $19,000 was actually collected on). I felt good about what had just happened--that such a commitment could be raised from such a relatively small group of people. However, Floyd held some of the frustrations that I expressed earlier regarding the people who didn't show. Some of whom were very conspicuous by their absence. There were two persons in particular who Floyd called "the two Marks." He was talking about Mark Whitlock and Mark Ridley-Thomas, who Floyd thought were my friends. At that point, I didn't consider Mark Whitlock a friend. I did consider Mark Ridley-Thomas a good friend and perceived him as sincere. He sent me a note after the NAACP election, telling me to move on with my life and do what's best for my family. I really appreciated him for that. The card was signed "your friend, Mark." I believed Mark to be principled in our relationship, though he curiously didn't return my call to lend his name to the fund-raiser invitation. I really didn't give it a second thought, but it really troubled Floyd, who had seen Mark a few days prior to the event, and got a commitment out of him to come.

He called Mark the day after. I don't know what he said to Mark, but Ridley-Thomas ended up calling me. Mark was real tentative and deliberate in his speech, like he was trying to choose his words. He apologized for not making the event, and then went into a real generic discussion about how he and Avis (his wife) had always perceived me as an acquaintance who was supportive of him and he wanted to do the same. At that point, I completely blanked out. Acquaintance? Is that what Mark thought of me? As an acquaintance? In the few minutes we were on the phone, I reflected on some of my more intimate experiences with Mark. How we talked on the phone late at night, most every night, for two years, about community and personal issues. I don't do that with acquaintances. I thought about the special gatherings Mark had invited me to: his wife's baby shower, his (first) celebration for receiving his Ph.D.

Those were very close and intimate settings where only Mark's family and friends attended. I don't recall any acquaintances in attendance. I recalled the people surrounding Mark in his decision to run for the Los Angeles Unified School District Board, after Rita Walters (the incumbent and then school board President) recanted on her decision to leave the school to run for the 10th District council seat. Mark was too proud to drop out of the race. I remember Mark sat in my Lakers season seats and for two hours vented how he couldn't be disrespected like this and so on and so on. The discussions we had I don't think he'd have with too many acquaintances. And even though we knew Rita was going to kick his ass (his own polls told him that) because Walters was the second most recognizable name in the community, second to Tom Bradley, we stuck by him. I gave him $350 knowing he was going to lose. The most I'd given a politician, up to that point, was $50. If I'd known I was an acquaintance, he would've gotten just $50 (if that much). I give my money to friends, win or lose.

Now this friend was telling me I had been a "rather supportive acquaintance." This hurt me more than any personal betrayal I had felt, at that point. What Mark was saying was he didn't have the integrity to stand by a friend in trouble. Our friendship was one that lasted as long as was it publicly convenient, but not one that could survive personal tribulation. Once he said that, I didn't even hear the rest of his conversation. He said something about sending me a check. My response was something like, "Uh, yeah, Mark. Whatever. I gotta go." That was the last personal conversation Mark and I had as, what I thought we were, friends. He did send me $100, and I acknowledged his donation, as acquaintances do.

* * *

Four days before the trial a number of events had taken place.

Janet had rejected the government's offer to lie for them. Conversely, they retaliated and hit her with one count of false statement. Furthermore, they had decided to pursue the charges against me associated with her loan, even though they had no proof of my involvement other than alleged guilt by association. The government's premise was if I had looked at Caldwell's taxes, I should have known they were false based on her full claims on properties she half-owned. So what did they do with her current business income and capacity guarantee payment? Absolutely nothing and the government knew it.

The second set of charges were as light as the first set, but it threw the case in a different light. It's called "snowballing" charges. They know they'll get some jurors to think that if the defendant did all of this, then he must be guilty. You have about as much of a chance of coming out of this "not guilty" as you have of stopping a growing, speeding snowball rolling downhill. It's a straight out bum- rush on the government's part. We knew it, too. They were filing charges when they should have been preparing for trial. So they weren't confident with what they had. The second superseding indictment consisted of another count of bank fraud, three more counts of false statement and one count of aiding and abetting. All connected with the Caldwell loan. I wasn't necessarily moved by this, until Ramsey called Bowers and asked why they were still digging. Bowers cited my refusal to cooperate, as the major reason. Also my refusal to accept responsibility for what they said I did (not what I actually did).

In trying to feel him out, Ramsey asked if there would be any more charges.

"Probably," Bowers replied.

"On what?" said Ramsey.

"We're looking at the Margaret Davis loan right now. Charges will probably come from it." Ramsey looked at me.
Since they were on speaker phone, I whispered, "Call him back."

Ramsey said, "Terry can I call you right back. I may have something to offer you."

When Bowers hung up. I told Ramsey, "Cut the best deal you can, without me pleading to bank fraud, if possible. I can't let them come after my mother. She had nothing to do with this. She can't handle that pressure, and I wouldn't let them put her through this. It wouldn't be fair to her, particularly if they decided to charge her.

My mother bought the house with the intention that she'd move in it with my sister, Shawn. When my sister moved out of state, she didn't want the house. Meanwhile, it qualified as owner occupied. The house was eventually sold. It would have been a terrible predicament to put my mother in, and I wasn't going to think of putting her in that situation. That Monday, the day after my fund-raiser, the papers ran the news on the superseding indictment. The day before the trial was to start, they ran the news on the 11th hour plea agreement.

Again, as in the NAACP reprimand, what should have been a victory hit like a bomb. The plea bargain I would agree to did not include either of the major counts of bank fraud. Of the eight remaining counts (seven false statements and one aiding and abetting), I pled to three (which were really one too many). The government had maintained all along that I had to take a major count to plead out. Then they said I'd have to take half of the remaining counts. I didn't do either. I pled to exactly what I did. Then the government made me take one count of the superseding charges, claiming that they couldn't just dismiss them all. It was a stretch, but I could live with it, given the alternative. In exchange for my pleas, they couldn't come after me or my mother criminally, or come after me on any other loan associated with Founders. Furthermore, they expected me to cooperate with the feds on the impending criminal investigation of Peter Dauterive, the President of the bank. If I refused to cooperate, all deals were off. When the plea bargain broke in the paper, only the *Los Angeles Sentinel* reported a fair and balanced account of the facts. Everybody else took it "off the wire," including some Black press. The community "grapevine" wasn't much kinder. The responses ranged from "I was being made an example of" or "I was a scapegoat for Founders' failure" to "I knew he did it" or even that "I sold out and let the community down." And to my surprise, some of my so-called friends and supporters were now helping to fuel the fire. Now that the admission had been made, it was no longer "save Anthony" but "damn Anthony."

While I thought I had won by taking on any charge that wasn't warranted, I had really lost, because both the government and the white press had accomplished their objective, which was to breakdown community trust in me, and then isolate me in the community. The game was over, in the opinion of many. In the best case, all support was effectively neutralized. Nobody was stepping in front of a moving train, now that my admission had tied me to the tracks. It was every man for himself. Good luck, Anthony. Wish I could help you but...

* * *

My sentencing was set for June 29, 1990. Prior to my sentencing, the federal probation department would conduct what was called a pre-sentencing investigation or a PSI report. This report was supposed to give the court some insight on my background and the likelihood of recidivism. The report was supposed to assess my ability (and willingness) to contribute to society and become a productive citizen again. It would document what the community thought about me and merge this data into data compiled regarding the seriousness of my crime, issues that caused the crime to come about and the condition under which the crime occurred (when there are guns and/or drugs involved, etc.). This was all done to come to a determination of what my sentence should be. Given my background, this being my first criminal offense and my community service history and the low severity of the crime (the supposition being no losses in the case), the presumption was that I would receive a sentence that didn't involve incarceration. Almost everybody I talked to thought I would receive either probation, community service or be forced to restitute money. Jail wasn't even a consideration. I talked to over a dozen prosecutors and attorneys and at least six judges, and they told me it would be a probation or community service case, if it were in their courtroom. Up to that point, I really felt that the PSI would come back in my favor.

My friends and I have to smile when I recall this, because they weren't leaving anything to chance. A friend, Sharon Clerkley and her prayer partner, Antonia Nogurea were holding a daily prayer session for me. Floyd, Daryl and Ron were gathering community letters in my support. One friend named Laura DeBats introduced me to her psychic, a very popular woman named Reverend Tooks. Scripture teaches us that God puts people on earth who see into the future. Though I was cynical, I figured it couldn't hurt.

When I went to Rev. Tooks' home, there were four people already waiting. After about an hour, my turn came. She had me come into her kitchen, which I guess was her sanctuary. The room had candles and incense burning all around it and was covered with silky shades to create a dark room effect. The only thing missing was the crystal ball, I thought to myself. I watched the woman go through a ritual to prepare herself while all the time wondering "why am I here?" I could barely contain my cynicism, almost wincing with every motion of her preparation. Finally, after what seemed like an hour, but in reality, was only a few minutes, she took my hand and spoke to me. "You have a very sensitive spirit. Are you some kind of water sign?" I nodded, yes

(Pisces). "I see a lot of writing in your life. Are you a writer, or writing something?"

Having written the first draft of this manuscript, I nodded yes.

She responded, "Whatever you are writing is going to be enormously successful."

I responded, "I hope so."

She replied, "No, it will be."

"What else do you see?" I was becoming somewhat impatient, though this was a very important revelation.

As grateful as I was to hear such a prediction, it wasn't what I was there to hear. I wanted to know if she saw any "bars," as in jail bars, in my future.

She continued. "You're going through a stormy period right now." She could have picked that up in the paper, I thought. "Are you in the midst of some tribulation right now?" she asked.

"You tell me," I responded sarcastically.

"I can't really see what it is, but someone is really praying for you," she said. I winced, looking like, "is this what I'm paying for, prayer talk." She saw the look on my face and said, "I mean that literally. Someone is actually holding a congregational prayer for you, at this very moment."

I looked at my watch. It was five minutes after noon. I looked up and asked, "What else do you see?"

She said, "You are a very calm man, in good health and sound mind. You have a good life ahead of you."

While these revelations were true blessings that most people would love to hear, I was like, "Is that all?" Surely seeming unappreciative, but in reality, unsatisfied, I must have looked real crazy to her. Rev. Tooks looked at me like, "Ain't that enough?"

Finally, she asked, "Is there something specific you want to know?"

I said, "Yes."

"Are you looking for me to tell you something related to a particular event or circumstance you are experiencing?" she asked.

"Yes," I said.

She closed her eyes and squeezed my palms. Keeping her eyes closed, she said, "Are you concerned about your safety?"

"Yes and no," I said. She took a deep breath like she was now becoming exasperated with me. "If your concern is danger, I don't see any."

"Well, what do you see?" I asked.

"I don't see anything that will harm you, or cause you extreme discomfort," she said. Well, it was a stretch but that could have been the answer I was looking for, I thought to myself. "You want to tell me what you're looking to know," she asked.

"I thought you would already know?" I said.

"You're confusing me with a mind-reader. I'm a seer, but no one sees all things but God," she said.

"I'm in a little trouble and I wanted to know if jail bars were in my future," I said candidly.

She said, "So, this is the tribulation you're going through?"

I nodded yes. She closed her eyes again. This time for about two minutes. Then she spoke, "I don't see any jail bars. That's not to say you won't receive any form of punishment, but nothing restrictive like a jail cell. Nothing to that extreme." I breathed a sigh of relief, half-heartedly wanting to believe what she was telling me, but knowing I gave her more help than I should have. Still, I saw this experience as a pleasant form of therapy, but not as a substitute for prayer and faith. As I paid her and prepared to leave, she gave me some oils and several bible verses to read with the instructions to read them upon entering the courthouse on the day of my sentencing. She wanted me to come back to see her, after I had been sentenced. I thanked her for her time and her sincere effort. While she may have thought to the contrary, I wasn't as cynical when I left, as I was when I came. Rev. Tooks was really a nice woman, and I could sense her spirituality was real. This psychic definitely wasn't a fluke. But it was no substitute for faith and prayer.

This was confirmed later that evening when Sharon called to see how my day was, and to recount my experience with the psychic. I relayed the blow-by-blow details of my reading. When I finished, Sharon went on to tell me about her day and how she and her prayer partner prayed for me at lunch today. In my account of the reading, I omitted telling Sharon that part about how Rev. Tooks said "someone was literally praying for me." I asked Sharon about what time that was."

"A few minutes after noon," she said.

"How long did you pray?" I asked.

"About five minutes." I got silent for about a minute. Thinking I had hung up, Sharon asked, "Are you there, Anthony?"

"Yeah, I'm here. Sharon, you won't believe this. During the reading, this woman said that someone was literally praying for me at that very moment. I know it was five after noon because I looked at my watch. What do you think of that?"

Sharon only relayed what I already believed--that God blesses some people with the power to "see."

The PSI investigator was a young, Jewish guy. My sources had told me that he was one of the more fair investigators in the federal probation system. When he came to my apartment, I noticed him looking at all the (Ramses) renderings I had on the wall of Muhammad Ali, Marcus Garvey, Elijah Muhammad, W.E.B. DuBois. I also had two laminated posters: one from Jesse Jackson's 1984 campaign, and one of The Honorable Louis Farrakhan promoting the premiere of P.O.W.E.R., in a 1985 speaking engagement. Minister Farrakhan and Jesse Jackson were public enemy number one and number two, as far as, many in the Jewish community were concerned. I really didn't deal with it at the time, though. We sat in my office. He proceeded to ask me questions about my past, my childhood, my family and my education. I answered directly and non-engagingly. He asked me if I considered my crime serious. I told him yes, to the extent that it was. He asked what I meant. I told him it wasn't as serious as the government was trying to make it. It was wrong but not pre-meditated. I wasn't seeking to defraud the bank. I was seeking to buy a home, and that was the process at the time. He asked would I do it again. I said no. He asked if I had anything else to say. I said, "No, other than I hope this process is truly fair." He didn't respond to my last statement. He just said goodbye.

Waiting for the PSI report was like sitting on pins and needles. To pass the time, I wrote poetry and short stories (which I hope to publish one day). My community interface had been reduced to one meeting a week. The meetings were basically surrounding two upcoming events, both of which were controversial. The first was regarding a visit to Los Angeles by then African National Congress revolutionary and freedom fighter (later President of South Africa) Nelson Mandela, who had been freed from a South African prison after 27 long years of political imprisonment. The release of Nelson Mandela was historic indeed and certainly cause for joy and celebration. However, the extent of the celebration in South Africa was directly related to the extent of sacrifice and suffering made by the South African people.

The effort to keep Mandela's struggle for freedom alive in America was largely a grassroots movement effort, though Martin Luther King, Jr. called out the injustices of apartheid as early as 1960.

It was a most subversive movement until the mid-1980s when South Africa thought it was going to be commercialized with the rest of the European world. Community activists throughout the country began to press elected officials on the South African question. As a result, the nation's conscience level was heightened, and in singular instances, legislation was passed to impose economic sanctions on South Africa, for as long as apartheid existed. However, with the exception of a few elected officials (Maxine Waters on the state level and Congressman Ron Dellums on the federal level), it was the grassroots community that maintained the call for Mandela's release in America. Not the Negro bourgeoisie.

Yet, when the historic moment came, most of the grassroots players were pushed in the background while all the mainstream Negroes, many who did little (or in some cases, none of the work) were running through the community, talkin' bout, "Mandela is free, y'all" while dancing and singing. Hypocrisy at its best.

These Negroes were dancing for Mandela's freedom, while Blacks in America were virtually in the same situation-- a pluralistic society based on race. Hell, in some cases, Mandela was a lot more free than we, here in America, were. His was a physical imprisonment, but his dignity and purpose remained intact. The dignity and purpose of the American Negro has been broken and compromised but, until this day, you can't get them to say shit about it. South Africans were fighting to rid themselves of their "day passes," while the American Negro would rather take the pass, than fight for true equality. Avoiding the real question of freedom in America, all Negro leadership could say then was, "Yeah, but at least Mandela is free. Many of our grassroots people, looking at their silly leadership, were thinking, "Yeah, Mandela is free, but what about me?"

This sentiment would play out a couple years later, when L.A. would go up in smoke. Once Mandela's visit to America was announced and the travel itinerary was formulated and confirmed, it was discovered that Los Angeles would be one of the designated stops. The grassroots people were elated and began organizing for Mandela's arrival.

When the community looked up, the Congresswoman had all of her operatives running the process, headed by a sister named Brenda Shockley. The Los Angeles Coliseum was secured for the public event and the preliminary program had been planned. In the beginning, the affair started looking more like a celebrity TV awards show and rock concert. This infuriated the community who saw this as the commercialization of a fellow revolutionary. Shockley had a hostile community on her hands the first couple of meetings. The people insisted she get Maxine back from Washington to straighten this out or the community would plan its own Mandela activities. Several of the grassroots players had asked me to attend the meetings to help them mediate the situation, if necessary. I appreciated that position. The congresswoman relented to have a greater grassroot involvement, including input and approval of the Coliseum program event. The flavor of the program was culturally centered (as it should have been from the start) and the program went off in front of 50,000, who came to see what a free man looks like.

The same couldn't be said for the other meeting I had been asked to attend, a community advisory committee created by the L.A.P.D. to pacify the Negro leadership. After the Oliver Beasley killing and the Miami riots over a police shooting earlier in the year, Police Chief Daryl Gates decided it was time to interface directly with Black leadership so that he could monitor the temperament of the community. As history will recall, the last time Miami burned (in 1965), Los Angeles was the next to burn. This was Gates' little joke to try to ensure that history didn't repeat itself (at least not immediately). Since Beasley's killing, the department made sure that the Nation of Islam (Muhammad Mosque #27) was included in these community meetings as a part of an effort to improve police-community relations. After the first few meetings, Minister Wazir asked me to attend the meetings saying it was difficult for him to read the sincerity of the Negro leadership. "Since you know most of them Bro. Anthony, you can get a better read on them than I."

My attendance at those meetings clearly antagonized the Negroes, both on the community and the police sides of the table. Mainly because I saw this process for what it actually was--counterfeit. And I said so. Yet, the rest of the Negroes, more than a few, were just glad to be sitting at the table with "the chief," and Gates knew it. So he stroked the Negro leadership, while his deputies massaged department policy to the group's appeasement. Just as the feeling got good I'd usually say something to break up the moment, and they'd have to start over.

All of this came to a head when, in a particular meeting (after I had pleaded on my case), one of the policy modifications the L.A.P.D. was proposing was called into question. In the heat of discussion, Mark

Ridley-Thomas looked at me, huddled with Urban League President John Mack, then asked Gates specifically, "Have the Muslims bought off on that?"

Gates responded, "Yes, we have the Muslims support on that." Well, that response was a half-truth, but within the context that it was asked, it was a straight out lie.

In referencing Muslims, the community (for the most part) is making reference to the Nation of Islam. In this instance, given the most recent conflicts with local law enforcement, they most certainly were making reference to the Nation of Islam. More directly, the Los Angeles Mosque of the Nation of Islam, Muhammad Mosque #27, who had not agreed to support this particular policy modification. Yet, Gates, in his response to the Muslim buy-off question, was referring to another sect of what they call "World Community" Muslims,whom he had brought to the table, when organizing the advisory panel. The representative of that Islamic group, who was in attendance, confirmed that they supported the modification. However, he wasn't speaking for the Nation,who hadn't bought off on anything like what Gates was talking about, at that point. I took issue with Gates' manipulation of this process, and his attempt to misrepresent the position of the total Muslim community, in general, and the Nation of Islam in particular. He, in turn, responded by saying that one of his captains, Noel Cunningham, would probably disagree with me, given the work Cunningham had put in on this project. This was Gates' way of diverting the community's attention away from the real issue, his attempt to gain their support on this policy, by misrepresenting the truth. Aside from the mental gymnastics that were now taking place, I re-emphasized to the group that the Nation of Islam hadn't bought off on this, and we moved to another topic. While the meeting concluded amicably, Gates and his then deputy chief (later L.A.'s Chief of Police, Bernard Parks, who was responsible for assembling the advisory committee), were clearly perturbed. This would be the last meeting I would attend. Parks called Minister Wazir, at the request of the Chief, to ask that I not attend any future meetings because of my pending trouble. He said it made the other members a little uncomfortable, according to Wazir's recollection. Minister Wazir, after defending my case as lightweight and politically motivated, agreed to send someone else. My assessment of this whole process, however, would be vindicated a year later.

* * *

My PSI report was in. Ramsey called me in a rather grim voice. "It's a rather strange report," Bob stated.

"What do you mean?" I asked.

"Well, in terms of representing your background, your community work and your potential for recidivist behavior, I've never seen a better report. This is the kind of report that would normally bring a recommendation for community service or probation," Ramsey said.

"So, what's the problem?" I asked,

"He's recommending jail time," Bob said sternly. After a long pause, I asked,

"How much time?" "18 months," Bob said.

"Damn." "Why'd he say I needed jail time?"

"For deterrence purposes." Bob said.

Deterrence time is what the courts give you to teach you a lesson. It's supposed to make sure you don't do it again. Black people get a lot of deterrence time on first offenses. White boys not only get felony charges reduced to misdemeanor counts on such menial charges, they get probation or community service on first offenses. "What's the likelihood of this recommendation being carried out?" I asked Ramsey.

"Well, the prosecution now writes a memorandum to the court bringing forth their recommendation. We will also write the memo to the courts. The judge is supposed to take all three under submission. Depending on what the U.S. attorney asks for and how effective we can counter it, we have a chance. For Keller to go against the prosecution, we'd have to put together a very substantive packet, but it's not over yet," Bob consoled. He suggested we start gathering letters of support. He would need them in preparation of the sentencing memorandum recommendation he had to put together. We had to get it to the judge, as soon as we could.

I had contacted friends and associates nationwide to write over 200 letters on my behalf, including letters from Fred Rasheed, then the NAACP's Economic Development Director, actress and businesswoman, Marla Gibbs, fraternal groups and civic organizations. Receiving over 200 letters, Bob and I selected 50 of the letters to go in the sentencing report, and had the rest sent directly to the judge. Once Bob wrote his report, all we could do was wait to see what the U.S. attorney wrote and recommended.

The last few weeks before sentencing offered a last chance effort to solicit opinions regarding my predicament. The overwhelming majority of opinions favored my receiving a relatively light sentence, meaning one without jail time. Still I couldn't help but wonder what other factors would come into play. One factor, that I had completely forgotten about, was brought to my attention, just when I began to feel this would be resolved, without a major disruption in my life.

A good friend of mine named Linda Bernard was visiting Los Angeles to attend an American Bar Association Conference. Linda was Executive Director of one of the largest legal aid support organizations in Detroit. She had been following my case, as a friend and advisor, prior to my plea bargain. We hadn't talked since then. Linda asked me to come downtown to "do lunch," when she had a break in the conference. I met her at the downtown Hilton outside of where the conference was convening. We hugged, and she immediately began telling me how great the conference was, who was there, and just as she said, "Thurgood Marshall," he walked by us and nodded (with a flood of people behind him). We were both star struck. One of the first things Linda and I learned we had in common was our hero-like appreciation for Thurgood Marshall. His courage was a civil rights example for me, and his legal brilliance was a mentoring model for her. He was indeed an awesome presence, and we felt it as he passed by us.

On the way to lunch, I brought her up to speed on my case. I told her about the government's blackmail move a day before the trial. I told her about the conditions of the plea bargain, and the results of the PSI report. Linda got very contemplative. After we ordered lunch, I asked, "What do you think?"

"When was your judge appointed to the bench?" She asked quizzically.

"In 1989," I replied.

"So he's a Bush appointee, she stated. "You pleaded to multiple felonies?" I nodded. "You're going to do some time. Not much, if he's fair about it, but he's going to send you to jail," she said buttering her roll and taking a bite.

"How can you be so sure?" I asked.

Linda tilted her head to the side, as if she was saying, "Anthony you should know this." I thought she was going to give me some legal mumbo-jumbo. Her response was very strategic and logical. "He's a Borker," she said.

"What?" I asked puzzled.

Repeating it, she said, "If they're a Reagan or Bush appointee, then they're most likely a 'baby borker.' Borkers follow the intent of the law, to the letter of the law. And they hardly ever go against the hardline recommendations of the government, particularly since they're virtually considered political partners in the courts with similar ideologies. I'd be shocked if a Borker let you off without doing any time. It's not in their make-up." As the server brought our lunch, I just stared at her. While she was right about one thing, I thought to myself, I should have known what to expect from a Borker. "Eat your lunch and let's talk about something else," Linda said. That was the last time we mentioned my case during the meal, but I heard what I needed to hear.

A week before sentencing, we received a copy of the U.S. attorney's sentencing memorandum. Schetina was asking for jail time according to what would be required, if this was a federal guidelines case, which it wasn't. He was asking for between 10 and 18 months, depending on how the judge felt that day. His reasoning and justification played to the sentiment of public outrage surrounding the hundreds of millions of dollars lost in the savings and loans industry, and how inside abusers must be sent a message that S&L crimes will not be tolerated by the courts. Schetina managed to tie the collapse of the whole S&L industry on my home loan. And while Neil Bush and many others cost the industry billions and settled out, with barely a civil fine, the government was asking that this little L.A. activist do jail time even though the industry lost nothing. Schetina maintained that the loss in my case would be the $50,000 (plus interest) on the Caldwell loan, even though there was sufficient equity in the house to cover both loans, totaling $171,000.

Three days before the sentencing, I received a call from Janet, wishing me luck on my sentencing. As I wished her luck (she was to be sentenced a few days after me), we began discussing how I thought my sentencing would go. I mentioned Schetina's memorandum and the loss projected on her loan, as the reason for requesting jail time. Janet immediately said, "What?" As I repeated what I had said, she interrupted. "Anthony, I paid the money."

"What?" I said. I paid $42,000 two days ago. The rest will be paid by my sentencing date," she said.

I asked her to fax copies of those checks to me. Sure enough, two checks in the amount of $35,000 and $7,727.28 had been paid to the lawyers of the Resolution Trust Corporation. Schetina had lied to the court in his report.

I immediately called Ramsey and faxed the checks to him. He

called Schetina who claimed he had no knowledge of the payment. We felt this was bullshit, since he was prosecuting both cases. The payment was what had been negotiated by Janet's attorney, with the hope that the feds wouldn't prosecute, but they did anyway. Janet had now made good on the payment on the advice of counsel to avoid a harsh sentence. Although we thought jail was out of the question for her, she wasn't taking any chances.

Schetina had managed to manipulate the case in a way that caused Janet and me to have different judges, even though we were considered co-defendants. It was highly improper, but this way he wasn't required to share information with each judge on the other co-defendant's activity. Co-defendants should always share the same judge so one judge would know the status of all defendants involved in related cases. Had we had the same judge, Schetina wouldn't have been able to use his "loss argument" in his sentencing memorandum for me. The judge would have also had Janet's sentencing memorandum that would have noted that she had made restitution on a loan on which Schetina was claiming a loss.

The whole purpose of the loss argument was to justify the appropriateness of his jail recommendation. Without a loss, a jail time recommendation was highly inappropriate. Regardless of how Schetina wanted to make a case of what the loss might have been, a "real" loss was what he needed to show, as the basis for even trying this case. Schetina intended to manufacture a loss, by hook or crook, for this law and order judge.

Meanwhile, Ramsey's position was to move forward to deal with the issue of Schetina's misrepresentation at the sentencing. Bob felt we needed to deal with my "air of defiance" in the face of the court. To date, Bob felt I hadn't humbled myself enough to convince Schetina or the PSI investigator that I was truly remorseful for my wrongdoing. Both of them somewhat stated so in their memos to the court. Their perception was that I could and would do it again, given the chance. While such a position couldn't have been further from the truth, there was a bigger issue. The issue of submitting to this wicked and crooked authority, who had manufactured a case against me, and now wanted me to beg off on it, was something I just wasn't going to do.

Ramsey felt that even in my letter to the court, while I had accepted responsibility for what I had done, I hadn't admitted that I had done wrong. His opinion was that my tone in the letter wasn't particularly apologetic. I had a slightly different perspective on this.

While I wasn't particularly proud of what I did, because it was wrong, was it as criminal as the government was trying to make it out to be? This prosecution wasn't about what I supposedly took or caused any damage for, it was about the fact that, in their opinion, I had the mind to do so and the audacity to do so. If I lied every day for the rest of my life, I could never be a bigger liar than the government of the United States of America, nor a bigger liar than those who set up the U.S. government; the immoral aristocrats who built their wealth on the backs and souls of a wicked and immoral (and indefinite, as far as Blacks were concerned) involuntary servitude. And if I stole something every day for the rest of my life, I could never be a bigger thief, with no greater audacity, than the government of the United States of America and the people who control it, who have stolen and cheated the "American public," ever since they set it up and are still stealing today. And whatever crime I may have committed, I'll never be more criminal in the eyes of the world than many of the social behaviors perpetrated by the government (and the immoral social majority) of the United States of America. Anytime a slave was caught running off, he was brought back, tied to the back of a wagon, paraded through the slave quarters and whipped in front of the rest of the slaves, while either apologizing for his wrongdoing or begging the master for forgiveness. The slave's only crime, in a land of criminals, is to want what massa has, and to get it like massa got it. America's true legacy as taught to the American Negro. That was my perspective of what was going on here. They were going do this irregardless of how "humble" or "repentant" they perceived me to be.

My crime, in my opinion, was trying to play a white man's game, the way whites in this country play it. And the way I know they play it, because I've seen 'em play it that way, firsthand. I know that wealth and social rights in America is a game of "do as I say, and not as I do." The rich and powerful make the rules and there's no rule they can't break and remake. My punishment wasn't the whippin' they were proposing by sending me to jail. My punishment was the public parading that took place after they caught me (or after I was handed over to them by my own people). The newspaper articles and the public discussions were the wagon I was tied to and dragged through the streets. The public degradation was the example by which the government demonstrated to the other slaves, what could happen to you if you tried to run away, too.

Now it was whipping time and my attorney wanted me

to humble myself, beg this devil not to "whip me too bad." He also wanted me to apologize for "running away" and say "I'z never do it again." My argument to that was I knew America like he knew America. Blacks could apologize a thousand times and it would never be accepted. That was the bigger principle at issue here.

Because this was never about showing or accepting remorse, why should I play that game? This was about reinforcing dominance and superiority, that a nigger's place is not to be forgotten in this society and when you forget, we will remind you. Pure and simple. The reinforcement of racial superiority and economic dominance is what the return to "original intent" is all about. And Blacks could beg whites from now until forever and it's not going to change their positions. The bottom line is that there is a price to pay for niggahs who play by white man's rules, particularly in the violation of those rules.

My attorney's position was that we needed to make a statement to the court on sentencing day that could possibly change the judge's mind. What Ramsey was telling me was that we were going to have to change Judge Keller's mind to change the recommendation, given the PSI report and the U.S. attorney's memorandum. But subliminally, he was telling me to go in humble, beg this judge and maybe my whippin' will be light. I resented this with all my heart for a few reasons.

First of all, no whippin' that the government could give me could be worse than what it had already done, which was publicly decimate my character and reputation. The whippin' is the momentary pain but his documented reference of his mark against the prosecuted and his public record of it, is the long-lasting one. So in that sense, a whippin' was a whippin'. The damage had already been done.

Second, I really couldn't see it making a difference. I didn't want any part of such pretense. Lastly, I knew the press would manipulate any statement I made public and make it look like I was begging what I now knew to be my enemy. They would then take it to the people and say, "See, he's not the courageous man you thought he was. He begged us not to, but we whipped his ass anyway." My biggest fear was that they would use any humility in my statement as a demonstration of weakness.

Bob thought I was being unreasonably philosophical and totally insensitive to the needs of my family. His position was, "Anthony, you have a young family that needs you. You don't need to be doing three to five years somewhere, because you decided to take a stand. This is not the time to rebel. This judge can run your terms consecutive, and put you away for 15 years, if he wanted to. Don't push him." I asked him if he really thought this would make a difference. He said he thought it would. I told him I didn't think it would, but to show him, I'd write a statement, if he promised me one thing. When he asked what, I stated that he would remember this conversation we had when it was over, and how the media would use my own words against me. He agreed. We proceeded to draft a statement. Twenty-five times. Each time I came with one, Bob would say "Not humble enough. Try again." It took us three days. Finally, the day before the trial, he accepted one. The statement read as follows:

"Your Honor:

I would like to express to the court my deepest regret and remorse for my wrongdoing, for breaking the law. I recognize the seriousness of my offense, and I sincerely apologize for these criminally libelous mistakes. As God is my witness, I vow never to do this again.

The private and public suffering has been long and painful to me, my family and many of those whose trust I've earned over the years.

This experience has been horrifying and one I will remember all of my life. I ask that as you decide my fate, that you temper justice with mercy, and I ask for leniency in your sentencing of me.

Thank you."

That same day I went to see the psychic, Rev. Tooks, again, as I had promised. Since the last time I had visited her, she had found out who I was and expressed her concern over such a miscarriage of justice. I appreciated her acknowledgment. It seemed our interface was elevated to a more personal level, like she had taken my well-being to heart. This time she rubbed my hands with some oils and gave me scriptures to read. She told me to read them that night, to find a secluded place in the courthouse to read them in the morning, then surrender my will to the will of God, and I would be protected. I thanked her and left. I slept all of two hours the night before the sentencing, mostly due to calls from well-wishers and friends. I read the Qu'ran and the Bible and prayed a lot that night. I also read the scriptures I was given.

Morning came quickly on June 20, 1990, but I wasn't tired. I had this adrenaline rush, like I was in anticipation of a big sporting event (and I was the game). I made Fujr prayer and made two additional rakas, asking God for protection against this beast of a government. I read the scriptures given to me by the psychic, then I just meditated and tried to relax my spirit. The phone started ringing around 6:30. The first call was mom. The second call was Deb. The third call was Ramsey, telling me to meet him at his office at 8 a.m., and not to be late. I got to Bob's office at 8:10. After a brief discussion of how the process would go, we left his office to make our way over to the courthouse. As we walked up to the court, we saw a group of television cameras and news reporters ahead of us on the sidewalk. A few more were on the courthouse steps. We both walked through them without comment.

As we went up the elevator to the floor of my designated courtroom, I reached in my pocket, pulled out the praying hands, kissed them and put them in the palm of my right hand. As the elevator doors opened, I saw a crowd of people standing in the hall. More reporters. But then I saw my family and friends who had come down to support me. Mom, Miss Shirley, Sharon, Henry F. Davis and his son, Hank, Floyd, and... Taurece. Ramsey wanted the whole family there, but I told him that I didn't want the children there. He then suggested that "T" be there for appearance sake, even if we didn't want the children there, and even if we weren't talking. He thought a "family appearance" might make a difference with the judge. As we approached the group, I gave an assuring nod, and a half smile. We stepped in the courtroom at 8:50 a.m. A chill went over my body. The courtroom was cold, very cold; at least, to me. The mood was almost spooky, very evil. I whispered in Ramsey's ear, "I have to go to the bathroom."

He looked at me and said, "Be back by 9 a.m. Don't keep the judge waiting." I walked out to find the bathroom. I found a stairwell where I knelt down and prayed the Al-Fatiha and read the 23rd Psalms and a few other scriptures aloud. After praying, I immediately returned to the courtroom. It could only seat about 40 people. After the press, that only left about 20 seats. They were all filled with family and friends. The judge was in his chambers with the probation officer who prepared the PSI report.

While we waited, Ramsey passed me a fax that he had received from Schetina that morning from the FDIC supporting his recommendation of a jail term, based on a loss from the Caldwell loan. Though the loan was now paid, Schetina had no intention of letting the judge know, and intended to play this little charade all the way out. When Keller came out of his chambers, he was flushed beet red. All I remember was seeing the side of his neck. The term "red-neck" became real that day. Not only did Keller look like one, he acted like one. Clearly pumped in front of the media, Keller hit the bench in his "take charge," "law and order" mode. He gave a little speech about how I had failed to uphold the public trust by feathering my own nest and pretending not to, and not only for myself, but for another person, how I sat in loan committees meeting knowing that there was fake data in the file (we later brought to his attention that this wasn't true, as documented in depositions; but it didn't matter at that point) and went on to default on the loan, and how the court will not tolerate such behavior from S & L officials, regardless of how large or small. Clearly, Keller came out leaning with the prosecutor. "Mr. Ramsey," he said, "your client's community service record is commendable, but he's not going to walk, OK? Keller stated that this was the type of self-dealing that created chaos in the industry, and warranted more than a slap on the wrist. Then Keller stated something to the effect, "Mr. Essex, $171,000 is a lot of money, and we can't let you get away with this." The implication was, of course, that's a lot of money "for a nigger," because anyone in the finance industry knew we weren't talking about big money in real dollars. But now it was a matter of how much time.

Just then Ramsey, who I had accused of being too soft with the U.S. attorney, went into a rage. "Your honor, there are several issues being misrepresented here, and my client is being falsely accused of. First of all, there is no loss here. Caldwell paid her loan back, and the bank will make money on the house. Secondly, Derick Payne's deposition clearly states that Essex wasn't in committee on the day his loan was approved. Lastly, my client is being lumped in with people who stole millions and millions of dollars, losses that can never be recovered, and with people who lined their pockets with gold. Your honor, this man didn't put any money in his pocket. He lived in this house with his family for five years and made payments. The house went into default after a marital separation. You're trying to compare him to others, when there are people in Orange County driving his and hers Rolls Royces (referring to two bank failures where the major players bought twin Rolls Royces with their fraudulent haul). I really don't think this is fair, Ramsey finished in a clearly disgusted tone. I believe for the first time, Ramsey recognized that Keller had come in with his mind made up, and not having at least the opportunity to argue the merits of a light sentence, pissed Ramsey off more, than what Keller had to say.

This was bias of the worst kind, and Ramsey and everybody in the courtroom recognized the arrogance of this bias from the time he hit the bench. But he did back Keller up for a minute. Keller then turned his attention to issues raised by Ramsey. In addressing the prosecutor, in a lot softer tone (like they were buddies or something), Keller asked Schetina, "Is it true that the money was paid back?" Schetina, who went from the growl of a bear to the purr of a (pussy) cat, said sheepishly that they had received payment of $42,000 on the Caldwell loan. Keller looked at him like, "How could you let me step out like this on such a high-profile case, knowing that the money has been paid?" Keller then asked Schetina how did our cases get two different judges. Schetina again shrugged and gave some answer, as though he thought it was unintentional. Then the discussion turned to what was he asking for. Schetina had asked for 10 to 18 months in his memorandum, but asked for one year in the courtroom. His reasoning was that I tried to minimize my involvement, even after I pleaded guilty. Bob and I looked at each other like, "What kind of shit is that?" You can only minimize your involvement to the extent of what you accept responsibility for, no more, no less. I interpreted Schetina's statement to mean that I didn't cooperate like he wanted me to, so he asked for jail time. That's all it could mean.

Keller appeared to be calculating something, as he asked Ramsey if he had anything else to say. Ramsey, a little more composed, again reiterated that I was not responsible for Founders' insolvency, and taking me out of society would do more harm than good, because I had a family and three young children to support.

Keller was unmoved and responded, "Doesn't his wife work? She can take care of the children for a little while." There was a moan from the small audience in the gallery behind us. Looking back, most everyone was just shaking their heads at the callousness of Keller's statement. The atmosphere was as evil as most had ever witnessed. Keller then asked me if I had anything to say.

For a moment, I said nothing. Bob leaned over and said, "Read the statement."

I whispered back, "For what?" Because you want to stay with your family, he responded. Silent to this point, I cleared my throat and read the statement.

Keller's response to it was, "I hope you truly feel that way, Mr. Essex. However, I'm going to give you a little time to think about it. You're going to be off the streets for a while." With that statement, he proceeded with my sentence.

"I sentence you to five years in prison, four and a half years suspended on count two. On counts three and 10, the imposition of a five-year prison term is suspended, and you are to be placed on five years probation. I order you to pay the amount of $63,745.50 to Founders Savings, credit being given for any payments already made. And I sentence you to 640 hours of community service. You shall surrender yourself to the Federal Bureau of Prisons, on or before August 1, 1990."

With the slam of his gavel, it was over. Mom came up and hugged me. Taurece and several others had tears in their eyes. Several press people came up to us outside the courtroom and in front of the courthouse where the cameras were. They all caught us coming out. Bob spoke to all of them. I had nothing more to say, and I didn't want to go on camera. Ramsey commented that this was a very unfair sentence, and that he was disappointed, because he felt I didn't deserve jail time. He was disappointed?

Shell shocked was more my feeling. In my first appearance ever before a judge, I was given every form of punishment at his disposal. Judicial discretion allows a judge to use his judgment in dispensing the most appropriate sentence that would encourage the defendant's rehabilitation. Oftentimes it's a combination of two penalties to ensure social correction. Usually, a jail sentence and probation, or a jail sentence and a fine. For first-timers it might be probation and restitution, or restitution and community service hours (which is a form of restricted labor, because if you don't complete it in a certain time, you go to jail). This judge did not sentence me conducive to encouraging rehabilitative behavior, it appeared as if this judge was trying more to burden me, than deter me. Not only did he give me all four forms of punishment, but tied me to repaying the loan of a customer, which was virtually unheard of. Restitution is repaying of money you took and benefited from, not money loaned to somebody else. It set a very dangerous precedent.

The 640 hours of community service combined with the six-month sentence made up the difference of the 10 months the prosecutor had asked for. The probation was just a tail to track me, just because he wanted to. Ramsey said it was outrageous, but within the authority of the court. It was difficult for me to rationalize this abuse of such discretion, maybe because it was happening to me. Clearly, Keller performed for the cameras and print media to reinforce his position as a

"Borker," and I was the residual benefactor of such public posturing.

After Ramsey made all his statements, we drove back to his office in virtual silence. There was nothing else to say. He agreed that the sentence was harsh and as we parted, he stated that he'd start looking at ways to either stall or have the sentence set aside. It really was more of a discussion to try and smooth my momentary disappointment. It was 10:30 a.m. I went straight home and got in the bed. The phone started ringing off the hook around noon. One of the radio stations had picked up off the news service that I had been sentenced to go to jail. It was the lead-in story for most of the community stations. My phone message tape ran out within an hour, but the phone kept ringing. I didn't answer it once. After falling asleep, I woke up in time for the 4 o'clock news. The story ran on the 4, 5 and 6 o'clock hour on every station. Around 7 o'clock, Mom came over asking why I wasn't answering my phone. "What for?" I asked.

Mom knew my attitude wasn't right. "Have you eaten today." I didn't answer but she knew I hadn't. "I brought you some snapper and some salmon cakes (I love my mother's salmon cakes.)

I said, "Thanks" and went to get back in the bed.

She followed me in the bedroom. "What are you going to do now?" she asked.

"I dunno." I responded. "I need to rest, to think through it," I said.

"Promise me you won't do anything dumb. I know things look bad now, but they won't be that way always," she said, always the eternal optimist.

"Yeah, Uh-huh," I said looking away. She hugged me and told me she loved me and left. I turned off all the lights in the house. It was dark except for the light of the television. I just laid there, staring into space until dawn.

By the following morning, I had fallen into a deep depression. I sat in front of the window of my living room eating cold salmon cakes and wondering to God if he was trying to destroy me. If so, couldn't he do it another way. Just take me without the misery. Clearly, I had lost perspective in relation to my understanding as to how God tries man. I spent the whole day in isolation, just praying and reading the Quran. The phone rang all day but I didn't answer it. Several people came by and knocked on the door but I didn't answer it. I didn't want to hear anything anybody had to say. I just wanted to be by myself. The following two days after the sentencing, I was clearly wandering down a tunnel bordering self-pity.

There was a knock on my door. I ignored it. Whoever it was knocked again. I still didn't respond. The knocking went on for about five minutes, then finally the person shouted, "Hey, good brother. I know you're in there. Open up." It was Floyd. I got up opened the door, unlocked the gate and went to flop back down in my chair at the window. He pulled up a wicker chair beside me and said, "You're the talk of the town, good brother. People are trying to reach you. Why haven't you answered your phone?" I didn't say anything and just continued to stare out the window. "People are talking everywhere. Nobody thought you should've gotten jail time. Even a few of your enemies felt that way. Even the *L.A. Times* felt that way," he continued as he pulled out the newspapers from the past two days. He handed me the paper on the day after my sentencing. I took it and read the headlines: "Former President of NAACP gets Six-Month Sentence for Loan Fraud." I frowned. My sentence was for false statements, not loan fraud. As I read the article I got madder. In quoting my statement to the court, the *L.A. Times* took selected portions of the statement, ran them together and made it read as follows:

"I would like to express my deepest regrets for my wrongdoing, for breaking the law. As God be my witness, I will never do this again...I ask that you temper your decision with mercy."

This wasn't my statement, but the devil *L.A. Times* used selected words in my statement to make it look like I begged this devil for mercy. The first thing I did was to reflect on Ramsey and my decision about this statement. All I could think of was, "He begged us not to, but we whipped his ass anyway." I threw the paper on the floor without finishing the rest of the article. Floyd opened the second paper, that morning's newspaper and read aloud the little Op-Ed piece the *Times* ran that essentially said that my sentence was disproportionate to the crime, that if I got six months for what I did, then others like (Michael) Milken and Ivan Boesky, who served three years and no fine for masterminding Wall Street's biggest insider trading fraud (in history), should receive several lifetimes behind bars.

After Floyd finished reading, I shouted at the top of my voice, "Fuck the *L.A. Times*." They were the ones that heightened the profile of the case. They were the ones working hand in hand with the prosecutor to misrepresent the facts. They just got through saying I begged this motherfucker for mercy and now they want to stroke me. I'll show you what I think of the fuckin' *L.A. Times*." Just then I snatched the paper from Floyd's hands, balled it up, threw it on the floor, jumped up and down on it, picked it up, went into the bathroom, took a shit, wiped my ass with the newspaper and flushed it down the toilet. Washing my hands (and butt), I dried my hands on the rest of the newspaper, telling Floyd, "That is what I think of the fuckin' *L.A. Times*."

Thinking that I had surely lost my mind, Floyd just laughed and said, "It's good to see you haven't lost your spirit, good brother." I forced myself to laugh with him, realizing how crazy my little tantrum must have looked. Sitting back in the chair turning serious again, I looked out the window and asked Floyd, "What am I going to do now, Floyd?"

Without hesitation, he responded, "You gonna continue what you been doing. You ain't gonna miss a beat. I'll stay in your house. Sharon and Debra said they will run your business, and take your messages. Nobody will know you're even gone. By the time they think you're gone, you'll be back. And keep on swinging. I'm convinced by the response of the people on your sentence that you have more support out there than you think you do. You'll see." I was touched by Floyd's offer, though I didn't believe that. I felt like the whole world fell down upon me. But with Floyd's presence and reassurance, for the first time, since the sentence was handed down, I could see something positive. I was reminded of something Maya Angelou wrote: "Just when it looked like the sun wasn't going to shine anymore, God put a rainbow in the sky."

In my first public statement since my sentencing, I was allowed to give the lecture at the Mosque, the following Sunday. Before a packed house at Muhammad Mosque #27, I gave insight to my experience that they hadn't read in the papers. For the first time, I made public the squeeze that the feds put me in, by threatening to prosecute my mother. It was the first time she, herself, had heard it. I talked about the dual standard of justice we lived under every day, and how the biggest theft and liar the world had ever known was now calling me one, for no other reason than to discredit whatever truth I had worked to expose, while with the Colored People's Association. I helped those who didn't understand the relationship of the government, the courts and the press, see how easy it was to take something that happened over five years ago, and make it seem like it happened yesterday, and convince the public that it was larger than it really was. That it was really nothing more than a "trial by pat hand," because there is nothing fair about how these charges were brought out, how they were kept out and how they were played in the media and in the courts. I clearly understood what this was all about, and if it meant that I'd have to go to jail, rather than be one of their Negroes; lock me up. I'll just be teaching and speaking the truth from wherever they locked me up. My lecture was well-received, and I appreciated Minister Wazir giving me the opportunity to respond to the events of the week. The lecture was taped for community distribution.

After this appearance, I pretty much kept to myself, holding out hope for some legal maneuver that would either stay or rescind the jail sentence. The anxiety of knowing that I was going to jail couldn't be any worse than actually being in jail. Ramsey filed a reconsideration motion that was scheduled to be heard some time in mid-August after my surrender date. He claimed he was going to try to get it moved up.

In the meantime, the stark realization that the inevitable was near came when I was called in for my introductory meeting to my federal probation officer. That was another process I absolutely dreaded but, in comparison to jail, I could deal with it. The woman that was to be my probation officer was named Carol Jones. A very professional Black woman with a stern disposition, Ms. Jones had a reputation for being very straightforward and hard, when necessary. Your probation could be as easy or as difficult as you made it, according to Ms. Jones. However, she could be pleasantly engaging and kind, when she felt you were being fair and honest with her.

In our initial meeting, which was the purpose of getting to know me, I went to her office as if it would be the starting point, completely denying that I would actually be going to jail. Interrupting my rhetoric about appeals and delays, Ms. Jones slapped me out of my state of denial by saying, "Mr. Essex, this is just an introductory meeting. According to my file, you will be going to a correctional institution. Short of a miracle, you will be going to jail."

Sitting there with this shocked look on my face, all I could say was, "I believe in miracles." But reality had set in. After that visit, I began to put my affairs in order, in the event the miracle didn't happen. That last month, I went out in public only once, and it was the hardest thing I had ever done in my life. But I did it for a friend.

The NAACP held its national convention in Los Angeles in July 1990. I still had some support in the NAACP and a few good friends in key places. Some of those supporters had called to find out if I was attending "my convention." They called it, "my convention," because most of them felt I should have been the host President, given the pre-planning and funds positioning I had been involved with. Be that as it may, I had no intentions of going anywhere near the Colored People's Convention. I didn't feel it was an appropriate place for me to be, nor did I have any personal inclination to want to be there. The primary reason I can never totally regret my NAACP experience is because of the associations I established during my involvement. One such association was Fred Rasheed. Because of our close working relationship on the Southland investigation, Fred and I had become very close friends. We developed mutual respect, in spite of, national's continually estranged relationship with the L.A. branch. As a professional civil rights strategist, Fred is as cool as they come. Highly respected as a negotiator and a mediator, Fred, who is an attorney by training, had turned the Economic Development program into the organization's prize plum.

Our perspectives on civil rights are very similar, which brought us close. Our perspectives on life, which are also similar, made us friends. I consider brothers like Fred, Joe Powell, Floyd Frazier and Carter Womack, not so much as father figures, but like big brother figures. Fred was like the older brother I never had. Whenever I am on the East Coast, or he's on the West Coast, we see each other. I had intended for it to be no different this time. Debra and I had made arrangements to pick Fred up from his hotel the night before the convention. We took him to dinner and to a concert (the Budweiser Superfest at the Rose Bowl). We had a great time, and Fred got some insight as to what we had planned to do at the Coliseum, had we (in the branch) gotten the chance. Only the proceeds would have gone to the organization. We talked about a lot of things that night, the organization, my situation, family, life. At the end of the evening, I told him I knew he'd be busy, but asked if we could get together toward the end of the week. Fred and his wife, Delores, were heading for Hawaii. Fred casually said, "Well, I'll see you some time this week at the conference, right?"

I responded, "No, Fred. I won't be coming to the conference."

"So that means you won't be coming to my workshop," Fred said. I didn't say anything. Fred then turned more serious than I had ever seen him and said, "Anthony, are we friends?"

"Yes, of course we are," I responded.

"Then if we are friends, why would you insult our friendship, by not coming to my workshop?" he said.

"Well, Fred, that's not my intent," I stated.

"But that's exactly what you're doing, if you put this L.A. bullshit ahead of supporting a friend. Is your feud with the branch more important than our friendship?" he asked.

"No," I said.

"Then I'll see you at my workshop tomorrow," he concluded. I just nodded, not being able to refute anything he had said. As he got out of the car, he turned back and said, "I don't take too kindly to having my friendship insulted. Friendship is friendship, and bullshit is bullshit. Remember that, OK," he said, in a warm but admonishing tone.

"Lesson learned." I said. He kissed Debra on the cheek, and ran into the hotel. The ride home was very quiet. Finally, Debra broke the silence. "You know he was right, don't you?"

"Yeah, I know," I acknowledged, feeling despondent. It only made this situation worse. I still didn't look forward to it.

The main meetings were held at the old L.A. Convention Center. The convention was in the midst of its usual pomp and circumstance. I took a deep breath, put my head up, and walked in like I belonged there. I entered where the branch set up its table. They looked at me like, "What are you doing here?" I looked at them like, "I'm a life member. Twice paid. I belong here," and kept on stepping. The first test went OK. I went upstairs to see where the Economic Development Workshop was going to be held. It was a quarter of two. The workshop started at 3 o'clock. Some of the earlier workshops were just concluding. I stuck my head in the workshop on the destruction of young Black men given by Jawanza Kunjufu. I asked him if he had seen Fred. He directed me to a meeting he had just left, saying Fred was in the meeting. I went to the room and walked through the door.

Fred looked up and smiled. "It's good to see you, brother."

"Good to be seen," I responded. We hugged.

Fred knew how difficult this was for me, but he also knew I could and would rise above it. He stated he had a meeting with the Chicago branch on some urgent issues, which he had to deal with. We agreed to meet downstairs in a half-hour. Suddenly, I had a dilemma: do I stay upstairs, go downstairs, or partake in the convention. I really didn't want to hang around looking like some old left shoe trying to find the right, but I didn't want to be downstairs wondering around like some lost puppy with his nose pressed against the window looking like I really wanted to be a part of this thing. I decided to take a walk outside and come back in 30 minutes. Foolish pride makes you do dumb shit. I ran into more people outside, than I probably would have inside.

While walking about the Convention Center, I ran into Berlinda Jamerson from Southern California Gas Company, who you remember was my Corporate Relations Committee Chairperson for the branch. It was through Berlinda's committee that we had lined up close to $200,000 for this convention. There was a sadness that our community would never see the fruits of our labor, not because a transition took place, but because of the way it took place. In a way that wasn't conducive to the spirit of continuity. And that clearly was on my part. I wasn't inclined to be dragged through the mud, prosecuted and jailed, only to turn over the map to buried treasure to the ones that started this shit. I wasn't that much of a team player, and I don't know anyone who would be. So much for my momentary sympathy for the branch. The branch would never see any of the money identified for branch projects, including the convention, nor access resources through my contacts. Never.

As we entered the Convention Center, it was almost time for Fred's workshop to start. Berlinda kissed me on the cheek, and said she'd see me in there. I immediately saw another friendly face that eased the anxiety of being at the convention. Sharon Bernard, Linda's sister and a civil rights activist in her own right, came over accompanied by another woman.

Flashing her warm smile, we hugged. Sharon was the board chair of the Detroit Urban League and the NAACP local convention chairperson for the 1988 NAACP National Convention, which was held in Detroit. I had some pre- planning discussions with her on convention ideas for the Los Angeles convention, and had intended on going to her convention, but instead made the trip to Egypt. She also referred to the conference as "my convention," expressing surprise at my attendance. I guess I was full of surprises that day. We walked toward the main hall where the workshop was about to start. Fred was already up on stage, but he saw me walk in and nodded. The workshop topic was getting our fair share of the entertainment business, and the discriminatory issues that go along with it. I took a seat in the front row, stage left. There were four women in the second row who watched me as I sat down. It felt like their stares were piercing the back of my head. Then again, it could have been paranoia. I heard one of them say, "Isn't that Essex?" I peeped around, only to see them stop talking and stare at the stage. I turned back, and they started talking again. "The nerve of him to show up here," one said. I turned around again, before the other could respond. They stared back up at the stage. Then I acted like I was going to turn around, and turned back real quick, only to catch 'em all with their mouths open, in the middle of their little gossip session. I knew I wasn't crazy, but I didn't say anything. I just put my fingers up to my mouth and said, "Shhh!" They all rolled their eyes and looked back up to the stage. I chuckled and turned around.

On stage, the speaker was football Hall of Famer/actor/activist Jim Brown. Jim was schooling the audience on the five "isms" of the entertainment industry: racism, sexism, nepotism, cronyism and classism. He talked about how these five "isms" shut Blacks and other minorities out of the production and distribution ends of the business. The next speaker, Atty. LeGrand Clegg, took the discussion one step further, and outright named "Jews" as the controlling influence in Hollywood that continued to perpetuate the negative stereotypes of Blacks in degrading roles, as well as, the lack of roles for Black women. These statements were, or course, picked up by the national media, and ended up being the controversy of the convention, but no less the highlight of the convention. Afterward, I met Fred by the stage as he walked his panel guests to the outer hall. He just shook his head and said, "Think we're gonna be quoted in the paper tomorrow?"

"You'll be quoted on the 6 o'clock news tonight, if not sooner," I responded. "Jews don't play that," I continued. We both laughed.

"I'm glad you came, brother," Fred said grabbing me around the shoulder. "I refuse to let them Negroes run you away." As we stepped into the hall, Fred handled his workshop wrap-up, while I was being approached by a small group of familiar faces.

Leading the group was a guy named Tony Nicholas. Nicholas was a 7-11 franchise owner, who came into the system as we were concluding our involvement in the Southland investigation. He was one of those let in to refute our claims of 7-11 stores being closed to Blacks. It was a good damage control move for Southland, but now Nicholas and a third group of Black franchisees were experiencing difficulties, similar to what the first two groups had experienced. The first words out of Tony's mouth was, "Boy, Anthony ... we sho' miss you as President of the L.A. branch. Southland can do anything they want to, now that Joe's President."

"Oh!" I said, trying to act like I really gave a shit. I mean, I liked Tony and all of 'em, but that wasn't my problem anymore.

Still, I listened as Tony continued, "Yeah man, we met with Southland, Larry Irvin and Joe Duff, and Joe told us that Southland was the best thing to ever happen to us, and we should be glad they allowed us to be franchisees. Anthony, it was the craziest shit we ever heard in our lives."

"I've heard crazier, Tony," I said nonchalantly.

"Oh, yeah. What?" Nicholas asked.

"How about 300 different people all telling you they forgot when the branch election was (Tony was one of those; now he was paying for it)," I said, looking him dead in his eye like, "So what do you want me to do now?" He knew what I meant and just shrugged his shoulders.

Fred was ready to go back to his hotel. He asked me if I wanted to go to a couple of receptions with him, after he rested for a couple hours. I agreed that I would. I went home to change, relieved that this little experience was over, but still anxious about a second encounter.

Upon my return to the Bonaventure Hotel where Fred was staying, we were due to go to three receptions. On the way to the first reception sponsored by the Chicago delegation, we talked about the events of the day. Sure enough, Legrand Clegg's comments had made the 6 o'clock evening news. They ran a little blurb on him, followed by a blurb on Hooks denying the Association's connection with any of Clegg's comments.

When we got to the reception, Fred moved around the room greeting delegates. I just moved from one spot to another trying not to look bored. This was absolutely the least enjoyable thing I could think to be doing, seemingly having done it a million times. The suits, the tight dresses, the fake laughs, the cleavage in your face, the attitudes where everybody was somebody, even if they were nobody. All of it was a tired reminder of the niggah merry-go-round I had come to hate. It made me absolutely sick, but for Fred's sake, I bore it.

After walking in circles a half dozen times, having had my fill of buffalo wings, fruit, cheese and crackers (the standard menu for receptions), I sat at a table with a young woman that looked about as bored as I was. Her name was Linda Byrd-Harden, the Executive Director for the Virginia State Conference. She was very quiet, petite and beautiful. Without introducing ourselves to each other, we just began to talk about different issues and subjects. Fred came over and introduced us to each other as two of "the brightest young people I know." We both appreciated the comment, but moreover, appreciated the conversational diversion. The reality was I didn't know how brilliant this young sistah was. As the first female Executive

Director of the Virginia State Conference, she was clearly one of the NAACP's brightest young stars, and one of the most dynamic speakers you'd ever want to hear. Many I talked to that night, when her name came up, felt she'd be national Executive Director one day, if she could hang in with the bullshit. Still, she was humble and unassuming, not like many in the organization, who try to wear their position on their sleeves.

As the evening progressed, it was clear we had similar views on advocacy, on the state of the Black community, on Black leadership and even the future of the NAACP. It did my heart good to know there was hope for the old dinosaur. She made a very tense evening very pleasant. Fred was ready to go over to the chairman's reception, an invitation only affair, so it was "so long" for now. I didn't have any real apprehensions about going to the reception for then Board Chairman, Dr. William Gibson.

"Doc" Gibson, in spite of all the controversy coming out of Los Angeles, always treated me cordially and with respect. Dr. Gibson was one of the few high level NAACP officials who knew "both" sides of the story, involving my ouster and subsequent prosecution, and it never swayed his view of me, nor his willingness to solicit my input on civil rights and economic issues. Whenever he was in Los Angeles, even though I wasn't active in the organization, I'd be invited to a strategy meeting or two he often had in his suite. In Dr. Gibson's effort to stay up on prevailing issues the NAACP sought to address or to get the "real" inside scoop on certain issues, I would be allowed to attend, when appropriate. I really appreciated Dr. Gibson for his fairness in dealing with me.

Ben Hooks was another story. He avoided contact with me like the plague, even though I had more contact with him, while I was in the organization than I had with Gibson, and he had more knowledge of what had actually transpired with conflict in the branch. I guess, because it wasn't "politically correct" to be seen in my company, Hooks followed that script. At the Chairman's reception, he stood within two feet of me for about 10 minutes and conversed with everyone who was in my conversation circle. Yet, when it came time to speak to me, he turned and went the other way. It really didn't faze me one way or another. Neither did stopping to speak to the "L.A. bunch" (including Mallory) standing out in front of the chairman's reception. They were more shocked to see me, than I was to see them, particularly since I was on the way in, and they were trying to figure out how all of them were going to get in. Fred stopped to greet them and I cordially nodded to them, hypocrites included. Now wasn't the time to fight that fight.

We made our way over to the Chairman, stopping several times along the way. Dr. Gibson seemed appreciative that we stopped through, though in that element, he was constantly meeting and greeting people. As the evening closed down, Fred and I had a very frank discussion once we got back to the hotel. He said he was proud that I had stuck the evening out. The whole purpose of him asking me to come out was to show those in L.A. that I had support far and beyond a small clique in the L.A. branch. Fred said he wanted to let the L.A. branch know that people around the country knew what happened to me was because a few in the branch chose to play it dirty. But, if it was left up to him (and a few others), he'd bring me back, in a second, with no questions asked, and wouldn't think twice about it. I really appreciated Fred for looking past my shortsightedness, and forcing me to deal with this in the way he had. Then he broke the sentimental moment when he said "In fact, I'm going to bring you back in the Association, in due time."

"It's time to go, Fred. We're getting carried away now," I said. We both laughed, but I knew he was serious. I told him I'd try to see him on the morning of his departure to Hawaii. We hugged, and I left with a feeling of relief that the evening was over, not because of the potential for conflict, but because I felt a chapter in my life had closed. I had shown my face at "my convention," not in the way I had imagined, but in a way that sort of vindicated me, both personally and organizationally. Still with a great deal of anger and hostility directed at the organization, there was no refuting its influence nationwide. And it was satisfying for me that Fred felt I could still contribute to that.

The morning Fred was due to leave town, I met him at the airport. Not knowing what the next few months would bring for me, this parting had an added sentimentality to it. During a recent trip out his way, Fred had complimented me on a leather Kenti cloth Kufi and scarf set that I wore last time I was on the East Coast. I had one made up for him. Upon arriving at the airport, I met Fred at his gate. He was standing there with Paul Brock, Dr. Gibson's administrative consultant. We all spoke. His flight was due to leave within 15 minutes. I told him how great it was to see him and gave him the Kufi and scarf set. He then told me he had something for me, reached in his pocket, pulled out a gold charm and put it in the palm of my hand. When I looked at it, I saw it was the gold, religious charm Fred used to wear around his neck. Before I had converted to Islam, I had once asked Fred what the charm meant. On one side it had "ALLAH" written in Arabic. On the other side in small writing, it had the first sura of the holy Quran, Al-Fatiha written in Arabic. Al-Fatiha is arabic for "Opening Chapter" and is the only prayer all Muslims are required to start with in each raka of every one of their five daily prayers. It says the following:

1. In the Name of Allah, Most Gracious, Most Merciful
2. Praise be to Allah, the Cherisher and Sustainer of Worlds.
3. Most Gracious, Most Merciful.
4. Master of the Day of Judgment.
5. Thee do we worship, And thine aid we seek.
6. Show us the straight way,
7. The way of those on whom thou has bestowed thy grace,
   Not those whose (portion is thy wrath, nor of those who go astray.

"Keep your prayers only to Allah. Even in trial, my brother, Allah protects the righteous," Fred said.

I could barely compose myself. We hugged and I told him, "Thanks, gotta go."

"Call me and let me know where you are," Fred said, without giving Paul a clue as to what we were talking about (though it wouldn't have been too hard to guess).

"You bet," I said trying not to tear up. I left my friend, Fred Rasheed.

I immediately went to buy a chain to put the charm on. It is still one of my most prized material possessions today, and one of the nicest gifts I've ever received from another brother. With this gift, the uncertainty of the future wasn't important. I felt suddenly empowered to face friend, foe and hypocrite alike. In what appeared to be a trial by pat hand, I now had a different perspective. I felt like now I had the pat hand. Though I didn't know it, I actually had it all the time. But now I had put my hand in the hand of ALLAH, the beneficial, the merciful, the lord of all the worlds.

* * *

16

139 Days In the Devil's Dungeon:

Myths Behind Societal Correction

"The dictum that truth always triumphs over persecution, is one of those pleasant falsehoods which men repeat one after another 'till they pass into commonplace, but which all experience refutes."

-John Stuart Mill

August 1st finally arrived. There were no last-minute delays, or reprieves. It was time to "do my time" in this devilish system's dungeon. I don't think I would have wanted to delay it any longer. Waiting was turning out to be more stressful than the thought of actual punishment. It was like waiting on your mother to come and give you a whippin.' Fear of the unknown is generally a good cause for high anxiety, but I was ready to take my medicine and get it behind me. I couldn't "psyche" myself up anymore than I already had. Six months wasn't my whole life. At least, I hoped it wasn't. I had been hearing horror stories of people being framed in prison, having something pinned on them to extend their stay. They'd go in with a little time, and end up with a lot. The choices were to either take the rap for some government plant, or not come out at all (meaning death). Of course, never having been in this situation, it was difficult for me to separate truth from fiction.

Since the NAACP convention, I had pretty much kept to

myself. The past couple of weeks had been spent in seclusion, just writing and reflecting, except for around mid-evening, when one of my friends would fix dinner for me and provide some late night comfort. No one can comfort a man, even in the midst of trial and tribulation, like the Black woman. It was almost like having "a last dinner" every night for the past two weeks, which I deeply appreciated. But now it was time to deal with reality, and that reality was leaving my family for six months. I purposely chose not to tell my children where I was going, which my estranged wife thought was a mistake. But it wasn't until the day before (July 31) that I actually owned up to the realization that I was leaving the next day (or be reported missing). Regardless of the fantasies we sometimes create of ourselves and our revolutionary causes, this wasn't a serious enough case or that much time to even consider running. It didn't make any sense to resist this momentary surrender. I was determined to get this little piece of bullshit out of the way. My eternal optimism wouldn't allow me to act like I was ready to go.

It wasn't until Debra flew down the day before, to drive me out to wherever I was suppose to show up, that I actually had gotten into that frame of mind. Coming in from Sacramento, she saw that I hadn't packed my clothes away, hadn't organized my office (so somebody would be able to find something while I was away). I hadn't rearranged the house or the closets to make room for Floyd's stuff, nor hadn't done the dishes for a few days. I just hadn't done anything, as if I wasn't planning on going anywhere. Of course, she went off, and we handled most of it that night. Leave it to Debra to bring me into a reality check. A good number of my friends started calling to say good-bye. Around 8 o'clock that night Mom was preparing the "last dinner" of my choice for the next six months. .

We did not get over to Mom's house until 9:30 p.m. The kids were there, so we talked "in codes," in hopes that they wouldn't understand. I knew Kellie understood, though she never said anything. Just before we left, Mom asked me to stop by the church for a prayer meeting with Chip. It took all the strength I had to restrain myself. My first thought was an impulsive rejection, expletives included. I didn't have any confidence in Chip and I didn't want him to pray for me. But trying to honor the wishes of my mother, I said, "OK Mom," and kissed her on the forehead. I had no intentions of doing that. I just couldn't tell her that.

On August 1, I woke up at 5:50 a.m., showered and prayed. I

read for about one hour and went back to sleep around 7:30. Debra woke me up again at five past nine. "What time are you supposed to be there?"

"I dunno. I guess I need to find out where there is," I said.

Nobody had notified me of anything. I called Ramsey, and he didn't know. I called the probation department, who gave me the Federal Department of Corrections, who didn't know. "Maybe I'll just wait until they come and get me," I told Ramsey, after calling him a second time. He promised to find out and get back to me.

About 10:30, he called back and said, "You're going to Boron."

Boron was a closed Air Force base in the higher Mojave Desert that was being used as a minimum security prison. Minimum security prisons on the federal level, called Prison Camps, generally don't have bars or fences. Such freedom of movement has caused critics of the federal correction system to call these camps, "Club Fed," because some of the camps, like Lompoc, tend to have a "resort-like" atmosphere. It was still jail, as far as I was concerned. I thanked Bob, who assured me he was trying to get my sentence changed to electronic home monitoring. Electronic home monitoring is what the federal system uses to prevent prison overcrowding. They strap a monitor to your leg, and it tracks your movement. You can't go more than 100 feet from your home, without permission, or the monitor goes off, and federal marshals come and check on you. It's only for the lowest minimum offenders, for which I qualified. He promised I'd hear from him in a couple of weeks.

It was time to pack. I suddenly went into a procrastination mode. I had an urge to see my children again. I went past the summer daycare facility they attended and checked them out for lunch. While at lunch, I explained to them that they'd talk to me every day, or as much as possible, and not to think I'd be too far away to give them advice and guidance. I told them to help their mother and grandmothers, and I'd see them as soon as I could. After about an hour, I returned them to summer camp and picked up Debra. We made our way over to the church. Mom was standing outside. I could tell she was disappointed, but relieved I had at least come. She said Chip had to leave. I asked her, "Does Chip pray to the same God we do, Mom?"

She said faintly, "Yes."

"Then we really don't need an intermediary, do we?"

She just looked off like, "Anthony, I don't need this today." But my point was that our parents and grandparents had always brought their trouble back into the church for some handkerchief-head preacher, who was no more principled or no more sincere than the person that was troubled, to lay hands on their troubled souls. Well, I needed that like I needed a hole in my head. I no longer viewed Chip Murray as a moral authority. If nothing else had come out of this last- minute procrastination, it allowed me to avoid another moment of hypocrisy, in exchange for moments of sincerity with my family. Breaking the silence, I put my arm around my mother and said to her, "Mom, it would actually mean more to me, if you and I prayed together before I left." She just nodded, with tears in her eyes. Together, she, Debra and I went into the church, got down on our knees, and prayed to the highest moral authority, the most high and merciful GOD.

* * *

Debra and I finally hit the road at 3:15 p.m., for what was supposed to be a two and a half hour drive to the Federal Prison Camp Boron, in Boron, California. There were periods when we conversed like we were heading out for a weekend vacation. Other times, there were long periods of silence, which was also nice. One of the things that Debra and I had in common was we both hated forced conversation. The last hour of the drive was up a lonely two-lane highway called I-395. "395" was a strip of pavement surrounded by desert. It was the only lifeline between civilization and "Death Valley," the other name for Mojave Desert. Part of the folklore contributed to Death Valley is largely due to the number of fatal accidents on 395. Many were due to "crossing the line" on the two-lane highway by falling asleep, drinking, swaying trucks or getting caught in a cross-wind or a sandstorm. "395" was "all that" and more. Finally, we pulled up to a side-winding road, with a sign that said, "UNITED STATES BUREAU OF PRISONS--FEDERAL PRISON CAMP, BORON, CALIFORNIA."

I took a deep sigh as Debra made the left hand turn across the highway. "This is it," I thought to myself. My last few moments of freedom. As we drove up to the gate, we could see what would momentarily be my fellow inmates engaged in their after-dinner softball game. The last conversation Debra and I had, before I exited the car, was a dream she had about a softball game in the middle of the desert. She said it was strange to her at the time, but became crystal clear when we pulled up to the gate. Deb got out of the car and walked me up to the check-in entrance. The guard pulled the window. "I'm Anthony Essex, and I'm here to serve my sentence." I intentionally said nothing about surrendering.

The guard responded, "Better late than never, huh," referring to my late arrival. "It's about time. This ain't the Hilton," he continued. It was now 6:10 p.m. I didn't respond. "Just a minute. You'll have to leave now, ma'am," he said to Debra as he slammed the window shut. As we hugged, we heard the guard yell, "Late self-surrender," the sound of which made me cringe and squeeze Debra tighter.

"You have a plane to catch. You better get on back," I said.

"I don't care about the flight. I don't want to leave now," she said.

"Well, you got to go. Let's not make this harder than it already is," I said. We hugged again and kissed. She got in the car, waved and drove off.

Just then, I heard the locks on the door pull up. Two guards escorted me into a room where another five people were waiting for me. This seemed like an inordinate number of people to check in one person. (I later found out that it was.) I felt like a spectacle of some sort. In the room were four men and three women. Two white males, a Black man and an Asian man along with two Black women and a white woman. It was clear to me that this late in the day wasn't an appropriate time for such a gathering. This was a diversity demonstration for the radical NAACP President who tends to see such things in Black and white and call them out.

One of the Black women, mid-40ish, attractive, but motherly in appearance, named Officer Robertson, spoke to me. "Welcome Mr. Essex. We've been expecting your arrival. Do you have identification?" I handed her a small pocket wallet with my driver's license and family pictures in it. She looked at my I.D. and handed it back to me. "Well, this appears to be you," she said smiling slightly. Turning serious again, she continued speaking. "From this point on, you will be known as Inmate Essex. Your identification will be 92768-012. Your counselor will be Mr. Frank Wilson (the Black man in the room). You will direct any concerns that you have to him. We will now go directly to the search procedure after which time you will be directed back here for registering of your personal items." Looking into the faces of my brother and sisters, I could see the discomfort in their eyes. This was painful. Maybe not as painful for them as it was for me, but painful nonetheless. I felt their sympathy for me and I had sympathy for them. I had done what I had done and now they had jobs to do. The white woman, who was the silent authority, was there to make sure no favoritism was shown toward me. And there wasn't.

After the indignation of the customary "strip search," I returned to the room where everything I had brought with me was inspected and accounted for. One pair of eyeglasses (Black framed), one address book (personal papers), seven family photos, one pair of Black underwear, one pair of Black shoes (Adidas), one pair of Black socks, one Black plastic bracelet, one Black watch (Seiko), two books, (Muslim prayer book, New Testament), and two religious medals (Allah pendant, praying hands). I then was asked to sign a document that none of the above items were worth more than $100. Of course, a couple of the items were worth more, but if I wanted to keep them, they were worth less than $100 (if you know what I mean). The other Black female was now "checking me in." She commented on my watch and asked if I was sure it was only worth $100. I said, "Yes." She asked to see it. I took it off and handed it to her. She then showed it to the white woman who was all the time acting like she was ignoring me by continuously shuffling paper.

Briefly scanning the watch, she coldly said, "Send it back," and went on doing what she was doing. "Mr. Wilson will take you to your quarters for the evening."

Wilson gave me a laundry bag to put all of my personal items in, including the clothes I wore in. I was given an ill-fitting pair of beige khaki pants and a faded khaki shirt. I was also given some blue rubber-soled deck shoes to wear. I would receive my standard issue in the morning. Over 50 inmates had been transferred in from Lompoc Federal Prison, earlier in the day. Camp housing was estimated at close to capacity, which was around 500 inmates. It would take a couple of days to finalize housing. Until then, I'd have to stay in the overflow accommodations, the gymnasium. When I got there, some seven or eight transfer inmates were already there. I took the open bunk on the far end of the room, putting my "stuff" under my head because, there was no pillow (just an itchy gray wool blanket). I laid face up on my bed and just stared at the ceiling. I could hear the other guys talking, but it was as if I was in another world. My first night in jail; I didn't sleep a wink.

Morning came quickly. That's because all the new surrenders and transfers who didn't have a work assignment had to report to GMC (General Maintenance Crew) at 6 a.m., two whole hours before everybody else had to report for their duties. You stayed on general maintenance, until you found another work assignment, which was sometimes never. A "CO" (camp officer, which is the same as a cell officer or prison guard) came to get us to show us where to go. From then on, we'd be responsible for getting there on our own. While walking over, I had a chance to get a clearer view of the total campgrounds. It was basically a bunch of two-story bungalows and dirt, in the middle of nowhere. There was a long and winding concrete walkway in the middle of the campground, which made it resemble an Army base or small community college campus. The walkway was lined with 2-foot curbs made of loose rocks. I thought to myself, "Who takes the time to stack those rocks like that?" I would soon find out. Upon arriving where the GM crew is "counted," in front of an old garden tool shack, I saw another three dozen or so men waiting for further instructions.

A young Black man with the name Johnson on his badge began looking at little cards with pictures on them, and calling out names. For every name called, someone answered, "Here." One name was called and the person didn't answer. Johnson called it again. No answer. He sent another guard to see if the inmate was still in his bed, while the other inmates yelled "AWOL" or "Walk-a-way." I asked the inmate standing next to me what that meant. He told me it meant just what it said. The inmate may have walked off. This was possible, because Boron had no bars and no fences. An inmate could just "walk-a-way" anytime they wanted to. More on this later. The guard came back with an inmate dragging behind him, stuffing his shirt in his pants and zipping them up along the way. "Next time you're late, that's a 'shot.'" Another jail term, I thought. I wanted to ask the guy next to me what a "shot" was, but he was so edgy on the last question, I just held it for later. Johnson finally called me in the last few names and "the count" was over.

Then they passed out garden rakes and trash bags. The inmates' GMC duty was to clean up the campgrounds before 6:45 a.m., which was the time breakfast was served. Since the campground was mostly dirt and rocks, with a little grass around the administration and cafeteria areas (and two of the housing units), that's exactly what you raked -- dirt and rocks. You not only had to rake dirt and rocks, but you had to rake them a certain way, where all lines were straight and went the same way. I learned that morning (one of my first jailhouse lessons) that many fights have broken out over stepping on an inmate's "lines" before they've been inspected and cleared. As I raked rocks and tried to get my lines together, I thought to myself, "This makes no damn sense at all." What is the benefit to the inmate of raking rocks?

Is raking rocks part of the re-disciplining or the societal correction process? I started getting pissed then.

Just as I stopped raking, a guard came up and said, "Them lines ain't too straight. You must be new. Let me show you how lines should be done." He took my rake, and gave it to an inmate he'd caught sitting down somewhere. As the guy raked delicately, the guard watched for a moment, before walking across the guy's "lines." I thought that was pretty messed up. The inmate cursed the guard under his breath. Minutes later, a horn went off, meaning you could turn your tools in and go to breakfast. I really didn't know where the cafeteria was, but I didn't really want to get into asking too many questions, or looking like I was lost, so I just followed where everybody else went. Soon, I found the line. Not knowing the process, when I got up to the food counter, I waited for a dish to be "thrown" at me (just like in the movies).

Well, that didn't happen. I was supposed to get my own plate. So, what I was doing was holding up the line. Just then, a big fat bearded redneck, about six persons behind me, screamed at the top of his voice, "Come on, move the line. What the fuck are you doing up there?"

The guy in front of me was a Black guy named Michael, who came in the day before on a transfer from Lompoc. "You're Essex, aren't you?" I nodded yes, "I've been following your case in the papers. Just do what I do."

He showed me where to get my tray, plate and utensils. He put his plate up, I put my plate up. Down splashed what looked like powdered eggs. Another guy plopped down what looked like potatoes. Another guy had two strips of bacon in prongs. I waved off the bacon. Mike took an apple from a big box of fruit.

"Ahhh, fruit," I thought. I took two apples.

The guard at the end of the counter shouted, "Only one piece of fruit."

I put one apple back. I got a glass of orange juice and a glass of milk. I followed Mike to one of the dining tables. "Thanks," I said, "I'm still trying to find out what's what."

"Yeah, I know how that is. Nobody told me anything when I first came in either," Mike said while chewing his food. He proceeded to tell me how my case was "the talk" of the Black inmates at Lompoc. Most saw the situation as political scape-goating. However, Mike made a point that was a consistent observation among inmates -- that nobody goes to jail for a case like mine, and that I was being held up as an example.

True to what I had heard (and seen in the movies), merging into a prison population is a real delicate situation. It's touch and go, until people know what you're about. If you go in trying to make friends (talking too much), they think you're a plant, or a snitch. A snitch is the second worst person you can be in prison (we'll discuss the worst later). If you go in too silent, you set yourself up for "a little attitude adjustment," from both the inmates and the guards. You view every situation differently, speak when you're spoken to, move about your own business, and stay out of other people's conversations.

I listened to the other inmates talk. "What you in for?" is a subject that almost always comes up. The question is put to everybody in the immediate circle of conversation. And as I had experienced the night before when the question was put to me, there was relative shock and disbelief over my response. "What you in for?"

"False statement."

"How many millions?"

"One Hundred Seventy Thousand."

"Well, how much do you get to keep?"

"None!?"

"Hey man, you hear what this guy is in on ..." and it went from there.

I later found out there was not one sentence of my kind in the whole prison camp. Almost every sentence involved either a monetary crime where "actual" dollars were lost (and kept in many instances), like income tax evasion, mail fraud, racketeering, banking and credit card fraud (where millions, not thousands, of dollars were involved), stock and securities fraud, and political fraud. Most of the inmate population was white collar criminals who weren't considered a "threat" to the general population. And most were white males, middle-aged, high level executives. Most of the drug cases were young Blacks (and a few Latinos) under 25, who were street dealers. There were a few Black "white collar" inmates (I was considered one of them), and a few white drug dealers. The sentences for each were highly disproportionate to what others received, according to what race they were (in spite of the mandatory sentencing guidelines). My sentence soon became the joke of the campground. It was good in a way, because it supported my position (and the position of others) that I was unfairly jailed. It was bad because of what being jailed meant to my family and me. Since my sentence was published, those who followed the case knew I was coming in "short." Short is a term for inmates with less than a year's time left on their sentence. Regardless of the fact that my sentence was short, the consensus was amazement that I got any time at all.

Mike was one of the first few to express what inmates generally knew as justified or unjustified time. We were both housed in the overflow "gym" housing and had not yet gone through the incoming "merry-go-round" for new inmates. This is where you get your standard uniform and toiletries issued, your physical, your permanent housing, and your permanent work assignment. There was also an orientation you'd have to attend. But to do all of this, you'd have to bring it to the attention of the supervising guard, so you could be formally excused, using a written request form called a "Cop Out" to document your movement. No one was going to bring it to you. You'd just be in the temporary clothes, the temporary housing, and on the General Maintenance Crew, until they found somewhere to put you, which could be never. All of this I learned over breakfast. Breakfast was over at 7:45 a.m. All inmates were required to be at their work assignments for the 8 a.m. "count." Since we had no work assignments, it was back to GMC.

After roll call, the real madness of the GMC work assignment started. GMC was just what it said, "General Maintenance," which meant wherever they needed manual labor, a runner, a flunky, whatever, the General Maintenance Crew did it. When they didn't have any use for a flunky, then you gathered rocks to build rock walls and curbs, or you raked rocks (and dirt) all day. What I didn't know was that the inmates paired up with inmates who had continuing work assignments, telling the assignment supervisor that they needed "an assistant," to help them to get out of raking rocks. By the time all the work assignments were given out, there were about seven of us left to rake and gather rocks. The guard handed out seven rakes, instructing us to spread out over the campground, and to rake until 10 a.m., when the trucks would be ready to gather rocks. No sooner than the guard could finish the instruction, the other six inmates broke out, leaving me the area within the guard's station. (I later found out getting out of the CO's immediate supervision was one of the inside tricks of surviving prison life.)

Being the only one left, of course, I had this area. As I raked rocks with all the excitement of a funeral march, I heard the guard say, "Pick it up a little, inmate." I kept my same pace, just moved to a different spot.

Just then, a white camp guard drove by in a golf cart-like vehicle and shouted at Johnson, "Hey, Johnson, I see you're an equal opportunity employer," no doubt a dig at my former civil rights affiliation.

Johnson responded to the little charade, "That's right, we treat everybody the same at Federal Prison Camp Boron." They both laughed.

I didn't even bother to look up, but was clearly annoyed. As the pace of my raking became more hastened and volatile, noting the dust I was kicking up, Johnson yelled, "Inmate Essex, you kickin' up too much dust. Go rake that patch of grass over there," pointing toward the cafeteria. I think he took more pleasure in giving the instruction than in trying to avoid the dust. It had become clear between last night and this morning that the little notoriety I'd received hadn't gone unnoticed.

I tried to comprehend what I was to benefit from coming here. Humiliation possibly? This certainly was humiliating, but no more humiliating, than a public persecution. Social Correction? The point of my error had long been made and acknowledged. And certainly there were more significant ways to demonstrate to society that I'd learned my lesson. I could have talked to youth, or other non-violent, first-time offenders about the negative impact of criminal negligence, or how small-time crime ruins lives, etc. How could raking rocks in the desert, or being verbally abused by camp guards lead to societal correction? Just in my first day in prison camp, I was able to see the myth in societal correction, even at the minimum security levels.

If a person makes a mistake and has to go to jail, if the person wasn't criminal before they went in, there is a greater likelihood that they will be, when they come out. Why? Because they're made criminal in jail. They are made more vicious, more cunning (to survive) and more incorrigible, due to the treatment and constant provocation. All you have to do is spend a little time in a so-called correctional environment, to understand why young men come out so vicious. Prison has become a tool politicians and prosecutors use to make a name for themselves, not to correct the wrongs of society. You just have to look at the sentences given to the treasurer of Orange County (CA), who was responsible for bankrupting one of the largest and richest counties in the nation (he received a daytime sentence at the local sheriff's station), to understand how American's take care of their own, even when they're wrong. But those who are forced to go under the guise of societal correction (particularly the non-violent), understand more than ever, the exploitation of America, as opposed to the rehabilitation of

America. Because America is becoming less redemptive in its attitude regarding the acceptance of those who may have stumbled, there is less of a concern as to what happens to them while one is doing "their time." If one makes a mistake, pays his debt to society, he is supposed to get a clean slate and a fresh start. Yet, he must bear the mark of the beast, and society stands ready to exploit him (or her) further. Where is the benefit in societal correction? There is none. Prisons in America, therefore, manufacture criminals. All of this evidenced itself to me that morning, just in my first interface with "the process."

It was a few minutes after ten. The temperature was already 106 degrees on its way to a high of 114 degrees. It was time to go gather rocks for building walls. Mike, another guy and I were taken about 100 yards outside the campground. The guard then warned us to watch for snakes. "Snakes?" Mike said.

"Yeah, they hide under the rocks to avoid the heat," the guard said. We all looked at each other like, "This is bullshit." Just then another guard came out with three more inmates, saying he needed three inmates to dig some ditches to the water main in front of the cafeteria. Immediately, he had three volunteers. In a choice between snakes and ditches, ditches won out.

After two hours of digging ditches, it was lunch time. I had a much easier time getting through the line, than I did that morning. I saw a lot more of the inmate population, than I had that morning, including the prison camp's other celebrity inmate, former California State Senator Joseph Montoya, who was convicted of political corruption and was forced to surrender, while his case was on appeal. (which he eventually won). We spoke briefly. On my way out of the cafeteria, I was approached by a very familiar face. It turned out to be one of my high school classmates, who was doing time on a drug charge. Though a little embarrassing at first, we reacquainted ourselves. His name was Larry. Larry offered to help me in anyway he could, which I appreciated. He explained all the little nuisances of camp life. What the "out of bounds" signs meant, times to use the phones and other inmates looking to provoke you. He told me who to go see to get my housing situated, and what I needed to do to get my mailbox and visitation papers straight. "They'll tell you this in orientation, but that might be another week or two," he said. They played ball after dinner and invited me to come out.

After lunch, it was back to digging ditches. The heat was now at a full 114 degrees. It was almost unbearable. They made us take turns digging, as opposed to digging all at once, like we did during the morning. We took water breaks every 30 minutes to prevent heat stroke and dehydration. We finished up around 3 p.m. I immediately asked for a "cop out" to go see about my housing. The guard acted surprised that I knew what a cop out was, but told me where to go get one, and to bring it back for his signature. I went to the counseling office where I met another counselor, whose name was also Johnson, and who was also Black. He was cordial, almost friendly. He told me they were still overcrowded, but in the next day or two, my permanent housing would be in place. I asked him if he knew where I could get my visitation packet. He told me to come back tomorrow, he'd have one for me.

By the time I returned from my trip to the counselor, it was time to call it quits for the day. All inmates had to return to their quarters for 4 o'clock count. After count, it was dinner time. During dinner I got to see the full scale politics of the campground. How they decided who ate first, how the total camp population interfaced with each other, and how they related to the camp authorities. I had the same thing I ate for lunch, a salad, that I served myself from a salad bar. (Really, a salad bar in prison camp.) Sitting with Mike for dinner, I was surprised to see how segregated the seating was. There were about 150 Black inmates (a surprisingly large number for the federal camps) who, by and large, sat together at about eight tables, at the south end of the cafeteria. There were the so-called radical elements sitting together, the "bangers," the klaners (big white boys with tatoos all over them), the dealers (as in drug dealers) and the socialites (a group of bank Presidents and corporate elite who had been sent away). The cafeteria mix was almost a direct reflection of the larger society that would probably have nothing to do with each other on the outside, but tied to each other by a common penalty, prison camp.

Walking around the camp after dinner, I ran into a man who looked like a cross between a hillbilly and a farmer, with overalls and the bill of his hat turned up. Real strange dude. "I'm the Chaplin," he said. I just looked at him. "Bible study is on Wednesday nights and Sunday service is at 10 a.m. Please feel free to join us. What denomination are you?" he asked.

"I'm a Muslim," I replied thinking to myself, "This is one goofy so and so."

"Well, we have an Iman on the camp. He is an inmate, and his name is Halim. I'll let him know you're here." With that he turned around and walked off. Strange dude.

About 20 minutes later, a very distinguished brother with a salt and pepper beard, wearing a white kufi came up to me and said, "As-Salaam Alakum, brother."

"Wa-lakum Salaam," I replied. "Anthony Essex," I continued extending my hand.

As he shook my hand, he replied, "I know who you are. We've been expecting you. I hope you will join us in prayer and study. There are about 25 Muslims on the camp. We pray together every day for "Asr" (pre-sunset prayer). It is the only time of the day we all are permitted to come together, besides Juma on Fridays at 1 p.m. Sunday nights we have Quran study."

I told him that I would be involved in the Islamic worship activity while I was there. "Inshallala," Halim replied (meaning be it the will of Allah). The Iman then handed me a book. "I know you're trying to get settled in. Read this. Then when you finish, I have some other books for you to read. Take care," he concluded, as we shook hands. He walked away.

I looked at the book. It was John Oliver Killen's *A Black Man's Burden*. At 6:30 p.m. it was still 100 degrees. I wandered down to the basketball courts and the softball diamond. I moved past the weight pile, it was mostly brothas working on their "buffs." I later found out most of the white inmates exercised at a different time. On my way back up to my quarters, I noticed a long line down the middle of the campground. I asked an inmate, "What's that line for?"

He said, "You must be new. That's the phone line."

As I looked farther ahead, I saw 15 phone booths. "Maybe I'll try to call home," I thought. I stood in line for about 30 minutes. It barely moved, and there were about 25 guys ahead of me. Another 30 minutes passed. There were now about eight guys ahead of me. It was now about 8:10 p.m. The phones cut off at 8:30. The phone use rules were supposed to be 10 minutes maximum. I saw guys that were on the phone at least 40 minutes with the guard standing right there. I finally got to the phone at 8:25. I told the operator my mother's phone number. It seemed to take forever for her to hook us up. Of course the call was collect.

When Mom accepted the call, she seemed relieved that I was OK. She said she didn't sleep at all last night. "Isn't that a song?" I asked trying to make her laugh. She chuckled a little, but not like I knew she could. I could tell her heart was heavy. As I was telling her that I hadn't received my mailbox number, but would give it to her as soon as I got it, there was a dial tone. Then silence. Before I could get it out of my mouth, the line was dead. I could tell by all the groaning and cursing that it was 8:30. They don't ask you to say goodbye and hang up in prison camp, they hang up for you.

I stood in line for an hour and 15 minutes to talk five minutes, but hearing Mom's voice did me good. The next inmate count was 9 o'clock. Then we would be allowed free time from 9:30 p.m. until midnight. Phone hours were from 9:30 - 10:30. After the count was confirmed, inmates would be excused according to their unit ranking from the weekly housing inspection. The same is done for mealtime. Because we were overflow housing, we automatically went last. By the time I got down the hill, the line was winding along the walkway, with some 50 inmates. I was in line for about ten minutes, when I caught my first drift of Mojave Desert night winds. The same desert that was 100 degrees, just three hours earlier, was now 60 degrees, windy and the temperature was falling. The low desert temperature would get into the 40s, even the low 30s during the change of seasons (summer to fall). I hated cold weather.

Still in my temporary khakis, with no coat and boat shoes, I complained about how cold it was. One of the guys in line replied, "Wait until winter, when it drops to 14 degrees at night. Better get yourself a coat and some long Johns. The line hadn't moved. I suddenly thought that I might be better off inside, instead of being outside freezing to death, and still not being able to use the phone. I returned to my quarters, pulled *A Black Man's Burden* out of my knit possessions (laundry) bag, and began reading.

* * *

I didn't sleep the second night either. When guards came in for the midnight count, I was looking at them. When they came back for the 4 a.m. count check, I was looking at them. I even met them on the way out to GMC duty for the 6 a.m. count check. Inmates were counted seven times a day, at 6 a.m., 8 a.m., 1 p.m., 4 p.m., 9 p.m., midnight and 4 a.m. After raking, rocking, and having an apple and milk for breakfast, I was excused to get my standard issue of clothes, sized to fit, what looked like combat boots (required daily wear during work hours), an old green Army jacket (even though the newer issue was a wool P-coat), five pair of boxer shorts, three pairs of socks, and a wool pullover cap. The khaki pants were all somewhat new. One of the shirts was worn down. The other two were in good condition. In watching the processing of the clothing and who gets what, I came to understand the power of an inmate's work assignment. Just like on the outside, it's about relationships (who you know). Who gets "hooked up" and who gets "anything period" is about reciprocal deals that enhances an inmate's influence, according to their need to survive. Bartering down to its most elementary levels, but necessary so as not to be totally consumed, in a system that tends to be strict and overbearing. A new shirt, for an extra serving of meat at dinner. A new pair of boots, for a hook-up at the commissary (materials when its not your day). A P-coat, for a small loan (non-payable, of course). It was about what one could influence, and what one could deliver.

It was real easy to see who the "haves" and "have-nots" were. The choice work assignments, the leniency on contraband (contraband was anything you didn't buy or wasn't approved for you to have), who got furloughs (approved leaves from the camp) and just the general treatment of inmates (levels of respect) ran along color lines, with a few exceptions (just like on the outside). However, the perception of favorable treatment wasn't handled very well by other inmates, and had to be kept ever so discreet. The notion that an inmate was receiving any unjustifiable preference, put the inmate in a position of being considered suspect by other inmates. An inmate that received justifiable considerations meant that the inmate had been around awhile or had come in from one of the higher level prisons, where they had earned their respect. A suspect inmate is an endangered inmate. Getting "too much," "too soon," like on the outside, had a downside. The downside here was that you could be labeled a "prima donna," or a "plant" (translation: "snitch"). Inmates in their thorough understanding of how the system works, know how hard it is to get anything light or easy in a correctional institution. Nobody has anything coming that they haven't earned. That's the way of this world. So anyone "in the yard," who gets something they haven't earned is not to be trusted, and is in possible danger, even at the appearance of a breach of inmate trust and confidence. This was explained to me through a series of events. Everything happens for a reason. While I am a firm believer in divine intervention, these events happened so fast, I had to just stop, watch and assess the impact of this sudden benevolence.

On the third day of my sentence, a guard named Johnson approached me. He said that he had appreciated the effort I'd given him the last two days on GMC, and asked if I had any administrative skills. I said that I did. He then asked me if I could type and use the computer. I told him I could. "How fast?" he asked.

"Bout 40 words a minute," I responded.

"Go up to the Powerhouse at the top of the hill and ask to see Barry Howard," Johnson concluded.

"How will I know him?" I asked.

"You'll know him," he said as he turned away.

When I got to the top of the hill, I went into a big building that looked like a cross between a science laboratory and a storage facility. A white man in inmate attire, sitting at a typewriter behind a desk, asked if he could help me. I asked to see Barry Howard. He asked if I had a cop out (which was permission to be up there). I told him no, but that Correctional Officer Johnson had sent me. He looked at me a little sideways, said "Excuse me," and left the room for a minute. When he returned, he took me down a hall into a small business office where a spectacled Black man with a part down the middle of his head sat behind a desk, plucking on a computer. The name plate on his desk said Barry A. Howard, Chief of Utilities.

"Have a seat," he said. After completing whatever work he had up on the screen, he turned from his computer to his office desk. I watched him as he watched me, spinning in his executive chair.

"I understand you got some skills I could use," he said. I nodded. "Tell me a little bit about yourself," he continued, as he leaned back.

"Finance management background, Master's from USC in Public Finance, my own business for five years. That's about it," I said.

He nodded his head, like he knew that I knew there was a little more to me than what I was willing to acknowledge. "What you in for?" he asked.

"False statement on a loan application," I responded.

"How big?" he asked. "$170 thou," I said.

"Is that all?" he said with surprise.

"Yep," I said, taking in a deep breath.

"Hummm," Howard said like he was thinking about what we had just discussed. "Any stolen cash, drugs or guns involved in your case," he continued.

"Nope," I said.

"So all you did was lie on a loan ap and you ended up here?" he asked again in disbelief.

"That's basically what I'm here for," I said.

"That's not what you're here for, but we won't get into that now. I have an administrative position open. I need you to come up starting tomorrow. I have some reports that are due. The inmate I had doing them was recently paroled, so your timing is great. What unit are you in?" he asked.

"I'm not in a unit yet," I said.

"Here, take this cop out to Counselor Johnson, and tell him I sent you down to get your housing together," Howard said, as he turned back to his computer desk.

I thanked him. Looking out the corner of his eye, Howard responded, "No problem. I understand you also have a background of standing up for your people. So do I." This was his way of letting me know he knew more about me than what I had told him. We both smiled a little bit, then I left.

Upon arriving at the counselor's office, the other Johnson, a real pleasant brother, already had my housing unit and room assignment available. I would be going into the Joshua housing complex, Unit 3, Room B-2. I was allowed the rest of the day to move my belongings. I could see the other GMC inmates looking at me as I dragged my laundry bag down the hill. I wondered what that was all about. I later found out that news around prison (camps or otherwise) travels fast. Many of the inmates knew I had already gotten an inside work assignment. I had gotten out of the 114 degree heat, after only two days, which was virtually unheard of. The usual process is two weeks (or more) on GMC, then a mandatory 60-day stint of cafeteria duty. Then, you get to seek out a work assignment. I never did a day in the cafeteria, so now it was perceived that I had gotten some sort of preferential treatment. But it didn't stop there. I also found out that no less than 25 inmates had requested the Powerhouse work assignment. Howard was the adviser to the Black inmate cultural group, many of whom had inquired about the work assignment. The talk was that such positions are coveted and highly competitive. For the assignment to be given to a two-day inmate didn't sit well with some of the other inmates. Then there was the housing assignment.

The Joshua housing complex was the newer housing on the camp. It was air-conditioned and generally perceived as the more preferential housing assignment. Of the 240 or so inmates in the Joshua complex, only about 25 were Black. The rest of the Black inmates were up the hill in the older complex, which wasn't air conditioned, so any time a vacancy came up in Joshua, there was a rush of requests to fill it, and inmates generally knew when that was. But this ain't all of it. I was put in Unit 3.

Unit 3 was the unit that housed the volunteer firefighters, those charged with assisting the Highway Patrol "scrape up people off 395 after an accident," as one of the inmates put it. As stated earlier, 395 was one of the most dangerous highways in the state, so there was always activity among the firefighters. But for the non-firefighters who were housed in Unit 3, (which were about 30 or so inmates), it was perceived as a privilege. There was a waiting list to get into Unit 3, because it usually rated first in the weekly housing inspections, which meant they ate first, used the phones first, and generally were given less supervision. Unit 3 wasn't required to cut the TV off at midnight and could shower after 10 p.m. Such leniency made Unit 3 a reward for inmates, who showed exemplary behavior. An assignment in Unit 3 was a judgment call so there was definitely some consideration given to my placement there and, of course, my fellow inmates knew that.

So, for all this to come together in a matter of a day, seemed so much more than coincidental. I had great apprehension about being the recipient of so much "good luck." Given the attitudes of some of my new "mates," I knew this could be potentially hazardous at some point. So how was I to take all this? My perception was that one of two things was happening: either the Black correctional officers were looking out for me, or I was being set up to have some inmate's wrath come in my direction. Truth to be known, I felt it was more the former, than the latter. However, I wasn't in much of a position to refuse it. I just had to be cautious as to how these acts of benevolence played out. But for right now, given my circumstance, it was a welcome relief.

* * *

The first two weeks were the loneliest of my life. I couldn't have any visitors until my visitors' list was approved. A few people had come out to see me but had been turned away. The Bureau of Prisons made a point of letting every inmate know that "they were in charge." They didn't care who you were, which meant any talk about your lawyer, etc., didn't mean shit to them. It had been an interesting two weeks, to say the least. I had met my new roommates, Mark, Craig and Dave. Mark, who was Jewish, was doing time for a combination of charges involving the record industry. He made a point of letting me know that his biggest hit was "Double-Dutch Bus" and that

Black people were OK with him. Craig was a white boy, also a banker, from Utah. He was doing five years probation, when he was arrested and convicted of drunk driving, in the last month of his sentence. His judge violated his probation, and sent him away for three years. He was the quietest of the three, wore a long beard, and read all the time (when he wasn't playing softball). Craig was always very cordial and respectful toward me. His position was, "I'm just here to do my time." Dave, who was also white, considered himself a social "blue blood" and was a straight out racist. He was in a major real estate fraud case and had more charges pending. Dave was clearly the most disturbed about my presence. He took it upon himself to acquaint me with the "room rules." The first thing out of his mouth was, "In this room, we take a bath every day." I looked at the other two, who looked at Dave in amazement. Mark apologized for him later, saying he had a lot of nerve, given that he worked in the shit pond (the sewage outlet for the camp).

On my first day in the room, a 12x12 room with two bunk beds and four 7-foot lockers for personal possessions, I was assigned the bunk over Dave. Beds were assigned according to seniority, so the new guy takes what's left. When a guy leaves, other inmates will trade mattresses, bed boards, pillows and anything else. I had a soft mattress and no bed board (for three weeks), so my bunk dipped lower than it should have. Every time Dave sat up he'd brush his head against the dip in my bed, (which was basically my butt) and he'd get up cursing and mumbling under his breath. Not a week had passed when it had gotten back to me, through another Black inmate, who got it from his white inmate, that Dave was looking to trade rooms. He couldn't stand livin' with that "Moos-lim nigger." He eventually got the unit manager to move him, just before they shipped him back to trial again.

But for the most part, we all got along pretty well, as did most everybody in Unit 3. I was surprised at how polite the whole camp environment was overall. In talking with another inmate who had made a similar observation, if the society on the outside was as polite, the world might be a better place. What made the camp environment so polite was that in prison, to disrespect someone, intentionally or unintentionally, could cost you your life; regardless of the level of security of the prison. It was a real study in sociology and psychology, to watch grown men respect the personal boundaries of other men. Most had more respect for other inmates, than the prison authorities. It wasn't that prison authorities had any less juice, the freedom of a prison camp was such that almost every inmate preferred it to the next step up, which was the medium security prison at Terminal Island (T.I.). The next step up was jail, for real. Any fighting, insubordination, failing a urine test, failing to return from authorized leave, was cause to be shipped out. But while most inmates didn't want that, it wasn't going to stop them from "getting their respect." There were fights on occasion, mostly over the television. To turn the television while somebody else was watching, almost guaranteed you an "ass-whippin'." The other thing that got you in trouble just as fast, was stealing from another inmate. The only thing worse than being labeled a thief was the label of snitch. Both brought on severe consequences. An inmate could leave most anything around the TV room, and it would stay there for several days, until the owner claimed it. These codes of ethics were largely self-imposed and self-regulated. It made for a somewhat peaceful existence.

I began to see the immediate benefit of being in Unit 3. Being the first to eat and use the phones, I had a chance to use the phones, almost every day. It was during this period that I began to understand how important support systems on the outside really were. People say "call me if you need anything," but most don't really mean it. I was fortunate enough to have several friends that did mean it, and they never rejected my collect calls. Collect calls from Boron were expensive as hell. Still, there were about a half dozen friends that took my calls.

There were also some people I thought were friends who didn't take my calls. If this whole experience taught me anything at all, it taught me the understanding of love and friendship. My loyalties, even today, are driven by how people dealt with me during this most difficult period in my life. However, while I was at Boron, I came to understand how really lucky I was to even have people to call. There were many people there, who had nobody to call, and who had no outside support systems to give them encouragement and hope. In the short period that I was at Boron, it was not uncommon to hear grown men cry and plead with their women, loved ones or external support systems, who threatened to discontinue such support by breaking off the relationship or the communication, simply telling the inmate to stop calling them. Some had been in four or five years and had nothing to look forward to on the outside but a friendly voice. Without that they had nothing. Just to be able to talk to somebody often made me feel I had nothing to complain about, regardless of how lonely I actually was.

By the end of the first week, I had received my P.O. Box. I was fortunate enough to have received mail from the very first day. Of the

139 days I was at Boron, not counting weekends , I received mail every day, except two days. Most days I received several pieces. Mail pick-up was after 3 p.m., and it was clearly the highlight of my day. Every day. I never thought I'd be so overwhelmingly excited about something so simple as receiving mail. I looked forward to receiving my mail. However, just as with the phones, there were inmates who never received mail, or whose hopes hinged on getting that letter in the mail that had been sent "a week ago," according to the sender.

Some inmates even displayed anger and hostility toward those that got mail. The jealously was so bad at times, you almost felt embarrassed that you had someone that cared enough about you to send you something. Some guys would look in the box, see mail and come back later to pick it up, just to escape the gaze of the envious, scrutinizing the daily mail run. You could literally make enemies because you got mail and somebody else didn't. The fact that you had support systems didn't make you better, but of course in the envious eyes that didn't have support systems, it did, so you had to be real low-key over anything you might have received in the mail. "Get any mail today?" you might be asked by some "mate" with a suspecting gnarl.

"Just junk mail," might be your best response. Even if you got the letter of your life, and were excited as hell about it, you better not show it, lest it be mistaken for flaunting.

It was the same with visits. I knew I would have some soon, so I watched how those inmates interacted after coming back from "visit highs." They could barely talk about it, other than to a roomie or a close confidant, because those inmates who didn't get visits, didn't really want to hear how you enjoyed seeing a loved one or kissing your woman. And it wasn't long before the conversation evolved to, "So you think you're all that ..." A visit that meant everything, had to be treated as if it was no big deal, although it was. You could see guys beaming on the inside from excitement after a visit, like they were going to bust--though they dare not. That was jail life.

Then there was the issue of money. Many inmates didn't have anybody to send them any money from the outside (although many did). The camp gives you a commissary card and a purchase account. You couldn't spend any more than $125 per month, which broke down to about $31.25 a week. Most inmates came in making 7 cents per hour on their work assignment. That's $2.80 a week to take care of one's basic necessities, not including extras. This meant that an inmate had to find other ways to earn money. "You got to find yourself a hustle," as my roomie Mark would say. Some inmates ironed clothes for other inmates. Some inmates cleaned rooms to pass inspection. Others typed legal papers for inmates working on their own appeals. Mark painted pictures and made cards for inmates to send to their loved ones.

The bottom line was that some inmates had money to buy things -- watches, tennis shoes, and sweat suits -- sold by the commissary. Others didn't, just like on the outside. And, of course, just like in the hood when you show up with something new, eyes roll and people mumble, "You think you're all that." Jealousy and envy permeates, successful circumstances notwithstanding. Capitalism makes some have to "hustle" inside and out, just to make-do.

I came in with money in my commissary account, plus a week didn't go by when somebody wasn't sending me $25 here or $40 there. Then, if I really needed something, I'd call Sharon Clerkley, and have her take it out of my business account. I figured I wasn't going to be there long enough to have to get a hustle, which was another reason not to like me. I came in "short," meaning I'd soon be leaving. What seemed like an eternity to me, was light at the end of the tunnel for most. You could virtually see it in their faces, when an inmate had been in for three or four years, and still had more time left than I had coming in. Some inmates had 2001 release dates, and this was in 1990 (because they had 10 and 15-year mandatory sentences). When you said six months, it was like "why'd they bother to send you." It also meant people weren't inclined to get too close to you. Inmates with short time were also in jeopardy of having fights picked with them by someone not leaving anytime soon. If found fighting, the "short" inmate would have his date moved back (release date deferred). The best thing a "short" mate could do was stay out of the way of trouble. Many inmates have been put to the jailhouse "pride" choice of what's more important, respect or going home? This is when you knew what an inmate had to go home to, depending on the choices one made. Many inmates chose to stay "a little longer" to prove this point. Some inmates are even baited into proving they "ain't no punk." I was one.

After going to orientation, and receiving my initial sentence computation, I found out that I wouldn't have to do all six months, but four and a half months, 139 days. Even if my home monitoring didn't come through, I'd be home for the holidays. One day, while playing basketball, the game took a rougher tone than usual. Three times straight, I got hit with an elbow. The last time in the face, under my right eye. It was obvious, at that point, that a provocation was in effect.

The guy throwing the elbows was called "Truck." That's because he was as big as one. He weighed about 340 pounds and had 22-inch biceps. I asked what the problem was.

His response was, "You ain't all that."

"All what?" I asked. Next play, he hit me again in the back of my head. Everybody just walked away. They knew Truck was picking a fight. Just then, a guard walked up.

"Is there a problem?" he asked. I had major choices: tell on an inmate and start a war, take a swing in front of a guard, and get time added, or take the shot for now. I could see Truck watching to see what I would do, as were the other inmates.

"No problem," I said. Now wasn't the time to fight that fight. I took a shot, walked around with a Black eye for a week, but gained the respect of my Black inmates. Not because I took the shot, but because I didn't snitch. From that point, they would come up and talk to me, unlike before the provocation. They let me know that it was because I had short time, and had been shown favoritism that the incident occurred. And they wanted to see how I'd respond to a little rough-housing. Would I give up my time over a senseless point in a basketball game, or would I endanger myself for the rest of my stay, by hiding behind the guards? I walked a very fine line that day. It was a turning point in how I was perceived by both inmates and by the guards.

I chose to side with my mates. I did get a chance to redeem myself a week later. Larry and I teamed up to play in a two-on-two basketball tournament, and so did Truck and his roomie. First prize was a case of sodas. The defending champs of the last three tournaments played us in the first round. We beat them easily and coasted to the finals. Truck's team had a relatively easy road to the finals. The match-up was after dinner. Almost all the brothers gulped down their dinner and were outside sitting on the sideline when we (Truck, his partner and I) got there. Larry had kitchen duty, and had to eat late. The game was supposed to start at 6 p.m. It was now 6:05. The opposition was calling for a forfeit, when Larry walked up. "Lets get started," the inmate referee called out.

Larry looked at me. "Do I need to warm up?" he asked.

"Nope," I said. He smiled and winked. The rules were called out. Straight 13 by one, call your own fouls, winner take out and shoot the die for outs. I stepped to the top of the key to shoot.

Truck said, "I'll shoot it." I handed him the ball. He missed. Our out. It was seven-nothing before anybody could blink, our favor.

I hit two. Larry hit three in a row. I hit two more. Then we missed. Truck came in, elbows and knees flying, Barkley style. Basket. Jump shot from the right perimeter. Basket. Truck rebounded a missed jump shot. Basket. He drove again for a lay-up, block.

I rebounded the block, dribbled to the top of the key and whispered to Larry, "This is kind of personal, mind if I take over?"

Larry said, "Handle it." I took the ball and went into the post. The score was 7-3. Larry dumped it down to me. Pump fake. Truck flew, a reverse lay-up, 8-3. Jump shot from the right of the key, 9-3. Jump shot from the top of the key, 10-3. Jump shot from the left corner, 11-3. Fake shot from the right perimeter. Truck flew. Easy lay-up, 12- 3. Point game. Larry threw the ball in. Truck charged and ran into me. No harm, no foul. He was up on me, hand on my waist to keep me from going around him. Everybody knew by then that I was going to take the last shot. Truck knew that if we were going to win, I'd have to shoot it over him. And he wasn't going to give it to me. I was about 25 feet out. I faked the drive, stepped back to the left perimeter like I was stepping behind a three point line, only there wasn't one. I raised up, 22 feet out. Truck charged like a bull, waiting for me to flitch up. I didn't. Swoosh. Nothing but net. Game, 13-3. I went over and shook Larry's hand. Then Truck's, then his partner's. The side line was quiet after cheering for Truck's three baskets. That was before I made the last six shots. Our differences had been settled in a way most of them didn't expect. Before I would leave Boron, Truck would apologize to me privately about the whole incident. But on this day, the theory of jailhouse intimidation didn't pan out. As I walked off the court to collect my sodas, I walked past Iman Halim, who had been watching from afar.

"You are a pretty talented brother, Bro. Anthony. Allah allowed you ... no, used you to demonstrate a lesson today. But did you learn yours?"

I looked at him in a perplexed manner. "What do you mean, Bro. Halim?"

"Allah didn't put you here for sport and play. Recreation is fine, as long as it's well-intentioned. Do you think all of those brothers were out there to watch recreation? They were out there to see confrontation. But Allah always protects the righteous. The lesson for you is to use both your time and temperament more wisely. Foolish pride makes us do foolish things, and opens us up to danger. Refrain from putting yourself in those situations where the danger is great, and benefit is little. Lest you risk your life for little or nothing," he explained.

I understood what he was saying. I didn't come to Boron to play ball, especially after being warned that basketball was almost a surefire way to bring on conflict at the camp. I thought about why I had went on to play ball, in spite of the risks. Why did I want to play that bad, to risk fights, heat stroke, ankle and back injuries? I concluded that I was in a period of high anxiety and going through my own form of culture shock. Though my main preoccupation had been reading, writing and praying about six hours a day, I was still very anxious over not hearing from my attorney, not being able to have visitors, and just being overly cautious about what I said, who I talked to, who I was with, who to trust, and who not to trust. I was indeed in shock.

Since I was a child, basketball had been a favorite form of relaxation for me. I was here trying to make the best of a bad situation. Playing ball, at least for a moment, made me forget my surroundings, my problems and my pressures, as it always had. It was the only way I could explain my getting caught up in these little jailhouse games, and the hazards that they brought on. But Iman Halim was right. I couldn't want to play so bad that I could get sucked up into somebody else's plot. After all, that's how I ended up here. Not because of what I did, but because somebody else used what I did against me, in advancing their own plot. And because I wanted so badly to change an organization, I ignored the plot and brought danger to myself.

I never again can ignore another person's motives. Never again, as the Jews say. Even those that seem well-intentioned; like a little recreational B-balling, for example. This was an excellent lesson, brought full circle by the Iman's insight. "Why don't you wash up and join us for Asr prayer," Halim asked.

I said "OK. I'll be right up." When I came up to the camp chapel, there were about a dozen brothers getting ready for prayer. I had seen most of them before at the two Juma services I had attended, but now I got to greet most of them personally. Within minutes of my arrival, Halim asked one of the brothers to perform the Adzan (call to prayer). The brother proceeded, in Arabic, to call the brothers to prayer. Lining up on our prayer rugs behind the Iman, everyone performed their four rakas of Asr prayer, some remaining behind to perform some supplemental prayers, including me.

As Halim turned to leave, he said, "Seven o'clock every day, Bro. Anthony. Prayer keeps us out of trouble and makes us stronger."

"Yes sir. I will be here," I responded. I went outside of the chapel and sat on the bench out front. The chapel was on the highest point in the camp. From there you could see the whole desert until it just disappeared into the horizon. The only visible means of escape was that narrow strip of pavement called Highway 395. Watching cars come and go, evaporating from view, was an imposing sight. You really understand the meaning of freedom when you can't go anywhere. With the sun at my back, I virtually watched the moon come up. I thought about why I was really there, watching a desert sunset that I would have probably never seen or thought to look for, had I not been forced to be there.

In our everyday lives, we often lose track of time or misunderstand its value. But in confinement, you can literally watch seconds and minutes go by, each seeming as long as hours, even days. You repeatedly find yourself checking the time. Damn, it's just 7 o'clock? What time is it now? Damn, it's just 10 after seven? In what seems like an eternity, is just a moment in time. Once you become conscientious of time and its relative value, then you suddenly understand the real penalty of incarceration. Taking something from you that you can never regain. A moment in time. More precious than gold. It can't be measured quantitatively for value, but when it's gone, you know it's gone. Gold and possessions can be replaced. How do you replace time? You don't.

This whole experience was about a lesson in time value and its rate of return. If you do nothing with time, you get nothing in return. When you misuse time, you lose more time trying to get on track. When you abuse time, you lose track of time altogether. Wasted or idol time (as our parents used to say) is the devil's workshop. How does all this time talk tie into my first three weeks in Boron? Up to then, I had just been passing time. No, actually I was wasting time, and had wandered into the devil's workshop. As I was sitting on this hill after prayer, things became more clear and unclogged. Now I felt that the monkey was off my back. The lesson is that "the place to be" is not necessarily where everybody is, but where you know there is something substantive and enriching. I liked the feeling. It was almost a high. My anxiety was gone, because I realized nothing could be taken from me, including time, unless I gave it willingly. The thought that I was losing or missing something in L.A., turned to thoughts that I was actually gaining something, if I took the time to examine it. My anxiety was nothing more than "niggah merry-go-round" withdrawal. You know how you still feel you're spinning, even after the ride has stopped? You may even walk in a circle or two. Well, on a merry-go-round, you feel you have to be some place, just to say you were there. This last little experience was symptomatic of merry-go- round withdrawal: the need to be somewhere, not necessarily to my benefit, or the need to prove something to people to whom you owe nothing, or the need to say you were there. But now that I had a chance to think about it, to pray over it, to assess it and to rationalize it, I understood what this was all about. I committed myself to advance myself with focus and purpose, not with wanting to conform to the whims and attitudes that just run people in circles.

* * *

The following week, then my fourth, was quite eventful. My mailbox was full every day, with my friends and loved ones keeping me laughing in an effort to keep my spirits up. On some days, I'd have more than a dozen pieces of mail, which really made me feel that people thought about me. A core group of my friends would always accept my phone calls when I wanted to talk. The few that didn't really disappointed me, helping me see that adversity was a clear barometer of who my friends were. At last, I could have visits. Almost a month after I arrived, my visitors list was approved. You could only have 15 people on your list at any one time. Everyone to whom I sent an application, said they sent them back within two days. It must have taken another two weeks for the feds to investigate my requests. No one on my list was rejected. The last weekend in August, I had five visits: three on Saturday, two on Sunday. My first visitors were Sharon Clerkley and Colin Mitchell. They came early Saturday. It was great seeing friendly and familiar faces. We talked about what was or wasn't happening in Los Angeles, how business was going and how clients were being handled. Just as Sharon and Colin were leaving, Debra pulled up. We all met at the door. Debra and Sharon hugged. Colin and I hugged each other. I hugged Debra. It was really great seeing her.

Debra, always being so analytical, methodically went down the list, "How's your spirit? How's your health? How's your attitude? Have you been eating? Have you been sleeping?" Answering fine, fine, fine, yes, yes, to all of her questions, we just sat and talked light for a couple of hours. She spent much of the time talking about her adjustment as a California Senate Fellow, the behind-the-scene antics of legislative politics and the tedious task of fashioning public policy. While Debra was somewhat venting her frustrations over making up the legislative learning curve, I still sensed her hidden excitement about being in the program. Combined with the Sacramento change of pace, I knew she'd rather be there, than anywhere else, at the time. Especially since I was here. We both were in a change of life adjustment period, and it was for the better for both of us. Both of our patience, mental fortitude and psychological toughness were being tried, and it was not without frequent trial. We laughed about each other's personal reflections, encouraged each other to hang in and dream about better days to come. It seemed like the three hours we spent together flew by. It was time for the noon count, which meant visitations were interrupted for about 30 minutes. Debra, down for the weekend, had to do the family tour. It had been about a month since she had been down. She planned to spend the rest of the day in L.A., spend the night in Riverside with her parents, come back to see me tomorrow then fly back up to Sacramento. We hugged and kissed (it's the only time you're allowed to kiss at the end of visits--there are no conjugal visits in the federal prison system). It was the best I'd felt, since this whole nightmare began. I was in seventh heaven.

Going back to my room, it was all I could do to keep from busting out with joy and laughter. I jumped into my bunk and just stared at the ceiling for what seemed like hours, when I heard over the muzzled loud speaker, "Essex, report to the visitation room. Essex report to the visitation room." I thought I was dreaming, so I ignored it. About 10 minutes later, someone stuck their head in the room, when the loud speaker repeated a similar gurgle, "Hey Essex, you have a visit." I ran back over to the visitors room thinking Debra probably left something, only to see Ron Carter and Steve Bradford. Daryl Sweeney was outside, but they wouldn't let him in, saying his name wasn't on the list. We all hugged and went outside to visit. I went over to the wall by the parking lot, where Daryl. We hugged over the brick fence. We sat by the fence where the four of us talked about 15 minutes, before a guard came and made Daryl leave. There was no waiting for visitors on the parking lot. You're either a visitor, or you're not. It was great just to see Daryl though, as well as Ron and Steve. Their sense of urgency to get out to see me will never be forgotten. Ron and Steve let me know that I wasn't missing anything in L.A., and that several radio discussions had indicated overwhelming sentiment that I was a prime example of judicial bias and sentencing discrimination against Blacks. I was glad to hear that somebody was at least saying something. But more than that, I appreciated the support system that appeared evident as my friends sought to keep me in high spirits. When Ron, Steve and Daryl left, I knew I had real friends. We underestimate support systems sometimes, particularly when we're feeling low. At least I did. However, at the conclusion of that day, I had a peace of mind that was just unparalleled. At "ASR" prayer, I performed an extra "raka" for each friend who had come to see me that day, asking Allah to bless them and protect them.

Sunday, Debra came back early. Floyd Frazier, accompanied by his friend, Rochelle Butler, came out around noon. They let Rochelle stay, even though she wasn't on the list. Sunday was every bit as pleasurable as the day before. As the time for visiting concluded, I learned another valuable jailhouse lesson. It was about a quarter to three, and most of the inmates were wrapping up their visits and getting out of the visiting room. Since visits end at 3 o'clock, I stayed until 3 o'clock. As I started to leave, I was held up, along with five other guys who came out after me. It was about 10 of us in all. What I found out was that the guards were supposed to randomly select 10 inmates to strip search after their visits. The guards instead would search whoever was left over at the end of the day. Most of the guys were relatively new and unsuspecting of this process. "Not no more," as we say in the hood. That would be the final time it would happen to me, but it still couldn't dull the feeling I had after seeing my friends for the first time in a month

The social and political aspects of incarceration are very similar to those on the outside, only more magnified. While inmate rights are stated in the Bureau of Prisons Manual, and there are processes to express and resolve problems, actual recourse is selectively applied. Plainly put, the racism one experiences in prison is much more deep-seeded, almost raw, in its establishment of power and privilege. If you ever really want to know what slavery was like, go to jail. Someone who's never been in this position can never communicate to one who has that "I know how you feel" inference. You can never know how one feels to be openly denigrated on a daily basis. To literally have no rights. Unlike any other institution in American life, the military included, incarceration is the reincarnation of involuntary servitude. And there is a selective application of favoritism shown to those in servitude. The privileges afforded to some, at the discretion of some twisted taskmaster, is greatly disparate and runs consistently along racial lines. Moreover, there's not a damn thing, in most cases, an inmate could say or do about it.

In the final analysis, just like in slavery, it's the master's word against the slaves. And in terms of credibility, when the race component kicks in, it's the Dred Scott decision all over again. The Dred Scott decision stated that Blacks had no rights that whites were bound to respect (when ex-slaves were recaptured and brought back across state lines from "free" territories back into slavery). So while the inmate population co-existed, their interface with the prison management was where power and privilege played out, even though, we were supposed to be treated equally as inmates. In my somewhat enlightened state, I was able to see, very clearly, the disparity in treatment among the general population. From an advocacy perspective, this experience was invaluable because it gives a greater insight, a more personal insight to the fallacy behind societal correction. Societal correction is actually perpetual rejection of those who were ordered to pay a debt to society for committing social wrongs. The reformed are treated so unjustly in terms of the exploitation one suffers, the correction never takes place, and recidivist behavior is actually nurtured in place of corrective behavior.

If a Black is on the bottom of the social rung on the outside, then that is where he is likely to remain on the inside. While he's locked up, he's to be treated no better than he would be treated, if he were on the outside. With this supposition as the operating basis for prison environments, I began to see disparities in how inmates received certain privileges and sought to justify those disparities. There was no reasonable justification, other than the inference of race. Who decided how furloughs came about, who received halfway house or parole consideration, how did one get recommended for privileged job assignments like the fire crew or off-base duty at George Air Force Base, how was it decided that a person's time is taken, when several inmates are equally liable, who gets piss-tested and who doesn't, or whose locker gets "tossed" or shaken down. The prevailing attitudes among the Black inmate population were that "things were the way they were" and that's it, never really knowing why or understanding the process of recourse. Then again, because of the subversive race politics, many may have felt that pursuing processes of recourse brought more trouble than they were worth, meaning retaliation or intimidation was the cost to pay for challenging unfairness. Their attitudes were why make "easy time, hard time." For the length of time most had to spend there, it just wasn't worth the challenge. As one young brother told me, "The system always wins in the end. Always."

"Anthony, you're short on time, you're a recognized activist, you understand the processes and you're smart. There's not a lot they can do to you. Once you're gone, what about the rest of us? They pick us off one by one until there's no one left to even raise a question."

It was absolutely true. The Federal Bureau of Prisons had so many leverages to control an inmate, it wasn't even funny. Not just control an inmate's behavior, but also manipulate any integrity one might develop while under the authority of societal correction. Anything from threats, to a higher security prison to withdrawal of halfway house consideration, to furlough delays, and to shots (a write-up) for the hell of it.

All of these leverages were enough to conveniently modify an inmate's behavior, attitude or recall at an appropriate moment or allow themselves to be abused by a power hungry, $500 a week, toy guard (the mates called them) without a gun (minimum security prison guards carry walkie-talkies). It was deep to watch inmates be told "they ain't got nothing coming," to watch them congealed into telling on someone or to watch them be locked in "the hole" (solitary confinement). But most disgusting was to see that this wasn't consistent treatment across the board. It was selective treatment very selective applications, "color selective." Not always, as is the case with the rest of American society, but disparate enough so that you'd notice. Though nobody wanted to say anything, Club Fed (the federal prison system) was having a culture shock of its own.

Minimum security prisons were traditionally reserved for white collar criminals, mostly fiduciary or tax breaches uncommon to most Blacks. It was very rare, at one time, to see Black so-called white collar criminals, in a minimum security federal prison. Largely because Blacks haven't been in white collar positions in significant numbers for very long, and if they were in such a capacity, they rarely had the juice to take on anything of substance. The federal prison camp environment was where this country sent the privileged to do their time. Like most systems in America, it was a system set up to create the illusion of incarceration, but it was actually just a place, a "handslap" penalty box, they sent their own where they could publicly represent that justice was being served. In actuality, it was like five minutes "time out" in a hockey game. In the process, justice (as in the American justice system) was serving them. So from the Nixon clan to the Reagan sleaze factor (where over 400 insiders were investigated and/or indicted), to the billionaire's boy's club--including the one who "broke" Wall Street, Michael Milken, none of them ever did a day of "hard time" in their lives.

Some of America's most diabolical "mastermind criminals, those who made their living and their wealth on "beating the system" that most Americans are forced to abide by, or manipulated the people, by virtue of privileged positions in government, did nothing more than sit in a resort-like environment for a few years, and lived the lives of the commoners that they never were, nor ever wanted to be. They were rarely treated as a criminal, even though many of them committed greater crimes against the public trust, than the most notorious murderer. A murderer may have had one victim, or several, if they were a mass murderer. Some of the most notorious white collar criminals literally destroyed thousands of lives, bankrupted whole systems, and did less time than a petty robber, and in many, many instances never, ever saw jail bars in their lives. When they left jail, they were never treated like criminals, and the only thing they can say they learned from their experience is that they know what its like to be treated as a common. America, a system of privilege set up by privileged for the privileged, has always found a way to take care of its own.

The federal prison system's problem came in the federal government's so-called "War on Drugs," which really hasn't been a war on drugs, but a war on street dealers. The sweep has not been at the borders, at the ports, or at the top of the cartels, but at the end, the dealer and the user. The crackhead, the "slanger," the "banger," the driver, the "bag man," anybody who ends up on the tail end of this illicit drug train, which to nobody's surprise, is mostly poor people of color. Since the late 1980s, with the combination of sentencing guidelines and Reagan's "crime stand against the mob" (to deflect attention away from Reaganomics and the Iran-Contra scandal), the federal court system has taken in literally thousands of young Black and brown men (and an increasing number of women) on "drug possession, with the intent to sell" charges. Many of them were first-time offenders, others were carrying a bag for a friend, others were driving the car, when stopped by police while someone in the car was carrying, and a whole host of circumstantial situations. Next thing they knew, they were before a federal judge, with no representation, a conviction, and a sentencing guideline for an automatic five years. The point: what was once an "away from home retreat" for America's white collar "bad boys," those still covering for the system and sure to be taken care of once they did their time, was quickly becoming an experiment in forced integration on another level. The resistance was great, because unlike the society at large, most of the men kept there (at least in the past) were men of accomplishment, who never had to see a Black, if they didn't want to. Now they were eating with them, working with them, and rooming with them on a daily basis. Some were vocal about it--to prison management no less--like this was the Hilton resort or something.

While all inmates were supposed to be treated equally, there appeared to be some empathy for some inmates' little social adjustment. Not necessarily (always) at the higher levels of prison management like warden, assistant warden, etc., but at those rank-and-file levels that interfaced with the prison population, particularly those who had the power to recommend furloughs and paroles to the counselors. They had their asses kissed on a regular basis and some were quite discriminate with whom they dealt. A few "CO's" at Boron were power drunk with this authority and were almost retaliatory toward anyone who chose to challenge their decisions.

The parole policy of the Federal Bureau of Prisons allows for any inmate sentenced six months or longer to be eligible for supervised parole within 60 days of their parole date. Sometimes that period can be longer. Supervised parole is more commonly called a halfway house. This is where the inmate goes to work in the public, but must return to supervision, by a designated time at a designated location, where a person sleeps and sees visitors. This is supposed to serve as an inmate's transition back into society. While any inmate may be eligible (according to the severity of their crime), it is up to the counselors, to decide who gets considered for the next halfway house opportunity. Because this process is highly selective, it helps to be in the good graces of those who make the decision. I decided that since my sentence wasn't going to be commuted, that I'd apply for halfway house consideration. The inmates that I was talking to felt that my offense was light enough to merit immediate consideration, given most felt I probably shouldn't have been there anyway. I set up an appointment to see my unit counselor, a guy named Pacheco.

Although he was a Latino, Pacheco had a reputation for flexing his power. Similar to what Blacks term as an "Oreo," Pacheco was similarly labeled, for whatever Latinos call those who act more white, than the white man himself, or act worse on his own and other minorities, than the white man would have acted. Word was Pacheco was tough on Black inmates, and nobody would appeal his decision. Why? Because if you did and lost, you could kiss furloughs and early parole goodbye. When I met him, he appeared to be disinterested in my request or what I had to say. "You ain't got nothing coming, Essex. We have guys who have been waiting for a halfway house for three years. What makes you think you should go before them?" he said.

"Because I qualify to go. The policy says one qualifies within 60 days of a release date on a sentence six months or longer. Do I qualify or not?" I reiterated.

Pacheco held firm saying, "Yeah, you qualify but you don't merit."

"What constitutes merit?" I asked.

"Paying your dues like everybody else," he said.

"I'm paying my dues as we speak, or I wouldn't be here," I said. "Are you the final decision?" I asked.

"Yep," he said. I turned to leave and noticed Pacheco laughing and shaking his head. I thought to myself that his view of paying dues was kissing his ass, until he was ready to recommend a halfway house placement, which I wasn't about to do.

"I can see you enjoy your job," I said.

"What's that supposed to mean?" he said, turning serious.

"Just what I said," walking out the door. I went back to my work assignment, and began picking other inmates about what my recourse options were. That's when the appeal process came to my attention. I filed an appeal on Pacheco's decision to deny me an opportunity to receive halfway house consideration. A few weeks later, the appeal was returned in my favor. When I went back to Pacheco, he was a lot humbler, but still just as disingenuous. I later found out that this was part of the psychological game played on inmates to get their hopes up, only to have them crash, when the date for halfway house release came about and guess what -- no halfway house, no release.

Some of the Muslim inmates advised me on what to expect as my date got closer. If certain things happened, I was on my way out. If they didn't, I wasn't going anywhere. Another ironic thing happened, after my appeal came back. My locker was tossed. That's when two guards come to your room and search your locker for contraband. This occurs about once a year, though they could do it every six months without cause. It occurred three times for me, in the four and a half months I was at Boron. Usually, after I appealed a decision by prison management (which I did on two other occasions). Generally, the guards would do it during the work day when nobody was in the room or during free time. They usually wouldn't disturb anybody if they were in the room. However, whenever they tossed my locker, they put everybody out of the room, closed the door and did whatever they had to do. On the first search, they found a radio that had been given to me by one of the inmates, who had since been paroled. This is sort of an inmate tradition, to give all their stuff away to other inmates, so they wouldn't have to buy them from the commissary.

I was on the yard shooting hoops when over the loudspeaker I hear, "Inmate Essex, report to Lieutenant Steele's office, right away." Everybody was like, "Oh shit, what'd you do?" Word was, the only time you got called to Steele's office was when your urine test came up dirty or you were about to receive a serious write-up. Since I didn't have a urine test, I even wondered what was up. Steele was the biggest intimidator on the camp and the only guard to wear a gun. His bullish demeanor and cold personality left a lot to be desired among the inmate population. You could barely talk to him, much less kid with him, like some of the inmates tended to do with some of the other guards. With him, he only had one reason to talk to an inmate--that was to bust `em. The inmates called him "the toy cop" too (but not to his face).

When I got up to his office, they had me stand outside his office for about ten minutes. I could hear him yelling obscenities at someone else, then yell, "That's two days in the hole for you."

Escorting the inmate out, Steele yelled, "Next." I came into his office and stood in front of his desk.

"Who are you?" he asked with a deep stare.

"Essex," I said.

"Ahh, so you're Essex. Our equal opportunity man." I ignored the comment, nodding my head. "I didn't hear you," he snapped.

"I'm Essex," I repeated.

"Well, Essex, we found a radio in your locker you didn't buy. Is it yours?" he asked.

"Yes," I said.

"Where'd you get it?" he continued.

"I found it," I said.

"Ohhhh, you found it," he said acting in mock surprise.

"I found it," I repeated.

"Where'd you find it?"

"On top of the ice machine in Unit 3," I answered. He looked at me with this real devilish stare, shook his head and started filling out the violation form. Completing the form, he put it in front of me to sign. "In possession of contraband" was the violation. "Inmate counseled" was the corrective action taken. Solitary confinement and transfer to another (which usually ment higher) facility and "other" were the choices listed below the counseling line marked.

Tearing off my copy, Steele said to me in a very stern manner, "Don't find nothing else."

Without responding, I took my copy of the write-up and left. Upon returning back to my room, my roomies wanted to know what happened. Mark said he just knew I was a goner. Most of them thought that it was highly unusual to have this search come up the way it did, so closely after my meeting with Pacheco. It was clear retaliation. After that incident, I was labeled by some of the "elite" inmates (if you could imagine such) a NWA (Nigger with an Attitude), but I had made my point. And they made theirs. Inmates are just squirrels in their world; without nuts. Squirrels don't fuck with wolves in their den.

As it came closer to the time I thought I would be leaving, I began to somewhat enjoy the camaraderie I had established with my fellow inmates. After a couple of months, you had pretty much heard everybody's story. The camp's law library was always full with inmates working on appeals, researching case law, and typing responses to the court or to attorneys. I was in there quite often making copies of material I sent out, in case they got lost (on purpose). Some of them would ask my opinion on certain issues, and I would ask them their opinion on legal points. One would expect an inmate or two to maintain their innocence in their charged offense, but at the minimum level federal camp I attended, there was an overwhelming number of people maintaining their innocence.

The fact that they were in prison had nothing to do with guilt or innocence, but the inability and capacity to defend themselves against the Fed's. A federal charge brings on unimaginable expenses, most of which the defendant is unprepared to deal with. The federal court is no place for the disadvantaged. Money is the name of the game in the federal courts, and you have to have money to match the government dollar for dollar, in the extremely expensive federal court system. Many just "buy-down" their charges and do their time. At least they'll still have some of their money upon their release. That's why "super criminals" can steal or cost tax payers billions of dollars while getting rich themselves, and only do one to three years, until they are released back into a life of luxury. Others choose to defend themselves and lose, not so much because they were proven guilty, but because they ran out of money; can't counter the government's expert witnesses who provide the kind of testimony that biases juries. Many innocent men have gone broke by challenging the United States of America's federal court circuit. And most end up in federal prison camp, working on their appeals pro bono, after paying some attorney their life savings.

With relatively few exceptions, my observation of the profile of the average minimum level federal offender in the late 1980s was white male, college grad, 35 to 50, earning between $60,000 and $100,000, as a middle management executive, who was "in the loop" as former President Bush once denied he was, when queried about his role in the Iran-Contra scandal. The average federal offender was not the primary target of the federal investigation, but was either snitched on or indicted for not snitching. The average dollars involved in their offense was a million plus. The average time of a white collar offender is 18 to 30 months.

Yes, the feds pick up a bank President, or a major securities player, every now and then, but the federal prison camps are filled with fringe players the feds picked up, because they failed in their attempts to successfully prosecute their original targets. Most everybody else, like myself, were virtually dropped in their lap. While some had knowledge that they were walking a thin line, in their white collar activity, many had no idea what their superiors were up to. Those who did, couldn't get out in time. So, as a result of blind ambition (blind meaning refusal to see or question impropriety or unethical behavior), many careers were ruined (or at least put on hold) behind the feds' shotgun approach to criminal investigation or prosecution. Yes, if you shoot in a crowd, you are bound to hit somebody, though it may not be the person you intended to hit. Government prosecutors can be just as irresponsible in their random prosecutions, as the gang member that randomly shoots in a drive-by. You can be hit for being in the wrong place, at the wrong time. Whether you knew or didn't know doesn't matter. If you didn't know, you should have known, is the government's position. If you know or don't tell, you deserve to go down, is the other side of the government's coin. For many of the federal offenders, not telling and going to jail was the better choice. In some cases, it was the only choice. But it didn't make the government right. In fact, it proved how misguided government investigations tend to be.

Frustrated prosecutors, in over their heads and needing to justify expensive investigations, retaliate against those they can intimidate or compromise, and lives are ruined in the process. Federal prison camps are filled with the horror stories of this type of treacherous prosecution. The biggest gangster in this country can be the U.S. government, in its often unjust pursuit of suspects. The government seems like, at times, they could care less about being right. Few get to see or even hear about government witch hunts (many that came alive in the 1997 IRS hearings), where the more frustrated the government gets, the more desperate it gets, and the more irresponsible it becomes in how it achieves what it calls justice. The people see the end result but don't see what the original goal was. When the government goes on television or in the newspaper to tell the public about the three little fish they caught, they don't tell you about the six big whales they went after. The "ones that got away." Nor do they tell you that they went whale fishing, and ended up guppy fishing. Guppies just got caught up in the net put out for whales and couldn't get loose. Federal prison camps are like guppy holding tanks, gettin' more filled every day, while the government continues to prove itself more inept at whale fishing.

The same analogy can be applied to its increasing drug prosecutions. Federal drug prosecutions are like a Black man's parade. The profile, I observed, of the average federal drug offender in the mid to late 1980s was a Black male, 18 to 25 years old, high school education (or less), sporadically employed and makes between $12,000 and $24,000 annually, when employed. The average offender was most likely a street dealer of crack cocaine. The amount of crack seized at the time of arrest was likely to be less than $1,000 in value and less than 25 grams in weight. Many times it's less than $200 in value. Just a few rocks in your possession is all its takes. There were no kilos or suitcases of money involved in their arrests, but because of the federal sentencing guidelines, the mandatory minimum sentence is five years. Of the three dozen or so Black males I met at Boron in on drug convictions, two-thirds of them were first-time offenders, never having been in jail before in their lives. Most had sold drugs for less than a year before getting caught. It's usually the young fish who don't know how to avoid the net. Most of these young men were not above the first or second level of the drug food chain. Most probably bought their stash from someone they knew, another Black, meaning they didn't have a clue, as to who the distributor or the manufacturer was, much less the controllers of the drug organization. Yet, the government would have you believe that the war on drugs has been successful due to the number of arrests and a big haul that they show on TV every once in a while. The guppy is about the lowest you can go on the fish food chain. The U.S. government has become a guppy connoisseur, in terms of how it seeks out prosecutions and who they eventually prosecute. The one thing I noticed at Boron was a lot of inmates (like several dozen) walking around in a zombie-like state of mind unable to figure out how they ended up in jail.

Many, like myself, just tried to fit in and made the best of it. One of those "get in where you fit in" situations. During Sunday and Monday night football games, camaraderie among the "mates" ascended in our "dorm." I guess male bonding around sports knows no boundaries. Everybody would bring something -- chips, nuts, sodas, etc. The only thing missing was the beer. But there were some "moonshine" makers on the campgrounds, for those who needed that. Watching the games was the highlight of the week for many and it crossed class and race lines. I saw inmates actually curse, because they had a visit during the games. Others would arrange their visits on Saturday or another day of the week (other than Sunday or Monday). I never got so heavy into the games that I didn't want to be disturbed by a visitor. I always wanted visitors. And thanks to my friends, I was most always in the company of outside associations. Still the peaceful internal bonding of inmates was something to see.

The other times that were particularly special for inmate-bonding was Thursday and Friday nights, for one hour each night. These were known as nights for "the brothers hour." It was where the Black inmates watched what was considered "Black programming" because Black people were in the shows. "The Cosby Show" virtually raised the quality of prime time programming single-handedly, but it was considered a Black show to the white inmates. It was followed by "A Different World," another so-called Black show. So during this hour, both TVs in our dorm were conceded to the Black inmates (and those whites that wanted to watch). But when 9 p.m. came, there would be a stream of white inmates flooding the room in time for "Cheers." The transition was almost immediate, like a shift change of some sort. Then it was back to your regular programming, until Friday night at 11:30 p.m. when a rap formatted show called "Pump it Up" came on. It was real popular with the younger Black inmates. They never missed a Friday night to stay up on all the latest street sounds. One night, a fight almost broke out, when two white inmates thought they were going to come in and turn the television while "Pump it Up" was on. They wanted to watch that day's "U.S. Open" tennis highlights. Inmates downstairs were watching a movie and because there were only a handful of inmates upstairs, they thought they could come upstairs and impose their will.

This was a clear case of a couple of elitists, who usually don't have to deal with Blacks on the outside, except to impose their will upon them. They obviously forgot where they were. They reached to turn the television. "Aye man, what you doin'? You know this is the brothers hour to watch 'Pump it Up,' and we always watch it. So if you don't want to start something, we'd advise you not to turn the television," one of the young brothers stated. The two inmates negotiated to watch "the Open" results during "Pump it Up" commercials. Watching these two "highly educated" white boys sit humbly in the midst of young "street" brothers watching 20 minutes of rap, to get two minutes of tennis results was probably the funniest thing I saw while at Boron. But the young brothers made their point and held their ground on a matter of principle. Brothers hour on Thursday night got expanded to two hours when a show starring James Earl Jones and the late Marge Sinclair about an ex-cop jailed for murder and is released back into a changing society, came to the attention of the Black inmates. It caused a problem at first with the white inmates but once they got into the programming, "Gabriel's Fire" became the most popular show on the campground (after football). It was something every inmate could relate to, plus James Earl Jones played the hell out of his part. The show just expanded the camaraderie of the inmates.

I felt the same camaraderie with many of the Muslim inmates. We prayed together every day, studied together on Sunday nights and learned prayers in Arabic. The week I was supposed to leave (in October), I was selected to give the Kumpa, the teaching lecture of Juma prayer. I felt it was an honor and an acknowledgment of my acceptance in the group. The Muslim community, of any prison, is one of the most respected segments of the prison population. Muslims are generally model inmates and are often called on to mediate inmate disputes. But sincere Muslims often have to deal with inmates not necessarily interested in the faith but looking for some form of inmate protection against the perils of prison. The word on the street is for "prison protection" (not to be taken advantage of) to "get with the Muslims." So when brothers come in talking As-Salaam Alakum, it may or may not be sincere. And the brothers know this, but it is an opportunity to bring the dead to life, with the truth of Islam. Muslims in prison find themselves having to deal with disbelievers and hypocrites, many who are converted in the process, but are not righteously seeking Islam. As one grows in Islam, through study and practice, however, Muslims are able to discern the true believers. On this occasion, I felt my fellow Islamic inmates were rewarding my work by asking me to give words of encouragement. Acknowledging their requests, I spoke on what Allah put in my heart -- how to use the trials that Allah puts in front of us to improve ourselves and be used as an example to exhort others to the truth. I helped many of the brothers understand where I came from, and how I perceived this experience, in the larger context of life as a basis for future achievement. The Kumpa was well-received and the brothers appeared legitimately happy that I was leaving. Only it didn't come to be.

October 19 came and went, without a mention of a halfway house. The camp's Muslim brothers called it right. I saw Pacheco the day after I was supposed to leave. "Two other inmates who had more coming were shipped out yesterday, but you're on the list," he said, as he winked at me. It was his way of letting me know that he had the power, no matter what I thought. From that point, I resigned myself to stay, until the end of my term, and not allow my expectations to be falsely raised and dropped again.

One night in mid-November, I woke up right after the 4 a.m. count. I thought I heard somebody being called. "Asad Samad." "Asad Samad." I looked around and saw that my roommates were still sleep. Figuring I was just hearing things, I went back to sleep. Again around 5:30 a.m., I heard that same name being called "Asad Samad." "Asad Samad." "Asad Samad." This time I just laid in my bunk with my pillow over my head, trying to ignore the disturbance. After about the fifth call, I felt something shake me, like they were trying to awake me out of my sleep. I sat straight up in my bunk, making enough noise to wake up my roommates. "Did you guys hear somebody being called? A something Samad?" Everybody looked at me like, "You had a nightmare, go back to sleep." But I couldn't. I knew I had felt something or somebody shake me. I got up, showered, made Fujr prayer and went on about my day, discounting this experience as a bad dream of some sort. The following night, I heard this name called almost all through the night, jumping up again around 3 o'clock, after feeling something shake me. I sat up for about an hour, thinking I was really tripping or losing my mind. I really don't believe in ghosts and thought someone was playing a trick on me. It was really messing with my sleep, and I was becoming somewhat agitated. I managed to go back to sleep and ignore the calling of that name, "Asad Samad." The next time I felt somebody shake I ignored it. Only that time, it was real.

I had overslept and missed 8 a.m. count. It was one of the guards coming to get me. Reporting late to your work station, and missing count is a major no- no. I told Howard that I had felt ill through the night and hadn't got much sleep. He chose not to write me up, which I appreciated. When you're missing on the number count, it usually causes a lot of drama around a prison camp. When the count is off, it usually means someone has escaped. To escape a federal prison camp, all you have to do is walk off the grounds. Over the previous weeks, about six inmates had walked off. When they are caught, they are placed behind bars. It added an automatic five years to your sentence. But if you had five years or more, some felt the chance was worth it. I didn't. After the third night of the same, I asked an Arab Muslim inmate, who I'd been joining in Isha (late night) prayer, if he knew who Asad Samad was. I explained to him how I kept hearing this name in my sleep, even to the extent that it shook me awake. It was his opinion that Allah was calling out to me.

"Allah calls out to his righteous servants and he calls to them in their true names. This is a blessing, Bro. Anthony. You should receive it gracefully," he said.

"What does the name mean?" I asked him.

He really didn't know, but when I put the question to the Iman, he told me Samad was one of the 99 supplications (names given) of Allah. "There can be no better blessing bestowed on a Muslim than to receive one of God's names," Halim continued. As for the meaning of Asad, he advised me to seek out its meaning, before I considered adopting the name. I immediately called Sharon Clerkley, and asked her to find a book of Muslim names and to express mail it to me.

Waiting at the mailbox the next day, I tore open the envelop and purged the book for the meanings of the names that had come to me. Asad meant "Lion" or defender of the faith. Asadullah (Lion of Allah) was the premier bodyguard of Prophet Muhammad (peace be upon him). He was given that name because he not only protected the Prophet, but he defended the belief against those who were trying to supplant the work of the Prophet, by spreading lies and falsehoods to stop the growth of Islam. The lion is the defender of nature and attacks only out of provocation, but when the lion does attack, it restores all order. Samad is an attribute of Allah, meaning an existence that is faithful eternally (forever) and one who is free from want and desire.

The book said behind every Islamic name is an Islamic spirit to fit the name. Both names I felt fit the spirit in which I had dedicated my life to, defending the rights of Black people. I had, and continued to be, faithful in that fight, by the grace of God.

In fact, there is no more a faithful defender of the rights of Blacks in Los Angeles, than myself. I defended our rights according to the faith and belief God instilled in me, not according to the beliefs that compromise our existence, and in many cases, forfeits our rights as a collective body. In many instances, I had been a lonely voice in Los Angeles for the expansion of Black involvement. Everybody claimed they wanted Blacks to benefit and prosper, but when it came to defending Blacks against many of the injustices, particularly when the police or Negro politicians were involved, there were generally few takers. In a couple cases, like the Crenshaw Mall and the County Jail investigations, there were no takers other than myself, backed by the power of Allah. I came out right on both issues, defending the faith and rights of our people, who had been treated wrongly. Once I understood what these names meant, I felt truly blessed and inspired. Blessed that God would find me in the midst of this personal trial, in the dungeon of my open oppressor, and call to me as his servant.

Inspired that I would even be found worthy in my present condition to be visited in spirit like this, I thanked Allah, over and over again for this experience and this blessing. After talking to the Iman, I called Debra and told her of the experience. She didn't say much, other than she loved me, no matter what I called myself. She said that she felt I was in the best spirits she'd seen me in. I called Mom, and told her of my experience. She said, "Well, I named you Anthony and I will always call you Anthony." She silenced me like only a mother could. She was less excited, and more concerned about putting this Boron experience behind me. After long consideration, I decided that I would keep the name my mother gave me but would change my middle and last names. Anthony Asadullah Samad was what I felt I had been blessed to be called. After Thanksgiving Day, I would sign all letters in Samad.

The last week of my sentence had come. The previous two weeks had produced some interesting events. Mom had brought Taurece out to surprise me during a visit. Of course, Debra was there, and it made for a very awkward situation. I really didn't care, at that point, about how the situation would be perceived. What Mom didn't know was that I had filed for divorce, since I had been at Boron, and

Taurece had been served, which may have inspired her visit. Heretofore, she had expressed no interest in coming to see me, and was extremely cavalier when I raised the issue. Debra, meanwhile, had been extremely faithful and attentive to me during this period, even though she was now living in Sacramento, and had no intentions of coming back to L.A. She was flying down on weekends making the two-hour drive to Boron, staying in roadside motels to avoid having to go back into L.A. on Saturdays, and coming back on Sundays. Along with Sharon, she was handling my business, better than I ever could have imagined. She truly was turning out to be the godsend that I always thought her to be. We were closer than ever now. I didn't think twice about Taurece's apparent level of discomfort for being in Debra's presence. If there was any feeling left from our years together, much of it had dissipated with this experience. Our level of understanding and sensitivity about real world issues never reached anywhere near where Debra and I were. What I was going through was a real life experience that Debra was deeply involved in, in a way that Taurece and our historical preoccupation with the trivial, petty issues never allowed us to be. This experience represented another level of growth for me, one that would only separate us even further. It was best we separated on this eventful note.

Four months represented a lifetime to me. It seemed each day was a year, filled with new observations and discoveries that added a greater base of knowledge and understanding. And I was finding it in a most unusual place. Not because the environment was so educational, but because I was forced to search for answers from within, for questions about situations from without. One's understanding, a combination of knowledge and experience, has the greatest bearing on their interpretation of things. A person can't talk about what they don't know and they can't lead where they haven't been (experienced firsthand or from the benefit of someone else's sincere wisdom). This was an experience I would've rather not had. But never having gone through it, nobody could have ever explained to me, how I saw what I saw, how I heard what I heard, and how I felt what I felt.

It was like taking a test. A test of tolerance and patience. A test of resolving complex issues or of even mastering deceit and trickery. The closer it came time to leave, the more thankful I became of this experience. Like high school, you don't necessarily want to repeat it, but you eventually come to understand the value of what you learned in preparation for the real world. As far as I was concerned, this was an American history lesson. You really don't know America until you've been in its dungeon. A synonym of the term devil is "archdeceiver," one which purposely deceives and does wrong. America is an archdeceiver in the eyes of many nations of the world, because of its conflicting faces on world and race politics. Those who don't agree with America, both domestic and abroad are banished to its dungeons, where they can be silenced.

There is no formal redemption process coming up out of America's dungeon; a system more geared to carrying out punishment, than it is fostering societal correction. There is no aid to reformation other than to submit to slavery-like, inhumane treatment; the penalty of violating selectively applied laws. The whole purpose of which, is not about societal correction but a subliminal indoctrination into a social underclass, from which most will never recover. An indoctrination that breeds recidivism, even dependency, in some cases. To take the prisoner's mind, not to a higher level but a lower level. In reality, the dungeon mentality, for most, will remain forever in the mind of the prisoner. The key to the devil's dungeon and the prisoner's mind are the same. The goal of societal correction, it appears (in numerous cases), is not to help an offender of society's laws and protocols find his (or her) right mind, but to help them lose their mind altogether. Or at least, leave them without control of their mind. What good is it if America sets you free, but keeps the key to your mind in its pocket?

Such is the societal correction experience in America. For anyone who experiences it, the goal is not to just escape the dungeon itself. The goal is to leave with your mind intact and the key to your mind in your own pocket, to unlock the challenges and hurdles of life that often face those who carry the mark of this beast(ex- felon, ex-convict, parolee, ex-offender, etc.). The objective is to try to forget what everybody tries to remind you of, as you walk to each and every door of opportunity that improves ones life and heals one's mind from such a harrowing experience. In an opportunistic world, life is hard enough. However, the mark of the beast is a constant reminder, not of what you did, but what America has done to you. Not correcting the error of your ways nor preparing you for re-entry into society, but branding you and targeting you for future exploitation.

* * *

My last week at Boron was almost uneventful. I was still on a high from a one day furlough I managed to get, on appeal, to take the Graduate Records Exam (GRE). I had decided I wanted to go back to school to get my Ph.D. in political science--that I might better understand America's race policy. The last eligible test date available for most of the application deadlines was December 9, 1990. I had gone through all the steps as before, A). See Pacheco. B). Pacheco decline. C). Appeal. D). Wait and see what happens. While my appeal sat on the warden's desk, something happened in my favor. The warden took sick and the assistant warden, who prided himself in communicating directly with the inmates, was now in charge. After Pacheco took particular delight, it seemed, in this last decline, I became more determined to test the sincerity of the process. In hearing that the assistant warden was taking up appeals, I waited for the opportunity to make an inquiry on his decision.

That opportunity came one day during lunch, when the assistant warden was making his routine appearance among the inmates. Pacheco was standing next to him. The acting warden's name was McAfee. I walked straight up to him. "Warden McAfee, may I have a word with you?" He nodded his head but didn't say anything. I continued, "Is it true that because you have a short term, you are not as eligible for the same furlough and parole considerations, as inmates with longer sentences?"

McAfee looked at me through his spectacled blue eyes and said. "Who told you that?"

"Why, Mr. Pacheco did, sir." Pacheco by that time was beet red looking in the other direction, pretending not to have heard the conversation, but hearing every word of it.

Not looking at Pacheco, McAfee said, "That is not true. Every inmate is entitled to receive the same consideration, according to their eligibility."

"Have you had an opportunity to review the appeal complaint I submitted to Warden Taylor on November 29th?" I asked, ignoring the line that was forming behind me.

"What appeal?"

"I appealed a decision for a one day furlough to take the Graduate Admissions Examination, so that I may attend school when I leave here."

McAfee just stood there silently, like he was thinking. Finally, he said, "Bring me a copy of what you sent to my office this afternoon. I'll take it under consideration."

I thanked him and walked away. Not before passing Pacheco, who had eased away from the "hot" conversation focusing on his acts of impropriety. He was past red, almost purple, furious that an inmate had the nerve to question his wicked use (abuse) of authority. Within 24 hours, my furlough had been accepted. I would be allowed to take the test. My furlough would be on December 9th from 6 a.m. to 8 p.m. I would be released only to my mother. While processing my papers, Pacheco didn't say one word to me. He wasn't his usual smart-ass self. And, of course, a day later, my locker was tossed again. For the third time in four months, when the normal process is once every six months. Some inmates had been there over a year and had never had their locker searched. Only this time, it was of a much greater intensity than the others. It was also with a sense of purpose. That purpose, of course, was to find (or plant) some contraband in my locker, and use it as a basis to overturn my appeal. It was a pretty tense situation, because we all knew that if they (corrections) wanted to find something, they would. Whether it was yours or not, is another story. Retaliation in prison isn't just an inmate thing. The officers took worse offense to their authority being challenged, and their code of silence was much more stringent. Mistreatment of inmates is much more prevalent than you can imagine.

The Bureau of Prisons talk about inmate's rights and reporting abuse, but for an inmate to actually do so, puts them at great risk. The inmate is likely to be the loser in the end, because in a dispute with a prison employee, it's your word against theirs. An inmate versus an employee. Us against them. Then you see what kind of rights an inmate really has. It becomes an issue of whose more credible, the inmate or the prison official. In actuality, many inmates have a lot more integrity than the prison officials. The inmates know this, but they also know that while they may win a battle over the integrity of a single issue, they are more likely to lose the war of surviving a compromise down the line. The inmate knows that retaliation is not only likely, it is probable.

Pacheco lost the battle, because he failed to uphold the integrity of a single issue. But now he was out to win the war, which at best was to take back the furlough, and at worst, move back my release date. My roommates thought I was crazy making such a stink ten days before release, but they knew I was right. Some of them began taking bets, as to whether I would actually receive the furlough. It was hairy, up until the last moment. I was ready to be picked up at 6 a.m. at the checkout window, when I was told by the guard that he wasn't expecting anyone to be furloughed this morning, and that I was to go back to my room, until he could check it out. I knew if I went back to my room, I wouldn't hear back from him until later in the day. Too late for the test, which would mean no reason to be furloughed. I refused to leave until a supervisor or the Warden came. He said, "Wait a minute." Fifteen minutes later, he came back all apologetic saying they had misplaced my furlough papers.

"Yeah, I bet," I said to myself, choosing not to escalate the conflict any further. By the time he finished processing me, it was 6:30 a.m. and test time was 8 a.m. The test site was the University of Southern California, a full two hours and 15 minutes from Boron. Debra had driven my mother out to pick me up. I could not drive myself. It was against my furlough instructions. With Debra driving like she was in the Indy 500, we pulled up on campus at 8:10 a.m. The last of the test applicants were being seated.

After taking the test, Debra and I went to eat and rested, before attending a historic community event that was, coincidentally, taking place at the Los Angeles Coliseum. The Honorable Louis Farrakhan was making his third "Stop the Killing" appearance, in a city that had become the "gang murder capital of the nation." Minister Farrakhan had given significant attention to trying to save the youth organizations in Los Angeles. Despite these efforts, the activity in Los Angeles continued to produce many senseless killings. Minister Farrakhan, growing wary of this activity, had stated that this would be his last appearance in the city for a long time. A crowd of about 40,000 attended the event. Regional Captain Wali Muhammad had made arrangements for my attendance and podium seating. Debra and I arrived about the same time Minister Farrakhan entered the arena, so access to the stage was sealed. We were seated in the second row of the field seating. Minister Farrakhan lectured his heart out to a very receptive audience. Everyone left feeling great. However, the lead story on the evening news was "Drive-by shooting at Farrakhan event." A total misrepresentation of the day's event, and an unfair association of the Minister to a regular occurrence that the city was very familiar with.

On the way back to Boron, I discussed how "dead" our people seemed to me. I couldn't put my finger on it, but Los Angeles had taken on a tainted perspective of a city that had accepted death and shootings as part of its reality. The people appeared uninspired, even at the minister's lecture, to change this reality. All sense of self-determination seemed to be gone. South Central seemed to be a reflection of a community plagued by death, controlled by a dead mentality that things were the way they were, and that's life in the big city. Being in the midst of the living dead was a real awakening for me. It was almost like there was nothing to come back to, in my returning to Los Angeles.

Debra had long seen what I now realized, and had no intention of coming back to L.A. Her hope was that I would agree to leave L.A., and also get a new start elsewhere. I couldn't agree with that, not with having a five-year tail (probation). I'm going to get a new start somewhere else as a parolee on federal probation. I don't think so. It's not the kind of start I wanted to make, if I decided to leave Los Angeles. Plus, there were some issues that needed to be rectified. Some integrity to be regained, credibility to be re-established, and some history to be corrected. Then, if I chose to, I could put L.A. behind me, with no loose strings, and no strings attached. If I were to leave L.A., it would be on my own terms. All issues would be resolved and all misconceptions about my compromise would be settled. Until then, I knew I had to come back to Los Angeles. But based on what I had just seen, I knew L.A. was a ticking time bomb. A major transformation would have to take place.

I got back to Boron at 7:50 p.m., and was immediately called in to take a urine test. I was pumped up from the events of the day. For the first time, I gave some extensive thought to spending the rest of my life with Debra. I appreciated what she had done. I wrote about my thoughts and feelings late into the night.

* * *

December 18, 1990 finally came. I was up and packed by 7 a.m. In tradition with other inmates who had left, I gave away most of the clothes I had acquired during my stay. I also exchanged numbers with many of the inmates I had met, though I would be precluded from contacting anyone while on probation. As I went on my merry-go-round, the exit process for paroled inmates, I thought about the many days I wished for this time. 139 days, to be exact. Now after 4 months, 17 days and "a wake-up", I could fathom the possibility of returning to a "normal" life. Not a totally free life, but a life a lot freer than the last 139 days. I never thought I'd see the day when I could appreciate something as simple as walking out a door, or a kiss and a hug, or the rising of the sun, moon and the stars, all emotions that I had come in touch with over the past 12 hours, in anticipation of this moment. I couldn't get excited, because I didn't want to be let down, if the Bureau of Prisons was to come up with some last-minute trick. Something like, we miscalculated your time, or we took some days, because you failed your urine test. They had been known to do it. I moved very tentatively, almost waiting for something to jump out from behind every door. Nothing did.

At 8:20 a.m., I heard on the loud speaker, "Inmate Essex, report to control." Gathering my possessions, I said goodbye to Craig. The other roommates were at their work assignments. I looked around the Army barrack that had been my cell block. As harmless as it looked, it represented a time and place I never wanted to see again. There was no sentimentality attached, whatsoever. Walking to the control center, I stopped and spoke to Barry Howard. We actually hugged, which was improper for an inmate and a prison official to do. But Howard had made this experience tolerable, first by giving me a preferred assignment, but most importantly, never making me feel like an inmate or less of a man, just because I was doing time. He never referred to me as "Inmate Essex," or imposed his authority upon me unduly. He asked for eight hours work, and he got eight hours work. If I did my work in less time, it was fine with him. He didn't try to exploit the "slave wage" situation. We talked about life, community, religion, beliefs and culture, as equals sharing common interests and a common bond. He was a good brother, as far as I was concerned, and I let him know that.

Inventory was taken on my personal items. I surrendered my commissary card. The officer gave me several papers to sign. I carefully read the papers before signing them. The last document was the BP-114 form, Notice of Release and Arrival. Here it was in writing that I would be released at 9 a.m. on December 18, 1990. It was now 8:44 a.m. Right over inmate's name, I conscientiously signed for one of the last times in my life (save a few probation reports after that date), ANTHONY ESSEX, 92768-012, 12/18/90.

I was told to sit outside on the bench until 9 a.m. The last 15 minutes seemed to go in ultra-slow motion. Tick-tock, tick-tock. I watched my fellow inmates, for another ten minutes, walk up and down the campground. They now seemed to be transfixed in the daily routine of coping with life in a federal prison camp. As I watched many of the men I interfaced with on a daily basis virtually ignore me sitting on the parole bench, I understood that it had nothing to do with me. It had more to do with the practice of coping. One of those practices is blocking out inmates leaving. The toughest thing an inmate experiences is watching another inmate be set free. Emotions range from anger to sadness, from gladness to hope. In minimum security prisons, almost every time a group of inmates leave, an inmate would go AWOL (absent without leave), unable to cope with having to stay caged. Freedom becomes a foreign commodity to a caged man. Only when he sees another man walk, does he realize it's not so foreign, but it is a close reminder of his continuing debt, not yet paid. To see another man settle his debt, makes you want to settle yours all the more, but time is not like money, where you can borrow future dollars now, or call on past savings to resolve present debt. There is no borrowing of time. It can't be rushed, before it's due.

It was 9 a.m. I looked out into the parking lot. Debra was waiting. I could see the reservation in her eyes saying, "Is this real? Are they going to let you go?" At that moment, a prison officer came out the control center door.

"Mr. Essex, you have served your sentence, as ordered by the Federal Courts of the United States of America. By order of the warden of this federal prison, you are hereby released." He handed me an envelope with my release papers, and the cash balance of my commissary account. He shook my hand and said, "Good luck and report to your probation officer within 72 hours." The door then slammed shut. I picked up my box of possessions and walked toward the car. As we drove down the long dirt road that led to Highway 395, I asked Debra to stop. We just sat by the road for about five minutes and prayed. From that moment, I knew my life would never be the same again, and it would only change for the better.

* * *

17

Rebel On Pause:

Reality Turns to Chaos

"Chaos is the score upon which reality is written"
- Henry Miller

When I returned to Los Angeles, I sensed that the reality of compromise had pretty much settled over the Black community. South Central was still every bit as depressed, but it seemed as though I was seeing the city through a different pair of eyes. Things seemed a lot slower. Everything appeared normal; the depression just seemed so much clearer. Back at my apartment, Floyd and a few of my friends were there to welcome me home. While I appreciated the gesture, I had mixed emotions, at that moment. I didn't know what to say to them, and they didn't know what to say to me, so nobody said anything for a while. In the middle of the party I decided to take a walk. I walked about two miles down Crenshaw to Jefferson, over to Western, up Western to 54th Street, and back over to Crenshaw. During that walk, I looked into the faces of Black people. Brothers begging at gas stations. Two young sisters, both of them pregnant and appearing to be less than 20 years old. Each pulling a two-year-old and pushing a stroller with a 6-month-old child in it. Old ladies were walking in fear every time a young man approached, expecting some sort of assault, rather than a helping hand. On almost every face I saw, there was a look of resignation. A kind of "this is the way it is" resignation. Our community was in a state of desperation.

I finally realized, halfway through my walk, why things appeared so different to me. I was finally looking at the community through a pair of fresh eyes. "Real eyes." This was reality. Our people's reality. A reality differently perceived by someone who now had another perspective to compare against the distorted realities I'd grown to know. Not from a hierarchical (I'm better than you) perspective that community leadership tends to see things from. I saw the world moving past me, and saw compromise manifest itself in the faces of our people. I tried to understand what I was seeing, and processed my assessment in relation to what I knew my community had become, a land of the living dead. Literally.

I had prided myself as one who tried to identify and represent the issues of the disadvantaged, the oppressed and the suffering, while on the merry-go-round, taking time to look over to the side every once in awhile. Most of the community leadership just looked straight ahead, taking tokens along the way. You tend to do that when you're dizzy. But as much as you try to pay attention to the small details, when you're dizzy from going in circles, reality is distorted and skews the accuracy of your account. What the Negro leader in Los Angeles felt was helping many, was actually helping a relative few. And the rest of the community was going to hell while its leadership was on the take. One looks straight ahead to keep from falling off the ride. In L.A., the leadership looked straight ahead to avoid noticing the suffering. When the community is spiraling downward, and you're being pampered with guilt money for your community organization, of course it's difficult to tell what's, real versus what is not. The suffering of people in the Los Angeles Black community was so distorted that those on the social and political merry-go-round really believed that there was little wrong in the community. I had been following community events in the *Los Angeles Sentinel* and the *L.A. Times* from Boron. I had seen, from afar, that nobody was speaking up. Few were advocating for the poor, or going against the grain. An obligatory comment against an obvious offense, every now and then. But for the most part, the control of the people was complete.

There was no problem that the police, the banking redliners, or the corporate contributors couldn't deal with through the Negro leadership. There was nothing that a little Negro meeting with the masses couldn't resolve. Not only did the Black leadership have a distorted perception of reality, but the bourgeois and the wanna be's were beginning to co-sign such sentiments and become a part of the facade. My "welcome home" walk through the community was very, very revealing. There was, in fact, something very wrong with the resignation on the faces of the people. It took many forms: anger, disgust, embarrassment, hopelessness and fear. They all said the same things though -- that they were now prisoners of their environment and prisoners of social conditions. Looking through a new pair of eyes, I now saw what they saw and I saw it as they saw it, as an imprisonment of a different kind. Our people were prisoners of the compromise of organizational leaders, elected officials, churches and educators. It was now clearer to me than ever before, the condition that had been created in inner-city Los Angeles. Not necessarily because I had any greater sympathy or because of any kinship by way of my own personal experience, but because I was no longer looking through glazed vision. I could no longer deny what I saw and it was even more blatant than before.

I could now see past the propaganda, and the rhetoric of the so-called leadership, and could make contact with the reality of the people's condition. The only benefit I could now see to my 139 days of social isolation was that it subsided my dizziness. By taking me out of the circles of illusion and confusion that our people call prestige and success, my head was so clear and my mind was even clearer. No amount of glitz, glamour and fool's gold, as Flavor Flav of Public Enemy once said, "can stop reality from being real."

When I returned home, everybody was gone but Floyd and Debra. Debra had a big night on the town planned. I told her to cancel it. I just wanted to spend a day or two alone. Then I wanted to see my children. But for now, I wasn't in the mood for a bunch of drama. We had dinner "in the hood" that night. But before dinner, Debra had one surprise she couldn't cancel. She had bought me a Jeep Cherokee that she wanted to show me. Three weeks before my release, I had told Sharon to give Debra a check for a Jeep Wrangler that I saw for sale in the Recycler magazine. After seeing it, she decided that the Wrangler didn't have enough room for the kids. "It was just enough room for them to fight," she said, and bought the Cherokee instead. It was a nice surprise and a good common sense move. We then went to dinner at the Marie Callenders restaurant in the Baldwin Hills/Crenshaw Plaza. When I asked why we were stopping there, Debra said there was a Black restaurant one of her board of directors at Watts (Health Foundation) owned, and she wanted to support him.

The restaurant had become the meeting and eating place for a community trying to support its own. In the process, we indirectly supported the developer and the illegitimate process used to acquire the mall. The legitimization of the community's compromise was now being validated by sincere efforts to support good community people like Gil, Louise and Jim. Still I saw Debra's point--that our people still had to be supported even in the midst of a raw deal. She was indirectly talking about me and my situation.

The first few days I spent alone, just writing and thinking about how I wanted to get back out in public. I knew I didn't particularly want to jump back on the merry-go-round. However, "Essex sightings" were getting around, and people were calling to get me "back in the mix." Most of the calls were about either supporting some community project or getting back involved with advocacy, neither of which I was particularly interested. I was just interested in writing and seeing my children. My third day back, they came over to my mother's house to see me for the first time in almost five months. They were unusually quiet when they came in, like they didn't expect to see me there. I'll never forget the look on my son's face like, "You better not leave again." But I felt in his hug that he had missed me. The girls were more reserved in their emotions, but they missed me, too. However, I missed them more than they could ever miss me. And from that point, we became almost inseparable. I wanted them to know there was nothing more important than them in my life. From now on, they'd be at the center of it.

When my children weren't around, I'd write, sometimes all day and all night, for two or three days straight. But the happiest time in my life was learning to appreciate fatherhood for really the first time in my life. Things like doing what they wanted to do, watching what they wanted to watch, going where they wanted to go, and just being with them, for as long as they wanted to be together. Seeing Kellie play chess with me, letting Gabrielle read to me, letting Tony, Jr. teach me to play Nintendo (feeling like I was the only father on the face of the earth who didn't know how to play) -- these became my reality, real pleasures in my life. Anything that came up while they were over got canceled. People were setting up meetings to generate new business for me. Others were just trying to get me out, providing the support system they thought I needed at the time. I had lost the feeling of being obligated to anything or anybody, except my children. Over the years, their time always got cut short, because I always had to run off to a meeting. Not now. Everything else got cut short or canceled when the children were over, and I missed them when they had to leave. Anyone who associated with me, had to have children activities at the center of their time with me. I ended up getting close to a sister named Debrah Fontenot because her boys, Roy and Ryan, were my children's age, and were just as rambunctious. Debra, who didn't want me feeling obligated to her, encouraged me to see other people. While several sisters were trying to interest me, they weren't interested in trying to interest my three children. It made going out with Debrah and her boys easier. Of course, she knew about Debra and always showed great respect for our relationship. Still, the times we spent with the five of our children were invaluable both to the children and our friendship. Debrah was a great complement in her knowledge of single parenting, which was really new to me. I could never really show my appreciation, and she knew that, because my heart and mind were deeply committed to Debra, but neither of us could help but wonder, what if ...

Other than being out casually with the children, I kept my interface with the community to a minimum. Other than going to the Mosque, the store, or out to dinner, a concert, or a movie, I was pretty much still away from anyone not an intimate part of my life. I was in regular communication with Western Regional Minister, Wazir Muhammad. One of my first requests upon my return was to meet with he and the Regional Captain Wali Muhammad to find out how they wanted me involved. Wazir was very specific about my continuing to do advocacy work, as well as, helping with the Mosque's financial planning. All the mosque officials gave me the time and space I needed to re-acclimate myself. I also discussed with them my wish not to use my given surname anymore. Most believers still use their given surname (slave name) in public, even after they receive their "X." While reinforcing the Nation of Islam's policy on holy names, I would be permitted to use another name outside of the Mosque. Inside the Mosque, I would continue to be known and referenced as Anthony 2X, until the Messenger's servant Minister Louis Farrakhan chose to give me another name -- if Allah moved him to do so (Minister Farrakhan gave all registered believers the holy names at Saviour's Day 1997). But at that time, I proceeded to legally change my middle and last name to the ones that came to me in my sleep, while at Boron. In 1991, my legal name would become Anthony Asadullah Samad.

My first highly visible public appearance was three weeks after my release, at longtime Los Angeles City Councilman Gilbert Lindsey's funeral. Lindsey had been very supportive of my leadership in the branch. I was a young undergraduate who came into his fraternity. We used to man his annual Easter parade, named after his wife, Theresa Lindsey. Lindsey's nephew had contacted Oscar Morgan about the Phi Beta Sigma members being pallbearers. Oscar called me, knowing how close I was to Gil. He had been told that the Prince Hall Masons were handling the pallbearer duties, but would be honored if the duties could be shared. They were having problems contacting members of Gil's lodge. I called one of my best friends, Hank Davis III, to see if he could assist me with locating the master of Lindsey's lodge, only to find out he was the Worshipful Master of the lodge that Lindsey was a member of. I explained the predicament. Hank gladly accepted our offer, due to the fact that his lodge was small and may not have had the number of pallbearers needed, anyway. The night before Lindsey's funeral, both Phi Beta Sigma fraternity and the Masonic bodies (Consistory & Shriners) all had their memorial services. Being a member of all three, I participated in all three.

At the funeral the next day, I was very low key, but the buzz was that I was there. A couple of people, including my convenient associate, Mark Whitlock, thought they had seen a ghost. My friends couldn't have been prouder, telling me to keep my chin up and to keep on stepping. The *L.A. Times* ran a picture of me as a pallbearer on the front page of the *Metro Section*, almost as if they were trying to serve notice. I got over 125 phone calls over the next three days. My answering tape ran out four times. Yes, I was back, but not in a way most had come to know. I was pretty much on pause, as far as any community activism was concerned. I'd done my time; in more ways than one.

1991 was a very telling year for Blacks in Los Angeles. The acts and events of that year basically reinforced that the Black community had become prisoners in their own communities to social, political and economic compromise. But how deep the compromise had become entrenched, in terms of the level of human indignation and tolerance Blacks were prepared to take, was unknown, until this period. 1991 proved that the Black community had fallen so low in its own demand of self-respect, that no one else was prepared to respect us either. Since the Lindsey funeral, I had pretty much been in seclusion for two months. Just writing, reading and spending time with my children. I had a select group of clients I continued to service from my financial services business, which allowed me to pay the government, child support and my bills (usually in that order) with some to set aside. But I pretty much worked when I wanted to. I was getting about a dozen calls a week to get involved with different things, to which I gave them all the same response, "For what?" I did, however, recognize that there was a market for paid advocacy in our community. People didn't even want to call the civil rights groups anymore. That was usually the end of the conversation. I did make an effort to stay on top of issues through several newspapers, TV and cable news shows. I'd often get into real in-depth discussions with Debra over how leadership responded to this or that, or how the ball was dropped here or there. Sometimes she'd be interested, other times she could care less. Clearly, she could see the advocacy was still in my blood, but sitting on the sidelines was fine with me, at that point in my life.

The year started out as a year perceived by many as one of political change for the Black community. Almost immediately following Lindsey's death, another Black City Councilman, Bob Farrell, unexpectedly announced his resignation. For the first time since Lindsey was appointed to the City Council, and Tom Bradley was elected to the council a few months later, in 1963, the Black community had a chance to put two new faces in local government. Young turks who basically had been put off for a generation, while the older leadership swapped seats and passed over them, began lining up. The running joke in Los Angeles and around the country was that L.A. Black politicians sit forever and die in office. At that time, prior to Lindsey's death and Congressman Gus Hawkins' retirement, we had two elected officials over 80, several in their late 60s, the rest were 50 or older. The youngest was Farrell and Marguerite Archie-Hudson who, in her late 40s, was now a state assemblywoman. In the last couple of years, three had died in office. The other two, Compton Mayor Walter Tucker and Inglewood Assemblyman Curtis Tucker (non-related), died in office prior to Lindsey, and were succeeded by their sons (both of the same name as their fathers). But beyond nepotism, by and large, the rest of the Black leadership had not mentored any new leadership. Lindsey had come the closest, entrusting senior aide, Bob Gay, with running his district in his last years. Bob, a contemporary of ours in his mid-30s, had done 15 years at Lindsey's side and was truly prepared to inherit the mantle of leadership. Only Lindsey stopped short of endorsing him (anointing him as we called it in L.A.) as his successor. Still Bob was clearly the most skilled player of our generation in the area of governmental affairs. He knew the city through and through, as well as where the money was (usually a problem for neophyte candidates). Most thought Bob would step right into the 9th District seat. The 8th District was another story.

Farrell's unexpected resignation was perceived as a combination of two things: burnout and increasing conflict of interest allegations that were being raised about contracts let to Farrell's former wife. The inside discussion was that Farrell's decision was being hurried, in a flex move, by Congresswoman Maxine Waters, who politicos saw as looking to establish herself as the "queen of L.A." To do so, she needed a local operative on the City Council, which she had identified as her longtime aide, Rod Wright (who is now a member of the California Assembly). Farrell, in choosing not to fight the allegations, after having been the victim of a re-call campaign three years earlier, chose to give up the seat. But before doing so, he endorsed SCLC executive director, Mark Ridley-Thomas, as his choice to succeed him.

Of the 20 plus candidates that filed for the seat, the race figured to be a four-way race of second generation community players. The other two players were Billy Mills Jr., whose father (of the same name) was one of the real first generation Black politicians. Billy Mills, Sr. held the council seat prior to Farrell, before he gave it up to become a superior court judge. Mills Jr., an attorney, really didn't have a real community activist presence, but had his father's name I.D. The last of the four front horses was Kerman Maddox. Kerman anonymously ran the re-call effort against Farrell, then he came out as the opposition choice candidate, which everybody perceived as kind of underhanded. Since that time, Kerman was now perceived as "Chip's boy" at First A.M.E., which had more minuses than pluses in the church community, where access to pulpits and congregations tend to bolster candidacies. Still, Kerman's community involvement brought him a following. But none of them, at that point in time, were in the class with Mark. Mark was a seasoned advocate, tried and true, with the practical experience of running a community organization, SCLC-West, for 10 years. His academic accomplishments were a plus, and allowed him to show depth, on more than one front. The biggest attribute of Mark's was that he was a proven fighter in community activism. There's a difference between watching somebody fight, and being in a fight. Mark had been at the center of the ring on some key community issues and had played a significant role in their resolution. For what all the others possessed (and I worked with all these brothers in some formal or informal capacity), they weren't prepared to lead the way Mark was prepared.

In spite of the fact that our friendship was now estranged, I had to give favor to Mark, because I knew what he knew, and knew what he could do with what he knew. How did I know? Because in the advocacy circles, in which Mark and I moved about in mid-1980s, we were the only ones under 40 at the table. Being around the old guard, and the wisdom that comes out of doing battle with and against them is invaluable. Eventually, the skills developed by the battles Mark had been involved in, would later rise to the top. All things being equal, and Mark's sometimes cynical personality (which was often perceived as arrogance) not getting in the way of his candidacy, he'd be hard to beat. This was Los Angeles "Black" politics, however, where anything is not just possible, but probable. Politics would not be the center of change this time. The focus would shift to landmark social conflict, which shook the very foundation of the Black community and its practice of passe politics, not just in Los Angeles, but around the nation.

The first landmark conflict would be the unveiling of the most vicious and brutal public beating of an individual, since the march on Selma. Only this had nothing to do with marching for voting rights. It did have everything to do with civil rights. Many in the Black community had long been saying that the Los Angeles Police Department was the most violent and vicious law enforcement agency in the country (outside of the L.A. County Sheriff's Department). Both agencies were (and still are) reputed to be among the nation's most abusive. Hundreds of people who came forth with horror stories of L.A.P.D. encounters, and could get no one to believe them, were vindicated in one night. On March 3, 1991, America got to see what many in the Black community had known all the time -- brutality at its worst. The Rodney King beating. The chilling videotape revealed a Black man being beaten senseless, while almost 50 law enforcement officers stood by and watched. Not one of the officers filed a misconduct report. Not one felt that there was any sense of wrongdoing. The attitude was, "The nigger ran, the nigger got beat." The real miracle in all of this was that King survived to tell about it.

In the meantime, the Los Angeles Black community leadership had nothing to say beyond the usual admonitions. Black leadership tried and would defend just about everything that Gates or the L.A.P.D. officials put out around that time. It was a leadership that was in bed with LAPD, and had been in bed with Gates for over a year. Now it had to picture how foolish they must have looked to have been stroked and poked at the same time. Gates had the Black leadership in pocket, expressing all the while that police relations were improving. This was because Gates was now regularly interfacing with so-called Black leaders which, mitigated calls for police abuse. Then the King beating happened. Gates interaction with Black leadership was no longer "an interface." It was more like pissing in their face, and they all had urine on their faces. Los Angeles Negro leadership, particularly those on this little advisory council, in March, 1991 could do nothing now but wash the stench out of their mouths.

The Negro leadership stumbled around the question of what to do for about a week. After all the shocking and appalling statements and the pleas for peace and calm played out, the statements of Gates' resignation began floating out. Sort of like trail balloons. But there was one problem. Gates wasn't about to resign. So what should we do, fire him? That wasn't likely either. Gates had continually received good performance ratings in recent years' job evaluations. Seen as a performing civil service employee with lifetime protection, Gates was literally untouchable. Firing the chief of police would require a majority vote from the police commission, a recommendation to the City Council, a majority vote from City Council with affirmation from the Mayor. Gates' "FBI surveillance" style of policing and his secret policing units had gathered intelligence on the Mayor and virtually every City Council member. Without extensive justification, City Council wasn't about to fire Gates. When it was first proposed, the council refused to even give it any serious consideration. They didn't feel it "was appropriate" at that time. It was widely known that the council was lining up for a political battle. Gates probably had as many City Council votes as the Mayor. Maybe even more. And, those he didn't have, the police dossiers he kept on council members provided a little extra comfort (or security--depending on where your vote fell).

The Negro leadership was also in a quandary. When in a quandary, what do they do? Call a meeting, of course. This is not to be sarcastic or anything, but crisis management in the Black community is so predictable. It's almost as if they all read from the same book; Negro Leadership 101. There's the meeting on what to do. Then there's the meeting with the entity that did it to us. Then there's the meeting at Rev's (the church) where everybody and their mama get up talking about what we need to do, and what "Whitey" better do, or we'll sic God on 'em when we get to heaven. Then there's the march down to where "Whitey" is, walking slow and humming low singing,

"We shall overcome, some day." Then when we get there, we hold a candlelight vigil for the victim, (or our own victimization) and we pray for the perpetrator to come into their right mind or for justice. Then everybody goes home, and it's back to life on the plantation, until it happens again.

It's the same ole' play. White folk have to be laughing their ass off, because for them it's like watching a rerun on television. They probably sit up and say, "This is what the niggahs gonna do next," or "This is the part where they march." "Those niggahs sure do sing pretty, don't they?" Knowing at the end of the show, some of the Negroes names will appear on the credits for throwing a rock at the Big House, while nobody was home, which makes them look big in the eyes of the other slaves, but wasn't about shit, as far as, the master was concerned. And the niggahs better be off the master's lawn by sun up, when he comes to work, or there'll be some real shit in the game. This is the way the process goes, and it was going that way again. This time, the Negro went in knowing they'd already been played by the city of Los Angeles' resident "whitey," LAPD Chief Daryl Gates.

Minister Wazir called me and requested that I attend this meeting with him. He had stated that he wanted a perspective that he could rely on, since he didn't run in their circle and that I knew their language. It would be my first meeting with the established Negro leadership, since my return from Boron, and I really didn't feel like being bothered with it. But I was in the Nation of Islam now. It wasn't about what I wanted anymore. I followed my instruction and attended the meeting. Upon arriving at the Los Angeles Urban League office building (Negro Headquarters for this meeting), the first thing that came to my mind was that our problem wasn't downtown at Parker Center (police headquarters), it was right here in this room. Not trying to be mean-spirited, but I saw this meeting as tantamount to a class reunion. A Negro class reunion, of sorts.

Urban League; John Mack - "Here"
SCLC; Ridley-Thomas - "Present"
NAACP; Duff - "Here"
Baptist Ministers Conference; Higgins - "Here"
Second Baptist Church; Kilgore - "Present"

With the exception of the 100 Black Men represented by Dr. Warren Valdry and former City Councilman David Cunningham, Jr., there was nothing different about the faces and philosophies around the table, with the possible exception of the elected officials (of which there were none), in attendance at this meeting. However, almost every party at the table had been part and parcel to the L.A.P.D. community advisory charade over the past year. I certainly did not expect this meeting to take a different flavor than any of the others. One move that was very curious, but smart on Mark's part, was that the Negro elders put Mark out front on this issue, representing the SCLC and the civil rights community. This was a first. Generally, everyone spoke in consensus, but autonomous of one another. However, in an effort to heighten Ridley-Thomas' viability in the 8th District council race, he was allowed to be the spokesperson for the coalition, as an affirmation of support from this select group of community leaders. The play was questionable, from a representative standpoint, because Mark was actually on leave from the SCLC while involved in the campaign. Yet he was using his post in the organization (while on leave) to launch this issue. It would be weeks before any of his competition realized what he was doing -- getting free publicity for his council race. By the time Rod Wright finally called it out, Mark had received over dozens of "media hits;" immeasurable publicity one couldn't buy for a million dollars. The "hits" were media sensitive (frequent as the hot issue in the city) carried on every channel three times a day (at 4p.m., 6p.m. and 11 p.m.) as well as in the print media. The media was under no obligation of "equal time" laws. Mark knew what to do with what he learned from the civil rights game. The others had never been in the game, so they were learning as the game moved along, and it lost them.

At this particular meeting, Mark was at the head of the conference table with civil rights legend (and pastor emeritus of Second Baptist Church), Dr. Thomas Kilgore. I walked in, just as the meeting focused on "the Gates problem." Most appeared surprised to see me, but showed little emotion. Minister Wazir gave me an affirming nod, which I took to mean "jump in with both feet." The discussion went around the table. Much of it had to do with calling Gates into the group, for an explanation of his comment: "Why was everybody so upset over the beating of a criminal, and the department's lack of response over the request for an internal investigation, of the officers that stood by and watched?" Other discussions centered on what to do from this point. Other than demonstrate and call for the officer's firing (they had already called for Gates' resignation), they weren't talking about any immediate solutions to solving the greater issue of police misconduct in the LAPD. If it was left up to Gates, who was now on record as wanting to take the lead on any department reform, a master cover-up would come into play, long before reform would. When Minister Wazir's turn to speak came up, he deferred to me, saying I was his adviser on this issue. Clearly annoyed, most around the table looked at Joe, NAACP representative, because they never knew how our personal politics would come into play. I completely ignored him.

"I am not inclined to recommend any participation in a process that was counterfeit from the start," I said referring to the Gates community advisory committee. "In fact, the L.A.P.D. has very little credibility on the street right now and that's not going to change with Gates at the helm. I would recommend an action that would facilitate Gates' ouster. Something like telling the people not to stop for police, unless they drive to the closest police station, where the process and procedure can be observed." My position was that civil disobedience had always been an excellent tool to advance civil rights advocacy. I was also trying to direct the group to an option they apparently hadn't explored -- a hidden clause in the city charter that said, if the public loses confidence in the services of law enforcement, the chief of police may be removed to restore the public trust. In order to do that, we, as the community, would have to demonstrate that public confidence had been lost. Such an announcement would not only create hysteria about the possibility of anarchy, it would flood police stations throughout the city. By jamming the process and forcing police administration to address the credibility problem, the politicians would evoke the charter and dismiss Gates in a matter of days. You would have thought I said "kill whitey," or something, with the silence that fell over the room. After a few moments of them sitting there with a "that's the craziest shit we ever heard" look on their faces, Rev. Higgins stated that he wouldn't participate in anything that would encourage people to break the law. Could you have imagined Dr. King rejecting the civil disobedience option, because it "broke the law?" Higgins suggested we try to legally remove Gates through the police commission or some other avenue. It was obvious they weren't looking to fire Gates anytime soon. The discussion reverted back to meetings and marches. Of course, everybody had to think about it, and they agreed to meet again.

On the way out of the meeting, I told Minister Wazir that this process would not get rid of Gates, but produce some sort of compromise that would not satisfy the community. Not until this thing blows up altogether, will they (Negro leadership) understand how deep this misconduct had affected the community. Minister Wazir appeared to be stunned at the way the others brushed off the strategy of civil disobedience. "How can you break the law, when the beating clearly showed there is no law? Our people take their lives in their hands when they stop for the police. It's only common sense to tell our people to drive to safety," he continued. "Brother, what do you perceive coming out of this?"

"Not an immediate resignation of Daryl Gates, and not any quick action on any type of change in police policy," I said. "And expect the same ole', same ole' from the Negro leadership," as I looked up at the Urban League sign in the front of the building, "Some things will never change. This is one of 'em." Minister Wazir nodded and thanked me for coming. We gave each other the greetings and parted. The police assault on Rodney King was just the beginning of confrontations in the Black community.

About a week later, one of the coldest executions of a human being ever witnessed on tape occurred, when a Korean merchant shot a 15-year-old Black girl in the back of the head. I never thought the community could be anymore enraged than they were after seeing the Rodney King beating. However, the murder of Latasha Harlins took outrage to the bottom of the well. It was a clear demonstration of disrespect for Black life, at the most immaterial, infinitesimal levels of existence. It was unimaginable that one could even equate the life of a child to a bottle of orange juice, which cost $1.79, yet this is what it had come to. This type of insensitivity masked in a "merchant defending their wares" was absolutely inexcusable. This was the defense Korean merchant, Soon Ja Du, chose to use, until the community saw the tape.

Young Latasha had gone into Du's market to purchase some orange juice. She put the juice in a bookbag, and made her way directly to the cashier counter. The tape showed her saying something to Soon Ja Du, as she extended her hand with money. Du grabbed her, and grabbed the bookbag in a very aggressive manner. Latasha responded aggressively, in defense of the attack on her person, hitting the woman several times, until she let go of her bookbag. Latasha then took the juice out of her bookbag, and put it on the counter, turned and proceeded to walk out of the store. Du pulled a gun from under the counter, pointed at Latasha, and shot her in the back of the head. The gun was later found to have a hair trigger, rigged to go off with the slightest pull of the gun's firing mechanism.

The community's response, as expected, was anger and outrage across the board. Negro leadership; the so-called "traditional" leadership, was as equally appalled as the grassroot "street" segment of the community, which has its own leadership. That wasn't the case with the King beating. Even in spite of what they saw, many of the Negro leadership felt there was some culpability on the part of Rodney King -- that he must have done something to merit such a beating. There was no such perception of culpability on the part of Latasha's murder. Short of coming in with a gun and saying, "Stick 'em up," there was nothing in the market that Latasha could have stolen that merited her life being taken. There was nothing in the whole store worth a life; much less a child's life. Nothing. Latasha's murder, again, raised the question about the tenuousness of the Black-Korean relationship, and how explosive this interface had become over the past few years. With this issue being the first advocacy case I'd worked for the NAACP, I knew firsthand that the conflict had come full circle in five short years. Korean merchants, after losing four merchants in 1986, began to take a more aggressive position with respect to using deadly force (guns) in their stores. What they weren't doing was exercising good judgment, in whether deadly force was appropriate.

Robberies and pilferage are part of providing retail services, not just in the Black community but in any community. In a robbery, the merchant has the right to protect his life, but there are laws to protect the merchant against thievery and pilferage. Korean merchants, in addition to not understanding the Black community's culture, didn't understand the laws of this country. They had gotten into the mode of taking the law into their own hands, which caused them to react in the extreme, in less than life threatening situations. Some merchants are shell-shocked from previous robbery experiences, which was the excuse used for Soon Ja Du's reaction. Others were acting as they would react in their own country's culture. In the few months after Latasha's murder, two other Black males would mistakenly be shot by Korean merchants. One, who ran into a store after seeking cover from a drive-by. The other, Lee Arthur Mitchell, was killed when the merchant thought he was being robbed, though no gun was found, nor was there any evidence that a confrontation even took place. Korean merchants were now operating from an "expect the worst, and deal with the consequences later" premise. Well, later arrived.

The Negro leadership went through their usual 1-2-3 routine. One, press conference; two, march; three, candlelight vigil, then it was back to sleep while the system does its thing. "Let justice take its course," was their position. The courts will bring justice to Latasha. Well, as much as we would have liked to believe that, the Harlins family put together a justice committee to act in the meantime. Daily protests were held in front of the market, ensuring that it would never again open for business. It remained closed. That wasn't the case for the merchant on 79th and Western that killed Mitchell. He intended to do business as usual. Danny Bakewell and the Brotherhood Crusade, along with Bethel A.M.E. Church and other community residents, called for a boycott on the store. The merchant was able to stay open through the donations of the Korean Merchants Association, who helped subsidize the business to minimize the losses being incurred from the boycott.

I followed both of these events from the sidelines, by attending community meetings, but declined any spokesperson roles that were offered, largely on the advice of Minister Wazir and Debra. Both of them felt it was too soon for me to get out in the public eye. I was also pre-occupied with satisfying the conditions of my probation, specifically the community service portion, which was 620 hours. My probation officer, Carol Jones, allowed me some flexibility in selecting a community-based group, as long as, the hours could be verified, and it was an organization they could recognize. My first choice was the Mosque. It was rejected on the basis that the service couldn't be something I'd normally do anyway. My next choice was the Sugar Ray Robinson Youth Foundation. It was pretty much arranged where'd I'd do some flexible hour, and could work with the youths.

Three days before I was to start, the part-time activities director was overheard telling one of the foundation employees that he would be supervising "that big-time NAACP guy who got caught with his hand in the cookie jar." It turned out he also worked with my ex-wife, so he had a little of the "job gossip" to run on. It was his intent to work me on Saturdays, during his little league games. I specifically said I'd prefer weekdays. My weekends were for my time with my children. The employee was a Black woman, who knew an associate of mine named Mike Henderson. We called him "Wood" for Hollywood. He's one of the nicest brothers I'd ever met. She tipped Wood what he was up to, and told him to tell me not to come, unless I wanted to slave for some chump who ain't never did nothing for Black folk in his life. To me it was community service, and it was going to be done when I wanted to do it, and how I wanted to do it. I decided to give my time to Daniel Freeman Hospital, discharging patients and sticking labels on hospital supplies. I could come any time, day or night. So much for the community benefiting from my mandated hours.

* * *

There were some real interesting turns in both the political campaigns for council seats, and in the campaign to fire Daryl Gates. In the 9th District race, an expected walk over victory for former Lindsey chief of staffer, Bob Gay turned into a war when Los Angeles Unified School Board President Rita Walters moved into the district to enter the race to succeed the late councilman. Not only would she enter the race, but she would receive Tom Bradley's instant endorsement, a sure fire clue that Walters' decision to run wasn't coincidental.

In the 8th District council race, every candidate was "ahead in the race," if you let them tell it. It was the race with all the flash and dash. Kerman was trying to grab the headlines with a recall (another one) on Gates' campaign, based upon the city charter clause I brought to the attention of the Negro leaders, at the meeting called the month before. Billy Mills was using the Masonic order and the legal community to reintroduce himself to seniors (high propensity voters) in the district who remembered his father. "This is Judge Mills' boy," was the intro line. Placating, but effective. Rod Wright had surprised everyone with his ability to raise money, and he hadn't even played his trump card yet -- the Maxine Waters connection. Mark was still getting plenty of free press coverage on the Gates issue.

The issue was actually taking a favorable turn, based on Mayor Bradley's bold appointment of Melanie Lomax to the Los Angeles Police Commission. Melanie was appointed on the basis of understanding her mission: to shake up the commission, and get to the bottom of the police misconduct. An issue that was largely being denied by both the L.A.P.D. and the Negro leadership. The weeks of hearing on police abuse activity produced several major discoveries: First, hundreds of complaints, maybe even thousands of complaints filed with the L.A.P.D. either were never submitted, or never followed up on. L.A.P.D. had basically developed an internal policing system "amongst the ole' boys" to divert abuse complaints. If a complainant was smart enough to ask for a supervisor, the L.A.P.D.'s officer code of silence would then take over, meaning they'd take your complaint, demonstrate their public relations skills by stroking the person into believing the complaint would be reviewed and acted upon, but very few were.

The second major discovery was the number of historically abusive officers that were allowed to stay on the street and the number of officers who were not disciplined for such acts in the past. The third major discovery were the flaws in the L.A.P.D.'s training processes that taught officers to heighten confrontation, rather than defuse confrontation, which contributed to the L.A.P.D.'s hostile "take control, shoot and ask questions later" attitude. The last and most damaging discovery, the one that gave the council the break they needed, was that several key senior personnel came forth and testified that Gates had been made aware of the abuse problems on numerous occasions, but did not take any action. Loyalty to the ranks and the ranks' loyalty to him was first and foremost with "Chief" Gates. Anyone taking any major act against "the family" was seen as betrayal by Gates, and his second in command, Assistant Chief Robert Vernon. Vernon, a Christian fundamentalist, was perceived by many as more of a racist than Gates. Between Gates and Vernon, the L.A.P.D.'s "do what you have to do" form of policing was condoned, not just in their willingness to turn their heads to abuse and misconduct, but in their strong arm retaliatory attitude at the top of department that virtually dared any senior officer to violate "the family's code of silence." Deputy Chief Thomas Rathburn took the chief of police assignment in Dallas, largely because he didn't agree with the L.A.P.D.'s "different form of policing," and he couldn't see it changing. But when three key senior officers and 11 ranked deputy chiefs broke protocol and violated the "code," the commission, headed by Melanie, moved quickly in tying the activity of the L.A.P.D. to a compromised style of management, which was not in the best interest of the citizenry.

The Southern Christian Leadership Conference-West, headed by Ridley- Thomas, was preparing to file a lawsuit against the city of Los Angeles to force them to place Gates on administrative leave, based on the ever-increasing discoveries coming out of the police commission deliberations. The position of the SCLC-West was that Gates had compromised the trust of the citizens of Los Angeles who had lost confidence in his leadership. Until further investigation was completed and the confidence of the people restored, Daryl Gates should not be allowed to run the Los Angeles Police Department.

There appeared to be the necessary votes on City Council to put Gates on leave. The members of the council had been following the police commission hearings. With evidence of Gates' knowledge of certain behavior virtually confirmed, and the documentation of the commissioners corroborating the sentiments that abuse of authority could be tied to the permissiveness of the chief's office, no one would be too afraid to challenge Gates, now that the snowball was rolling. The intimidation over "secret dossiers" had subsided. The moment of truth was upon the council. It appeared that the SCLC-West had forced the vote down with their lawsuit, and the community was about to experience a small win, when a major turn of events spooked the whole plan. It broke in the press that Melanie Lomax had breached the confidentiality of the commission, and the city, indirectly, by allegedly leaking what the press termed "confidential documents" to the SCLC. The SCLC used the documents as the partial basis for its claim that Gates had breached his leadership trust. It added substantial credibility to the SCLC's suit, largely because the contents of the documents were firsthand matters of fact. Members of the City Council were livid that a city representative would leak documents on such a sensitive matter. How did they know she passed SCLC the documents? The lawyer for SCLC put it right in the complaint, stating that their allegation was based on documents received from a Los Angeles Police Commission. They traced it right to Melanie, because no one else was that close to the community. It was the dumbest move so-called community strategists had made in a long time. The first rule of advocacy investigation is you never give up your source of information. All that really matters is if the information is factual, not how you obtained it. The press, the police, politicians--none of them ever give up their sources. Conspirators of racism are so effective, because they never give their source. The validity of the information is all that matters. How Mark or the SCLC advisers could let Melanie be incriminated like that was beyond anyone's sense of reason. Mark was smarter than that. It caused the whole dynamics of the attack on Gates to change. Gates, a master of media manipulation, now was effectively able to put the spin on the fact that illegal and unethical means were being used to try to take his job, and that his "due process" was being violated. He was threatening a lawsuit of his own, if the City Council insisted on carrying out the vote to place him on administrative leave.

The members of the City Council were spooked again. Votes against Gates had fallen from an anticipated 10 or 11 to seven or eight. Eight was the magic number required to get Gates placed on leave. But the council vote had almost become secondary. The focus had become Melanie, and the two other police commissioners who had "allegedly" conspired to get Gates. Members of the Police Protective League, the

City Council and citizens of the other community were calling for the President of the police commission to resign. The talk was that the police commission couldn't be trusted to negotiate reform of the department, after exhibiting behavior deemed as lacking integrity. Melanie, now all but condemned, had been served up twice in five years. Only this time, she was her community's hero, as leader, after leader stood up for her honor and integrity. Melanie had done what she was put there to do, expose Gates from the inside, unlike our community had ever been able to do before. She played her hand marvelously.

However, our allies on the City Council were questioning the Black community's sense of right, in its continued denial of any wrongdoing on Melanie's part. They weren't about to be a part of any action that would bring another lawsuit, because they chose to ignore alleged wrongdoing on the part of one of their own commissioners. The deal was now that the police commission would have to be purged. The three commissioners that were part of the internal investigation would have to resign. The commissioners, former assistant police chief, Jesse Brewer, Sam Williams and Lomax (all Black) agreed to do so, if Gates resigned immediately. Gates was insisting that he would resign when the reform of the department was complete. The commissioners then said, if Gates wasn't stepping down, they weren't going to step down. The council's position was that if the commissioners didn't step down, the process wouldn't go forward, and if it did, it would go in favor of Gates. The Mayor and his community advisers felt that they could hold the right votes needed to put Gates on administrative leave. So even if the commissioners stepped down, they didn't need Gates to commit to leave immediately. The council would just send him home early. The longer the commissioners stayed, the more Gates was able to fuel the fire, and the more difficult it became to hold the eight votes on the council. The commissioners agreed to step down under the premise of allowing the process to move forward. The real deal was to allow the council vote to move forward.

When it came time to rumble, all predictions were that the votes against Gates were good to go. South Central was in, East L.A. was in, the Westside was in and Hollywood was in. That was eight votes--all day. Yet, when the time came to vote, the results were seven to eight in favor of keeping Gates on the job. Everybody's biggest fears became reality, the Black community gave up the seats on the commission, and Gates stayed. Somebody flip-flopped, rolled over, sold out, whatever you want to call it.

True to form, the betrayal was, once again, in the Black community. City Councilman Nate Holden, an African American who rejected the sentiments of his own district, voted to appease conservative white voters in the San Fernando Valley, who had voted for him in the last Mayoral election, as a protest vote against Bradley. Holden's momentary delusions of grandeur were influencing his decision to run again for Mayor, and target that same constituency. In the same pull of the lever, he compromised the community's will and best interest. Holden's action was perceived by many, as absolutely inexcusable. Months of community planning came down to what many perceived as one man putting his personal ambition ahead of the community's desire.

From that point, all hell broke loose in our community. Of course, there was the community meetings. I attended one immediately following the Gates vote at the African American Unity Center. For the first time in, at least, five years, the grassroots community applauded Tom Bradley's appearance, for his bold stand against Gates, the LAPD and for appointing Melanie Lomax, now being called the mother of LAPD police reform. Didn't stay long, though. The meeting turned into a circus of political speeches and finger pointing. I walked out as Councilman Holden was trying to explain himself over the shouts of 500 people. Whatever justification he put forth, it had little to do with the best interest of the community.

* * *

In the midst of this social and political change that I was following, like soap operas on television, I suffered a very personal tragedy that moved me unlike I had never been moved before. On July 5, 1991, I got a call from my friend Greg. "Hey Es (that's what he'd called me since we were kids), they got Kevin man. They found him dead in his car, shot to death. "Kevin" was our good friend, Kevin Thomas. He was one of the nicest brothers I had ever met in my life. He was a good brother.

Kevin was my line brother, when I pledged Phi Beta Sigma Fraternity at Cal State, Los Angeles. He, Greg and I, along with Derrick Taylor, Rick Kelly, Waveland Wilkins and Butch Howard pledged Delta Gamma Chapter's reactivated charter line in 1976. Kevin was the smallest on the line. Since Greg and I had developed a reputation for fighting, at the drop of a hat, the "big brothers" would go to the end of the line and pick on Kevin, in an effort to provoke us in to fighting them, in defense of our line brother. Kevin would always refuse to let us get in the middle of it. He took a hell of a lot of abuse, all for keeping the line together. No one came to another brother's aid quicker than Kevin. We all lived a lot faster than Kevin. None of us expected him to be the first to die. Not that any of us wanted to go first. It just seemed that Kevin should have gotten a better break than the rest of us. But then again, maybe he did. Sometimes Allah uses tragedy to save the rest of us.

Kevin had come to see me about once a month since I returned from Boron. The five or six times we saw each other in 1991 was more than we'd seen each other the last 10 years. Kevin came to see me in January, upset at himself that he had lost touch, to the extent that he had no idea how my case had ended up, until he attended a rededication ceremony at the fraternity house in December, about a week before my release. He had noticed my name was listed on a giving plaque and asked where I was. He said the brothers got real quiet like they didn't know, but they did. Greg pulled him aside, and told him where I was. Kevin felt like that was something the brothers (at least on our line) should have known about, and should have been able to contribute toward any help for my family or legal defense. The last time I saw Kevin, he had dropped by in June. He had a real serious demeanor. We talked about everything happening in politics, sports, his work and his business, and my new business. Then the discussion turned to our personal lives. Kevin asked about Taurece. They had always gotten along quite well. He was sorry to hear about our impending divorce. He'd known us both since college. He admitted that he was considering making a move of his own. None of us knew her, but if she could make Kevin, the most dedicated of bachelors, consider marriage, she must have been very special. I felt very happy for him, and told him I looked forward to meeting her. We both just kind of bonded in Kevin's revelation, for a moment. Then he asked me if I thought I'd try marriage again. I told him I didn't think so. "Marriage is a lot of work, brother," I told him. And I just don't know when I'll be in the space for that again." I said. "I don't know when I'll be in the space for anything Kevin. I kind of like taking it day by day."

As he got up to leave, Kevin said something to me that I'll remember all my life. He asked, "How long do you plan to sit on the sideline."

I asked him, "Did it matter?"

Kevin responded, "This is not what we trained you to do, Governor." Kevin used to joke in college about my drive and ambition, saying I'd be Governor one day. I'd say, "only if you are my treasurer." "You're too much of a player to waste your talent like this," Kevin continued. "You took your shot and had your rest. It's time for you to get back in the game. It's never going to change. If you don't stand up, they'll play somebody else, like they played you. Who better to stop it, than somebody who knows its effect, firsthand." Kevin could tell I wasn't interested in hearing what he just said. In his joking, jovial way, he said, "Well, maybe we'll let you sit just a little longer, but we will have this conversation again. Maybe next month?" We both laughed.

I said, "Yeah, OK" as I was rushing him out the door. It would be the last time I'd see him alive. The story was that Kevin was shot collecting rents on the 4th of July, at 7 a.m. Kevin used to manage apartments, his own as well as income property for other people. The property management company was his business he ran in addition to his regular job. Some of the units were in some pretty tough areas of South Central. We used to warn him about going in those areas anytime of the day or night, for safety sake. Kevin used to say that if he didn't go get the money when they (his tenants) had it, they wouldn't have it when he finally made time to get it. That was a rule he lived by for the 15 years I knew him. It was the rule he died by when he was ambushed off of 50th and Vermont. All I could remember at Kevin's funeral was his parting words, "When are you going to get back in the game." There would be no more games for Kevin.

A few weeks later, I got a call from Skip Cooper. "Anthony, I want you to come to my luncheon this week. I got someone I want you to meet."

"Who is it?" I asked.

"I'm not going to tell you now, but it'll be someone that will motivate you to get back in the game. Time to get off the sidelines, brother. Just be at the V.I.P. reception, before the luncheon. Your ticket will be at the door."

Skip would tell me how I'd pick up a whole constituency that had a different level of sensitivity toward incarceration having been incarcerated themselves, had a relative or loved once incarcerated, or had a close friend that's been incarcerated. These discussions made me realize that like it or not, I had earned the common Black man's "badge of community service." In many street circles, you ain't shit if you've never been to jail. As twisted as that seemed to me, and as much I would have preferred not to have gone that route, it was something I'd had to reckon with.

When I got to the luncheon reception, I saw a lot of friendly faces. And some not so friendly. I wore a full three-piece traditional African dress, called a Grand Abada (some call it a "1,500"). I pretty much only wore European suits when I had to, which was when I worked at a client's site or, when I attended the mosque. Of course, there were some very ignorant snipes like, "Oh, I guess you African now, huh? The positive comments, on both my appearance and my attendance, greatly outnumbered the negative.

One such positive response was from John Holoman. John, then a senior Vice President of Home Savings, was a supporter of the branch, when John McDonald was President. He discontinued his association with the branch when Ray became President, then began to support my efforts. I considered John a serious player, because not only was he a real (as opposed to being a figurehead) corporate executive, but he was also a successful entrepreneur and a socially responsible advocate. Holoman's entrepreneurial success came as a result of the dozen or so Church's Chicken franchises he owned. His advocacy was a result of being the publisher of one of L.A.'s oldest and most historical (and radically responsive) newspapers, the *Herald Dispatch*. The legacy of the *Dispatch* included pre-*Muhammad Speaks* articles of Malcolm X, and other so-called radical writings of the 1960s and early '70s. Holoman had successfully demonstrated more than any person I'd met in L.A.--that you could be a part of a corporate environment, as well as, a part of your community.

We spoke for about ten minutes, after which time John said to me, "Now, remember Anthony, I have a newspaper you can use when you need to."

Curious as to what I would need to use his paper for, I asked him, "Why, John?"

He responded in his usual quick (and curt) manner, "Because I think you have something to say that will benefit the community. I know I would, if I had been through what you had."

I thought for a second about what he had said. "Thanks, John. I appreciate that," I replied, and turned to leave. By that time, Skip was on his way to get me. "Glad to see you out," he said. He took me to a table of people who were talking with their backs to us, but I recognized one brother from his hair before we got there. It was boxing promoter/manager Don King. Skip introduced us. Don was kind in his comments about my dress, acknowledged it was a pleasure to meet me, and went back to his conversation. I'm sure I was just another face in a crowd of so-called "V.I.P.s" he met that day. And quite frankly, given a chance to meet somebody, Don King wouldn't have been my first choice, particularly if you were inclined to believe media representations of the man. My opinion was greatly changed, however, once I heard King speak.

On the way up to the main ballroom, several others approached me for various reasons, all positive. It felt good to be missed and supported by people who seemed to understand what I went through and why. Most importantly, many wanted to know where I was now. I stood at the rear of the ballroom another 25 or 30 minutes talking to people, while the program started. As I finally made my way to my seat, a woman grabbed me by the arm from behind. "Young man I need to talk to you," she said. I turned around, and it was California State Senator Diane Watson. We hugged and exchanged greetings. Senator Watson was one of three elected officials that supported me to the end of my persecution. Diane said, "I need to meet with you today. It's very important."

"What is it, Senator?" I said with some reservation.

"We can't talk here. Can you meet me at my office at 4:30 today?" she said.

"I can arrange to, if necessary. Is it really that urgent?" I said.

"Yes, it is. I'll see you at 4:30?"

"Yes, Senator. I'll be there," I said, as she was being pulled away.

As she turned to the line of people that had gathered behind her, she turned back. "Anthony?"

"Yes, Senator?" I responded looking over my shoulder.

"You look good! Great to see you out with us again," she said winking.

"Thanks, Senator," I said, as I walked away.

Don King gave a very impressive luncheon keynote, discussing some of the pressing issues in the boxing game around the topic "The niggah did it." The topic was King's personal insights on some problems he was being blamed for in the fight game, most critically the continuing personal problems of former heavyweight champion, Mike Tyson. Tyson, who was managed by King, was under a rape investigation stemming from his attendance at a beauty pageant, associated with the Indiana Black Expo. Of course, as history now reflects, Tyson was eventually convicted and served time for a rape allegation he, to this day, maintains he never committed. King gave the audience some insight in to what he perceived as the motives behind the continued attack on him. He quite frankly reduced it to a power struggle in boxing, particularly around the departure of Tyson from his former management. Tyson was the top draw in the game, and he was now with Don King. In fact, King then had the top two draws in the fight game with Caesar Chavez. However, the heavyweight division is where the dollars are, and King had the plum prize. Therefore, he was king of the fight game. King stated they wanted to challenge his integrity and criticize his control over his promotions, but it was no more than what they do when they're in the driver's seat. King said they play with their people, hire their referees, promote their own fights, and you don't see "a niggah in site," other than in the ring. He gave propers to Muhammad Ali for changing much of that, and prided himself as the biggest employer of Blacks in the fight game.

King talked about how even though he promoted some of the most successful fights in boxing history, he can't get banks to put up the kind of credit lines for him that they do for white boys. He talked about how he had to bankroll his own pay per view event, because the boxing establishment, claiming that he was locking them out, dried up the money sources. Yet, no one said anything when they were locking him and other Blacks out. The most fulfilling part of King's discussion came when he talked about the integrity issue associated with his fights. He first dealt with the fact that boxing didn't have the most honest reputation, before he came to boxing, nor before he got to the top of the fight game. Nor did Don King make the rules. Nor were they really an issue, until Don King became Mike Tyson's manager. Now all of a sudden, its "the niggah did this, and the niggah did that..."

Then King asked the audience to name another sport or business industry for that matter, that is controlled and dominated by whites, with a Black at the top of it. After a small pause he said, "You can't, can you? So while the niggah is doing everything else, he's doing that too, so he must be doing something right." To this comment, he received rave applause.

King then turned very serious when he talked about the public's perceptions of him in. He said its not whites, who buy off on negative perceptions of him. They know it's business, and even while coming after him, they frequently show respect for him. King said it was Black people, who don't know him, the fight game, or what he has to deal with, that take what the press writes about him at face value.

"They even add a little bit to it, when it's not bad enough."

I couldn't help but testify out loud when he said that. I hollered, "That's right. That's what they do."

Don King received a very warm standing ovation from the sell-out crowd that day. It was certainly a different kind of message than what most of us had expected to receive. I left the Bonaventure Hotel on a real high. Don King did change my perspective, in more ways than one. Whatever I did or didn't do, people would talk and believe what they want to believe.

In a conversation I had with Skip later that day, he reminded me of where I'd been, who I knew and what I could do. We got into a discussion of what was reality and what was illusion. My position was that I did in fact, have a network of contacts that exceeded most. That was real. The illusion was getting past those who say they are with me, and those who really were, and most importantly, being able to clearly identify those who were against me. Leadership is a 50/50 proposition. At anytime, 50 percent of the people will be with you, and 50 percent will be against you. Skip, rushing off the phone, wanted to make one last point. "Anthony, that may be true for an average brother, but you're not an average brother. You got a lot of chips out there. Half of your Rolodex is more resourceful, in terms of access to important people, potential business and continued advocacy, than most people I know. The lesson for you in this is for you to determine which half is with you. When you come back, as I believe you will, the same people will be up in your face that talked about you in the public, in the press, in the back room, behind your back and anywhere else they could talk about you. Only you can determine how you identify who is sincere, and who's looking to trap you again. It happened once. Shame on them for doing it, but if it happens again, shame on you for letting it happen. But I think you're under estimating yourself," he stated. "You have more chips in your pocket than you may think. As many people as you helped both in the bank and the NAACP, when nobody else would help them, many will still remember that, and they'll help you, when it appears nobody else wants to," Skip concluded.

As we hung up, I had to acknowledge that the brother made a lot of sense. I had pushed everyone away from me, except a select few and had been distrustful of almost everyone who had tried to reach out. It was now time to reach back. It just might be my call to get back in the game.

As I drove over to Senator Diane Watson's office, I began to think about how I wanted to get back in the game. Was it too early to take a visible role in the community politics, or should I take a background role? I had set up an urban affairs company to address that very question. When I entered the Senator's office, it certainly was a Kodak moment. The Senator's staff just stared at me, and I stared back at them. Of course, most of them knew whom I was. I broke the silence, "I'm here to see the Senator."

The Senator's chief deputy, Charles Stewart, stepped up acting very official. "Do you have an appointment?" he said, refusing to acknowledge that he knew me.

"I think so?" I replied. He looked at me cynically, doubting that I had one, as he looked in the Senator's appointment calendar. I don't see your name, he said.

"Is the Senator in?" I asked thinking to myself, "this is the kind of bullshit I don't know if I can deal with."

"Yes she is, but she's very busy," he said.

"I'm here at her request. Why don't you tell her I'm here," I said, becoming very annoyed. He looked at me as if I was sending him on a goose chase. After a few seconds, the Senator came right out.

"Anthony, good to see you, Come right in," she said as we embraced. Everybody just stared, as I walked behind the Senator back into her office. I felt like giving them all "the bone." I almost did, but settled with a wave of my hand. Charles and I would get along and work well together in the future, but right then, it wasn't going well.

Once seated in front of the Senator at her desk, she went into a succession of questions, many of which I wasn't really prepared for. So how have you been? Where have you been? You really look good. So what are you doing now? Are you ready to get back out there ? Have you talked to anybody about some of the politics around here?

I tried to answer them in the order they came. "Fine." " Just taking it easy and trying to stay out the Negro circles." "Thank you, you look fine yourself." "I'm doing some consulting, mostly strategic planning and urban affairs stuff." "I've just been watching some of the council stuff in the 8th and 9th districts, and some of the "back and forth" on this Gates stuff but that's about it." I think I answered everything.

The Senator looked out her window. "Has anybody approached you on anything having to do with the supervisor's seat?" she said as she looked around.

"Well, I'm being approached by a lot of people these days about a lot of different things, Senator," I responded.

"Yeah, I could tell by that line around you today at the luncheon," she smiled, "But seriously," she continued.

"No Senator," I said.

"Then I need you as part of my brain trust," she said.

"Brain trust for what?" I said.

Then as bold and direct as I had heard anybody make reference to it, Sen. Watson said, "I'm running for Kenny Hahn's seat. I need you with me."

I looked at her with surprise. Not so much at the announcement, as unexpected as it was, but out of her proclamation that she needed me to be with her. After a moment of silence, I came back just as straightforward, "Diane, how can you say that. What do you mean by that?"

"There are only three young players in this city that really know what's goin' on. The other two are running for office." She was talking about Bob Gay and Mark Ridley-Thomas. "It's time for you to come back in and play. You have too much talent to be out of the loop. You're a star. You made a mistake, but that doesn't diminish your talent. You've learned your lesson, haven't you?" she snapped back. I nodded. "Then I want you with me," she said leaning back in her chair. I felt I was being placated and I let into the Senator's response, "Senator, what about all I've been through."

She responded, "Anthony, I'm not concerned about those few people who may want to drum up some of that dirt that caused you to lose a branch election. And as for the jail time, everybody knows what that was about. Everywhere I went, people were talking in your favor. Anthony, the people weren't talking about you, they were talking for you. I want you to bring that grassroots following into my campaign. Nobody knows the issues that impact our people like you do."

I really appreciated her saying that. I really never thought she had taken the time to notice. I became silent again. Now able to focus on the whole purpose of this meeting in the first place (her running against Kenny Hahn), this was political blasphemy in Los Angeles. In L.A. political circles, you usually made the cross over your heart and head, at the mention of Los Angeles County Supervisor Kenny Hahn. To run against the prophet of pothole politics was unthinkable.

The last time someone mounted what they thought was a serious challenge, it was popular former L.A. City Councilman turned local Judge, Billy Mills. Mills was the third Black elected to City

Council (after Lindsey and Bradley) and was the first to challenge the notion of Hahn's "plantation politics." Years later, the Mills challenge came up, in a 1987 clandestine meeting, so secret that people refused to sign in, because of fear of Hahn's reprisal-- if he ever got a hold of the list. A dozen or so of us met at First AME. The meeting was attended by most of the old L. A. political vanguard, H. H. Brookins, Tom Kilgore, Bill Elkins (for Tom Bradley), Maxine Waters, Diane Watson, Nate Holden, Chip Murray and some of the new vanguard, namely Mark Ridley-Thomas, Danny Bakewell and myself. Everybody made Holden swear to secrecy, because he was a Kenny Hahn player, and warned if it got back to Hahn, they would assume it was him. The purpose of that meeting was to discuss if Black leadership was prepared to step forward to ask Kenny Hahn not to run again. Hahn had suffered a stroke in the middle of his current term.

The Supervisor's district was being run by staff, while Hahn took almost a year to recover. Bound to a wheelchair, he could only attend one or two meetings a week, couldn't really meet with constituents, and the services in the district were deteriorating. Hahn's office had went into a P.R. mode to try to allay the increasing levels of concern about the district's lack of representation. Hahn's aides were putting the word out at every appearance, "If Roosevelt could run the country from a wheelchair, Kenny Hahn could run the 2nd District from a wheelchair."

Well, of course, most everybody in the community's leadership circles was saying, "That's bullshit," but were keeping it to themselves. The real facts were Black leadership was extremely concerned about Hahn's health status. To watch a once brilliant and articulate public servant stumble five minutes over the simplest of statements was scary," some stated in the meeting. It damn near killed Kenny Hahn every time he opened his mouth. It was very clear that this was cause for concern. The basis for such concern was that most of the leadership did not expect Hahn to survive the term. In California, a vacant County Supervisor seat is filled by the Governor. The Governor at the time was George Deukmejian, the man that defeated Tom Bradley (twice) for the governorship. Most of the L.A. Black community had a very poor relationship with Deukmejian, a republican. Certainly, an appointee would not come from a community recommendation, so the only logical move was to pre-empt any such event from occurring. The choices were few. In fact, only three. One, run someone against Hahn. Two, ask Hahn not to run. And, three, let Hahn sit, and pray he survives.

The choices were reduced by process of elimination. Running against Hahn was eliminated first. That's when the Mills race came up, and the last time a major player underestimated the Hahn influence in our community. Bishop Brookins recalled how the very popular Mills ran a great race, until voting time came. Bishop said he never saw so many people in wheelchairs, walkers and respirators in his life. People left hospitals and got up out of sick beds to vote for Kenny Hahn. Old ladies cried at the mention of his name, and cursed the nerve of someone running against Kenny Hahn. In the Bishop's words, "Hahn killed Mills at the polls, getting twice the number of votes."

The issue was how much of that influence was left. It was largely acknowledged in political circles that Kenny Hahn was now just bankrolling "favor chips," to use for his son's future political aspirations. Nobody knew how many there were. But (then) 36 years in a seat where the size of sole source contracts had the capacity to make a dozen millionaires every year, in his district alone, was something to consider. As a flex of his power, insiders talked about a recent luncheon Hahn had where he invited 50 people, and raised close to a half-million dollars. Hahn called in ten grand a pop, at the blink of an eye. He didn't have to follow-up on one invitation. His supporters just "knew what to do." The thought was that Hahn would need very few chips for himself, and still would have plenty left over to godfather his son's political career. Then, there was the issue of who would run against him. No one, including those in the room, could think of anyone who could, or would, take on Kenny Hahn. Even, if he was incapacitated, thought to be half-dead, one foot in the grave, no one was going to take on the wrath of Hahn (no pun intended).

Then came the choice of asking Hahn not to run. Of course, the question again was who was going to take it to him. The room was dead silent. Everybody knows the golden rule of power politics, you wait your turn, until the incumbent decides what they want to do, and allow him (or her) to choose their successor. Anything else is an assault on their power seat. Marlon Brando said it best, in "Godfather I," as his character Don Carlone transferred the power of the family business to his son, Michael, played by Al Pacino. He capsulized the perception of betrayal in one line, "The one that brings you the deal, is the one that will betray you." Whether its true or not, plenty of messengers have been shot carrying such a message. And if they survive to talk about it, they most certainly fall out of favor. No one was prepared to fall out of Kenny Hahn's trust, by trying to force his hand. Someone tried to suggest to Nate that he be the one, he didn't even let 'em finish. Holden said his support was with Hahn and would always be with him, because of what Hahn has done for him.

We moved on from there. Talking through this process, Black leadership in Los Angeles began to realize how vulnerable they really were. Whether we liked it or not, "wez (in the Los Angeles 2nd Supervisorial District) was Mr. Hahn's property," for the moment and nobody was prepared to "steal away" to freedom. Not this term. In a moment of resignation, those in the room considered the third option. All of us joining hands, the Bishop began with, "Lord, let us pray..."

Recalling that meeting, as I listened to the Senator's intentions, raised several questions in my mind that I immediately put to Diane. The first one was, "Is Black leadership ready to back such a move?"

The answer to that was a resounding, "Yes." Hahn did survive the term, but the services in the district had declined so sharply that constituents were now very dissatisfied. Moreover, access to Kenny Hahn had become extremely limited. The district was being run by Hahn's chief aides Mai Fukai, a Japanese male, and Carmen Perez, a Latina. Neither was perceived as having a high level of sensitivity to Blacks.

Many felt it was time for a change, even if Hahn was healthy, because of the nature of the politics. Many felt Hahn was not in a position to play ethnic politics for Black people. It never was the nature of his political style. Gloria Molina, the first Latina elected to the board, was having no problem running over the other three white males on the board. She might have hit the horn once or twice for Hahn, in deference to his seniority, but no one was standing in the way of her pro-Latino politics. Had he chosen to oppose her, Hahn at that point, would have just been another victim. The sentiment of tip-toeing around "the Hahn issue" four years earlier was gone. Not because any feeling toward Hahn had mellowed, but because the fight had changed. Hahn could sit for us, but he couldn't fight for us. That made a big difference. Diane had clearly been in touch with Hahn's constituency.

The next question was, "Is Hahn running?" In the eyes of many, Kenny Hahn was beginning to exploit the people's loyalty, and stretch their benevolence with this "wait and see" game he was playing. Hahn had gone past several self imposed deadlines, where he was to announce whether or not he was going to run. Hahn was playing his hand to the final card, while pushing the patience of everyone who had the greatest respect for him. Senator Watson tried to talk to him on several occasions to try and get an idea of where he was, but Hahn was too cagey a player to tip his hand. The community was now growing tired of trying to wait on Hahn, while Molina was moving through his district and county departments picking on Black interest. Many felt the seat was almost being held hostage. I asked the Senator if she felt Hahn would run. She said, "No, I hear his health is declining and his wife wants him to quit."

"What if he doesn't quit? Will you run against him?"
Diane still stated, "I'm running for the seat, not against Kenny Hahn."

I looked at her sarcastically like, "OK, we'll see how far that gets with Hahn." "Do you think you can sell that?" I said.

"I'm gonna try," she said.

"Where you gonna get your money?" I asked.
She stated that she already had several commitments that amounted to a half-million. "It'll take a million and half to win." (Former California state Senator) Art Torres spent almost two million," she said.

"And lost (against Molina)," I reiterated.

"Do you see anyone else in the race?" She stated that Julian (Dixon, the congressman) is said to be interested and Maxine (Waters) was said to be looking to come home. "But I don't see either of them moving," the Senator said. "So, getting to the chase, "Are you in? This is a historic opportunity, and I need the cream of the crop to play," she said.

"Thanks, Senator but I need a minute to think about it. It's not like I'm talking to a lot of people in your circle these days, but I promise not to share our conversation," I said.

"My kitchen cabinet is meeting next Thursday night. If I see you there, I'll count you in," she said. We hugged, as I left.

When I walked up to the Senator's home, her sister Barbara answered the door. She invited me in. There were about 20 people in the room. They were in a very intense discussion. Everybody stopped momentarily to watch me take a seat. I knew some of the faces. Others I didn't remember right off, but associated their names with some of the city's power politics during the course of the discussion. Still most had taken note that I was there and reacted in various ways. A stare, a tilted eyebrow, a slight glance. The Senator nodded and I nodded back. The meeting lasted about 90 minutes. Much of the discussion had to do with Hahn now being perceived as holding everyone qualified to succeed him at bay, while the deadline for filing approached. Being pushed too close to the filing deadline, while Hahn was deciding what to do was a concern, because it limited the options of any real challengers. If a challenger was going to wait on Hahn, they'd almost assuredly have to have his endorsement to make up for lost time. If the challenger was going to challenge Hahn, they'd need the time to amass the huge amount of resources they'd need just to compete with Hahn, not to mention match, or exceed his enormous name recognition. It was decided that since the Senator's plan did not hinge on Hahn running, benchmarks would be developed to determine where the line in the sand should be drawn. She was trying to wait for Hahn's announcement, as long as she could, as a courtesy to him for his 40 years of service. It was late July. Mid-September was set as the drop-dead date for making a decision on an announcement. Until that time, we were to spread out into community circles and measure the sentiment of the masses. After the meeting, the Senator came up to me. "I'm glad to see you here," she said. "Welcome aboard," she continued amid the looks of concern of those standing behind her. She gave me a "don't worry about them, I'll handle it" kind of wink. She asked me to begin to develop issues around abuse in the County Sheriff's Department, and the decreasing number of Blacks in county management positions. I was well-acquainted with both issues. I had just begun consulting to an employee's rights coalition called the Black Organizations Alliance. The population parity issue the Latinos were pushing was at the top of their agenda. As I left the meeting, a couple of people did come up to me and acknowledge that they were glad I was getting involved. However, I knew this was just a sample of the response I would receive stepping back into some of the "Negro circles." But I felt good about why I had to do this.

* * *

There was significant movement on the Black national scene. Thurgood Marshall, the nation's first Black solicitor general and Supreme Court Justice announced his retirement. If I ever had a hero, Thurgood Marshall was it. His contribution to the changing of America's race politics is immeasurable. Much of his effort predated the Civil Rights Movement, which many historians officially began in 1955. But the victory of Brown vs. the Board of Education of Topeka, Kansas in 1954, which Marshall litigated, was the board from which the call for civil rights sprang. Prior to 1954, it was very dangerous to be a civil rights advocate. And it wasn't very popular. Black people stayed away from the "troublemakers" that brought on that "civil rights talk," riling up white people. Yet that's what Thurgood Marshall did. He was litigating civil rights before we could appeal to white folks' sense of moral right to legislate civil rights. Thurgood Marshall would clearly be the most important figure of the 20th century, in terms of challenging America's race politics in courts. He busted up the "Jim Crow" laws in "their" courts, and made the way for the many legal challenges in the succeeding civil rights movement. And, he integrated America's most prestigious closed circle, the Supreme Court: the last word in American democracy.

For the first time, since he'd been there, Black America realized the importance of not having him there. Whether Blacks wanted to admit it or not, Justice Marshall's seat was our seat, the Black seat. A seat we had earned. Not to have a seat at the last bar of justice, in this day and time, would definitely be a reversal of fortune for Black people. Our Supreme Court seat was the most prized reward of our struggle in America, and with the constitutional fundamentalists trying to redefine and re-interpret the constitution, we had to be at the table to forestall this return to racial aristocracy. The question was, who would replace Thurgood? Black America, who never had a good relationship with President George Bush, was now at the virtual mercy of a man charged with ushering in the "New World Order." Which, by most accounts, didn't include us. Bush was having enough problems of his own, though, and couldn't afford the kind of social anarchy a non-Black appointment would bring, if he chose to go that way. And he was considering it. Bush, instead, chose to do something much worse; something that really did more to demonstrate how unaffected "power in America" is by the current corps of so-called "Black leaders." Instead of trying to appeal to the masses of Blacks and the Black leadership, which the Republican party hadn't done, but claimed it was trying to do, Bush went with a party ideologist--in a Blackface--and challenged Black America to either accept it, or get nothing. Bush's selection of former Equal Employment Opportunity Commission Chairman (EEOC), then federal judge, Clarence Thomas, was not just a shrewd move, it was a wickedly cruel move.

Thomas, was not only unknown to most Blacks, he was unpopular on Capitol Hill. He was not considered a legal scholar and was accused of being ineffective at the EEOC, the civil rights policy arm of the government. He didn't have a lot of friends out there from jump street. The slightest opposition from the major civil rights community would be enough justification for the Senate to vote along party lines and kill the nomination. Bush had said Thomas was it. Blacks wouldn't get another choice. So then the debate began. Should we or shouldn't we support Clarence Thomas. This, of course, thrust the NAACP back into the national news. Everybody wanted to know where the NAACP stood. The national organization initially stated that it would remain neutral. It eventually made comments that gave indication that it was not in support of the Thomas nomination, though it made no official proclamation one way or another. For the first time, in a long time, I agreed with the "Colored People," not so much on their statements. I was like most people who felt "the brother" couldn't be that bad. He was doing what he had to do in "playing the game" and would "come around" after confirmation. History would prove that we were all so wrong, but hindsight is 20/20. We had no way knowing this then. I also felt, like most Blacks, that this was no time to gamble with "the Black seat." But like the NAACP, I felt that Thomas' politics wasn't our fight. That if we couldn't outright support him, we shouldn't say anything at all. Let white folk get him by themselves, without our help. We'd have a better chance of going back to Bush and saying you put up a nominee that couldn't win, versus Bush saying to Blacks "you helped defeat the nominee for your seat." We couldn't be part of Bush's justification for either Thomas' defeat, or for not considering another Black nominee. It would be the only way we could appeal to Bush's sense of fairness, if he had any.

There were some branches in the NAACP that wanted to support Thomas, in spite of national's position. One branch in Compton, California officially came out in favor of the Thomas nomination. Once this happened, NAACP director of branch services, Bill Penn, immediately demanded that the branch change its position, or have its branch charter snatched and its officers removed. Same ole' Penn, was the sentiment of many in Los Angeles.

It was being perceived in the national media, as a bully move by the one organization that professed to defend democracy and civil rights of others. Penn eventually backed off his position. However, the damage had been done. Again, the NAACP was made to look like it was out of step with the sentiments of the people. Moreover, it was made to look like it overreacted to the Compton branch's position. It was the second time that year the NAACP had made a major decision that was perceived as not in it's best interest.

Earlier in the year, many felt the NAACP had shot itself in the foot, when the national board of directors decided to seize control of the NAACP Image Awards show. The Image Awards started by the Hollywood-Beverly Hills branch, had grown from a local industry award presentation to a nationally recognized prime time awards show, and it was hugely profitable. The branch President, Willis Edward, and his First Vice President, Sandra Evers-Manley, were largely responsible for the show growing to success. It was year-round work by the branch that made it successful. Willis not only got the show picked up by NBC, after a few years of running in the late night (middle of the night in some cities), he convinced them to run it in primetime. A crowning achievement. The positive media the image awards received from prime-time was more than it received all year. And it brought the NAACP in over a half million dollars. The NAACP (national) decided to seize the show when it found out that NBC had paid Willis a $25,000 consulting fee on the project. Of course, a NAACP member is not supposed to receive outside compensation on NAACP fundraising projects, without permission. Supposedly, Ben Hooks knew, but when it went public, Hooks denied it. The national board voted to take over the show. Willis announced his resignation the night of the awards, in the program booklet, not only without giving Hooks any forewarning, but severing ties with the show. Most people felt that the NAACP, again, threw the baby out with the bath water.

Most fundraisers charge 10 percent or more on projects like these. Willis not only raised a half million dollars, he saved the organization another $25,000 to $35,000 (even after the $25,000 he took) they would have otherwise had to pay out. He deserved to be paid for his effort. What did the NAACP end up doing? Hiring a consultant (at 10%), producing the show out of Florida, at almost twice the cost. The show was back on late night, and losing money. They eventually ended up selling the rights to produce the show to "Soul Train" producer Don Cornelius, for a lot less than they would have, if they had let Willis continue to handle the show. The Image Awards move coupled with the attack on Compton was only some of the NAACP's public posturing. The organization was in the midst of a civil war that had turned ugly and very public. Ben Hooks and the NAACP board chairman, Dr. William Gibson, were now publicly warring. Gibson's term was due to expire, and it appeared Hooks was trying to usher him out by trying to block a resolution that Gibson supporters had put forth that allowed the chairman to succeed himself. The Clarence Thomas episode only added more discussion to the NAACP relevancy question.

Aside from the NAACP controversy, Thomas escaped any further damaging criticism, passed the confirmation of the Senate Judiciary Committee, and was on the verge of being confirmed by the full Senate. The night before Thomas' confirmation vote was to take place, a staff member of one of the Senate Judiciary Committee members leaked Anita Hill's sexual harassment allegation to the press. The press ran it and the confirmation vote was jeopardized. The judiciary committee, 14 white males, had seen the allegation in file, but didn't note it as substantive enough to raise issue with it. Of course, the U.S Senate may have contained only the foremost "booty-pinchers" in the country. Known as the one of last "white male" chauvinistic boys club, the U.S. Senate was certainly not going to be the one to initiate a sexual harassment discussion, much less pass judgment on someone. However, the racial implication of the leak was very apparent.

The assumptions were that the Democrats couldn't raise the issue without appearing to be dirty, so they leaked it, causing alarm in the party, and cause to investigate the allegations. The pressure of Hill's allegation was so great, the Senate ordered hearings on them immediately. Not only did they order the hearings, they ordered them televised. During the course of the hearings, the whole nation witnessed the most humiliating propagation of racial stereotypes since Amos and Andy aired. Everything from Black men having big dicks and uncontrollable sexual desires to Blacks lie and can't be trusted, from Black women always wanting sex, and therefore can't be harassed, to Blacks play games on the job, from allegations that he played her, to allegations that she played him, all staged before this panel of very political white males who were hardly in any position to judge anybody's behavior. Then the hearings turned into a "Black on Black" thang; about whose character was more credible, and who could attest the most. In the end, it was his word against hers, as it was from the beginning, but the integrity of Blacks, as a people had been set back a hundred years.

There was nothing more than a whimper about who leaked the information, in the first place. Where was the Black leadership on that issue? Dead Silence. Meanwhile, America's feminist organizations, who've never seen a bandwagon they couldn't catch and jump on, hailed Anita Hill for her stand, and criticized the Senate Judiciary Committee for its examination of Ms. Hill. This was more publicity and more progress on the sexual harassment issue, than white women had been able to conjure up in the history of their movement. Thus, the year of the woman was born, on the back and trampled reputation of a Black man and a Black woman. It was appalling.

The racial implications of the Thomas-Hill hearings infuriated me so, that I couldn't stop talking about it. Even though I was beginning to get out more in public, Debra had largely become my sole confidant. I talked frequently with others, but I really opened up to her. It was like my old self in terms of being about to assess and articulate my views without fear of "who I could really trust." After a few days she got tired of talking about it. She said to me, "You know, you really know the intricacies of these race issues. I've noticed that. Not just on this issue but others, too. You need to start writing about it, sharing your views with others also." I initially took that as a "You ain't gonna talk my ass to death, every time I come over here" kind of statement. However, a few days later while dropping her off at the airport on her way to the annual Congressional Black Caucus (party) weekend, she raised the issue again. "You really need to consider writing a column. I think you'd do quite well. Didn't you say someone said they'd give you a chance to write?" Debra asked.

I nodded, "Yeah, I'll think about it." She said, "Good, I'll see you Sunday," as she kissed me goodbye.

When Debra returned, I was driving around the airport terminal when I saw John Holoman. I pulled over and approached him. He had also just returned from the Caucus. I asked if that offer to write in his paper was still good. He said that it was. I made an appointment to see him later that week. After a couple of meetings and some extended negotiations, John allowed me to begin submitting my weekly column in his paper, the *Herald Dispatch*.

The first week of November (7th) 1991, my by-line "Between the Lines" was born, and it took off. Never could I have imagined that in six months, the column would be running in over 75 papers nationwide. It was (and still is) a hard-hitting column dealing with the social, political and economic realities of America's race politics. It was formatted as an issues-based column, very topic- driven, which took the personalities out of the mix. I had long understood the power of the opinion page in newspapers.

Editorials check runaway segments of society (like politicians and police), and tend to shape public policy and social politics by the benefit of public discussion. Opinion writers are the watchdogs of society; the "testers" and "enforcers" of the first (and last) legitimate right, free speech. A right that many Blacks have abdicated, in their fear, or their willingness to capitulate and compromise. The power to advance public sentiment, be it large or small, and advocate for the voiceless, is our last protection against tyranny. Opinion writers can influence opposition or support for a certain position. Politicians and bureaucrats understand this and they know they're being watched and being held accountable.

White folk have long understood that the pen is mightier than the sword (though they don't hesitate to use either), which is why their editorial pages are the most important pages in their newspapers. They use their editorial pages to "check" their own. Editorialists are generally the leading "talking heads" in the news, and their opinions drive public affairs television and "talk" radio. That's exactly what Black people, particularly Blacks in Los Angeles, needed to understand, at this critical time in the city's history. The Black community had now become a cliché of power hungry drones, who intimidated second generation leadership where visionary thought and new ideas were born. In Los Angeles, Negro leadership was "eating their young" and killing ideas for social change, before they were even born. We needed someone to discuss, expose, agitate, arouse and check what was going on in our communities. Who better to do it than someone who has had a history as social agitator and had nothing to lose.

I committed myself to doing nothing but telling the truth -the real truth on social and political issues of social consequence, on a weekly basis. And by the grace of Allah, I'd spend the rest of my life being a truth teller -900 words a week. All the truth the enemy of freedom, justice and equality can stand. That includes all enemies, including those trying to hide behind their Black face. In fact, they are now considered the worst of our enemies, in my humble opinion.

November 7 was a bittersweet day for me. It was a day that brought news that shocked the world. While sitting in Coley's Jamaican Restaurant (on Slauson Avenue) reading my new column and eating jerk chicken, programming both on television and the radio was interrupted. The Los Angeles Lakers were holding a press conference. Magic Johnson was announcing that he had contracted the HIV virus (the virus that supposedly leads to AIDS) and, therefore, had to retire, effective immediately. The restaurant went dead silent. It hit me like a gunshot. One of the waitresses started to cry. Suddenly, I wasn't hungry anymore. This was tragic. Earvin "Magic" Johnson brought respectability back to professional basketball. He changed the game and changed the lives of Los Angelenos and the world. In the day of Reaganomics, when Blacks were just trying to hold on, Magic gave our people a reason to smile, with his smile. His winning attitude and down home personality brought people together around basketball. I was a fan of Magic. He was the connection I had with my childhood game of choice, which I still played, just as serious on weekends.

I went over Debra's house to watch the 6 o'clock news, and all the after-specials. We both were particularly quiet that night. I sat there thinking how fate turns suddenly, (like I hadn't thought of it before) having everything one minute, and seemingly nothing the next. I thought that tomorrow is guaranteed to no one. I thought about my life, and how I would want to spend the rest of my life and who I'd want to spend it with, if I only had a short time to live. And why. All I could think of was bible verses, and other small but meaningful sayings like "What does it profit a man to gain the whole world and lose his own soul" or "What good is success, if you have no one to share it with."

After a couple of hours of silence, I turned to Debra. "So you want to do that thing?"

What thing?" she asked.

"You know, that thing you been saying you've been wanting to do."

Debra looked at me as seriously as she ever had, and said, "Boy, don't play with me."

I said, "I'm not. All I can say is I'm willing to try if your are."

Debra said, "You know I don't believe you. You're just emotional right now. I'll give you a 60-day recision clause. Come back, and ask me again in 60 days."

I knew what I wanted right way. Sixty days later wouldn't have mattered. I loved Debra and I knew it. I was in that male denial. All denials ended on November 7. Life is too precious and too short. Reality has a crude way of waking us up. I was ready to marry Debra, and spend as much of my life with her as God would permit. It wasn't about perceptions anymore. It was about reality and truth. In reality I knew I wasn't perfect, but if she was willing to love me, in spite of my faults, I was willing to do the same for her. In reality, she made me happy. In truth, I loved her and loved the time we spent together, so what else was there. It was time, in truth, to live the reality I dreamed. Debra was that reality.

* * *

The past couple of weeks had been very interesting. L.A. County Supervisor Kenny Hahn had gone past his self-imposed "end of October" promise, to decide whether he would run for a 10th consecutive term. He was clearly painting any potential challenger into a corner. Not only would the challenger have to overcome Hahn's influence, but time was even a bigger opponent, and everybody knew that. If he could push his opposition into 1992, nobody would have enough time to overcome his name recognition and resources (war chest) in six short months or less. Knowing what she had to do, Senator Watson called Kenny Hahn the morning of November 1, and told him she was running. She announced it to the press that same day. Even though Hahn was gracious in his statements that "Diane Watson would make a fine supervisor," behind closed doors, he was said to be furious. His hand had been forced. He was said to be livid, and expressed that he had earned the right to make his announcement, whenever he made it. He felt like he had been stepped on, some insiders said. "Diane would regret this," he was said to have commented. Hahn's position being that no one without his endorsement would succeed him. For the moment it looked like a one horse race, but there were several major players rumored to be interested. Congressman Julian Dixon, who eventually declined, and Congressman Maxine Waters. Waters, who had just gotten to Washington, was said to have been influenced by their family to stay there. However, word of Hahn's anger got around the community, and the word was sent out that Diane Watson would not run unopposed. You (Hahn's sources stated) could guarantee it.

In the meantime, the manifestations of unbridled race insensitivity in the courts had finally reached the public eye. In what was perceived, by even many legal experts, as one of the most blatant abuses of judicial discretion, since the 1960s; the killer of Latasha Harlins, Soon Ja Du, who was convicted of second degree murder, received a sentence of five years probation, and a one dollar fine. The judge in the case, Joyce Karlins, a known conservative who is married to an arch conservative in the U.S. attorney's L. A. office, was filling an appointed term that was due to expire. She would soon have to run for reelection.

Clearly, the community was incensed. It also understood the impact of partisan politics on the court. As Reagan's and Bush's judicial appointees became increasingly strong in their numbers and more settled in their judicial philosophies, they became known for their boldness in rendering political decisions. Karlins' use of discretion in the Du sentencing, was an example of how ridiculously far such power could be taken, and how selective it could be used. The decision also raised the more frequent question as to how others perceive the value of Black life. During that same time a Glendale (CA) man received a 30-day jail sentence for kicking a dog. This added insult to injury in the Du case. The disparities in judicial sentencing discussed earlier barefaced this out.

It was being played out, to the fullest. The community leadership, again, came out with its ole' "three step" dance. "Public dismay, call for peace, march and pray (candlelight vigil). One-two-three, one-two-three, one-two-three. Only this time, the public outcry was a little louder, the march for justice was a little stronger and a new generation of grassroots advocates emerged who didn't wish to be stroked. Talk about "brothers and sisters, be cool!" wasn't even heard. It was with the soft sentencing of Latasha Harlins' killer that the nation first heard the battle cry of a new generation, "No Justice, No Peace." There were frequent demonstrations that so marked the holiday season, that for the first time in a long time, even the "feel good hypocrisy of Christmas didn't soothe the hurt and anger of the Los Angeles Black community. The new year, in Los Angeles was marked by what would have been Latasha's 16th birthday. It was held on 92nd and Figueroa, in the heart of South Central Los Angeles, in front of the store where Latasha was killed. About 150 people attended. Her aunt, Denise Harlins, held a silent prayer vigil, after which time the attendees had birthday cake. In a brief speech, Denise vowed that this merchant would never open this market again. The market, to date, has never reopened again.

* * *

Then, L.A.P.D. police chief, Daryl Gates, was going around the community to calm "the masses." In his most humble public relations mode in years, he was trying to convince the people that the beating of Rodney King was, in his words, "an aberration" and that he was the one to lead the department's police reform effort. First on his list, of course, were Negroes, "the so-called leaders," that had been a part of the bogus community advisory panel he had made up. Gates was pulling on the community organizations that bought into this advisory process, to now advance his interest in staying out front on police reform. He was definitely calling for his pay off (in the quid pro quo sense of any arrangements), and was expecting Black leadership to comply at all cost. No excuses, even if it meant Black leadership had to go against the will of its membership and constituency.

One very disgusting example where this occurred was with 100 Black Men of Los Angeles, Inc. The board of directors for the L. A. 100 Black Men had received a request from Gates to come speak to the organization. The board overwhelmingly declined the request. Chapter President, Warren Valdry, however, was part of the advisory panel. Valdry defied the decision of the board that sets the meeting agenda and brought Gates to the monthly membership meeting. Gates walked in like he owned the place, leaving two undercover cops standing at the door, as if they were guarding his back and prepared to draw on anyone that moved. One of the members asked Gates to ask the cops to take a seat. But no one said a word about why the hell Gates was there. In the midst of a half-stunned membership, Gates proceeded to do his thing on Rodney King, that he was working with the department to calm the community, and how he wanted to be the one to lead reform. The members sat dead silent while Gates spoke. Those of us who knew what was going on, couldn't believe what was happening. You had judges, lawyers and doctors in the room who argued for hours on the least little breach of protocol, sitting silent in the midst of an obvious compromise of a stated organizational position. Gates took questions from the group.

There was a question about the privatization of police services by the owner of a private security service. Former Councilman Dave Cunningham asked "the chief" had he called Rodney, which we all knew he was legally prohibited from doing, because of the pending criminal and civil cases against the city of Los Angeles. The timidness of the so-called most influential group of Black males in the city was shocking and almost unbearable. I stood up and said, "The activity of the department has been corrupt for years, and the lead your officers have taken is from you. You got a lot of nerve coming up in here. You need to resign." I thought Valdry was going to faint.

Gates looked at me, knowing who I was, and said, "That's your opinion," and took the next question.

A couple other members stood up in objection but, by and large, it was 100 Black Wussies that night. After a few more questions, Gates walked out of the meeting with a look on his face that I will never forget. He had just "batter-rammed" a meeting of the so-called "Black male elite," said whatever the hell he wanted to say, and walked out virtually unscathed. It was like someone walking in your house, kissing your woman, looking at you like, "What you wanna do?" and leaving the door open on the way out. He looked at his two officers, they all smiled at each other, and left it like, "Which organization do we do next?"

Ironically, at the next meeting, the 100 Black Men were back to biting and barking at each other over a Black college charity football game. The same ones that had a squeak in their voice when dealing with Gates were barking loudest, when dealing with each other. As much as I respect the work the organization does, I discontinued my affiliation with 100 Black Men after that meeting. I still highly respect many of its members and associate with them, on occasion as individuals, and may affiliate again in the future. But it was a major conflict for me, at a time in my life when I was trying to be "true to self" and push social compromise out of my life. If there's supposed to be strength in unity, I couldn't see affiliating with a group that can be strong at a Christmas party, but weak when standing up against one white man. Hell, I could be weak by myself, or strong by myself. I could also be stronger with a group committed to strength, not one committed to weakness. This wasn't the one.

* * *

State Senator Diane Watson's campaign for Supervisor was now in full swing. Her primary opposition had finally been announced. It would be former Congresswoman Yvonne Braithwaite-Burke. Ms. Burke, once the darling of California politics, had been out of public office almost eight years since losing a re-election bid to the County Board of Supervisors in 1984. Governor Jerry Brown appointed her to the board, in 1981, to fill the vacancy in the fourth district seat. In 1984, challenger Deane Dana played the race card, in a mostly white affluent district, took the seat in a close election, and retired California's first Black Congresswoman, for what many thought, was for good. Ms. Burke, since that time, was a law partner in a very prestigious law firm. There wasn't a lot that anyone could say bad about Ms. Burke, who was very well-liked during her stay in politics. Everyone admired her, including many in the Watson camp. I thought it was very unfortunate that two of Los Angeles' most prominent Black women were being forced to run against each other and, of course, this wasn't by mistake. The information we were receiving in our camp was that Ms. Burke was being coerced out of political retirement, and in time she would receive Hahn's blessings. If anyone had anything critical to say about Ms. Burke, it was that she was too nice, and might not be up to the Board's increasing confrontational style of ethnic politics. Still, when you asked most people in the community whom they preferred, the response most often received was, "I like 'em both." But when it came to what Black people needed most, at that time, Diane would be more likely to get the nod, due to the fact that she was perceived as more confrontational.

Moreover, Sen. Watson had much of the Black community support. It was in the outlying areas of the district, where non-Black voters lived, that she had the weaker base of support. And that happened to be where a candidate like Yvonne Burke and her easy non-confrontational style, went over the best. Political operatives with less than favorable reputations get plenty of work, because they know how to trick voters and win elections. And it seemed many of them were either in, or on the fringe of Senator Watson's campaign. Some, of course, were playing both sides, and we knew it. Others were trying to make a name for themselves. Others had no loyalty to the mission, but as "hired guns" were there just to "get paid." This really soured my taste for politics, as a primary solution for the problems of Black people. However, for many of us in the Watson campaign, it wasn't about running against Ms. Burke, or Hahn, or anybody else. It was about electing someone who had an extreme level of sensitivity for her people, and a tireless will to serve them. One of the people that I most enjoyed working with was a man considered a legend in his own time, promoter, producer, writer and social commentator, Booker Griffin. Booker was a walking historian, when it came to Black life in Los Angeles.

Booker was the campaign's media/communications consultant. For years, he was the city's number one public affairs commentator with KGFJ, then L.A.'s oldest (and only) Black radio station. Booker was also a very astute political consultant. He'd have us bustin' up laughing with his unique historical insights of damn near anyone in Black leadership over the last 30 years; not just in Los Angeles but around the nation. Booker pulled no punches and was straight as an arrow, when it came to giving his assessment of a situation.

Booker was also invaluable in his historical account of the L.A.P.D. The Rodney King beating trial was about to begin, where four policemen had been charged with going beyond the call of duty in trying to subdue and arrest Rodney King, after a police chase. Booker knew the history of the L.A.P.D. backward and forwards, including many of its unwritten codes. Most of the nation thought King got beat, because he allegedly resisted arrest, but Booker confirmed what many of us, particularly Black males in "the hood", already knew. In Los Angeles, if the cops, L.A.P.D or L.A. County Sheriff's, put the lights on you and you didn't stop, it was cause to get your ass whipped. And if you made them chase you, you were definitely gonna get your ass whipped. That was the standing practice of both the L.A.P.D. and the L.A. County Sheriff's Dept. "Rodney King was any Black man, on any given night in Los Angeles. Rodney didn't get beat because he broke the law; he got beat, because he ran from the law," Booker said on several occasions. King had a benefit that all the rest of us never had, a video camera and a helicopter light. One without the other (no video or no light), Rodney was just another nigger beat in the dark by some lyin' ass cops, who would swear King either fell down or whipped his own ass. Booker gave us "youngstas" the history of who started that practice in the L.A.P.D. in the Parker administration (longtime police chief and segregationist, William Parker). When the defense for the cops moved for a change of venue, most of us felt that it wouldn't make a difference, because we had the videotape. Booker was the only one to say that a change of venue would get these guys off. "They'll never find a jury that would convict them," Booker said. "The move is solely to allow a greater sensitivity to the cops.

It's a race play and they can always find enough racists to tie up a jury," he continued. Booker was, of course, referring to a hung jury scenario that would allow for a mistrial. The community in which the trial was to take place was Simi Valley, a lily white bedroom community in Ventura County, about fifty miles north of Los Angeles. "They might as well have taken it to Mississippi or Alabama," Booker said. "It's the same thing. Simi Valley is where many police live. They are not going to convict a cop of beating a runaway niggah in Simi Valley."

We all thought it was time for Booker's insulin shot (he was diabetic), because he was talking a little crazy. Turns out Booker wasn't very crazy at all. Booker Griffin died in 1993 after falling into a diabetic coma. When Booker Griffin died, a significant part of L.A. history went with him (and he is sorely missed in the activist community). As Booker predicted, both California and Los Angeles would eventually pass term limits legislation to curtail this pattern of state and local incumbents serving in one public office "for life."

* * *

The NAACP was back in the news. The civil war inside the organization had finally busted loose and gone public. Ben Hook's move to oust William Gibson as chairman had backfired and several key Hooks supporters were ousted instead. Hazel Dukes was removed as national President. Julian Bond, Herbert Henderson, and Percy Sutton lost their board seats, as did a few others. The contract extension Hooks was seeking was countered with an offer he deemed unacceptable. At the conclusion of the board meeting, Benjamin Lawson Hooks, the 15-year executive director, announced he would resign after the annual national convention. Julian Bond would respond to the board's action in the national press as "a bunch of niggah business."

On the local front, things were just as hairy. The Los Angeles branch was perceived as leaderless. In the three years since Duff took over as President, the membership dropped faster than a thermometer in a snow blizzard. The 8,400 members the branch had at the end of my administration was now below 1,500. Duff claimed that half of the members we brought in during that campaign period was theirs, meaning they should have at least 4,000 members. Yet, the membership was back to where it was when I took over, after Ray's resignation. Moreover, the branch had become a tool for a spirit of cooperation with corporations that represented compromise in the eyes of the people. The Los Angeles NAACP was no longer in the business of advocacy. It was more into seminars and workshops on issues totally unrelated to civil rights work. The NAACP was literally dead in Los Angeles. Why? It had lost all of its life's blood, new members who had a sincere interest in advocacy.

One evening at the Watson campaign office, one of the community mothers approached me. I had known Audrey Quarles since my college days, through her affiliation with Zeta Phi Beta Sorority. She was a very active member of the NAACP women's auxiliary, and a supporter of mine during my involvement in the branch. She knew that many of the seniors in Second Baptist weren't with me, before Joe Powell had confirmed it, since she was a member there. "Sit down, baby," Soror Quarles (as I had always called her) said as she patted the seat next to her. "I hear you doing a real good job for Diane," she said.

"Thanks, I'm trying to do my best."

"And the community really loves your column. It's the type of discussion we need to make things right around here," she continued.

"I appreciate that Soror Quarles," I said.

She then said, "Now baby, I'm going to ask you something.

Don't get up and don't interrupt, OK? Promise?"

"Yes, ma'am," I said.

"People aren't happy about what's going on in the branch. Joe's not a leader, and there are no young people in the branch," she said.

"I understand there's still a few," I said sarcastically.

"Yeah, but most of them left with you. You know that," she said looking at me seriously. Then she got to her point. "Would you consider coming back into the branch? I assure you, the seniors would be with you this time."

My breathing increased to the point where I thought I was hyperventilating. I could feel my jaw tighten. Then I looked back into Soror Quarles' calm, sincere face. "Soror Quarles, who put you up to this?" I asked.

All she would tell me was that it had been a continuing discussion among some of the members for some time. Whoever it was, they knew enough to send someone I respected enough not to cuss out or beat up. Certainly, Soror Quarles was that person. I have nothing but the highest respect for her. After thinking a moment and calming down, in my most polite voice, and with all the temperament and restraint I could muster, I then said, "Soror Quarles, I could never go back into that branch. Any branch, for that matter."

She interrupted me, "Is it because of what happened to you before?"

"Partially." I responded. "Soror Quarles, nothing will ever change in the NAACP based on volunteer advocacy. The days of volunteer advocacy are over."

"So, you're saying you'll never work with the NAACP again?" she said.

"I'll never say never, because I still have friends in the NAACP. But I can truly say that I will never serve in the NAACP at the branch level, nor any other level, as a volunteer. It's not an effective issues resolution position, and there's too much conflict in the branches. Over what? Nothing. I don't have the time for it. But thank those who were blind, but now see, Soror Quarles," I said.

"Too bad we couldn't see at the same time," Soror Quarles said. She stated how she appreciated my position, but felt obligated to give me my chance if I wanted it. I kissed her on the cheek, and we parted. On the way home, I thought about what Soror Quarles and I had discussed.

I couldn't help but feel proud that she would even consider my coming back, but why wouldn't they. The branch hadn't headed one major issue, since I left. It was now in bed with Southland. It was now in bed with the Baldwin Hills/Crenshaw Shopping Plaza. It had even gotten in bed with Daryl Gates, to the point that Gates called Joe by name, when Black leaders met with the L.A. police chief to call for his resignation. As the group of Black leaders concluded their meeting on the King beating, and his need to step down, by several accounts, he looked Joe Duff right in the face, and said, "I'm very disappointed in you, Joe."

Duff responded, "I'm disappointed in you, chief."

It was a discussion that shocked the room, almost confirming that there had been some on-going relationship. With many of the same old antiquated minds still in control of the NAACP, I don't think so. The week of Soror Quarles' request, I got about another dozen calls either requesting that I come back or clarifying rumors that I was coming back to run against Joe. I told them I had no interest in coming back to the NAACP, not then and not in the future.

The saying "what goes around, comes around," and "you reap what you sow" couldn't have been more true than in the case of the Los Angeles NAACP. What could have been reaped as a rich harvest of second generation advocacy was sown by the seeds of jealousy and ignorance. The L.A. NAACP was tantamount to a biblical analogy; while branch hypocrites were trying to call out the stick in my eye, it looked past the bigger board in its own, and a movement of vision for the future was now blind in both eyes, without a harvest to look forward to.

* * *

April 1992, in Los Angeles was a strange, but telling month. It was a month of revelations. Many of the injustices revealed were ones that so adversely impacted the quality of life for Black people. Coming into the month, it was reported that the city's two largest banks, Bank of America and Security Pacific, now in the middle of a merger discussion, had basically strangled the Black community, economically. An investigative report by *L.A. Sentinel* writer Frank McRae, disclosed that six branches of each bank (12 in all) located in South Central Los Angeles, while holding $631 million in deposits combined, made a combined total of 87 loans for an aggregate amount of some $11 million in 1991. This was absolutely outrageous.

We had long been saying that banks were redlining South Central. I was on a committee with Melanie Lomax, who first raised the issue in 1985, about banks not lending in our communities. But even though, there were the Home Mortgage Disclosure Act (HMDA) of 1975 and the Community Reinvestment Act of 1977, passed to ensure that low and moderate income communities received their fair share of loans, there was no enforcement, and banks weren't required to report their activity. So, we had no proof. But in 1989, HMDA was amended to include the Financial Institutions Reform Recovery Enforcement Act (FIRREA). Under FIRREA, banks were now required to document and make public their mortgage lending activity by race, gender, income, location and census tract. The first reporting was due December 1991. They were made public in late March 1992. The results confirmed what we knew all along. It went beyond redlining. This was economic rape. Even the banks, who usually always had some kind of excuse for not being able to do something in our community, could say nothing. The numbers were in Black and white, and the disparity was startling, even to them.

There was barely a peep out of the traditional Negro leadership. Many of them had their homes, but didn't conventionally qualify. They leveraged relationships. But for the common Black man and Black woman, who didn't have the "connections," this report demonstrated that they had been clearly wronged. That wasn't the end of the discussion. As few as the number of mortgage loans were, the number of commercial loans (usually made to businesses) were even less. In fact, there wasn't one major bank that made more than a dozen commercial loans in Los Angeles. Of the loans that were made, it was either to a church, or in an amount less than $50,000. There were several banks that made no commercial loans, at all. Yet, they were doing plenty of business in the Black community, soliciting deposits, issuing credit cards, charging higher rates of interest on car loans. But with no money for businesses or commercial development, in the midst of a national recession, Black business in Los Angeles was in a depression, losing businesses almost every day.

The last key revelation was that there were was no job growth for Blacks in Los Angeles County. In fact, there was significant job reductions in the African-American labor force, largely due to 31,000 jobs cut in the defense industry in 1991. Ethnic minorities were 53 percent of those, according to a L.A. County Aerospace Task Force report that predicted 420,000 jobs and $84.6 billion in personal income would be lost, by the turn of the century. Latinos, because of the language barrier and educational transition, had not immigrated into aerospace, in significant numbers, to this point. Meaning, Black people lost the overwhelming majority of the jobs. Not only was aerospace downsizing, but corporations were leaving Los Angeles at an enormous rate. Nationwide unemployment was 7.3 percent according to the 1991 U.S. Labor Department statistics. It was 8.7 percent in California, the highest it had been since September 1983. In Los Angeles, it was 9.9 percent, but for Blacks, it was 13.8 percent, highest of any ethnic group. Teen unemployment was 20 percent countywide but for Black teens, conservative estimates were 40 percent. Realistic estimates, according to several sources, were closer to 60 percent.

The environment that had been created for Blacks in Los Angeles was unlike any elsewhere in the county, with the possible exception of a few small cities in the rural South. Certainly, there was no place in any major urban city, where so-called progressive Blacks lived, where so-called influential Blacks supposedly prospered, and where so-called astute Blacks had sufficient political representation to bring about social and economic changes. Yet, none of that was evident in Los Angeles. There were a very, very few singular examples of achievement, and they were, by and large, held up as the models of success for the entire Black community. In reality, the Los Angeles Black community had become the victim of its claim to fame, a facade. Hollywood, the facade-maker, is where fiction is real, and reality is what you make it. If you went strictly on appearance, Blacks in Los Angeles would appear to be more successful, based on where they lived, what they drove and what they wore. Based on appearance, Blacks in L.A. would appear to be more progressive, based on the many circles Blacks deal in. Based on appearance, Blacks in L.A. would appear to be astute, in terms of dealing with the race politics that selectively and conveniently discriminates against ethnic minorities. And based on appearance of the significant number of Black elected officials, at all levels of government, one would think that Blacks would be able to influence social and economic benefits for the masses of people in their community.

However, none of that was real. Los Angeles, for Blacks, was a place where there was little opportunity to make money (if you depended on municipal contracts or bank financing), little chance of buying a home (without being creative), little chance of getting a long-term good paying job, or keeping a short-term low paying job. Then, there was the constant para-military behavior of law enforcement, where Blacks rights where frequently violated, the double standard prosecutionary practices of L.A. courts, and the apparent double standard of the use of judicial discretion in criminal sentencing. Blacks in L.A., by and large, had no money, no business, no jobs, and no justice. More crucially, Blacks had little conscience and no concerted form of advocacy. And it all became publicly noted in April 1992.

* * *

April 29th was a day of reckoning. It started out as a day filled with extreme tension. There just appeared to be a hum in the air. Something like if a missile was enroute, and you knew it was going to hit any time. You didn't know when--but your senses allowed you to pick up the hum, like today would be the day something significant would happen.

Jury deliberations of the King trial were now in their sixth day. The trial had been a circus. First, the change of venue. Then a jury selection process that produced no Black jurors. Seven white males, three white females, an Asian woman and a Latino woman. No men of color. Ethnic minorities were in the overwhelming minority. Of the two minorities, both were very docile and worked in jobs where they were required to be passive. The Asian was a staff nurse, the Latino was a housekeeper. Not the kind of jury one would hope for in a case with racial implications. Moreover, all six alternate jurors were white. This deck was stacked to the hilt, exactly what a change of venue move was supposed to do. The prosecution team, a Black male and a white male, had argued the case soft--in the opinion of many.

Their strategy was largely reliant on the tape, not the historical and pervasive attitude of the L.A.P.D. They did manage to bring out the tape transmissions that produced the infamous "gorillas in the midst" comments. Testimony of a nurse who treated King the night of the beating brought out how the officers joked with King at the hospital. She stated how they kidded about "playing a little baseball on his head." Still the prosecution didn't effectively go to the issue of intent, or how these officers, and the ones who stood around, intended to reinforce old adages of how police treat Black males. The community felt that the L.A.P.D.'s history in all its wicked splendor, should have been hung around these officers' necks. Much like when one Black is on trial, a whole race, many times, is on trial. The sword should cut both ways. This wasn't the case, however, and the prosecution argued that these individual officers' broke from established police policy. A policy that was as flexible as a plastic straw, when it came to an officer's discretion to use deadly force. And they didn't shoot him (when on many occasions, Blacks had been shot for doing less).

The question of justifying the right amount of force suddenly became a very objective issue. One that the defense argued was sufficient, given what the officer said they thought at the time. And they threw in all the curve s: He (King) was a monster of incredible strength. He was thought to be on PCP. He wouldn't lay down and resisted order. He continued to resist arrest after he was stopped. So, these actions justified King being struck 56 times. This argument was coupled with the fact that the prosecution couldn't conclusively determine that King was struck in the head with the batons, even though eyewitnesses said that he was. The tape was at such a distance that it appeared King was struck "around the head area," which the defense argued as the shoulder area. The broken bones in King's face and eye socket were said to be from King's fall to the ground. None of this was significantly countered by the prosecution. It just appeared, when the prosecution needed to be aggressive, it wasn't. When they needed to respond, they didn't. When the Black prosecutor was supposed to be up; the white one was, and vice versa. The "salt and pepper thing" never quite worked out to the benefit of the prosecution. They spent more time trying to convince the press that they were winning than showing the jury, and it showed.

The people in the Black community knew what was up, though. Many had spent enough time in front of a judge and a jury to know when things were or weren't going our way. Clearly, the sentiment in this case wasn't going the people's way. In fact, most felt it was slipping away. The streets were buzzin' about it. The Negro leadership was still espousing the company line, "Justice will prevail." "We're gonna be vindicated in the courts." "We have to give the system a chance to carry out the process." "We shall overcome," and stuff like that. They even went as far as to plan a victory party of sorts. Mayor Bradley was so sure that the courts would vindicate the people that a justice celebration was planned at First AME Church, whenever the verdict came back.

However, when the jury didn't come back with an immediate verdict, the community's anxiety rose. By the second or third day, people on the street were visibly concerned, and they weren't listening to all that cheerleading coming out of the politicians and so-called community leaders. By the fifth day of deliberation, the Negro leadership began taking a different approach. In their first admission that everything wasn't going hunky-dory, they began to interject that in the event the officers are acquitted, the people should remain calm, and meet at First AME in solidarity. The victory meeting would become a solidarity rally. In solidarity of what? Nobody ever said what, but it became obvious that the people weren't responding in a manner to which the leadership had become accustomed. It was a case of Black leadership trying to run out front and stay ahead of the people, but it was by no means, a lockstep. The more the politicians and preachers pleaded for calm, the stronger the signal was to the people that this case wasn't going to favor them.

History has demonstrated the only time so-called leaders pleaded for calm was when things were about to go awry, after the people had been misused and abused. This was probably one of the more traditional carryovers from slavery. Someone ballyhooing the actions of the master. Well, they were now in an advance mode in L.A., expecting the worst out of a horrible situation. The people watching this movement of their so-called leadership began to talk. Their talk wasn't about the acquittal of the cops, as outraged as they would be, should that occur. It was about the passivity of the leadership. The people on the streets were sick of Black leadership co-signing injustice, by blocking any outlet of community frustration with the same old peace talk. After everybody calms down, everything stays the same and the people are left to simmer in their frustration.

The community talk this time was that there wouldn't be a bottle big enough to cap the people's frustration, and those so-called leaders would go down with their masters, if they loved them so much. The people had a plan of their own. The City Council gave the L.A.P.D. a million dollars for a post verdict contingency plan. Daryl Gates spoke to his rank-and-file officers (by video tape) on the possibility of an acquittal, and according to the *L.A. Times*, told them "not to display their feelings in a manner that will evoke any kind of reaction from the public." I guess that meant for them not to cheer an acquittal. The hum in the air had intensified.

It was around 2 o'clock when the news came that the jury had reached a verdict. If there was ever a moment when it seemed like time stood still, that was the moment. Whatever people were doing, they stopped at that very moment. People were scurrying to get in front of a television, like there was no tomorrow. It was almost as if they knew there would be no tomorrow. That is to say, no tomorrow, the same as today. For many, this decision would change the face of the Black community one way or another. If they only knew how much.

It was time to read the verdicts: Officer Stacey Koon, the officer in charge of the scene, on the charge of assault with a deadly weapon, NOT GUILTY, on the charge of excessive force by an officer under the color of authority, NOT GUILTY; on the charge of filing a false police report, hung jury; on the charge of being an accessory to assault, NOT GUILTY. Officer Laurence Powell, on the charge of assault with a deadly weapon, NOT GUILTY; on the charge of excessive force by an officer under the color of authority, NOT GUILTY; Officer Timothy Wind, on the charge of assault with a deadly weapon and excessive force by an officer under the code of authority; NOT GUILTY. Officer Theodore Briseno, on the charges of assault with a deadly weapon and excessive force by an officer under the color of authority, NOT GUILTY. I sat in front of my television stunned. I could hear several of what sounded like Black men at my neighbor's house, yelling, I'LL BE GODDAMNED. I DON'T BELIEVE THIS SHIT. THAT DAMN GATES DONE WON AGAIN.

To add insult to injury, the officers were chuckling with each other and hugging one another, like they had, in fact, a right to do what they did. This was frankly the most hateful scene I had ever personally witnessed in my life. It was beyond outrageous. My feeling at that moment was that the justice system had said, to the world, that Blacks are fair game, do what you have to do to control them, and it will be defended in court. This is America, and Blacks have no rights that whites are bound to respect. The Dred Scott decision said this some 130 years ago, and it was about to happen all over again. I felt a nakedness that said whatever cloak of protection I felt we might have had under the law, had just been taken. Simi Valley was supposed to represent a random sampling of America, at its best, to show the world that a failure to uphold injustice anyway, is a failure to uphold injustice everywhere (a paraphrase of Dr. King's quote). Instead it showed how far America would go to maintain control. The people of South Central had something else in mind. "Racism wouldn't win again" was the Black community's sentiment. Not this time.

I got a call from Nick McClure, the Senator's campaign manager to meet them at First AME church at 5 p.m. When I got there at about 4:45, the church was three-quarters full. As I moved through the church's little security post at the front of the church, the church was in a stir. The program hadn't started yet, but the people were definitely buzzing. Sort of edgy in their behavior. This wasn't FAME's regular congregation. It was more of people who had heard this was the place to come and (constructively) vent, if the verdicts hadn't gone in favor of the community. They were out in droves. By 5 o'clock, the church was packed with about 300 people outside waiting to get in. The program was about to start. I wanted to advise the Senator prior to her taking the stage. I felt it might have been best to catch her outside at the curb. The security said they couldn't assure anybody that left would get re-entry. Since she could come in any number of ways, I just stayed in the church and waited. Chip Murray took the mike to tell the people why we were there but, of course, we all knew. He asked the choir to sing a song. The choir stirred as if it didn't quite know what to sing. They came up with some song that somehow seemed inappropriate. Music, period, seemed inappropriate. While music supposedly soothed the savage beast, it could only antagonize this situation. Any minute, I expected them to break out in "We Shall Overcome" and sure enough, they did. The crowd booed. Then Mayor Bradley entered the church and went straight to the rostrum. He received the loudest boo I had ever heard the Mayor of a city endure.

Mayor Bradley had addressed the city right after the verdict. In one of his more emotional addresses, the distressed Mayor expressed that a jury had just told us that what we all saw with our own eyes was right, though we all knew that this verdict was, in fact, unjust. It was the first time, as Mayor, that I had seen Tom Bradley express anger for his people. The Mayor had made a career of playing the color blind role, the "not so much as what's good for Blacks, but what's good for the city" role. This time, his distress didn't appear to be a neutral, distant distress. The kind of distress white folk express when they say "they know how we feel," never having been Black or having done to them what has been done to us, in such continuously blatant fashion. Bradley, an ex-athlete, ex-cop and in the eyes of many--an ex-Black man in one swift moment, was forced to reckon with his former self and what he had become. He could no longer separate himself from what he once was, and what he had become. The former Tom Bradley knew the pain his people had endured. He knew how his people had been treated by law enforcement. He knew how his people had been treated by society. He had once shared such a pain, such treatment before his achievements and notoriety allowed him to separate himself from the burdens of his people. But in this one brief plea for peace and restraint, in all dignity and grace of his stately posture, Tom Bradley, in ever such a slight expression, remembered. For just a moment, the Mayor of Los Angeles remembered the pain of being Black and being powerless to a system of racism. A system he was the figurehead for and, therefore, had to sustain. I'm sure it was very difficult being Mayor of all the people, at that very moment.

Now recomposed, Bradley, in the church pulpit, tried as best he could to re-instill faith in the justice system and uphold the dignity of his people, at the same time. The people in the audience weren't hearing any of it, though. The day of serving two masters was over. On this evening, Bradley couldn't come home again. Waving the flag of a tainted system of governance and, at that moment, the people couldn't separate him from the master he had served for the last 20 years. City Councilman Mark Ridley-Thomas had become kind of an unofficial master of ceremonies. The crowd had received him politely, because regardless of what people said about him, he was of the people. He admonished the crowd of how they had treated the Mayor, who had now left the church. The crowd momentarily turned on him, booing him for his unsolicited admonishment.

The rally was now being televised nationwide. True to the Negro spirit, the so-called leadership played to the cameras. Only to be booed off the rostrum. It was virtually a unilateral rejection of leadership. Most of them were talking as if their speech was preventing some people from taking action, but the people were already taking action. Those of us on the side of the pulpit could see some of the television media's portable monitors. While many of the stations were carrying the rally, a few had a split screen where half the screen was showing the rally and the other half showed the activity going on at Florence and Normandie in South Central, where a crowd had gathered, pulled a man (later identify as Reginald Denny) out of his truck and beat him. The media was also reporting that the L.A.P.D. had been ordered to retreat from the scene.

Senator Watson arrived at the church. We huddled on the side of the pulpit. She was distraught. They had just driven through several areas of the city. "The streets were hot," in her words. People had already begun to demonstrate violent behavior. Bottles and rocks had been thrown at her state car. I told her it was no less hostile in the church.

At that time, the NAACP's Joe Duff was being booed off the

mike. Another speaker came up and the same happened. The only speaker to receive the full applause and appreciation of the people was Minister Charles X, Assistant Minister of Muhammad Mosque, #27 from the Nation of Islam. Brother Charles, a very humble and unassuming man, had the spirit of God in him that night, and the people felt it. He warned the people that the system would use this verdict and our outrage to declare war on our youth. What Minister Charles was referring to was several accounts that the Nation had received from gang leaders that when the verdicts returned, if there was violence, gang members would be targeted first and killed outright. They were being told this by the police.

Ironically, two days before the verdicts, I had been approached by a young man, who requested a meeting with the Senator. The young man claimed he was a leader of a Westside Blood sect, based in an area of the Crenshaw district called "the Jungle." He claimed the police were getting ready to "move" on gang members, and that somebody needed to help them, if they wanted things to change. The Senator met with about four of them, and agreed to facilitate a larger meeting, if they were sincere. However, the major focus of the discussion was this "police threat" on gangs, when the verdicts came in. To add fuel to the fire was a piece of police intelligence that was intercepted by NOI regional captain, Wali Muhammad, claiming that the Nation of Islam was training gang members for para-military attacks on police, when the verdicts came in. Captain Wali immediately called Noel Cunningham to vehemently deny the news. The L.A.P.D., surprised that the Nation was in possession of such a memo, claimed the memo was a hoax. Clearly, though, it appeared that a hidden hand was trying to target the two most powerful (and organized) community groups, youth organizations (called gangs) and the Fruit of Islam.

Minister Charles wasn't just engaging in Black talk and the community knew it. So did the Senator, who looked out at me, when he said it. As Minister Charles finished his talk, the media on the portable monitors were reporting some looting was taking place. Still everybody in the church was operating in a virtual vacuum. By the time Senator Watson took the mike, word had gotten around that some fires had started. Senator Watson received polite applause. She raised her fist in acknowledgment. Nick and I looked at each other in surprise. The Senator proceeded to talk about the unfairness of the verdict, and how we had to pull together to hold the process accountable. She ended by saying this city can't expect any peace without rendering justice, to which she was cheered.

Another speaker got up to speak, at which time, a young woman got up in the audience and said, "All you so-called leaders do is talk. What are we going to do about not receiving our rights?" The crowd cheered. Ridley-Thomas ran to the podium, grabbed the mike and told the sister to respect the speaker and have a seat. The young woman responded with, "The people have something to say, and I'm not going to be sat down."

The crowd jumped to their feet yelling, "Let her speak. Let her speak." Clearly, the rally was turning more hostile. The movement of the crowd was real strange, like the door of a lion's cage had been left open, and it didn't know whether to come out or stay in. The spectators outside the cage (the so-called leaders) were now as cautious of the lion's (crowd) movement as the lion was of theirs.

Everybody was in attack mode, but nobody was making any sudden moves until then. As the confrontation appeared to heighten, Chip Murray grabbed the mike and said, "OK sister, we hear you. We're all in this together. Young lady, come up here and speak your mind." The young woman was given a standing ovation. The first of the night and only for one of their own. "This is happening because the leaders don't hear the people anymore, because they don't represent us anymore," the young woman said, to a huge applause. Ridley-Thomas was pacing on the sidelines, looked at me like "this is out of control" and shook his head.

"What were you going to do Mark? They would have torn this place down if you tried to stop her. You had to let her speak," I said. It was the first real personal conversation we'd had since our estrangement. We both knew what was about to follow. He gave a sigh of resignation and went back on stage. The young sister was thundering, "kicking knowledge" to the crowd, as the youth say.

Just then, there was a shout from the back of the church. "The building across the street is on fire. So is the market on Adams (and Hobart, next to the historical Golden State Mutual Insurance Building)." There was a hush over the audience. The press started scurrying for the door. Chip grabbed the mike, before the audience created a stampede. He asked the people to remain calm, exit slowly and go directly to their homes. The word was "there are some disturbances taking place around the city." Disturbances. That was the understatement of the last quarter century.

The Senator had a look of panic on her face. Willis Edward

grabbed her and rushed her to the car. "Meet us at Diane's house," he shouted as they pulled away. My Jeep was right in front of the building that was on fire. People were yelling that there may be people still inside. I ran over to the building. A brother ran out with a Latino woman and two children. He said everybody was out. There were people running everywhere. There was smoke everywhere. People were driving off, almost hitting people running in the streets. As I drove off, I could see fires in every direction. Going west on Adams Blvd., I figured Crenshaw Blvd. wouldn't be the way to go. I made a left on Arlington Blvd. I hit the downhill double-dip the same slope we called "Arlington Double," when we rode our go-carts down it as kids. The signal lights were out at Jefferson. I could see several places on fire. The closest was a pawn shop people were looting. As I pulled across Jefferson, I could see a crowd gathering at Exposition Street. The crowd was throwing rocks and bottles. Cars were running lights to avoid the angry crowd. There had already been one collision. The owners were chased from their cars. In the car in front of me, a Black man barely avoided being pulled from his car. Several young men ran up on his car, busted the driver's side window with a stick and began throwing punches in the car. They got his door halfway open, before he furiously started fighting back. Then he suddenly turned his car right (from the left hand lane), and sped west on Exposition. The crowd came running for my Jeep. A bottle cracked my windshield. I put it in reverse, then hit the peddle with a VA-Roomm of my engine, speeding toward the crowd coming at me. They parted enough to allow me to make a U-turn up and over the curb. As I came off the curb going north back up Arlington, I heard several rocks and another bottle hit the Jeep. Going left on Washington, I passed over a dozen buildings on fire, before I hit Crenshaw. At Washington and 11th Avenue, the supermarket was being looted. Fire trucks were speeding down the street, and there was not a cop in sight.

I couldn't get down Crenshaw for all the people rioting in the street. I got on the 10 Interstate Freeway West, and got off at La Cienega going north. There was looting all up and down La Cienega Blvd. But the complexion of the looters had changed. It was mostly Mexicans and white people, running down the street with jeans and stereos. South Central had now spread to the Westside. I went down Cadillac west, to check on Taurece and the children. They were okay. I gave them the number to Debra's house and left. Debra lived on the Westside of Motor and Palms. It was still calm over there.

When I got to Debra's house, she was sitting on the couch with tears in her eyes, watching all the fires on television. We hugged and just sat there watching the chaos. Anarchy was what it was. Caused by a justified insurrection. Justified because the law failed to protect the people. When the laws do not hold true for the people it was designed to protect, why should the people obey any law. There can be no selective application of constitutional rights. Either it's all good, or none of it's good. But there was no law now. Hell had come to Los Angeles. It was time to meet at the Senator's home. I'd have to drive through hell to get there. Debra wouldn't let me go back out into the lawless fires of hell. It was hard to imagine anything worse. Hell is the price you pay for total and complete compromise. The devil was now claiming his debt, the many souls that had been sold for momentary benefit, material gain and the chaos that results from giving in to everything and standing for nothing. There was now no harvest to reap. Only the release of a rage that had been placed on pause for 27 years. Los Angeles was reaping exactly what it had sown, the score being the reality it had created.

* * *

18

Why L.A. Had to Burn Twice

*"When the government violates the people's rights,
Insurrection is, for the people and for each portion of the people,
the most sacred of rights and the most indispensable of duties."*
- Lafayette

"A Black man will never be free until he wants LIBERTY more than anything else. More than money, more than power, more than fame. When he says "I want to be free; Give me liberty or give me death, we would be free overnight."
- Minister Louis Farrakhan

*It's winter in L.A. and I'm about to die from the heat
ninety degrees outside and I can't go out on the street
Snowed under by the smog like a quiet Buffalo blizzard
I'm coughin' and wheezin,' ain't got no cold but I'm sneezin'
It's so cold my ride won't start
homey felt obliged to relieve me of some parts
There's a big chill in this city, folks hatin' one another
nawh-we-can't-just-all-get-alooong with each other
In a place so hot I ain't never felt so cold
icy stares from perfect strangers -hummph
It's winter in L.A., City of Angels is the name
nineteen million degrees outside -but it's winter just the same.*
-"Winter In L.A" Kamau Ramsey, 1992

The Los Angeles 1992 rebellion was the biggest and most costly man-made disaster in this country's history. It has been ten years, since the disturbance, yet the perceptions of why it happened have been simple-minded in scope, complexity and clarity. Los Angeles had become, and still is, such a collection of contrasts and conflicts, with each contrast promoting a form of conflict, and each conflict resulting in a form of compromise. In 1992, the circumstances and events that preceded this explosion made life in Los Angeles for the African born in America, almost unbearable. Subsequently, insurrection was virtually inevitable. However, when sincerely examined, to look beneath the overt causes given for the rioting, burning, looting and if Blacks are ever honest enough to admit it, they would see that the people's reaction to unjust laws was about more than "what whitey did to us." And it wasn't about hate or rage, which is what society loves to say, when oppressed people react to injustice. American society never admits to succumbing to anger, hate or rage nor does it even acknowledge the actions that precipitate emotion-driven behaviors, such as racism. After the rock has been thrown, this society hides its hand and wants to talk about how Blacks should stop "being so angry," or reacting with "hate." American society is always quick to lecture how "two wrongs don't make a right," but the wrongs on the front end never seem to stop.

Well, the Los Angeles rebellion really wasn't about "hating whitey" or Koreans, or hating anybody else. The L.A. rebellion wasn't about Rodney King, or four white cops, or Reginald Denny. It wasn't as simplistic as a symbol. People damn near laughed their asses off, when white folk pulled Rodney out of a closet to stumble through his now infamous, "Can we all get along?" statement. It's not like Black people are so simple that this whole thing was about justice for Rodney King. A lot of us said, "they still don't get it," and time has proven this to be the case. Most of the Los Angeles leadership community (Black and white) still don't understand what the underlying causes for the civil disturbance were, nor what the ramifications were (and still are) for abdicating the laws of fairness, social equity and economic parity. This blindness to the social perils of the inner city set the scenario for social outrage, and social outrage is often the basis for anarchy. This momentary anarchy came to be known as the "Los Angeles Riots; Revisited" or "the L.A. Rebellion," the second time around.

Walking through the rumble of buildings with community leaders and those who professed to be the leadership, I noticed the people weren't necessarily moved about any more talk. They appreciated the assistance, but weren't moved by it. The activities of, not just the previous months during the trial but, the past few years had been compromise, after compromise, after compromise, after compromise. The circumstances in the people's lives, who lived in South Central had eroded away any bit of progress or dignity that had been salvaged from the ashes of 1965. And this time, the people understood who the real betrayer of their trust was. The verdict was just the signal used to expose their dissatisfaction. And the leadership of Black people was, all at once, relieved of their assignment, particularly where fidelity to their masters appeared to be greater than that to the people. What more could be done to Black people that hadn't already been done in the five years prior to the 1992 civil unrest. The police in South Central, the most vicious law enforcement of any municipality anywhere, had wilted away the very integrity of what the law was supposed to represent. And in the eyes of the people, who co-signed its behavior? Black leadership. The economics of South Central were as crooked and wickedly disparate as you'd find anywhere in the country.

In 1999, the United Way published a report called, "Los Angeles: A Tale of Two Cities," where it documented the city's growing wealth disparity. The city's top 50 wealthiest residents had a combined wealth of $60 billion dollars, more than the combined wealth of two million working class residents of the inner city. Much of this was already in place, prior to 1992. No loans, no insurance, no capital for business, just opportunities for predator lenders to exploit the absence of competition, with higher yield products (pay more, earn less) and limited services that made those outside the community rich and prosperous. More jobs left South Central in the 10 years prior to the 1992 rebellion, than in the rest of the state combined. Yet, the leadership of Black people were in total denial about it, and they allowed whites to deny that jobs were leaving the city. On every level of political leadership, in the Black community, there was a leadership void. Two thirds of the political leadership had been serving since the mid 1970s, half of whom had sat since the 1960s. Pothole politics, known in political circles as the "politics of remedy" had ruled, and plantation or "compromise" politics was its successor. The quality of life in the Los Angeles Black community had been reduced to levels of unbearable stagnation. Leadership was bankrupt of vision and stigmatized in its inability to mentor future leadership.

The church, the spiritual and moral guide of the family and community, were no more than competing social clubs--more committed to entertaining members than redeeming souls. Spirituality in South Central was reduced to "the largest congregation, the biggest choir and the loudest band." Preacher rivalries were as fierce as gang rivalries, and gang rivalries were only outdone by the pseudo-social classism among Blacks, who perpetuated and sought to replicate the materialism for which L.A. had become known. Who lived where, who drove what, who dictated to whom, who they did it with, and how they did was how you rated in the Black community. A pecking order in a subordinated, sub-cultural reality.

The Black community, as we knew it in 1992, really didn't exist anymore. We were really only a gathering of Black faces now. No Black places, hotels, grocery stores, movie houses, restaurants, to speak of. Individual interest drove the community. Any spirit left in the souls of Black people, were sold to white people, by their own people in Los Angeles. -Black people who, by and large, had become the buffer for change, the buffer for progress, the buffer for opposition, the buffer for objection. Black leaders' real purpose was to maintain a peaceful co-existence with whites, from which they, as individuals, could sustain relationships that would be rewarded. Rewarded for loyalty to them, not to their own people or community interest. They were paid handsomely. Their desire for notoriety and closeness to whites allowed Black leaders to do whatever they had to, to keep the community in check, and stay in favor with the so-called powers-that-be. Even if it meant compromising their own to do it.

Social progress during the 1980s, in economically impoverished areas of Los Angeles, had been only to the extent corporations would give to civil rights and social advocacy organizations. This conditional social progress also applied to any aggressive forms of economic or business advocacy. Advocacy had now been relegated to those who provided forums for proponents of racism to show token efforts to massage their conscience, or to floorshow. Such activity is now a cost of doing business for the racist. They will avail you all the minority business opportunities you can stand to see. However, to access those opportunities is a different story. And as we've witnessed, in the 1990s, the levels of racial sensitivity required to bring about economic parity are not at the front of the social change agenda. The prevalent opinion is that race is no longer a factor that needs to be addressed when dealing with parity issues. To raise issue with the amount of progress, or questions related to the need for monitoring access to equal opportunities is to jeopardize the gratuity of the corporation. In that sense, most of the Black community's civil rights groups, social and business advocacy groups also became buffers for progress. No matter how much these organizations claimed their programs were directed toward "change," or how much more money is poured into poor communities, the "collective" social progress of the Black community only regressed. Economic disparities between Black and white became greater, thus magnifying "the great divide." The poor got poorer, and the rich got richer.

Certain civil organizations and community groups who were considered "safe bets" in the 1980s, helped facilitate the widening of that divide. Regardless of how racially recalcitrant whites and their economic interests are, and how much they may be perceived as part of the problem (verses being part of the solution), Black organizations, be they social, business or religious, continuously receive (and accept) funding from interest adverse to the Black community's collective survival interests. Whether or not Black communities saw whites as rational actors, acting out of self-interest, in the prevailing "best" interest of America, or just engaging in token benevolence; they took their money, as its safest bet, the hedge against social upheaval. Who really stood to win in the final analysis of these acts of insincerity? The exploiter, or the exploited. Most certainly, it was the one that had the option to give and do good, the exploiter. Limited acts of kindness may be fine enough for the exploiter. But where does that leave the exploited; licking their wounds, while a few sellouts count their tokens. Was the giving sincere or done to create the perception of sincerity? Or as in an overwhelming number of cases, was the giving only about damage control or control, period. Perception was reality in L.A., and in other cities around the country, where a smile and a checkbook virtually puts community leaders in the pocket of the enemy, regardless of what the company may be doing on other fronts.

Calling a community leader's loyalty into question, was never raised, in context of building economic and social infra-structure in the Los Angeles Black community, during the 1980s. To raise issue with so-called leadership about progress for the benefit of the people, or even their level of conscience movement in defending the rights of the people was to bring oneself under attack. The level of preparedness for leadership in Los Angeles was being compromised, at the most basic levels. To even engage in a conversation of progressive social advocacy oftentimes seemed an act of futility. The discussion always seemed to turn toward comparing levels of Blackness or self-interest. Misguiding the discussion was done by directing attention on someone else, other than one's self and the question at hand. It wasn't about "who was right--Black or white," or "who was the Blackest," or "not being no punk," or "who sold out," or not even "who did what to whom," but "was there benefit?" Was there individual benefit, or church benefit or benefit by somebody's business. Clearly, Black leadership in Los Angeles was afraid to ask the question of their right-minded white associates (and there are many who try to be right-minded), while many built the Los Angeles "skyline" we see today. Why they were not more vocal on issues of social change and economic parity? Giving their money in anonymity, or secluding themselves in social gatherings, while absolving themselves of the city's problems, was enough. It did not allow all in the city to prosper. Not pressing the social change agenda in the 1980s; sitting silent (both Blacks and whites) while systemic and institutional racism took hold, caused a compromise of a new generation of urbanites.

There were some very real questions that needed to be called in to account, for what happened on April 29th, 1992. Guilt ran beyond the release of four white cops. Guilt also included the failure of Black leadership to accept responsibility for not defending Black "community" interest. Black leaders were bought and sold in Los Angeles, to where the definition and integrity of true "interests" were lost. The expectation that Black leaders would defend altruistic interest of a community, versus accepting the tangible benefits of self-interest was a discussion Black leadership never was prepared to have in Los Angeles. Yet, it was a very crucial reality of the community politics. In the meantime, those who were benefiting, a select group of Blacks, were not necessarily doing what was in the best interest of the people. Foresight and hindsight has proven this to be true. While a second generation of Black leaders was trying to call out compromise and create change, while their hands were shaking the "progress tree," who was catching the fruit of that effort? It was many of those same so-called leaders, who called themselves "mentors," "advisors" and "leaders" of the social change movement.

If Tom Bradley, as mayor of the nation's second largest city for 20 years, was truly an agent of change (for his people); there should be hundreds even thousands of people, our people, in our community alone, who should have benefited. Just as those in other parts of Los Angeles benefited with tangible legacies, like the buildings and high-rises and multi-million dollar businesses built elsewhere around the city. It didn't have to be a "brother thang" but it could have (and should have) been a progress thing, with our people in the middle of it. Somebody else benefited from the Bradley legacy. When you look at how downtown, the Westside, the Airport Area, and even parts of the Valley were developed over 20 years, you know somebody else benefited from his legacy. As bad as developers wanted to build in the '70s and '80s, you mean not one of those projects could have coattail clauses that would have tied an inner city five or 10-story building to the cost of a fifty or sixty-story downtown development. Over 20 years and not one major Black construction company could have built one of those high-rises, even if they had to be mentored to do it. Not one credible youth employment project that could, continuously, over 20 years employ youth, so as to deter gang violence.

These were many of the questions that were never answered, when it came to discussing the benefits of leadership. Conversely, Blacks in Los Angeles became alienated, not by whites or Latinos, but by their own leaders. Leaders who never recognized the benefit of building for eternity. They instead built for "their run." To empower their cronies, and to share the benefits of political power with their few associates. What should have been the "Black power and social elite" in Los Angeles, the talented tenth that W.E.B. DuBois predicated Black progress upon, instead became another level of bourgeois; of Blacks imitating white culture and values. Los Angeles was "the clique" capitol of Black America. Everybody who thought they were somebody, had a camp. Tom Bradley had a camp. Former Congressman Mervyn Dymally had a camp. Former Assemblywoman turned Congresswoman Maxine Waters had a camp. County Supervisor Kenny Hahn (who wasn't Black, but godfathered many Black elected officials) had a camp. Then their were the mini- camps; the democratic clubs, the Urban League camp, the NAACP camp, the SCLC camp, the Brotherhood Crusade camp, the UNCF camp, the 100 Black Men camp, the Links, the Masons, Jack 'n Jill, the fraternities and sororities, and it went on and on. Some working together on the surface, while others were working in a vacuum. But all of them were cutting their own deals on the side, self-preservation being the first law of man (and woman). And none really grooming any leadership for succession of the charge that would keep us all free, social progress.

When it comes to the Los Angeles Black community, self-preservation never stopped, nor did it ever defer to community preservation. Everybody, including the so-called "players of the 80s," threw a nickel in the pot and kept on stepping. If you belonged to a camp, you couldn't sign off on community projects, because of conflicts your camp leader had. And for that reason, community consensus could never be reached because if Tom (Bradley) was involved, Merv Dymally couldn't be involved. If Merv was involved, Maxine (Waters) couldn't be involved. If Maxine was involved, Diane (Watson) couldn't be involved. If Diane was involved, Rita (Walters) couldn't be involved. And this madness went on and on and on, at even intermediate and lower levels of the community.

It bred feuds between political aides and other community protégés, who were looking to those leaders to mentor them and lead them in the right direction, only to find out, if you wanted to "play in the game, you had to play out petty jealousies." Many young players in Los Angeles (there were, at least, three sets of L.A. young professionals in 1982, 1986, and 1989) were forced to declare loyalties, and act out these loyalties by maintaining conflicts initiated by their mentors, at all levels. What it produced was another generation of foolish conflict, while the community stagnated. Stagnation in the Los Angeles Black community became deterioration. After a while, Black community interests--because of the fractionalization of its leadership--were put on the shelf, for the most part, while these petty feuds played out.

Everything perishable will spoil, if you leave it on the shelf too long. The lives and communities of Black people in Los Angeles were basically allowed to perish by a political gangsterism that failed to change the quality of life for its constituents. The type of gangsterism that took place in these feuds had no boundaries. The Crips and the Bloods, for all their killing and robbing in their ignorance, have caused nowhere near the damage of these political wars that cost the Black community hundreds of millions of dollars in lost opportunities. And the "preacher wars" were just as bad.

The biggest assassinator of a preacher's character in Los Angeles was generally another preacher. And money was their God too. At least, the so-called gangbangers have a code of conduct, ethics and laws that guide their behavior (honor among thieves). There was no such honor among the traditional Black leadership in Los Angeles, in the mid and late 1980s. And because of it, leadership had become tribalistic, and tribalism then turned to cannibalism, where

Black leaders, both old and young, were feeding off each other, biting and chewing each other up, to the demise of the community. If one person couldn't be out front, then they couldn't be involved. If one leader couldn't be "the favorite Black" (of white people), they criticized the one who was. Fighting for the seat closest to the former slave master, for personal prestige and benefit, while the community wasted away.

So arrogant had many of the socially and politically affluent become, in Los Angeles that they were neither receptive to more moderate perspectives, nor respectful to the repeated warnings that things weren't right in their communities. For years, at least five or six prior to the 1992 rebellion, the traditional leadership--inclusive of political, civil rights, social and religious officials--had been made aware of civil, social and economic injustices in the Los Angeles Black community. So adamant was the quickly fading leadership about their "positions of authority and notoriety," that most never bothered to look back to see the ever-increasing gap between them and the people they were supposed to be representing. Most relied on the perspectives of aides and contemporaries. Many were getting the same obsolete perspective, because their confidants were of similar age, interest and perspective. The leadership (collective) and their aides were never willing to acknowledge that they were out of touch, and almost out of time. Instead, the insistence was to deny reality, reject "radical" perspectives (which were only closer, more real perspectives), and continue to run the leg of another generation's race. A race many of the leaders had long been out of. Instead of handing off the baton, or coaching a successor, the Black leadership chose to stay in the race twice as long, run twice as slow, and without regards to the end result. To the majority of Black leadership, it didn't matter if the community won or lost, as long as they could say they were on the field. This attitude caused Blacks in Los Angeles to lose ground, while every other cultural ethnicity gained ground. Inner race conflict compromised Blacks in a race for progress, and ultimately caused the energy of Blacks to be misdirected on issues of little or no consequence. Black burnout resulted before their collective benefits could be realized (or the race was won). Crash and burn was more like it.

In a race to make-up social, political and economic progress, the public policy of the last quarter century was fashioned to favor equality for a change. Blacks got out front first, in the race for parity and equity, but as the current status of social and economic affairs will attest--Blacks are finishing last. Much of it having to with its inability to transition generational leadership. Because leadership (in most cases) never handed off the baton in the fight for social change, the "gap" widened. Some passed (the baton) off; but not until the competition was way out front. Succeeding Black leadership could never hope to make up "the gap" created by our generation of leader's selfish, short-sightedness.

In fourteen years (1988-2002) of the selling of souls in Los Angeles, younger leadership was oftentimes forced to eventually challenge older leadership, after continually having their more accurate perspectives disregarded and disrespected. And, of course, the youngsters took their lumps, not because we were wrong, but because we had the audacity to challenge visionless, stubborn-ass leadership, who were too insecure to bring a fresh (and oftentimes unconventional) perspective to the table. Those they brought to the table were either whites, who gained invaluable experience (like Tom Bradley's 36-year-old deputy mayor Mark Fabiani, for example, who ended up in the White House as a senior staffer to Bill Clinton), while having little regard for the Black community or young Black interns who didn't know any better, and had better not bring a perspective to the table, not consistent with their boss' view.

In effect, many Blacks staffers in local and state politics just had jobs fetching messages and carrying proclamations. Real issues in the community were excused as isolated instances, instead of fundamental breakdowns of the systemic, bureaucratic and legislative processes. Civil and racial abuses of social and economic public policy systems were constantly and consistently excused and cosigned by Black leadership.

Accountability for the continuing violation of South Central Los Angeles lay with no one, in particular; but can be attributed to everyone, indirectly. Repetitive violation of the people in the Los Angeles Black community were trivialized, both in frequency and velocity. Not until Rodney King was violated in such a blatant manner, on tape, did Black leadership, in unison, recognize how far removed they were from the street realities of the people. The Los Angeles Chief of Police (at the time) still tried to use what he had always used to comfort "his out-of-line niggahs," calling the King beating "an aberration," even though many of the same violations, though probably never having subsided since 1965, were well known and documented, as early as 1986.

It took five years, a video tape, a public hearing, a special commission, a public trial and another judicial violation for Black leaders in Los Angeles to understand the significance of the compromise. Even as Los Angeles started burning a second time, some of those same leaders had the audacity to try and play out the same hand they've been playing, since the city burned the first time. Their acts of foolish audacity, in the face of betrayal and rage, was televised worldwide.

The refusal of Black leadership to accept responsibility for community compromise only fueled the flames for an eventual insurrection. They certainly could not expect to find the people so tolerating of another civil violation. Especially in light of a jury condoning the most vile public behavior of law enforcement, in the last quarter century. Black leadership in their persistent denial of the reality of our people's condition probably did more to fan the fires of frustration, than to calm them.

The sickening sight of Black leader, after Black leader advancing the company line, "Let's have peace, brothers and sisters--We shall overcome, one day," on the night insurrection broke, made one thing clear to all who watched, both live and on television. Time had run out on Black leadership in Los Angeles. With nothing else to say, and no justification for what happened or why it was happening, Negro leadership went with the only hand they knew, placation.

Black people (and others) recognized that there were no rules, when it came to dealing with Blacks. There was no law, and there was no recourse, for which Blacks could turn to, for a fair and satisfactory resolution of the injustices facing the Los Angeles Black community. Black leadership had been given five strikes to defuse a ticking time bomb: a community in social and economic crisis. The signs were all around us: the Oliver X Beasley murder, the King beating, the Latasha Harlins killing, the Soon Ja Du trial and finally the King Beating trial. All occurred in less than 24 months. The resolution in each case was to continue to buy in to a system of inequity, injustice and intolerance, all at the expense and compromise of Black people. Yes, Latinos and others had suffered, but Blacks have been and always will be the litmus test for social change. Only this time social change would not come at the expense of only Blacks, and it would not come with a buy-in. Change in Los Angeles had to come with the outward rejection of injustice and the total rejection of Negro compromise. Given the alternative, a continued buy-in from a leadership of compromise, the people had an obligation to express their displeasure, or continue to suffer at the hands of their oppressor and their hand-picked overseers.

Los Angeles had to burn twice. Not solely because of a judicial or a jury's decision. The system was only doing what it was set to do, and had done all along. The city had to burn again, because the combination of a very hazardous mix of disparate social and economic conditions in South Central Los Angeles, made for a very dangerous toxic situation. The rags placed around the heads (minds and eyes) of Black leaders gave little room for the people to ventilate. The doors to vision and hope (for future change) was closed and locked. South Central had no way to bring fresh air in, and no way to let contaminated air out. The Los Angeles Black community had been locked in a closet of compromise. Its own leaders not only refused to use their key (access to the system) to let 'em out of the closet, they placed their foot against the door. Los Angeles burned out of a leadership futility the people didn't know any other way to correct, so it exploded from within. Internal combustion doesn't just apply in the physical sciences. It also applies in the social sciences, thus is the lesson of Los Angeles.

1992 was the same dangerous mix as 1965, only more magnified, and it produced a similar, but more magnified result. There are no band-aid solutions to social crisis. Band-aid approaches have been (and continue to be) transition remedies, where race and social change are concerned. The scar never healed in Los Angeles, because the city's real wounds, social justice and economic parity, were never treated properly. Band-aids were used. And instead of putting them on for the short term, they were put over the leaderships' eyes for the long term.

Whether you were Black or white, part of the problem or part of the solution, colored (obsolete) or ex-colored (progressive) in your thinking, it really didn't matter in the eyes of the oppressed. All deals were off and all we could do was watch the souls that had long been sold set fire to a community built out of compromise.

Twice in 27 years. It may not be the last time. Why? Much of the same leadership mindset that caused the rebellion has run to the head of the line. In many cases, the very same faces that compromised the community in 1965, in 1992, call themselves speaking for the community today. Fork tongue wagging one way, begging hands wagging another. The fires of the L.A. night didn't burn the corruption of leadership away.

Their purpose wasn't purified by the fires of their people's frustration. The selling of new souls, and in many cases--the same old souls, had already started the day after April 29th. The redlining, the exploitation, the predatory policies that create social and economic disparities between whites communities and communities of color, the compromise of people's lives; moreover, the excuses for why things remain the same in the South part of the city, while the rest of the city evolves in a state of constant change. Yes, the excuses, the compromise of soul-selling have begun, all over again.

* * *

'Revolutions are apt to take their color from the regime they overthrow."

-Richard H. Tawney

"When you win---you have a story to tell; lose and you don't have a story to tell. Only winners have a story to tell."

-Dr. Maulana Karenga

"History is the past written by the winners."

-Alex Haley

"We must use time creatively, and forever realize that the time is always ripe to do right."

-Nelson Mandela

Epilogue

Time Heals All Wounds

...Sometimes

Some of the best lessons we ever learn, we learn from our mistakes and failures. The error of the past is the wisdom and success of the future.

-Tyron Edwards

We are all witnesses of time, each in our own contexts, reflecting the events of time as they have bounced off our respective lives. Our recollections are often reflective of the full spectrum of thoughts and interactions, based on varying degrees of insights and experiences, direct and indirect, positive and negative, that cause us to view life based on what we understood, at a particular time and place in life. It is often in hindsight that we recognize the true meaning of the trials we experience. Very few of us, (Blacks in particular), view life as history, or recognize the events of our lives as history unfolding on the rolling scroll of time.

Like history, life is a succession of events, private and public, stories told and untold, which we may or may not make public. Every event, every public story, every success and even every failure has two sides. Be it sacrifice, pain, trial, tribulation, elation or elevation. The ultimate result has a hidden factor that influenced, changed, and fashioned the result that forged an outcome that could have been different, had one or more factors of a particular event varied. Change a point in time, and you, in fact, change the course of history. Social engineers decide how others live, if by doing nothing more than framing history in a Eurocentric context. It is these people who document the time and comment on what is said, what is done and determine the outcomes of events in a cultural perspective. These are the people who are most likely to direct how history is written.

Rarely do we get to see history played out in its redemptive context. Nor are we rarely fortunate enough to witness the vindication of wrongs experienced over time, in our time. There's a saying that "time heals all wounds." This may be true. Much of the bitterness and emotional pain that came out of the writing of Souls for Sale: The Diary of an Ex-Colored Man has subsided. As we seek to move on, advancing ourselves and our communities toward redemption, we can and should forgive much of the conflict second-generation advocates have had to endure, in the post-civil rights era. We can't, nor should forget the compromises the conflict forged, largely because many of the realities of the social compromise that has caused so much of the material pain of the Los Angeles Black community still remain. Historical events, and the outcomes of history, are always bigger than one person. Many personal conflicts rose out of that fight against social and economic compromise in the Los Angeles Black community. Both the individual and collective pain this community suffered, and this author has experienced are reflected in the continuing presence and behaviors of the players still on the scene and the circumstances that still exist. This was recently represented in the 10th anniversary of the 1992 Los Angeles civil disturbance-the most expensive engagement in social protest in American history. This behavior of conflictive leadership succession is not unique to just the Los Angeles Black community, but in Black communities all over America where young leaders seek to emerge and are forced to challenge a generation that "won't pass the ball," as some of my younger colleagues like to say. When they do pass it, it's passed to another generation of "new Negroes" who see conflict of social change as an inconvenience to their "status quo" politics of materialism and race neutrality.

Whenever diversity issues, equity issues, and/or quality of life issues are called into question, for the old (and new) Negro, social and economic compromise is the answer. Compromise becomes an answer, because social and economic circumstances are permitted to exist. Somebody sits silent and rationalizes its existence. Somebody looks the other way. This book provided instance after instance of people looking the other way. But people don't sit silent, or look the other way for nothing. Just as painful as watching others ignore racial suffering and social injustice was to watch those who suffer because of socioeconomic compromise

It's painful when a community's talent or brain-trust becomes a part of the compromise. Sipping champagne, or eating finger-foods, these neo-Negroes act as if they or the people they represent--poor and oppressed people--haven't a worry in the world. Stepping into many Negro social circles is like bathing in galleys of hypocrisy. Fake smiles, fake dialogues, fake sincerity and fake remedies for the pain and despair that ails Black people. An evening of "Negrolizing" generally requires time to detoxify one's self from the stench and stigmatization of "hob-nobbing" with those who choose to do nothing in the face of genocide. I am a believer that support is reciprocal, if for no other reason than providing one a "free look" in a circle of compromise, and offering a presence of a free mind and a conscience spirit of liberation before the Negro and a new generation of compromisers, that they may one day have the courage to emulate someone disconnected from the politics of pretense. The Negro leadership in America desperately needs to be free from the trappings of this compromise. The parties, receptions, dinners that now significantly outnumber the days of advocacy and sincere struggle. The "race" man or woman, as advocates of racial inequality were once called, no longer exists in America's second post-reconstruction period. The second post reconstruction has been deemed America's Colorblind Era. The Negro and his mentee, the new Negro, have bought this line.

After completing "Souls" in 1993, many of the issues discussed in this diary were either still unresolved, or too "new," and too painful to discuss. The wounds had not yet healed. Nothing aggravates the healing process more than scratching an open or partially healed wound. Most times, doing so impedes proper healing and leaves an even bigger, more infected scar. We (my wife and I) waited for the scar to close, and in the process many of the issues resurfaced and played out in some very interesting ways. In many cases, positions I took in my advocacy days that were thought to be incorrect, were later found to be correct. Yet at the time "Souls" was completed, it was premature to step out on many of those issues. History has proven the positions correct.

Still, as we have often witnessed in competitive sports, the anxiety and greater damage one often experiences in wanting to compete "too soon," after sustaining an injury, forces one to pace the sideline needlessly. Athletes often overlook the potential damage to be done from coming back too soon. Though we hardly realize it, this is also true for real life. While I was enjoying the subtleties of family life, the complexities of parenthood and the normality of anonymity; I too was anxious of wanting to have this story told. I wanted the community to really understand why social and economic circumstances had hardly changed in 27 years. I wanted to correct history (not reject history or HIS-story), not necessarily in terms of what happened to me but, in what happened to the Los Angeles Black community in the 1980s that caused it to be the national focus of everything that was wrong with urban cores in the 1990s. Coming back too soon would have been painful, but I was willing to take the chance, just to be a part of the discussion of how and why Blacks continue to be compromised. My wife, in her God-given wisdom and understanding of me suggested that "we (this is her story, too)" hold the book until I was ready to disrupt the calmness of my life as it's been reestablished, but also ready to relive the pain, without re-injuring my psychological and spiritual state of mind. Her position, aptly stated, was. "Why should you defend the truth? Let history defend the truth, and you defend history."

"Plus", she said, "God is vindicating almost everything you discuss. Wait it out and receive all of your glory." So that's what we did. She was correct about some things, but some of the wrongs discussed in this experience, like in history, seem to go on forever. Yet, as we live, we learn that God does vindicate right. But there can be no healing without injury; no redemption without failure; and most importantly, no resurrection without crucifixion. Each injury that occurred during this period of personal betrayal has been followed with a very public vindication. All of them taking place over the past ten years, closing some chapters in this experience, redeeming others, while allowing me, by the grace of Allah, to rise again to speak out for truth, justice and righteousness. Where I was once a witness of (and served to some extent) man's world--one not always of truth and factual reality, I am now a witness of (and serve) God's world; a truth-teller for justice and reality. One of the things I can bear witness to is that man cannot serve two masters. Most of our people still try to "fit in" a world that has become increasingly more hostile to our societal inclusion. The personal redemption that has come of this experience is that I no longer see the value of being a part of the superficial existence set aside for the "Negro" reality of second class citizenship, or stereotyped homogeneity set in America's desire to return to the race caste of America's past. The new Negro is misled by his relative comfort.

The parties, the corporate sponsored dinners, the disingenuous discussions do little to change the reality of disenfranchised communities. The new Negro reality is tantamount to an assimilating sub-culture in an unrighteous counter-culture. It's like stepping into a cloud of smoke; I come out coughin' and gaspin' for air--the bullshit is so thick. Just bein' around 'em clouds the mind, confuses ones logical thought process, and requires time just to get back into relevant mind and space. The Negro was (is) not of his natural mind, particularly in Los Angeles. I know who my master is and it is not the Negro or his master that causes us to accept this caste reality. Allah, and he alone, is sufficient for me.

* * *

It has been a full ten years since the 1992 civil insurrection in Los Angeles. Rebuilding has been just that, re-building half of what was already there. That's if any rebuilding took place at all. Any rebuilding that needed to occur, was not so much brick and mortar, as it was rebuilding feelings of frustration and despair-a point missed by the Negro leadership of Los Angeles. And much of the same Negro leadership that brokered despair prior to April 29th, 1992 are brokering despair now. Negro leadership is back to offering excuses for a system of compromise that has not only been rebuilt, but re-enforced. The funny thing about time is if you live long enough, it has a way of correcting injustice. Maybe not in the same way it was put out there, and maybe not by man's law or those who consider themselves moral guides. But, in the end, the scales of life and God's law are eventually balanced. Life is bitter and life is sweet, but hardly at the same time. And just as good times don't last always, neither do bad. As King David said in Psalms (32:1), "blessed is the man whose sins God hides."

Many of the sellers of souls in Los Angeles (and other parts of the country) got away in the eighties. Got clean away. Maybe they were blessed, or maybe they are a sign of things to come. Maybe their time will (or may have already) come. Only time will tell, but one thing we do know is that Los Angeles has become an increasingly unfriendly place for Blacks to live; hostile to the notion of continued mainstream participation. It's as if Black participation is a passing fancy of days gone by. The city's changing demographic has Latinos sitting in the batter's box, and they let you know "their turn is next," every chance they get. The conservative turn in social attitudes that L.A. Blacks face is disputably more hostile, than in any urban city in America.

The land of the rebellion, the nation's social laboratory by which the problems of the urban core are now measured, has been subplanted by the rage of the O.J. Simpson verdict. The arrogance of a rich white republican Mayor who, in a matter of months, came into office and uprooted much of the diverse social (human) infra-structure established by the 20 years of the Bradley administration. (who was Mayor longer than any Mayor in the history of Los Angeles) His replacement got on the backs of Black voters by using his father's name-only to turn his back on the community's choice for Chief of Police. A tree with shallow roots is easily toppled. With California's "return to yesterday," in a time when Blacks in Los Angeles needed access the most, there was little access to be had. As L.A. reverted back to the way things "used to be," the rush to become "the head nigga'," "the house nigga"-whatever you want to call 'em in the 1990s-it became more obvious that the "sale on souls" went bargain rate.

As I reflect on the many faces and places that were part of this time in my life, some issues have been vindicated, but much of the personal hypocrisy still remains. The post civil rights era has been particularly hard on the City of Los Angeles. The second post reconstruction period has been re-enforced to where the United Way published a report in 1999 called “Los Angeles: A Tale Of Two Cities,” outlining the increasing gaps in wealth and income between the rich and poor. It is not difficult to understand why the rest of the country perceives Los Angeles (and most people from Los Angeles) as conflicted, confused, even crazy. The lack of stability in L.A. social culture is a direct reflection of its people and their distorted and conflicted views of the city--of one another (in terms of understanding different races and cultures), a misguided sincerity (direct insincerity, in many cases) and a pretense about its reality that boggles the mind. LA-LA land represents a clear perception (by outsiders) as a place of distortions. People who see Los Angeles as not being rooted in any sense of a common reality, or a place where people don't have a mutual respect for cultural differences. Los Angeles has proven to be a reinforcement in cultures that run counter to what the rest of the world sees as right and just (where rightness and justice exists). Blacks in Los Angeles, in overwhelming numbers, have taken on the behaviors of the L.A. counter-culture--a fake and pretentious way of life--not rooted in culture, nor in cooperative equities. Community is just a figure of speech for Blacks in Los Angeles. Plainly put--Blacks in Los Angeles are more confused than the counter-culture it chooses to practice. Blacks practice counter-cultural behaviors on each other with fervid regularity. Subsequently, the collective Black community in Los Angeles suffers because of it. You can't take on another's values, take their guilt money and expect to remain "true to self." Los Angeles, the city--at the same time, has not gone without punishment for its corrupt ways.

After the 1992 civil insurrection, the city moved to heal itself racially by moving to oust LAPD Chief Daryl Gates. He left almost a year later, on his own terms. Philadelphia Police Chief Willie Williams was given a five-year contract to begin implementation of the police reforms called out in the Christopher Commission report (named for Warren Christopher, who was later tapped in President Bill Clinton's first administration as Secretary of State). Two of the four cops in the King Beating trial were found guilty in a federal trial, while the infamous "L.A. Four," the four young men seen at the flashpoint of the 1992 rebellion (Florence and Normandie), were acquitted of attempted murder charges (though found guilty on lesser charges). This only caused to further racially polarize the city.

In January of 1994, a major earthquake hit Los Angeles (Northridge is a suburb of Los Angeles). It was considered one of the deadliest and costliest natural disasters in U.S. history, where dozens of people lost their lives and billions of dollars of damage was caused ($26 billion at last estimate). Later that same year, Los Angeles experienced major floods and fires.

The biggest public spectacle of all; one that demonstrated hypocrisy, arrogance and incompetence of the Los Angeles law enforcement and legal system, was the O.J Simpson trial. The prosecution put forth a case that was both stumbling and bumbling. They took on some unnecessary gambles (the glove test), the biggest of which was to put on the witness stand an LAPD officer named Mark Furhman, who was a known racist and claimed he "found" O.J.'s leather glove. It set the stage for the biggest racial "bumrush" in the history of television. When the smoke cleared, the police officer who the prosecution hung its case on, lost the case for 'em. Furhman, who claimed he had never used the word, "Nigger," was on tape using "the N-Word" (America's new social decorum for a hateful tag it hung on Blacks for 200 years--

and is still the most used word in many whites reference book for Blacks) forty times--talking about the judge's wife (and everybody else). Furhman has since written his own book and has made it big on the lecture circuit. A true injustice. As Don King says, "Only in America."

Bottom line was, the prosecution put on a poor case and tried to seal their case with falsehood, (a cop's lie) and it didn't stick. We'll never know if truth prevailed, but the system (as white folks have played it out all these years) worked for a Black man this one time, in the most publicized trial of the century. A year later, the other man's "revenge" came about, as a nearly all white jury tagged O.J. Simpson for civil damages, to the tune of $33.5 million dollars. Los Angeles hasn't stopped there. Unbeknownst to the rest of the country, Los Angeles was in the middle of a "white riot" that used public policy (ballot initiatives), and the voting process to turn back the clock on Blacks, and other people of color quicker than you can say "revolution." Many of the Black city and county department heads, who came to power under Tom Bradley, were either put out (of their jobs), or put under siege by succeeding Mayor Richard Riordan.

Los Angeles County voters overwhelmingly supported the anti-affirmative action initiative, Proposition 209, recently upheld by the state courts as constitutional. This was only after the University of California Board of Regents, headed by then California Governor Pete Wilson put forth a motion to end affirmative action as a consideration for UC admissions. Consistent with the theme of Souls for Sale, most of the lobbying for both the UC Regents action and Proposition 209 was advanced by a blackface; some silly Negro named Ward Connelly, who is convinced that race has no place in American society. As the "conservative right's colorblind mascot, he is now pushing a second initiative in California, on the ballot for November, 2002, to remove race from all government employment and education applications. Economic strangulation continues in Los Angeles, as much of the post-riot activity that produced entities like Re-Build L.A., the L.A. Community Development Bank (which subsequently failed), and dozens of "EDCs" (economic development centers) and SBDCs (small business development centers) produced little results, but lots of people got high priced jobs out of these relief efforts.

Job training opportunities have provided little relief, as Los Angeles continues to lose industry to more "business friendly" cities. Business flight and the corrupt politicalization of major federal transportation projects have caused minority contracting opportunities to stagnate. California's adoption of welfare reform threatens the social safety net of many low-income communities, in a matter of three years, with no real solution in place. With the Hispanic immigrant influx, Latinos now represent close to 50% of the Los Angeles population, and the city's growing Asian Pacific influence now outnumbers Blacks, and has cash to burn (long before Asians were buying influence in the White House, they had bought influence in Los Angeles).

Black influence in Los Angeles was sliding quicker than an elevator drop. Blacks have gone from being the second largest ethnic population to the fourth largest, in L.A.'s diversity mix. Throw in white women, and L.A.'s closet (and openly) gay population, and Blacks probably fall from the "social radar" altogether. Blacks have gone from the largest social "minority" to the fourth largest "minority" (behind white women, Latinos and Asians).

Black culture's contribution to Los Angeles has been greatly undermined by an increasing slew of entertainment buffoonery. Between Black television shows, and white-owned and controlled urban formatted radio that have little regard for Black cultural dignity and ethnic sensitivity, Blacks are projected to the whole world as gangstas, hoochies, fools and buffoons. This return to Amos n' Andy type mimickery has Blacks looking "real crazy," and much of it is originated out of Los Angeles, where the entertainment culture is only interested in making money--no matter what price Black dignity has to pay--a second generation of "Black-plortation." Unlike the first generation--a mix of Black heroes and pimps (Shaft, Foxy Brown, Superfly and the Mack), the second generation is either extremely violent or sexual degenerate. There is no shortage of blackfaces willing to play the fool for, what they call, entertainment sake. Los Angeles has also been the center of "gangsta' rap" wars that have caused the death of rappers Tupac Shakur and Notorious B.I.G. (Biggie Smalls). The manifestation of "commoditized filth," as scholar Maualana Karenga calls it, what the industry calls music-everybody else calls madness. A filth glorified for the riches it brings our youth, while making them social outcasts. The renewed hostility toward Blacks, framing of Black youth as maniacal and dangerously hostile, can be attributed to this genre of rap music. Los Angeles is where much of it started (N.W.A.) and has brought us, as James Weldon Johnson wrote in "Lift Every Voice and Sing," "treading our path through the blood of the slaughtered."

Los Angeles is even more misleading, in terms of sincerity in promoting racial harmony. Some Negroes may disagree to agree, but only because they go along with "the new race politic" to get along (and not get shut out totally). Irrespective of these sentiments, the facts bear out this new reality called Los Angeles. Recognizing that the 1992 rebellion has been removed from the conscience of the city's "fathers (and step-children)," two things haven't changed about Los Angeles. One, many whites, particularly those in power and influence of the social politic, are still pretending to be liberal and smiling in the faces of Negro leadership, while re-enforcing the "red-line" around South Los Angeles, in capital and in homeownership. Two, Negro leaders are still taking their money to hold favor with the power elite, in spite of the Black community's compromised existence, and despite clearly token efforts to pacify the community en mass. So ten years after outrage personified grabbed the attention of the world, souls are still being sold in Los Angeles. All day, every day. And the Negro is still out front, co-signing the compromise and being paid for it.

Time heals all wounds, vindicates all wrongs.....sometimes.

* * *

The Los Angeles NAACP has been reduced to a bit player in L.A.'s civil rights advocacy agenda-a cameo role that occasionally finds a mere mention in the local news. The branch launches very few issues and generally coat-tails on other organizations' issues. Many call the L.A. NAACP to their press conferences to legitimize themselves. The NAACP can still legitimately draw press interest, as the branch did some seven years ago, when it called two different press conferences to take a stand on both sides of the Chavis firing issue, proving there's still no buffoonery like L.A. buffoonery. Niggershit for real. Most of the progressives, who really understand real advocacy, are not in the branch. Membership, as recent as June, 2002 was down around 1,100 members, down from the over 8,000 members that were involved during my presidency. The national membership was also down under 100,000 for the first time in 50 years. It had to run television commercials to recruit members. The Los Angeles branch's active membership is less than 75 members, most of which are on the Executive Committee.

The branch's advocates are basically novices trying to get their faces and quotes in the press, not for the sake of the NAACP, but for themselves.

The Negro opposition that banded together to oust me finally showed their true colors (as coloreds) and turned on each other. Tired of four years of stagnation under Joe Duff, Henry Dotson, who was President in 1974, decided he wanted to be President again in 1994, with no plan and no vision. The same Second Baptist Church "swing vote" contingent that voted against me, voted against Joe, and the branch took a twenty-year step back into yesterday. Unable to inspire members with his abrasive personality and dictatorial style, Dotson resigned after six months. The former head of the branch's Womens Auxiliary, Geraldine Washington, took over as head of the branch as interim President. That term has been filled with conflict and petty politics that was almost an exact repeat of the experience written about in this book. Two years later, she defeated a young man that became active in the NAACP, inspired to ascend to the leadership of the branch's First Vice Presidency after witnessing my compromise and defeat in the branch election. His name was David Allen. Many of the same tricks to confuse and manipulate the membership took place that was used to defeat me, including holding the membership list from Allen, while Washington mailed to the members three times. Again National Director of branch services, Bill Penn (who has since retired), was in the middle of the election. Ms. Washington is a very nice lady, but not a change activist. Her interim presidency has now lasted eight years. Time heals all wounds....sometimes.

* * *

After the 1992 rebellion, the First African Methodist Episcopal Church became a literal clearinghouse for the crisis response to help repair "the Black community. Much of it was corporate "guilt money," and the church (collective) became the central focus for economic efforts that white folk didn't trust to set up anywhere else. The community had no economic infra-structure or depositories to receive "social change" dollars, beyond the Negro organizations that were themselves lobbying for the conscience of white America. The irony of First AME's placement in the breakdown of social change in Los Angeles is that it was the very place that second generation leadership was compromised. But because it was the meeting place for the Negro establishment (Tom Bradley's church), the church got worldwide visibility for "the victory party" it staged on the night of the riots.

The church set up FAME Renaissance, an economic development corporation set up to monitor and fund small businesses. The fund was endowed with a one million dollar grant from the Walt Disney Company and supplemented by other corporate donations. FAME Renaissance was supposed to train existing and "wanna-be" entrepreneurs on succeeding in business, by having them write their own business plans, before they would lend them $20,000. This was tantamount to having people operate on themselves, after taking a six-week course in medicine. Many of the businesses failed, or were not able to repay their loans, because of controversial conditions placed on the money, or not enough money to do anything with. The church also has expanded into housing development ventures, an employment agency, a school named after Cecil "Chip" Murray, and a newly renovated "entertainment" incubator. But its economic thrust beyond the church-based interests has had minimal success. FAME Renaissance is headed up by my NAACP supporter who betrayed me, Mark Whitlock, also now in the ministry. I've always liked Mark, and maybe his soul has been saved now, but time hasn't totally healed my wounds with him. We manage to deal in a cordial, but mostly "distant" manner.

In 1999, the church was the center of controversy over harboring and protecting a known FBI informant named Julius Butler, whose testimony was the key evidence in the conviction of former Black Panther Geronimo Ji Jaga (Pratt). Butler, who now claims to be saved, and was Chip Murray's chief operative as Trustee Board Chairman, has had his testimony totally discredited and was given every opportunity to recant, even in the face of Johnnie Cochran's cross-examination at Geronimo's hearing for a new trial later that year. Butler stuck by his story, even after it came to light that he was also an informant for the Los Angeles district attorney who brought the case against Pratt. Had this information been known during the trial, Butler would have not been considered a credible witness by the jury, and wouldn't have been allowed to testify, as he did. Chip Murray, again, didn't act as a moral authority to prompt Butler's repentance, and in an act of the highest hypocrisy, Chip Murray went on public record in support of a new trial for Geronimo Pratt, while the man the whole world knew as Pratt's framer, sat at his right hand, as his top assistant in the church. When Geronimo Pratt was granted a new trial, and released, because of Butler's incredible testimony, Butler was unceremoniously "kicked to the curb." First AME Church, in spite of the good work it's doing, has a problem being a moral authority on real issues of spiritual integrity. Time vindicates all wrongs....sometimes.

* * *

Both the Los Angeles Police department and the L.A. County Sheriffs Department still suffer from internal strife and misconduct problems, in spite of, the public's call for police reform, after the 1992 civil insurrection. The Los Angeles Department hired former Philadelphia Police Chief, Willie Williams, to head the department's reform efforts. Most of his five-year tenure was spent trying to break the internal "crony" network deeply embedded in the department, and countering allegations generated from internal leaks and breaches of confidentiality. These allegations were made from the police commission, the police union and insiders who never wanted Williams there in the first place. It's tough to "do your job," when you have to spend your time defending your actions, or your decisions, or your integrity, as Williams found out. In spite of all these allegations and attacks, Williams had done a decent job, given what most knew and understood to be a damn near impossible charge--cleaning up L.A.P.D.

Several "mini" controversies that highlighted a superfluous scrutiny that followed the chief during his five-year contract undermined the authority, and ultimately, the longevity of Willie Williams. This activity, much of it unrelated to his performance as chief, created the needed justifications to jam Williams contract renewal. A very strategic and deliberate approach that has been used before, but not without the help of the mainstream press. Specifically the *Los Angeles Times* and the *Daily News* (a San Fernando Valley based paper). What compromise would be complete without the help of house Negroes, who felt they would benefit by scapegoating one of their own. Williams' ongoing feud with then LAPD Assistant Police Chief Bernard Parks, also "a brotha'" (the top ranking insider to replace former chief Daryl Gates), resulted in Williams having to demote Parks, only to have it overridden by the Los Angeles City Council. But in taking such action, he made an inside enemy of Parks who, by many inside accounts, had made ousting Williams a full time preoccupation. Given Williams couldn't "be every place at one time," the leaks, the morale issues, the (police) commission conflicts, and the level of scrutiny only increased after the Parks incident, and was compounded by a "no confidence" vote by the police union. In spite of, Chief Willie Williams being the most popular public official in Los Angeles, and the department being credited for a reduction in crime in the city, as well as, a reduction in abuse complaints, Mayor Riordan's stacked police commission recommended to not rehire Williams. The Los Angeles City Council laid down behind the commission's decision, and

Williams was "finis complet."

Ironically, five years later, the exact same thing happened to the man that replaced Williams, Chief Bernard Parks. Parks, who had restored some credibility to the department, while overseeing the biggest scandal in the department's history, the Rampart Scandal, was not the choice of the new Mayor, James Hahn. Mayor Hahn, elected by a strange coalition of Valley conservatives and Black loyalists (to the Hahn legacy), ousted Parks in mid-2002, without so much as a wimper by anybody outside the Black community.

L.A.'s biggest bombshell happened in June of 1996, when a reporter from the *San Jose Mercury News*, Gary Webb, investigating the drug trade, stumbled upon a source that confirmed what I publicly stated in January of 1989 (during our interviews with gang members on county jail police abuse), that the government was providing drugs (and guns) to gang members for sale and distribution. Webb's story placed government involvement at the feet of the Central Intelligence Agency, when, in the early and mid 1980s, it used Columbian drug operatives, with the cooperation of local law enforcement, to flood South Central L.A. with drugs, took the profits from the inner city drug sales (other urban cities were involved also) and assisted in the financing of weapon purchases for Contra rebels. The notion that American lives and communities would be sacrificed for the sake of financing an illegitimate war to overthrow a legitimate government is unconscionable. This is the same Iran-Contra scandal that made Ollie North a national hero. The CIA has vehemently denied that this ever happened. However, anyone who knows the history of American covert operations, know that denial is the first line of defense. The CIA line has been that "we have no proof or evidence that this ever happened." Well, of course they don't. That doesn't mean it didn't happen, and the trail of destruction that has been left on the streets of America are indicative of the casualties of war.

The drug invasion occurred literally "overnight" (in a few years, relatively speaking) though the mainstream press, academic and urban specialists attempted to manufacture an "earlier window for the crack invasion (the late '70s) to sustain their rebuttals. They also tried to defray the focus on government activities during this period, claiming "no one person" was responsible for the "crack explosion." They were right about that part. More than one person was responsible. Try a whole nation who abdicated its responsibility to a segment of its population, and was now denying it. Yet, they wanted the world to believe that nobody knows how it happened, and why it ended up targeting the poorest communities of the country. Not likely.

At the time we interviewed gang members, they could only say they were getting drugs and guns from "the police," because they couldn't discern federal law enforcement from local law enforcement. What they could attest to was that on many occasions, local law enforcement knew the time, the place and the quantity of drugs that were being delivered, and most of the time, they served as "lookouts" for the Fed's. Local law enforcement permitted this activity and even engaged in the skimming of profits, which came to light when the Fed's turned on the local sheriffs that were providing their cover -- prosecuting them for stealing drug money. In hindsight, our little jailhouse investigation came very close to uncovering a major covert operation, which many people now connect to the feds aggressive (and swift) prosecution of me. Our intent was to bring civil rights charges against LAPD, and LACS would have given gang members (and others) a public forum to discuss this major cover-up that devastated communities nationwide. But God permitted it to come to light anyway. Under police chief, Bernard Parks, LAPD suffered its biggest corruption scandal ever, when it was discovered that its Rampart Division officers were stealing cocaine out of evidence lockers, dealing drugs, robbing banks, planting evidence on gangs members and even shooting and killing citizens during planned "routine" stops, and then falsifying reports. To Parks credit, he initiated an investigation of one division that soon spread to four. The city of Los Angeles has paid out over $200 million dollars in settlements over corruption lawsuits against LAPD.

Time heals all wounds, vindicates all wrongs....sometimes.

* * *

The Baldwin Hills Crenshaw Mall is one of the wrongs that has yet to be vindicated. After the 1992 rebellion, the mall was one of the biggest beneficiaries of rebuilding efforts. Tenancy has risen from 65% to almost 80%. Disney put a store in the mall, as well as Household Finance (finance companies are historical compromisers of poor people), Macy's and Taco Bell. However, the biggest investment was made by Sony Pictures, who in a joint venture with former Laker Ervin "Magic" Johnson, brought a 12-screen first run movie theatre called "Magic Theatres." The deal was financed and constructed with $11 million from the city of Los Angeles. Most accounts felt the theater could have been built for $3 million--$5 million maximum. The theater revived the mall for a minute, bringing foot traffic back to the mall.

In 1994, it was disclosed that the Alexander Haagen Company had sold the city's 50% interest of the mall to a company owned by himself. After the city threatened to freeze the theatre financing, he gave it back. Magic's company has ownership in the theater parcel, but as for the mall itself--there is still no Black ownership in the mall. Taxpayer money still supports one man's payoff.

I finally surrendered my one-man lifelong protest against the misuse of public redevelopment funds by agreeing to take a public discussion forum that I co-founded and hosted to a Black-owned business, Gumboz Restaurant located in the mall. It was a difficult decision, but it was for the better good of the community. Still within six months, Gumboz was out of business-another victim of the mall's skewed financing scenario. Time heals all wounds....sometimes.

* * *

An entity created by the federal government to manage the multi-billion dollar S&L scandal, the Resolution Trust Corporation, in July, 1993 filed a $10 million dollar lawsuit against the former board of directors and senior management of Founders Saving. In March of 1992, an attorney for the RTC by the name of Robert Heltowski called me. He wanted me to cooperate with him on the government's civil case against the rest of the Founder's defendants. I told him the Founders saga was behind me, and I wanted no part of any "civil litigation." He tried to tell me that it was a condition of my probation, and that he would violate my probation if I didn't cooperate. I told him the only condition of my probation was that I cooperate on any criminal prosecution case against future Founders principles, but not any civil case. He called my probation officer to try to get her to make me cooperate. She refused, saying what I had said, that it wasn't a condition of my probation. He then asked her had I completed all the requirements of my sentence; the community service, and was I current on my restitution, looking for something to hang over my head (to go to the judge to request a violation of my probation). She told him I was. That was the end of this little inquiry for a minute.

Justice never has and never will be served in the Founders Saving case from a criminal position. Founders was compromised long before I got there, while I was there, and long after I left. There were principles in the bank that either misdirected and/or mis-managed more money than they could ever recover, much more than the $10 million dollars the Resolution Trust Corporation was suing for. Prosecutions never came about for the ones who should have gone to jail, the ones most responsible for the failure of Founders Savings, and the government knew who they were. Some got clean away. That's how I know to this day my prosecution was never about justice for the taxpayers. It was about silencing me with what little they could use. A home loan at Founders was just the excuse. But now the feds were looking to recover the losses, under a civil lawsuit. Another waste of government time and money.

Just before the civil case was filed, Heltowski called again. This time he threatened to include me in the lawsuit, if I didn't cooperate with their civil case. This time, I got hostile and told him "I'm the only one that has paid a price in this whole situation, and I'm not about to be screwed twice by the government. Your threat only makes me more determined not to cooperate, so "Go fuck yourself." Three months later, I was served as a defendant in the civil suit. I made a conscious decision to represent my self in the case, for several reasons. One, I wasn't about to give some attorney $25,000 to $50,000 to defend a federal case of frivolous claims. Secondly, I wasn't about to hire some attorney to plead me out again, and bind the rest of my financial future in some unjust settlement (like some of my co-defendants ended up doing). The third reason was a very fundamental premise; if I'm to be screwed this time, I'd do it myself--to myself. And I'd do it playing the hand all the way out-no compromise.

The RTC ended up getting a jury award claim in excess of $700,000 against Dauterive (which the RTC appealed, because they felt it was too low) and a $30,000 claim against Art Meadows. Not one word of it appeared in the *L.A. Times*. The RTC's case against me was non-existent, as I proved in pre-trial settlement conferences. The RTC also recognized that I'd spend more time attacking them, than helping, which threatened to let their big fish (Dauterive) off the hook. In the end, they recognized that trying to frame a second case against me wasn't worth it. They had nothing on me. Never did, other than my notoriety, and a file somebody sent them, and the hope that they could intimidate me into telling on somebody. They couldn't press me, because there was nothing to tell that they didn't already have. Defending myself, I settled out of the case, on the day before trial for $5,000, the lowest of all the defendants, except Jarone Johnson.

Jarone also settled for $5,000 which was peculiar, because he was the board member that recommended the loan that turned into the biggest loss on one deal, in the history of the Founders Saving ($1.7 million). Turns out, Jarone was the one that took the case to the RTC. His reward was the $5,000 settlement. As an aside, it was estimated that the RTC spent over $10 million dollars trying the former officers and directors of Founders Saving in this civil suit. They recovered less than $2 million in judgments and settlements (if you include the estates of two of the former directors that died, prior to the case going to trial). Is that justice? Probably...Capitalist style. Is it fair? Probably not, but then what is fair in America. A country that won't admit to the injustices in its social construct is not going to advance a discussion about prosecutorial fairness. Founders Savings and Loan ended as it began, an institution of ill repute, where no justice prevailed.

On August 16th, 2002, less than a month before the release of this book, the most wicked man I've ever met--one who tried to destroy my life (save God's grace), Peter W. Dauterive, died at home of natural causes. His obituary in the *Los Angeles Times* lauded him as a trailblazer, never mentioning his misdeeds at Founders Savings or the many people those deeds ruined. The Bible says in Psalms 32:1, "Blessed is he whose transgression is forgiven, whose sin is covered." The Quran says it a little differently Surah 45 Ayat 15, "Whosoever does a good deed, it is for his ownself, and whosoever does evil, it is against (his ownself). Then to your Lord you will be made to return."

Time vindicates all wrongs....sometimes.

* * *

After becoming an activist, City Councilman, Mark Ridley-Thomas has been an avid supporter of community-based involvement in urban economic development. His efforts in building community-based infra-structure has been recognized nationally. Many in the Los Angeles community have developed a healthy respect for Ridley-Thomas' progressive politics and coalition building, but have raised questions about his personality. What was once thought of as confidence, has now been perceived, by his own people, as an elitist attitude. It's the same kind of person, we once despised in our twenties and early thirties, when Mark and I used stay up late talking about what when wrong with "the struggle." At the time, we felt that the problem was a lack of respect for a community perspective. It was "them" (distant political insiders, insensitive outside financing interests) against "us" (community people).

My perception of his non-support of me caused me to keep my distance from Mark, in his early years on the city council. Our friendship was never readdressed. We just sought to maintain a cordiality that was neither close nor distant, mainly keeping an eye on each others activity, for "old times sake." In. 1998, Mark took the lead in Los Angeles' bid to bring professional football back to the city. The city leaders had tabbed then Dodger owner Peter O'Malley to head an ownership team to develop the stadium that would convince the NFL to return to Los Angeles. Ridley-Thomas, on the other hand, took the position that if football was to return to Los Angeles, it would be in the L.A. Memorial Coliseum, or no place at all. His demand came at a critical time for Mayor Riordan, who was trying to get city council support for a municipal bond issue, on a new downtown arena for the Lakers and Kings (Staples Center). In exchange for Mark's vote, the Mayor agreed to abandon O'Malley's football proposal, and throw his support behind the Coliseum, which most informed players thought the NFL would never, ever accept.

So disillusioned was O'Malley over the city's abandonment of his proposal, in the opinion of many, that it was a major factor in his decision to sell the Dodgers. Meanwhile, Los Angeles still didn't have a clear shot at football, when a competing proposal came from the neighboring city of Carson, headed up by entertainment mogul, Michael Ovitz. The lead person for the city of Carson was one of my best friends, Daryl Sweeney, who had now become a city councilman. I had a great loyalty to Daryl for the loyalty he had shown me during my times of trial. Plus, Carson had a better proposal, and I said so, publicly, in my editorial column. When the decision was announced, as to whom would receive the NFL franchise, Houston had outbid both Los Angeles and Carson, by $100 million dollars.

A week later, during a going away party for newly appointed Ambassador to the Republic of Micronesia, Diane Watson, at Melanie Lomax's home, Mark and I saw each other. We just stared at each other momentarily, like two lost brothers who had just recognized each others weaknesses--our division. After another year or so, we slowly began to talk again, after I took the first step to send my prayers and well wishes during a life threatening medical crisis involving his wife, Avis. We cautiously opened up about different things we had done to each other, without each other over the past ten years. We never talked about my persecution, or his non-support of me during that period, and why we stopped speaking after that. It no longer seemed as important as it once did. I perceived Mark as one of the most vigilant fighters for Black inclusion in the city, and I wanted to be of help to him. We couldn't do that distrusting each other. In this regard, it was time to move on, and Mark and I have become friends, the best of allies, again. This is the truest sense of time healing all wounds.....sometimes.

* * *

Consistent with the outrage expressed over my jail sentencing for a very minor offense was a more public controversy that arose out of perceptions of my sentencing judge, William D. Keller's racial intolerance. In 1993, a Jewish civil rights attorney considered highly competent by his peers, Stephen Yagman, assaulted Keller's less than professional behavior, in a letter to legal newspaper publication, the *Daily Journal*, expressing what he felt was the federal judges unethical behavior, extreme political leanings, lack of legal scholarship and his obvious racial biases.

Yagman charged that Keller was "dishonest" and called him "ignorant", "a right-winged fanatic," "a buffoon," and "a bully" who is one of the worst judges in the United States. Yagman's letter was in response to a sanction Keller placed on Yagman for overzealously arguing a case for a client. Yagman stated that Keller "has a penchant for sanctioning Jewish lawyers: me, David Kenner and Hugh Manes. I find this to be evidence of anti-Semitism." In response to this article, Keller acted in a manner most perceived as retaliation against Yagman, a very credible (and popular) attorney, for writing the letter, charging him with" impugning the integrity of the case" and filing a grievance before a special federal court disciplinary committee, who in turn brought the charges before a panel of federal trial judges. The panel, who attempted to back Keller, ruled in July of 1994 that Yagman violated an attorney code of conduct, and issued a two year suspension preventing Yagman from practicing in the Los Angeles Federal Courts. The suspension was overturned on appeal, ruling that it violated Yagman's 1st Amendment rights. During that same time, my probation officer had confided in me that he and several other probation officers noticed Keller's tendency to violate Black probationers (sending them back to jail) and felt that he was unjustly biased toward Blacks. My victimization wasn't Keller's first, and won't be his last. The perception held by my attorney and I that Keller mishandles his judicial discretion, abuses his authority and has disparate racial leanings (depending who's who and what color or creed they are) has since played out in some (not so) private and public circles. And even though many of his peers and legal practitioners know these views exist, there is nothing the public can do about it. Keller, who will use his demented discretion to render judgment and decide the fates of many lives to come, is still a federal judge for life. Time heals all wounds, vindicates all wrongs...sometimes.

* * *

In 1996, Basil Kimbrew was identified as a key operative in a political scandal that rocked the city of Compton. One that caused both former City Councilwoman Pat Moore and former Mayor and then sitting Congressman Walter Tucker, III to be convicted and sent to jail. Basil was the government's witness against Moore, who as her former campaign manager and alleged "bag man" recounted the cash-for-votes schemes that caused Moore and Tucker to be prosecuted. The prevailing thought throughout the L.A. political community was that Kimbrew "gave up" Moore to save himself. Amidst many protestations, Kimbrew is now a member of the bankrupt Compton School Board, the only school board in the state of California in receivership, and was a congressional aide for Congresswoman Juanita Millender McDonald, who succeeded Tucker, and launched her political career out of the "Black Santa Claus" issue in Carson, in 1988.

He's still labeled, by many, as one of the most unethical players in Southern California politics. And he still receives plenty of work for his willingness to engage in the kind of unethical (dirty) politics that helps candidates win political offices, at all cost. Others hire him to keep him out of the opponent's camp. His latest victim was controversial (but much loved) Mayor of Compton, Omar Bradley, who was ousted in a close run-off election in June, 2001. The deciding factor for many of the voters of Compton was a "hit piece" sent by Kimbrew, who was a candidate for Mayor in the primary. Kimbrew took to wearing a bulletproof vest during the election, in fear of his life. He was soon thereafter arrested for having lied about his residency in Compton. Either way, Kimbrew's involvement in public service is a travesty to the notion of "public service." Time vindicates all wrongs....sometimes.

* * *

The last fourteen years have offered many lessons, many observations and many revelations that have allowed me to grow in knowledge, wisdom and understanding. This period has allowed me to (both) witness and become a witness to testaments of faith we often speak with our mouths, but don't believe in our hearts. To pass the test of "belief," you have to step out on faith; most times, believing in the unseen and in the "substance of things hoped for." If we, as a people, believed in our hearts what we speak with our mouths, and opened our hearts and our minds to the miracles of life, even in conflict and despair, we would find the answers to the questions we seek; about life, about America's race politic, about our social standing in America and about our ability to change our own future.

As Africans in America, we have to become cultural realists, understanding the nature of what we are dealing with here in America and recognize (and acknowledge) the nature of the people we're dealing with in America. Our unfounded eternal optimism and our self-defeating pessimism are opposite extremes of misguided perceptions about why, when and how America will change. Perceptions often rooted in assumptions that we are dealing with a principled, right-minded, fair-minded society who sincerely want to see Blacks in this country live out an uncompromised reality. Blacks in America can no longer assume that a system set up for the benefit of one segment of the population is all of a sudden going to come self-correcting, self-forgiving and self-sacrificing. Even in the face of thousands, maybe even millions of fair-minded white people. Many of whom may not have a racist bone in their body, but are not going to disrupt an injustice system that is structured in their favor. Plainly put--whites, no matter how fair-seeming, are not going act against their own self-interest, nor seek to correct institutions and systems that represent "trap" doors and closed doors for the historically excluded.

There is nothing in the contemporary mainstream discussion focusing on rectifying past racial injustices, or on the social, political and economic revitalization of America. There is no mainstream discussion that indicates any massive societal movement toward racial equity and parity. None whatsoever. In fact, it is the reverse. They call it "race fatigue," where discussion on the race divide is no longer a desired public discourse. Therefore, it is incumbent upon us to be principled and rational about the realities of our predicament and the solutions that will bring about a change in our destiny. Certainly not one tied to any real change of heart on the part of whites.

Those whites who are right-minded, and well intentioned, will continue to be right-minded and probably will try to make a difference where they can, while not placing themselves in harm's way (society's resentment for pushing this "racial equality"). However, they will also continue to be a relative few, a micro-minority in and of themselves, insignificant to the overall population, which has historically and continually moved toward self-interest and eurocentric empowerment. Rightminded or not, the masses of whites will continue to be indifferent to the race politic, or be misguided in their perceptions of the race politic, because of the enormous benefits of "white privilege" in America. A massive change of heart of the masses of whites would require an act of God and a demonstrative act of God's power to humble the majority of American whites into becoming right-minded about its racial past. Even then (as September 11th, 2001 demonstrated), it's inclined to bring on a greater patriotism that would only reinforce America's whiteness. The state of race relations in America does not favor honest dialogue and truthful recognition of social and economic disparities. Nor, does it concede that remedy is eminent in an active effort (on their part) to rectify Black people's inferior social and economic situation, or offer recompense.

Blacks, conversely, must become realistic in their view of "where whites are" at this point in history, and where this society is heading, in their attempts to re-enforce their superior position in America. Blacks must also become more realistic in their view of our community's circumstance, and in their recognition that our community's social and economic recovery will not be tied to any sense of social benevolence, on the part of whites. Our "coming ups" will be as a result of strategic and well-thought out approaches to proving our worth to society (i.e., whites), and offering principled justifications, as to why they should even care about the "Negro Problem."

Our self-worth (collective), which is no longer seen as a significant value beyond singular contributions of individual talents that can be promoted and exploited, is not recognized by our own--much less the larger society. Our community's waste of human capital can't be rationalized solely based on what society has or hasn't done for us. There is plenty of culpability on our part, because we give up so easily on ourselves and our youth, when they stumble, or don't do what some of us think they are supposed to do, the way they want them to do it. Our (Black people's) impatience with one another, often translates to our refusal to recognize the larger mission, or the barriers that impede our mission.

Nation of Islam leader, Honorable Minister Louis Farrakhan has a saying that he communicates to the believers (members of the Nation) from time to time, that "we shouldn't be so quick to throw away our brother or sister (when we get impatient with them or they don't perform as "we" feel they should). The American Negro, like American society, is good at rationalizing why we shouldn't use some talented person (based on some historical view), when they're the best available, or why we shouldn't give someone a chance (or a second chance). We'd just as soon 'throw someone away" and start from scratch, then to use the benefit on one's experience (be it successes or failures, both are better than no experience at all). Our communities have many talented people, whose talents and gifts are being wasted, because the so-called "players in the community,' generally in no position to judge--do so, sidestep real talent to prove some meaningless point. The Black community will rise overnight, when it overstands how to "get ours" in the collective, and convert its most precious commodity, its human capital. Time heals all wounds....sometimes.

* * *

The solution to America's race problem, and to the "Negro problem" in particular, is in seeking God's face in three ways: Healing, Living and Loving. We, sometimes, never get to see how much certain experiences mean to us, until we view them in retrospect. I've learned in this experience that if you "live to love," you'll "love to live," and loving life is a healing experience, in and of itself. Sometimes we get so occupied in trying to "live life," we forget how to love life. We get so preoccupied with what's wrong with the world, that we don't find time to pursue all that's right with it. Living to love doesn't mean you ignore the inequities and injustices that make life unbearable. Living to love means living in pursuant of a peace that only God can provide. A peace as we seek "God's face" to guide us, and in asking for his love, guidance and protection in pursuit of that which is right and good for us, we pursue justice--not as a cause but--as a way of life. When we say "God is love," we acknowledge that God is the highest level of spirituality that we can obtain, and can only be obtained by pursuing a balance that brings peace. God tells us in Second Chronicles (Verse 7, Paragraph 14) when he appeared before King Solomon, that "if my people, who shall be called by my name, will humble themselves and pray, and seek my face and turn from their wicked ways, then will I hear from heaven and will forgive their sin and will heal their land." God re-enforces this in the Qu'ran, Sura 8, Ayat 29, saying that, " O you who believe! If you obey and fear Allah, He will grant you a criterion (to judge between right and wrong) making a way for you to get out from every difficulty, and will expiate for you your sins, and forgive you, and Allah is the Owner of the Great Bounty."

We often forget who is the sustainer of life and the deliverer of all blessings. We think the "in-crowd," or the aristocrats, or the social bosses, or our so-called friends determine our lot in life. But if you seek God's face, you'll have it all without ever submitting to anybody, but God. "Loving life" means that you embrace and submit to God's law, and allow him to direct the life that he, and only he, has given you. You permit him to lead you to the bountiful blessings that he promised, those that would seek his face, humble themselves, pray and do God's will. God's will is a natural pursuit of freedom, justice and equality for all his people; not what society thinks, or what the Negro thinks, or what the cowardliness of friends and associates think. Those who believe and whom he allows to see his face in the modern day miracles he ordains and permits to come about, stand for truth and right (not one or the other). And by his permission, they allowed to exist and must bear witness to the truth, and become warners to the disbelievers and the hypocrites. "God's face" is that divine intervention that all common sense and logic and theoretical interpretation tells you that somebody, other than those physically present, had a hand in the outcome of some event, some circumstance, some trial and some unforeseen victory. How we seek to re-enforce God's will is the difference between success and failure. Giving God the glory is putting "God's face" before others, on the blessings and achievements he permits us to accomplish. Once God permits you to see his face, you can't help but to become a living witness for God. A witness to his greatness, his benevolence and at all times, his grace and his mercy (not necessarily one in the same). Black people are good for calling on God in times of peril and despair, and when he appears, we often think it is to "save us" from others, when it is really to save us from ourselves, and to reinforce faith in what we should believe, a true higher power. After we submit to that faith, the blessings of heaven are open unto us. It's a tough lesson to learn, but if you're going to get your "butt kicked," who better to do it than the God that will elevate you as an example of redemption, when you submit to his will.

There are two instances in which God permitted me to "see his face" through his grace, power and mercy. Both were personal experiences, though one involved family and the other community, that were key in fashioning my insight for recognizing the blessings of the trials experienced through this book. The first was the birth of my youngest daughter, DeShawn Keren Olivia Samad. DeShawn was considered a "miracle baby," because she wasn't supposed to be here. Debra's uterus had turned in a way that doctors had told her it would be impossible for her to conceive and if she did--she would miscarry, or the complications of the birth would be a danger to her (Debra's) health. This was combined with a reluctance on my part to want to "start over" with the fatherhood piece. In trying to mend my relationship with my other children, and the travel involved in building my business; Plainly put--a baby "wasn't in my plans," when Debra announced that we were expecting a new addition to the family. Debra, who has the spirit of God in her anyway, was prayerful the whole nine months. On the eve of DeShawn's birth, complications arouse. Debra had to have a Caesarean birth.

In what appeared to be a painful and highly stressful process, in the bloody, hectic and rapid-fire confusion of a delivery room, DeShawn was delivered. As she was pulled from Debra's abdomen, she had a look on her face that produced a look of amazement on my face. Debra looking at me thought something was wrong with the baby. She called me to ask what's wrong, and I couldn't answer her. DeShawn had the look of an angel on her face, a peaceful calm that even the doctor's spank couldn't disrupt (he had to tap her twice). She made a brief whine then stopped, just like that. She had big eyes that were clear and alert, and that ran deep into the soul, not the kind of blurry, cloudy eyes babies usually have. Her stare was long and deliberate, as if she knew what she was looking at, and was trying to discern its place and relevance. This perception was more than the biased excitement of a doting father. I clearly remember my first impressions of all my children.

This is my proudest accomplishments; being present for the births of each of my children and maintaining a constant and continual presence in their lives, by having custody of them and raising them through high school. My children are the center of my life and I study each of them, so that I can share their "essence," and their beauty can be ingrained in me, and the benefit of my experiences can be ingrained in them. Kellie was a very happy baby that smiled all the time and was very, very smart. Gabrielle was a brooding baby with a temper to match. Anthony was very indifferent, and went along with the flow dictated by his sisters. But all did the things babies did, had attention spans of babies and offered the kind of behaviors that went along with newborns. DeShawn was (and is) different. It was like she was a grown person in a baby's body, like she was sent to us and had been here before. She rarely blinked and would only close her eyes to turn her head and focus on something else. Her attention span far exceeded most babies I've ever seen (including my first three), as she studied objects around the room. Mind you, she was only a few minutes old.

The miracle of DeShawn's birth and the subsequent joy she has brought to Debra and myself as well as the rest of the family, in spite of what I thought I wanted (or didn't want), has been immeasurable. Every time I look in my youngest daughter's face, I think about what I might have missed, had I tried to force my plans over the miracle God has allowed us to experience. I see God's face when I look at her, and I am constantly reminded that no matter what we plan, it's God's plan that always wins out. As man plans, God plans and "God is the best of planners."

The other opportunity to see "God's face" was through my involvement in the greatest demonstration of faith, a true modern day miracle, "the Black man" has ever been involved with here in America, the Million Man March. The Million Man March was an expression of faith unseen before by Black men. The notion of "a million men" coming to the nation's capital was a threatening proposition to white America. The press created an environment of hostility that tried to manipulate the intent of the march, and cast aspersions on its convener. All over the country there were threats of "what would happen on this day," if we carried out the march. Philosophical extremists predicted everything from the government "bombing us," to "a violence breaking out from Black men turning on each other." The government closed down that day preparing to have to use force to restore order. The atmosphere for confrontation had been set, and none of us was sure what to expect, but if we had listened to the "devilish" predictions that were being circulated, either death or embarrassment (including not reaching the projected "one million men) was all we could look forward to. All any of us had on this day was our faith that Allah, and Allah alone, would be our salvation and our protection against forces of evil, regardless of race. If there was any day that I was prepared to die, it was on this day--a day the "Black Man" was on the world stage, atoning for their sins and asking God (not the government) for justice, freedom and equality. Yet, in the midst of over 1,000 death threats there was a calm of peace.

By the grace of God and the permission of the Honorable Minister Louis Farrakhan, Claudette Muhammad (his National Chief of Protocol) appointed me (from among her seven regional protocol representatives) to be the lead protocol representative for the Million Man March. My responsibility was to insure the proper timing and facilitation of the many participants on the program from the holding rooms to the stage, as well as, to coordinate the protocol team's handling of the many, many dignitaries that wanted stage seating for that day. Everybody who was anybody was a "VIP" that day. We had to rotate people on and off the stage several times an hour, during the course of the day, which became increasingly more difficult, as the program culminated with the appearance of its convener, the Honorable Minister Louis Farrakhan. We were on our post at 4 a.m. on October 16th, 1995, and held post until its conclusion at 5 p.m. that evening. There were already over 250,000 men on "the mall" for "the Adhan" (the pre-sunrise "Call to Prayer.") By 10 a.m., there were over one million men on the mall. Faces for as far as the eyes can see. By 2 p.m, there were over 2 million men that ran beyond the space graphed out to hold one million. Beyond the Washington Monument. Beyond the Lincoln Memorial. Behind the stage area, up both Independence and Pennsylvania Avenues. I caught myself several times during the day, just looking out, in awe, into the faces of a virtual "tidal wave" of Black men. This was truly "God's face" looking back at me.

Black men that had no malice in their hearts, no anger toward each other on this day. Black men, who have been stereotyped as insensitive and unaffectionate, hugging each other, feeding each other, praising each other, and telling each other, "I love you, brother." It was unlike any feeling I've ever experienced. Never have I been in the presence of Black men I didn't know, where I didn't feel any hostility, jealousy or envy waged toward me, "just for looking at another brotha'." Never have I been in the presence of so many Black men, and not feel I had to be concerned about my life and personal safety. Never have I ever experienced being in the presence of Black men telling each other that they were sorry for "not lifting up our families and communities," or for not being "the best that we could be, "as lovers and as friends" to our women. Never have I ever experienced Black men making commitments to each other to stop killing and exploiting each. Never have I ever felt like I belonged to a race, a culture, a people, a community like I felt on October 16th, 1995. Every Black man should feel this way; an indelible love, an uncontrollable appreciation for culture and self-pride, at least one day in his life. In fact, this love was so incredible, every brother who attended should spend every day of his life trying to hold on to it, passing on to the brothas who didn't get there what "true love for self and your people" really feels like. Any description of the feelings one experienced on that day is not sufficient . The "love just kept coming, pouring out with endless bounty. A love that kept Black men, who have been framed as "anti-social," and who society has branded as one who can't come together in groups of 20 without fighting and shooting each other, in check, where not one incident (relating to the march; only two total-- probably the most "crime free" day in D.C's recent history) broke out. A love that paralyzed the Capital police and military reservist there to move on us at a moment's notice. They were largely ignored all day. Police and Black men sharing the same space in peace and harmony (imagine that). A real love that fed and sustained every soul present, all emanating from one man who God placed both his hands and his protective hedge around, gave him the vision and the desire to make the unthinkable real. In a country that never taught them how to love or showed him how to love. The "Black man" loved on that day.

You could now imagine being a part of real miracles, like how Jesus fed 5,000 with five loaves of bread. God makes all things real, done in his name. The "Day of Atonement" should have been proof to all that God is real, that he is present in the world, and that he raises one from amongst us to "bear witness" to his supreme authority. The Million Man March was America's clearest demonstration of how God empowers and protects the true and faithful believer. In spite of falsehoods and fears that tried to prevent this miracle from coming about, faith brought forth truth and truth vindicated faith. We, as believers, just have to know the face of God when we see it, and follow his will. If we don't, he will "know us not" on the day of Judgment.

* * *

The lessons learned from being lifted from the lowest depths I've ever felt are many. But what I learned most is that God is merciful and oft-forgiving. As I began to rebuild my life, there was never any uncertainty as to "if" I would rebound. It was just a matter of "when"

I would rebound. I never felt that God was trying to destroy me, as much as, I felt he had to test and mold me into something, by his supreme wisdom, more perfected than I was. I knew, if I sought "God's face," I would be successful, by Allah's permission. I re-established my consultancy in 1990, focusing on strategic planning and issues management consulting. The key to my so-called "comeback" was not a re-embracing of the counter-culture's value system or the re-adoption of the Negro (im)mortality approach to social acceptance. My reemergence was (by the grace of Allah) rooted in the same principled advocacy that "got me in trouble with white folks (if you listen to some)," but what was never anything more than wanting for Black people what they should have wanted for themselves. The commentaries that I write and are published weekly (and have become highly popular amongst young adult and older readers (ages 18-35 and 50 and older) are rooted in the truths of the inequities and injustices Blacks face. They offer discussion regarding the refusal of our leaders to offer revolutionary approaches (in thought and action) to a continued social and economic compromise that paralyzes our communities nationwide. My business consulting efforts help small businesses and community organizations in developing sustainable infrastructures and viability approaches in (and through) tough operating environments.

Crises in our communities are still ignored by mainstream Negroes, who oftentimes speak with their tongue what they do not believe in their hearts. That is, of course, until it affects them personally. So many people have embraced my vigilance, while many a Negro leader continue to be embarrassed in their roles as compromisers. Basking in their roles as "house niggas," indirectly holding the rope that's hanging their own people, these niggas try to excuse my commentary to their masters as a "cry in the wild," as opposed to a voice of principled reason on issues of social and economic inequity. Holding fast to my beliefs that systems and institutions in this country are inherently unfair, and are still "separate and unequal, has allowed me, through my editorial commentary, to partake in the discussion of the destiny of the Negro. I have been able to do so without having to deal with flawed Negro reason and unprincipled, irrational defenses that Negroes often put forth as justifications for social tolerance. Or even Negro simple-mindedness that only clouds and frustrates efforts for self-determination beyond what white people underwrite as benefactors of our social and economic compromise.

Equal rights, access to economic power, social justice

and political fairness (in representation) is the basis of community, and what everybody else has--except us (in few and singular numbers). Furthermore, we just can't seem to find opportunity among our societal counterparts, except the very ones who seek to exploit conditions of compromise. So we surrender to inferior materiality, inferior existence, create false barriers to justify mainstream involvements and offer excuses for "being there." Right is right, and real is real. There's no justification for the social and economic conditions our people live in, nor for the continuing compromises they must endure just to live a minimum standard of life that everyone else enjoys; free and without peril.

I have learned that, oftentimes, progressive Negroes who question the reality of the "racial divide," who challenge the legitimacy of a peaceful racial co-existence as a facade, are rebutted through the counterculture's media and social defenses, and have to end up coming back, with their tail tucked, to the same systems of oppression that compromised them, in the first place. They are unable to withstand the constant bombardment of counter acculturation that makes it seem as if wrong is right, and right makes no difference. The call for a "brotha to work within the system," being nothing less than a call to surrender to the system. A system of compromise that represents the proverbial "crumb" laid out for Negro life. And sometimes the crumbs are quite lucrative, in the individual scheme of things. But individuals don't run countries (not in a democracy); collective communities do. Therein lies the compromise. The individual reward will never save our people. Nor will the individual perspective. So we're stuck, paralyzed in individual desires to escape the madness, with no collective desire to affirm what is right for our people, nor an unified approach to escape.

One thing is for sure. Coming back to a master/slave relationship is not the answer. I'm glad I didn't have the kind of Negro relapse that would cause such a regression of thought and principle. Huey Newton once said, "I'd rather die on my feet, than live on my knees." The Negro has created the advent of permanent knee pads. Still, some of us stand in the face of social oppression and Negro regression to the challenge we know amounts to social compromise.

* * *

I have learned that revenge is not something that vindicates you, it only further indicts you, and causes you to act in ways that only bring more danger. God permits man to avenge, to bring justice upon the violation of his law (according to his will), but never does he permit revenge as an act of his hand. Revenge is the judgment of man to get even for the acts of other men. God avenges right by guiding the acts of people he selects to correct wrong. To avenge something is to correct a wrong, to vindicate it by an act of right. Not to "get even" for a wrong by committing another wrong. Man trying to "play God" is casting judgment and bringing about punishment termed as revenging God's will. Revenge is never God's will. Revenge is a manmade concept; a "wrong for a wrong" devil inspired behavior borne out of "a eye for an eye, a tooth for a tooth" mentality that leaves us all crippled and blind, as Martin Luther King once said. Most importantly, it takes us all out of God's good graces and jeopardizes our own protection. God stands with us in righteousness, but when doing wrong you're on your own and, except for God's grace, are exposed to the dangers of the devil's world. God avenges some of the wrongs we experience, but despises those who do wrong to "get even" and bring about the fate of another by their own hand. That kind of judgment is not ours to render. I have learned that God evens the score in his own way, and oftentimes that is demonstrated by the failures and falls of your opposition or enemies. Other times its demonstrated in the rise of one's self in the face of blatant enemy opposition. Success is God's revenge to the wicked.

God vindicates you, unlike anything you can do of your own hand. He vindicates you with his blessings and makes your successes known, in spite of, the efforts of your enemies to hold you back, and many times in spite of, our own faults. God is a great God, beneficent and oft forgiving. There is no greater truth than the saying, "Success is the best revenge." Your enemies truly "gnash their teeth in anger," when they can't figure out how you managed to "come back" without their help, without their permission and, in many cases, even without their knowledge. It frustrates them greater, when you do it with their knowledge. The disbeliever and the hypocrite doesn't understand that "as they plan, Allah plans; and Allah is the best of planners."

I've also learned that all wrongs aren't vindicated. Not because God wants to cover up wrong. He never does that. God covers people's faults and he redeems those who repent and seeks to atone for their sins. The lord of all the worlds is a forgiving God, who believes in redemption for those who change their ways, and he rewards those who atone by lifting them up, as positive examples of what the "redeemed" can do. God throws away no one who doesn't want to be thrown away. And he shows time and time again, just as he has redeemed many, he can redeem all who seek "his face." No matter how wrong you were, a sincere confession and a pure desire to atone will bring about Allah's redemption, in time, should he permit it. Why does he allow some people's sins to go covered?

God is a just God, who weighs one's faults with the good one does. Some of the wrongs certain players in Los Angeles (and other parts of the country) may never come to light, because he has excused their sins from the judgment of man. That's not to say those sins won't be judged, because God will judge all of our acts, good deeds and bad ones. But God's grace and God's mercy allows those whom he feels will make a difference to escape judgment for the moment. One of God's greatest Prophets, King David--who returned the blessed kingdom of Israel to God. David recognized his faults and how God spared him. David acknowledged God's blessings when he wrote in his Psalms (Book 32, Verse 1-3), "Blessed is the man whose sins God covers and whose transgressions is forgiven." God from the beginning of time has protected the righteous, in spite of their faults. God protected David from his many enemies and from his many personal faults.

What God chooses to uncover will be revealed in its proper time, under proper circumstance. However, what God chooses to cover, no man can uncover, and whatever God has forgiven, no man can bring judgment upon. No matter what people chose to "bring up," or dig up," if it's not God's will, he will turn it into a blessing, a benefit for the believer, and use it as proof of the power of his redemption. This is the testimony of a living witness, who has received the benefit of God's grace and mercy and who has been redeemed by a beneficent and merciful judge.

Lastly, I have learned to trust again. Not that it's easy. But God has put me with a living example of trust and goodness, in my wife, Debra. A woman who understands my flaws and my faults, who had no reason to trust me, or had no justifiable basis to believe that I could, or would, recover from this period of tribulation, or make a commitment to seek my happiness and contentment with her, other than a well-founded faith in God. She knew what I was made of, and had personal insight to the facts, not the fiction. Debra is a true believer. As a young man embroiled in public controversy, recently separated with three young children, I recognized I wasn't exactly at the top of "the most eligible bachelors list." Covered by the mud and defilement of conflict and compromise, she still was able to recognize my God-given brilliance and resilience, that of a ten karat diamond laying on the ground-in the mud. She took it home, washed it, buffed out the scratches and polished it up, and now wears it proudly, in spite of, the nicks and scratches that were present, at one time. The cornerstone is no less valuable, and even increases in value, as time moves on. Only a trained eye, one that looks deep below the surface of something, can discern the true value of anything, including people. Our society "throws away" human resource quicker than a material resource. Life is more precious than any "thing." So they say. Healing broken bones is one thing, healing the broken spirit is another. In a time where glitz was everything and substance meant little, I'll forever love my wife, Debra, for being trained, true and trusting enough to believe that what she had found, laying on the ground, was in fact "real" and helped to heal my wounded soul.

It's this trust that vindicates truth. A truth (not falsehood or F.E.A.R.--false evidences appearing real) that vindicates faith and faith vindicates, period. For faith is the evidence of things unseen--the substance of things hoped for, and is the basis for true salvation of every soul, who believes in the true power of God, a belief that can never be challenged, compromised or bought. For God is sufficient for those who believe. Only the true believer can show the disbeliever and the hypocrite what the power of God can do, including saving and redeeming lives, simply based on faith. Faith and fear cannot occupy the same space, so it is the faithful that can face all things--even death--when all others, who claim they are faithful, are overtaken by fear. Fear is the truest sign of the unfaithful, the disbeliever. Black communities are run by those who fear men, more than they fear God. Even preachers, the so-called "Men of God," now bow down to the modern day deity. The "Caesar" we call the United States of America.

Irrespective of what people believe--time, given to each of us, only by the grace and mercy of Allah, heals all wounds and vindicates all wrongs, sometimes. All things are revealed and corrected by his will, and only for purposes he commends. Due to God's grace and protection, I survived this experience and won, not the games of men, but in the games and lessons of life. For God tests those who say "they believe." I am truly grateful for my test. Praise God, forever.

* * *

INDEX

Reflections

Reflections

Reflections

Reflections

Reflections